An
Emily Dickinson
Encyclopedia

AN
EMILY DICKINSON
ENCYCLOPEDIA

Edited by

Jane Donahue Eberwein

Greenwood Press
Westport, Connecticut • London

Library of Congress Cataloging-in-Publication Data

An Emily Dickinson encyclopedia / edited by Jane Donahue Eberwein.
    p. cm.
  Includes bibliographical references (p.) and indexes.
  ISBN 0–313–29781–9 (alk. paper)
    1. Dickinson, Emily, 1830–1886—Encyclopedias. 2. Women and
literature—United States—Encyclopedias. 3. Women poets,
American—19th century—Biography—Encyclopedias. I. Eberwein,
Jane Donahue, 1943– .
  PS1541.Z49E47   1998
  811'.4—dc21   97–39723

British Library Cataloguing in Publication Data is available.

Library of Congress Catalog Card Number: 97–39723
ISBN: 0–313–29781–9

First published in 1998

Greenwood Press, 88 Post Road West, Westport, CT 06881
An imprint of Greenwood Publishing Group, Inc.

Printed in the United States of America

♾™

The paper used in this book complies with the
Permanent Paper Standard issued by the National
Information Standards Organization (Z39.48–1984).

10 9 8 7 6 5 4 3 2

For Bob

Contents

Preface

When Emily Dickinson responded to one of Thomas Wentworth Higginson's questions early in their acquaintance by remarking, "All men say 'What' to me, but I thought it a fashion—" (L271), she found a graceful way to alert her mentor that she was accustomed to arousing curiosity but had developed defenses against self-revelation. Now that her poetry has taken its place at the heart of America's literary canon, readers continue to raise questions about the poet herself, the environment that sustained and challenged her, her artistic choices, and the implications of her poems. Some of these questions can be decisively answered within this book's encyclopedic framework. Others continue to provoke speculation. Those who consult this encyclopedia can count on learning, for example, which of her Sweetser correspondents were related to the Dickinsons and which of them were neighbors but should expect no definitive identification of the person she addressed as "Master." Even though one turns to an encyclopedia for distilled nuggets of factual information, one must recognize in this case the continuing fact of Emily Dickinson's amazing ability to keep us rejoicing with Higginson in the "sparkles of light" emerging from the "fiery mist" in which she hid herself (L330a).

This encyclopedia provides succinctly informative entries on people important to Emily Dickinson: family members, friends, neighbors, and persons who influenced her. Other entries report on places and institutions familiar to her and aspects of nineteenth-century New England culture. There are also entries on the editing history of her poems and letters, reception of her work in the United States and other parts of the world, and the impact of various scholarly and critical methodologies on Dickinson scholarship. Readers may also consult entries on Dickinson's stylistic traits, her use of such poetic devices as metaphor and oxymoron, and her relation to various literary traditions. Because Joseph Duchac's annotated guides to *The Poems of Emily Dickinson* 1890–1977 and 1978–1989 already provide invaluable reviews of critical commentary on each individual Dickinson poem, this book makes no attempt to duplicate those existing references but provides entries only on the ten poems published in the poet's lifetime and those that appear virtually without exception in anthologies currently used in American colleges. These serve as models demonstrating approaches applicable to other poems. Contributors to the encyclopedia refer to many additional poems, however, and readers are encouraged to consult the Index of Poems Cited to locate these citations.

Although entries provide useful information when read alone, this book will prove most enlightening and even entertaining to those who explore connections among its entries. The General Index and cross-referencing guides within entries call attention to linkages that may themselves open up further associations. An asterisk * following a name or term calls attention to a separate entry within the encyclopedia. The referenced term may refer to a different form of the base word, however (e.g., *The Bible*, biblical; Editorial Scholarship, edition, editing, editor). It seems fitting that this tribute to a poet who read her dictionary with the enthusiasm others reserve for novels should be a reference designed to encourage browsing. As Dickinson scholars repeatedly discover, everything connects.

Still, this encyclopedia remains only a starting point for research. None of us who have contributed entries imagine that we have presented the last word on a given topic or satiated an eager reader's curiosity. Recommendations for further reading accompany most entries, and the Bibliography provides further guidance. Beyond that, researchers are referred to existing and ongoing bibliographies. For those contemplating archival research, Appendix B provides information on major research library holdings and the hypermedia textual archive.

Two additional reference works scheduled for publication at about the same time as this encyclopedia will also be much appreciated by Dickinson scholars. The *Emily Dickinson Lexicon*, edited by Cynthia Hallen (Greenwood Press), documents Dickinson's knowledge of words in terms of dictionary definitions available to her as well as her own artful applications of particular words. The *Emily Dickinson Handbook*, edited by Roland Hagenbüchle, Gudrun Grabher, and Cristanne Miller (University of Massachusetts Press) provides chapter-length reviews of the current state of knowledge on key issues in Dickinson scholarship. Consulted in connection with this encyclopedia, these references open revealing perspective to the active reader. The most important and rewarding reading, of course, remains the direct experience of Dickinson's poems and letters. The goal of this book is to send readers back to those primary sources with heightened appreciation and renewed wonder.

The encyclopedia reflects where the scholarly community stands today and the directions in which we are moving after a little over a century of Dickinson study. Since *Poems by Emily Dickinson* appeared in 1890, readers have been raising questions about the poet, her environment, and the poems and letters that have established this reclusive woman, America's patron saint of neglected genius, as a world-famous literary figure. Factual knowledge has largely supplanted the mythic image that was already established in Amherst lore before the poet's death. Thanks to biographers and cultural historians, we have considerable information about Dickinson's life circumstances and the Connecticut Valley environment that stimulated her. There are gaps in that knowledge, however, and this book reflects the willingness of scholars at the end of the twentieth century to live with doubts, avoiding claims to definitive knowledge where none exists. It also reflects our willingness to disagree respectfully on matters of emphasis and interpretation when consensus eludes us.

Also evident is the current disposition of many critics to focus attention on subtle aspects of Dickinson's poetic artistry and thus on the texts that represent her poems to readers. Some of the most animated critical conversations among Dickinson scholars today concern editorial practices—both historically regarded with attention to the varying forms in which poems and letters have been represented in print and theoretically regarded as we confront doubts about the possibility of honoring the poet's intent. Such questioning, initiated by R. W. Franklin's facsimile reproductions of fascicles and sets in *The Manuscript Books of Emily Dickinson* (1981) and spurred by Susan Howe's poetic response to the physical evidence of Dickinson's creative process in *My Emily Dickinson* (1985), focuses research on fascicle study and scrutiny of holograph evidence in ways that will be apparent throughout this book. Her poems and letters are shown to be multiple, open-ended, resistant to closure, and forever in process. The same can be said of the poet who emerges through these pages.

Given the unsettled state of textual scholarship, any decision about representations of poems within this book presents critical challenges. To achieve a common base of reference, I have asked contributors to cite Dickinson's writings as they appear in Thomas Johnson's three-volume compilations of *The Poems of Emily Dickinson* (1955) and *The Letters of Emily Dickinson* (1958). Although no longer regarded as "definitive" or even fully authoritative, these remain the standard scholarly texts. Poems and letters are still identified by the numbers Johnson assigned. To supplement Johnson, Appendix A provides a full listing of poems in each of Dickinson's forty fascicles so that readers may benefit from Franklin's findings in *The Manuscript Books* about her groupings of poems, in effect her self-publication. A new edition of the poems, prepared by Franklin and published by Harvard University Press, will appear at approximately the same time as this encyclopedia and was unavailable to those preparing entries. It, along with the hypermedia archive initiated by Martha Nell Smith and several related editing projects, may well transform Dickinson scholarship in the way Johnson's editions did half a century ago.

If this book conveys the excitement of Dickinson's admirers around the world about those emerging prospects as well as transmitting information as clearly and accurately as possible, it will reward the efforts of its contributors. I feel a deep sense of gratitude to the many people who assisted me in preparing the encyclopedia. I appreciate Greenwood Press' invitation to edit this book and the wise and helpful assistance of George Butler, Maureen Melino, Norine Mudrick, and Carol Lucas at various stages in the publication process. Present and former board members of the Emily Dickinson International Society provided guidance and encouragement for me to launch this project at the August 1995 Innsbruck Conference. Approximately a hundred contributors shared their knowledge; the identifying notes that conclude the encyclopedia only begin to suggest their talents and range of knowledge. I am grateful as well to Rebecca Roberts, who has joined me in painstaking details of preparing the manuscript while representing the "intelligent general reader" in the editing process, and to Oakland University's Department of English for goodwill and considerable practical support. In particular, I thank Joan Rosen for her encouragement of this project, June Fisher and Nola Puvalowski for their stalwart, cheerful, and resourceful secretarial help, Martha Hammel and Donald Morse for useful information, and John Coughlin for computer rescues. David Jaymes of Oakland's Department of Modern Languages also provided assistance. Students in undergraduate and graduate Dickinson seminars over many years have reminded me of the poet's gift for engaging curious readers while calling my attention to questions this encyclopedia may help to resolve. Calliope sustained the tradition of feline editorial assistance set by Clarence, Echo, and Daphne. My greatest debt, as always, is to Bob, to whom this book is dedicated.

Jane Donahue Eberwein

Chronology

1828	Marriage of Emily Norcross and Edward Dickinson.
1829	Birth of William Austin Dickinson; death of grandmother Betsey Fay Norcross.
1830	Edward Dickinson family moves into the Homestead, sharing half the house with the Samuel Fowler Dickinsons; Emily Dickinson born, 10 December.
1831	Grandfather Joel Norcross marries Sarah Vaill; Emily Norcross Dickinson joins Amherst's First Church.
1833	Lavinia Dickinson born; Samuel Fowler Dickinson family moves to Cincinnati; Edward Dickinson's family shares the Homestead with new owner, David Mack.
1835	Emily begins schooling; Edward Dickinson named treasurer of Amherst College.
1838	Grandfather Dickinson dies in Ohio; Edward Dickinson elected to Massachusetts legislature.
1840	Dickinson family moves to North Pleasant Street; Emily and Lavinia enter Amherst Academy; grandmother Lucretia Gunn Dickinson dies.
1844	Emily visits Norcrosses in Boston after Sophia Holland's death; meets Abiah Root at Amherst Academy.
1846	Death of Grandfather Norcross; Emily visits Boston; frequent letters to Abiah Root.
1847	Emily completes program at Amherst Academy, enters Mount Holyoke.
1848	Leaves Mount Holyoke after a year's study, interrupted by home stay for sickness; friendship formed with Benjamin Newton.
1849	Newton leaves Amherst; Lavinia away at school.
1850	Dickinson's first publication, "Magnum bonum" valentine (L34) in Amherst College *Indicator*; she sends a valentine poem, "Awake ye muses nine" (P1) to Elbridge Bowdoin; Emily's and Austin's friendships begin with Susan Gilbert; Emily makes first written reference to her dog, Carlo;

Newton sends gift of Emerson's *Poems*; Austin graduates from Amherst College, begins teaching; Edward and Lavinia Dickinson and Susan Gilbert join Amherst's First Church during religious revival.

1851   Frequent letters to Austin, teaching in Boston, and Sue, teaching in Baltimore; Emily and Lavinia visit brother; Dickinson meets Josiah Holland.

1852   "Sic transit gloria mundi" (P3) appears in the *Springfield Republican*.

1853   Austin at Harvard Law School; he enters into secret engagement with Sue; Ben Newton dies; Emily and Lavinia visit the Hollands in Springfield; Edward Dickinson elected to U.S. Congress; Newman cousins become wards of Edward Dickinson.

1854   Emily remains at home with Sue Gilbert and John Graves while mother and sister visit Edward Dickinson in Washington; she and Lavinia visit the Hollands; Sarah Vaill Norcross dies.

1855   Emily and Lavinia visit father in Washington; probably meet Charles Wadsworth while visiting Coleman cousins in Philadelphia; Edward and Austin Dickinson enter into law partnership; family returns to the Homestead; mother begins long period of invalidism.

1856   Austin joins church; marries Sue Gilbert and moves with her to the Evergreens; Emily's friendship begins with his friend Samuel Bowles; her rye and Indian bread wins prize.

1857   R. W. Emerson lectures in Amherst, stays at the Evergreens.

1858   Dickinson writing poetry intensively; begins assembling fair copies into fascicles; *Republican* prints "Nobody knows this little Rose—" (P35); first "Master" letter (L187); Newman cousins move next door with Austin and Sue.

1860   Charles Wadsworth visits; Helen Fiske Hunt and her husband visit; Aunt Lavinia Norcross dies.

1861   Second and third "Master" letters (L248, 233); "I taste a liquor never brewed" (P214) appears in *Republican*; Civil War begins; a year of personal suffering and poetic productivity.

1862   Dickinson's most dazzlingly productive year as a poet; "Safe in their Alabaster Chambers—" (P216) printed; she begins correspondence with Thomas Wentworth Higginson; Ned Dickinson born; Charles Wadsworth accepts call to Calvary Church in San Francisco; Bowles in Europe.

1863   Lorin Norcross dies, leaving daughters Frances and Louisa orphans.

1864   *Round Table* prints "Some keep the Sabbath going to Church—" (P324); *Drum Beat* prints "Blazing in Gold and quenching in Purple" (P228), "Flowers—Well—if anybody" (P137), and "These are the days when Birds come back—" (P130); *Brooklyn Daily Union* prints "Success is counted sweetest" (P67); *Republican* reprints P228 and P137 (the latter also picked up by the *Boston Post*); Emily in Cambridge with Norcross cousins for seven months of eye treatment.

1865   Eye treatments again in Boston, after which Dickinson remains at home for the rest of her life; Civil War ends.

1866	Carlo dies; "A narrow fellow in the grass" appears in the *Republican*; Martha Dickinson born.
1870	Higginson visits Dickinson for the first time.
1873	Edward Dickinson elected to the legislature; Austin replaces him as Amherst College treasurer; Rev. Jenkins finds Emily spiritually "sound."
1874	Edward Dickinson dies suddenly in Boston; Bowles returns to Europe.
1875	Emily Norcross Dickinson paralyzed; Thomas Gilbert Dickinson born.
1876	Helen Hunt Jackson encourages Dickinson to publish.
1877	Deaths of Mary Higginson and Elizabeth Lord.
1878	Samuel Bowles dies; Helen Hunt Jackson, who visits in October, includes "Success is counted sweetest" (P67) in *A Masque of Poets*.
1880	Charles Wadsworth pays his second visit; Austin develops malaria; Judge Lord presents Christmas gift.
1881	Lord visits at the Evergreens; Mabel Loomis Todd and her family move to Amherst; death of Dr. Holland.
1882	Wadsworth dies; Judge Lord seriously ill; Emily Norcross Dickinson dies; Austin and Mabel Todd begin their affair, which results in tension between Sue and his sisters.
1883	Gilbert dies; grieving Emily extends comfort to Sue; Austin and Lavinia ill.
1884	Judge Lord dies; Emily stricken with illness.
1885	Helen Hunt Jackson dies.
1886	Dickinson dies 15 May.
1890	*Poems by Emily Dickinson* published by Roberts Brothers, edited and promoted by Mabel Loomis Todd and T. W. Higginson.
1891	*Poems*, second series.
1894	Todd edits *Letters of Emily Dickinson*.
1895	Austin dies.
1896	*Poems*, third series, edited by Todd.
1898	Todd discontinues editing after Lavinia sues her successfully in controversy over Austin's will; Ned dies.
1899	Lavinia dies.
1902	Martha Dickinson marries Alexander Bianchi.
1913	Susan dies.
1914	Martha Dickinson Bianchi brings out *The Single Hound*.
1924	Bianchi, assisted by Alfred Leete Hampson, edits *The Life and Letters of Emily Dickinson* and *The Complete Poems of Emily Dickinson*.
1929	*Further Poems of Emily Dickinson*.
1930	*The Poems of Emily Dickinson: Centenary Edition*.
1931	Mabel Todd renews her claims with *Letters of Emily Dickinson*.
1932	Bianchi responds with *Emily Dickinson Face to Face*; Todd dies.

1935   *Unpublished Poems of Emily Dickinson.*

1937   *Poems by Emily Dickinson.*

1943   Bianchi dies, leaving the Evergreens and rights to Dickinson materials to Alfred Leete Hampson.

1945   Millicent Todd Bingham brings out *Bolts of Melody*, edited with her mother.

1951   Theodora Van Wagenen Ward edits *Emily Dickinson's Letters to Dr. and Mrs. Josiah Gilbert Holland.*

1955   Thomas Johnson edits *The Poems of Emily Dickinson* in three-volume variorum that stimulates critical attention and artistic recognition.

1958   Johnson and Ward edit *The Letters of Emily Dickinson.*

1981   R. W. Franklin's facsimile edition of *The Manuscript Books of Emily Dickinson* launches a period of intensive textual study.

1986   Dickinson centennial celebrated in the United States, Canada, and Japan.

Abbreviations

L   A letter from *The Letters of Emily Dickinson*. Ed. Thomas H. Johnson and Theodora Ward. 3 vols. Cambridge: Harvard University Press, Belknap Press, 1958. The number following refers to Johnson's chronological numbering system for the letters.

P   A poem from *The Poems of Emily Dickinson*. Ed. Thomas H. Johnson. 3 vols. Cambridge: Harvard University Press, Belknap Press, 1955. The number following refers to Johnson's roughly chronological numbering system for the poems.

PF   A prose fragment from *The Letters of Emily Dickinson* (1958). The number following refers to Johnson's chronological numbering system for the letters.

AB   Bingham, Millicent Todd. *Ancestors' Brocades: The Literary Debut of Emily Dickinson*. New York: Harper & Brothers, 1945.

FF   Bianchi, Martha Dickinson. *Emily Dickinson Face to Face: Unpublished Letters with Notes and Reminiscences by Her Niece*. Boston: Houghton Mifflin, 1932.

Life   Sewall, Richard. *The Life of Emily Dickinson*. New York: Farrar, Straus, and Giroux, 1974.

LL   Bianchi, Martha Dickinson. *The Life and Letters of Emily Dickinson*. Boston: Houghton Mifflin, 1924.

Ly   Sewall, Richard, ed. *The Lyman Letters: New Light on Emily Dickinson and Her Family*. Amherst: University of Massachusetts Press, 1965.

Years   Leyda, Jay. *The Years and Hours of Emily Dickinson*. 2 vols. New Haven: Yale University Press, 1960.

A

"A narrow Fellow in the Grass" (P986)   This poem was anonymously published under the title "The Snake" in the 14 February 1866 *Springfield Republican*.* Dickinson's unhappiness with editor Samuel Bowles'* changes to the poem is reflected in a letter to T. W. Higginson* in which she enclosed a clipping of the poem: "Lest you meet my Snake and suppose I deceive it was robbed of me—defeated too of the third line by the punctuation. The third and fourth were one—I had told you I did not print—I feared you might think me ostensible" (L316). She referred to the published copy that was transformed into three eight-line stanzas in which a comma was added to the end of line 3 and "instant" substituted for "sudden" in line 4. Scholars conjecture that Susan Dickinson* forwarded her own copy of the poem (received from Emily in a note) to Bowles; his surprised response to the first lines of the third stanza reportedly was, "How did that girl ever know that a boggy field wasn't good for corn?" (*FF*27).

"A narrow Fellow in the Grass," generally considered one of Dickinson's nature* poems, has become a standard text in classrooms and anthologies. It is one of her more accessible poems by virtue of its visually precise description and its loosely narrative form, but it goes beyond her poetry, celebrating the "transport" one often experiences in nature to explore the mystery of its cold-blooded, unknowable aspects. Critical attention has focused upon a number of the poem's features, including the phallic nature of the snake's description, the identification of the speaker as a "Boy" (see also P389), and the singularity of the striking final image ("Zero at the Bone—").

RECOMMENDED: *FF*; *Poems*; Rebecca Patterson, "Emily Dickinson's 'Double Tim': Masculine Identification"; Martha Nell Smith, *Rowing in Eden: Rereading Emily Dickinson*; Cynthia Griffin Wolff, *Emily Dickinson*.

Mary Jane Leach-Rudawski

"After great pain, a formal feeling comes—" (P341)   was transcribed by Dickinson into Fascicle* 18 (Appendix A). The second stanza is written out in the order in which Johnson* prints it, but Dickinson had placed the numbers 1, 3, 2, and 4 before lines 1, 2, 3, and 4. Thus an alternative version of the stanza would read:

> The Feet, mechanical, go round—
> A Wooden way
> Of Ground, or Air, or Ought—
> Regardless grown,
> A Quartz contentment, like a stone—

The poem was published in the *Atlantic Monthly** (February 1929) and again that same year in *Further Poems of Emily Dickinson.**

Critical commentary has focused on the poem's analysis of pain and suffering; on its depiction of the relationship between psychic trauma and external conditions, such as time and space; and on the tropes and figures Dickinson uses for depicting these themes. Indeed, the poem may be viewed as an exemplar of Dickinson's figurative technique, a dazzling display of linked and embedded figures, carrying information like the chains of nucleotides that form the double helixes of DNA. Altogether, it operates as a poetic parable, imaging a psychological* condition through a rhetoric of objects, actions, and situations pertinent to the "after"math of "great pain."

What follows great pain is a "formal feeling": the poem describes its initial occurrence, then the memory of it. What pain? Whose feeling? The poem does not say. Rather, it tells of how the nerves sit, how the heart questions, how the feet go round. It speaks of ceremonies, tombs, ground, air, ought, quartz, stone, contentment, lead, and then snow. It describes a lack of attention or regard—a memory of how this formal/stiff/mechanical/wooden/ contented feeling, this stupor after chill, could become a letting go.

The feeling under survey is "formal." Commentators like Joanne Feit Diehl stress the loss or lack of feeling that marks this internal crisis*; all of the tropes in the poem, she says, are versions of death,* "the single trope which can convey this merging of self* into stone." For Vivian Pollak the trauma inaugurates a loss of identity, an imperviousness to externality, resulting in the poem's peculiar figurative structuring, a "subversion of analogic function" (208). Rather than yoking disparate elements, these figures compare like to like, as in "A Quartz contentment, like a stone—."

Thus not only the images but their very structure give form to the experience under surveillance. The extravagant appositionality of the terms of description— until the poem's final two lines, all of the figures modify one another, and all of them modify "formal feeling"—creates the redundancy of stasis that defines the peculiar formality with which mind and body respond to trauma. Dickinson's variations for the second stanza serve to reinforce the prevailing principle of appositionality: placement of the images seems interchangeable. The poem concludes by questioning the possibility of returning to "life" after such a "death." The ambiguity* of the final "memory" allows commentators to interpret the concluding stage in the aftermath of pain variously—as either a return to life or a giving in to death.

RECOMMENDED: Sharon Cameron, *Lyric Time: Dickinson and the Limits of Genre*; Joanne Feit Diehl, *Dickinson and the Romantic Imagination*; Suzanne Juhasz, *The Undiscovered Continent: Emily Dickinson and the Space of the Mind*; Vivian Pollak, *Dickinson: The Anxiety of Gender*.

Suzanne Juhasz

ALDRICH, THOMAS BAILEY (1836–1907)   Eminent New England poet, critic, and arbiter of literary opinion as editor of the *Atlantic Monthly** (1881–1890), Aldrich championed Genteel formalist aesthetics and condemned Dickinson's "versicles" as the "ungrammatical thought[s]" of a "half-educated recluse," marred by utter disregard for conventional uses of meter, rhyme, and syntax (Buckingham 283–84). He illustrated his understanding of poetic form by an exemplary revision of P214.* His 1903 review partly reconsidered Dickinson's "formlessness" as "deliberate affectation." (*See*: Critical Reception)

RECOMMENDED: Thomas Bailey Aldrich, "Un Poête Manqué," *Ponkapog Papers*; Willis J. Buckingham, *Emily Dickinson's Reception in the 1890s*; Klaus Lubbers, *Emily Dickinson: The Critical Revolution*.

Marietta Messmer

AMBIGUITY   Dickinson's poetry contains many types of ambiguity, including those kinds of enrichment of language William Empson describes and ambiguities by the more commonly understood definition, double meanings that may contain an element of accident.

Dickinson uses puns frequently, providing a layered poem. Syntactic* ambiguity often results from her elliptical style. Many of her poems also have open, ambiguous endings that give rise to multiple, often incompatible, but individually defensible readings. Another factor contributing to multiple interpretations is her occasional affectation of a childlike* voice.* Are these poems ingenuous or disingenuous? Moreover, is this question to be answered for all such poems, or is the answer different for each individual case? The ambiguity of the poetry is increased by the circumstance of Dickinson's having provided so many textual variants,* making editors choose from among preferred synonyms and even alternative stanzas. Thus there are both intentional and apparently accidental ambiguities.

Of the recurrent puns, one of the most common is her use of the word "feet" to refer both to physical feet and to metrical feet. She explains and justifies her rebellion against conventional form in P326: "I cannot dance upon my Toes—/ No Man instructed me—." A number of other poems expand this theme, and once identified it can be found in still more. "Sewing" and "sowing" blur and merge in P617: "Till then—dreaming I am sowing / Fetch the seam I missed." The "sowing" might be considered a simple spelling mistake (spelling not being one of Dickinson's strong points), but for the "furrow" earlier in the poem, which suggests a subtle merging of the two activities of sewing and sowing as a metaphor for poetry.* Wordplay may spark double readings as in P328: "And then he drank a Dew / From a convenient Grass" prompts the reader to substitute "adieu" and "glass" for the last words in the lines, enhancing the image.

Open-ended poems like "Because I could not stop for Death—"* (P712) illustrate the possibility of variant readings. After the speaker has passed through scenes that suggest the morning, noon, and evening of life, she concludes that although centuries have passed, the time "Feels shorter than the Day / I first surmised the Horses Heads / Were toward Eternity." The conclusion can be read either as an affirmation of Immortality,* who is, after all, personified as sharing the carriage with the speaker and Death,* or as suggesting merely the telescoping of time into blind eternity at death.

The child poems have a double vision.* P585 ("I like to see it lap the Miles") in its childlike admiration for the locomotive, compared throughout the poem to a horse, may also be read as an ironic comment on "progress" if the enthusiastic voice is perceived as naive and the implication of the horse-train comparison is explored.

Two versions of P216 ("Safe in their Alabaster Chambers"*) illustrate problems of unintentional ambiguity. The second stanza of the first version has a very different tone, an almost playful evocation of the ironic contrast between natural continuity and human death. The second stanza of the second version is startling in its complex, evocative image of the void. Some editors have combined the two, producing a three-stanza poem with a marked inconsistency of tone between the second and third stanzas.

Syntactic leaps and gaps are present throughout Dickinson's work, and, with her idiosyncratic use of punctuation* and capitalization,* they contribute to ambiguity. The lines "Like one in danger, Cautious, / I offered him a Crumb" (P328) may be read with the "Cautious" assigned to the speaker, to the bird,* or perhaps to both.

The various ways in which Dickinson's poems resist closure enhance their appeal to contemporary readers and identify the poet as a precursor of modernism. Her verbal tricks are sometimes playful, sometimes serious attempts to represent the lack of facile answers in her experience. The confusion in meaning caused by multiple versions may represent shifts of thought on questions that preoccupied her.

RECOMMENDED: Richard Benvenuto, "Words within Words: Dickinson's Use of the Dictionary"; Cynthia Griffin Wolff, *Emily Dickinson*.

Janet McCann

AMERICAN DICTIONARY OF THE ENGLISH LANGUAGE   Between 1812 and 1824, Noah Webster* lived in Amherst* while he worked on the dictionary. Published in New York by S. Converse in 1828 in a two-volume quarto edition, Webster's dictionary contained 70,000 words, 12,000 more than earlier dictionaries, and approximately 30,000 new definitions, including scientific,* technical, and vernacular words. An abridged octavo edition, edited by Joseph Worcester in 1829, became a standard dictionary at Amherst Academy* and Mount Holyoke Female Seminary,* attended by Dickinson. Webster published a revised and enlarged two-volume octavo edition of his unabridged 1828 dictionary in New Haven in 1841. In 1844, after Webster's death, J. S. and C. Adams of Amherst, using their imprint, bound unsold sheets of the 1841 edition with a thirty-five-page "Supplement" to the second volume. In 1845 George and Charles Merriam acquired the rights to the remaining unbound sheets and published an imprint that added a six-page addendum to the 1844 Amherst issue. Subsequent editions published by the Merriams, beginning with Chauncey Goodrich's revision in 1847, represent works markedly different from Webster's 1828 and 1841 editions and are not reliable examples of dictionaries like those Dickinson used.

In her second letter to T. W. Higginson* in 1862, Dickinson called her "lexicon" her "only companion" (L261). Though an overstatement, she identified an important source for her poetry, a source also revealed by references in letters and poems to words,* lexicons, and philology. Her poems frequently offer her own definitions of abstractions (e.g., faith,* fame,* and exhilaration). Given Dickinson's creative use of language and sense of the power of words, critics have long turned to dictionaries to understand her poetic practices.

In a letter to Joseph Lyman,* Austin Dickinson* described the family's kitchen table filled with "Webster's big Dictionary," pens, and paper (*Ly* 12). While critics have speculated about which dictionary the poet used, the family dictionary (inscribed by Edward Dickinson* in 1844 and now housed at Harvard's Houghton Library) was the 1844 Amherst imprint of Webster's unabridged 1841 edition. Before its purchase and during her school years, she probably had access to the abridged version of Webster's dictionary recommended by her schools.

Research on Dickinson's use of the 1844 version suggests that by working closely with the dictionary, she used etymons, synonyms, antonyms, and collateral words as well as words located nearby on the dictionary's page to create semantic relationships (termed "webplays" by Hallen) between words in poems and dictionary entries. Given the rarity of both the 1841 and 1844 versions, scholars are often forced to use the more available 1828 edition of the dictionary but should not use editions after Chauncey Goodrich's 1847 revision for the Merriams.

RECOMMENDED: Richard Benvenuto, "Words within Words: Dickinson's Use of the Dictionary"; Willis J. Buckingham, "Emily Dickinson's Dictionary"; Cynthia L. Hallen and Laura M. Harvey, "Translation and the Emily Dickinson Lexicon"; Carlton

Lowenberg, *Emily Dickinson's Textbooks*; Richard Sewall, ed., *The Lyman Letters: New Light on Emily Dickinson and Her Family.*

Jean Carwile Masteller

AMHERST   Dickinsons were associated with Amherst, Massachusetts, from the onset of settlement in 1745. Under the direction of her father and brother, Amherst saw various physical changes during Emily Dickinson's lifetime. The coming of the railroad was an event that Edward Dickinson* did much to ensure, and Austin* later directed the planting of trees, the draining of the Commons, and the planning of Wildwood Cemetery. With the arrival of Irish immigrant families, the town's character became more diverse, yet Amherst retained villagelike qualities that are still evident.

Social life was a prime feature of the poet's references to the town in early correspondence. At eighteen she commented favorably, even enthusiastically, on its stir and bustle: "The last week has been a merry one in Amherst, & notes have flown around like, snowflakes" (L27). Signs of the poet's pleasure in socials and parties disappeared by around 1861; yet when Mabel Todd* came as a newcomer twenty years later, she similarly delighted in the combination of country life with "refined & educated society," noting that "Amherst is in many respects quite ideal" (*Life* 172).

The poet's writings name "Amherst" and "New England" as shorthand for herself as citizen, much as she uses "Mr New Bedford Eliot" (L750) or "our sweet Salem" (L751). Thus when the poet asked, "Do they know that this is 'Amherst'—" (P215), she engaged in self-reference, just as when she styled herself "his Amherst" (L751). It is as if she regarded herself as a character in a Shakespearean* play, with the locative functioning as an act of almost hyperbolic self-dramatization in keeping with that aristocratic sensibility we could attribute to Emily Dickinson as the daughter of a Whig* squire.

A draft of a letter to "Master"* posits "New England" and "Amherst" as interchangeable terms: "Could you come to New England . . . would you come to Amherst—" (L233). When she wrote to Higginson,* declining an invitation, the poet said, "I am uncertain of Boston.* . . . Is it more far to Amherst? You would find a minute Host but a spacious Welcome—" (L316). The "minute Host/spacious Welcome" would apply equally to how Emily Dickinson would style both herself and the town to a new acquaintance.

Emily Dickinson could be quite critical of the piety and gentility that characterized the inhabitants of Amherst, the Connecticut Valley,* and—by extension—New England. Even in her self-description as "see[ing] New Englandly," she offered the synonym "Provincially" (P285). The poet poked fun at the "New England Farmer," described as "punctual" and having "oblique integrity" but (again with reference to vision*) lacking "a Vista vastly warmer" (P1483).

Like her ancestors and immediate family, Emily Dickinson looked out on the landscape of Amherst and lived in the climate of New England. Yet her poetry and letters offer what none of her ancestors did, a record of nearby flowers and fields, roaming birds, and distant hills. Hers was a unique sense of belonging to and in a landscape that others passed unseeing, as appears in the poem she entitled "A Portrait of the Parish" when she sent it to her convalescent nephew (P1407). In that "Field of Stubble," her Amherst is the landscape "often seen— but seldom felt, / On our New England Farms—."

RECOMMENDED: *Life; Years*; Jane Donahue Eberwein, "Dickinson's Local, Global, and Cosmic Perspectives"; Polly Longsworth, *The World of Emily Dickinson*.

Elizabeth Horan

AMHERST ACADEMY   As its incorporation papers state, Amherst Academy was established "for the purpose of promoting morality, piety and religion, and for the instruction of youth in the learned languages, and in such arts and sciences as are usually taught in other Academies." One of New England's many classical schools preparing young persons for higher study, it opened on 6 December 1814, in a three-story brick building on Amity Street. Among its most prominent founders were Noah Webster* and Samuel Fowler Dickinson.* Prominent students included Mary Lyon,* Sylvester Graham, Henry Ward Beecher, and Helen Hunt Jackson.*

Both Emily and Lavinia Dickinson* began studying at the academy in September 1840. In August 1847, Emily's seven years of attendance (with some time lost to ill health) ended. Emily studied in both the English and classical departments, which offered courses in Latin, Greek, German, ancient and modern geography, history, natural and intellectual philosophy, mathematics, chemistry, and rhetoric.*

The academy's religious and moral leanings were evident throughout its program. Two-thirds of the members of the founding board were Congregational* ministers. The majority of principals under whom Dickinson studied were either ordained or training for the ministry. The academy catalog of Emily's first year states, "All the Pupils are also expected regularly to attend Morning and Evening Prayers in the Chapel, and Public Worship at one of the Churches in the village on the Sabbath." Many textbooks, such as Isaac Watt's* *The Improvement of the Mind* and Thomas Cogswell Upham's *Elements of Mental Philosophy*, had a religious orientation.

According to Richard Sewall, the influence of Edward Hitchcock,* the famed geologist of Amherst College,* was pervasive. Thus almost half of Emily's references to her studies reveal enthusiasm for courses in the sciences.* She wrote to Jane Humphrey* that "I am in the class that you used to be in Latin— besides Latin I study History and Botany I like the school very much indeed" (L3) and to Abiah Root* announcing her classes in "Mental Philosophy, Geology, Latin, and Botany" (L6). Though it is unknown whether Dickinson participated, students of the natural sciences were allowed to attend lectures at Amherst College in such subjects as chemistry, natural history and mineralogy, geology, botany, and astronomy.

In 1821, the academy's trustees also founded Amherst College. By the mid-1850s, Amherst College was well established, while Amherst Academy barely functioned. Its building served as meeting place for a variety of purposes. (In 1856, for example, Edward Dickinson sponsored Miss Brewster's School, which met there for a few terms.) When Amherst built its first high school in 1861, the academy closed. The building was sold to the town in 1867 and razed the following year.

RECOMMENDED: Catalogs of the Trustees, Instructors, and Students of Amherst Academy. Special Collections Dept., the Jones Library, Inc., Amherst, MA; Frank Prentice Rand, *The Village of Amherst, a Landmark of Light.* Amherst, MA: Amherst Historical Society, 1958: 42–55; Frederick Tuckerman, *Amherst Academy: A New England School of the Past, 1814–1861.* Amherst, MA: Printed for the Trustees, 1929.

Daniel Lombardo

AMHERST COLLEGE   For three generations, Amherst College played a crucial role in the lives of the Dickinsons. Established in 1821, when Harvard was seen by the Connecticut Valley* as too liberal, the college had as its object "civilizing and evangelizing the world by the classical education of indigent young men of piety and talents." Samuel Fowler Dickinson,* Emily's grandfather, gave years of his life and much of his fortune to its founding. Her father, Edward,* attended the college in its first year, before transferring to Yale. More important, he became its treasurer in 1835, a post he held for thirty-eight years. Emily's brother, Austin,* graduated from Amherst in 1850 and succeeded his father as treasurer in 1873.

On a rise overlooking the town, Amherst College was omnipresent in the cultural and economic life of Amherst. It attracted brilliant minds to its faculty and hosted lecturers like R. W. Emerson,* Bronson Alcott, and others from the fields of science,* politics, and theology. Emily was profoundly influenced by, and had profound differences with, Amherst men, such as Edward Hitchcock,* Heman Humphrey,* and William Stearns.* Dickinson's first known published piece was her valentine* letter (L34, "Magnum bonum, 'harum scarum' ") written to Amherst College student George H. Gould* and published in the *Amherst College Indicator*, February 1850.

While attending Amherst Academy* (1840–1847), the poet's association with the college community deepened. The academy and college shared trustees, and most of the former's teachers were graduates of the latter. Moreover, it is likely that Dickinson attended Amherst College lectures, which were open to students of the Academy—male and female alike. At least one connection made at this time had lasting effects on Dickinson's poetry. As Richard Sewall points out in "Science and the Poet: Emily Dickinson's Herbarium and 'The Clue Divine,' " Dickinson read with great appreciation and may have attended the lectures of Edward Hitchcock, botanist, geologist, astronomer, and president of Amherst College.

RECOMMENDED: Claude Moore Fuess, *Amherst: The Story of a New England College.* Boston: Little, Brown, 1935; William Gardiner Hammond, *Remembrance of Am-*

herst: An Undergraduate's Diary, 1846–1848. Ed. George F. Whicher. New York: Columbia University Press, 1946; W. S. Tyler, *History of Amherst College during Its First Half Century, 1821–1871.* Springfield, MA: Clark W. Bryan, 1873.

Daniel Lombardo

ANTHON, CATHERINE (SCOTT) TURNER (1831–1917) was the recipient of five extant Dickinson letters and a number of poems. The recently widowed Kate Scott first met the poet in Amherst* in 1859 while visiting Susan Dickinson,* her former Utica Female Academy schoolmate. A friendship developed during Anthon's later visits in the 1860s, but the women's close acquaintance apparently ended with Scott's second marriage in 1866. Dickinson's letters* to "Condor Kate" (L222), which in their playful intimacy bear a rhetorical* resemblance to the earlier correspondence with Jane Humphrey* and Abiah Root,* form the basis of Rebecca Patterson's controversial thesis that the two women were lovers. (*See*: Lesbian Approaches)

RECOMMENDED: *Letters*; Rebecca Patterson, *The Riddle of Emily Dickinson.*

Robert McClure Smith

APHORISM The history of rhetoric* recognizes no stable distinction between aphorism and other pithy, memorable, and generalized forms of expression: proverb, gnome, sentence, and so on. Equally shadowy is the difference between prose aphorism and poetic epigram, since the latter, in the great English tradition of Jonson and Herrick, reproduces the "point," the sharp focus, of Martial's Latin grammar through the use of poetic rhyme* and meter.

Emily Dickinson's lifelong bent for condensed and oracular statement falls in line with the generic uncertainty bequeathed to us, and her, by history. It is impossible to place a single source, old or new, high or low, at the center of her aphoristic practice. Thus William H. Shurr includes under *New Poems* hundreds of "fourteener epigrams," "trimeters," and short "riddles" culled from her prose, and some of her brief freestanding "verses" are formally irregular. She inherited the tradition in all its flexibility.

Whatever its form, an aphorism or epigram works on the basis of three qualities evident in many Dickinson poems (e.g., P185, " 'Faith' is a fine invention"): generalization, compression,* and memorability. The meaning of an aphorism should be so broad that it comes across as folklore or established wisdom rather than personal observation. The expression should be compressed beyond the point of immediate accessibility; an aphorism should require figuring out and thus promote reflection. The form should be memorable—balanced, clever, or vivid. The pontification characteristic of aphorism is often leavened by wit or self-parodying irony, as in P1641, "Betrothed to Righteousness might be."

More important than Dickinson's incessant production of verse and prose aphorisms is the centrality of the aphoristic spirit to her art. Many of her poems, like "Publication—is the Auction" (P709), begin with aphorisms and then reflect on, and unfold, them. Others, like "To pile like Thunder to it's close" (P1247), come to powerful aphoristic conclusions. Some are logical, some witty and rhetorical, and some vividly imagistic.

In Dickinson's rhetorical milieu, as defined by the textbooks in use at Amherst Academy* and Mount Holyoke Female Seminary,* liveliness was a key discursive goal, and she used the full range of aphoristic techniques to make her verse more "alive." She also used aphorism to add wit, authority, and conclusiveness to her pronouncements. Indeed, to an important extent it is because Emily Dickinson is a surpassingly great aphorist that she is a great poet.

RECOMMENDED: Karl Keller, *The Only Kangaroo among the Beauty: Emily Dickinson and America*, ch. 6; Carlton Lowenberg, *Emily Dickinson's Textbooks*; William H. Shurr, ed., *New Poems of Emily Dickinson*.

Bryan C. Short

"Apparently with no surprise" (P1624)   was written about 1884, a few years before Emily Dickinson's death. Titled "Death and Life," it was separated into two quatrains in *Poems* (1890).* She may have written it remembering when the family gardener said, "Squire, ef the Frost is the Lord's Will, I dont propose to stan in the way of it" (L692) in reaction against her father's urging him to harvest winter vegetables before frost would fall.

There are typically Dickinsonian ambiguous* expressions and ironic humor,* though this is ostensibly a familiar autumn scene representing nature's* relentless process. Even the first word, "Apparently," is ambiguous. Either the innocent flowers apparently accept their death by whimsical force, or the poor flowers are apparently not given time to know danger. "At its play" may also have two meanings. Frost kills flowers while it is playing or while flowers are playing, or frost kills flowers and is likewise killed by the unsympathetic sun. Both forces can be personified as "blonde Assassin." "The Sun proceeds unmoved" is a very interesting and important expression or pun. The sun is emotionally unmoved to see frozen flowers, though it is too late to save the flowers' life by the power that can melt frost and that moves forward to measure out the day for God,* who controls everything except the sun's movement. God seems only to approve of the natural process.

Unlike Melville in *Moby-Dick*, Dickinson does not write about sudden death seriously. Her generally regular stanzas and meter give the poem a gentle, easy feel. She also uses plays on words, comical personification, and a detached point of view to emphasize God's inexplicable cruelty that befalls man as well as nature. From the perspective of a religious critic,* this poem addresses the problem of Job; from that of a feminist* critic, however, it can also be read in terms of the struggle between female fertility and potentially destructive male power.

RECOMMENDED: Charles R. Anderson, *Emily Dickinson's Poetry: Stairway of Surprise*; Wendy Barker, *Lunacy of Light: Emily Dickinson and the Experience of Metaphor*; Betsy Erkkila, "Emily Dickinson on Her Own Terms"; Inder Nath Kher, *The Landscape of Absence: Emily Dickinson's Poetry*; Cynthia Griffin Wolff, *Emily Dickinson*.

Michiko Iwata

ASIAN RESPONSES TO DICKINSON (outside Japan) Dickinson's poetry has aroused varying degrees of interest in Asia, with Indian scholars emerging as the most prolific producers of works relating to her. C. Vimala Rao suggests that the universality of themes such as nature,* life, love,* death,* and immortality* renders Dickinson's poetry accessible to all. N. Sahal hypothesizes that Dickinson's refusal to publish* all her poems during her lifetime represents a modesty that followers of Eastern religions find attractive. In 1961, C. D. Narasimhaiah urged Indians to worry less about translation issues and more about formulating a recognizably Indian response to Dickinson's work. Salamatullah Khan theorizes that Dickinson's attitude toward death, symbolized by her ability to write of a funeral procession transformed into a bridal procession, is characteristic of her work and especially appealing to the Oriental mind-set.

This may help explain the growing interest in Dickinson's poetry in the People's Republic of China, Hong Kong, and Taiwan. Several editions of Dickinson's poetry have been published in book form in the People's Republic of China, and in December 1995, seven of her poems appeared in *Readers*, a Chinese periodical that reaches an audience of 48.8 million. Dickinson has been the subject of several B.A. and M.A. theses in that country. However, a complete edition of her poems has not yet appeared in Chinese, and only a pamphlet-sized publication has been released in Hong Kong. Thai scholar Chanthana Chaichit has reported that the Vietnamese have been studying Dickinson since the 1960s, and Koreans have been writing about her since 1986. In Thailand, Dickinson has been taught in universities and studied since 1979, and some of her poetry appeared on-screen during program breaks on an international cable television channel. (*See*: Canadian, Japanese Responses)

RECOMMENDED: Chanthana Chaichit, "Emily Dickinson Abroad: The Paradox of Seclusion"; Salamatullah Khan, "Emily Dickinson on Death"; Temple Peng, "Singing Along with Great Masters"; C. Vimala Rao, "The Poetry of Emily Dickinson"; N. Sahal, "Emily Dickinson on Renown."

Susan Biscella

THE ATLANTIC MONTHLY, A MAGAZINE OF LITERATURE, SCIENCE, ART, AND POLITICS came to the Dickinson household from its first issue in 1857 through 1886, the year of the poet's death. Editors included James Russell Lowell, James T. Fields, William Dean Howells,* and Thomas Bailey Aldrich.* Among its prominent contributors were Ralph Waldo Emerson,* Henry Thoreau,* Louis Agassiz, Henry James, Oliver Wendell Holmes, Lydia Maria Child, Rebecca Harding Davis, and Harriet Beecher Stowe.* In April 1862 Dickinson initiated her friendship with Thomas Wentworth Higginson,* who wrote regularly for the *Atlantic* (e.g., "Negro Spirituals," "The Greek Goddesses," "Sappho," "An Evening with Mrs. Hawthorne"), when she responded to his "Letter to a Young Contributor" published in the April issue.

Intellectually and socially progressive, the *Atlantic* featured substantial essays on artists and philosophers from the canonical (Dante, Shakespeare,* the Elizabethans) to the contemporary with extensive coverage of nineteenth-century American, English, and European writers (including "Charles Baudelaire, Poet of the Malign" in 1868). Its articles on critical social issues ranged from "Outside Glimpses of English Poverty," "Reconstruction and Negro Suffrage," and "Various Aspects of the Woman Question" in the 1860s, through "Immigration," "The Righteousness of Money-Making," and "The Relations of Labor and Capital" in the 1870s, to "Caste in American Society," "The Rapid Progress of Communism," and "Some Phases of Idealism in New England" in the 1880s. Extensive coverage of religion featured such titles as "The Saints and Their Bodies" (1857), "The Eleusinia" (1859), "The Confessions of a Medium" (1860), "The Jesuits in North America" (1867), "Buddhism; or, the Protestantism of the East" (1868), "Mohammed and His Place in Universal History" (1869), "The Trustworthiness of Hebrew Tradition" (1883), and "The Religious Aspect of Philosophy" (1885). Essays on nature included "Weak Lungs and How to Make Them Stronger" (1863), "The Darwinian Theory" (1866), "The Blue Jay Family" (1870), "Can a Bird Reason?" (1871), and "Volcanoes" (1883). The *Atlantic* also featured fiction and poetry (including Nathaniel Hawthorne's* *The Dolliver Romance* and Henry James' *The American, The Europeans*, and *The Portrait of a Lady*), along with extensive literary notices and book reviews that contributed to Dickinson's reading formation. (*See*: Bibliography for books and reading)

Joan Kirkby

AUSTIN   Dickinson, William Austin

B

BATES, ARLO (1850–1918)   New England poet, critic, editor, author of grammar books, professor at the Massachusetts Institute of Technology, and house reader for Roberts Brothers,* Bates was invited by Thomas Niles* to provide an appraisal for the manuscript of *Poems* (1890).* Balancing his censure for technical imperfections with praise for the "originality," "power," and "genius" of Dickinson's thoughts, he reported to Niles: "There is hardly one of these poems which does not bear marks of unusual and remarkable talent; there is hardly one of them which is not marked by an extraordinary crudity of workmanship" (*AB* 52). He cut the editors' original selection (ca. 200 poems) in half (objecting primarily to instances of playful tone and semantic repetition), insisted on some "absolutely necessary" changes, and recommended printing a small number of carefully edited copies. This mixture of praise and critique is also echoed in his later reviews, which moved from formal criticism to an admiration for the "gleam of genuine original power, of imagination, and of real emotional thought" while quoting appreciatively from thirteen poems on nature,* love,* life, and religion* (Buckingham 29). In addition to granting Dickinson's poems the status of a "new species of art," Bates was the first to situate her within a nineteenth-century American literary and cultural context, explaining her technical imperfections—like Whitman's*—as inextricably linked to America's rapid intellectual development. (*See*: Critical Reception)

RECOMMENDED: *AB*; Willis J. Buckingham, ed., *Emily Dickinson's Reception in the 1890s: A Documentary History*; R. W. Franklin, *The Editing of Emily Dickinson: A Reconsideration*.

Marietta Messmer

"**Because I could not stop for Death—**" (**P712**)   was first published in *Poems* (1890),* edited by Mabel Loomis Todd* and Thomas Wentworth Higginson.* The editors titled it "The Chariot," omitted the poem's fourth stanza, and changed the wording of four lines. Subsequent reprintings continued to omit the fourth stanza and change Dickinson's wording until Thomas H. Johnson's* 1955 *The Poems of Emily Dickinson,** which restored the fourth stanza and the wording of the handwritten* copy in Fascicle* 23 but did not follow the poet's original lineation (Appendix A).

For most modern readers, the long-omitted fourth stanza contains the emotional center and the turning point of this poem. Beginning as a properly Victorian romance, in which the speaker describes the moment of death* as a leisurely carriage ride and "Death" as a kind suitor, the poem later takes on gothic* elements of suspense.

The first three stanzas portray the moment of death as genteel, complete with chaperon ("Immortality"*) to ensure the speaker's safety from any untoward advance. In the fourth stanza, however, the speaker sees her situation differently. First, she realizes that it is the "Setting Sun" that passes her, rather than they who proceed: this realization calls the fiction* of the carriage ride into question. Second, the speaker realizes that she is inappropriately dressed: her "Gossamer" gown and "Tulle" tippet (materials suggesting both wedding apparel and a shroud) do not keep her warm. The physical "chill" she announces here suggests that death may also be more chilling in other ways than she had anticipated. The final two stanzas present the carriage "paused" before a grave* and then the speaker reflecting that this pause seems to have lasted for "Centuries"—a period that, despite its length, "Feels shorter than the Day" on which she "surmised" that the horses were pointed "toward Eternity" but not apparently getting any closer.

This poem's haunting quality stems from its never fully articulated suspicion that Death's courtship may never lead beyond the limbo of the grave, that is, that Death may be as sinister as "He" is suave. The "Horses Heads" remain "toward Eternity—"; but, as there is no evidence that they will arrive, even that good chaperon "Immortality" may not deliver the clarity and comfort promised in Victorian accounts of Christian death or marriage* with God. Dickinson makes no overt claim that death is frightening or heaven* unreachable, but she effectively undercuts the apparent calm certainties of the first three stanzas through the understated "chill" of the final three.

Without the pivotal fourth stanza, one might read this poem as a genteel portrait of a courtly Death: the unsettling "surmise" of the final stanza does not resonate so fully because it is not anticipated by the speaker's earlier realization that she has been inadequately prepared and that her carriage no longer moves. With the fourth stanza, one must read the poem's beginning as ironic. The poem becomes a satiric portrait of Victorian gentility and repression, in which even the terror of eternal displacement in death is shown as an ambiguously represented possible jilting by a gothic suitor, who appears to follow all the rules of propriety but, in fact, abandons his brides to endless limbo, never bringing them to the promised wedding ceremony and new family fold.

RECOMMENDED: Vivian Pollak, *Dickinson: The Anxiety of Gender*; Barton Levi St. Armand, *Emily Dickinson and Her Culture: The Soul's Society*; Martha Nell Smith, "The Poet as Cartoonist"; Daneen Wardrop, *Emily Dickinson's Gothic: Goblin with a Gauge.*

Cristanne Miller

BIANCHI, MARTHA GILBERT DICKINSON (Mattie) (1866–1943)

Martha Gilbert Dickinson Bianchi, daughter of Austin* and Susan Dickinson* and the poet's niece, was an intimate part of Emily's life for nearly twenty years. Among those "who saw [Emily] face to face in her later years of seclusion" (*FF* xxii), she was the most prolific writer. As a family member and as the poet's editor* and biographer, Martha's role is significant.

Mattie, or Madame Bianchi, as she came to be known, was born in Amherst* and educated there at the private schools of Miss Howland (1879–1880) and Miss Marsh (1882–1883) and by tutors from Amherst College.* After attending Miss Porter's School in Farmington, Connecticut (1884–1885), she studied music at the Smith College School of Music (1885–1889).

In the Dickinson genealogy, Mattie holds the distinction of being the last of the Edward Dickinson* line. Her older brother Edward* never married and died of a heart attack at the age of thirty-seven. Another brother, Gilbert,* died at eight of typhoid fever. The poet's letters give insight into this only niece's development. She characterized the little girl at three as "stern and lovely—literary, they tell me—a graduate of Mother Goose and otherwise ambitious" (L333). A wry comment in an 1877 letter* reflects something of Mattie's relationship with her father at the age of ten: "Austin said he was much ashamed of Mattie [after a visit to the Hollands*]—and she was much ashamed of him, she imparted to us. They are a weird couple" (L492). In June 1885, Emily said of Mattie that she "fast becomes an imperial Girl" (L987).

In a letter to Mattie on 7 October 1884, Ned described his sister as having very little of "the infernal Dickinson reserve" and commented, "thank the Lord for that" (St. Armand 377). Mattie's life would prove this true, from her accomplishments as a musician (studying for four years with noted teacher Agnes Morgan in New York), to her marriage to, and travels with, Count Alexander Bianchi.

Although her love of Amherst is unquestioned, Martha sought wider circles. In 1902, she and her mother left home to spend a year in Europe. Friends read in the newspapers that on 26 July, while in Dresden, she had married a captain of the Russian Imperial Horse Guards stationed in St. Petersburg. The couple had actually married in Carlsbad, Bohemia, on 19 July. Born in Odessa in 1873, "Count" Alexander Bianchi was transferred to Boston* in 1903, and the couple reached Amherst that fall. Later Amherst Town Directories list Alexander and Martha Bianchi as living in the Evergreens* on Main Street, but the count is never listed as a resident taxpayer. He became the source of much local speculation, some of it spurious. According to a contemporary, Smith College English professor Mary Jordan, Bianchi posed as a Russian but was actually an Austro-Italian. Alexander Bianchi spent time in a New York jail on fraud charges in 1907. He abandoned his marriage the next year, and Martha divorced him in 1920.

In the early 1890s, well before her European ventures, Martha began publishing poetry in magazines such as *Harper's,** *The Century, The Atlantic Monthly,** and *Scribner's.** In 1899, *Within the Hedge*, the first of her many books, appeared. Others include *The Cathedral* (1901), *The Cuckoo's Nest* (1909), *A Cossack Lover* (1911), and *The Wandering Eros* (1925). The latter includes "T. G. D.—'Deare Childe,' " dedicated to Gilbert's memory; the poem ends: "Gone back to dust—/ Or infinitely on—somewhere—/ All that was love and eagerness / And golden hair."

Bianchi's most important literary contributions, however, began with the publication of *The Single Hound: Poems of a Lifetime by Emily Dickinson** (1914), the first book of Dickinson poems since Mabel Loomis Todd's* *Poems by Emily Dickinson, Third Series** (1896). Martha essentially began a revival of her aunt's posthumous literary career with this book, which collected poems sent to Martha's mother, Sue, and other members of the family. In 1924 she published *The Life and Letters of Emily Dickinson** and *Complete Poems of Emily Dickinson.** The latter collected the body of work that had appeared thus far.

After Lavinia Dickinson's* death in 1899, Martha inherited the poetry that had remained in Lavinia's possession. From these manuscripts, she and Alfred Leete Hampson* published *Further Poems of Emily Dickinson: Withheld from Publication by Her Sister Lavinia** (1929), *The Poems of Emily Dickinson, Centenary Edition** (1930), and *Unpublished Poems of Emily Dickinson** (1935). Bianchi's *Emily Dickinson Face to Face** (1932) included unpublished letters and Martha's substantial reminiscences. Thus Martha Dickinson Bianchi shaped the popular and critical interest in Dickinson for the first third of the twentieth century.

Martha's relationship with her aunt gave her unique access: "My first definite memory of my Aunt Emily," she wrote, "is of her coming to the door to meet me in her white dress—looking to me just like another little girl—when I was to be left with her for safe-keeping on Sunday mornings while the grown-ups of both households went to church. . . . On regular days she was quicksilver. On Sunday, by some divine law of the holy day, she was mine" (*FF* 3–4).

For Martha, her aunt was a simple, unself-conscious, natural poet, without a thought as to who she was, how she related to the world, or what the world thought of her. One of Martha's strongest images is of Emily in "her flying wild hours of inward rapture over a beauty perceived or a winged word" (*LL* 5). Whatever complexity she saw in the poet was, she felt, caused by terror of the evil that might "overtake her loved ones." The niece's perspective was condensed into the following portrait: "Before one thinks of her as a poet and philosopher or mystic, one must in honesty remember her as an adoring and devoted daughter, a sister loyal to blows, a real nun of the home, without affectation or ritual beyond that of her gentle daily task, and all that she could devise of loving addition to the simple sum'' (*LL* 4).

Through much of her adult life, Martha spent winters in New York or abroad and summers in Amherst. When she died in New York City after an attack of influenza, her will left the Evergreens and its contents (including all Dickinson manuscripts and memorabilia) to Alfred Leete Hampson, her literary assistant. The will's stipulation, however, that the house be razed when no longer occupied by Hampson and his family was later overturned in court. The Dickinson papers in the Evergreens (the largest collection then extant) were sold by Hampson to attorney Gilbert H. Montague, who transferred them to the Houghton Library of Harvard University in 1950. When Mary Hampson,* who had lived alone in the house after her husband's death in 1952, died in 1988, her will established the Martha Dickinson Bianchi Trust to preserve the Evergreens as a charitable and cultural facility associated with the work of Martha Dickinson Bianchi.

RECOMMENDED: *FF; LL*; Elizabeth Horan, ''To Market: The Dickinson Copyright Wars''; Barton Levi St. Armand, '' 'Your Prodigal': Letters from Ned Dickinson, 1879–1885.''

Daniel Lombardo

THE BIBLE   Though almost any educated New Englander of the mid-nineteenth century could be expected to know the Bible well, Emily Dickinson's ''knowledge of certain sections of the Bible, especially the Gospels,'' says Jack Capps, ''was extraordinary'' (41). Biblical ideas, subjects, allusions, and imagery abound in her work. As Capps' *Emily Dickinson's Reading: 1836–1886* (1966) demonstrates, ''biblical quotations in her letters and poems far exceed references to any other source or author'' (30). Often inexact or deliberately altered, these quotations reveal not only a deep familiarity with Scripture that resulted from lifelong study, but also, as Richard Sewall noted, ''a recklessness and humor* quite unbecoming her time and station'' (*Life* 700). One of her last letters to Thomas Wentworth Higginson,* for example, inverts Jacob's demand of the angel with whom he had wrestled all night: ''Audacity of Bliss, said Jacob to the Angel 'I will not let thee go except I bless thee'—Pugilist and Poet, Jacob was correct—'' (L1042). Three poems that mention Moses question God's* fairness in denying his entry into Canaan after he had led God's people there (P168, 597, 1201). In a poem given a draft title ''Diagnosis of the Bible, by a Boy,'' Dickinson described the Bible as ''an antique Volume—/ Written by faded Men / At the suggestion of Holy Spectres—'' and suggested that didactic Bible stories could use ''a warbling Teller—'' (P1545).

In questioning the Bible's literary style, Dickinson may not have been so out of touch with her time as Sewall suggests. During her lifetime, biblical scholarship was shifting from the textual analysis that came to be called ''lower criticism'' to a ''higher'' form that applied scientific methods to the reading of Scripture. The more radical of the scholars in the higher biblical criticism movement asserted that, far from being the received Word of God, the Bible was instead a sometimes flawed record of Hebrew experience. Yet Dickinson need not have read D. F. Strauss' controversial *Life of Jesus* (translated in 1846 by favorite author George Eliot*) to find support for her close readings of Scripture. Such encouragement could be found in the more conventional texts in her family library, such as William Jenks' *A Companion to the Bible* (1838), which included "A Guide to the Reading and Study of the Bible; being a Comprehensive Digest of the Principles and Details of Biblical Criticism, Interpretation, Theology, History, Natural Science, Usages, Etc."

Rather than leading her to reject the Bible as useless or inaccurate, Dickinson's careful reading may have caused her to see it as a boon companion. In a letter to Joseph Lyman,* Dickinson wrote, "Some years after we saw each other last I fell to reading the Old & New Testament. I had known it as an arid book but looking I saw how infinitely wise & how merry it is" (*Ly* 73). In other letters she characterized the Bible as speaking "portentously" (L558), "joyously" (L796), "boyishly" (L889), even "roguishly" (L562). For Dickinson, it seems, the Word* had indeed been "made Flesh," that it "dwelt among us" was a "loved Philology" (P1651).

Critics differ widely in their assessment of Dickinson's use of Scripture in her life and work. Some view her questioning approaches as evidence that she rejected traditional Christianity entirely. Others identify that apparent irreverence as following in the tradition of mystics and other Christian poets, whose work reflects an intimacy with God that allows serious, probing questions, mockery, even rage, as attempts to comprehend God's purpose and word. Still others try to find a middle ground between these two views. Dickinson put the Bible to so many and varied uses that it may be impossible to codify her approach.

There can be no question, however, that the Bible was an important source for her. When asked by Higginson in 1862 to identify her favorite reading, Dickinson singled out from the Bible the Revelation of St. John the Divine (L261). As Rebecca Patterson's *Emily Dickinson's Imagery* reveals, Dickinson seems to have been especially fond of Chapter 21, the "Gem Chapter." Given Dickinson's interest in heaven,* this fondness is not surprising. If the number of allusions is any indication, other favorite books included the Gospels, especially Matthew, which figures in the poems and letters more than twice as often as any other biblical book. Most frequently used from the Old Testament are Genesis, Exodus (the clear favorites for poetic subjects), Psalms, and Isaiah.

In addition to identifying and exploring the many allusions to Scripture in her letters* and poems, several critics have suggested that Dickinson's language, even her syntax,* is biblical. In *Emily Dickinson: An Interpretive Biography*, Thomas Johnson* asserts, "Even when she draws her figures of speech from the language of the sea, of trade, of law, or of science,* they usually suggest that they have passed through the alembic of the King James version of biblical utterance" (151). Capps concludes that Dickinson's "affinity for Scripture is reflected in her choice of words* and metaphors* as well as in her aphoristic* style'' (58). Cristanne Miller notes a number of stylistic parallels between Dickinson's grammar and that of the King James Bible. Beth Doriani traces Dickinson's ''prophetic voice'' to its roots in biblical prophecy.*

In a letter written less than two years before her death, Dickinson declared, ''The Bible dealt with the Centre, not with the Circumference*—'' (L950). Among the books now housed in the Dickinson collection at the Houghton Library of Harvard University, Capps lists an 1843 Bible inscribed, ''Emily E. Dickinson a present from her Father 1844'' (Capps 148). Well-thumbed, even mutilated in places, this Bible withstood a lifetime of study and serves now as a tangible reminder that the Bible stood at the center of Emily Dickinson's life and work. (*See*: Congregationalism; Faith; Religion)

RECOMMENDED: Peggy Anderson, ''The Bride of the White Election: A New Look at Biblical Influence on Emily Dickinson''; Beth Maclay Doriani, *Emily Dickinson, Daughter of Prophecy*; Thomas H. Johnson, *Emily Dickinson: An Interpretive Biography*; Cristanne Miller, *Emily Dickinson: A Poet's Grammar*; Rebecca Patterson, *Emily Dickinson's Imagery*; Dorothy Huff Oberhaus, '' 'Tender Pioneer': Emily Dickinson's Poems on the Life of Christ.''

Emily Seelbinder

BINGHAM, MILLICENT TODD (1880–1968)   Between 1945 and 1955 Mrs. Bingham published one volume of Dickinson's poems and three biographical studies that added substantially to what was known about the poet. Raised in Amherst* from age two and often in the Dickinson Homestead* as a child, Bingham brought to her work firsthand knowledge of personalities and circumstances surrounding the poet and an unusual relationship to the Dickinson family.

Bingham's father, David Peck Todd, professor of astronomy at Amherst College* from 1880 to 1920, was a friend of college treasurer Austin Dickinson,* the poet's brother. Bingham's mother, Mabel Loomis Todd,* was even more intimate with Mr. Dickinson. The passionate, clandestine love affair this winsome, multitalented woman conducted with Austin from 1881 to 1895 aroused no jealousy in her husband but attracted considerable enmity from Austin's family and cast an incomprehensible pall on Millicent Todd's childhood, by her later account. Two years after the poet's 1886 death, Mrs. Todd began a ten-year involvement in editing* and publishing Dickinson's poems and letters, work that dominated the Todd household during Millicent's upbringing.

Educated in private schools in Amherst, Millicent also made lengthy visits in Washington, D.C.,* with her maternal grandparents, Eben J. and Mary (Molly) Wilder Loomis.* She absorbed Eben's strong amateur interest in the natural sciences and Molly's old-fashioned moral rigidities, although the latter instilled lifelong uneasiness toward her parents' values. Protected from notoriety surrounding her mother's 1898 lawsuit with the Dickinson family by being sent away to school, Millicent subsequently attended Vassar College and graduated a member of Phi Beta Kappa in 1902.

For three following decades Millicent thought and heard little about Dickinsons. She was engaged in accompanying her father on astronomical expeditions to the Dutch East Indies, Tripoli, Chile, and Russia, in teaching French at Vassar and Wellesley colleges, and in studying in Paris and Germany. She also earned her master's degree in geography from Radcliffe in 1917 and a doctorate in geography from Harvard in 1923. Between these two degrees, Millicent spent a year in France teaching French to American soldiers and helping in a World War I field hospital. In 1919, when her father was eased off the Amherst faculty because of increasingly bizarre behavior that led to his eventual institutionalization, she helped her mother, partially paralyzed from a 1913 stroke, move the family home to Florida. In addition, in 1920 she married Walter VanDyke Bingham, a psychologist with the Carnegie Institution.

Mabel Todd had stored away the Dickinson materials in her possession after 1898 but in 1931 was provoked by Martha Dickinson Bianchi's* misrepresentations of her role in editing Dickinson's poetry into republishing, with Millicent's help, an expanded version of her *Letters of Emily Dickinson* (1894). When Mabel died the following year, Millicent assumed her mother's agenda of publishing the rest of Todd's Dickinson holdings. She avoided the disturbing evidence of her mother's love affair among these materials in preparing manuscripts for *Ancestors' Brocades: The Literary Debut of Emily Dickinson* and *Bolts of Melody: New Poems of Emily Dickinson.** Both publications were delayed by Harper until 1945, after Bianchi's death, when copyright challenge was less chancy, for Bingham and Bianchi each claimed rights to Dickinson's poems.

Harvard University acquired Bianchi's Dickinson materials in 1950 and began pressuring Bingham for the manuscripts in her possession so that Thomas H. Johnson* could edit Dickinson's poems and letters under Harvard's imprint. Bingham's resistance, which she termed "The Deadlock," persisted while she completed two biographical studies: *Emily Dickinson: A Revelation,** in which she disclosed the poet's late love affair with Judge Otis Phillips Lord,* and *Emily Dickinson's Home*, an authoritative account of the poet's family life and physical milieu based on Dickinson family documents. Both were published in 1955, after she had provided Harvard with photocopies of her Dickinson manuscripts and had acknowledged (but publicly challenged) the university's copyright claim. She gave her Dickinson manuscripts themselves to Amherst College.

To divest herself of her mother's "shameful" love affair, which had "hung as a shadow over me all my life," Bingham gave her own family papers to Yale before she died in 1968, entrusting Mabel and Austin's love letters to Richard B. Sewall for his 1974 biography, *The Life of Emily Dickinson*. Bingham felt her struggle "to set the record straight" had been a torturous one, that "Dickinsons have reached into every crevice of my life."

RECOMMENDED: Polly Longsworth, "Millicent Todd Bingham (1880–1968)." *Emily Dickinson International Society Bulletin* 6, 2 (1994): 4+; Millicent Todd Bingham Papers, Yale University.

Polly Longsworth

BIOGRAPHICAL SCHOLARSHIP As of the end of the twentieth century, biographies of Emily Dickinson fall into four chronological groups, each with a characteristic emphasis.

The Earliest Studies. Until about 1930 the predominant tone was set by Susan Dickinson's* *Springfield Republican** obituary and Mabel Loomis Todd's* lectures. As Klaus Lubbers demonstrated in *Emily Dickinson: The Critical Revolution*, Dickinson's earliest readers were most attracted to her sentimental* poems, and the earliest biographers reinforced this predilection. In the first full-length study, Martha Dickinson Bianchi's* *Life and Letters** (1924), the sweet cartoon figure of "Our Emily" takes its completed form as summarized by Jay Leyda: "unaware of community and nation, never seeing anyone, never wearing any color but white, never doing any housework beyond baking batches of cookies for secret delivery to favorite children . . . jotting down little verses that help to keep alive the great love she renounced many, many years since" (*Years* xx). This creature, created by a process of altering dates and withholding information, was a work of biographical art comparable to the retouched daguerreotype* of her aunt that Bianchi presented as the family's preferred image.

Biographies of the Modernist Period. Associating Emily Dickinson with Isadora Duncan, Hart Crane's *The Bridge* (1930) may be taken as a representative reading during the years when, as Lubbers observes, Dickinson began being read by people who were also reading T. S. Eliot. In the same year two other poets produced desentimentalized biographies that still have some value: Josephine Pollitt's *Emily Dickinson: The Human Background of Her Poetry* and Genevieve Taggard's *The Life and Mind of Emily Dickinson*. But the two masterpieces of this generation, Allen Tate's "Emily Dickinson" (1932) and George Frisbie Whicher's *This Was a Poet: A Critical Biography of Emily Dickinson* (1938), achieved their enduring power by referring Dickinson to what was now perceivable as a vanished past. Envisioning nineteenth-century New England as a culture, Tate and Whicher read Dickinson's language as a translation of that culture's meanings into words.

Johnson, Leyda, and Sewall. Thomas H. Johnson's* *Emily Dickinson: An Interpretive Biography* (1955) derives in obvious ways from Whicher's book. But by giving readers Dickinson's actual words* for the first time, Johnson's editions of the poems and letters instantly rendered Whicher and every other biographer obsolete. At about the same time, Millicent Todd Bingham's* studies in history and documentation were bringing much valuable material to light.

The major biographical result took the form of two massive, fundamentally different biographies. Leyda's *The Years and Hours of Emily Dickinson* (1960) is a fascinating trove of raw data: everything Leyda could find about Dickinson and her world, laid out on the page in chronological order, without commentary. Rigorously anti-New Critical,* Leyda's object was to prevent readers from "using [Dickinson's] device as *your* device to make the letters and poems mean what you want them to mean'' (xxii). However, a collection of unmediated facts must necessarily remain sui generis.

Richard Sewall's magisterial *The Life of Emily Dickinson* (1974), for counterexample, undertakes biography's traditional task of presenting its data under interpretation. Building on Bingham's posthumous revelation of her mother's affair with Austin Dickinson,* Sewall chose to write in the style of a Whicher whose historiography has darkened into cultural anthropology.

After Sewall. Since the late 1970s, feminist* rereadings of the biography have helped us to conceive of a Dickinson less fey than we once imagined, more at home in a world of women whose voices we had barely heard before. In the enormous volume of that reinterpretation, the most influential studies were clearly Adrienne Rich's ''Vesuvius at Home'' essay (1976) and Sandra Gilbert and Susan Gubar's *The Madwoman in the Attic* (1979). Overshadowed by the feminist work, Cynthia Griffin Wolff's religiously oriented critical biography, *Emily Dickinson* (1986), seems worthy but old-fashioned. By the 1990s, however, older ways of reading the biography, such as Betsy Erkkila's political analysis in ''Emily Dickinson and Class'' (1992), had thoroughly assimilated feminism's influence.

Nevertheless, Emily Dickinson's life still lies just beyond readability. Susan Howe's narcissistic equation of textual analysis with autobiography in *My Emily Dickinson* (1985) and *The Birth-Mark* (1993) carries the readerly act of identification with the text to its excitingly fanatical extreme, and in her insistence on imputing a specific intertextual meaning to *this* ink mark on *this* manuscript page, read at precisely *this* fugitive moment, Howe certainly shares one of the moods of the poet who said, ''Forever—is composed of Nows'' (P624). But, as we have learned, that is only one mood among many. What remains from a century of biographical scholarship is perhaps only the somehow satisfying news that the life of Emily Dickinson remains definitively unknown. (*See*: Historicism; Reader-Response)

RECOMMENDED: Martha Ackmann, ''Biographical Studies of Emily Dickinson''; Jonathan Morse, ''Memory, Desire, and the Need for Biography: The Case of Emily Dickinson.''

Jonathan Morse

BIRDS   According to *The Poems of Emily Dickinson** edited by T. H. Johnson,* there are around fifty birds used as subjects among Dickinson's 1,775 poems, most of which could have been seen around her Homestead.* The bluebird, blue jay, bobolink, crow, hummingbird, lark, oriole, owl, phoebe, robin, sparrow, woodpecker, and wren are mentioned specifically; however, many other bird poems ignore individual names. She began writing bird poems in her twenties and often included them in letters* (e.g., P5 in L173 to Susan Gilbert* and the well-known P1463 in L770 to Mabel Loomis Todd* when thanking her for a panel of Indian pipes).

Although Dickinson's avian representations are always based on ornithological reality, her treatments of birds sometimes distilled them metaphorically* through gnomic and abstract creative imagery. Her birds sing to imply love,* death,* God,* or other things, the interpretation of which is left to the reader's* imagination.

To T. W. Higginson,* Dickinson wrote, "I had no portrait, now, but am small, like the Wren" (L268), likening her own persona to that bird. Regarding "For every Bird a Nest—" (P143), Eberwein has suggested that the wren, "which was small could rise, especially if nurturing sublime* ambitions" (13). For Dickinson, a hummingbird's flight symbolized elusiveness, as in "A Route of Evanescence" (P1463), which Porter uses to exemplify her kinetic imagery. The destination of her birds is some unknown circumference,* not on the earth. Anderson has said with respect to P328 and 500, "All winged things seemed to her to live in another world" (119).

Bird poems as well as Dickinson's other poems have recently been reexamined from humorous* and feminist* perspectives as well as through psychoanalytic* eyes. For instance, Juhasz reads "Split the Lark—and you'll find the Music—" (P861) in comic terms, while Cody emphasizes that its theme derives from potential Eros.* (*See*: Lesbian Approaches; Nature)

RECOMMENDED: Charles R. Anderson, *Emily Dickinson's Poetry: Stairway of Surprise*; John Cody, *After Great Pain: The Inner Life of Emily Dickinson*; Jane Donahue Eberwein, *Dickinson: Strategies of Limitation*; Suzanne Juhasz, Cristanne Miller, and Martha Nell Smith, *Comic Power in Emily Dickinson*; David T. Porter, *The Art of Emily Dickinson's Early Poetry*.

Midori Ando

BLACK CAKE   Dickinson baked this special fruitcake for the Christmas holidays. An astounding quantity of raisins—Emily used five pounds!—created its density and distinctive dark color. In 1883, the poet sent Mrs. J. Howard Sweetser* a cake sample and the recipe with a thank-you note for flower* bulbs (L835, 835a). William Luce borrowed her list of ingredients and instructions for baking the cake in a milk pan to craft the witty opening of *The Belle of Amherst*. As adapted by Margery Friedman, black cake is served at the annual Dickinson birthday tribute at the Folger Shakespeare Library. (*See*: Dramatic Representations)

RECOMMENDED: *Letters*; Nancy Harris Brose, et al. *Emily Dickinson: Profile of the Poet as Cook with Selected Recipes*. Amherst, MA: Newell, 1976; Margery K. Friedman, "Remembering Emily with Rhyme and Raisins." *Washington Post*, 29 Nov. 1995: E1+.

Jonnie Guerra

BLAKE, WILLIAM (1757–1827)   The complex works of this self-educated, visionary, English engraver-poet-painter did not gain wide critical recognition until the twentieth century. Although Dickinson probably never read Blake, a

diffused Blakean influence may have reached her through R. W. Emerson,*
whose reading of Blake is documented in his journals. Since Thomas Wentworth
Higginson's* comparison of Blake and Dickinson in his preface to the first
edition of her poems in 1890, comparisons of the two poets' visionary* and
epigrammatic qualities have become commonplace in Dickinson criticism.

Among the diverse group of writers who have pointed out Blake–Dickinson
parallels are William Dean Howells,* Christina Rossetti, Hart Crane, Amy Lowell, Louise Bogan, Northrop Frye, Thomas Johnson,* Harold Bloom, and Camille Paglia.

RECOMMENDED: *Life*; Jack Lee Capps, *Emily Dickinson's Reading 1836–1886*;
Michael Ferber, *The Poetry of William Blake*. Harmondsworth: Penguin, 1991; Paul
Ferlazzo, *Critical Essays on Emily Dickinson*.

Rosa Nuckels

"Blazing in Gold and quenching in Purple" (P228)   The prime defining
features of P228 are its dynamic, explosive energy and color that springs to the
eye in words like "Blazing," "Leaping," "tinting," "Leopards," and "Juggler." This poem, originally published in *Drum Beat*,* appeared shortly
thereafter in the 30 March 1864 *Springfield Daily Republican** as "Sunset";
that title, however, misses much, even though it suggests the molten gold just
before the sunset's purple. Higginson's* title for *Poems* (1891),* "The Juggler
of Day," only hints at the poem's essence, which is more narrative than descriptive, even though one hesitates to assert precise correspondences between
that narrative and transitions either in nature or in the mind.

The poem's "Leopards" have the medieval color of heraldry; "old Horizon"
suggests ancient mythology as well as Dickinson's "Circumference"* theme.
For some, the "Otter's Window" may suggest an illustrated tale for children,
though a yet more meaningful link could be the almost surreal "Banks of Noon"
(P328). Yellow and purple images call to mind other Dickinson sunset poems,
especially P1650.

Although the poem's colors are breathtaking in their strength ("Blazing/
quenching") and delicacy ("Touching/tinting"), the key is less painting as col-
oring than as showing the artist's mastery. We have, too, the mastery of the
"Juggler" as artist, whether the performer be Dickinson herself or the sun. The
action of l.7 suggests the artist's satisfaction, nonchalance, and affection. In
"Laying her spotted Face to die," we see humility, also evident in "Stooping
as low." Or perhaps "spotted" is tinged with imperfection, and "Stooping"
refers to the poet's generous condescension. The "spots" may be in the eye of
the beholder, who may also be the speaker, or may refer to spots in the setting
sun.

In l.1 Dickinson may have availed herself of one of the uninflected English
language's greatest resources: the reader's frequent uncertainty as to whether
sentence structures are transitive or intransitive. The primary sense is generally
taken as the intransitive "blazing golden" or "suffused with blazing gold."

However, the artist may also be "blazing/quenching *in*" color as the craftsman might "burn *in*" enamel pigment (cf. P1387, "With spots of Burnish roasted on"). With the poem's final line, 1.1 is seen to have not only its single trajectory (or perhaps the half-trajectory from noon to sunset) but also another rhythm—twin trajectories, corresponding to a juggler's repeated masterly tossing of ball(s), plate(s), or disk(s).

While Johnson's preferred version is more "finished," the poem's textual variants* provide valuable evidence and are satisfying in themselves. Dickinson appears to opt for "Touching" over "Flooding." Even if "oriel window" were shown to be place-specific and grounded in reality, readers might be glad that it was discarded for the bold choice of "Otter's Window." Like Dickinson's greatest poems, P228 satisfyingly defies definitive explication. (*See*: Ambiguity; Appendix A (Fascicle 13), *Complete Poems*; Nature; Time; Visual Arts, as Influence)

RECOMMENDED: Charles R. Anderson, *Emily Dickinson's Poetry: Stairway of Surprise*; Jane Donahue Eberwein, *Dickinson: Strategies of Limitation*; David T. Porter, *The Art of Emily Dickinson's Early Poetry*; Barton Levi St. Armand, *Emily Dickinson and Her Culture: The Soul's Society*.

James Fegan and Haruko Kimura

THE BODY, IN DICKINSON'S POETRY   While one won't find anatomically correct, drawn-to-scale human bodies in Emily Dickinson's works, one will find figurative representations of the body that register subjective experiences of living in a body during the nineteenth century. Critics disagree about the degree to which Dickinson's representations of the body indicate she is capitulating to her era's ideologies of the body and the degree to which she is resisting them. However, most agree that Dickinson's representations of the body propose that the so-called objective human body is a dynamic concept negotiated between real or fantasized individual experiences of the body and contemporary social ideologies.

Robert McClure Smith and Cristanne Miller maintain that Dickinson resists nineteenth-century gender ideology by making her body pervasively present in her works. Smith argues that, despite the Christian doctrine that the spirit should transcend the inferior body, Dickinson insists that the body and mind/spirit draw upon one another for definition. For instance, in "I felt my life with both my hands" (P351), Dickinson represents the soul by invoking human body parts. The bodiless narrator needs the body parts to articulate her new form and to delineate her soul by contrasting it with her bodily form. Just as the body in Dickinson's poetry is the product of the subjective mind, so is the mind a product of the body.

Miller interprets Dickinson's excessive bodies as arising from a tension between her typical experience of self and the culture that defines her "deviant" experiences of self as monstrous. One such excessive body is the volcano in "A still—Volcano—Life" (P601). Here, Dickinson employs the volcano as an absurd and grotesque metaphor* for the sexually potent woman poet. This metaphor offers an image of woman so tremendous it would defy any attempt to reinscribe women in impoverished linguistic terms. Her society might have sought to repress women's bodies, but the pleasures and complex difficulties of living in a nineteenth-century woman's body live as well in Dickinson's poetry. (*See*: Eroticism; Women's Culture)

RECOMMENDED: Sylvia Henneberg, "Neither Lesbian nor Straight: Multiple *Eroticisms* in Emily Dickinson's Love Poetry"; Cristanne Miller, "The Humor of Excess"; Robert McClure Smith, *The Seductions of Emily Dickinson.*

Robin E. Calland

BOLTS OF MELODY: NEW POEMS OF EMILY DICKINSON (1945) Published by Harper & Brothers and coedited by Mabel Loomis Todd* and Millicent Todd Bingham,* this volume introduced 668 poems, about half of which Todd had originally prepared for editing* in the 1890s before her quarrel with Lavinia Dickinson.* Like *Ancestors' Brocades, Bolts of Melody* reasserted Todd's claims as Dickinson editor and interpreter over the recently deceased Martha Dickinson Bianchi.* With readers already prepared to accept Dickinson's stylistic idiosyncrasies, Bingham followed the poet's text more faithfully than her mother had previously felt free to do, and she replaced the four topical categories by which *Poems by Emily Dickinson* (1890, 1891, and 1896)* had been organized with twelve flexibly allusive groupings such as "The Far Theatricals of Day" and "An Ablative Estate." Although *Bolts of Melody* was probably drawn mainly from manuscripts relegated by Todd and T. W. Higginson* to their "C" group of poems judged too unfinished or obscure for early publication, the collection included "Circumference thou Bride of Awe" (P1620), "Four Trees—upon a solitary Acre—" (P742), "I would not paint—a picture—" (P505), "Tell all the Truth but tell it slant—" (P1129), and "The Soul has Bandaged moments—" (P512). Bingham ended the book with "If I should cease to bring a Rose" (P56) in tribute to her deceased mother. Her introduction paid tribute to Todd's pioneering editorial achievements and acknowledged the continuing challenge Dickinson presented for editors and anthologists. Although some poems might be seen as "incomplete, fragmentary, or trivial," Bingham preferred to let posterity select the poet's canon; meanwhile, she declared that "the poems should be given an equal chance at survival." George Frisbie Whicher's prepublication review, excerpted on the book's jacket, hailed this collection (unexpected in light of Bianchi's claims to complete representation of her aunt's poetic legacy) as "the most stunning surprise in the history of American literature."

RECOMMENDED: *AB*; Polly Longsworth, "Millicent Todd Bingham (1880–1968)." *Emily Dickinson International Society Bulletin* 6, 2 (Nov.–Dec. 1994): 4+; Joel Myerson, *Emily Dickinson: A Descriptive Bibliography.*

Jane Donahue Eberwein

BOLTWOOD, LUCIUS and FANNY Neighbors and friends to the Dickinsons and pillars of the Amherst* community. Lucius, a lawyer and one of the founders of Amherst College* along with Samuel Fowler Dickinson,* married Fanny Haskins Shepard, a cousin of Ralph Waldo Emerson,* in 1824. Despite the closeness of the Amherst community, there seems to have been no strong personal tie between Dickinson and the Boltwoods, though the poet did send flowers* and a letter* to Fanny when her son, Charles Upham Boltwood, died in 1880. Charles had been Emily's schoolmate, and she wrote, "I thought the flowers might please him, though he made like Birds,* the exchange of Latitudes" (L363). Letters and notes between the Dickinsons and Boltwoods indicate a neighborly relationship, in which Emily and Lavinia* exchanged household goods with Fanny: butter, pies, peaches, and flowers.

RECOMMENDED: *Letters*; *Years*; Charles F. Carpenter and Edward W. Morehouse. *The History of the Town of Amherst, Massachusetts*. Amherst: Carpenter and Morehouse, 1896.

Sara Eddy

BOOKS AND READING Dickinson shared her culture's reverence for the word* and its power to make the unseen visible. Reading inspires "Conversion of the Mind" (P593). "By Chivalries as tiny, / A Blossom, or a Book, / The seeds of smiles are planted—/ Which blossom in the dark" (P55). A book is a "Bequest of Wings," the bearer of "Liberty" (P1587), a "Frigate," "the Chariot / That bears the Human soul" (P1263); moreover, the word is immortal*: "A Word dropped careless on a Page / May stimulate an eye / When folded in perpetual seam / The Wrinkled Maker lie" (P1261). Dickinson's "Kinsmen of the Shelf" (P604) included her textbooks at Amherst Academy* and Mount Holyoke*; periodicals that came to her house; books borrowed from the local lending library and from friends in her Reading Society; and the Dickinson libraries in the Homestead* and the Evergreens* (now held by Harvard University's Houghton Library and Brown University's John Hay Library in its "Martha Dickinson Bianchi Bequest").

The "Handlist of Books Found in the Home of Emily Dickinson at Amherst, Massachusetts, Spring, 1950" includes almost 900 titles and specifies thirty books "most clearly associated with Emily Dickinson" (including her Bible*; Lexicon; Emerson's poems, given to her by Ben Newton*; Huntington's* *Christian Living and Christian Believing*, given to her by her father), but many more books have pencil markings, pages folded in half, corners turned down that many Dickinson scholars ascribe to Dickinson. The library includes literature with a wide selection of nineteenth-century American, English, and German writers (E. B. Browning's* *Aurora Leigh* is heavily marked, as is von Arnim's *Gunderode*); religious history, sermons, and philosophical works (including Thomas Brown's *Lectures on the Philosophy of the Human Mind*, Edward Hitchcock's* *The Religion of Geology*, Dugald Stewart's *Elements of the Phi-*

losophy of the Human Mind, Thomas Upham's *Principles of the Interior or Hidden Life*); and artists' lives (including Charlotte Brontë,* Michelangelo, and Byron,* which from markings would seem to have been of particular interest to Dickinson); miscellanies—collections of essays and poems on diverse topics having a particular affinity with the vast, diverse, kaleidoscopic nature of Dickinson's project, including *Salad for the Solitary* by Frederick Saunders as "one that sucks his sustenance . . . through a quill," Washington Irving's *Salmagundi* ("a mess [or mix?] of chopped meat and pickled herrings, seasoned," handwritten on the first page), James Fields' *Household Friends for Every Season*, John Brown's *Spare Hours*, Ralph Waldo Emerson's* *Miscellanies*, William Hazlitt's *Table Talk: Opinions on Books, Men and Things*, James Jackson Jarves' *Art Thoughts*, John Ruskin's *Precious Thoughts*, James Russell Lowell's *Among My Books* (Lessing's words "I wish to do nothing more than scatter the *fermenta cognitionis*" are marked), Martin Tupper's *Proverbial Philosophy*, John Wilson's *Noctes Ambrosianae*, and William Elder's *Elegant Extracts: A Copious Selection of Instructive, Moral and Entertaining Passages, from the Most Eminent Poets*. (*See*: *American Dictionary*; *Atlantic*; Bible; *Harper's*; *Scribner's*)

RECOMMENDED: Jack Capps, *Emily Dickinson's Reading 1836–1886*; Joan Kirkby, "Dickinson Reading"; Benjamin Lease, *Emily Dickinson's Readings of Men and Books*; Daniel Lombardo, "What the Dickinsons Read"; Richard Sewall, "Emily Dickinson's Books and Reading"; Robert Scholnick, " 'Don't Tell! They'd Advertise': Emily Dickinson in the *Round Table*"; Martha Nell Smith, *Rowing in Eden: Rereading Emily Dickinson*, ch. 2.

Joan Kirkby

BOSTON, MASSACHUSETTS   Dickinson visited and stayed in this city at least five times. She stayed with the family of her mother's sister Lavinia Norcross* for a few weeks in 1844; for about four weeks in 1846, when she saw a Chinese Museum exhibition and attended concerts; and for about two weeks in 1851, when she attended *Othello*, saw the Railroad Jubilee, climbed the Custom House tower, visited her Uncle Joel Norcross'* store on Milk Street, and consulted Dr. Wesselhoeft on Bedford Street. In 1864 and 1865 she underwent eye treatment with Dr. Henry W. Williams at 15 Arlington Street, while staying with her Norcross cousins in Mrs. Bangs' Boardinghouse* in Cambridge.* She saw the growth, industrialization, and urbanization of the city in the 1840s, 1850s, and 1860s.

RECOMMENDED: *Years*; Hiroko Uno, *Emily Dickinson Visits Boston*.

Hiroko Uno

BOWDOIN, ELBRIDGE GRIDLEY (1820–1893)   graduated from Amherst College* in 1840, taught school for five years, then studied law with his father. Upon admission to the bar in May 1847, he joined the law offices of Edward Dickinson,* with whom Bowdoin had differences of opinion arising from his liberal political viewpoint. Bowdoin was friendly with the Dickinson children and lent them books frowned upon by their father; in particular, he initiated them into the *Jane Eyre* fever that was then sweeping the country. Emily enjoyed a certain banter with the gentleman ten years her senior and sent him a lively verse valentine* teasing him about his bachelorhood and asserting that "the Earth was *made* for lovers" and that "God hath made nothing single but *thee* in His world so fair!" (P1). In 1855, Bowdoin and Emily's father dissolved their partnership, whereupon Bowdoin moved out to Iowa, established himself in real estate, and later became the representative for Floyd County to the state legislature. He kept Emily's valentine for forty years, then shortly before his death sent it back to Amherst, where it ultimately was included in the 1894 *Letters.**

RECOMMENDED: *Letters*; *Life*; *Years*.

Mary Carney

BOWLES, MARY SCHERMERHORN (1827–1893)   knew Emily Dickinson primarily through her husband's relationship with the Dickinson family. She married Samuel Bowles* in 1848, and much of her married life was dominated by ten pregnancies. She bore seven healthy children but suffered three stillbirths in the late 1850s. Mrs. Bowles met Dickinson in 1857 or 1858, when her husband's newspaper work took him to nearby Amherst,* where they started visiting both Dickinson families. The visits were supplemented by correspondence. Emily Dickinson wrote more often to Samuel Bowles but did write sixteen letters to Mary that have survived. She also sent her a poem, " 'They have not chosen me,' he said" (P85).

Mary's quiet, unassuming ways were a contrast to her husband, a nationally known journalist, influential in many areas, attractive to both men and women. Wolff and Sewall have commented on her jealousy regarding his close friendships with women, especially with Susan Dickinson* and Maria Whitney.*

Dickinson's letters often acknowledged small gifts or accompanied such offerings. Among the most poignant were notes of condolence over a stillborn child, "Don't cry, dear Mary. Let us do that for you, because you are too tired now" (L216) or responses to Samuel's death: "I hasten to you, Mary, because no moment must be lost when a heart is breaking" (L536).

RECOMMENDED: *Letters*; *Life*; Cynthia Griffin Wolff, *Emily Dickinson.*

Ronald Palosaari

BOWLES, SAMUEL (1826–1878)   Journalist, author, social reformer, and owner-editor of the Springfield, Massachusetts, daily newspaper, Bowles was born to Huldah Deming and Samuel Bowles, publisher of the *Springfield Republican.** Public education was followed by classical tutoring at Eaton's School. As a youth, "Sam" (as most friends except Dickinson called him) showed enthusiasm for botany, gardening, and reading, together with a susceptibility to illness and a physical beauty that he retained throughout life.

Denied a deeply desired university education, Bowles joined the *Republican* staff at seventeen, reporting on Amherst College* commencements, fires, or major political conventions with equal zest and exactitude. As editor from 1851, he promoted the paper's conversion to the "new journalism" of the 1850s, which provided social, political, and cultural ideas as well as news. Vigorous, ebullient, constructive, "practical rather than speculative" but willing, he said, "to die" for his dream, Bowles attracted sophisticated assistants like Josiah Holland* and worked to transform the *Republican* from a sleepy provincial paper into one of the six most influential in America (Merriam 1:34, 67). He bravely supported the antislavery movement, helped to establish the Republican Party in New England, defended Lincoln during two administrations, denounced the carpetbag regime, and fought against what he (as a Christian humanist/ Unitarian*) considered immoral, whether local prizefighting or Indian treaties.

Bowles' personal charm was widely acknowledged. Contemporaries praised his "deep magnetism" and candor or "whiteness of soul." Despite a crusty temper that was especially roused by "shams," he was celebrated for his compassion and tender sensibility. Indeed, that he had "the hand of a warrior [but] the heart of a woman" (Merriam 447, 446, 443) was offered in explanation for Bowles' extraordinary appeal for many "intense," "refined" women (*Life* 471). Holland's superficial assessment, "I think that his strongest passion was the love of power" (*Life* 470), was probably prompted by Bowles' executive brilliance, crusading interests, and notable determination to seem masculine—that is, superior and dominating—despite a vulnerability to illnesses provoked by excessive labor. Among Bowles' many causes was woman suffrage. (Dickinson's 1860 apology for "smil[ing] at women" [L223] probably alluded either to a witty sally against frivolous women or possibly to her deprecation of women's genius intended to curry favor with Bowles but earning his rebuke.) Bowles encouraged women reporters but scolded those who let their "rhetoric get borne off . . . on the sea of silks" (gorgeous imagery) and who ignored "the art of punctuation . . . the clear-starch of composition" (Merriam 2:334).

Socially prominent, Bowles knew Dickens* and Thackeray, but his favorite writer was Charlotte Brontë,* and his chosen novels *Shirley*, which he claimed he read yearly, and *Jane Eyre*, a copy of which he gave to Susan Dickinson.* In 1848, Bowles married a former schoolmate, Mary D. Schermerhorn* of Geneva, New York. He would declare the marriage fundamental to his success: "I married early, and I worked with all my might" (Merriam 1:56); but it became strained by clashes in temperament—both Bowleses were moody—and by Mary's depressions after the birth of three stillborn children and her debility after seven other births. Bowles' civic, political, and literary labors and his intermittent, patiently borne illnesses of the 1850s and 1860s (sciatica, dyspepsia, eyestrain, arthritis, depression) increased his desire for lively society. The shy, homely Mary was irritated by her husband's gregariousness and his open attraction to and for such urbane men and women as Austin* and Susan Dickinson, Kate Anthon,* and her own cousin, Maria Whitney.* After apologizing for Mary's "peculiarities" of behavior toward the Dickinsons in a note to Austin, Bowles usually visited their home alone after 1858, when, in June, Emily Dickinson commemorated a visit with both Bowleses in the only letter she ever addressed to them as a pair. (Tactfully, she directed sixteen of her fifty extant Bowles letters to Mary, though most appear intended for the man she demurely, if often archly or fervently, addressed as "Mr Bowles." The Dickinson–Bowles letters survive from a much larger, lost correspondence, Dickinson herself indicating its voluminousness when she told Mary in 1859, "my cheek is red with shame because I write so often" [L213].)

Bowles' relationship with Emily Dickinson began seriously during her participation in Sue and Austin's evening parties of the 1850s—"magical," Anthon called them—which included dancing, dining, shuttlecock (a game he played with Emily), and recitation. After 1860 until Bowles' death, it continued by means of Dickinson's eloquently shaded correspondence and his earnest if intermittent replies and visits. Analyzing the dates, number, intensity, common imagery, and often daringly passionate or erotic* character of Dickinson's letters* to or about Bowles, some commentators associate him with "Master"* and the "Master letters" (see Farr, Higgins, Miller, Sewall) and/or hypothesize that Dickinson was in love with Bowles, at least until the early 1870s. (Thus, Bowles' nicknames for Dickinson were "Queen" and "Daisy,"* while "Master" also employs "Daisy.") The speaker in the "Master" letters wants the "Queen's place" at his side (L233); and many "Master" poems and letters either quote or repeat tropes and imagery from Bowles' preferred *Jane Eyre*, while Dickinson used for Bowles her poetic love metaphor,* "Eden." Other scholars regard Bowles as Dickinson's close "Friend,"* a salutation she characteristically chose for him. Dickinson showed Bowles marks of special favor and confidence. She invited him to sit alone with her in her bedroom during her father's funeral in 1874; to him she acknowledged her mysterious misery in 1860 (L219). During his trips to Europe or New York in the early 1860s, she complained to him of their separation: "I tell you . . . it is a Suffering, to have a sea . . . between your Soul, and you" (L272). From Bowles, she tolerated both boisterous teasing and searching criticism, especially on the subject of her reclusion.

Bowles' behavior toward Dickinson has sometimes been regarded as crude or obtuse. Sewall cites as insensitive his greeting through Austin "to the Queen Recluse my especial sympathy—that she has 'overcome the world' " (*Life* 474). Wolff calls attention to his printing of an 1865 column (probably written by Holland) that ridiculed women writing out of a "need of sympathy" as likely to have discouraged or wounded Dickinson (245). Although the *Republican* published six Dickinson poems (P3,* 35,* 214,* 216,* 228,* and 986,* her "Snake" poem of whose altered punctuation she complained), some scholars lament that Bowles failed to recognize her genius, merely bidding the Dickinsons to "tell Emily to give me one of her little gems!" (*Life* 475). Yet Bowles' habit of sending her flowers yearly on the anniversary of her father's death (until his own death, which she called an eclipse of the sun) provides a kinder view of his thoughtfulness. A glimpse of what he may have sought to offer her— decided interest, bracing masculine affection, and hearty common sense—ap- pears not only in his inquiries about her health* and happiness but in a well- known incident of summer 1877. The poet having refused to leave her room when he called on her, Bowles shouted up the stair, "Emily, you damned rascal! No more of this nonsense! I've traveled all the way from Springfield to see you. Come down at once." These words, like Bowles' remark about the "Queen Recluse," were perhaps provoked by his concern over what he judged Dick- inson's extravagant or (to him) unhealthy behavior. That she came down and later sent him P1398 illustrates their complex relationship and Bowles' ability, quite simply, to *affect* her.

Bowles traveled widely in midlife, summering in Maine (from which he wrote the Dickinsons that he was "row[ing]" in "Eden") and the West and compos- ing the travel books *Across the Continent* (1865), *The Switzerland of America* (1868), and *The Far Western Frontier* (1869). Bowles collected landscape paint- ings and showed the poetic eye of an Emersonian* nature* lover in his descrip- tions of flowers* such as "the painter's brush [like] a beacon . . . [that] would make a room glow" (*Frontier* 104). His activities were extensive: he was trustee of Amherst College (1866–1878), a permanent director of the Springfield Li- brary, and the organizer of Massachusetts civil service reforms. Bowles died on 16 January 1878 after three paralytic strokes and a long illness, cheerfully con- fident of immortality and surrounded by loving friends and family. At his me- morial service, Rev. Washington Gladden* read from Scripture, and Dr. Josiah Holland gave a eulogy praising Bowles' generosity and integrity. The title of George S. Merriam's 1885 biography was chosen to capture him as "a child of his age." In it, Bowles is summarily described as "a lover"—of nature, of people (2:459). In 1884, Dickinson sent to his son Samuel, Jr., a spray from the jasmine plant Bowles had given her twenty years earlier, commenting that his father constituted "the whole of Immortality"* (L935; P1616).

RECOMMENDED: *Life*; Judith Farr, *The Passion of Emily Dickinson*; David Higgins, *Portrait of Emily Dickinson: The Poet and Her Prose*; George S. Merriam, *The Life and Times of Samuel Bowles*. New York: Century, 1885; Ruth Miller, *The Poetry of Emily Dickinson*; Cynthia Griffin Wolff, *Emily Dickinson*.

Judith Farr

BRIDE ROLE   This role is assumed by female speakers in Dickinson's poetry who voice the cultural mythos that marriage* is essential to the development of a complete self.* The majority of bride poems typically originate in the present and oppose expectation with actual experience, concluding with the speaker's discovery that marriage may not coincide with self-fulfillment. Poems like "I'm 'wife'—I've finished that—" (P199), "A Wife—at Daybreak I shall be—" (P461), and "The World—stands—solemner—to me—" (P493) reveal how the reality of marriage falls short of the dream engendered by society. An important early identification of the danger marriage poses for "simple trusting spirits" comes in Dickinson's famous June 1852 letter to Susan Gilbert* in which she contrasts the joys of the "plighted maiden" with the disappointment of the *"wife forgotten"* (L93). Whether a speaker actually is married matters less to her status as bride than her trust that formal commitment to another can transform and fulfill her. For this reason, unmarried speakers who imagine marriage or commit themselves to spiritual union with Jesus* can equally participate in the role of bride. Poems like "Given in Marriage unto Thee" (P817) and "I am ashamed—I hide—" (P473) illustrate this range of possible brides. Though the speaker's relationship to marriage may vary, the more than forty poems that feature the bride consistently illuminate the socially sanctioned discourse on marriage, holding up for scrutiny its implications for female self-fulfillment. (*See*: Voice; Women's Culture)

RECOMMENDED: Joanne Dobson, *Dickinson and the Strategies of Reticence: The Woman Writer in Nineteenth-Century America*; Susan Harris, "Illuminating the Eclipse: Dickinson's 'Representative' and the Marriage Narrative"; Elizabeth Phillips, *Emily Dickinson: Personae and Performance*; Vivian R. Pollak, *Dickinson: The Anxiety of Gender*; Cynthia Griffin Wolff, *Emily Dickinson*.

Paul Crumbley

BRIGHT'S DISEASE   For the last two to three years of her life, Dickinson was treated for a form of glomerulonephritis (or simply nephritis), which was then called Bright's disease in honor of Dr. Richard Bright (1789–1858), who first described its symptomatology in 1827. Though the term "Bright's disease" is still used, it is usually considered a generic name for various diseases of the kidney. According to current medical science, the three successive stages of glomerulonephritis are (1) acute, (2) subacute, and (3) chronic. The disease does not necessarily progress beyond the acute stage, and acute symptoms may occur only once or recur without ever progressing to the second and third stages. In a March 1886 letter to her Norcross* cousins, Dickinson gives a clue that she may have suffered from recurring bouts with nephritis: "I have twice been very sick, dears, with a little recess of convalescence . . . and have lain in my bed since November" (L1034). Symptoms leading her doctors to this diagnosis probably included edema, hypertension, severe back pain, renal insufficiency, and swelling, possibly with fever, rash, vomiting, and respiratory difficulty. The fact that Dickinson slipped into a brief coma on the day she died (15 May 1886) suggests toxic uremia as the final cause of death. (*See*: Health)

RECOMMENDED: Horst Oertel, *The Anatomic Histological Processes of Bright's Disease and their Relation to the Functional Changes*. Philadelphia: W. B. Saunders, 1910; James Tyson, *A Treatise on Bright's Disease and Diabetes with Especial Reference to Pathology and Therapeutics*. Philadelphia: Lindsay & Blakiston, 1881; H. von Ziemssen, and Albert H. Buck, eds. *Diseases of the Kidney*. Trans. Carl Bartels and Wilhelm Ebstein. *Cyclopaedia of the Practice of Medicine*. 15. New York: William Wood, 1877.

Charles M. Erickson and Marianne Erickson

BRONTË, CHARLOTTE (1816–1855) Dickinson read and admired this nineteenth-century British novelist. Genevieve Taggard notes that the two women bore similarities in both their experiences and appearance; Dickinson obviously sensed a personal affinity, craving personal details such as she found in Elizabeth Gaskell's *The Life of Charlotte Brontë* (1857). Her own P148, "All overgrown by cunning moss," was written in commemoration of Brontë's death and is filled with biographical particulars, including Brontë's pen name (Currer Bell) and home (Haworth), and concludes "Oh what an afternoon for Heaven, / When 'Bronte' entered there!"

Dickinson was also very familiar with Brontë's novels, first reading *Jane Eyre* (1847) when she was nineteen; it not only is mentioned in her letters* (e.g., L28, 475) but may also have inspired various poems. Elizabeth Phillips is convinced that Dickinson used Brontë's novel as " 'raw' material" for explorations of love* and self*-awakening (99–108). Walsh argues that at least twenty poems can be traced to scenes in *Jane Eyre*, suggesting near plagiarism. Similarly, Jane Crosthwaite shows how various "letter poems" parallel the descriptions of letter writing and reading found in Brontë's *Villette* (1853): examining, in particular, Polly Home's reading of a letter next to Dickinson's "The Way I read a Letter's—this—" (P636), she concludes, "Dickinson must have composed her poem in response to, under the inspiration of, or in order to improve the Brontean selection" (163). Farr argues that Dickinson used Brontean references in her "Master* Letters" to code her sexual feelings for Samuel Bowles,* a great reader of Brontë's novels. (*See*: Books and Reading)

RECOMMENDED: Jane Crosthwaite, "The Way to Read a Letter: Emily Dickinson's Variation on a Theme by Charlotte Brontë"; Judith Farr, *The Passion of Emily Dickinson*; Elizabeth Phillips, *Emily Dickinson: Personae and Performance*; Genevieve Taggard, *The Life and Mind of Emily Dickinson*; John Evangelist Walsh, *The Hidden Life of Emily Dickinson*.

Alisa Clapp-Itnyre

BRONTË, EMILY (1818–1848) Like her sister Charlotte,* the author of *Wuthering Heights* (1847) and various poems was well loved by Dickinson, who characterized her as "gigantic" (L742). Reading A. Mary F. Robinson's *Life of Emily Brontë*, Dickinson wrote to Mrs. Holland,* "I wish the dear Eyes would so far relent as to let you read 'Emily Bronte'—more electric far than anything since 'Jane Eyre' " (L822). Dickinson described Mrs. Holland as like Emily, "of whom her Charlotte said 'Full of ruth for others, on herself she had no mercy' " (L742).

Emily Brontë's poetry was particularly meaningful to Dickinson, for she quoted "No coward soul is mine" in various letters* (L873, 940, 948); T. W. Higginson* read it at her funeral.* The courage of the poem's speaker both in clinging to faith* ("Faith shines equal arming me from Fear") and in revolting against orthodox religion* ("Vain are the thousand creeds") may have appealed to Dickinson. Dickinson seemingly realized an affinity between herself and the

Brontës' poetry; when Thomas Niles* asked to read her poems, she sent him a copy of the sisters' *Poems* (1846) instead. Her poems and Emily Brontë's, especially, show striking similarity: compare Brontë's "Hope was but a timid friend" to Dickinson's " 'Hope' is the thing with feathers—" (P254), or Brontë's "I see around me tombstones grey" to Dickinson's "Safe in their Alabaster Chambers—"* (P216). Recent scholarship has increasingly focused on their literary kinship. Peeck-O'Toole makes Dickinson and Emily Brontë the focus of her study on nineteenth-century women poets' anxious preoccupation with poetic voice. Howe explores how a "close reading of [Emily Brontë's] life and work is crucial for understanding Emily Dickinson" (213). However, Homans argues that in her comments about Emily Brontë, Dickinson "treats Brontë the poet as a rival and distances her, while at the same moment welcoming an affinity on the personal level" (165). Loeffelholz, too, views Dickinson's poetry as in conflict not only with the male Romantic* tradition but also with the literary tradition of Emily and Charlotte Brontë. (*See*: Canadian Responses)

RECOMMENDED: Margaret Homans, *Women Writers and Poetic Identity: Dorothy Wordsworth, Emily Brontë, and Emily Dickinson*; Susan Howe, "Part Two: Childe Emily to the Dark Tower Came"; Mary Kay Loeffelholz, "The Compound Frame: Scenes of Emily Dickinson's Reading"; Maureen Peeck-O'Toole, "Lyric and Gender."

Alisa Clapp-Itnyre

BROWNING, ELIZABETH BARRETT (1806–1861)   Dickinson greatly admired the British poet Elizabeth Barrett Browning, author of *Aurora Leigh* (1856). She named Browning and her husband, Robert,* along with Keats,* as her favorite poets (L261). Browning's verse offered proof to many nineteenth-century readers that women could become great poets, and at the time she was the better known of the two Brownings.

Studies have shown the influence of Browning's *Sonnets from the Portuguese* (1850) and *Aurora Leigh* on Dickinson's choice of themes and diction. "I'm 'wife'—I've finished that—" (P199) is thought to have been inspired by Browning's sonnets #13 and #27. Dickinson identified strongly with the character Aurora Leigh, who felt a kinship with nature* and struggled against Victorian biases to define herself as an artist. The renunciation* and physical suffering of Marian Erle in *Aurora Leigh* also had an impact on Dickinson. She referred to Marian Erle's illness in two letters (L372, 696), and the poem "I stepped from Plank to Plank" (P875) is one of several thought to have been influenced by Marian Erle's experiences. In addition, Romney's blindness in Book 9 of *Aurora Leigh* may have inspired Dickinson's dramatic poem "Before I got my eye put out" (P327). She also admired Browning's "Catarina to Camoens" (1843), which she quoted in two letters (L491, 801).

Dickinson wrote at least two poems in honor of Browning. In the elegiac* "Her—'last Poems'—" (P312), Dickinson declared that "Silver—perished—with her Tongue—." She used the language of a conversion narrative to describe the overwhelming experience of reading* Browning for the first time in

"I think I was enchanted" (P593). Dickinson's respect for Browning was so well known that three friends sent her pictures of the poet, and in her later years she hung a portrait of Browning along with ones of George Eliot* and Thomas Carlyle* in her bedroom. Browning's death in June 1861 occasioned personal bereavement for Dickinson, who later asked Samuel Bowles* to visit her grave and "put one hand on the Head, for me—her unmentioned Mourner" (L266). At her first meeting with T. W. Higginson* in August 1870, she gave him a picture of Browning's tomb. (*See*: Books and Reading)

RECOMMENDED: S. Diane Bogus, "Not So Disparate: An Investigation of the Influence of Elizabeth Barrett Browning on the Work of Emily Dickinson"; Jane Donahue Eberwein, *Dickinson: Strategies of Limitation*; Ellen Moers. *Literary Women*. Garden City, NY: Doubleday, 1976; Frederick L. Morey, "Two Major Sources: Emblems and *Aurora Leigh*"; Elizabeth Phillips, *Emily Dickinson: Personae and Performance*.

Denise Kohn

BROWNING, ROBERT (1812–1889)   Emily Dickinson named the British poets Robert Browning and his wife, Elizabeth,* along with Keats,* as her favorite poets in an early letter to T. W. Higginson* (L261). She also asked her friend Mary Bowles* to name her son Robert in honor of the poet, whom she called "the bravest man—alive" after his wife's death in 1861 (L244). Dickinson praised *Men and Women* (1855) as a "broad Book" (L368), and in the table of contents of her own copy of the book the poems "Evelyn Hope," "In three Days," and "One Way of Love" are marked. In her letters Dickinson frequently alluded to Browning, including references to "Evelyn Hope" (L669), "The Last Ride Together" (L1015), "Love Among the Ruins" (L891), and "Sordello" (L337, 477). His dramatic monologues are thought to have influenced her own dramatic verse and adoption of different personae. Unlike many contemporary readers, Dickinson was not disturbed by what was considered Browning's obscure and abrupt style.

RECOMMENDED: *Letters*; Jack L. Capps, *Emily Dickinson's Reading: 1836–1886*; Jane Donahue Eberwein, *Dickinson: Strategies of Limitation*; Elizabeth Phillips, *Emily Dickinson: Personae and Performance*.

Denise Kohn

BULLARD, ASA (1804–1888) **and LUCRETIA GUNN DICKINSON** (1806–1885)   were prominent Congregationalists* in Cambridge,* Massachusetts, from the time of their marriage in 1832 until his death. Asa Bullard graduated from Amherst College* in 1828 and was ordained in 1832. That same year, he married Emily Dickinson's aunt, Lucretia Gunn Dickinson, who was Edward Dickinson's* eldest sister. Bullard, who was affiliated with the Congregational Sunday School and Publishing Society, wrote and edited a number of religious* publications, including such society periodicals as *Sunnybank Stories* and *The Children's Album of Pictures and Stories*. His younger brother, Ebenezer, boarded with the Dickinsons in 1829, and, through him, Bullard grew more familiar with the family. Dickinson refers to Lucretia in only two letters (L194, 656), which, not surprisingly, offer only a thread of insight into the fabric of their relationship. According to Leyda, Dickinson and the Bullards corresponded faithfully for years; however, not one of these letters has surfaced.

RECOMMENDED: *Letters*; *Years*; Millicent Todd Bingham, *Emily Dickinson's Home*.

Dean Rader

BYRON, GEORGE GORDON, LORD (1788–1824)   Dickinson's interest in this English Romantic* poet seems limited to his monologue "The Prisoner of Chillon" (1816). It is based on the ordeal suffered by François de Bonnivard, who was imprisoned for about six years in the Chateau of Chillon. During his imprisonment, Bonnivard almost loses his sanity. By the last verse, the prisoner feels that his cell has become his domain. When liberty comes, he regains "my freedom with a sigh" because he can never feel free again. He can no more escape the boundaries of earth than leave the walls of his prison.

Dickinson alludes to Byron or this poem in six letters*: L227 (1860), 233 (1861, a "Master"* letter), 249 (1862), 293 (1864), 1029 (1886), and 1042 (1886). The latter three were written either when Dickinson was quite ill or after the death* of a friend* and allude to the difficult juxtaposition of captivity and liberty that the Prisoner of Chillon encountered.

In addition to these allusions in her letters, Byron's poem is a source for three poems: "If any sink, assure that this, now standing—" (P358) and "My Life had stood—a Loaded Gun—"* (P754) are based on lines 225–30 and 386–88, in which the narrator has the power to kill but cannot die; "No Rack can torture me—" (P384) applies Bonnivard's ability to keep his soul free despite physical incarceration to the narrator's ability to keep *her* soul free by remaining true to her convictions.

RECOMMENDED: *Letters*; *Poems*; Jane Donahue Eberwein, *Dickinson: Strategies of Limitation*.

Marcy L. Tanter

C

CALLED BACK   In January 1885, Dickinson described *Called Back* as "a haunting story . . . 'greatly impressive to me' " (L962). This popular novella written by British novelist John Frederick Fargus (1848–1885) under the pseudonym Hugh Conway was probably given to her by Mabel Loomis Todd*; it had a profound enough influence on Dickinson that she used its title in her last known correspondence (L1046), a note to her Norcross* cousins that read simply "Called Back." It is tempting to speculate that she might have identified closely with Conway's protagonist-narrator, Gilbert Vaughan, who shared not only the forename of her beloved nephew, whose loss she still grieved, but the poet's own reclusive tendencies and compromised eyesight. The intricate mystery tale begins with a flashback to Gilbert's temporary blindness, and the narrator's confession that "I have been looked upon by my neighbors as a man with a history—one who has a romance hidden away beneath an outwardly prosaic life" is a striking anticipation of Dickinson's own critical history. Austin Dickinson* had the epitaph "Born December 10, 1830. Called Back May 15, 1886." carved on his sister's headstone. (*See*: Health; Spiritualism; Vision)

RECOMMENDED: *Years*; Hugh Conway. *Called Back*. New York: H. Holt, 1884; Ida Fasel, "*Called Back*: A Note on Emily Dickinson"; Josephine Pollitt, "Called Back," *Emily Dickinson: The Human Background of Her Poetry*; "Three Young Novelists." *Blackwood's Edinburgh Magazine* 136.827 (Sept. 1884): 296–316.

Marianne Erickson

CAMBRIDGE, MASSACHUSETTS   Dickinson must have driven through this town, where T. W. Higginson* was born, and Austin Dickinson* studied at Harvard Law School, when she took a tour of Mount Auburn Cemetery in Watertown with her Aunt Lavinia Norcross'* family during her stay with them in Boston* in 1846. For about half a year in 1864 and again in 1865, during eye treatments in Boston, she stayed with Fanny and Loo Norcross* in Mrs. Bangs' Boardinghouse* at 86 Austin Street (now 124 Bishop Richard Allen Drive), Cambridgeport. This area was then the boundary between the residential area and the commercial area along Main Street (Massachusetts Avenue); it was very close to Haymarket Square, then the terminal of the horse railways.

RECOMMENDED: Hiroko Uno, *Emily Dickinson Visits Boston*; Anna Mary Wells. *Dear Preceptor: The Life and Times of Thomas Wentworth Higginson*. Boston: Houghton Mifflin, 1963.

Hiroko Uno

CANADIAN RESPONSES TO DICKINSON Critical and creative interest in Dickinson began in the 1890s and remains lively to the present, with articles and reviews in major Canadian journals and nearly a dozen dissertations defended in Canada. Notably, Inder Nath Kher's important study, *The Landscape of Absence*, was first undertaken as a doctoral dissertation at the University of Alberta.

In the 1890s, Canadian-born poet and journalist Bliss Carman (1861–1929) wrote three articles on Dickinson, including one of the first parodies of her poetry (Buckingham 450). More seriously, he speculated that Dickinson, like Emerson,* may well have acquired her "exquisite ear for cadence" from the "English mystic," William Blake.* Two Dickinson poems were also included in J. E. Wetherell's *Later American Poems* (1896), an anthology of American poetry intended for use in Canadian high schools (Buckingham 453).

In the 1930s and 1940s, Dickinson held particular interest for Canadian modernist poets like Leo Kennedy (b. 1907) and Dorothy Livesay (1909–1996). Livesay, who privately studied Dickinson, H. D., and Katherine Mansfield, figured Dickinson in her poem "The Three Emily's." Livesay contrasted her own conflicts reconciling life as poet and mother with the lives of three childless and solitary Emilys: Canadian painter Emily Carr, British novelist Emily Brontë,* and Emily Dickinson.

Following publication of Johnson's* biography of Dickinson and the *Poems of Emily Dickinson* (1955),* Northrop Frye wrote an influential article that emphasized Dickinson's self-imposed isolation.* He argued that she led a "carefully obliterated" social life to preserve "[t]he intensity of her ordinary consciousness"* necessary for her poetry.

One frequently cited article in Dickinson bibliographies is a comparative reading of the poetry of Emily Dickinson and Canadian poet Sarah Binks. In "A Haunting Echo," C.C.J. Bond purported to demonstrate Dickinson's literary influence on the "Sweet Songstress of Saskatchewan." Binks, a Canadian poet rivaling Twain's Emmeline Grangerford, is actually the fictional creation of Paul Hiebert. Bond continued Hiebert's humorous conceit by praising her Dickinsonian slant* rhymes in such lines as "Barley in the heater, salt pork in the *pantry* / How nice that you never feel cold in this *country.*'' (*See*: Latin American Responses)

RECOMMENDED: C. C. J. Bond. "A Haunting Echo." *Canadian Literature* 16 (Spring 1963): 83–84; Willis J. Buckingham, ed., *Emily Dickinson's Reception in the 1890s*; Northrop Frye, "Emily Dickinson"; Dorothy Livesay. *Collected Poems: Two Seasons*. Toronto: McGraw-Hill Ryerson, 1972: 202; Inder Nath Kher, *The Landscape of Absence: Emily Dickinson's Poetry*.

Nancy Johnston

CAPITALIZATION Dickinson's capitalization is extremely idiosyncratic in that she capitalized not all but many nouns, not all but a fair number of modifiers and verbals, and only some function words. Though it is not always possible to make clear distinctions between uppercase and lowercase letters in the manuscripts, and although there exist in-between sizes of letters (e.g., see P216), it is safe to say that the capital letters consistently appear at the beginning of lines and sentences and may additionally emerge anywhere within Dickinson's lines, sentences, and, as some critics hold, words. Arguing that Dickinson herself would have desired "correction" of her misspellings or that her inconsistencies are an unacceptable distraction, editors* like James Reeves and the German Kurt Oppens have, in the past, proceeded to regularize Dickinson's capitalization. Today most editors agree, however, that all textual eccentricities should, as far as possible, be preserved. The editions that come closest to maintaining Dickinson's irregular capitalization are Thomas H. Johnson's* *The Poems of Emily Dickinson** and, of course, Ralph W. Franklin's* *The Manuscript Books of Emily Dickinson.**

Scholars and editors have made various attempts at explaining Dickinson's inconsistent capitalization. Thomas Wentworth Higginson,* Dickinson's adviser and publisher, suggested early on that she followed the Old English and present German method of capitalizing every noun substantive. This is clearly inaccurate, and other critics have consequently argued that Dickinson's capitalization follows no pattern at all, that it is, instead, accidental, random, whimsical, capricious, spontaneous, uneducated, or overcivilized. Such views are reinforced by the fact that there are differences in capitalization between various extant copies of certain poems (P67) as well as between words incorporated in a poem and their variants (P627, 640). Dickinson's irregular capitals may also be a matter of habit, as they occur in letters,* recipes, and notes alike. They might reveal Dickinson's attempt to imitate nineteenth-century epistolary fashions that encouraged a relatively liberal use of capitals and punctuation, or they can, as some have argued, represent the poet's deliberate creation of an original stylistic signature, a defiant and deviant standard of her own. Scholars who believe the eccentric capitalization is intentional contend that it lends dignity or at least emphasis to a given word and that it sometimes serves to mark grammatical units (P19; Franklin 125) or to intensify the pause a dash* causes (P534). Several critics, among them Cristanne Miller, have also suggested that the capitalization results in the allegorization or personification of a given thing or quality (P754; Miller 59). More recently, scholars like Jerome McGann have foregrounded the visual aspects of Dickinson's writing, pointing out that her poetry was imagined and executed as a scriptural rather than as a typographical event. Applying McGann's ideas specifically to Dickinson's capitalization, one might see her capitalized words not only in terms of their content but in terms of their textuality as such. Capitalization thus contributes to lending the text of her writings a radical self-identity. (*See*: Textual Variants)

RECOMMENDED: Ralph W. Franklin, *The Editing of Emily Dickinson: A Reconsideration*; Jerome McGann, "Emily Dickinson's Visible Language"; Cristanne Miller, *Emily Dickinson: A Poet's Grammar*.

Sylvia Henneberg

CARLO   For at least sixteen years, Emily Dickinson's dog Carlo was her constant companion. He is first mentioned in a prose valentine* in 1850, when Dickinson was twenty. He was probably a Newfoundland, though he may have been a Saint Bernard. Also the name of Ik Marvell's* dog, there were five Carlos in Amherst* in 1858. In her second letter to T. W. Higginson,* Dickinson identified her companions as "Hills—Sir—and the Sundown—and a Dog—large as myself, that my Father bought me" (L261). According to neighbors' reports, Carlo always accompanied her on errands. He appears by name or reference in over forty poems and letters.* Dickinson refers to him as her "mute Confederate" (L319), her "Shaggy Ally" (L280), as "dumb, and brave" (L271). She remembered Major Hunt because he said "her great dog 'understood gravitation' " (L342b). He is the only animal in her entire corpus given human emotion and intelligence. Early in 1866, Dickinson sent Higginson a one-line letter, which read "Carlo died—," followed by a postscript, "Would you instruct me now?" (L314). One neighbor recalls walking in 1860 with Dickinson "while the huge dog stalked solemnly beside them. 'Gracie,' said Miss Dickinson, . . . 'do you know that I believe that the first to come and greet me when I go to heaven* will be this dear, faithful old friend Carlo?' " (*Years* 2:21).

RECOMMENDED: *Years*; Mary Allen. *Animals in American Literature*. Urbana: University of Illinois Press, 1983; Dorothy Waugh, *Emily Dickinson Briefly*.

Margaret Freeman

CARLYLE, THOMAS (1795–1881)   Martha Dickinson Bianchi's* recollection in *The Life and Letters** that Carlyle's portrait hung alongside those of Elizabeth Barrett Browning* and George Eliot* on her Aunt Emily's bedroom wall suggests that Dickinson must have admired this Scottish Romantic* historian and essayist. Yet she made no poetic allusions to his distinctive prose nor referred to him in letters.* Carlyle's reputation in the United States, which began with R. W. Emerson's* Transcendentalist* circle and gradually extended to other readers, drew attention to his writing in the Amherst* of her youth. George Gould* delivered a speech on Carlyle at the 1848 college commencement, and

William Howland lent his copy of *The French Revolution* (1837) to Lavinia Dickinson* three years later. The Dickinson family copy of *Heroes and Hero Worship* (1853) is classified by the Houghton Library among books "probably" marked by the poet herself. That collection of lectures included "The Hero as Poet," which Gary Stonum cites as a possible influence on Dickinson's poetics through its celebration of the sublimely* masterful "Carlylean poet," a figure to whom she responded with characteristic ambivalence.

RECOMMENDED: *Years*; Gary Lee Stonum, *The Dickinson Sublime*.

Jane Donahue Eberwein

CARMICHAEL, ELIZABETH (Mrs. Daniel)   was a close friend of Lavinia Dickinson* and the mother of Lizzie Mather, whose husband was a professor of classics at Amherst College.* She lived in the Mather household until Richard Mather* remarried following Lizzie's October 1877 death. She then moved in with her sister, Mrs. Skeel. Carmichael sent sweets as a gift to the Dickinsons on two occasions as well as a recipe for coconut cake.

RECOMMENDED: *Letters*; *Years*.

Monica Chiu

CARTOONS   Although Dickinson was not a cartoonist in the twentieth-century sense of the term, referring to producers of comic strips and animated television shows or movies, she did enliven her words with visual designs. Layouts attaching engravings or text scissored from books,* flowers,* or stamps adorn many poems and/or letters to make humorous* points, as do drawings (including the shaping of alphabetic letters so they illustrate their meaning). Several cartooning layouts survive among Dickinson's writings: cutouts from Charles Dickens'* *The Old Curiosity Shop* attached to "A poor—torn heart—a tattered heart—" (P78) comment on novelistic sentimentalities that make a cartoon of love* and its dedications. A cutout of a robin from *The New England Primer* attached, along with a flower, to "Whose cheek is this" (P82) similarly comments on the mawkishness of some popular poetry even as Dickinson's lyric queries whether poetry* kills life into art or renders some semblance of a new lease on life. Another cutout of "Young Timothy / Learnt sin to fly" from the *Primer* jokes about her father's having summoned her home from a late evening at the Evergreens* (L214). Cutouts from a three-cent stamp featuring a loco-motive and from a *Harper's New Monthly Magazine** review of George Sand's* *Mauprat* critique patriarchal privilege as she "visually and textually dramatizes . . . joyful play with writing's construction of the body (Holland 141); and in-numerable attachments of a flower or some other object now lost, like that of a pine needle that topped (or dressed) "Of Brussels—it was not—" (P602), em-phasized, ironized, or satirized a text's meanings.

Likewise, several drawings on which Susan Dickinson* and Macgregor Jen-kins* remarked can be found among Dickinson's papers. Drawings around the embossed Capitol Building on Edward Dickinson's* congressional stationery show her father, a Whig* representative to Congress, "flipping his wig" as he strides away from Washington (L144); and in a note about the "Music of the Spheres" sent to Sue, accompanied by a drawing that featured a slightly altered musical staff, Dickinson even joked about the Pythagorean maxim to forestall flatulence by avoiding beans. Displaying political and religious irreverence as well as poking fun at seemingly unremarkable frustrations of everyday life, her cartoons mocked a range of subjects, from the institutions of family, state, and school in which most have a stake, to quotidian comings and goings that everyone recognizes. Similarly, Dickinson's range of subjects in her sketches and layouts paralleled those treated in cartoons—from lampooning familial tensions to deflating national literary and political figures (Smith 65). Also, exaggerated calligraphies that mimic her linguistic sense began to emerge dramatically in the 1860s, when the poet appears to have been most engaged in copying and sending out her poems (Howe; Sands). Complementing her comic verbal dexterity, Dickinson's "cartooning" strategies reveal the "witty humorous" qualities Susan Dickinson bemoaned as missing from *Poems by Emily Dickinson* (1890).* (*See*: Fictionality; Handwriting)

RECOMMENDED: Jeanne Holland, "Scraps, Stamps, and Cutouts: Emily Dickinson's Domestic Technologies of Publication"; Susan Howe, "These Flames and Generosities of the Heart: Emily Dickinson and the Illogic of Sumptuary Values"; Margaret Sands, "Re-Reading the Poems: Editing Opportunities in Variant Versions"; Martha Nell Smith, "The Poet as Cartoonist"; Marta Werner, *Emily Dickinson's Open Folios*; Katharine Zadravec, "Emily Dickinson: A Capital Visitor."

Martha Nell Smith

CATHOLICISM Dickinson's droll comment on a sermon that announced "several facts which were usually startling" about "the Roman Catholic system" (L96) reflects the staunchly Protestant atmosphere of her Connecticut Valley* environment. Her knowledge of Catholics and their church was limited to Irish immigrants in Massachusetts, including those her brother taught in his year with the Boston schools, and impressions transmitted from Europe by American travelers. Servants in the Dickinson household worshiped at St. Bridget's Church, Amherst,* after its dedication in 1871. The role of "nun" the poet assigned herself in a few poems, references to the Madonna, and some surprisingly un-Calvinistic sacramental imagery suggest that there were elements of Catholic piety to which her imagination responded, and her attentiveness to *The Imitation of Christ*＊ shows her openness to elements of pre-Reformation Christian spirituality. The Anglo-Catholic tradition would have reached her through readings in English literature and through the growing Episcopal movement in the United States. Amherst's Grace Church was founded in 1864, and Bishop Frederick Dan Huntington* was a family friend. Awareness of the Oxford movement is suggested by an 1859 reference to "Puseyite" with regard to her brother's reading (L213). (*See*: Maher)

RECOMMENDED: Frances Bzowski, " 'Half Child—Half Heroine': Emily Dickinson's Use of Traditional Female Archetypes"; Jane Donahue Eberwein, "Emily Dickinson and the Calvinistic Sacramental Tradition'' and '' 'Siren Alps': The Lure of Europe for American Writers''; Patricia Leal, ''The History of St. Brigid's Church'' (unpublished University of Massachusetts student paper, Jones Library, Amherst).

Jane Donahue Eberwein

CHICKERING, JOSEPH KNOWLTON (1846–1899)   Lavinia Dickinson's* friend exhibited special concern for the Dickinson sisters when their mother died in 1882. Emily Dickinson responded to his words of sympathy, ''I do not know the depth of my indebtedness'' (L784). During this time, Chickering requested permission to call on Dickinson, which she granted but later canceled, along with several other similar requests. Thus, she met Chickering only through their correspondence. Chickering graduated from Amherst College* in 1869, where he taught English for twelve years before accepting a position at the University of Vermont in 1885. Early in the 1880s, he, along with Thomas Higginson,* may have encouraged Dickinson to contribute poems to the Mission Circle, which supported children in the Far East and India.
   RECOMMENDED: *Letters*.

Monica Chiu

CHILD ROLE   Dickinson assumed the role of the child as a way of contrasting the wonder of childhood with the social constraints imposed by the adult world. In this way, her representation of childhood innocence became an important tool in her critique of nineteenth-century American culture. This characteristic of the child role is particularly clear in the harsh analysis of biblical* religion* presented in ''Abraham to kill him'' (P1317), the depiction of familial indifference of ''I was the slightest in the House—'' (P486), and the nightmarish parental interrogation conveyed in ''Who is it seeks my Pillow Nights—'' (P1598). The rejection of adult authority by child speakers like the one in ''So I pull my Stockings off'' (P1201) is all the more scathing because it comes from speakers whose fear and uncertainty appear unmediated and absolute.
   Writing about the child provided a relatively safe avenue for social critique for women writers such as Dickinson because children were viewed as part of the proper, domestic* domain of women's lives. However, from the relative haven of this socially accepted topic, Dickinson deliberately challenged domestic ideology by introducing into the child role speakers who refused to submit quietly to socially assigned scripts. The speakers of ''I'm ceded—I've stopped being Their's—'' (P508) and ''We talked as Girls do—'' (P586) aspire to levels of authority totally out of keeping with domesticity. (*See*: Voice)
   RECOMMENDED: Joanne Dobson, *Dickinson and the Strategies of Reticence: The Woman Writer in Nineteenth-Century America*; Sandra M. Gilbert and Susan Gubar, *The Madwoman in the Attic: The Woman Writer and the Nineteenth-Century Literary Imagination*; Barbara Antonina Clarke Mossberg, *Emily Dickinson: When a Writer Is a Daughter*; Cynthia Griffin Wolff, *Emily Dickinson*.

Paul Crumbley

CIRCLE IMAGERY   Dickinson used circle images to focus the gaze and develop perspective. She did this with cycles, processes of examination, and round objects. Cycles signifying rebirth include the times of day and seasons* of the year, the growth cycles of plants and people, and the movements of heavenly spheres. In these analogies, night precedes dawn, death* rebirth, seed fruit, and pain ecstasy. Dickinson recognized the comfort of design, wholeness, and abundance in a fallen world and celebrated them where she could see them. However, her poems tend to place a speaker on a segment of a cycle; whether the speaker celebrates life or suffers from it, the reader* must often imagine the whole cycle to position the speaker in it.

Many poems use a direct or inferred image of Jesus,* which implies the old circular sun/Son narratives of death and resurrection. Dickinson wanted to believe the circular biblical* narrative of paradise regained through union with Christ in heaven* and examined it from many perspectives.

The circle and its parts—including diameters, arcs, crescents, centers, and even degrees, angles, slants, and the elusive disc—form a portion of Dickinson's geometric imagery. Using spatial imagery to articulate her ideas, she imagined God* in "the Stupendous Vision* / Of His Diameters" (P802); she portrayed risk in "She staked her Feathers—Gained an Arc—" (P798) and represented loss in "Each that we lose takes part of us; / A crescent still abides" (P1605).

Dickinson drew a provisional "circle" around something actual or imagined to examine it, intensifying her subject, clarifying its nature, and ultimately revealing its connections to the larger world. Her numerous definition and riddle poems use this technique. The poet as observer concentrated her microscopic eye on the near and small and her telescopic eye on the faraway.

Yet Dickinson realized the dangers of the static circle: "A Prison gets to be a friend . . . a Demurer Circuit . . . The narrow Round" (P652). While familiar circles offer comfort, they could also constrain. She used several circular images to express various stages of constraint, freedom, pain, comfort, and value, including the drop, tear, jewel,* seed, flower,* crown, wheel, and round as noun, verb, adjective, and preposition. (*See*: Circumference)

RECOMMENDED: Ralph Waldo Emerson, "Circles." *Essays and Lectures*. New York: Library of America, 1983; Dorothy Huff Oberhaus, *Emily Dickinson's Fascicles: Method and Meaning*; Vivian Pollak, *Dickinson: The Anxiety of Gender*.

Joanna Yin

CIRCUMFERENCE   Dickinson declared, "My Business is Circumference" (L268). Although circumference forms the outside of a circle,* Dickinson used the term dynamically to describe the limit of something and then violently enlarge it, expanding the speaker's knowledge.

A favorite Dickinson position, often terrifying but always exhilarating, was on the edge of a circumference: "I alone—/. . . . Went out upon Circumference—/ Beyond the Dip of Bell—" (P378). Her expansions of circumference informed journeys toward possibility, from the known toward the unknown. She tended to work from the specific to the general, from the concrete to the cosmic. She saw New Englandly but outward to the universe and eternity. Her expanding circumferences show the reader* where she wrote from and what she wrote toward. Ultimately, the enlargement of circumference creates "vaster attitudes" (P290) that cross, blur, or erase boundaries and barriers such as those that separate bipolar concepts like inside/outside, life/death,* earth/heaven,* male/female, and ruler/ruled.

She dramatized and complicated the Christian journey with the encompassing image of circumference: "The Bible* dealt with the Centre, not with the Circumference—" (L950). Dickinson applied central biblical narratives and images to life on earth. Whether overtly Christian or lacking specific biblical reference, experiences of circumference are sacred revelations. The soul ripens, the brain widens, the spirit intoxicates, the imagination surges, the self* radiates ecstasy or awe, the ocean engulfs; Dickinson's many images of enlargement serve as sublime* analogies of immortality,* her flood subject.

Poems in the same fascicle* expand their circumferences as similar images interact. Similarly, her poems enrich each other. They show ways to see, learn, and know. As she pushed the limits of language and thought, Dickinson strained against the boundaries between knowing and not knowing with a "Sweet Skepticism of the Heart—/ That knows—and does not know—" (P1413). (*See:* Vision)

RECOMMENDED: Albert Gelpi, *Emily Dickinson: The Mind of the Poet*; Suzanne Juhasz, *The Undiscovered Continent: Emily Dickinson and the Space of the Mind*; Mary Loeffelholz, *Dickinson and the Boundaries of Feminist Theory*; Dorothy Huff Oberhaus, *Emily Dickinson's Fascicles: Method and Meaning*; Gary Lee Stonum, *The Dickinson Sublime*.

Joanna Yin

CIVIL WAR   Emily Dickinson's most prolific writing period coincided with the years during which America's Civil War was fought. Between 1861 and 1865 Dickinson wrote 852 of the 1,656 poems that have been assigned dates. While Dickinson did openly mention the war in personal letters, scholars disagree about the impact it had on her poetry. A few agree with Edmund Wilson, who declared in 1977 that Dickinson never referred to the war in her poems. Others support Daniel Aaron, who argued in 1973 that the Civil War created an entire nation of people experiencing intense emotions and that Dickinson fed from that outpouring of emotion to create her most intense, urgent, and anguished poems. As evidence of this, scholars agreeing with Aaron point to Dickinson's use of martial analogies and imagery in poems apparently unrelated to the war. Still others—such as Thomas W. Ford, who in 1965 first raised this issue, and Shira Wolosky, who in 1984 wrote the most authoritative work on the subject—point to select poems as direct commentaries on the war. Ford argues that, while not commemorating any one person, the poem "It feels a shame to be Alive—" (P444) is recognizably a tribute to all who died in the war. Wolosky has taken Ford's idea and expanded on it, noting that the poem "My Triumph lasted till the Drums" (P1227) is not only Dickinson's reflection on the war but also an expression of the way her struggle with the war parallels her struggle with religion. Dickinson left behind letters* proving that she knew both friends and relatives who were fighting and dying in the Civil War. More and more, scholars are agreeing that this sensitive poet could not have ignored the cataclysmic events occurring around her and must have addressed them, in some fashion, in her poetry.

RECOMMENDED: Daniel Aaron. *The Unwritten War: American Writers and the Civil War*. New York: Knopf, 1973; Thomas W. Ford, "Emily Dickinson and the Civil War"; Edmund Wilson. *Patriotic Gore: Studies in the Literature of the American Civil War*. New York: Oxford University Press, 1962; Shira Wolosky, *Emily Dickinson: A Voice of War*.

Susan Biscella

CLARK, JAMES D. and CHARLES H.   Dickinson's brief, twenty-one-letter correspondence with the Clarks began in August 1882 and ended with a letter* written a month before her death. Initiated by James, the correspondence continued with Charles after James' death in June 1883. The Clarks' lifelong friendship with Charles Wadsworth* constituted the basis for the correspondence and thus makes these letters relevant to Dickinson scholarship on two counts: Dickinson's relationship with Wadsworth and her ideas about death.*

Written shortly after Wadsworth's death, these letters reveal an intense, emotional bond between Dickinson and Wadsworth, a bond that Dickinson may have tried to commemorate by writing to those "who knew him" (L766), a unique joy she acknowledged in the letters. As Dickinson ascertained facts about Wadsworth's family's sorrow and his final days, and as she received copies of sermons and other remembrances from the Clarks, her gratitude, sympathy, and affection for the Clarks grew. These letters clearly indicate that Dickinson was drawn to Wadsworth because of his suffering, eloquence, mystery, and "Grandeur" (L776). Included with this letter, P1543 compares Wadsworth's grandeur to Jesus's* power in effecting his own resurrection. In Dickinson's last letter to Charles Clark, she recalled her final meeting with Wadsworth and Lavinia's* characterization of him as "the Gentleman with the deep voice" (L1040). Wadsworth was in some way important to the end of her life.

In addition to Wadsworth's death, the time period of this correspondence recorded the deaths of four other people important to Dickinson: her mother, her nephew Gilbert,* James Clark, and Otis P. Lord.* So it is not surprising that these letters contain powerful reactions to death, including a touching eulogy-like statement about her mother: "Her dying feels to me like many kinds of Cold—at times electric, at times benumbing—then a trackless waste, Love has never trod" (L788). The images of "Cold" as "electric" and "benumbing" reveal the profound hurt death causes, and loss is evident in the image of "a trackless waste." When James died, Dickinson wrote with sympathy to Charles:

"I wish I might say one liquid word to make your sorrow less. Is not the devotion that you gave him, an acute Balm?'' (L859). Again, she acknowledged the extremity of pain that accompanies death; and, as in her larger discussion of death, she could not be certain she believed in immortality.* In L872, she sent a poem to Charles that questions, "The Spirit lasts—but in what mode—'' (P1576); but Dickinson did consider the comfort of reunion with those she loved as she wrote, "To be certain we were to meet our Lost, would be a Vista of reunion, who of us could bear?'' (L896). On these themes of death and immortality,* the correspondence with the Clarks serves as a microcosm of Dickinson's macrocosmic discussion: about them, she was ambivalent, skeptical, acquiescent, angry, and believing. Perhaps this is because thinking about death, remembering those who died, and considering her own death gave Dickinson "a bliss of sorrow" (L827), a powerful oxymoronic* expression of strong emotions in bereavement. (*See*: Elegy)

RECOMMENDED: *Letters*; *Life*; *Years*; Cynthia Griffin Wolff, *Emily Dickinson.*

Susan Rieke

COLEMAN, ELIZA M. (1832–1871)   was Dickinson's close friend and second cousin. Coleman's mother, Maria (Flynt) Coleman, was a first cousin of Dickinson's mother. Her father, Lyman Coleman,* was the principal of Amherst Academy* when Dickinson and her sister attended. In an 1854 letter to John Graves,* Coleman expressed concern about Dickinson, stating, "I know you appreciate her & I think few of her Amherst* friends do. They wholly misinterpret her, I believe'' (*Years* 1:319). It has been speculated that Dickinson wanted to marry John Langdon Dudley,* and, after Coleman hastily married him in 1861, their union may have distressed the poet. Coleman's health began to decline in the early 1860s; she succumbed to consumption in 1871. Dickinson took kind interest in her ailing cousin's situation and was in regular communication with Fanny and Loo Norcross,* who moved to Wisconsin to assist the Dudleys until after Eliza's death. (*See*: Flynt)

RECOMMENDED: *Letters*; *Life*; *Years.*

Marisa Anne Pagnattaro

COLEMAN, LYMAN (1796–1882) **and MARIA** (1801–1871)   Principal of Amherst Academy* (1844–1846), Lyman Coleman married Maria Flynt, a cousin of Emily Norcross Dickinson.* At the time of their move to Amherst,* the Colemans had two daughters, Olivia, seventeen, and Eliza,* twelve. Emily and Eliza became close friends and continued their friendship after the Colemans moved to Philadelphia, where the Dickinson sisters stayed with the family for two weeks in March 1855 during their trip to Washington.* It may have been during this visit that Emily met Charles Wadsworth,* who was then minister of the Colemans' church. Despite evidence of careful parenting, Olivia succumbed to consumption at age twenty; Eliza died of the same disease at thirty-nine.

RECOMMENDED: *Life*; *Years.*

Mary Jane Leach-Rudawski

COLLOQUIALISM is a term derived from Latin words for informal conversation and speech; Dickinson's daring colloquialism was an almost insurmountable barrier to publication* during her lifetime. In 1866, Dickinson called attention to the inability of an editor* to fathom her colloquial style when a manuscript copy of "A narrow Fellow in the Grass" (P986)* was printed anonymously in the *Springfield Republican**; in a letter to Higginson,* the poet expressed annoyance about its unauthorized publication and faulty punctuation, as the interpolation of a question mark in the middle of a line changed the poem's conversational flow and meaning.

Dickinson saw the world around her "New Englandly—" and "Provincially—" (P285). Provincialisms and laconic wit are central features of her poems. "Elijah's Wagon knew no thill" (P1254) ponders the fact that the prophet's* chariot of fire was not a New England buggy (thills being the regional term for the shafts of wagon wheels). Some poems deploy a feminine (never ladylike) vernacular of domestic* tasks. In "She sweeps with many-colored Brooms—" (P219), a sunset is personified as a careless "Housewife in the Evening West—" who should "Come back, and dust the Pond!" Other poems speak in a voice* not readily identifiable as regional or feminine. "It feels a shame to be Alive—" (P444) pays tribute to the Civil War* dead while asking questions about a world that requires such sacrifice; images are evoked of corpses stacked up like dollars, of an "Enormous Pearl" of life dissolved "In Battle's—horrid Bowl." After Frazar Stearns* was killed at Newbern, Dickinson wrote, "It dont sound so terrible—quite—as it did—" (P426), a poem that poses disturbing questions about war and about the lifeless euphemisms that shield us from an awareness of the "Murder" that has been done: "Put it in Latin—left of my school—/ Seems it dont shriek so—under rule." In "The Auctioneer of Parting" (P1612), the coarse language of the marketplace is deployed to dramatize the agony of separated lovers—an agony likened to that of the Crucifixion: "His 'going, going, gone' / Shouts even from the Crucifix, / And brings his Hammer down."

Dickinson's colloquialisms expose and pierce the shields of genteel usage; it is not surprising that the posthumous publication* of selected poems in the 1890s (timidly edited by Higginson and Todd*) smooths away hundreds of Dickinson's uncompromising unconventionalities. The famous slant of light "That oppresses, like the *Heft* / Of Cathedral Tunes—" (P258) is changed to the more refined "*weight* of cathedral tunes"; in "I never saw a Moor—" (P1052), genteel substitutions weaken a powerful expression of religious faith: "And what a *Billow* be" is changed to "And what a *wave* must be" (emphasis added); in the concluding lines of the poem ("Yet certain am I of the spot / As if the Checks were given—"), the Higginson and Todd version substitutes the more dignified *chart* (showing the way to heaven*) for Dickinson's *checks*. Checks are stubs exchanged for tickets by a train conductor who marks them in a way that validates a passenger's destination. "Tickets, please!" is a call familiar to all who have traveled on a train—but the word "checks," in this sense, did not make its way into any dictionary during Dickinson's lifetime. Her lexicon was important; but her ear for the vernacular was, on occasion, a more reliable guide. Not until Thomas Johnson's* 1955 variorum edition did readers encounter for the first time in print the range and power of Dickinson's colloquialism. (*See*: Linguistic and Stylistic Approaches; Words)

RECOMMENDED: *Letters*; *Poems*; Benjamin Lease, *Emily Dickinson's Readings of Men and Books*; Brita Lindberg-Seyersted, *The Voice of the Poet: Aspects of Style in the Poetry of Emily Dickinson*; Cristanne Miller, *Emily Dickinson: A Poet's Grammar*.

Benjamin Lease

COLTON, AARON MERRICK (1809–1895) Minister of the Dickinsons' church in Amherst,* the First Church* of Christ, from 1840 to 1853, Colton surely influenced Dickinson's conception of faith* and perhaps even her choice of rhetorical* devices. Colton was known for hard-hitting, personally challenging sermons. He participated in some Amherst revivals*: during the summer of 1850, for example, he influenced at least 150 individuals, including Dickinson's father, to profess conversion. Dickinson described Colton as giving "eloquent addresses" with "calls of *now today*" and preaching with an "earnest look and gesture" (L46). She called his sermons "enlivening," but apparently the term is not wholly complimentary. Compared to his successor, Edward Dwight* (whom she also found "alive"), Colton seemed less loving, perhaps more frightening—but not at all boring.

RECOMMENDED: *Letters*; *Life*; *Years*; Beth Maclay Doriani, *Emily Dickinson, Daughter of Prophecy*.

Beth Maclay Doriani

COLTON, SARA PHILIPS of Brooklyn, New York, was a close friend of Martha Dickinson Bianchi* for most of her life. Although she never met or saw Emily Dickinson, Colton received two letters from her during a visit to Amherst* (L1010, 1011). According to a story that appeared in the *Hartford Daily Times* in 1937, a story for which Colton (then Mrs. A. L. Gillett) supplied information, on two occasions Dickinson placed her favorite flower,* the jasmine, in a basket and "sent them to the young girl in her brother's home. And each time she sent one of her cryptic and characteristic notes" (*Years* 2:457).

Perhaps unknowingly, Colton Gillett also made other contributions to Dickinson studies that dispel the fiction that Dickinson was dour, loveless, or lifeless. For instance, in the story just mentioned, she recalled that while she was staying in Lavinia Dickinson's* house, "she heard laughter and gaiety from the rooms at the back, and knew that the voice was that of Martha's other aunt."

RECOMMENDED: *Letters*; *Years*.

Dean Rader

THE COMPLETE POEMS OF EMILY DICKINSON (**1924**) Even though some critics questioned its completeness, Martha Dickinson Bianchi* assembled in this one volume what she identified as "a final complete edition" that included five previously uncollected poems and all four published collections of Dickinson's poetry: *Poems* (1890)* and *Poems, Second Series* (1891)* edited by Mabel Loomis Todd* and T. W. Higginson*; *Poems, Third Series* (1896)* edited by Todd; and *The Single Hound* (1914)* edited by Bianchi. Organizing the 597 poems in five parts, Bianchi combined the poems of the 1890, 1891, and 1896 editions in their four original categories of "Life," "Love,"* "Nature,"* and "Time and Eternity," adding only the poem "Title divine—is mine!" (P1072) to end the section "Love." Concluding the volume with "The Single Hound," Bianchi reprinted the poems from her 1914 collection with four additions: "A little overflowing word" (P1467), "Give little Anguish—" (P310), "The Bible is an antique Volume—" (P1545), and "Through lane it lay—thro' bramble—" (P9). Three of these additional poems (P1072, 1467, 1545) Bianchi earlier published in *The Life and Letters of Emily Dickinson* (1924).*

By gathering Todd's earlier collections after the copyrights lapsed, Bianchi claimed literary rights as sole heir of Dickinson's poetry and copyrighted the poems in one volume. In the process, she removed any reference to Todd's work in the first three collections. Publication of Bianchi's *Life and Letters* and *Complete Poems* encouraged the "discovery" of Dickinson in the 1920s as part of the American literary canon.

RECOMMENDED: *AB*; R. W. Franklin, *The Editing of Emily Dickinson: A Reconsideration*; Elizabeth Horan, "Mabel Loomis Todd, Martha Dickinson Bianchi, and the Spoils of the Dickinson Legacy"; Klaus Lubbers, *Emily Dickinson: The Critical Revolution*.

Jean Carwile Masteller

THE COMPLETE POEMS OF EMILY DICKINSON (1960)   Published by Little, Brown, this was the "reading text" Thomas H. Johnson* provided as a complement to *The Poems of Emily Dickinson* (1955).* Johnson retained the variorum's chronological arrangement, numbering system, editorial* practices, and indices but represented only one version of each poem. His introduction acknowledged questions of poetic judgment that confront anyone making editorial choices in cases where Dickinson herself left no preferred version. In "Blazing in Gold" (P228),* for example, his choice of "the Otter's Window" may be less pleasing to one or another reader* than "the kitchen window" or "oriel window" that the poet employed as options. In general, Johnson retained Dickinson's wording from semifinal drafts unless her own underlining of options suggested a preference. Although he retained Dickinson's dashes* and capitalization,* Johnson silently corrected misspellings and misplaced apostrophes. Consequently, this one-volume edition cannot be substituted for *The Poems* as a source of quotations to be used in scholarly writing. In 1961, Little, Brown published *Final Harvest: Emily Dickinson's Poems*, which provides a compact selection of 576 poems from *The Complete Poems*, along with a Biographical Note and Johnson's essay "The Vision and Veto of Emily Dickinson."

RECOMMENDED: R. W. Franklin, *The Editing of Emily Dickinson: A Reconsideration*; Joel Myerson, *Emily Dickinson: A Descriptive Bibliography.*

Jane Donahue Eberwein

COMPRESSION, AS ARTISTIC DEVICE   Dickinson employed compression in three realms: form, syntax,* and content. Critics claim, albeit from different theoretical perspectives, that compression is the most striking characteristic of Dickinson's language; it accounts for most of her poetic effects, which include ambiguity,* multiple meanings, multiple referents, concealed or withheld power, density of narrative, and her often teasing or ironic tone.

Compression of form, in line, stanza, or poem length or in meter, distinguishes Dickinson from most nineteenth-century poets. With or without the temporal context, this physical compression is striking. As Eberwein states, Dickinson's poems are "ode aspirations in nursery rhyme shapes" (143). For example, P1127 suggests an event of epic proportions: "Soft as the massacre of Suns / By Evening's Sabres slain." The formal compression occurs in its brevity; Dickinson gives us half of a hymnal* or common measure stanza (a tetrameter line followed by a trimeter); it is not possible to tell which without the remaining rhymes.* Even the "simple melodies of American Protestant hymns" that "guided her verse forms" were "adapted mainly by compression" (Eberwein).

Compression of syntax occurs in both obvious and obscure ways in Dickinson's language. Miller presents a detailed analysis of the mechanisms of grammatical compression, stating that compression occurs in three categories: (1) recoverable deletion in which words are elided but understood grammatically; (2) nonrecoverable deletion in which compression is caused either by parataxis—"The blank *and* replaces temporal or adverbial connectives, thereby marking that some connection exists but omitting to clarify it"—or by syntactic* doubling in which a word or phrase functions in two unparallel syntactic roles; and (3) patterned contrast with polysyllables—"latinate abstraction defined by monosyllabic, native words representing concrete objects or actions" (30, 41).

P1127 contains two examples of syntactic compression. What does "Soft," the word on which the simile is constructed, modify? Compression of the subject into this adjective creates the possibility of multiple referents and thus ambiguity. Syntactic doubling occurs in the second line: Does "By Evening's Sabres slain" modify "Suns" (explaining agency) or "Soft" (explaining means), or does it modify the elided referent and thus explain causality? The ambiguity of the referent for "Soft" intensifies the ambiguity surrounding this phrase's syntactic function; thus the phrase contains all the possible syntactic functions marked by the preposition "By."

Compression of content depends in part on how we read* any particular compression of form or syntax but is also a function of lexical and narrative choices. In a reading of P505, Wolff observes that the vocabulary suggests a "compression of sexuality, legal rights, and the power of art" within a "bombastically satirical and very funny" poem (173). Eberwein notes that even in her most narrative poems, Dickinson "distill[s] plot, character, and setting to release a radiance of suggestion" rather than revealing "what condition the speaker actually describes, how she got there, and how she emerged" (141).

Dickinson's use of compression has various theoretical implications. Porter would read the absent referent for the simile "as the massacre of Suns" as evidence of her lack of a poetic enterprise: "Willy-nilly, that decentered . . . stance constituted a perception of the world that was inevitably chaotic"; her "art [is] without a subject," and she "has pared away the very armature of meaning" (152–53).

Feminist* scholars, however, might read P1127 as a poem about gender confrontation. Miller claims that "compression allows for protective ambiguity [and] conveys a sense of the speaker's withheld power" (27). Wolff sees Dickinson's use of compression as a necessary part of the poetic voices* she used to explore subjects, such as female sexuality, that might otherwise have been taboo. Whatever the resulting theoretical implications, "just as steam results from compression of water subjected to intense heat, so poems result from pressure on language in the cauldron of imagination" (Eberwein 156). (*See:* Linguistic and Stylistic Approaches)

RECOMMENDED: Jane Donahue Eberwein, *Dickinson: Strategies of Limitation*; Cristanne Miller, *Emily Dickinson: A Poet's Grammar*; David Porter, *Dickinson: The Modern Idiom*; Cynthia Griffin Wolff, *Emily Dickinson*.

Lynne EFM Spear

CONGREGATIONALISM By far the largest denomination in Massachusetts, Congregationalism served Dickinson as the formal channel of language, concepts, and emotional responses generally associated with the New England Puritan* tradition. Distinguished by its covenantal form of church polity, Congregationalism originated in England and served as the established church of the Massachusetts Bay Colony.

Born into a family prominent in the Congregational church since the time of the Great Migration, Dickinson most likely was baptized in 1831. She attended the First (Congregational) Church* of Amherst* until about age twenty-nine but never made the public profession the church still required for membership.

At a time when a growing liberalism centered in eastern Massachusetts promised to divide the denomination, Congregationalists in the Connecticut Valley* defended a Trinitarian orthodoxy grounded in the tenets of the Westminster Confession, adopted with minor changes as the official expression of New England Congregationalism in 1680. Within Amherst, First Church was an integral part of the community; college faculty and visiting Congregational leaders frequently supplied its pulpit. The ministers whom Dickinson knew best received their theological education at Andover or Yale, institutions dedicated to promoting neo-Edwardsean orthodoxy.

Although recast over time, doctrines basic to the Covenant of Grace as enunciated at Westminster—divine sovereignty, original sin, and justification by faith* in Christ's* atoning work at Calvary—were still preached in Amherst. Baptism served as the "seal" of this covenant. Continuing an emphasis encouraged by early "covenanters" in New England and later heightened by the advent of revivalism,* orthodox Congregational churches in the Connecticut Valley also continued to give special prominence to the operation of "grace" as an inward force that could "convert" and afterward "sanctify" the soul.

While Dickinson consistently rejected any "contract" based upon original sin and consisting of a legal* "negotiation" (P1270), in her writing she acknowledged a fallen universe and revealed a strong need for spiritual reassurance. Her persona never doubts the sovereignty of God,* distrustful as she often is regarding His intentions. "Deity," also called "Omnipotence" or "Immortality," is ever close, evoking intense feelings of sacredness and awe. The search for "Redemption" persists; "Justification," while based upon a private "calvary of Wo" (P126), demands suffering. "Grace," though assuming the guise of human love* or nature's* beauty, is a gift of supreme significance that effects an inward transformation.

In a representative poem, "Mine—by the Right of the White Election!" (P528), terms and concepts such as "Election,"* "the Royal Seal," "the Scarlet prison," entitlement, and confirmation derive from the Covenant of Grace upheld by orthodox Congregationalists, and a tone of exultation arises from her assumption of a powerful and everlasting "Charter." (*See*: Edwards; Religion)

RECOMMENDED: *Life*; Jane Donahue Eberwein. " 'Graphicer for Grace': Emily Dickinson's Calvinist Language"; First Church of Amherst. *Articles of Faith and Government*. Amherst, MA, 1834; Rowena Revis Jones, " 'A Royal Seal': Dickinson's Rite of Baptism"; Williston Walker. *A History of the Congregational Churches in the United States*. New York: Christian Literature, 1894.

Rowena Revis Jones

CONNECTICUT VALLEY   European settlement of the Connecticut Valley began in 1635 in the Wethersfield/Windsor area of Connecticut. From there, William Pynchon traveled upriver and settled Springfield, Massachusetts, in 1636. There he found only 200 Native Americans left, thousands having been decimated by smallpox and bubonic plague. In 1659, Hadley, Massachusetts, was settled by a dissident group from Wethersfield, led by their minister, Rev. John Russell. In this group was Nathaniel Dickinson, whose great grandson, Nathan, would be among the first to settle the Third Precinct of Hadley. In 1759, this became Amherst,* where, eight generations after Nathaniel reached Hadley, Emily Dickinson was born.

Western Massachusetts slowly developed a distinct, independent character. Jonathan Edwards* awakened a storm of religious fervor in Northampton in the

1730s and 1740s. His "Great Awakening" swept the colonies. Northampton's reaction was quite in keeping with the history of the valley: it rebelled against such a confining philosophy and asked Edwards to leave. As the Revolution approached, most towns in the region were, at first, cautious about taking part. After winning independence, many in western Massachusetts lost their farms to Boston bankers (backed by the state) in the depression that followed. This led to Shays' Rebellion of 1786–1787, a little western Massachusetts rebellion that demonstrated the need for a U.S. Constitution.

The Hadley-Northampton-Amherst section of the Connecticut River Valley has been the home of a variety of true geniuses—and true eccentrics. Washington Irving sensed something unusual there in 1832, when he wrote, "I have had a most delightful excursion along the enchanting Valley of the Connecticut— of which I dare not speak at present—for it is just now the topic which I am a little mad upon. It is a perfect stream for a poet." Irving knew nothing of Dickinson, who was just then almost eighteen months old. She would make hardly a ripple in that poetic stream during her lifetime, but, in a way, she epitomizes the valley. Dickinson loved the land and wrote passionately of it: "This—is the land—the Sunset washes—/ These—are the Banks of the Yellow Sea" (P266).

RECOMMENDED: Edmund Delaney. *The Connecticut River: New England's Historic Waterway.* Chester, CT: Globe Pequot Press, 1983; James C. O'Connell. *The Pioneer Valley Reader: Prose and Poetry from New England's Heartland.* Stockbridge, MA: Berkshire House, 1995; William F. Stekl. *The Connecticut River.* Middletown, CT: Wesleyan University Press, 1972.

Daniel Lombardo

CONSCIOUSNESS, AS THEME   Consciousness, in Dickinson's view, is complex, vast, deep, and valuable when considered in reference to God,* death,* and immortality.* Dickinson grasps consciousness as her divided self.* Consciousness steadily observes the soul; even if the soul hides itself, it cannot be rid of consciousness. Functioning as God, consciousness punishes a deed contrary to God (P894). It reveals the self that is usually concealed. Suffering from haunted consciousness (P670), Dickinson found that consciousness of death leads the human being to be intensely aware of the self.* Consciousness is fully revealed in death, "Costumeless Consciousness" (P1454). Consciousness, Dickinson thinks, is far more important than the outer world. Consciousness, not any external force, decides whether the soul is free or captive (P384). Although consciousness attacks the poet's reasoning mind, the poet alone can subjugate it. If she controls her consciousness, it means that she can overcome any difficulties caused by the outer world (P642).

In 1870 Emily Dickinson celebrated Susan Gilbert Dickinson's* birthday with flowers* and a poem acclaiming one whose life occasioned joy "Without the date, like Consciousness or Immortality—" (P1156; L356). Later, she defined consciousness as "the only home of which we *now* know" in a letter to Maria

Whitney* that offered comfort to one struggling with belief, commenting, "That sunny adverb had been enough, were it not foreclosed" (L591). (*See*: Gothicism)

RECOMMENDED: *Letters*; *Poems*; E. Miller Budick, *Emily Dickinson and the Life of Language: A Study in Symbolic Poetics.*

Sahoko Hamada

COOPER, ABIGAIL INGERSOLL (1817–1895)   The widow of Amherst lawyer James Sullivan Cooper figures notably for her condolence letters on several anniversaries of Edward Dickinson's* death. The prevailing topic of Emily Dickinson's quite lyrical correspondence with Mrs. Cooper is nature*—flowers* in particular. Thus Dickinson communicates to this friend one of her most subtle observations on nature: "How strange that Nature does not knock, and yet does not intrude!" (L510).

RECOMMENDED: *Letters*; *Years.*

Jutta Fraunholz

COWAN, PEREZ DICKINSON (1843–1923)   Dickinson's favored "Cousin Peter." His grandfather, Perez Dickinson, was the brother of Samuel Fowler Dickinson.* After his family fled north from Tennessee through Confederate lines, Cowan attended Amherst College* from 1863 to 1866 and was close to the Dickinson family. He later became a Presbyterian minister. Of what is considered to be an extensive correspondence, only five letters from Dickinson to Cowan survive.

RECOMMENDED: *Letters*; *Years.*

Erika Scheurer

CRISIS   is integral to Dickinson's concept of poetry: "If I feel physically as if the top of my head were taken off, I know *that* is poetry" (L342a); "To pile like Thunder to it's close /. . . . / This—would be Poetry—" (P1247). Crisis was a state privileged by Dickinson because extreme moments expand consciousness* and teach it awe; they are "A Grant of the Divine" leaving the "dazzled Soul" in "unfurnished Rooms" (P393); "If we survive them they expand us" (PF49). In another poem she wrote: "A Bomb upon the Ceiling / Is an improving thing" because of its stimulus to "Conjecture" (P1128). Crisis is a liminal state, in her dictionary, "that change [of a disease] which indicates recovery or death . . . the point of time when an affair is arrived to its highth, and must soon terminate or suffer a material change." In P889 "Crisis is a Hair"—a hair's breadth between life and death,* knowing and not knowing, having and not having, loving* and not loving. Critics have cited biographical* explanations for the sense of crisis in her work, the early death of school friends, fear for her vision,* the loss of loved ones, fear of sexuality and gender roles. However, crisis was also a mode, Dickinson's way of winnowing out what was important and what was not. She had great confidence in the mind's power to survive its "larger—Darknesses" (P419). Her fearless explorations of all the data of human consciousness* contribute to the curious modernity of Dickinson's work and its affinities with the sublime* and negativity as privileged by theorists such as Kristeva, Bataille, and Bakhtin. (*See*: Psychological Approaches)

RECOMMENDED: Adrienne Rich, "Vesuvius at Home: The Power of Emily Dickinson."

Joan Kirkby

CRITICAL RECEPTION OF THE 1890s   The first decade of Emily Dickinson's critical reception was characterized by evaluative journalistic reviews rather than academic criticism. Between 1890 and 1897, the publication of three editions of poems and two volumes of letters elicited 600 notices—in addition to numerous private responses and creative tributes—from across the United States and Britain in a wide variety of daily newspapers; political, religious, academic, and family journals; as well as eighty influential literary periodicals. With more than 200 reviews, *Poems* (1890)* evoked the strongest response, while the effect of novelty gradually wore off after 1891, only to revive briefly with the publication of *Letters* in 1894. Impatiently awaited by the public as an explanatory companion to the poems, Dickinson's letters,* although praised almost unanimously for their "poetic" and humorous* style, nevertheless did not satisfy readers' curiosity about autobiographical data, and critical interest abated after only four months. Without further printings of Dickinson's poems after 1897, critical reception came to a temporary halt until the publication of *The Single Hound* (1914).*

The "broad spectrum of responses ranging from sheer enthusiasm through approval and dislike to parody and sarcasm" (Lubbers 22), often influenced by the critic's gender or geographical affiliation, illustrates that, while fame* indeed did not escape her, Dickinson nevertheless "was evidently born to be the despair of reviewers" (Buckingham 279). The most heated debates focused on the issue of poetic form, with Dickinson criticized for false rhymes,* irregular meter, and incorrect grammar. A small group of eminent arbiters of literary opinion (Thomas Bailey Aldrich* [Boston], Andrew Lang [England], and Richard Henry Stoddard [New York]), engaged in preserving elite literary standards based on genteel aesthetics of formalist perfection, castigated Dickinson's "balderdash" as "divorced from meaning, from music,* from grammar, from rhyme, in brief, from articulate and intelligible speech" (Buckingham 82). The majority of New England reviewers, however, adopted a more dichotomous position (foregrounded by T. W. Higginson's* promotional essay "An Open Portfolio"*) in balancing defects of form against merits of thought and admired the affective "force," "strangeness," "genius," and "originality" of Dickinson's poetry. Unqualified enthusiasm was sounded by female reviewers (Louise Chandler Moulton, Lilian Whiting) and nonprofessional readers, with William Dean Howells* emerging as Dickinson's most influential advocate. Celebrating her powerful "new language," Howells insisted that the "harsh exterior" is the "perfect expression of her ideals" (Buckingham 77).

Additional critical concerns included explications of verbal obscurities; bio-graphical* speculations (sympathy for Dickinson's life as custodian of female respectability and curiosity about the reasons for her "withdrawal from the world''); attempts at classification (comparing her to some ninety-five different authors, most frequently Emerson,* Whitman,* Thoreau,* and Blake*); and the-matic discussions. Frequent praise was bestowed on her choice of "feminine" topics (home,* womanhood,* human relationships, death*), with nature* poems as the most popular category, followed by her religious* lyrics* (sometimes regarded as disquieting). This wide range of critical responses turned out to be, as Higginson had predicted in 1891, a sure indicator of Dickinson's permanence well beyond the 1890s. (*See*: Fame)

RECOMMENDED: *AB*; Willis J. Buckingham, ed., *Emily Dickinson's Reception in the 1890s: A Documentary History* and "Poetry Readers and Reading in the 1890s: Emily Dickinson's First Reception"; Klaus Lubbers, *Emily Dickinson: The Critical Revolution*; Marietta Messmer, "Dickinson's Critical Reception."

Marietta Messmer

CULTURAL STUDIES, AS AN APPROACH   Since cultural studies chal-lenges the traditional literary canon and canonical readings of these works, ar-guing for appreciation of authors and traditions that resist cultural domination, reading Dickinson's poetry as a cultural critic has manifold applications. How-ever, as Berlin has put it, cultural studies "simply cannot be easily pinned down" (viii), and critics tend to debate the meaning of this field of study rather than agree on a single definition. Generally, it is interdisciplinary, adopting an-thropological and sociological concerns; it addresses linguistic, economic, and political issues; and it looks at cultural forces and how they are produced. Ray-mond Williams, a British Marxist critic who investigated society from the stand-point of the economic impact of the Industrial Revolution, suggests that "the development of the word *culture* is a record of a number of important and continuing reactions to . . . changes in our social, economic, and political life, and may be seen, in itself, as a special kind of map by means of which the nature of the changes can be explored" (*Culture and Society* xvii). Another primary theorist is Antonio Gramsci, an Italian writer who spent part of his life in prison for opposition to Mussolini's fascist government. Gramsci's emphasis on "hegemony," understood as power exercised by tacit or passive consent rather than by domination, is integral to this field.

Partial to the idea that "the personal is political," cultural studies tends to view everything as potentially political, theorizing on the very forms of cultural interpretation. Given her lack of engagement in the political and social events of her day, Dickinson has not been a writer generally viewed as an active cul-tural critic in the current sense. Because of her resistance to politicizing her topics overtly, combined with the tendency to personalize experience, Dickinson's poetry at first glance may seem to run counter to this field's theoretical attention to issues of marginalization and cultural hegemony.

But given the anguish she expressed about Connecticut Valley* religious culture, a case could be made that her poetry exhibits how she suffered under, and resisted, the religious hegemony current during her lifetime. From this standpoint, the range of past and current studies devoted to interpreting Dickinson's stances on economics (issues of class), gender (feminism* and patriarchy), politics (Whig* tendencies, abolition), religion* (Puritan heritage*), and other aspects of nineteenth-century American culture may equally qualify as cultural criticism. Also, Dickinson's general lack of publication and relatively recent inclusion in the canon present a perfect case study for the role of gender in the cultural production of literature in society. (*See*: Women's Culture)

RECOMMENDED: James A. Berlin and Michael J. Vivion. *Cultural Studies in the English Classroom*. Portsmouth, NH: Heinemann, 1992; Joan Burbick, "Emily Dickinson and the Economics of Desire"; Betsy, Erkkila. "Emily Dickinson and Class"; A. R. C. Finch, "Dickinson and Patriarchal Meter: A Theory of Metrical Codes"; Jim Philip, "Valley News: Emily Dickinson at Home and Beyond"; Karen Sanchez-Eppler, *Touching Liberty: Abolition, Feminism, and the Politics of the Body*, ch. 4.

Michael Strysick

CURRIER, ELIZABETH DICKINSON (1823–1886) was Emily Dickinson's aunt, the youngest sister of Edward Dickinson* and only seven years older than Emily. Elizabeth, whom Emily sometimes called Libby, lived with her brother William* in Worcester, Massachusetts, from 1839 to 1866 and frequently visited Amherst.* She married Augustus Nelson Currier on 10 October 1866 and was active in charitable and church work, belonging to the Union Church in Worcester.

Emily's letters make frequent reference to Libby's visits and her commanding ways; once Emily acerbically quipped that Libby was " 'the only male relative on the female side' " (L473). Elizabeth shared with Emily the practice of writing verses, not unusual for women of their education, and was, in effect, the family scribe, even writing a verse history of the Dickinsons for the 1883 reunion.

RECOMMENDED: *Letters*; *Life*; *Years*.

Mary Carney

CUTLER, HARRIET and WILLIAM Susan Gilbert (Dickinson)* lived with her sister Martha* at the home of her oldest sister, Harriet Cutler (1820–1865), and brother-in-law (an Amherst* merchant) from 1850 to 1856. The Cutlers must have been in somewhat close contact with the Dickinsons at the time, because Lavinia Dickinson* mentions several calls to and from the Cutlers in her diary of 1851. Apparently, Harriet and her husband tried a little too anxiously to replace Sue's parents, by trying to prevent her from taking teaching positions, for example, and criticizing her love for Austin Dickinson* as financially imprudent. This caused Sue to seek her independence on various occasions, thus winning Emily Dickinson's applause.

RECOMMENDED: *Letters*; *Years*.

Jutta Fraunholz

D

DAGUERREOTYPE   In 1862, when Thomas Wentworth Higginson* asked Dickinson for a photograph of herself, he was making a gesture expected by the etiquette of the era: offering his correspondent an opportunity to place herself on display in his photograph album. Used to facilitate conversation in the parlor, albums like Higginson's were typically filled with small, mass-produced photographic keepsakes known as *cartes de visite*—"the social currency, the sentimental 'green-backs' of civilization," as Oliver Wendell Holmes called them. These owed their vogue to the invention, in 1854, of the fully transparent photographic negative. Until then, the only practical photographic system had been the daguerreotype, whose direct-positive images were impossible to produce in multiple copies.

The daguerreotype, invented in 1839 and named for its coinventor, the French artist Jacques Daguerre, worked by depositing a film of mercury on photosensitized areas of a polished silver surface. When viewed straight on, the resulting mirrorlike image was beautiful, with brilliant whites and rich, deep blacks. But it was also elusive. As Phoebe says in Hawthorne's* *The House of the Seven Gables*, daguerreotypes had the disadvantage of "dodging away from the eye, and trying to escape altogether." They were also expensive, physically delicate, and unique. Perhaps Emily Dickinson felt at home among them.

At any rate, Dickinson declined Higginson's request (L268), and the only known photograph of Dickinson is a daguerreotype currently believed to have been taken in Amherst* about 1847. In its original state or in numerous retouched versions, this is the source of all other portraits of the poet as an adult. In addition to discussing the history of this image, Longsworth reproduces the three other known portraits of Dickinson: a painting and two silhouettes, all executed when she was a young girl.

In his 1974 biography, Sewall reproduces a mysterious fifth image: a *carte de visite* labeled "Emily Dickenson [*sic*] 1860." Subsequent forensic analysis has demonstrated, however, that this is not a picture of the poet. The attribution was apparently a hoax perpetrated by the eccentric bookseller Samuel Loveman.

RECOMMENDED: *Life*; Jane Donahue Eberwein, *Dickinson: Strategies of Limitation*; Polly Longsworth, *The World of Emily Dickinson*; Joe Nickell, "A Likeness of Emily? The Investigation of a Questioned Photograph"; Robert Taft. *Photography and the American Scene: A Social History, 1839–1889*. New York: Dover, 1964.

Jonathan Morse

"DAISY"   The term appears in twenty-six poems, mostly written in 1858 and 1859. Daisies are frequently grouped with other flowers or with other aspects of nature* and often evoke the cycle and transience of life. Dickinson and "daisy" become one in poems that speak of love* and of the imbalance of power between individuals. Critics have argued that because the conceit of the daisy is informed by the myth of Apollo and Clytie (in which the latter transforms into a daisy or sunflower to prove her unwavering devotion to Apollo/ Sol), the daisy represents a small, submissive, weak female who faces the power and condescension of a stronger male. The daisy's fragility in P72, her dependence on the sun in P106, and her unreciprocated love in P85 confirm this view. However, the daisy can also be seen as endowed with independence and strength. "Daisy" derives from the Old English *day's eye* and in that sense represents a force with which the male—the sun—must contend. "Daisy" in P106 thus becomes "daisies" who/which manage to steal the sun's power. In P124 "A Myriad Daisy," at first childlike and meek, succeeds in diminishing the "Immortal Alps," bringing them down to her level.

The relationship between "Daisy" and "Master"* is central to the second and third Master letters. Critics have not definitively identified the "Master," an individual who assumes almost God*-like proportions, as male or female, but they agree that "Daisy," the passionate, frustrated, subservient lover-writer, represents Dickinson. In L233 Dickinson challenges this image of herself, however: "if I had the Beard on my cheek—like you—and you—had Daisy's petals—and you cared so for me—what would become of you?"

RECOMMENDED: Judith Farr, *The Passion of Emily Dickinson*; Suzanne Juhasz, ed., *Feminist Critics Read Emily Dickinson*.

Sylvia Henneberg

DANCE RESPONSES TO DICKINSON   Most significant among choreographic works honoring Dickinson is Martha Graham's *Letter to the World*. Ironically, *Letter*, now considered among the important dance compositions of the twentieth century and a signature piece for Graham, disappointed the audience and critics who attended its August 1940 premiere in Bennington, Vermont. By January 1941, when Graham's revised *Letter* made its New York debut, the dance received unqualified praise as a work of genius. Among Graham's collaborators on *Letter* were composer Hunter Johnson and set designer Arch Lauterer. In particular, Lauterer's evocative stage scenery—an imaginatively sculpted bench and a trellised house front—underscored the dreamlike quality of Graham's representation and her emphasis on Dickinson's interior life and struggles rather than external events.

The plot of *Letter* grew out of Graham's knowledge of romantic legends that dominated early biographical studies of Dickinson, and Graham made the poet's own words central to the narrative. The role of Dickinson is split between a woman who dances and one who speaks. In the original cast, Jean Erdman played the speaking Emily; Graham herself, the dancing Emily. Other performers included Eric Hawkins as the Lover,* a role Graham intended as a symbol of worldly attractions rather than a portrait of a specific person; Merce Cunningham as the character "March," Graham's personification of Dickinson's own lively wit and imagination; and Jane Dudley as the Ancestress, a stern figure representing the poet's Puritan* heritage and preoccupation with mortality. The dance's thematic movement is divided into five sections, described by Graham with phrases from Dickinson poems: (1) Because I see New Englandly; (2) The Postponeless Creature; (3) The Little Tippler; (4) Leaf at love turned back; and (5) This is my letter to the world.* At the work's climax, the dancing Emily is reconciled to her solitary fate as a poet.

Letter to the World has inspired tributes by several visual* artists. Barbara Morgan translated significant moments of Graham's choreography into photographs and arranged these in an essay that recorded the dramatic sequence of the dance. Charlotte Trowbridge commemorated Graham's portrayal of Dickinson in a series of drawings. More recently, Michigan textile artist Ann Kowaleski has completed three art quilts that celebrate the affinity between Graham and Dickinson and use images from *Letter* as narrative features.

Since *Letter* and, perhaps, because of its stature, few choreographers have returned to Dickinson's life or poetry for the content of a major work. Heinz Poll, artistic director of the Ohio Ballet, choreographed a piece titled *Called Back.*—Emily* (1984), which the company performed in its regular season and as a featured part of its program for the Jacob's Pillow Summer Dance Festival in Massachusetts. Poll's dance, like Graham's, reinforces biographical legends about Dickinson and similarly casts two Emilys—one to say the poems and one to interpret them in movement. Also noteworthy is Warren Spears' ballet *Rowing in Eden* (1987), commissioned by the Royal Danish Ballet Company, which includes two movements based on Dickinson poems. (*See*: Dramatic Representations; Fiction; Musical Settings)

RECOMMENDED: Agnes de Mille. *Martha: The Life and Work of Martha Graham.* New York: Random House, 1991; Don McDonagh. *Martha Graham: A Biography.* New York: Praeger, 1973; Barbara Morgan. *Martha Graham: Sixteen Dances in Photographs.* New York: Duell, Sloan, and Pearce, 1941; Charlotte Trowbridge. *Dance Drawings of Martha Graham.* New York: Dance Observer, 1945.

Jonnie Guerra

DASH AND OTHER PUNCTUATION   Dickinson's favored and most original punctuation is the category of marks editors have consistently represented as "dashes." The degree of disjunction* signaled by dashes is much less fixed than the relatively standardized pauses or full stops indicated by commas, semicolons, periods, question marks, and exclamation marks. For this reason, Dickinson's use of the dash increases the level of reader participation in determining both the rhythm and meaning of a poem. Dashes also significantly influence gradations of inflection and tone that bear directly on interpretations of voice* and identity in both poems and letters. Dickinson indicates the importance she attributes to voice nuances of this sort when she observes to Higginson* in August 1876 that "a Pen has so many inflections and a Voice but one" (L470).

The "dash" entry in the 1828 edition of Webster's *An American Dictionary of the English Language** supplies both an early influence on Dickinson's thinking about the dash and a means to identify key issues related to it that figure prominently in her poetic project. In addition to describing the disjunctive function of the dash, Webster's citation of Virgil's *"quos ego—"* in his entry on the "dash" may have reminded Dickinson that Virgil frequently employed that punctuation within his *Aeneid*: "A mark or line in writing or printing, noting a break or stop in the sentence; as in Virgil, quos ego—: or a pause; or the division of the sentence" (55a verso). The words of Virgil literally mean "what," "I," or "you" and may have been translated as "what I am," "what you are," or "that which I am or you are." These meanings, in combination with the dash, suggest an assertion of self, but a distinctly inconclusive one: Virgil's fragment declares that the speaker or someone else is something but does not further designate what that something is. The appearance of Virgil's assertion within a definition describing the disjunctive function of the dash thus associates self-definition with syntactic* rupture. The dash, then, may have appeared to Dickinson as the form of punctuation best suited to challenging the linear progression of sentences while emphasizing the uncertainty of identity. In light of Dickinson's friendship with the Webster family, the existence of a family dictionary inscribed by Noah Webster,* and numerous references to her "lexicon" in her writing, we can readily accept Cristanne Miller's conclusion that Dickinson read her dictionary and that doing so freed her to be a more daring writer.

Familiar poems like "This is my letter to the World" (P441),* "I'm 'wife'— I've finished that—" (P199), and "You're right—'the way *is* narrow'—" (P234) readily demonstrate the way dashes extend reader options for determining inflection, tone, and meaning. Poems 199 and 234 also show that dashes can coordinate with quotation marks and underlining (italics) to dramatize further voicing possibilities. (*See*: Linguistic Approaches; Words)

RECOMMENDED: Sharon Cameron, *Choosing Not Choosing: Dickinson's Fascicles*; Paul Crumbley, *Inflections of the Pen: Dash and Voice in Emily Dickinson*; Brita Lindberg-Seyersted, *Emily Dickinson's Punctuation*; Cristanne Miller, *Emily Dickinson: A Poet's Grammar*; Martha Nell Smith, *Rowing in Eden: Rereading Emily Dickinson*.

Paul Crumbley

DEATH, AS SUBJECT   Although not her "Flood subject," a phrase Dickinson reserved for immortality* (L319), death certainly inspired an outpouring of poems. Many of her most discussed poems, such as "Safe in their Alabaster Chambers—" (P216),* "I felt a Funeral, in my Brain" (P280),* "I died for Beauty—but was scarce" (P449), "I heard a Fly buzz—when I died—" (P465),* and "Because I could not stop for Death—" (P712),* focus on death. In fact, one critic has stated that nearly every Dickinson poem has to do with death, at the least as an analogy for a finish. Dickinson wrote a variety of types of death poems, some of which follow and may overlap: the elegy*; its more sentimental relative, the consolation poem; poems describing deathbed scenes; and poems in which the speaker attempts to experience death and whatever follows it.

The last two categories are most controversial. Convention prompted nine-teenth-century Calvinists to observe deathbed behavior because it might offer clues to the afterlife. Some Dickinson deathbed poems acknowledge this convention. In P465, watchers wait patiently for "that last Onset—when the King / Be witnessed—in the Room—." Dickinson subverts the convention, however, because the poem fails to achieve a radiant, uplifting climax assuring the soul's salvation; instead, "the Windows failed—," and nothing more could be seen.

This poem also broaches the fourth category, the poem in which the speaker attempts to experience death and its sequel. Probably the most anthologized example is "Because I could not stop for Death—" (P712), in which the speaker journeys with her suitor, Death, beyond the "labor" and "leisure" of her life. Some critics have observed the importance of Emily Dickinson's Death as a character in American literature. Even more have pointed out the audacious move Dickinson makes in assigning a dead person as speaker. The fact that the accounts in both P465 and P712 are first-person contributes to the strangeness and freshness of these poems and, some would say, their morbid quality. Dick-inson's speakers' fascination with death can undoubtedly turn morbid and even grisly, when it focuses on the details of the corpse itself, as in "If I may have it, when it's dead" (P577). Not just grisly, however, Dickinson's poems are also seen as analogical. The figure of death allows her to plumb states of con-sciousness* and explore concepts that might not otherwise be representable— among them despair, spiritual doubt, meaninglessness, timelessness, and the ces-sation of knowing. (*See:* Gothicism; Grave; Immortality; Puritan Heritage)

RECOMMENDED: Jane Donahue Eberwein, *Dickinson: Strategies of Limitation*; Tho-mas H. Johnson, *Emily Dickinson: An Interpretive Biography*; Barton Levi St. Armand, *Emily Dickinson and Her Culture: The Soul's Society*; Robert Weisbuch, *Emily Dick-inson's Poetry*; Cynthia Griffin Wolff, *Emily Dickinson*.

Daneen Wardrop

DICKENS, CHARLES (1812–1870) This popular, prolific, sentimental* British novelist explored and defined many Victorian worlds—domesticity* and romance, children, institutions (poorhouse, court, prison), and other elements of lower- and middle-class life. Dickens was the most popular author in Dickin-son's family library, and she knew his work so well that both Wolff and Farr read her epistolary allusions to Dickensian characters and phrasing as a ''playful private code'' (Wolff 179), accessible to her correspondents.

After an idyllic childhood, Dickens' youth was frighteningly poverty-stricken. His father, John Dickens, entered debtors' prison; young Charles left school for a blacking factory and its dirty, strenuous work. Ever after, he worked unstintingly to avoid recurrence of privations he could barely speak about. As a clerk, court stenographer, and parliamentary reporter, he honed his sense of words and their specific meanings and power; in this attention to language he is similar to Dickinson, but their lives were extremely different. Dickens saw work in print by age twenty-one, then continued publishing prolifically until he died at fifty-eight, exhausted by public appearances reading his immensely popular creations. Paid by the word and usually published in installments, he was a mainstay of the great age of magazines, several of which he founded and edited (*Bentley's Miscellany, The Clock, Daily News, Household Words, All the Year Round*). He married and raised a large family, responded to a demanding audience, participated in literary and philanthropic circles, and continued his dramatic readings. Thus his art was prolific, public, and popular, in direct opposition to Dickinson's limited publishing, minimalist innovative poetry, and decades of retreat from ''society.''

Dickens collected early magazine pieces in 1836–1837 as *Sketches by Boz*, which achieved notice, but he became famous at twenty-five with *The Pickwick Papers* (1836–1837). Years of vigorous production followed (almost a novel a year): *Oliver Twist* (1837–1838); *Nicholas Nickleby* (1838–1839); *The Old Curiosity Shop* (1840–1841); *Barnaby Rudge* (1841); *Martin Chuzzlewit* (1842–1843); *Christmas Books* (1843–1848); *Dombey and Son* (1847–1848); *David Copperfield* (1849–1850); *Bleak House* (1852–1853); *Hard Times* (1854); *Little Dorrit* (1857–1858); *A Tale of Two Cities* (1859); *Great Expectations* (1860–1861); *Our Mutual Friend* (1864); *The Mystery of Edwin Drood* (unfinished, 1870); and other works.

Many memorable child* characters suffer evil but are rescued by noble, selfless adults, often of high economic or social class; but Dickens also showed the moral strength of working-class people, as in *Expectations* and *Copperfield* (his most autobiographical work). This last, like *Oliver Twist*, shows a boy struggling to remain good in spite of bad treatment. Tiny Tim, another variant on this theme, is the crippled child from ''A Christmas Carol,'' Dickens's famous story about Ebenezer Scrooge, whose name defines miserliness. Dickens' early sentimental vision, full of miraculous coincidences, gave way in the 1850s to a more ironic fiction, with fewer rescues, more realities, and unhappy or ambivalent endings, but also characters such as Pip who grow and develop. By his last decades, ''Dickens had arrived at his penetrating insights into the workings of society'' (Karl 131), which he treated with maturity, better character development, and more sophisticated irony.

Despite criticism for sensationalism, sentimentality, and difficulty portraying complex females, Dickens was the most popular writer of the century. Although

Emily Dickinson wrote in 1853 to Austin* that their father castigated Dickens as one of the " 'modern Literati' who he says are *nothing*" (L113), apparently Edward Dickinson* overcame his lack of enthusiasm; nine titles remain in the family library collection at Harvard. Dickinson read others not in their library; in early letters she alludes to *Pickwick Papers*, the Christmas stories, and *Bleak House*, while references to *Copperfield*, *Dombey*, and *Curiosity Shop* show that the family knew and used codes based on Dickens' works. Dickens' characters and phrases (especially from these last three works) turn up in her poems. Dickinson illustrated "A poor—torn heart—a tattered heart—" (P78) with "two illustrations clipped from her father's copy" of *The Old Curiosity Shop*; the poem may be based on Little Nell's grandfather, killed by grief. In "Trudging to Eden" (P1020), "Somebody's little Boy / . . . 'Trotwood' " (*David Copperfield*) is going smilingly to heaven* with the poem's narrator. Similarly, in P196, Dickinson's dying child narrator combines her own plea with one for Dickens' Tiny " 'Tim.' " Although Dickens' sentimentalized children fit closely with some poetic personae Dickinson created, both artists also wrote of another vision of life than that assured by popular Victorian religious and social ideals. (*See*: Books and Reading)

RECOMMENDED: Jack L. Capps, *Emily Dickinson's Reading 1836–1886*; Judith Farr, *The Passion of Emily Dickinson*; Frederick Karl. *Reader's Guide to the Nineteenth Century British Novel*. Rev. ed. New York: Noonday Press, 1972; Cynthia Griffin Wolff, *Emily Dickinson*.

Susan Kurjiaka

DICKINSON, EDWARD (1803–1874)   "His Heart was pure and terrible and I think no other like it exists," Emily Dickinson wrote after his death (L418). Later she referred to "his firm Light—quenched so causelessly" and "his lonely Life and his lonelier Death," remorseful last touches to her lifelong portrait of her father (L432, 457).

The poet caught facets of gentleness, ridiculousness, and black humor* few others saw in the authoritarian Edward. Ever respectful of her father's sternly controlled nature ("the straightest engine" that "never played" [L360]), Dickinson obeyed him as a child, rebelled or circumvented him as a young woman, but finally, with wit and sometimes exasperation, found accommodation with his unbending, autocratic ways. Her friend and literary mentor T. W. Higginson,* who bumped up against Mr. Dickinson's dislike of "modern Literati" during a call at the Homestead* in August 1870 (L113), thought him "thin dry & speechless," although "not severe I should think but remote" in "a house where each member runs his or her own selves" (L342a, b). The poet, however, came to think of her father as "Home"* itself.

Eldest son and the first of nine children of Amherst* lawyer and farmer Samuel Fowler Dickinson* and his wife, Lucretia Gunn,* Edward Dickinson was born 1 January 1803. He grew up in a white clapboard house that preceded the federal-style brick Homestead his father began building on his Main Street acreage in 1813. Largely due to the elder Dickinson's perseverance, Amherst Academy* opened in 1814, just as Edward exhausted the offerings of the district public school. A bright student, he afterward entered Yale College, graduating in 1823, although his father was so short of funds during the period that Edward spent one and a half of his four college years in Amherst, matriculating as a member of the junior class the year Amherst College* opened. Only one brother, Frederick, also had the privilege of college education.

After studying in his father's law office, Edward attended the Northampton Law School for a year, then passed the state bar and opened his Amherst practice in the fall of 1826. On 6 May 1828 he married shy, timid, pretty Emily Norcross* of Monson, whom he had courted for two and a half years. Their letters reveal Edward as a stiffish, overbearingly rational young man who distrusted emotional display, placed high stakes on his professional reputation, and was extremely sensitive to ridicule. Within five years their family of three children was complete: William Austin* (b. 16 April 1829), Emily* (b. 10 December 1830), and Lavinia* (b. 28 February 1833).

During the same decade, 1824–1833, Edward's father lost his property, having overcommitted it as collateral to help found the college. He removed to Ohio late in 1833, and Edward's family, which had owned and lived in the west half of the Homestead since before Emily's birth, rented the east part from new owner David Mack until moving to North Pleasant Street in 1840.

Determination to restore his father's ablated reputation apparently drove Edward to establish an irreproachable regional reputation, win back the family Homestead, and regain some lost family wealth. Fear of failure probably accounts for excessive self-control that suppressed his natural impulses, including a bent for pomp and circumstance, and distanced him from his emotions. He was able to repurchase his home in 1855, remodel it, and build next door the Evergreens* for his son Austin, whom he took into his busy legal* practice.

Edward's exemplary public career was framed by his thirty-eight-year treasurership of Amherst College (1835–1873). He served Amherst as representative to the General Court in Boston* in 1838, 1839, and 1874, was state senator in 1842 and 1843, became a member of the Governor's Council in 1846 and 1847, and was proposed but did not run for lieutenant governor of Massachusetts in 1861. During 1854 and 1855 he served in the Thirty-third Congress as representative from the state's Tenth District but lost the race for reelection. An avid Whig* who resisted a secret passion for political fray, Edward nonetheless attended several state and national political conventions and stumped for presidential candidates Henry Clay, Zachary Taylor, and Daniel Webster.*

He was an active member of the local Temperance Society, the Hampshire Colonization Society, and the three-county Agricultural Society. He also was lifelong trustee of the Amherst Academy from 1835 and frequently chaired the annual town Cattle Show and Town Meeting. Further, he served on the First Church* Parish Committee and the Northampton Lunatic Asylum board. A prominent citizen, driven by an outsize sense of duty but indulging, too, a flair for the best horses, his proudest achievement was the bringing to town of the nineteen-mile Amherst and Belchertown Rail Road, a spur that linked Amherst to the world in 1853. Over the years, Edward's civic involvements, his legal engagements, even his annual Commencement Tea and distinguished guests he attracted to his home provided the poet an intimate view of the larger world.

Within his home Edward kept tight rein on family activities and health* matters. Decisions more usually left to the mother of the family he took over from his less effectual wife, excepting only the religious* instruction of his children, an acknowledged area of deficiency until he joined the church in 1850. A firm believer in educating women, Edward provided his daughters a year each at the best schools, and he appreciated his elder daughter's intellectual superiority despite his bewilderment at meeting her mental attainments in a female. With neither daughter marrying and Austin's family living next door, Edward's domination as family patriarch continued intact until his death.

After she returned from Mount Holyoke Female Seminary,* Emily felt governed by her father's dictates and desires to an uncomfortable degree. Such incidents as his insistence that incoming letters be "family affairs" and his upset if she wasn't home from visiting friends punctually were described for her absent brother, sometimes humorously, sometimes with desperation. Gradually, she found ways to appease or get around her father. She baked all his bread and she kept at home to perform the little acts he might otherwise miss. Avoiding Father's "fumigations," she waited until he grew "too busy with his Briefs—to notice what we do" (L261). Edward, respectful of his daughter's requirements for time alone, seems never to have noticed she wrote poems. An inveterate haunter of bookstores, he purchased her many titles but begged her "not to read them" (L261). "Father . . . is in the habit of me," she told Higginson at age thirty-five, refusing an invitation by excuse of catering to her parent's needs (L316).

The father-daughter relationship was symbiotic. Edward provided the home and protection she needed in order to write. He was sympathetic to strange restrictions that hobbled her social interactions, having already met her symptoms in his wife. It was Father who gave Emily her great dog Carlo* that she might "ramble" in security, who did "not insist upon her coming" to Washington, D.C.,* with the rest of the family in 1854 (L157n), who created a nook among the trees behind their home where Emily could sit out-of-doors unobserved.

Dickinson's early fear of her father and her resistance slowly shifted to a mutual respect and finally subsided in pathos and awe. He was an isolated,* solitary figure, "the oldest and the oddest sort of a foreigner" (*Ly* 70) who read "lonely & rigorous books" (L342a) and who hid to watch the birds eat crumbs he distributed. But she also knew the man who led the railroad celebratory parade "like some old Roman General, upon a Triumph Day" (L127) and who could mimic the South's Jefferson Davis escaping capture in women's skirts. "Lonely" is the word she used most often, and his lonely death in a Boston boardinghouse from a toxic dose of morphine, administered after he collapsed while giving a speech in the state legislature one hot June day, seemed unbearable to the whole family.

The entire town closed down the day of Edward Dickinson's funeral; a nine-man delegation attended from the legislature. Among several poems Dickinson probably wrote in memory of this complicated man is "Lay this Laurel on the One" (P1393).

RECOMMENDED: *Letters*; *Life*; *Ly*; Millicent Todd Bingham, *Emily Dickinson's Home*; Vivian R. Pollak, *A Poet's Parents: The Courtship Letters of Emily Norcross and Edward Dickinson*.

Polly Longsworth

DICKINSON, EDWARD (Ned) (1862–1898)   was the eldest child of Susan* and Austin Dickinson.* Recurrent health problems prevented him from completing a degree at Amherst College,* and he became an assistant librarian in the college library. Following the pattern set by his mother and Aunt Emily, Ned was well read and a gifted writer. His school notebooks contain short pieces of exposition that further showcase his wit, a trait shared by his father and Aunt Emily. Ned's writing talent is also apparent in his intelligent, perceptive letters. He was the recipient of many notes from his aunt that indicate her affection for him; Martha Dickinson Bianchi* shows that the two often shared private jokes. Emily Dickinson named herself Ned's "Uncle Emily" when he was small (L315). After his father's death and prompted by many years of studying art and literature, he accompanied his mother and sister on their first "Grand Tour" of Europe in 1897. He never married but was engaged to Alice (Alix) Hill at the time of his premature death from angina.

RECOMMENDED: *FF*; Barton Levi St. Armand, " 'Your Prodigal': Letters from Ned Dickinson, 1879–1885"; Hampson Collection, Brown University.

Marcy L. Tanter

DICKINSON, ELIZABETH   Currier, Elizabeth Dickinson

DICKINSON, EMILY ELIZABETH (1830–1886)   Daughter of Edward* and Emily Norcross Dickinson,* the poet was born in Amherst,* Massachusetts, and spent all but a few brief interludes of her life in that Connecticut Valley* college town where she grew up during the period of revivalism* known as the Second Awakening. The education she received at Amherst Academy* and Mount Holyoke Female Seminary* gained reinforcement from extensive reading in the Bible,* Shakespeare,* authors of her own time both English (Dickens,* the Brownings,* George Eliot*) and American (Emerson,* Hawthorne,* Harriet Prescott Spofford*), and such periodical literature as the *Atlantic Monthly*ered* and *Springfield Daily Republican*,* to which her household subscribed. Two tendencies evident from Dickinson's teenage years, exuberant facility with language and withdrawal from any kind of public display, gradually resulted in her choice

of a reclusive life in the family Homestead* that allowed her to devote herself
to writing. Whether any romantic, medical, psychological, or spiritual crisis con-
firmed that choice in the years of her greatest poetic productivity during the
Civil War* remains in the realm of speculation.

The hidden nature of Dickinson's life, contrasted with the dazzling brilliance
of her poetic achievement, necessarily focuses attention on persons close to her.
These include her parents, her sister Lavinia,* brother Austin,* sister-in-law
Susan,* her niece and two nephews; family friends such as Samuel Bowles,*
Elizabeth Holland,* and Otis Phillips Lord*; schoolmates and other Amherst
neighbors; and friends to whom she reached out for spiritual guidance (Charles
Wadsworth*) or literary counsel (Thomas Wentworth Higginson* and Helen
Hunt Jackson*). Only ten Dickinson poems saw print in her lifetime, and those
appeared anonymously. When she died at age fifty-five, nobody guessed the
magnitude of her contribution to American literature. Lavinia, however, responded to discovery of her sister's manuscripts by enlisting Mabel Loomis
Todd* to initiate the publishing* project that has now established Dickinson as
one of America's literary giants and the best-loved woman poet yet to write in
English.

Insight into Dickinson's achievement may be gained through study of her
poems' and letters' editorial* history, as her writing has been successively represented by Todd and Higginson, Martha Dickinson Bianchi,* Millicent Todd
Bingham,* Thomas H. Johnson,* and R. W. Franklin.* Musical* settings of her
poems and responses to Dickinson in poetry,* dance,* drama,* fiction,* and the
visual arts* witness to the continuing creative energy unleashed by her poems,
as do poetic tributes* by twentieth-century authors and other manifestations of
her influence. Scholarly responses open varying perspectives on her work, particularly biographical,* editorial,* feminist,* psychological,* and poststructuralist* approaches. Study of literary influences on Dickinson, her relation
to many different literary traditions (Romanticism,* Realism,* the sublime,* the
hymn,* the elegy*), and her stylistic choices (use of the dash,* metonymy,*
oxymoron*) contribute to appreciation of her art. Focus on key themes of Dickinson's writing (death,* immortality,* consciousness,* gardens,* words,* God*)
aids in understanding. This book as a whole, then, distills what has been learned
about Emily Dickinson since *Poems* appeared in 1890.

Jane Donahue Eberwein

DICKINSON, EMILY NORCROSS (1804–1882)   has often been dismissed
as the unremarkable mother of a remarkable poet. But her part was indisputably
essential in the familial constellation out of which her daughter emerged as an
artist.

A native of Monson, Massachusetts, Emily was the daughter of Joel* and
Betsey Fay Norcross.* One of nine children, she was preceded by Hiram and
Austin and followed by two sisters and four brothers. Her capable mother ran
her expansive house efficiently and hospitably, while her father's business, ag-

ricultural, and civic activities brought local fame. Surrounded by siblings and an array of first cousins, Emily attended coeducational Monson Academy and studied in 1823 at the Herrick School "for Young Ladies" in New Haven, where a brother attended Yale. With parents who valued education, her opportunities clearly exceeded those of most women in the early nineteenth century.

For Emily, Monson proved both stimulating and secure. She and her sister Lavinia* became principal figures in a home alive with activity and visitors, despite their mother's declining health. Emily engaged in a multiplicity of civic events from attending concerts and academy lectures, to participating in a singing society, in Bible study, and in church associations. Her father's familial business alliances resulted in closer social contact with the extended family of Flynts, Packards, and Norcrosses. Yet Emily's societal security contrasted with the insecurity of illness and death in her family: Eli and Nancy died as children and Austin at twenty-one; Hiram struggled with tuberculosis.

Emily Norcross first met Edward Dickinson* in January 1826, when he came to Monson on business. Initially, she attended chemistry lectures with him. Their interest in each other was immediate, and Edward was soon introduced to her convivial relatives. Although his spontaneous and decisive efforts to head for marriage appeared rash, he saw her as "a person, in whom so many of the female virtues are conspicuous," intelligent, sensitive, socially graceful (Pollak 3). They had similar values and goals, an interest in books and religion, and complete conversational rapport. As rural New England gentry, both transmitted to their relationship concepts of formality and gentility. On her wedding day, 6 May 1828, Emily left Monson and her fragile family with real reluctance despite her unqualified desire to marry Edward Dickinson.

The Dickinsons spent the next two years in half of Jemima Montague's Amherst* house, only to move in 1830, when Edward bought the west half of his parents' Homestead.* Emily had various adjustments in her new life, having married a forceful husband. Her sphere was her home,* but she was determined to help Edward succeed professionally. The year 1829 was traumatic for her: William Austin* was born in April, but her brother Hiram died in February, and her mother in September. Sharing the Dickinson house with Edward's prominent family when they were in a precarious financial position made Emily and Edward partners in insecurity. This was the climate when Emily Elizabeth Dickinson was born.

Mrs. Dickinson's impaired health for a period after Lavinia's* 1833 birth coincided with the sale of the Homestead to the Macks* and the financial dissolution of the elder Dickinsons before their departure for Ohio. She presided over half a house for seven more years prior to acquisition of the North Pleasant Street residence and the final return to the Homestead in 1855.

Firm convictions she shared with her husband contrasted with her physical frailty. Regarding their children as superior, they agreed on the importance of education, discipline, and religious orthodoxy. Though he was overtly authoritarian, she was covertly so; thus her domestic directives especially annoyed her children. Within the patriarchal framework, she exercised perfectionist vigor in maintaining an orderly, immaculate house and a kitchen where delectable food was prepared. Edward's external commitments merely increased his wife's focus on familial care and her expectation that both daughters would acquire house-keeping and cooking skills, even though there was usually hired help. But by the time she was nineteen, Emily was exclaiming, "God keep me from what they call *households*" (L36).

To manage a house effectively involved, in Mrs. Dickinson's view, hospitality to extended family and friends. She was so drawn to the beauties of plants that she could never be without a splendid garden.* The mere sight of "elegant flowers" in Ohio caused Catherine Dickinson (Sweetser)* to want to "tie up a bunch and toss them over the mountains into [Emily's] flower pitchers."

Communicative and lively, the younger Dickinsons became boldly unitary. Austin referred to his parents in their forties as "the ancient people" (*Ly* 12); Lavinia reported "great commotion on maternal side" (*Years* 1:216); and Emily breezily observed that "father and mother sit in state in the sitting room" read-ing papers with "nothing carnal in them" (L63). Whether bemused or critical, both daughters turned permanently toward home, while Austin remained nearby. Their mother, far less dominant than their father, became a pervasive force in creating a sense that family equated with identity.

Mrs. Dickinson's prolonged ill health in the 1850s set the seal of privacy on the family for a time. Apparently both physiological and psychological, illness restricted her church, community, and social activities. Meanwhile, the evolution of her daughter Emily's intellectuality and poetic brilliance, apart from educa-tional and social stimulus, gathered momentum. Her mother had favored a bal-ance between learning and activity but did not expect her to focus so completely on the mind. Religion* became a major divergence, with the senior Emily com-mitted to a conventional Congregationalism,* and Emily destined to confront lifelong tensions of faith* versus doubt.

Individualism marked the family, with Austin as his parents' star. The Home-stead* and the Evergreens* side by side gave tangible evidence of faith that Austin and Susan* would perpetuate the Dickinson heritage, and traffic of grand-children between the houses provided reassuring confirmation. Yet Emily and Lavinia played essential roles. Lavinia observed that Emily "had to think—she was the only one of us who had that to do. Father believed; and mother loved; and Austin had Amherst" (Bingham, *Home* 414).

Edward Dickinson's death in 1874 was a thundering blow to his wife and family. A year later, Mrs. Dickinson suffered a stroke and lived for seven years, nursed by Emily and Lavinia. Their privacy intensified. After her mother's death on 14 November 1882, the poet observed, "When we were Children and she journeyed, she always brought us something. Now, would she bring us but herself, what an only Gift'' (L792). Actually, Emily Norcross Dickinson's gift proved to be Emily Dickinson.

RECOMMENDED: *Life*; Mary Elizabeth Kromer Bernhard, ''Portrait of a Family: Emily Dickinson's Norcross Connection''; Vivian Pollak, *A Poet's Parents: The Courtship Letters of Emily Norcross and Edward Dickinson.*

Mary Elizabeth Kromer Bernhard

DICKINSON, HARRIET AUSTIN, MARY TAYLOR, and MARTHA were sisters of Isabelle, William Cowper,* and Richard Salter Storrs Dickinson and daughters of Rev. Baxter Dickinson. The siblings were fifth cousins once removed to Emily and thus fairly distant relations, but Harriet, Mary, and Martha attended Amherst Academy,* where they befriended Lavinia.* Emily wrote to all three sisters, but a lengthy correspondence with Martha (including some verses) was burned at Martha's death in 1870.

In 1883, Emily wrote to Harriet (L871) thanking her for kindness to Lavinia, presumably at that summer's Dickinson family reunion. An earlier letter (L518) uses the poem ''Perhaps they do not go so far'' (P1399) to console the sisters on their father's recent death. Some disagreement exists over the date and recipients of this letter, but most convincing is Isabelle's son Austin Baxter Keep's remembrance that his aunts Harriet and Mary received it while visiting Amherst* in 1876. It was sent to them while calling at the Homestead,* where they ''espied Emily, all in white, among her flowers'' (*Years* 2:253).

RECOMMENDED: *Letters*; *Years*.

Sara Eddy

DICKINSON, LAVINIA NORCROSS (1833–1899) ''Sisters are brittle things,'' Emily Dickinson wrote, ''God was penurious with me, which makes me shrewd with Him'' (L207). Younger by two years and two months, Lavinia Dickinson was the poet's only sister and her closest consort for half a century. The bond the sisters shared was vital and proved to be, in Emily's words, ''early, earnest, indissoluble. Without her life were fear, and Paradise a cowardice, except for her inciting voice'' (L827).

Few studies have devoted attention to Lavinia and her integral role in Dickinson's biography. A pragmatic, intelligent, assertive, witty, astute, and creative woman, Lavinia possessed genuine humor, incisive intellect, furious devotion, and unwavering faith in her sister's genius. While Emily playfully referred to Austin* as ''Brother Pegasus,'' Lavinia was reverentially defined as ''all, so long'' (L110, 200).

As a young woman, Lavinia's social life was active; she traveled frequently, spending time in Boston,* Philadelphia, and Washington, D.C.* Despite several proposals, Lavinia never married. Of all the Dickinson romances, Vinnie's youthful relationship with Joseph Lyman* is the best documented. Lyman later romanticized his former sweetheart as a soft-lipped siren who wound strands of luxurious hair around his neck.

While Vinnie may have loved Lyman, she undoubtedly loved her garden,* her ménage of cats, her family, and her home* more. This devotion, tempered with pragmatism, enabled Vinnie to navigate the Homestead* effectively. When Edward Dickinson* died, Austin was so stricken that he was unable to remember the actualities of his father's funeral; afterward, he could not recall those who had attended from abroad, nor could he recollect who had served as pallbearers. Emily had sequestered herself upstairs, her door slightly ajar. It was Lavinia who comforted and wept with mourners because she was sure her father would have wished it. Although both Emily and Lavinia nursed their mother continuously throughout her lengthy illness, "Dont leave me, Vinnie" were the last words Emily said she spoke (L779). When beloved nephew Gilbert Dickinson* died so abruptly, it was Vinnie who nursed Emily back to mental and physical health*; it was Vinnie who comforted Austin in his profound grief despite the fact that she herself was treated for exhaustion one week later. It was Vinnie who endeavored to keep, as she said, "all that's left of this home" (*Life* 146).

Moreover, Lavinia loved Emily most of all. Her care of her older sister was maternal; her protectiveness fostered Emily's increasing dependence upon her "own dear Vinnie" (L154). Vinnie respected her sister's genius; her devotion to Emily and her art privileged Dickinson with the privacy and time necessary for her artistry. Lavinia's proficiency in domestic* routines afforded Emily the time to create, and her social skills, labeled "my courtesies" by Emily, liberated the poet from unwanted distractions (L200). Lavinia's "transact[ing] the commerce," as her sister wryly termed it, delivered a grateful Emily from a variety of domestic detriments (L176). Vinnie kept Amherst* and the world at bay when Emily desired, yet she served as a window to the world when Emily needed the view. Her influence was tantamount; her pragmatic role, crucial.

While Vinnie respected Emily's need to create, she also understood her sister's nature. Emily possessed, she wrote, "a joyous nature, yet full of pathos, and her power of language was unlike any one who ever lived" (*Life* 153). Emily embodied Lavinia as "Soldier and Angel too" who fiercely utilized language as her own " 'drawn sword' " to protect and defend (L861). Emily admired her sister's "special Mind," and Vinnie understood her sister's need to create because she too wrote poetry (L502). Her extant works, hauntingly beautiful creations, are found in Richard B. Sewall's *The Life of Emily Dickinson*, Appendix I. Friend Joseph Chickering* aptly noted that Lavinia's "conversational and literary gifts would have been more highly appreciated and more widely known, but for the extraordinary powers of her famous sister."

Not only did Lavinia play an integral role in Emily's personal and creative life, but she dedicated much of her own life to the publication* of her sister's poetry. After Emily's death, Vinnie, her undisputable heir, took the fascicles* first to Susan Gilbert Dickinson* and then to Mabel Loomis Todd,* who, with Lavinia's input, transcribed and edited the poems in conjunction with Thomas Wentworth Higginson.* After Austin's death, pressure from the Evergreens* influenced Lavinia to sue successfully for return of the land she had deeded to the Todds to satisfy Austin, reportedly in compensation for Mabel's editing efforts. While Todd has rightfully been credited for her dedication to the Dickinson corpus, were it not for Lavinia's unwavering belief in her sister's genius and her unswerving devotion directed to the publication of Emily's poetry, we may never have witnessed the brilliance of Emily Dickinson. Lavinia was eager that the "whole world have the opportunity to enjoy [Emily's] genious as she was too shy in life to take her rank" (*AB* 105). Before her own death in 1899, Vinnie had outlived all her immediate family, yet she witnessed three volumes of Emily's poetry and an edition of the letters* published as a result of her impeccable perseverance. Thus she could proudly afford to write Higginson: "I have had a 'Joan of Arc' feeling about Emilies poems from the first & their reception convinces me I was right" (*AB* 87).

RECOMMENDED: *AB*; *Life*; *Ly*; *Years*; Michele Mock, "Partnership in Possibility: The Dialogics of 'his efficient daughter Lavinia and his poetess daughter Emily.' "

Michele Mock

DICKINSON, LUCRETIA GUNN (1775–1840)   Dickinson's paternal grandmother was born to Hannah Montague Gunn and Nathaniel Gunn in Montague, Massachusetts, the second of their ten children. In 1802 she married Samuel Fowler Dickinson* and the next year gave birth to Edward,* first of her nine children. The family lived in Amherst* until 1833, when Lucretia moved with her husband and their youngest children to Ohio. After her husband's death in 1838, she returned east. When none of her children offered her a home, she stayed with relatives, living for at least the last six months of her life in Enfield, Massachusetts, with her sister Clarissa Gunn Underwood. (Clarissa's husband, Kingsley, is the heretofore unidentified "Uncle Underwood" to whom Dickinson referred in a reminiscent letter to Catherine Sweetser* [L478].) Lucretia died in Enfield and was buried there; her remains were later reinterred in Amherst. Dickinson made no known reference to her grandmother, though they undoubtedly had some contact during the last two years of Lucretia's life. In the letter cited earlier, Dickinson alluded to being with her aunt Catherine at the Underwoods' home—perhaps when her grandmother was there. (*See*: Genealogy)

RECOMMENDED: *Life*; *Years*.

Karen Dandurand

DICKINSON, SAMUEL FOWLER (1775–1838)   Born in Amherst,* son of Esther Fowler and Nathan Dickinson, Emily Dickinson's grandfather was five generations removed from his English ancestor, Nathaniel Dickinson, who came with John Winthrop's Great Migration in 1630. Samuel graduated second in his class from Dartmouth in 1795 and went on to become one of Amherst's most influential citizens. Upon graduation, he taught school for a year in New Salem, Massachusetts, then briefly explored a calling to the ministry (becoming a deacon of Amherst's First Church* at twenty-one) before deciding to read law in

Amherst in 1797 and becoming a highly successful lawyer. He married Lucretia Gunn* in 1802 and had nine children (Emily's father, Edward,* being the eldest). He served intermittently as representative to the Massachusetts General Court between 1803 and 1827, then became a member of the state Senate in 1828. His lasting contribution, however, was his work toward the founding of Amherst Academy* in 1814 and Amherst College* in 1821. He raised money, helped Amherst win out over thirty-seven other towns as site of the new college, and served on its first Board of Trustees. His dedication gradually brought him financial and emotional ruin, however: he staked his private property to gain additional funds for building when resources ran low, donated his own horses and laborers, often boarded the workers in his home at his expense, and sometimes even paid their wages. His neglected law practice suffered, and he was forced to sell the Homestead.* In 1833, when Emily was just two, he left Amherst with his wife and younger children for Lane Theological Seminary in Cincinnati, where he was to direct student laborers. In 1836 he became treasurer and building supervisor at Western Reserve College in Hudson, Ohio, then an isolated frontier outpost. Depressed, in poor health, and financially broken, he died there in 1838, when Emily was seven.

Emily Dickinson made only the briefest acknowledgment of her grandfather in the surviving records: when her father's sister, Catherine Sweetser,* asked her to send Samuel's Bible,* Emily replied that she was "reluctant to entrust anything so sacred to my Father as my Grandfather's Bible to public messenger" (L828). Evidence that Emily knew anything about her grandfather comes only from the fact that Austin* did, as his 1889 tribute at a First Church celebration shows. The Dickinsons spoke little about Samuel's failure, but apparently it cast something of a shadow over the family, for at sixteen Emily wrote to Austin that she dreamed her father had failed financially, their rye field "mortgaged to Seth Nims," the local postmaster (L16).

RECOMMENDED: *Letters*; *Life*; Cynthia Griffin Wolff, *Emily Dickinson*.

Catherine Carr Lee

DICKINSON STUDIES (1968–1993)   Frederick L. Morey founded this literary journal, the first to focus exclusively on Dickinson's life and work, with his 1968 circulation of a single-page, mimeographed bibliography of Dickinson materials identified during his dissertation research. Known originally as the *Emily Dickinson Bulletin*, the modest newsletter was distributed at Morey's own expense to academics who published on Dickinson. By the time it had evolved to the semiannual *Dickinson Studies*, the bulletin format had been replaced with issues of fifty or more pages, and Morey had acquired a list of paid subscribers that included libraries, scholars, and readers in almost twenty countries. In both its earlier and later formats, the journal retained a commitment to disseminating bibliographical information and publishing book reviews. In the 1970s, Morey initiated a valuable library project that led to the publication of surveys of Dickinson holdings at U.S. libraries with significant collections. Throughout the life of the journal, Morey's knowledge of eight languages for reading promoted it as a source of information on Dickinson scholarship outside the United States. Overall, the Dickinson material Morey published reflected a wide range of approaches to the poet and her work and included first-time publications from graduate students as well as contributions from prominent scholars. Despite these positive aspects, *Dickinson Studies* established a reputation for being, as Anna Mary Wells describes it, "a curiously idiosyncratic little journal, impossible to categorize" (19). Morey's editorial practices were notoriously eccentric, and the journal never achieved professional standards of editing and publication. In some instances, Morey used the journal to showcase his own work on Dickinson or to publicize his autobiographical concerns. In 1972, Morey inaugurated the *Higginson Journal of Poetry* and began sending it, free of charge, to all *Dickinson Studies* subscribers. The *Higginson Journal* was intended to honor Colonel Higginson through its publication of contemporary poetry and articles that related to Higginson's interest in all minorities. Morey's dedication to advancing knowledge of Dickinson continued for twenty-six years. Virtually single-handedly, he operated the Dickinson-Higginson Press until his unexpected death on 22 June 1993, after which both *Dickinson Studies* and the *Higginson Journal* ceased publication.

RECOMMENDED: Jonnie Guerra. "Profile: Frederick L. Morey." *Emily Dickinson International Society Bulletin* 2, 1 (May/June 1990): 3+; Anna Mary Wells. "In Memoriam: Frederick L. Morey." *Emily Dickinson International Society Bulletin* 5, 2 (Nov./Dec. 1993): 9+.

Jonnie Guerra

DICKINSON, SUSAN HUNTINGTON GILBERT (1830–1913)

DICKINSON, SUSAN HUNTINGTON GILBERT (1830–1913)   With Susan born nine days after Emily and only about ten miles from Amherst (in Old Deerfield, Massachusetts) and dying 12 May, almost twenty-seven years to the day after her, the sisters-in-law have been called "nearly twins" by Jean Mudge (93), and indeed they enjoyed many mutual passions—for literature, gardening,* recipes, music,* nature.* Their intense and constant relationship spanned five decades, and the poet sent substantially more writings to Susan than to any other correspondent. According to surviving documents of Dickinson's writing habits, Susan was the only reader at whose behest Emily changed a poem.

The youngest of six children born to Thomas and Harriet Arms Gilbert, Susan was orphaned by age eleven—her mother dying in 1837, and her father in 1841. From then until the late 1840s, when she came to live in Amherst* with her sister Harriet and brother-in-law William Cutler,* Susan was reared by her aunt, Sophia Arms Van Vranken, in Geneva, New York, where she attended Utica Female Academy. After teaching mathematics at a private school in Baltimore 1851–1852, she became engaged to Austin Dickinson in 1853; they married 1 July 1856 in a simple ceremony at the Van Vranken home. Though the young couple contemplated moving to Michigan, where Susan's older brothers lived, Edward Dickinson ensured their never leaving Amherst by making Austin a law partner and building them the Evergreens* on a lot next door to the Homestead.* A generous dowry from her brothers helped to make her home a showcase in its furnishings and art. Susan and Austin had three children: Edward,* Martha,* and Thomas Gilbert*; but both sons preceded her in death.

Variously praised and disparaged by Dickinson's biographers and critics, Susan was affectionately called "Dolly"* by the poet and with unfailing admiration characterized as an "Avalanche of Sun" (L755), a "breath from Gibraltar" uttering "impregnable syllables" (L722), even "Imagination" itself (L855); her words were of "Silver genealogy" (L913). Susan and Emily Dickinson's forty-year relationship has by all accounts been seen as one of crucial importance, even by those intent on calling Susan's character into question. A powerfully intellectual, vivacious, charismatic, sometimes arrogant, often generous, acutely and astutely well read woman and devoted mother, Susan Dickinson, her life stories, and their meanings for Emily Dickinson almost inevitably became sites of contestation in a culture with limited story lines for women.*

Yet what is most important about Susan Dickinson's decades-long involvement with Emily is what can be learned from Susan's writing and reading about the compositional, epistolary, and poetic practices Emily knew, participated in, and appropriated for her own art. Dickinson herself characterized their relationship in literary terms—comparing her love for Susan to Dante's for Beatrice and Swift's for Stella (L393) and comparing her tutelage with Susan to one with Shakespeare* (L757). Clearly, she valued Sue's opinions about writing and reading, and both women shared an affective theory of poetry evident when one compares Sue's response to "Safe in their Alabaster Chambers"* ("I always go to the fire and get warm after thinking of it, but I never *can* again") with Emily's comment to Higginson on poetics: "If I read a book [and] it makes my whole body so cold no fire ever can warm me I know *that* is poetry" (P216; L342a).

In a December 1890 letter to Higginson, Susan compared her relationship with Emily and the lifetime of writing exchanged between them to that recorded in *Goethe's Correspondence with a Child*, the intense dynamic of poet Karoline von Gunderode's correspondence with writer Bettina von Arnim. Underscoring their relationship's literary, intellectual nature, as well as the intensity of their emotional entanglement, Susan spoke with quiet but unassailable authority about his and Mabel Loomis Todd's* editing* of Emily's poems. Making clear that she was thoroughly acquainted with Emily's poetic corpus, Susan approved most titles* used in *Poems* (1890)* and, in a 4 January 1891 letter, corrected the printing of "afar" for "ajar" in "I know some lonely Houses off the Road" (P289). In subsequent editions "ajar" was printed.

We cannot help but approach this relationship with the assumption that Emily was always the writer, and Sue the reader; yet Sue constantly wrote essays, reviews, journals, poems, letters, and memorials, and she produced commonplace books along with scrapbooks of her own publications, of clippings about admired figures, and of favorite works by other writers, including Emily. In

April 1852 Dickinson enthused over "Susie" keeping a journal, exclaiming that she wanted "to get it bound—at my expense" (L88); and among papers found in the Evergreens is a journal Susan kept of a trip to Europe at age seventy-five. As an elderly traveler and inveterate writer, Susan took care to record her observations in a literary vein.

Besides a lifelong habit of keeping journals, Susan published several stories in the *Republican* in the early 1900s. A lengthy 1903 review of "Harriet Prescott's Early Work" cited Emily Dickinson to argue for its republication. In "Annals of the Evergreens," a typescript unpublished until the 1980s (abridged version in *Amherst* [Alumni Quarterly] Spring 1981), Susan first praised Prescott's "Pomegranate Flowers," then proceeded to describe an Evergreens life rich in cultural exchange: reading the Brownings,* Thomas de Quincey, Julia Ward Howe, Thomas Carlyle,* and Shakespeare and entertaining such distinguished visitors as Ralph Waldo Emerson,* Harriet Beecher Stowe,* Wendell Phillips, and Frederick Olmsted. Personalities more intimately associated with the Dickinson circle also grace these pages as Susan related luscious accounts of lunches with "fresh asparagus" and "salad from our own garden" and dinner of "very nice lamb and strawberries" with editor Samuel Bowles,* his wife, Mary,* friend Maria Whitney,* Josiah* and Elizabeth Holland,* and Otis P. Lord.*

Among Susan's surviving papers in Harvard and Brown University archives are hundreds of letters, numerous essays on subjects as diverse as nursing and architecture, and a review of the work of Thomas Hardy, which she found most "refreshing" because "it does not presuppose idiocy in the reader but makes a little demand upon a moderate equipment of mind and imagination" (a remark equally applicable to her appreciation of Emily's poems). Besides collecting paeans to Queen Victoria, Susan wrote tributes to strong pioneering women such as Elizabeth Blackwell, the United States' first female doctor.

Susan's writings witness care and passion for the word; drafts of essays and poems show careful searching for the most effective vocabulary and syntax. That she did not regard the printed word as final is obvious from the fact that several clippings of her own work placed in a scrapbook show her revising after their appearance in the *Republican*. That she was confident of her intellectual abilities and critical acumen is demonstrated by her correspondence about such matters not only with Higginson and Bowles but also with other leading editors. Moreover, "Annals" shows clearly that she was a most capable conversationalist who held her own with Emerson and was known by many for her ability to handle the most difficult, "hard reading" (*Years* 2:78).

Besides publishing critical pieces and stories, Susan published at least one poem, "Love's Reckoning," and wrote quite a few others. Though more conventional in form than Emily's, Susan's poems attend to many of the same subjects. "There are autumn days of the Spring" distinctly echoes both "These are the days when Birds come back—"* (P130) and "The Crickets sang"

(P1104), and "The Sun kept low as an oven" recalls both the "Stooping as low as the kitchen window—" of "Blazing in Gold" (P228)* and "The Sun kept stooping—stooping—low" (P152).

Although she has been roundly criticized for not seeing Emily's poems into print with good speed, Susan's own account in the 1890 letter to Higginson shows that she had projected a volume with "many bits of her prose—passages from early letters . . . quaint bits to my children &c &c" (*AB* 86). In a March 1891 letter to another editor, she elaborated her vision to include Emily's "illustrations," "showing her witty humorous side, which has all been left out of" the 1890 *Poems*. Susan described a much more holistic volume than the epitome of the late nineteenth-century poetry book produced by Higginson and Todd. Her outline for the production shows that she would not have divided the poems into conventional categories but would have emphasized poetry's integration with quotidian experience, Emily's intellectual prowess, and her philosophical interrogations of the spiritual, corporeal, emotional, and mental realms.

A profound love and deep appreciation for nature pervaded Susan's sensibilities, and she clearly favored literary and visual art* focused on the natural world's splendors, its "Eden, always eligible" (L391). In the Evergreens, John F. Kensett's *Sunset with Cows* (1856) bears Susan's name on the back, and one of her manuscript poems seems a direct response to the painting. Her regard for nature was intense enough to be characterized as religious or spiritual, and Susan was indeed devoutly religious from late teens throughout adulthood. Late in life, she turned toward the rituals of the High Church and even pondered becoming a Roman Catholic* but was dissuaded by Bishop F. Dan Huntington.* Yet her religious devotions were far more than ceremonial, for Susan spent almost every Sabbath for six years in the 1880s establishing a Sunday school in Logtown, a poor village not far from Amherst.

Susan's tasteful enactment of ritual for profound utterance is perhaps best displayed in the simple flannel robe she designed and in which she dressed Emily for death, laying her out in a white casket, cypripedium and violets (symbolizing faithfulness) at her neck, two heliotropes (symbolizing devotion) in her hand (St. Armand 74–75). This final act over Emily's body underscores "their shared life, their deep and complex intimacy" as well as their anticipation of "postmortem resurrection" of that intimacy (Hart 255; Pollak 137). Susan also penned Emily's obituary, a loving portrayal of a strong, brilliant woman, devoted to family, neighbors, and her writing, for which she had the most serious objectives and highest ambitions. (*See:* Appendix B; Biographical Approaches; Funeral; Lesbian Approaches; Publication; Spofford; Visual Arts; Women's Culture)

RECOMMENDED: *FF*; Ellen Louise Hart, "The Encoding of Homoerotic Desire: Emily Dickinson's Letters and Poems to Susan Dickinson, 1850–1886"; Jean McClure Mudge, "Emily Dickinson and 'Sister Sue' "; Dorothy Huff Oberhaus, "In Defense of Sue"; Barton St. Armand, *Emily Dickinson and Her Culture: The Soul's Society*; Martha

Nell Smith, *Rowing in Eden: Rereading Emily Dickinson*, Harvard University and Brown University Library Archives.

Martha Nell Smith

DICKINSON, THOMAS GILBERT (Gib) (1875–1883) was born shortly after his parents' nineteenth anniversary. Having a young child in the house again (Martha* being ten at the time of his birth) may have changed the tenor of the household. This is indicated by the redecoration of some rooms, including the nursery. Susan Dickinson* kept an extensive "baby book" for Gib, whereas none is known to have been kept for Mattie or Ned.* A bright, intelligent boy, he won the heart of everyone he met and was especially dear to Aunt Emily. As with his siblings, he showed a talent for writing. After his unexpected death from typhoid fever, his mother preserved Gib's letters and schoolwork, and left his clothing in the drawers of his dresser and his toys on the floor. From that point on, no other small child ever lived in the Evergreens.* Gib's death was probably the final emotional blow that precipitated Emily Dickinson's slow decline.

RECOMMENDED: *Life*; Hampson Collection, Brown University.

Marcy L. Tanter

DICKINSON, WILLIAM (1804–1887) William Dickinson, the poet's uncle, was the younger brother of Edward Dickinson* and second eldest child of Samuel Fowler Dickinson* and Lucretia Gunn.* Like Edward, he attended Amherst Academy*; but rather than enroll at college, he elected to train for a career in business, serving an apprenticeship in Amherst* paper factories. In 1829, he moved to Worcester, Massachusetts, where he lived out his life as a successful businessman. William Dickinson married Eliza Hawley of Andover in 1831. The following year, their son Willie (William Hawley Dickinson*) was born. Emily Dickinson visited that family in June 1844 and formed a lasting bond with her cousin Willie, who was the only member of his family to maintain a regular correspondence with Emily and Lavinia.* After his first wife's death in 1851, William married Mary Lou Whittier in 1852; they had two sons and a daughter. Thomas Wentworth Higginson* described Dickinson's uncle William as "a man of integrity and character, who shared her abruptness and impulsiveness but certainly not her poetic temperament, from which he was indeed singularly remote."

RECOMMENDED: Thomas Wentworth Higginson. "Emily Dickinson's Letters." *Atlantic Monthly* 68 (Oct. 1891): 444–56.

Marianne Erickson

DICKINSON, WILLIAM AUSTIN (Austin) (1829–1895) was the eldest child of Edward* and Emily Norcross Dickinson.* Of all the important people in her life, Emily Dickinson probably counted Austin as the most significant. From the earliest days of their childhood, Austin shared a special relationship with his sister Emily. They were confidants; indeed, he seems to be the only person other than Colonel Higginson* to whom Emily wrote directly that she desired to be a poet: ''Austin is a Poet. . . . I've been in the habit *myself* of writing some few things'' (L110). They shared a love of jokes, and he provided her with many books over the years. Emily's introduction to, and love for, poetry* are documented in her letters* to Austin. After graduating from Amherst College* (Phi Beta Kappa) and then Harvard Law School, he became his father's partner in the law practice in Amherst*; Edward built the Evergreens* for Austin and Susan* next door to the Homestead* as an enticement to keep them in town. Today, the house remains virtually unchanged following Susan's redecoration in the late 1880s.

Austin was well respected as a lawyer and businessman who also maintained an interest in collecting paintings and artwork. He developed a taste for architecture of both buildings and landscape. His love of landscaping was passed on by his grandfather and was a great boon to the town. He designed Wildwood Cemetery, where he, Susan, and their children are interred. The town sewage and lighting systems were pet projects of Austin's, as was the beautification of Amherst; he supervised the choice and planting of many trees. He became treasurer of Amherst College in 1873 and held the position for the rest of his life. Literary figures of the day such as Wendell Phillips and Ralph Waldo Emerson* stayed at the Evergreens, and Austin named publisher Samuel Bowles* among his closest friends.

Austin always maintained a large circle of friends, which included women. In 1882, he began a clandestine affair with Mabel Loomis Todd* that continued until his death. Lavinia Dickinson* provided the pair a meeting place at the Homestead; Emily's reaction to the affair is unrecorded, although she did communicate with Mrs. Todd by letter, sent her poems, and asked her to sing at the Homestead. When Todd eventually prepared Dickinson's poems for publication, Austin involved himself to a limited extent (perhaps even mutilating some manuscripts to excise affectionate references to his wife). Upon his death, Austin's attempt to compensate Todd for her editorial accomplishments through a bequest of land to herself and her husband precipitated a lawsuit brought against the Todds by Lavinia Dickinson (backed by Susan, Ned,* and Martha*) that has had long-term divisive effects both on the editing and disposition of the poet's manuscripts and on biographical* representations of her closest personal relationships. (*See*: Visual Arts, Influence of)

RECOMMENDED: *Life*; *Poems*; Barton Levi St. Armand, *Emily Dickinson and Her Culture: The Soul's Society*; Martha Nell Smith, *Rowing in Eden: Rereading Emily Dickinson*; Hampson Collection, Brown University.

Marcy L. Tanter

DICKINSON, WILLIAM COWPER (1827–1899)   A friend and distant relative of the Dickinsons, he graduated from Amherst College* in 1848 as valedictorian and was a tutor there, 1851–1852. His sisters (Harriet, Martha, and

Mary)* were friends of Emily's sister, Lavinia,* at Amherst Academy.* The son of clergyman and theology instructor Baxter Dickinson, he was ordained to the ministry in 1854, having probably experienced a public conversion in the midst of the 1845–1846 revival* at Amherst College. Emily addressed him as "Cousin William" in a valentine* letter of 1849, where she chided him for sending a valentine that was "a little condescending, & sarcastic" (L27). A year later she sent him five brief lines of verse about life as "strife," "bubble," and "dream," illustrated with small clippings from old books and papers (L33). Emily named him several times in the newsy portions of her letters* to Austin from 1851 to 1852.

RECOMMENDED: *Letters*; *Life*.

Catherine Carr Lee

DICKINSON, WILLIAM HAWLEY (1832–1883)   The son of Edward Dickinson's* brother William* of Worcester, Massachusetts, "Willie" was one of Emily's favorites when he was a student at Amherst College.* Willie was apparently lively and adventurous. One account tells of Emily's escaping a funeral for an elderly relative with Willie in his buggy. He took Emily home by way of a jaunt seven miles in the opposite direction, a stunt that brought her a lecture and tears from her mother, a punitive silence from her father. Willie evidently left Amherst* and graduated from Brown University in 1852; he lived in New York City for many years, where he practiced law. His widow destroyed his letters from Emily, possibly as many as a hundred.

RECOMMENDED: *Letters*; *Life*; Laura Benet, *The Mystery of Emily Dickinson*.

Catherine Carr Lee

DISJUNCTION, AS A CHARACTERISTIC   Disjunction is caused by any aspect of disjointedness or rupture in a text—even breaks in narrative or abrupt changes in tone. Characteristically, however, Dickinson's disjunction takes structural form. While for decades critics regarded such disruption as evidence of Dickinson's lack of training or ability as a poet, most now regard it as a significant, perhaps strategic, aspect of the verse.

Dickinson's verse seems particularly disjunctive because it remains relatively traditional in many ways, hence supplies a familiar norm as well as its rupture. One may see this most clearly in her meter and rhyme.* For example, "Wild Nights—Wild Nights!" (P249) begins with a stanza of four lines, each with four syllables, and a clearly iambic metrical grid, despite the spondaic "Wild Nights." The second stanza varies this pattern slightly, giving the third and fourth lines each five syllables. As Thomas H. Johnson* prints it, the third stanza contains no line of four syllables: the first line contains five; the second three; the third six, and the last two. As Dickinson writes the poem in Fascicle* 11, the third line does contain four syllables, but "Tonight—" appears on a line of its own, making the last stanza five lines long. The poem's rhymes reverse the metrical pattern of increasing irregularity: the first stanza contains an uneven rhyme (thee/luxury), the second a slant rhyme (port/Chart), and the third a perfect rhyme (Sea/Thee)—although the symmetry of the final rhyme is disrupted by the five-line structure of the handwritten poem. Most of Dickinson's poems provide a similarly strong normative regularity with multiple aspects of disjunction.

Dashes* disrupt rhythm, syntax,* and a sense of conclusiveness, hence have a particularly disjunctive effect in the poetry. Similarly, Dickinson's more conventional punctuation may be disjunctive: her many poems concluding with questions have an unsettled quality, and Dickinson frequently uses even the apparent certainty of periods and exclamation marks ironically.

More obviously disruptive is Dickinson's experimentation with form-class transpositions. For example, she uses verbs grammatically as nouns ("The Daily Own—of Love" [P580]) or as adjectives, frequently by adding the suffix "less": "postponeless," "Perturbless" (P390, 724). Adjectives become nouns ("farness" and "foreignhood" in P719); nouns become adjectives ("more angel" in P493); a plural or mass noun becomes singular, and singular nouns become plural (both reversals occurring in the line "a Glee among the Garret" in P934). Similarly, Dickinson frequently uses uninflected verb forms in what are, at best, questionably subjunctive contexts. Such unusual manipulations of grammar open up complex possibilities of meaning that contradict the apparent simplicity of her short, primarily metrical, often balladic verse forms.

Some syntactical patterns create disjunction in Dickinson's poems, in particular her juxtaposition of phrases, thoughts, and sentences through parataxis. For example, in "He fumbles at your Soul" (P315), Dickinson ends the poem with a two-line stanza that contains no obvious reference to the preceding lines. More typical is Dickinson's juxtaposition of the stages of an idea or story through "and" or line breaks, as in this stanza: "Life—is what we make it—/ Death—We do not know—/ Christ's acquaintance with Him / Justify Him—though—" (P698). Here the reader must link the disconnected lines through interpretation.

More radical instances of syntactic disruption stem from deletion: Dickinson occasionally deletes so many or such major words that multiple re-creations of the syntax become possible, each leading to different nuances of meaning (see "Further in Summer than the Birds," P1068). Equally disruptive is Dickinson's use of syntactic doubling, or use of a single phrase to cover two nonparallel, logically consecutive, syntactic contexts. For example, in "A Bird came down the Walk—" (P328), the line "Like one in danger, Cautious" may modify either the preceding "He stirred his Velvet Head" or the following "I offered him a Crumb," hence either the bird* or the speaker or both. Such disruption stems from the logical difficulty of holding more than one syntactic possibility in the mind at once.

Dickinson's use of variant word choices is the most unusual disjunctive aspect of her poetry. By leaving multiple possibilities for a thought or phrase in fascicle* or fair copies of her poems, Dickinson forces the reader to deal with radical ambiguity* even at the level of the poem's text.

Brita Lindberg-Seyersted regards disjunction as one of Dickinson's strategies to give her poetry a colloquial* tone. Disjunction also undercuts a reader's expectation of finding ordered form and meaning in a poem or in the world. In addition, however, Dickinson's repeated disruptions create possibilities of humor* and originality that suggest human capacity to respond significantly to a world without reliable order. (*See*: Linguistic and Stylistic Approaches; Textual Variants)

RECOMMENDED: Brita Lindberg-Seyersted, *The Voice of the Poet: Aspects of Style in the Poetry of Emily Dickinson*; Cristanne Miller, *Emily Dickinson: A Poet's Grammar*, "Dickinson's Language: Interpreting Truth Told Slant," and "Dickinson's Experiments in Language"; David Porter, *The Art of Emily Dickinson's Early Poetry*.

Cristanne Miller

"DOLLIE"   was a nickname for Susan Huntington Gilbert Dickinson* that originated in her family during her childhood. Letters from her siblings when Susan was in her late teens use this name, which stayed with her for life. In the early 1900s, she used the signature "Dolly" in letters and telegrams to her daughter Martha Dickinson Bianchi.* A scrapbook that remained in the Evergreens after Bianchi's death and is now in the Bianchi Collection at the John Hay Library at Brown University opens with the following inscription: "*Private 'Doings' of M. G. D.*—/ This book not for the inspection of the rabble—/ Dolly may *read* / others must *run*—." (Before her marriage Bianchi's initials were "M. G. D.": Martha Gilbert Dickinson.) This scrapbook contains articles from the *Springfield Republican** written by Susan Dickinson and by Bianchi between 1899 and 1908.

On five known occasions Dickinson used "Dollie" in poems from the late 1850s to early and mid-1860s to refer to, or address, Susan. (Dickinson varied the spelling of the name, as in the mid- and late 1850s she varied the spelling of her own name, "Emilie.") The language of these poems reveals the intimacy of the bond between Dickinson and Susan. The following lines appear in three poems in the *Manuscript Books**: "Cry 'it's I', 'take Dollie,' / And I will enfold!" (P51); "To find the windows dark—/ And no more Dollie—mark—" (P156); "Death wont hurt—now Dollie's here!" (P158). The version sent to Susan of "The Love a Child / can show—below" begins with the note, "*Excuse me—Dollie—*" (P673); an unpublished version of "The Overtakelessness / of Those" is addressed on the verso, "Dollie" (P1691).

Ellen Louise Hart

DOMESTICITY, AS SUBJECT   Similar to the work of other nineteenth-century women poets, Dickinson's verse is replete with images of domestic life, allowing the female poet to fuse her inner and outer lives. Domestic activity and the domestic locus inform much of her nature* poetry ("The Wind begun

to knead the Grass—/ As Women do a Dough,'' P824) and her explorations of
death* (''The grave* my little cottage is, / Where 'Keeping house' for thee / I
make my parlor orderly / And lay the marble tea,'' P1743). Domesticity is at
the center of her religious* contemplation (''To mend each tattered Faith / There
is a needle fair,'' P1442). Dickinson also depicts the artist as domestic woman
and describes poetic creation as housework (''That sacred Closet when you
sweep—,'' P1273).

Dickinson terms domestic activity ''the honorable Work / Of Woman, and of
Wife'' (P732), but for her it is also ''a prickly art'' (L907). That is, there is
often an ironic dimension to her insistence upon the domestic. The impossibility
of salvation is expressed in domestic terms in ''I saw no Way—The Heavens
were stitched—'' (P378), and the poet is described as the ''Indolent Housewife—in Daisies—lain'' (P187). Nature is most beautiful when it resembles an
untidy home,* as when Dickinson praises the exquisite ''litter'' of the fall season* in ''She sweeps with many-colored Brooms—'' (P219). Although domestic imagery informs her poetry, Dickinson frequently challenges the order of
housekeeping in her depiction of nature and the spiritual, emotional, and creative
lives of women. (*See*: Black Cake, Women's Culture)

RECOMMENDED: Dorothy Z. Baker, ''*Ars Poetica/Ars Domestica*: The Self-
Reflexive Poetry of Lydia Sigourney and Emily Dickinson''; Jane Donahue Eberwein,
''Doing Without: Dickinson as Yankee Woman Poet''; Sandra M. Gilbert, ''The Wayward Nun beneath the Hill: Emily Dickinson and the Mysteries of Womanhood''; Gertrude Reiff Hughes, ''Subverting the Cult of Domesticity: Emily Dickinson's Critique
of Women's Work.''

Dorothy Z. Baker

DRAMATIC REPRESENTATIONS OF DICKINSON   A tradition of biographical drama about Emily Dickinson can be traced within twentieth-century
American theatrical history. Plays about the poet first appeared on the Broadway
stage in the 1930s, a decade during which biographical drama became a vogue,
and continued into the 1940s. The second wave of theatrical interest arose with
the success of *The Belle of Amherst* in the 1970s and has been sustained into
the present. Consistently, dramatic versions of the poet's life have advanced the
central Dickinson myth: that a thwarted romance determined her personal and
poetic identities. Individual playwrights often have accepted the validity of a
particular biographer's* speculation about the identity of Dickinson's alleged
lover* and showcased the theory in a dramatic format.

Among the earliest Dickinson plays was Susan Glaspell's *Alison's House*
(1931), thought to have its source in Genevieve Taggard's *The Life and Mind
of Emily Dickinson* (1930). Although the poet's family denied Glaspell's request
to use the Dickinson name and to quote from the poetry, and Glaspell herself
cast Alison Stanhope—her Dickinson figure—as an offstage character, critics
received the play from opening night as a biographical drama about Dickinson.
Set eighteen years after Alison's death, the plot revolves around the dilemmas

that face the poet's family when a portfolio of Alison's unpublished poetry is discovered. Because the work is confessional, revealing the joy and agony of Alison's love affair with a married man, its publication would precipitate a scandal. In the final scene, members of the family gather in Alison's bedroom and read aloud from her poems. Ultimately, niece Elsa convinces her father, Alison's brother, that the poetry speaks to and for others, especially women, and that future generations should be endowed with Alison's legacy.

Although Glaspell pioneered the offstage character as a successful theatrical strategy in other plays, its use in *Alison's House* probably contributed to the unenthusiastic reception popular audiences and critics gave to the Broadway production. When the play unexpectedly won the 1931 Pulitzer Prize in drama, the jury that made the selection was severely criticized. Not only have scholars erroneously perceived the Pulitzer as a sign of the play's success, but also they have misjudged the purpose of Glaspell's dramatic project, failing to recognize the play's critique of the constructs proposed to explain Alison's (and, by extension, Dickinson's) life.

Other theatrical treatments of Dickinson's life during this early period are straightforward adaptations of other biographers' theories, portray the poet onstage, and quote from her work. *Brittle Heaven* (1935) by Vincent York and Frederick Pohl was inspired by Josephine Pollitt's *Emily Dickinson: The Human Background of Her Poetry* (1930). Like Pollitt's biography, the drama speculated that the key event of Dickinson's life was the poet's renunciation* of her love for Major Edward Hunt in deference to Helen Fiske Hunt [Jackson],* her childhood friend and his wife. Dorothy Gardner's play *Eastward in Eden: The Love Story of Emily Dickinson* (1945) presented the theory George Frisbie Whicher espoused in *This Was a Poet: A Critical Biography of Emily Dickinson* (1939) that another married man, Rev. Charles Wadsworth,* was the person Dickinson loved. Both works follow the pattern of the well-made play, and their highly melodramatic plots similarly climax with scenic portrayals of Dickinson's emotional devastation at her romantic loss. Dorothy Gish played the role of the poet in *Brittle Heaven*; Beatrice Straight, in *Eastward of Eden*. While neither play achieved critical success, both actresses were cited for convincing performances. The plays themselves retain interest because they document the nature of Dickinson's early reception.

With the appearance of William Luce's *The Belle of Amherst* in 1976, the trend in biographical plays about Dickinson shifted to the monodrama. Luce's work is the most influential Dickinson drama written and produced in the twentieth century and probably has elevated the general public's awareness of Dickinson more than any other single work since the publication of the poetry in the 1890s. *Belle* achieved an impressive Broadway run, including 117 performances and a fifth Tony Award for Julie Harris and was presented subsequently as a featured public television special. The play has maintained popularity with actresses and audiences in amateur and professional theaters around the globe and is revived frequently.

In contrast to the general public, Dickinson scholars view *Belle* with ambivalence. Among the limitations they point out are the play's adherence to the legend that Dickinson's creative life was compensatory when she failed to marry and its controversial representation of Dickinson as ambitious to become a published* poet and, thus, reduced to despair by Higginson's* alleged critical judgment that she should not. Luce's work also misleadingly recommends biographical readings of particular Dickinson poems despite evidence that contradicts such simplistic interpretations.

Whatever the play's flaws, the success of *Belle* confirms a change in the reception of Dickinson by nonacademic and international audiences since the early decades of the century. Luce's work also has been a major catalyst for other one-woman performance pieces about the poet. Belinda Heckler, Ruth McRee, Lavinia Moyer, and Caroline Ryburn are among contemporary U.S. actresses who have crafted original melodramas to interpret Dickinson's life. Their works have been produced extensively in regional theaters but remain unpublished. (*See*: Fiction; Popular Culture)

RECOMMENDED: Jonnie Guerra, ''Dickinson Adaptations in the Arts and the Theatre''; Anita Plath Helle. ''Re-Presenting Women Writers Onstage: A Retrospective to the Present.'' *Making a Spectacle: Feminist Essays on Contemporary Women's Theatre.* Ed. Lynda Hart. Ann Arbor: University of Michigan Press, 1989: 195–208; Maravene Loeschke, ''Challenges of Portraying Emily Dickinson in William Luce's Play *The Belle of Amherst*''; Klaus Lubbers, *Emily Dickinson: The Critical Revolution.*

Jonnie Guerra

DRUM BEAT Three Dickinson poems (P130,* 137,* and 228*)—nearly a third of those known to have been published during her lifetime—appeared in this Civil War* fund-raising newspaper. Edited by Rev. Richard Salter Storrs, Jr. (a founding editor of the *Independent*), the *Drum Beat* published 6,000 copies daily in conjunction with the Brooklyn fair to raise funds for the U.S. Sanitary Commission (22 February–5 March and 11 March 1864). Other contributors included Louisa May Alcott, William Cullen Bryant, and Oliver Wendell Holmes. Two of Dickinson's poems (P137 and 228) were reprinted in other newspapers; a fourth (P67)* appeared 27 April in the *Brooklyn Daily Union*, a local paper that gave support services to the *Drum Beat.* (*See*: Publication)

RECOMMENDED: Karen Dandurand, ''New Dickinson Civil War Publications'' and ''Why Dickinson Did Not Publish.''

Karen Dandurand

DUDLEY, JOHN LANGDON (1812–1894) A graduate of Amherst College,* Dudley married one of Dickinson's closest friends, Eliza M. Coleman,* in 1861. Dudley, who was said to be very liberal in his views, was the pastor of the South Congregational* Church in Middletown, Connecticut. There are rumors that Dickinson was romantically interested in Dudley and that his marriage* to her cousin troubled her. According to Norcross family lore, Dickinson "wanted to marry" Dudley. Based on this speculation, one scholar has conjectured that Dudley may have inspired Dickinson's "Master"* letters and lyric* love* poems.

In 1867 Dudley spent several months alone in Europe. When he returned, he left Middletown and became the pastor at Plymouth Church in Milwaukee, Wisconsin. After his wife's death from consumption, Dudley married Marion Churchill, a young journalist, poet, suffragist, and freethinker, in 1872. He resigned from Plymouth Church that same year after charges of heresy were brought against him for doctrinal liberalism and his embrace of Unitarians* and unchurched Christians. In 1877, Dudley accepted a pastorate in Boston* at Parker Memorial Church but resigned in 1879. He returned to Wisconsin and, for the remainder of his life, accepted preaching engagements upon request.

RECOMMENDED: *Letters*; *Life*; *Years*; Polly Longsworth, " 'Was Mr. Dudley Dear?': Emily Dickinson and John Langdon Dudley."

Marisa Anne Pagnattaro

DWIGHT, EDWARD STRONG (1820–1890) Minister of the First (Congregational*) Church* of Amherst* 1854–1860, Dwight was highly valued by the poet and her family. This grandson of Yale president Timothy Dwight was born in New Haven and graduated from Yale College (1838) and its Theological Seminary (1843); he later received a doctor of divinity degree from Yale also (1874). His preaching reflected significant features of the New Divinity tradition that dominated the Connecticut Valley* at that time. For example, Dwight strongly supported a settled ministry and argued the inseparability of faith* and learning. He shared in the valley's widespread rejection of the Halfway Covenant as a "false and dangerous position," insisting instead upon the necessity of an inward "conversion" of the "heart" toward God.* Although his delivery appears to have been more restrained than that of his predecessor Aaron Colton,* he continued with other pro-revivalists* to encourage "awakenings" such as occurred in 1857 under his ministry at First Church and in 1872 while he served the Russell (Congregational) Church in nearby Hadley. The doctrinal statement supported by Dwight before he left Amherst, while debated within the congregation and abbreviated and less specific in language, remained essentially unchanged from that originally formalized in 1834.

After a delay of several weeks because of his wife's ill health, Dwight conditionally accepted a call to First Church in July 1853 and was officially installed one year later. Dickinson was attracted to him immediately, declaring that she had "never heard a minister I loved half so well" (L123). She awaited his response in suspense (L127, 129) and remained enthusiastic after his arrival. Dwight preached "beautifully" and "wonderfully," she wrote Austin* that autumn (L140, 159). To Sue* she described his sermons as "precious," particularly one that dealt with unbelief (L176). Her respect and affection for the new minister were shared by her family, with whom he developed close ties.

Not only was Dickinson present at church services, but her attachment to both the Dwights also took her "weekly" to their home, where she professed to find "sunlight" (L176). Years later, following his wife's death in Maine in 1861, the poet wrote Dwight of the consolation she herself found in her memory of intimate winter evenings spent with them at the parsonage. Acknowledging the greater comfort Jesus* his friend could supply, she too even now would seek admission, knocking "on that far study door—that used to open kindly" (L243). The tone of her response when Dwight sent her a picture of his wife is poignant and heartfelt (L246).

Dwight was "dismissed" at his own request from First Church in 1860, about the same time Dickinson stopped attending. In 1864 he returned to the area to minister in Hadley for the rest of his life. A member of the college Board of Trustees from 1855 onward, he would have remained a familiar figure in Amherst, on hand for the annual commencement tea at the Homestead.*

RECOMMENDED: *An Historical Review: One Hundred and Fiftieth Anniversary of the First Church of Christ.* Amherst, MA: Amherst Record, 1890; *Obituary Record of Graduates of Yale University.* No. 50. 1891.

Rowena Revis Jones

E

EAST EUROPEAN RESPONSES TO DICKINSON   Interest in Dickinson's poetry is found in all East European countries (evidenced by Károlyi's and Havkova's translations of some of her poetry into Hungarian and Czech, respectively) but is particularly noticeable in Poland, where several selections of Dickinson's poems and one of her letters* are now available.

Discovery of Dickinson and interest in her poetry* date back to the 1960s and 1970s. Early publications included not only translations of individual poems undertaken by various poets, such as Ludmiła Marjańska, Artur Międzyrzecki, or Jan Prokop, to be found in various literary journals, but also two volumes of selected poems translated by another poet, Kazimiera Iłłakowiczówna (1965 and 1975). Although Iłłakowiczówna has the credit for making a wider selection of Dickinson's poetry available in Polish for the first time, she must also be held responsible for painting a largely conventional portrait of the poet as sentimental* and Victorian, a poet of the past. Thus the essential modernity of Dickinson's poetry had yet to be discovered. This was done primarily by Ludmiła Marjańska in her translations of individual poems and by Stanisław Barańczak, especially in his 1990 volume of Dickinson's poems. Barańczak's modeling of his translations on the meter and diction of Cyprian Kamil Norwid, a highly unorthodox Polish Romantic* poet, evoked a strikingly modern aura in Dickinson's poetry. However, occasional one-dimensional interpretations, elimination of some esoteric vocabulary, and overall regularity of meter and rhyme* (particularly evident in his second volume of selected poems published in 1995) sometimes resulted in yet another taming of Dickinson.

A major recent arrival is a selection of Dickinson's letters translated and edited by Danuta Piestrzyńska, which is the first publication of Dickinson's prose into Polish. While not always successful in handling some of the pitfalls of Dickinson's prose, this translation has generally been praised for rendering accurately some of the poet's complexity of meaning and boldness of imagery, as well as the general poetic quality of her prose.

In addition to translations of her poetry, Dickinson has been the subject of both biographical* and critical studies, primarily by Poland's Aleksander Rogalski and Agnieszka Salska, as well as Hungary's Károlyi Amy. Although much remains to be done (a volume of collected poems or collected letters remaining a dream for the future), all of these recent publications have succeeded in making Dickinson, if not quite a household name, yet increasingly present in East European culture. (*See*: French, German-Language, Scandinavian, and Slavic-Language Responses)

RECOMMENDED: Emily Dickinsonova. *Můj dopis světu*. Trans. Jiřina Havkova. Praha: Mlada fronta, 1977; Emily Dickinson. *Poezje*. Trans. Kazimiera Iłłakowiczówna. Warszawa: Państwowy Instytut Wydawniczy, 1965, and *100 wierszy*. Trans. Stanisław Barańczak. Kraków: Arka, 1990, and *List do Świata*. Trans. Danuta Piestrzyńska. Kraków: Wydawnictwo Znak, 1994; Amy Karolyi. *Emily Dickinson valogatott írásai*. Budapest: Magveto Konyvkiadó, 1978; Agnieszka Salska, *Walt Whitman and Emily Dickinson: Poetry of the Central Consciousness*.

Danuta Piestrzyńska

EDITORIAL SCHOLARSHIP Dickinson's handwritten manuscripts left without instructions for publication* continue to challenge editors seeking the best strategies for representing her work in print. Editorial approaches to Dickinson scholarship emphasize the following practices: study of manuscript features—lineation, punctuation, capitalization,* spacing—and ways of arranging text; examination of the complex relationship between Dickinson's poetry and prose; and evaluation of texts that constrict or subvert possibilities for reading* poems or obscure the poetic qualities of letters.

Editors can show how line phrasing or the angle of a dash* affect meaning, moving readers beyond confusion over unusual markings to an understanding of Dickinson's purposeful, expressive devices and an appreciation of her manuscript art. Thomas Johnson* leveled the dashes,* which Dickinson positioned at various angles, and he regularly altered her line endings. Lineation has become a central issue of debate since Susan Howe's exchange with Ralph Franklin* in the mid-1980s, where Howe argued that line breaks were Dickinson's visual strategies, while Franklin maintained that paper size and shape dictated the length of her lines. Howe's work has encouraged a number of scholars to look again at features previously termed "eccentricities," "idiosyncrasies," or "habits of handwriting"* and to conclude that Dickinson used symbols systematically to indicate emphasis, set pace, and help guide readers in determining meaning.

Like Franklin, some defend Johnson, arguing that his "understandable assumption" was that Dickinson's carry-over lines fill out her meter, that line endings are accidental, caused by running out of room on a page, that to fit words in, she would have had to cramp or crowd her script. Others point out that she often did cramp and crowd her script and frequently chose to disrupt meter. For example, the familiar four opening lines of Johnson's P712* look like this in Dickinson's writing:

> Because I could not
> stop for Death—
> He kindly stopped for me—
> The Carriage held but
> just Ourselves—
> And Immortality—(*Manuscript Books* 509)

Johnson's first line accentuates "Death"; Dickinson's first line accentuates "I." "The Carriage held but" is suspenseful and "just Ourselves" more chilling alone on the line. Her lines dislocate phrasing and disrupt meter to achieve visual, sonic, and dramatic effects. Mistranslations, where nuances and ambiguities are less recognizable or lost, result in misreadings and limited readings. Editorial approaches to Dickinson scholarship help readers recover options for experiencing and interpreting the writing.

Editing is a matter of individual reading. No editor can ever be "objective" or "disinterested," no edition "definitive." As Marta Werner writes in her "experimental edition" of late drafts and fragments associated with Otis Phillips Lord,* "Every reader is a bibliographer-poet finding his or her own way toward the future by striking out in a different direction through the past."

All editing "is more an act of translation than of reproduction," writes Jerome McGann (*The Textual Condition* 53). Three kinds of editions are currently being designed and produced: photofacsimiles, electronic texts, and new print translations. Facsimile editions have been published by Franklin, *The Manuscript Books of Emily Dickinson** (1981) and *The Master Letters of Emily Dickinson* (1986), and by Werner, *Emily Dickinson's Open Folios: Scenes of Reading, Surfaces of Writing* (1996). In electronic editions texts will be embedded in a network of related documents and critical materials. Martha Nell Smith writes of the hypermedia project she directs, "Editorial decisions are always interpretive, and happily, such an archive would enable many more of Dickinson's readers to make such decisions for themselves." These editions, monumental advances for Dickinson studies, are the closest readers can come to viewing manuscripts.

Editors using typography are currently experimenting with fonts, spacing, angled dashes, and sizes of minuscules and majuscules. Print translations, with commentary, are the most democratic texts—accessible, economical, and easily reproducible. Along with students, scholars, and academics, Dickinson has a diverse, popular audience that includes readers* of selected works, teaching texts, foreign-language editions, lines quoted in fiction and nonfiction, on greeting cards, posters, and T-shirts. New typographical representations will show

Dickinson to be a more approachable and less cryptic writer than she has sometimes been portrayed.

Illuminating connections are being made among textual studies, criticism, and
biography.* For example, Dickinson often referred to her writing as her
"Thought." The "T" may be uppercase or lowercase, but Johnson sometimes
overlooked the capitalization. This may be one reason the term has not received
more notice. When Dickinson writes, "My Mother does / not care for
Thought—/ And Father / too busy / with his Briefs / to / notice what we do,"
Johnson's omission of the capital "T" makes a subtle but significant difference
(L261). These lines are usually understood to mean, "My mother prefers to
remove herself from intellectual life," but they may also read, "My mother is
not interested in poetry and writing." "My father generally pays no attention
to what I do" has been the common interpretation; yet she may mean, "He
overlooks my work as a writer." New readings, made possible by new texts,
have important ramifications for all branches of Dickinson scholarship. (*See*:
Publication)

RECOMMENDED: Susan Howe, *The Birth-Mark: Unsettling the Wilderness in
American Literary History*; Jerome J. McGann. *A Critique of Modern Textual Criticism.*
Charlottesville: University Press of Virginia, 1993; Martha Nell Smith, "Dickinson's
Manuscripts."

Ellen Louise Hart

EDWARDS, JONATHAN (1703–1758)   Although Edwards lived fully two
generations before Dickinson, his religious* legacy thoroughly leavened her
western Massachusetts cultural environment long after his death. During the
Great Awakening of the 1730s and 1740s, Edwards and others had reignited
Calvinistic Christianity in the new light of Newtonian physics and Lockean
psychology; his project was immensely successful, as measured by the intense
religious fervor that swept the colonies. In the early part of the nineteenth century, Edwards' grandson Timothy Dwight led the Second Great Awakening
(joined later by Nathaniel Taylor, Lyman Beecher, and others), a continuation
of Edwards' efforts to adjust Calvinism to meet contemporary needs. Proclaiming the sovereignty of God* and humanity's absolute need for divine grace,
Edwards had attacked Arminian tendencies that had threatened what he saw as
orthodox Puritan* faith. In an ironic reversal, this third generation of revivalists*
expressed an "Arminianized" Calvinism that shifted attention away from God
the Father to emphasize the role of human volition in the salvation process,
apparently, in part, to soften the earlier image of God as a merciless tyrant—
an image against which critics see Dickinson rebelling. The centrality of a personal conversion, a quest for affective piety, and the renunciation of self* to
gain spiritual reward remained key tenets well into Dickinson's era.

Jones finds Dickinson continuing Edwards' sacramental view of nature*; yet,
from another perspective, the Edwardsian "pit" may dominate her poetry in
ways Keller finds consonant with Dickinson's tendency to express the fulfillment

that can emerge from tragedy. With the possible exception of his posthumous *History of the Work of Redemption* (a Mount Holyoke* textbook), Dickinson probably did not know Edwards' writings firsthand. At the end of an 1881 letter, she made her only explicit reference to him in a play of wit identifying Edwards with the austere side of Christianity (L712). (*See*: Congregationalism; Connecticut Valley; Religious Criticism)

RECOMMENDED: Joseph Conforti. *Jonathan Edwards, Religious Tradition and American Culture*. Chapel Hill: University of North Carolina Press, 1995; Beth Maclay Doriani, *Emily Dickinson, Daughter of Prophecy*; Rowena Revis Jones, ''Edwards, Dickinson, and the Sacramentality of Nature''; Karl Keller, *The Only Kangaroo among the Beauty: Emily Dickinson and America.*

Beth Maclay Doriani

ELECTION, AS THEME   Emily Dickinson continually battled feelings of religious* uncertainty. Whereas she probed for evidence of God's* having elected her for salvation, she was unable to achieve comprehensive assurance. Her conception of nature* as a ''haunted house'' (P1400) implied belief in a transcendent deity, but one who remains distant from creation. We are left in his empty house, groping among deceptive signs and emblems for clues to our eventual fate.

Dickinson's fusions of contradictory attitudes toward election presented an unremitting protest against the assumption that Christians could presume to know what happens after death.* Her upbringing in the latter-day Puritan* culture of Amherst* would have made her aware of the significance of deathbed behavior: if the person's manner was calm, chances were good that the soul could be sure of its election. Dickinson, however, denied the eschatological significance of last words and gestures. In P465 the dying woman's last moments, when she might expect a sign of immortality,* are lost to the petty annoyance of a fly's buzzing. Representing nature* in its least dignified manifestation, the insect* separates the dying woman from the light and foreshadows the body's eventual disintegration in the grave.*

Renouncing the pleasures of present reality, Calvinists concerned themselves with the question of election and the afterlife. The first stanza of P216 asserts that those waiting to be reborn are ''Safe in their Alabaster Chambers—.''* Like corpses, they remain enclosed in their chambers of dogma. The light breeze, the babbling bee, and the sweet birds* of this poem's second stanza assert the folly of worrying about a possible afterlife when a vital world is all around.

Dickinson loved this world too much to renounce it for an indefinite Heaven*—God's ''House of Supposition'' (P696). If her choice must be between a temporal world and Heaven, the poet/speaker in P1012 emphatically prefers the proverbial '' 'Bird within the Hand' '' to whatever the '' 'Bush' '' may yield or deny. Dickinson suggested that, if we would only look around us, we would realize that "Earth is Heaven—/ Whether Heaven is Heaven or not" (P1408).

Yet in P528, the speaker exults in the permanence she possesses: "Mine—by the Right of the White Election!" She has chosen to be a poet and as a result of this "Election" has been given the "Royal Seal." The speaker's re-iteration of the word "mine" is an imperial assertion of her right. A similar confirmation of self*-election can be heard in "The Soul selects her own Society—" (P303).* Rather than wait for God to author her fate, the speaker claims power to determine it for herself. (*See*: Legal Imagery; Religion)

RECOMMENDED: Paula Bennett, *Emily Dickinson: Woman Poet*; Rowena Revis Jones, "The Preparation of a Poet: Puritan Directions in Emily Dickinson's Education"; Wendy Martin, *An American Triptych: Anne Bradstreet, Emily Dickinson, Adrienne Rich*; Cynthia Griffin Wolff, *Emily Dickinson*.

Deborah Dietrich

ELEGY   Discussions of the genre seldom mention her poems, but Dickinson scholarship foregrounds thematic concerns central to the elegy: loss, grief, death,* and prospects of immortality.* If the nineteenth century was "the elegiac century" (Potts, *The Elegiac Mode*), Dickinson feels very much a poet of her time, even though the affinity remains unacknowledged by historians and theoreticians of the genre. The difficulty may lie in the poet's "slant"* relation to nineteenth-century developments in elegiac verse; for, whereas English elegists until Hardy translated grief into consolation (Sacks, *The English Elegy*), modern elegists demonstrate "fierce resistance to solace" (Ramazani, *Yeats and the Poetry of Death*).

For historical and practical reasons a clear-cut definition of elegy is almost impossible. A distinction has grown up in the English tradition between "elegiac" (i.e., meditative and reflective verse), and the elegy proper (i.e., a poem occasioned by the death of an actual person); Ramazani distinguishes additionally the subgenre of self*-elegy and mentions Dickinson in this context; yet "the boundary is by no means sharp" (Preminger, *Encyclopedia of Poetry and Poetics*). Coleridge defined elegy as "the form of poetry natural to the reflective mind." Thus descriptions of the genre more readily point to tonal and structural than to occasional distinctions: a seriousness (if not formality) in diction and mood and the movement of the poem from sadness to consolation or acceptance (Preminger; Lieberman, *A Modern Lexicon of Literary Terms*). In addition to those, it entails an intention, not so much for "an outpouring of personal grief as a generalization beyond the particular situation to reflections on living and the course of life. . . . Elegy is in the final analysis less for the dead than for the living" (Lieberman).

If the preceding characteristics are accepted as defining features, Dickinson's poems become problematic as elegies since they hardly progress from grief to consolation. For instance, Poems 389 or 1100, clearly occasioned by specific deaths, explore the shock of loss rather than seek reconciliation. Typically, Dickinson brings her most powerful poems to an emotional and intellectual confrontation with the void without suggesting means of transcending it. Her poems are hardly "lamenting" or "grieving," for they treat loss as the experiential given and strive, often with alarming curiosity, "To note the fashions—of the Cross—/ And how they're mostly worn—" (P561). Again and again in Dickinson's vision, "that White Sustenance—Despair" must suffice as life's nourishment (P640). Dickinson's recognition of dispossession as the ultimate reality places the poet much closer to twentieth-century elegists than to the elegiac mode of her own times. (Comparison with Whitman* is enlightening here.) Rilke's *Duino Elegies* are frequently cited as the modern example of the genre, in which lament over the human condition, motivated by metaphysical terror, reaches philosophical* heights. For all their grounding in individual experience, Dickinson's poems may be perceived in similar categories.

RECOMMENDED: Janet W. Buell, " 'A Slow Solace': Emily Dickinson and Consolation"; Elizabeth A. Petrino, " 'Feet so precious charged': Dickinson, Sigourney, and the Child Elegy."

Agnieszka Salska

ELIOT, GEORGE (1819–1880)   Marian Evans, the Victorian novelist who wrote under this pen name, inspired Dickinson through her life and works. Writing that "God chooses repellant settings, dont he, for his best Gems?" (L692) while awaiting a picture of Eliot, Dickinson nevertheless hung Eliot's portrait in her bedroom. Dickinson once wrote to her Norcross* cousins, " 'What do I think of *Middlemarch*?' What do I think of glory—except that in a few instances this 'mortal has already put on immortality.' George Eliot is one" (L389). For her, *Daniel Deronda* was "that wise and tender Book" (L974). In her letters,* Dickinson particularly invoked characters and events from *The Mill on the Floss* (L650 and 888), and Martha Dickinson Bianchi* recalled that "no one who knew Emily in life could ever forget her tenderness for Maggie Tulliver" (302).

News of Eliot's death* in 1880 seriously grieved Dickinson: she wrote, "The look of the words as they lay in the print I shall never forget. Not their face in the casket could have had the eternity to me. Now, *my* George Eliot" (L710). While eagerly anticipating Eliot's biography by John Walter Cross, she read Mathilde Blind's *Life of George Eliot*. Dickinson empathized with Eliot's isolation* and hardships (stemming from a "scandalous" relationship with a married man), writing, "The Life of Marian Evans had much I never knew—a Doom of Fruit without the Bloom" (L814). Dickinson also seemingly related to Eliot's religious* anxieties: "she lost her way to the early trust, and no later came" (L710).

Dickinson wrote two poems to commemorate Eliot. P1562 begins, "Her Losses make our Gains ashamed—/ She bore Life's empty Pack." P1564, "Pass to thy Rendezvous of Light" (originally written at her nephew Gilbert's* death), was included in a letter to Higginson* about Eliot, Dickinson prefacing the poem with the words "Biography first convinces us of the fleeing of the Biographied" (L972). Eliot's literary influence on Dickinson is more ambiguous; Pollak, for instance, senses a "contextless punishment motif" in P1562 (241). Other scholars, however, see Eliot's works, particularly *The Mill on the Floss*, as strong literary influences for Dickinson: Phillips relates Poems 401, 537, and others to themes in that novel, while Cary, noting the writers' similar water imagery and themes of renunciation, suggests that the novel "may well have stimulated the poet's imagination" (36). (*See*: Books and Reading)

RECOMMENDED: Martha Dickinson Bianchi. "The Books of Revelation." Appendix A in *Emily Dickinson and Her Culture* by Barton Levi St. Armand; Cecile W. Cary, "*The Mill on the Floss* as an Influence on Emily Dickinson"; Elizabeth Phillips, *Emily Dickinson: Personae and Performance*; Vivian R. Pollak, *Dickinson: The Anxiety of Gender*.

Alisa Clapp-Itnyre

EMERSON, FORREST F.   was the pastor of the First Church* at Amherst* from 12 June 1879 until he was dismissed on 21 February 1883. Thereafter, Emerson moved to Newport, Rhode Island. Dickinson wrote at least eight brief notes to Emerson and his wife, which are essentially expressions of gratitude acknowledging some thoughtful gesture. One such letter is a note of thanks for the transmittal of clippings on the death of Helen Jackson* (L1018). In that same letter, Dickinson also recalled Emerson's words of sympathy following young Gilbert Dickinson's* death.* The overall tone and length of the notes suggest that Dickinson's acquaintance with Emerson was slight. (*See*: Emerson, Kendall)

RECOMMENDED: *Letters*; *Years*.

Marisa Anne Pagnattaro

EMERSON, JOHN MILTON (1826–1869)   regularly called at the Dickinson home while he studied law in Edward Dickinson's* office and served as a tutor at Amherst College.* Valedictorian of the college's class of 1849, Emerson was a classmate of Emily's brother, Austin.* Emily found Emerson's visits tiresome and likened him to "Sir Oracle" from Gratiano's speech in Shakespeare's* *Merchant of Venice*: "he carries about the sail of a good sized British vessel, when he has oped his mouth I *think* no dog has barked" (L48). In 1856, Emerson moved his law practice to New York City, where he remained until his death in 1869. His obituary contains an intriguing reference to a lost love who "left this true lover lonely through life." Richard Sewall suggests the object of Emerson's affections was Olivia Coleman,* who died of tuberculosis in 1847 and whose mother was a cousin of Emily's mother.

RECOMMENDED: *Letters*; *Years*; *Life*.

Mary Carney

EMERSON, KENDALL   was one of Gilbert Dickinson's* playmates. Emerson and Gilbert were playing in the same mud hole when Gilbert contracted the typhoid fever that caused his death* in 1883. For three consecutive years following this disaster, Dickinson sent the child Christmas notes in her nephew's memory (L876, 956, and 1027). Emerson later graduated from Amherst College* in 1897, studied medicine, and became an orthopedic surgeon. (*See*: Emerson, Forrest)

RECOMMENDED: *Letters.*

Marisa Anne Pagnattaro

EMERSON, RALPH WALDO (1803–1882)   The principal figure of American Transcendentalism,* Emerson graduated from the Harvard Divinity School in 1826 and was called in 1829 to the pulpit of Boston's Second Church (Unitarian*), which he was asked to leave three years later. Starting in 1833, Emerson supplemented his inheritance from his first wife's estate by guest sermons and lectures. In 1835 he married Lydia Jackson and moved to Concord, Massachusetts, where he soon became Henry David Thoreau's* mentor and the leading voice in the Transcendentalist movement. His book *Nature* (1836) encouraged readers to build their own spiritual worlds out of the natural signs they perceived. In "The American Scholar" (1837) he proclaimed America's cultural independence, and in his "Divinity School Address" (1838) he attacked established Christianity as merely historical, asserting that Christ should be worshiped not as a historical figure but as an example of the divinity attainable by all men and women. Emerson's essays became more concrete and less prophetic* in the 1840s. In *Essays: First Series* (1841), he continued to argue for the presence of a Universal Mind underwriting man's relation to nature.* But at the center now was "Self Reliance": he considered nonconformity an inevitable result of what it meant to be a self.* *Essays: Second Series* (1844) continued Emerson's concern with the self. In "The Poet" he repeated the Romantic* trope that the poet was a bard recapturing an original unity that had been lost. But the other essays were less optimistic about man's ability to attain knowledge.

Dickinson was reading Emerson's work—particularly his essays—as early as the mid-1840s, and many scholars believe him to have been a major influence on her. Emerson's *Poems* (1846), given to Dickinson by her father's law student Benjamin Newton* around Christmas 1849, used rhyme* and meter in innovative ways. Dickinson called these poems "immortal," and she labeled his *Representative Men* (1850) "a little Granite Book you can lean upon" (L481). She marked her copies of Emerson's *The Conduct of Life* (1861, 1879), *Essays* (1861), *May-Day* (1867), and *Society and Solitude* (1879). Whether she attended any of the lectures Emerson gave in Amherst* in 1855, 1857, 1865, and 1879 cannot be determined, but she certainly knew of their content. On the occasion of his 1857 lecture Emerson stayed with Austin* and Sue Dickinson* in the house next door to where Emily was living. She wrote to Sue, "It must have been as if he had come from where dreams are born!" (PF10). During the last years of her life Dickinson copied out several scraps of Emerson's verse, something she did very rarely for any of her favorite poets. She enclosed the phrase

"Tumultuous privacy of storm" from Emerson's "The Snow Storm" in a letter that Lavinia* sent Mrs. Todd* in 1884 (PF116). Nonetheless, it seems that Dickinson never wrote to Emerson, went to see him in Boston,* or talked to him while he was in Amherst.

Both Emerson and Dickinson were rebellious, creative, and primarily concerned with humanity's relation to God* and nature,* regarding natural signs as symbols of what lay beyond them. However, Dickinson did not share Emerson's optimism. While he spoke of "nature," she spoke of a gothic* "landscape"; and while for Emerson the interpretation of natural signs brings the perceiver closer to the benevolent Oversoul, to Dickinson it revealed the presence of an awe-inspiring God.* Where one recognized the moral justification of everything, the other experienced painful doubt. For both writers, however, the soul was consciousness* and had to catch the ecstasy of the irrecoverable moment. But while Emerson's poetic circles reached outward, Dickinson's mostly plunged inward. Since Emerson believed in man's capacity to deduce meaning from signs, his language clarifies and liberates, while Dickinson's reveals the ambiguity* of signs and the predicament of the perceiver.

Although several borrowings from Emerson show through in Dickinson's work, the parallels have been judged by various scholars as parodies or inversions rather than imitations. However, contemporary readers may have seen little difference: when Helen Hunt Jackson* anonymously published Dickinson's "Success" (P67),* the poem was attributed to Emerson. (*See*: Philosophical Approaches; Romanticism)

RECOMMENDED: Joanne Feit Diehl, "Emerson, Dickinson, and the Abyss"; Karl Keller, *The Only Kangaroo among the Beauty: Emily Dickinson and America*, ch. 6; Roland Hagenbüchle, "Sign and Process: The Concept of Language in Emerson and Dickinson"; James E. Mulqueen, "Is Emerson's Work Central to the Poetry of Emily Dickinson?"; David Porter, *Dickinson: The Modern Idiom*.

Josef Raab

EMILY DICKINSON: A REVELATION (1954)   At the core of this collection are thirteen letter drafts written by Dickinson to Otis Lord* in the 1870s and 1880s and discovered among the poet's papers after her death. The drafts, though mostly fair copies composed on fine linen, have neither salutations nor signatures and do not appear to have been posted. Several have been heavily censored; many others are missing an unknown number of leaves. Mabel Todd* knew of their existence by the 1890s but considered them too private to publish at that time. Instead, she passed the cache of manuscripts on to her daughter, who finally printed them in *A Revelation*. Millicent Todd Bingham* initially conceived of *A Revelation* as an edition of the Dickinson–Lord correspondence; however, after a twenty-year search failed to uncover any additional letters,* the shape of her work changed. In addition to transcriptions of the thirteen letter drafts printed in sequence in part 1, she selected, apparently at random, sixteen rough-copy prose fragments for inclusion in part 2. No link between the two groups of documents has been established. Finally, in a further effort to add heft to the slim volume, Bingham printed redactions of twenty-three late poems, all previously published. The volume closes with a facsimile of Dickinson's transcript of stanzas two and three of George Herbert's* "Matins." The Herbert transcript, another textual non sequitur, provides a fitting epilogue to this editorially constructed "Master Passion." *A Revelation* was one of Bingham's last "editions" of Dickinson's work, and its eclectic nature may result from the fact that her store of unpublished documents was dwindling. The highly sensationalistic narrative has recently been revised by scholars focusing less on the uncertain biographical implications of the drafts and more on their complex history of discovery, mutilation, and publication.* (*See*: Editorial Scholarship)

RECOMMENDED: Marta L. Werner, *Open Folios: Scenes of Reading, Surfaces of Writing.*

Marta L. Werner

EMILY DICKINSON FACE TO FACE (1932)   Spurred by Mabel Loomis Todd's* 1931 revision of *Letters of Emily Dickinson,** Martha Dickinson Bianchi* edited this anecdotal biography,* which was published after many delays with a foreword by Alfred Leete Hampson.* Described in the subtitle as "*Unpublished Letters with Notes and Reminiscences*," the text presents itself as an "intimate study . . . of the habits, temperaments, and daily life of all the members of the Dickinson household" based on unpublished family letters and diaries along with reminiscences of friends. *Face to Face* contains Bianchi's first suggestion that the poet's seclusion was caused by an unhappy renunciation of the love* of a married* man. In support of her authority to present this as a faithful portrait of her aunt, Bianchi cast herself as "the one person now living who saw her [Dickinson] face to face in her later years of seclusion" (xxii). Hampson insisted that such a vantage point was necessary to Dickinson scholarship in the wake of renewed interest in Dickinson's life and poetry and the resultant wild speculation about her personality and character.

The book is arranged in five sections: personal reminiscences by Bianchi; a familial history complete with a reproduction of the Dickinson coat of arms; excerpts from letters between Austin Dickinson* and Susan Gilbert and from Lavinia Dickinson's* diary; extended portraits of the family interspersed with letter excerpts; and finally, excerpts of letters* and notes written by Dickinson herself to family members, most of them addressed to Bianchi's mother and Dickinson's sister-in-law, Susan Gilbert Dickinson.* The book also provides an appendix highlighting important moments in Amherst* history as well as in Edward Dickinson's* public life, followed by a remarkable series of obituaries.

Despite an attempt to claim interpretive supremacy over all other collections of Dickinson's work up to 1932, various inaccuracies and questionable editing* practices undercut Bianchi's achievement in *Face to Face*. Bianchi typically corrected what she perceived as inaccuracies on the part of other biographers, without saying who was being discredited and also without demanding the same rigor of her own work. There are numerous mistakes in the dating of poems and letters and, as in *The Life and Letters* (1924),* Bianchi took from Mabel Loomis Todd's published research without citing her source.

RECOMMENDED: Elizabeth Horan, "To Market: The Dickinson Copyright Wars"; Morris U. Schappes. Rev. of *Emily Dickinson Face to Face* by Martha Dickinson Bianchi. *American Literature* 5 (1933–1934): 82–85.

Jeanne E. Clark

THE EMILY DICKINSON INTERNATIONAL SOCIETY (EDIS) was incorporated in 1988 as a nonprofit corporation in the commonwealth of Massachusetts to promote, perpetuate, and enhance the study and appreciation of Emily Dickinson throughout the world. Among its objectives are to establish and support local chapters; to sponsor international conferences; to sponsor a journal; to establish a Center for Dickinson Studies; to secure the future of the Homestead* and the Evergreens* as cultural and historical treasures; to obtain by purchase, gift, or otherwise writings and materials relevant to Dickinson studies; to acquire, own, or lease and hold any real estate and buildings necessary or proper; to accept, hold, and expend money or property given it in trust (from *Articles of Incorporation*). With its numbers steadily growing, the society has members on almost every continent and from over twenty countries. It held its first two international conferences in Washington, D.C. (1992), and Innsbruck, Austria (1995). Society publications include the *Emily Dickinson International Bulletin** and *The Emily Dickinson Journal*.* Local chapters of the society hold regular meetings with a variety of activities scheduled throughout the year. Information about EDIS can be obtained by searching the World Wide Web.

Margaret Freeman

THE EMILY DICKINSON INTERNATIONAL SOCIETY BULLETIN Published twice yearly (May/June and November/December) since 1989, the *Bulletin* is distributed free of charge to members of the Emily Dickinson International Society (EDIS).* It carries news of EDIS, including annual meetings, chapter meetings, elections, conferences, participation in meetings of other scholarly societies, and Dickinson-related activities by individual members. It also includes reviews of recent books, exhibits, and performances (live and recorded) dealing with Dickinson and news and feature articles of general interest to the membership. Continuing series cover Dickinson library collections, important Dickinson scholars, the two Dickinson houses in Amherst, and twentieth-century poets and visual artists influenced by Dickinson.

Georgiana Strickland

THE EMILY DICKINSON JOURNAL sponsored by the Emily Dickinson International Society (EDIS),* was founded in 1991. It was published by the University Press of Colorado from 1992–1996; thereafter, by the Johns Hopkins University Press. The founding and current editor is Suzanne Juhasz. Published biannually, the *Journal* creates a forum for scholarship on Dickinson and her relation to the tradition of American poetry and women's literature. It publishes essays and review essays on Dickinson and Dickinson publications to showcase the poet at the center of current critical practices and perspectives. Since its first issue in 1992, it has published four Special Issues: the Conference Issue from "Translating Emily Dickinson in Language, Culture, and the Arts" (1993); the Special Issue on Editing and the Letters (1995); the Conference Issue from "Emily Dickinson Abroad" (1996); and the Special Issue, "Translators on Translating Emily Dickinson," guest-edited by Margaret Freeman, Gudrun Grabher, and Roland Hagenbüchle. The *Journal* is a member of the Johns Hopkins University Press's electronic Project Muse: http://muse.jhu.edu.

Suzanne Juhasz

EMMONS, HENRY VAUGHAN (1832–1912)   was attending Amherst College* when he started visiting the Dickinson home and became a friend of Emily Dickinson in early 1852. His introduction to the family was through John Graves,* his college friend and relative of the Dickinsons. Emmons and Dickinson began a close friendship, probably based on their mutual love of literature. The two took walks and rides together and exchanged short letters. Although their relationship apparently involved some flirtation (to use Wolff's term), Dickinson accepted easily his interest in another young woman in 1853 and his engagement to Susan Phelps in 1854. After that engagement was broken by Phelps, Emmons married Ann Shepard in 1865.

He graduated from Bangor Seminary in 1856 and was an active minister until 1902. In August 1854 Dickinson wrote Emmons a thank-you note for the gift of "the pearl, and then the onyx, and then the emerald stone" (L171), which has sometimes been interpreted as a book of Poe's* poems. This correspondence apparently ceased soon after his graduation.

RECOMMENDED: *Letters*; *Life*; Cynthia Griffin Wolff, *Emily Dickinson*.

Ronald Palosaari

EROTICISM   Although potential for such readings was recognized earlier, scholarly unpacking of erotic subtexts in Dickinson's poetry has been a recent development. In 1891, Higginson* worried that "the malignant" might read into "that wonderful 'Wild Nights' . . . more than that virgin recluse ever dreamed of putting there" (*AB* 127); but until Rebecca Patterson's *The Riddle of Emily Dickinson* (1951), scholars tended to scant such matters. The first to decode widespread erotic significance in Dickinson, Patterson contextualized her unorthodox readings within the poet's short-lived, intense friendship with Kate Scott Anthon.* In linking Dickinson's eroticism with lesbian* desire, Patterson laid out what has since become one of the most contested sites in Dickinson criticism. But further exploration of erotic themes in Dickinson's writing suggests that the very multiplicity of possibilities that can be drawn from her texts is the defining quality of her eroticism. Persuasive analyses have been developed attesting to her heterosexuality, her homoeroticism, her autoeroticism, even her necrophiliac and incestuous tendencies. Typically, these readings are internally coherent, becoming problematic only when brought together.

Part of the difficulty in defining Dickinson's eroticism derives from her habit (shared with such contemporaries as Christina Rossetti and Harriet Prescott Spofford*) of mediating sexual desire through inherently ambiguous* imagery. She depends on a network of female sexual images—fruits, flowers,* jewelry*—deployed in the Western literary tradition from *Canticles* on. As a result, given that her response to all forms of beauty was typically intense—indeed, erotic—one cannot be sure, in most instances, whether what seems to be there actually is. For example, Dickinson incorporated "All the letters I can write" (P334) in a letter to her cousin Eudocia Flynt,* together, presumably, with a flower. With its sexually weighted references to "Velvet," "Plush," "Depths of Ruby," "Lip[s]," and "sip[ping]," the poem seems to deal, on at least one level, with cunnilingus. But it hardly seems possible that Dickinson would send such a poem to a cousin with whom she was on friendly but by no means intimate terms.

So how can we know whether such poems are truly erotic? How can we be sure we are not reading into Higginson's "virgin recluse" more than she ever dreamed of putting there? The easiest answer may also be the correct one: we can't. Unlike sexual orientation, which is defined explicitly through object choice, eroticism can be, and often is, free-floating. In Dickinson's case, she appears to have eroticized many different kinds of relationships, including those to books,* nature,* God, and to any number of individuals, from her brother and sister-in-law, to friends such as Anthon, Elizabeth Holland,* Samuel Bowles,* and the elusive "Master."* She used (sexual) imagery deeply rooted in Western literary tradition to express the intensity of these sensually desiring relationships, but the exact nature of those relationships, how much—or little— we should read into them about her sexuality, will probably always elude our grasp. (*See*: Body; Love; Lovers)

RECOMMENDED: Paula Bennett, *Emily Dickinson: Woman Poet*; Margaret Homans, " 'Syllables of Velvet': Dickinson, Rossetti, and the Rhetoric of Sexuality"; Camille Paglia, *Sexual Personae: Art and Decadence from Nefertiti to Emily Dickinson*; Rebecca Patterson, *The Riddle of Emily Dickinson*.

Paula Bennett

THE EVERGREENS In response to his son Austin's* expressed interest in moving to the Midwest, Edward Dickinson* provided him with land and a house in Amherst* in 1855 as an inducement to remain close to home. "The Evergreens" (the first "named" house in Amherst) is a pale yellow, two-story, wood-frame house on a granite and brick foundation. It was designed in the popular Italianate style by William Fenno Pratt, a Northampton architect.

The house includes ten main rooms, several smaller spaces, a full basement, and two separate attics. It is set on a deep lawn set off by Austin's naturalistic landscaping. The setting originally included a small barn (no longer extant) and a long picket fence with monumental gate posts (portions of which are preserved on-site). The prominent three-story tower provides a strong visual focus and also serves to ventilate the entire house.

The Evergreens was occupied by Austin and Susan* immediately after their wedding in July 1856, and they raised three children there: Edward* (Ned), Martha* (Mattie), and Gilbert* (Gib). Susan's tastes and personality are expressed in the furnishing and decoration of the house. She made the Evergreens a center of social life in Amherst, entertaining such notable guests as Ralph Waldo Emerson,* Wendell Phillips, Frederick Law Olmsted, and Henry Ward Beecher.

After Austin's death in 1895, Susan lived at the Evergreens until her own death in 1913. The house then passed to Martha, Austin and Susan's only surviving child, who had remained there after her separation from Captain Bianchi. When Martha Dickinson Bianchi died in 1943, the Dickinson manuscripts and the Evergreens went to her coeditor and literary assistant, Alfred Hampson,* with the provision that when he no longer lived in it, the house should be demolished, and the property sold. Alfred's widow, Mary Hampson,* entertained few visitors but kept the house intact and sought a way to ensure its preservation. Her will (effective upon her death in 1988) directed the remaining Dickinson-related books and manuscripts to Brown University and established the Martha Dickinson Bianchi Trust to restore and maintain the Evergreens. The house and grounds are now being restored and will eventually be open to scholars and the general public. As fund-raising and restoration progress, the Evergreens will provide a physical context for appreciating the Dickinson household and the character of Amherst in the Victorian period.

RECOMMENDED: *Life*; Susan H. Dickinson. ''Magnetic Visitors: The Annals of the Evergreens.'' *Amherst* 33, 4 (Spring 1981): 8–15, 27; Gregory Farmer and Masako Takeda. ''The Evergreens: The Other Dickinson House.'' *The Massachusetts Review* 34 (Winter 1993–1994): 545–64; John Evangelist Walsh, *This Brief Tragedy: Unraveling the Todd–Dickinson Affair.*

Masako Takeda

F

FAITH That Emily Dickinson was intrigued by faith is evident in the many and varied ways she sought to define or characterize the term in her poetry. Identified variously as "a fine invention" (P185), "The Experiment of Our Lord" (P300), "the fellow of the Resurrection" (P491), and "Constancy's Result" (P969), faith is perhaps most memorably described in two instances as a bridge that lacks any visible means of support yet provides a strong and necessary link between this world and whatever lies beyond (P915, 1433). To gain even a glimpse of the world beyond, a personified faith "slips—and laughs, and rallies—" (P501) and "bleats to understand" (P313). Dickinson personae explore their own faith (P766, 1007, 1557) as well as that of others. The "faithful witness" (P260) and "everlasting troth" (P792) of martyrs receive special commendation, while the confident faith of the dying (P43) and the triumph of faith over "that Old Imperator—Death" (P455) inspire awe. Biblical figures such as Lot (P702) and the disciple Thomas (P861), even such nonbiblical figures as William Tell (P1152), provide opportunities to explore the nature of faith. Examples of faith in nature* include the lily that pushes "Through the Dark Sod" showing "no fear" (P392). Faith also serves as a link between lovers* or friends* (P205, 387, 440, 999). Tests of faith often appear unfair or unjust (P338, 497), even disastrous. The simplicity of "The Child [whose] faith is new" gives way to suspicion of both God* and mankind when the child* is exposed to the ways of the world (P637, P476). Perhaps that "tattered Faith" can be restored by "a needle fair" (P1442), but it may be, as another poem suggests, that once lost, faith can never be regained, and without it, "Being's—Beggary—" (P377). (*See*: Bible; Jesus; Religion)

RECOMMENDED: E. Miller Budick, *Emily Dickinson and the Life of Language: A Study in Symbolic Poetics*; Paul J. Ferlazzo, *Emily Dickinson*.

Emily Seelbinder

FAME, AS SUBJECT   In her 7 June 1862 letter to Higginson,* Emily Dickinson said she was not interested in achieving fame by publishing* her poems: "If fame belonged to me, I could not escape her—if she did not, the longest day would pass me on the chase—and the approbation of my Dog, would forsake me—then—My Barefoot-Rank is better—" (L265). She went on to indicate that she lacked the will to regulate rhymes* in her poems as Higginson had suggested. That is, she did not want to reach fame by writing her poems as the public expected. According to Rosenbaum's *Concordance,** Dickinson's poems use the word "fame" twenty-six times, "fame's" twice, and "fames" once. Dickinson viewed fame in this world ironically, regarding it as fickle and untrustworthy (P1475, 1659). Not relying on public estimation, she asserted that a person himself or herself judges the self* (P713). The fame that Dickinson had in mind is not conspicuous but simple and modest (P1009, 1232). She desired that her poetry be appreciated by those understanding its true value, even if they be few. The fame she sought was to be esteemed after death* (P431, 448, 675, 866, 883).

RECOMMENDED: *Letters*; Jane Donahue Eberwein, *Dickinson: Strategies of Limitation*; S. P. Rosenbaum, ed., *A Concordance to the Poems of Emily Dickinson*.

Sahoko Hamada

FARLEY, ABBIE COGSWELL (Mrs. William C. West) (1846–1932) Judge Otis Lord's* niece, Abbie Farley moved into Lord's home after his wife's death in 1877 and kept house for him until his death in 1884. A friend of Susan Dickinson's* and Lavinia's* "special aversion" (*Life* 232), she firmly opposed the attachment between Dickinson and Lord, perhaps with a view to her position as chief beneficiary of Lord's will. Farley's animosity toward Dickinson propelled her to destroy all letters from Dickinson in Lord's possession.

RECOMMENDED: *Letters*; *Life*.

Mary Jane Leach-Rudawski

FASCICLES   Compiled by Emily Dickinson between 1858 and 1864, the forty surviving books, called fascicles by Mabel Loomis Todd,* became available as reassembled in Ralph Franklin's* 1981 *Manuscript Books of Emily Dickinson,** which provide virtually the only unmediated means of reading the poet in her own context. Between 11 and 29 poems (814 in all) fill the pages of each book, made of four to seven prefolded stationery sheets bound with thread. Although seven of the books are incomplete, the fascicle collection has become the focus of intense and varied critical attention.

Why, readers wonder, did Dickinson prepare what Richard Sewall calls her "private substitute[s] for publication . . . her notion of the way her poems should be presented to the world?" (*Life* 537). At least five dissertations, four books, and many articles discuss possible answers to such questions. Critical interest may not yet have become what Rosenthal and Gall cite in *The Modern Poetic*

Sequence as "one of the great voyages of discovery in modern criticism" (73), but proliferating studies contest Robert Weisbuch's contention in a review of the *Manuscript Books* for *American Literary Scholarship: 1983* that reading the poems in fascicles "shows not a jot more coherence than one could derive from any random groupings" (94).

Likening the sequences to "long link poems" in *The Poetry of Emily Dickinson* (1968), Ruth Miller first urged readers to "let Emily Dickinson's choice guide them" (249, 8). Although Ralph Franklin himself declared in his introduction to the *Manuscript Books* that the collections were "a continuing workshop" (x), others, such as Buckingham, said the fascicles "may well constitute an intended sequence of interrelated poems" (614); Gerlach finds them crucial to those interested in Dickinson's methods.

Interpretations vary as to what each sequence—and the sum of the forty—implies about Dickinson. The first post-Franklin full-length study was William Shurr's *The Marriage of Emily Dickinson* (1983), in which all fascicles form a narrative of disappointed passion. Martha Nell Smith, however, argues in *Rowing in Eden: Rereading Emily Dickinson* (1992) that the fascicles represent Dickinson's strategy for a kind of self-publication that evaded the gender implications of print. Among those who have accepted Smith's challenge to devote time to the poet's gatherings, with divergent results, are those who liken the fascicles to devotional books. Oberhaus, for example, posits that fascicle 40, "a simple conversion narrative," is the culmination of the narrator's spiritual quest.

Others (Doreski, Heginbotham) find the nature of the linkages of poems and images within fascicles to be less consistently narrative or devotional but to be more like what Michael Riffaterre calls in his *Semiotics of Poetry* the "hypogram": "a structure's complex network of relations" (5–6). Sharon Cameron's fascicle study moves even beyond the notion that, while the fascicles may not suggest story lines or religious categories, they do show the poet's love of play, her self-conscious, if tricky, negotiations with the reader. Cameron sees the fascicles as evidence of Dickinson's choice "not to choose." For Cameron, the fascicles, particularly the poet's increasing use of variants within them, indicate her intentional resistance to closure.

These two approaches—one that queries the theoretical, textual implications in the fascicles, the other that finds something approaching a narrative of a personal or a religious* experience in the poems—exemplify the ongoing discussions of those who "hold a [fascicle] to the light" (P169). Threaded together, literally and figuratively, the fascicles are evidence of Dickinson's self-identification not only as a deliberate poet but also as an editor. (*See*: Appendix A; Publication; Textual Variants)

RECOMMENDED: Willis Buckingham. Rev. of *Manuscript Books. American Literature* 54 (1982): 613–14; William Doreski, " 'An Exchange of Territory': Dickinson's Fascicle 27"; John Gerlach, "Reading Dickinson: Bolts, Hounds, the Variorum, and Fascicle 39"; Eleanor Heginbotham, "Dwelling in Possibilities: The Fascicles of Emily

Dickinson''; Dorothy Huff Oberhaus, *Emily Dickinson's Fascicles: Method and Meaning*.

Eleanor Elson Heginbotham

FEMINIST APPROACHES   Recent feminist criticism of Dickinson can be classified into three types: works that locate Dickinson in a tradition of women's literature; readings of the particularities of her poetics as efforts to resist or revise patriarchal language; and studies of Dickinson's sexuality.

The criticism of the first type was more or less inaugurated by Gilbert and Gubar's influential *Madwoman in the Attic* (1979), which interprets Dickinson's isolated* and relatively eccentric life in the context of images of enclosure and escape, anorexia, agoraphobia, claustrophobia, and maddened* female doubles that characterize nineteenth-century women's writing. Gilbert and Gubar interpret these images as women's efforts to negotiate between the demands of authorship and the repressive ideal of woman as an "angel in the house." Unlike a fiction writer, Dickinson could not represent the repressed underside of the feminine ideal by describing such images, for, as Gilbert and Gubar demonstrate, the role of lyric poet demands the self-articulation of a strong central consciousness. They argue that Dickinson met the particular challenges of being a female lyric poet by acting out the roles of bride,* child,* and madwoman that female fiction writers merely described. A number of subsequent studies read Dickinson in the context of the female literary tradition Gilbert and Gubar identify. Cheryl Walker's *The Nightingale's Burden: Women Poets and American Culture before 1900* relates Dickinson to an American women's poetic tradition; Barton Levi St. Armand's *Emily Dickinson and Her Culture: The Soul's Society* assembles an array of cultural materials constituting "a biography of American Victorian culture"; Jane Eberwein's *Dickinson: Strategies of Limitation* and Joanne Dobson's *Dickinson and the Strategies of Reticence* both relate Dickinson's emphasis upon restraint, smallness, and reticence to nineteenth-century women's culture.

Homans' work has set the standard for the language-oriented deconstructive approach to feminist criticism of Dickinson. Her *Women Writers and Poetic Identity* draws an analogy between the functioning of language and the functioning of Western literary practice, in that both attempt to recapture a lost presence. The use of a word to represent a thing indicates that the thing is absent, but it also represents a hopeful though impossible effort to reconnect with that absent thing through symbolic representation. Just as words are both signs of absence and futile efforts to regain presence, so too, literary activity in Western culture is seen as both a sign of absence and an effort to regain presence. In our androcentric culture, Homans proposes, individuality is typically constituted through difference from the maternal presence experienced in infancy, and symbolic activities such as literary creation represent both a sign that maternal presence has been lost and a futile effort to regain that presence. Dickinson's poetry, however, subverts these "male" views of language and literature as systems that "mean" through difference from women and presence; it tends to assert the materiality of the signifier rather than alluding to an essential meaning "else-where"; it deconstructs binary gender opposition, and it denies the masculine assumption that hierarchy and opposition are necessary for linguistic meaning.

Joanne Feit Diehl's *Dickinson and the Romantic Imagination* also analyzes Dickinson's subversions of a male tradition as exemplified by major Romantics*: Wordsworth, Keats,* Shelley, and Emerson.* Revising Harold Bloom's theory of influence to account for gender, she argues that by conceiving of herself apart from this male line of poets, Dickinson creates a space that provides her the freedom to experiment. Loeffelholz develops the feminist deconstructive approach to Dickinson from a psychoanalytic perspective; her *Dickinson and the Boundaries of Feminist Theory* addresses Lacan's language-based theory of the formation of female subjectivity in patriarchal culture, a culture whose influence Loeffelholz traces in the male literary tradition. Cristanne Miller's *A Poet's Grammar* analyzes Dickinson's tropes, rhetorical* strategies, syntax,* and other poetic devices as antipatriarchal linguistic strategies, and Helen McNeil's *Emily Dickinson* provides an overview of Dickinson's work that is informed by deconstructive and feminist concerns. In *The Wicked Sisters*, Betsy Erkkila challenges many of these arguments for the feminist radicalism of Dickinson's linguistic* experimentation, arguing that they efface the material differences between women of different classes and races and have little political effectiveness. Karen Sanchez-Eppler agrees that Dickinson is largely an apolitical poet but credits her with understanding that conventional efforts to alleviate the suffering of oppressed others frequently collaborate in oppression by demanding conformity to dominant values.

Feminist critics have also focused extensively on Dickinson's sexual orientation. Rebecca Patterson's, Jeanette Foster's, and Lillian Faderman's early arguments for the poet's lesbianism* have been followed by Bennett's *Emily Dickinson: Woman Poet*, which describes a lesbian sensibility in general and identifies in particular a cluster of erotically* charged vaginal and clitoral images. Likewise, Martha Nell Smith's analysis of the original manuscripts indicates a startling, systematic pattern of erasures and substitutions of "he's" for "she's," bespeaking a "desperate" effort on the part of Austin Dickinson or an early editor to prevent public awareness of the lesbian sensibility that permeates the manuscripts. By contrast, in *Dickinson: The Anxiety of Gender*, Pollak describes a largely heterosexual sensibility thwarted by the limited possibilities for women's romantic fulfillment in the mid-nineteenth century. Suzanne Juhasz's collection of nine essays in *Feminist Critics Read Emily Dickinson* (1983) remains a groundbreaking resource for feminist approaches to the poet. (*See*: Fictionality; Poststructuralist Approaches; Psychological Approaches; Women's Culture)

RECOMMENDED: Paula Bennett, *Emily Dickinson: Woman Poet*; Sandra Gilbert and Susan Gubar, *The Madwoman in the Attic: The Woman Writer and the Nineteenth-Century Literary Imagination*; Margaret Homans, *Women Writers and Poetic Identity:*

Dorothy Wordsworth, Emily Brontë, and Emily Dickinson; Mary Loeffelholz, *Dickinson and the Boundaries of Feminist Theory*; Cristanne Miller, *Emily Dickinson: A Poet's Grammar*; Vivian R. Pollak, *Dickinson: The Anxiety of Gender*.

Marianne Noble

FICTION, DICKINSON IN   Some Dickinson critics call the commentaries of other critics "fiction," but the poet who claimed that her own first-person dramas involved a "supposed person" has figured in many frankly fictional works from her own lifetime on (L268). Earliest of the novels, Helen Hunt Jackson's* *Mercy Philbrick's Choice*, begins with a dedicatory sonnet's "gratitude and love" to the writers "Who serve before Truth's altar, in his name." Jackson, Dickinson's Amherst* contemporary and would-be agent, suggests parallels between Emily and Mercy: both live "in the ordinary New England town"; both are "slight," have "gentle, laughing brown eyes," "pale skin," and so forth. Mercy becomes a rather well known, "deeply affecting" writer as she is wooed through correspondence by an older man. After Mercy's death, she is mourned by a Jackson-like female poet.

Another neighbor, little MacGregor Jenkins,* to whom Dickinson wrote, "Please never grow up. . . . Please never 'improve' " (L717), did grow up to write *Emily*. The love* story it tells about his childhood friend and her minister lover claims to be "the picture of a beautiful young woman . . . as courageous as a crusader and as shy as a nun, threading her devious way through the mazes of a cyclonic experience." People from the actual life (Maggie Maher,* Lavinia* and Sue Dickinson*) blend with an imagined Emersonian* professor and a Rev. Hayward, who prompts "a sense of something impending."

Closer to the historical little Jenkins and his Amherst neighbor is the beautifully illustrated children's story *Emily* (Bedard and Cooney), in which the curious little narrator learns about gingerbread, plants, and poetry. Somewhat older readers could learn other lessons from Zibby Oneal's adolescent novel, *A Formal Feeling*.

Styron's Sophie, whose remembered and horrible "Choice" propels her to death, makes Dickinson's "Ample make this Bed—" (P829) poignantly relevant to postwar adult readers. Other recent novels include Jane Langton's romp of a periodic academic murder mystery in which "ardent tributes to Dickinson's memory are rudely interrupted by arson, forgery . . . and murder" and Jamie Fuller's "discovered" *Diary*, which struggles to equal the wit and dash of the real letters.* In *I Never Came to You in White*, Judith Farr presents a more complex network of seasoned research, imaginative empathy, and great fictional and poetic skills to provide a witty, suspenseful, and moving exploration of what really happened between Miss Lyon* and her puzzling young charge in 1848. Around that focus Farr weaves material from the poems and letters into a suspense story that moves from Dickinson's memories of childhood to 1932 as Mabel Loomis Todd* tells her story. "Letters" from the proud and still befuddled Higginson,* from the stolid English teacher, Margaret Mann, and others reflect the impossibility of knowing the truth behind the genius and the lover.* Anne Walter's French novel moves even more dramatically between two centuries as a would-be translator imagines Amherst, the Dickinsons, Lord,* and others.

More lighthearted fictions based on Dickinson have been offered on National Public Radio by Garrison Keillor and in a science fiction anthology by Connie Willis. In the former, Keillor has variously imagined a Dickinson rendezvous with Thoreau* and (in common meter) a posthumous pizza order; in the latter, Willis has her writing beyond the grave to repulse a Martian invasion of Amherst. Such varied embodiments attest to what happened because "fame* [did, indeed] belong" to Dickinson (L265). (*See*: Dance Responses; Dramatic Responses; Poetic Tributes; "Saxe-Holm"; Visual Arts Responses)

RECOMMENDED: Michael Bedard, *Emily*. New York: Doubleday, 1992; Judith Farr. *I Never Came to You in White*. Boston: Houghton Mifflin, 1996; Jamie Fuller. *The Diary of Emily Dickinson*. San Francisco: Mercury, 1993; [Helen Hunt Jackson.] *Mercy Philbrick's Choice*. "No Name Series." Boston: Roberts Brothers, 1876; MacGregor Jenkins. *Emily*. Indianapolis: Bobbs-Merrill, 1930; Jane Langton. *Emily Dickinson Is Dead: A Novel of Suspense*. New York: St. Martin's, 1983; Zibby Oneal. *A Formal Feeling*. New York: Fawcett Juniper, 1982; William Styron. *Sophie's Choice*. New York: Random House, 1979; Anne Walter. *L'Herbe Ne Pousse Pas Sur Les Mots*. Arles: Actes Sud, 1994; Connie Willis. "The Soul Selects Her Own Society: Invasion and Repulsion: A Chronological Reinterpretation of Two of Emily Dickinson's Poems: A Wellsian Perspective." *War of the Worlds: Global Dispatches*. Ed. Kevin J. Anderson. New York: Bantam, 1996.

Eleanor Elson Heginbotham

FICTIONALITY Dickinson located reality in the fictive; her engagement with the realm of imaginative relationship, from her early attachment to "lies," through her emphasis on the meaning-making process involved in coping with textual variants,* to her thematic concern, in poem after poem, with "Possibility" (P657), lay at the root of her poetic vocation. Yet Dickinson early on found her "ardor for the lie" (L315) at odds with her milieu. She wrote Austin* in 1851, "we do not have much poetry,* father having made up his mind that its pretty much all *real life*" (L65). Fiction was often confused with the frivolous and false: "Now my dear friend," Dickinson warned ironically, "let me tell you that these last thoughts are fictions—vain imaginations to lead astray foolish young women. They are flowers of speech, they both *make*, and *tell* deliberate falsehoods, avoid them as the snake" (L31). Her confession to another friend, "I have dared to do strange things— . . . I have heeded beautiful tempters" (L35), suggests that her pursuit of the fictive might be conceived as satanic. Dickinson, as Eve, celebrated her humanity because its "fallenness" required and permitted precisely the work of the imagination—meaning-making, loving, believing. In fact, in P861, she aligned literalists with inhumanity and death*: "Split the Lark—and you'll find the Music—/. . . . Scarlet Experiment! Sceptic Thomas! / Now, do you doubt that your Bird was true?" In reducing the bird's

"Music" to its blood, the biblical "Doubting Thomas" (who had declared to the risen Jesus, "unless I put my hand in your side . . . I will not believe") has failed to believe his ears, to let his relationship to the bird be imaginative.

More redemptively, Dickinson could make a point of being literal in order to demonstrate the fictive basis even of literality. She wrote to Ned* in May 1872, "Neddie never would believe that Emily was at his Circus, unless she left a fee—" (L373). Johnson* records that the impression of a coin remains in the note paper. Funnily, the coin acknowledged an imaginary circus as literal; it was enacted just like a "real" circus. Both literal events were "made up." Dickinson's absence (imagined to be literal), however, was also made up; the coin presented evidence of her participation. Whether an actual coin was sent, or just its impression, its literality produced a new fiction about "what happened." The imaginary itself is not at all unreal but, actually ("Neddie never would believe"), like the coin, produces real consequences (relationship, exchange), and this is the surprise and the joke. The other joke is that "real" money is an imaginary token for imaginary worth, like words.*

RECOMMENDED: Suzanne Juhasz, *The Undiscovered Continent*; Robert Weisbuch, "The House of Possibility," *Emily Dickinson's Poetry*.

Melanie Hubbard

THE FIRST CHURCH OF CHRIST, AMHERST   Established in 1739, when Amherst* was a precinct of Hadley, Massachusetts, this church is the Congregational* assembly that the Dickinsons attended. Beginning with strong Tory sympathizers during the time of the Revolution, the congregation continued its historically Puritan,* orthodox stance through the time of the Dickinsons' membership, when it held out against the liberal strains of Unitarianism* flourishing in eastern Massachusetts. These concerns were closely allied with the founding of Amherst College* at a time when the congregation was also experiencing a series of revivals.* The Dickinsons were active in the congregation's life: in 1868, when the present church building was dedicated, Edward Dickinson* delivered a speech; other records show how he and Austin Dickinson* participated in many decisions made by the congregation.

The church was certainly in Emily Dickinson's consciousness* throughout her lifetime, whether located in the building she first knew beside the Amherst College campus or in its new structure across the street from the Evergreens.* Many early letters recount her impressions of events during church services. However, Dickinson never formally converted and thus, in the Congregational tradition, could not be admitted to full membership as a participant at the Lord's Supper. At some time in her late twenties, she stopped attending church services, though she remained on friendly visiting terms with the Reverends Dwight* and Jenkins.* For many profound reasons, it appears that Dickinson simply preferred to live her religious* convictions on her own terms, terms in which her writing clearly played a part. (*See*: Faith; Religion)

RECOMMENDED: *Life*; *250 Years at First Church in Amherst 1739–1989*. Amherst, MA: First Congregational Church in Amherst, 1990; Regina Siegfried, "Bibliographic

Essay: Selected Criticism for Emily Dickinson's Religious Background''; Cynthia Griffin Wolff, *Emily Dickinson*.

Susan Rieke

FISKE, NATHAN WELBY (1797–1847) **and DEBORAH VINAL** (d. 1844) The Fiskes, like Emily Dickinson's parents, married and began housekeeping in Amherst* in 1828. Dour, pedantic Rev. Fiske taught Latin and Greek and, later, philosophy at Amherst College* for twenty-two years, beginning in 1824. His wife, pious yet intrepid and possessed of felicitous wit, struggled with consumption. The Fiskes lost two infant sons but raised daughters Helen and Ann, who were near age-mates and occasional playmates of Emily and Lavinia Dickinson.* That Helen proved a handful is apparent from family correspondence in the Helen Hunt Jackson* papers at Colorado College, a collection containing Rev. Fiske's diary and Mrs. Fiske's perceptive letters.

During the 1870s and 1880s, after Helen became the popular poet, essayist, and novelist known as H. H., she and Emily renewed an acquaintance interrupted when thirteen-year-old Helen left Amherst after her mother's death in February 1844. Deborah's funeral sermon was preached by Amherst College president Heman Humphrey.* Nathan took leave from the faculty in the autumn of 1846 to improve his own deteriorating health through travel. He died in Jerusalem the following May and was buried on Mount Zion.

RECOMMENDED: *Years*; Heman Humphrey. *''The Woman That Feareth the Lord'': A Discourse Delivered at the Funeral of Mrs. D. W. V. Fiske, February 21, 1844.* Amherst, MA, 1844, and *Memoir of Rev. Nathan W. Fiske, Professor of Intellectual and Moral Philosophy in Amherst College.* Amherst, MA, 1850.

Polly Longsworth

FLOWERS   Not only is flower imagery among the most pervasive image patterns in Dickinson's writing, but for Dickinson (as for most middle-class women of her period), the care and feeding of flowers were themselves a supremely important component of life. As a young woman she kept an herbarium, which, still extant, is distinguished for its beautiful and careful arrangement. As an adult, she maintained a conservatory, growing exotic flowers despite New England's forbidding weather. Summers, she, like her mother and sister, worked in the garden* outdoors. In her 1894 memoir of Dickinson, Emily Fowler* Ford recalled her in that garden, ''a flower herself'' (*Life* 376).

Dickinson's own comments on flowers are more pungent. To a friend, she wrote, ''Expulsion from Eden grows indistinct in the presence of flowers so blissful, and with no disrespect to Genesis, Paradise remains'' (L552). Flowers were, it seems, as close as she could come to heaven* on earth, and, conversely, she had no use for ''a Redemption that excluded them'' (L528). Given the large role flowers played in Dickinson's life, it is not surprising that floral references appear ubiquitously in her writing. Frequent references to flowers in the letters support the fact that they were fundamental to her daily life, the activities she engaged in, and the gifts (often a single bloom) she gave. In the poems there are approximately 400 references to flowers or their parts, such as "stem" and "sepal." The range of flowers to which she referred is unusually broad, even for her flower-obsessed period, covering wildflowers as well as cultivated blooms. But the rose was for her, as it has been for most poets in the Western literary tradition, the poetic flower of choice, appearing in over twice as many poems as its nearest competitor, the daisy—this despite the fact that Dickinson called herself "Daisy"* in a number of important texts, including the "Master"* letters. Like other American women poets of the period, Dickinson deployed flower imagery figuratively in a wide variety of ways. Flower images encoded references to poetry* and the poetic process, to individuals and to generic human beings, to Jesus* and the soul, to Eden and bliss, and, perhaps most important, to woman and the female genitalia, so these images substantially contribute to the notorious ambiguity* of her writings. (See: Nature; Women's Culture)

RECOMMENDED: Life; Paula Bennett, "Critical Clitoridectomy: Female Sexual Imagery and Feminist Psychoanalytic Theory," and Emily Dickinson: Woman Poet; Wendy Martin, An American Triptych.

Paula Bennett

"Flowers—Well—if anybody" (P137)   gives evidence that publication of Dickinson's work during her lifetime was wider than previously assumed. The poem appeared in Drum Beat,* 2 March 1864, and was reprinted in both the Springfield Republican* and the Boston Post. Poems 130 and 228 were also found in Drum Beat, causing their discoverer Karen Dandurand to conclude that it was Dickinson's own disinclination rather than editorial resistance that explains her failure to publish* more widely.

Beyond its unique history, P137 illustrates colloquialism* (the only instance of Dickinson's using "Well" as an intimacy signal) as well as a wry oxymoron* in "Half a transport—half a trouble." She challenges "anybody" (later specified as male) to define "the exstasy" and offers "all the Daisies / Which upon the hillside blow" should such a task be accomplished. Since she frequently described daisies as "modest," "low," or "small," particularly in contrast to powerful persons or forces such as a lord or the sun, and since ecstasy enables "flowers [to] humble men," the poem may shed light on Dickinson's sense of herself as a woman poet challenging traditional hierarchies. The daisies also echo the "Daisy"* persona of her "Master"* letters, the earliest of which is estimated to have been written in the late 1850s, around the time of this poem.

Defining ecstasy is equated with finding the source of floods (an untamable and often sexual force in Poems 530 and 861) whose "flow" is alliteratively connected with the flowers.* The poem takes on further sensual overtones with the purple line suggestive of love,* butterflies symbolic of the beloved, and St. Domingo, which Patterson interprets as "symbolizing the South of erotic happiness and freedom." Ecstasies of flowers and butterflies surpass systems of aesthetics or attempts at definition. Sherwood sees P137 as evidence of Dickinson's perception of the gulf between nature* and humanity. As in P97, where "My flowers turn from Forums / Yet eloquent declare / What Cato could'nt prove," Dickinson illustrates the ineffectiveness of systems of philosophy* or logical discourse when it comes to expressing the inexpressible. (*See*: Appendix A (Fascicle 4); Eroticism; Garden; Insects)

RECOMMENDED: Karen Dandurand, "New Dickinson Civil War Publications"; Brita Lindberg-Seyersted, *The Voice of the Poet*; Rebecca Patterson, *Emily Dickinson's Imagery*; William Sherwood, *Circumference and Circumstance*.

Terry Blackhawk

FLYNT, EUDOCIA CONVERSE   of Monson, Massachusetts, was Dickinson's first cousin once removed on her mother's side. She was the second wife of William Norcross Flynt, who was the brother of Mrs. Lyman Coleman.* In her diary, Flynt recorded details about Dickinson's funeral,* including the following observations: "private, no flowers, taken to the Cemetery—by Irishmen, out of the back door, across the fields!! her request—" (*Years* 2:475). (*See*: Kelley)

RECOMMENDED: *Letters*; *Years*.

Marisa Anne Pagnattaro

FOWLER, EMILY ELLSWORTH (1826–1893)   A granddaughter of Noah Webster,* Fowler was Dickinson's childhood friend. Born at Greenfield, Massachusetts, Fowler moved to Amherst* in 1838, when her father, William Chauncey Fowler, accepted a position as professor of rhetoric at Amherst College.* Fowler and Dickinson's friendship probably began in 1842, when they both attended Amherst Academy's* classical program. Both girls contributed to *Forest Leaves*, a school publication, and were members of the Shakespeare* Club, where they would meet to discuss literary works. According to Taggard, Fowler was also socially active in giving P.O.M. (Poetry of Motion) meetings, where she would gather her friends to dance. Fowler, like many of the girls her age, responded to religious revivalism.* In November 1842, at age sixteen, she joined the Amherst College Church on profession of faith.

Dickinson began corresponding with Fowler in the spring of 1850, before her correspondence with Susan Gilbert.* The correspondence ended in 1854, when Fowler married Gordon Lester Ford, a New York City lawyer. Then the Fords resided in Brooklyn, where they raised their eight children. In 1872, Ford published her first and only book of verse, *My Recreations*, which includes such headings as "Verses of Thought," "Flowers," and "Verses of Feelings." In the copy housed in the Amherst College Library's Special Collections, Ford handwrote a dedication of a preface poem to Dickinson, as she may have done to the copy she sent her friend. The last letter Dickinson sent to Ford thanked her for the book. Ford also wrote essays, stories, and a two-volume biography of her grandfather, *Notes on the Life of Noah Webster*, which was posthumously published in 1912. In 1891, she wrote "Eheu! Emily Dickinson," a poem that appeared in the *Springfield Republican.**

RECOMMENDED: *Years*; Genevieve Taggard, *The Life and Mind of Emily Dickinson.*

Michelle Tice

FRANKLIN, RALPH W. (b. 1937)   is the foremost living editor of Emily Dickinson's manuscripts. His *The Editing of Emily Dickinson* (1967) includes historical inquiry into the editorial* methods employed by those responsible for her posthumous publication*; reconstruction of packet contents and order; and a philosophical meditation on the need to reconsider authorial intent as the standard litmus in editorial decision making, since Dickinson never prepared her poems for publication. His groundbreaking publication in facsimile of the reconstructed fascicles* and sets in *The Manuscript Books of Emily Dickinson** (1981) spurred an unprecedented revival of interest in the physical appearance of Dickinson's manuscripts. Franklin is now preparing a new edition of Dickinson's poems for Harvard University Press. (*See*: Johnson, Thomas Herbert)

RECOMMENDED: Sharon Cameron, *Choosing Not Choosing: Dickinson's Fascicles*; Ralph W. Franklin, ed., *The Master Letters of Emily Dickinson*; Susan Howe, "These Flames and Generosities of the Heart: Emily Dickinson and the Illogic of Sumptuary Values"; Martha Nell Smith, *Rowing in Eden: Rereading Emily Dickinson*; Marta Werner, ed., *Emily Dickinson's Open Folios: Scenes of Reading, Surfaces of Writing.*

Melanie Hubbard

FRENCH, DANIEL CHESTER   The sculptor of the Lincoln Memorial lived in Amherst* as a teenager (1864–1866) and was slightly acquainted with Dickinson through Susan Dickinson* and Louise* and Frances Norcross.* When his statue of John Harvard was unveiled at Harvard in 1884, Dickinson wrote him a note of congratulation (L898) containing the poem "Circumference* thou Bride of Awe" (P1620).

RECOMMENDED: *Letters*; Joshua C. Taylor. *The Fine Arts in America*. Chicago: University of Chicago Press, 1979.

Jonathan Morse

FRENCH RESPONSES TO DICKINSON   In Europe, France was the first country to recognize Dickinson's genius and is now second only to Italy in publishing Dickinson criticism. The first French article on Dickinson was Jean Catel's "Emily Dickinson: Essai d'analyse psychologique" (1925). Yet it must be noted that in France Dickinson's poetry has not received widespread critical recognition. Writing in 1989, for example, Claire Malroux, a contemporary Dickinson translator, questions the reasons a poet considered so important in her own country remains comparatively disregarded in France. She concludes that in addition to the enigmatic character and difficulty of Dickinson's verse and, to the French ear, the relative unfamiliarity of Dickinson's biblical* and

Shakespearean* references, the determining factor is the lack of a translated edition of the complete poems.

Nevertheless, since 1925, some of the best French scholars have devoted significant attention to Dickinson's poetry. In the 1920s, for example, when he wrote on Dickinson, Régis Michaud was known as the best French specialist of English literature. Throughout the 1930s and 1940s, when he published his piece on Dickinson, Catel was considered the leading French Americanist. French Dickinson critics have frequently been scholars of significant European and international reputation: L. Bocquet, Charles Cestre, Cyrille Arnavon, Robert Goffin, Guy Forgue, and others. Moreover, highly respected poet-critics such as André Maurois, Alain Bosquet, and Philippe Denis have all translated Dickinson's poems and published criticism on her. Current French scholarship is active with several recent book-length studies on Dickinson (Savinel, Delphy) and a 1996 collection of critical essays (*Profils américains: Emily Dickinson*), the first of its kind to be published in France. (*See*: Fiction)

RECOMMENDED: Jean Catel, "Emily Dickinson: Essai d'analyse psychologique"; Francoise Delphy, *Emily Dickinson*; Claire Malroux, trans. and ed. *Emily Dickinson: Poèmes*. Paris: Belin, 1989; Andre Maurois, "Emily Dickinson, Poétesse et Recluse"; Christine Savinel, *Emily Dickinson et la grammaire du secret*.

William Dow

FRIENDSHIP, AS SUBJECT   Contrary to the myth that Dickinson was an isolated* recluse, connections with others were extremely important to the poet. Although, as she noted in an 1871 letter, "My friends are very few" (L223), Dickinson's small circle of companions formed her treasured "estate" (L193).

Dickinson's poetry* echoes both this valuation of friends and anxiety concerning their loss. As Jeffrey Simpson notes, intimate friendships offered her a safe haven from a menacing world. Verse passages such as "Her heart is fit for *home*—/ I—a Sparrow—build there / Sweet of twigs and twine / My perennial nest" (P84) and "An Hour is a Sea / Between a few, and me—/ With them would Harbor be—" (P825) describe friends as places of shelter and rest. In addition, her poems of friendship tend to use metaphors* that depict a close companion as "a Jewel"* (P245) or a "guinea golden" (P23), a possession as valuable as a pearl of great price. Although, as Thomas Johnson* notes in *Emily Dickinson: An Interpretive Biography*, Dickinson did not often meet her friends face-to-face; this was due to the intensity of her relations with, and her feelings for, them. In "The Soul selects her own Society—/ Then—shuts the Door—" (P303),* she expressed her choice to concentrate emotional energies on an important few. In spite of this diligence, lines such as "those who know her, know her less / The nearer her they get" (P1400) show Dickinson's fear that a close emotional connection is ultimately impossible.

So valuable were the friends who inhabited Dickinson's poetry that, as with those who inhabited her life, she expressed a constant fear of their loss. In "Are Friends Delight or Pain?" (P1199), Dickinson worried that they might "fly away''; while in "I should not dare to leave my friend" (P205), she showed concern about irrevocable loss. Death,* misunderstanding, or simple negligence might cause this loss, a familiar theme in her poems and letters. (*See*: Elegy)

RECOMMENDED: Christopher E. G. Benfey, *Emily Dickinson and the Problem of Others*; Paula Bennett, "The Pea That Duty Locks: Lesbian and Feminist-Heterosexual Readings of Emily Dickinson's Poetry"; Adalaide K. Morris, "Two Sisters Have I: Emily Dickinson's Vinnie and Susan"; Jeffrey E. Simpson, "The Dependent Self: Emily Dickinson and Friendship"; Michael E. Staub, "White Moth and Ox: The Friendship of Emily Dickinson with Helen Hunt Jackson."

Jennifer Hynes

FUNERAL   Held Wednesday, 19 May 1886, four days following her death, Dickinson's funeral was attended by a small group of intimates: family, friends, servants, and their children. Thomas Wentworth Higginson* read the poem "No coward soul is mine" by Emily Brontë.* Honorary pallbearers Dwight Hills, John Jameson, Edward Hitchcock, Jr., and Julius Seelye* carried the white casket out the back door of the Homestead,* whereupon her chosen pallbearers, six Irish immigrant Homestead workmen, took over. At Dickinson's request, Thomas Kelley,* chief pallbearer, and Dennis Cashman, Daniel Moynihan, Dennis Scannel, Patrick Ward, Stephen Sullivan, and/or Owen Courtney carried her coffin and flower*-bedecked bier front to back through the barn, over the grounds, always within sight of the house. Followed by butterflies, the procession wended irregularly through flowery fields to the family burial plot in the West Cemetery. At the grave, the Reverends Dickerman and Jenkins* performed a brief service. No flowers were bought or chairs and carriages hired for the occasion, yet the poet's funeral was among Amherst's* most expensive that spring ($121.75).

RECOMMENDED: Jay Leyda, "Miss Emily's Maggie" and *Years*; Daniel Lombardo. *Tales of Amherst: A Look Back*. Amherst, MA: Jones Library, 1986; Barton Levi St. Armand, *Emily Dickinson and Her Culture: The Soul's Society*.

Aífe Murray

***FURTHER POEMS OF EMILY DICKINSON, WITHHELD FROM PUBLICATION BY HER SISTER LAVINIA* (1929)**   This volume, edited by Martha Dickinson Bianchi* and Alfred Leete Hampson* and published by Little, Brown, apparently was created in response to the popularity of Bianchi's *Complete Poems of Emily Dickinson** (1924) and *Life and Letters of Emily Dickinson** (1924), which helped begin a Dickinson revival. *Further Poems* included some 182 poems from manuscripts that had belonged to Lavinia Dickinson* and had been passed down to Susan Dickinson* and then to Bianchi. Thus these poems had not been part of the Todd*–Higginson* volumes.

The only American edition of *Further Poems* appeared 8 March 1929 and sold for $2.50; this first printing of 2,000 copies was immediately followed by a "limited edition" second printing of 480 copies and six more print runs by the end of 1930. The book appeared in London in October 1929 from Martin Secker, Ltd.

Further Poems received blockbuster marketing; previews appeared in the *New York Herald Tribune, Nation, Saturday Review*, and *London Mercury*. Louis Untermeyer praised it as "Emily Dickinson's most beautiful, and from every standpoint, most important book" (Horan 115). However, critical commentary was less kind. Conrad Aiken's lengthy review argued that Bianchi and Hampson had obscured the source of the new poems and that the book should be reedited "by someone competent to do so" (797). Later criticism of Bianchi has come from R. W. Franklin,* who argues that *Further Poems* contained abundant misreadings of the manuscripts, committed in an attempt to excite public interest by presenting an excessively eccentric poetic form, and from Morris Schappes and Elizabeth Horan, who question Bianchi's editing skills. (*See*: Editorial Scholarship)

RECOMMENDED: Conrad Aiken, "Emily Dickinson and Her Editors"; R. W. Franklin, *The Editing of Emily Dickinson: A Reconsideration*; Elizabeth Horan, "To Market: The Dickinson Copyright Wars"; Joel Myerson, *Emily Dickinson: A Descriptive Bibliography*; Morris U. Schappes, "Errors in Mrs. Bianchi's Edition of Emily Dickinson's *Letters*."

Jennifer Hynes

G

GARDEN, AS SUBJECT   Dickinson often used gardens as microcosms of nature,* analogies of heaven,* and representations of her soul, home,* and New England culture. The gardens in Dickinson's poems are relatively safe and small places where speakers can experience a tamed nature and contemplate a flower,* bird,* or shadow or even "keep the Sabbath" (P324). As the locus of both delight and loss, the garden serves as a setting for musing on the sublime* and fallen mortal world and imagining the immortal.* The natural and supernatural mingle in gardens under the hand and gaze of Dickinson's speakers.

Dickinson's figurative gardens that she names Paradise and Eden recall and revise the narratives of Creation and the Fall in Genesis as well as the new heaven of *Revelation*. Her poems often contemplate the nature of God* and the gender relations he established in the paradise that Adam and Eve lost and also the nature of the paradise to be regained in heaven. Yet Dickinson often found paradise, Eden, and heaven on earth: she declared to Austin* that Amherst* "seems indeed to be a bit of Eden" (L59), and P1408 states that "Earth is Heaven." She knew that her Puritan* ancestors had struggled to create a Christian paradise in the New World.

The Dickinson family garden, which she called "my Puritan Garden" (L685) and "Vinnie's* sainted Garden" (L885), offered privacy yet also means of keeping in touch with the wider world. She often sent flowers and produce, along with a letter poem, to friends* and neighbors. In the glass-walled, south-facing conservatory that her father built for her off his study, which she called "the garden off the dining-room" (L279), she brought plants and poems to life.

Paradoxes bloom in Dickinson's poetic gardens, which contain sweet and bitter, promise and loss, growth and death. The Dickinsonian garden is a place of possibilities; the "unexpected Maid" that the speaker of P17 encounters in her garden may be nature, poetry,* and the speaker herself. She cultivated a peculiar and stunning strain of Puritan, Romantic,* and realistic* contemplation that probed her self* and her world.

RECOMMENDED: Jane Donahue Eberwein, *Dickinson: Strategies of Limitation*; Margaret Homans, *Woman Writers and Poetic Identity*; Jean McClure Mudge, *Emily Dickinson and the Image of Home*; Gary Lee Stonum, *The Dickinson Sublime*.

Joanna Yin

GENEALOGY The parents of Emily Elizabeth Dickinson and her siblings were Edward Dickinson* and Emily Norcross,* who were married 6 May 1828 at Monson, Massachusetts. Emily's grandparents were Samuel Fowler Dickinson,* Lucretia Gunn,* Joel Norcross,* and Betsey Fay.* Her great-grandparents were Nathan Dickinson, Jr., and Esther Fowler, Nathaniel Gunn and Hannah Montague, William Norcross, Jr., and Sarah Marsh, and Jude Fay and Sally Fairbanks. The next generation back were Nathan Dickinson and Thankful Warner, Nathaniel Gunn, Jr., and Dorothy Marsh, Richard Montague and Lucy Cooley, William Norcross and Lydia Wheeler, Seth Marsh and Rachel Ellis, Ebenezer Fay and Thankful Hyde, and Eleazer Fairbanks and Prudence Cary. Emily had many cousins as her contemporaries living in Massachusetts cities and towns such as Worcester, Andover, and Billerica. Others lived in New York City, Michigan, Alabama, and other locales in the South. None of her first cousins resided at Amherst,* although her second cousin, Henry Holland (born 1831 at Belchertown, Massachusetts), was a merchant there.

RECOMMENDED: Elinor V. Smith, *Descendants of Nathaniel Dickinson*. New England Genealogical Society. *NEXUS* 7, 5 (1978): 156–58; James Avery Smith. *Families of Amherst, Massachusetts*. Amherst: Unpublished typescript, 1984, and *Records of West Cemetery at Amherst, Massachusetts*. Amherst: Official records of the town engineer.

James Avery Smith

GEOGRAPHIC IMAGES Although Emily Dickinson hardly traveled, geographic images abound in her poems. The place-names she employed cover the world. She was keen on geography, writing in an 1850 letter, "We will talk over what we have learned in our geographies" (L34).

As for Asia, several place-names in the Bible* enter her poetry: Ararat, Bethlehem, Gethsemane, Nazareth, Jerusalem, and Israel. The images of these place-names usually resemble those in the Bible. India is related to wealth or richness. Himmaleh refers to gigantic size or strength. Other place-names are Asia, Burmah, Bosporus, Cashmere, Caspian, Circassian Land, Jordan, Oriental, and Tripoli. As for Europe, geographic names in Italy are most frequently employed. Volcano is the outstanding image in Italy, found in references to Naples, Sicily, Etna, and Pompeii. Some place-names present images of industry: steel in Birmingham; wine in Frankfort, Norway, and the Rhine; clock making in Geneva. Other place-names include the Alps, the Apennine, Aragon, Athens, Azof, Baltic, Dnieper, Durham, Finland, Ghent, Gibraltar, Mexico, Paris, Spain, Switzerland, Westminster, and Yorkshire. In Africa, Ethiopia is presented as a place in which civilization is not accepted. Related place-names include Africa, Red Sea, Sahara, Teneriffe, and Tunis. In North America, Dickinson presents New England and Amherst* as countryside, with reference to farmers and farms. Other place-names include America and the Potomac. For South America, she mentions jewelry and mines in poems referring to Potosi, Peru, Buenos Ayres, and Bolivia, though the most frequently used place-name from Latin America is Brazil. Related references include Andes, Chimborazo, Jamaica, and the Bahamas. Dickinson also employs frequent place-names in her letters.*

RECOMMENDED: *Letters*; Rebecca Patterson, *Emily Dickinson's Imagery.*

Sahoko Hamada

GERMAN-LANGUAGE RESPONSES TO DICKINSON   can be divided into (1) translations of, and (2) critical responses to, her poetry. The earliest translation occurred in 1898, when the German-American Amalie von Ende translated four poems (of which two are incomplete) in an essay published in *Der Westen*, a Chicago periodical for Germans. Though a number of scholars such as Rosey Eva Pool and Julius Bab translated some poems in the first half of the twentieth century, only after the Second World War did large-scale efforts become evident. Among them were Maria Marthi's 1956 translation of fifty poems and some letters* in *Der Engel in Grau* (The Angel in Gray) and Lola Gruenthal's translation of thirty-six items, published in 1959 in *Emily Dickinson: Gedichte* (Poems). The German poet Paul Celan contributed eight significant translations in 1961; the next two decades brought others by Gertrud Liepe and Walter Naumann among others, but critics have reacted most enthusiastically to a very recent translation of more than 100 poems by Werner von Koppenfels. No edition containing a German translation of the complete works of Dickinson yet exists.

German-language responses, as well as foreign-language responses in general, began with the previously-mentioned essay by von Ende. Comparing Dickinson to the German poet Annette von Droste-Hülshoff (1797–1848), von Ende established a tradition in which Dickinson was seen not as a specifically American phenomenon but in relation to such European artists as von Droste-Hülshoff, Rainer Maria Rilke, Heinrich Heine, the French symbolists, and the English metaphysical poets. In the sparse criticism from 1920 to 1959 (sparse despite Mathi's and Gruenthal's full-length studies), critics repeatedly praised Dickinson's unconventional poetics and extraordinary precision but sometimes called her technique "naive" or "imperfect." She was also frequently considered a pioneer of American poetry and a great influence on future generations. Since the 1960s, such influential Dickinson scholars as the Germans Kurt Oppens, Klaus Lubbers, Teut Andreas Riese, Hans Galinsky, and Katharina Ernst and the Austrian Gudrun Grabher have engaged in Dickinson criticism. The Swiss critic Roland Hagenbüchle, author of what are now considered classics of Dickinson criticism, has made perhaps the most significant contribution to Dickinson scholarship in German-speaking Europe. Writers of German-language responses generally tend to lean on philosophy* when analyzing the poet's work. Grabher's book, for example, deals with Dickinson's "I" in the context of German, American, and East Asian transcendentalisms.* An exception to this tendency is Ernst's book, which takes a thematic approach to *"Death" in the Poetry of Emily Dickinson* (1992). Discussing religion,* spirituality, and death* in Dickinson, Ernst addresses issues that have held the attention of German, Austrian, and Swiss Dickinson critics throughout the years. (*See*: French, Scandinavian, Slavic Responses)

RECOMMENDED: Gudrun Grabher, *Emily Dickinson: Das transzendentale Ich*; Roland Hagenbüchle, *Emily Dickinson: Wagnis der Selbstbegegnung*; Werner von Koppenfels. *Emily Dickinson: Dichtungen.* Mainz: Dieterische Verlagsbuchhandlung, 1955 (translation); Ann Lilliedahl, *Emily Dickinson in Europe: Her Literary Reputation in Selected Countries.*

Sylvia Henneberg

GILBERT, MARTHA (1829–1895)   was Susan Gilbert Dickinson's* older sister, although the two were often referred to as twins. Dickinson thought of both Gilberts as her "sisters," and Austin Dickinson* corresponded with Martha before courting Susan. Emily tried to urge Austin's attention toward Martha rather than Susan in the early 1850s, perhaps in an attempt to keep Susan all to herself, but by March 1853 it was already clear that Austin had made his choice. Martha ended the correspondence with Austin at that time, perhaps because she realized he was pursuing her sister, or perhaps she, being a pious believer, was scared off by his lack of faith.* She left Amherst* in 1853 and married John W. Smith. They moved to Geneva, New York, in 1857.

RECOMMENDED: *Life*; Martha Nell Smith, *Rowing in Eden: Rereading Emily Dickinson.*

Lena Koski

GILBERT, SUSAN   Dickinson, Susan

GILBERT, THOMAS DWIGHT (1815–1894) **and FRANCIS BACKUS** (1818–1885)   Susan Gilbert Dickinson's* older brothers were born in Greenfield, Massachusetts. During the 1830s they moved to Grand Haven, Michigan, where they engaged for two decades in merchandising and lumbering on Lake Michigan. After 1855 both became prominent businessmen and philanthropists of Grand Rapids. Frank was president of the Grand Rapids Gas Company at his death, while Dwight founded and was president of the City National Bank, then succeeded Frank as president of the Gas Company. A millionaire, Dwight was honored for integrity and public spirit by the erection of his bust in a city park.

Dwight's benevolent, fatherly role in the lives of his orphaned sisters included furnishing Sue with money and guidance as she grew up. Her regard for him is apparent from Gilbert correspondence within the Dickinson Family Papers at Harvard. The brothers' 1855 prenuptial gift of $5,000, together with Frank's underwriting of a fifty-volume library for her wedded home, undergirded Sue's enormous pride in her Michigan siblings. Emily Dickinson grew acquainted with both Gilberts during their visits to Amherst* over the years.

RECOMMENDED: *Years*; Polly Longsworth, *Austin and Mabel: The Amherst Affair and Love Letters of Austin Dickinson and Mabel Loomis Todd*; Obituaries in the *Grand Rapids Eagle* and the *Grand Rapids Telegram* of 25–26 May 1885 and 18–19 December 1894.

Polly Longsworth

GLADDEN, WASHINGTON (1836–1918)   Born in Pennsylvania, Gladden grew up on a New York farm. After graduating from Williams College, he was ordained to the Congregationalist* ministry in 1860. When he corresponded with Emily Dickinson, Gladden was pastor of a Springfield, Massachusetts, church.

A pioneer in the Social Gospel movement, Gladden moved to Columbus, Ohio, in 1882 and for the rest of his life used that pulpit to advocate liberal theology. Through sermons, lecture tours, and forty books, he brought religious teachings and influence to social problems. *Working People and Their Employers* (1876), *Applied Christianity* (1887), and *Social Salvation* (1902) prepared the nation to accept health and safety laws, child labor restriction, and labor unions. Gladden opposed both socialism and John D. Rockefeller's "tainted money" and was one of the first clergymen to endorse the labor union movement.

Gladden was one of several famous people with whom Dickinson corresponded, although there is no evidence that they ever met. On 27 May 1882 he replied to her letter* on the topic of immortality,* assuring her of that doctrine's truth.

RECOMMENDED: Jacob Henry Dorn, *Washington Gladden: Prophet of the Social Gospel*. Columbus: Ohio State University Press, 1967; Robert T. Handy, ed. *The Social Gospel in America, 1870–1920*. New York: Oxford University Press, 1966.

Peter C. Holloran

GOD   Present at the edges or at the center of a great number of Dickinson's poems, the subject of God the Father usually provoked a strong emotional response from her. Although her assessments and uses of the Christian faith* varied considerably throughout her poetry, Dickinson was remarkably consistent regarding her presentation of God. Most often, she portrayed him as distant, uncaring, even punishing and vindictive, as opposed to her softer, more accessible image of Jesus.* In one poem, for example, "God is a distant—stately Lover—" who, jealous that souls prefer his "Envoy," Jesus, "Vouches" in retaliation that he and the Son are "Synonyme" (P357). In another, God is a coldhearted murderer who sends the frost to assassinate an unwitting flower* "at it's play" (P1624). Over and over, Dickinson demythologizes God, calling him "Dunce" (P267), a heartless "Banker" who keeps her in spiritual poverty (P49) but who elsewhere gives her a precious "Crumb" (P791), a sudden intruder (P1462), an amputee without a powerful "Right Hand" (P1551). God seems to be a terrifying presence with power to give and take away, thus evoking in the speaker anger, desperation, and sometimes (as in P564) awe. In that poem, a curious but not fearful speaker attempts a personal visit to God only to find a faceless, silent "Infinitude" who, although he does not lash out at her, nevertheless silences her; the speaker "worshipped—did not 'pray'—." Overall, Dickinson seemed less able to trust God's power to save than the divine power of human love.*

On her religious* views, it is important to note that Dickinson was influenced by a number of religious cultures: the evangelicalism of Mary Lyons* and many preachers (Aaron Colton,* Edward S. Dwight,* Edwards Amasa Park, and others), the mild orthodoxy of Josiah Gilbert Holland,* the eucharistic Presbyterianism of Charles Wadsworth,* the conservative Unitarianism* (and, later, the Episcopal faith) of F. D. Huntington,* the more liberal Unitarianism* of T. W. Higginson* and Samuel Bowles,* and the Christian Spiritualism* of Higginson and Theodore Parker. (*See*: Congregationalism; Edwards; Prophecy)

RECOMMENDED: Beth Maclay Doriani, *Emily Dickinson, Daughter of Prophecy*; Rowena Revis Jones, "A Taste for 'Poison': Dickinson's Departure from Orthodoxy"; Benjamin Lease, *Emily Dickinson's Readings of Men and Books*.

Beth Maclay Doriani

GOTHICISM is a literary genre that depends on dread and fear of the unknown for its suspenseful effects. These effects are techniques Emily Dickinson utilized and transformed in a plethora of poems. The first gothic novels are generally agreed to be Horace Walpole's *Castle of Otranto* (1765) and Ann Radcliffe's *The Mysteries of Udolpho* (1794). *Udolpho*, with its protagonist trapped by a villain in a seemingly haunted castle, is the source of the female gothic, from which Charlotte Brontë's* *Jane Eyre*, in part, descends. *Jane Eyre* can serve as an exemplar of the female gothic, with its governess employed by a dark, strange master in a mysterious mansion. Dickinson may have read Radcliffe and certainly read Brontë. Other gothic-inflected authors she read include Emily Brontë,* Nathaniel Hawthorne,* Harriet Prescott Spofford,* and the graveyard poets.

Two of the most recognized staples of gothic fiction include the haunted house and doubling, aspects of setting and character, respectively. The spooky location is a staple that Dickinson borrowed from fiction to use for her own macabre effects in poetry. Her condition for art, in fact, involved such a frightening location: "Nature is a Haunted House—but Art—a House that tries to be haunted" (L459A). Setting is paramount in the gothic genre of literature because the gothic often contains a secret, hence, the need for enclosure. Enclosures— an obsession with windows, doors, drawers, sliding panels, trapdoors, and so on—prevail, so that the secret stays in the dark for most of the story. The secret may have to do with a family's lineage, which is often tainted because of incest, "illegitimacy," or the shadowy conditions of inheritance. Dickinson's sense of enclosure and withheld secrets informs many poems.

Dickinson likewise used a second main feature of the gothic novel, the doubling or Doppelgänger, the most famous being Dr. Jekyll and Mr. Hyde, where two characters exist as halves of one personality. In *Jane Eyre*, a somewhat more subtle doubling can be seen with the composed Jane and the insane Bertha Mason. Dickinson broached a kind of Doppelgänger in such poems as "I felt a Cleaving in my Mind—" (P937), where the self* splits into two such disparate selves that the speaker can't recombine them. Dickinson made liberal use of doubling in "One need not be a Chamber—to be Haunted—" (P670), where she detailed a scenario of pursuer and pursued only to designate them as "Ourself behind ourself, concealed—." P670 thus serves as an excellent example of both frightening setting and split self.

The gothic allowed authors living in the nineteenth century an opportunity to explore some states of mind not so well articulated or concepts not so available to authors before the ideas of Sigmund Freud and some twentieth-century psychologists. The "uncanny" gothic, as Freud was to see it, found most fearful and dreadful what was closest to home and had been repressed. Hence, authors like Dickinson, working with elements from gothicism, could sometimes target psychological* states more effectively with the help of techniques from that genre. (*See*: Consciousness; Death; Grave; Madness)

RECOMMENDED: Jane Donahue Eberwein, *Dickinson: Strategies of Limitation*; Sigmund Freud, "The Uncanny." *The Standard Edition of the Complete Psychological Writings of Sigmund Freud*. 17. Trans. James Strachey. London: Hogarth Press, 1953: 217–56; Sandra Gilbert, and Susan Gubar, *The Madwoman in the Attic: The Woman Writer and the Nineteenth-Century Literary Imagination*; Joan Kirkby, *Emily Dickinson*; Daneen Wardrop, *Emily Dickinson's Gothic: Goblin with a Gauge*.

Daneen Wardrop

GOULD, GEORGE HENRY (1827–1899)   was Austin Dickinson's* classmate at Amherst College.* After Emily Dickinson's death, Lavinia Dickinson* spread the unfounded rumor that Gould was the man Emily Dickinson had been in love with and addressed in her love* poems. None of the correspondence between Dickinson and Gould has survived, except for a valentine* Dickinson sent him, which was published in the Amherst College *Indicator* in February 1850 (L34). (*See*: Lovers)

RECOMMENDED: *Life*; Rebecca Patterson, *The Riddle of Emily Dickinson*.

Lena Koski

THE GRAVE   Clearly a major preoccupation of Dickinson's, the graves in her poems represent a strange conflation of life and death.* Often, Dickinson's graves are busy places where people get to know each other, make tea, and justify their lives. They are also mysterious houses in which the afterlife conducts its secret business. Dickinson's equation of "grave" and "house" is sometimes reversible; if to her the grave is a house, the confining elements of houses and other enclosed living spaces are like graves.

Dickinson wrote dozens of poems mentioning graves and more than a few with a tomb as central image. Her home library included several copies of a popular book on tombstone inscriptions; these may have fed her imagination, as did the many funerals she attended and the cemetery visits that were commonplace.

An early poem (P216) pictures grave inhabitants as "Safe" in "Alabaster Chambers,"* unaware of changes in time. The disturbing initial imagery is followed in the first version by images of sentient nature* going on without these sleepers, in the second by a terrifying suggestion of eternity: "Diadems—drop—and Doges—surrender / Soundless as dots—on a Disc of Snow."

Many of her grave poems employ the voice* of a deceased speaker; this "dead" voice provides no revelations about death but only about life's ironies. The dead child* in " 'Twas just this time, last year, I died" (P445) wonders how the holidays will be spent without him and concludes that the living will "some perfect year" join him in death.

A late, undated poem, "The grave my little cottage is" (P1743), sees a grave visit as a continued communication between two lovers, one above and one underneath the ground. If this poem was written after the death of her close friend Otis Lord,* the cozy tea it suggests may be a continuation of their satisfying relationship. Other poems speculate about the sentience of the corpse in the grave in ways recalling Baudelaire's poetry but with gentler irony and less physical imagery. In Dickinson's poems the grave is usually the point at which the physical challenges the metaphysical, and her response to this challenge depends on the state of her philosophy* and emotions at the time. Her last poems are more likely to imply faith.* She wrote her aunt in 1884, "I thought the Churchyard Tarrytown, when I was a Child, but now I trust 'tis Trans" (L892). (*See*: Domesticity; Gothic)

RECOMMENDED: Jerome Loving, *Emily Dickinson: The Poet on the Second Story*; Cynthia Griffin Wolff, *Emily Dickinson*.

Janet McCann

GRAVES, JOHN LONG (1831–1915)   was Dickinson's cousin, one year her senior, born in Sunderland, Massachusetts, and related through the Gunn family. He completed his undergraduate degree at Amherst College* in 1855, after which he taught at Orford Academy in Orford, New Hampshire. He married Frances Britton on 1 September 1858. Although ordained in the Congregational* Church several years later in 1860, he eventually turned to business-related activities in Boston.* While still an undergraduate, Graves, along with his friend and schoolmate Henry Vaughan Emmons,* was a frequent and anticipated visitor to the Dickinson home. In fact, Emily and Susan Gilbert* were left in Graves' care when the rest of the Dickinson family went to Washington, D.C.,* in April 1854. Graves was one of few people to offer comments concerning

Dickinson's piano talents, a creative interest that was a precursor to her poetry. He also presented her with an aeolian harp as a gift; she sent him wristlets in an appreciative gesture. (*See*: Coleman, Eliza; Music)
RECOMMENDED: *Letters*.

Monica Chiu

GREENOUGH, JAMES C. and JEANIE BATES   The Dickinson sisters met Jeanie Bates in Washington, D.C.,* in 1855, when all three stayed at Willard's Hotel while visiting their congressman fathers. Many years later, this lady recalled young Emily at that time as "a girl with large, warm heart, earnest nature & delicate tastes" (*Life* 446). After Jeanie returned home to Westfield, Massachusetts, and Emily and Lavinia* to Amherst,* there is no evidence of their corresponding until Jeanie and her husband moved to Amherst in 1883. An educator, James Greenough had administered the state Normal School at Westfield before being appointed president of the Massachusetts Agricultural College* (1883–1886). Three of Dickinson's four notes to Mrs. Greenough (L850, 887, 973) apparently accompanied small gifts reflecting welcome or remembrance; the last (L1022) extended sympathy on her mother's death* in October 1885, an event that linked these friends in autumnal bereavement.
RECOMMENDED: *Letters*; *Life*; *Years*.

Jane Donahue Eberwein

H

HALE, EDWARD EVERETT (1822–1909)   An influential American clergyman, social reformer, and writer, Hale became a Unitarian* minister in 1842 and went on to earn a national reputation as an early advocate of the Social Gospel movement to reform society through liberal Christian principles. He was chaplain of the United States Senate from 1903 until his death. Among Hale's major works are the *Ingham Papers* (1869); *In His Name* (1873); *James Russell Lowell and His Friends* (1899); and *Franklin in France* (2 vols., 1888), along with two autobiographies: *A New England Boyhood* (1893) and *Memories of a Hundred Years* (2 vols., 1902). In 1863 the *Atlantic Monthly** published his most memorable story, "The Man without a Country."

Hale's contact with Emily Dickinson occurred in 1853, when Benjamin Franklin Newton* died. Newton had been a law student in Edward Dickinson's* office from 1847 to 1849, and Emily Dickinson wrote to Hale as his pastor to inquire about her friend's death. She wrote again to Hale in 1856. This exemplifies the poet's tendency to seek reassurance from prominent spiritual counselors on death* and immortality.* (*See*: Clark; Gladden)

RECOMMENDED: *Life*; Edward Everett Hale, Jr. *The Life and Letters of Edward Everett Hale*. Boston: Little, Brown, 1917; Jean Holloway. *Edward Everett Hale, a Biography*. Austin: University of Texas Press, 1956.

Peter C. Holloran

HALL, EUGENIA (b. 1864)   was the daughter of George and Mary E. Montague Hall of Athens, Georgia. In 1868 Hall moved to Amherst* to live with her grandfather, George Montague,* who was a first cousin of Dickinson's grandfather. At the time of Hall's marriage to Franklin L. Hunt in October 1885, Dickinson sent her a short and somewhat curious note: "Will the sweet Cousin

who is about to make the Etruscan Experiment, accept a smile which will last a Life, if ripened in the Sun?'' (L1021).
RECOMMENDED: *Letters.*

Marisa Anne Pagnattaro

THE *HAMPSHIRE AND FRANKLIN EXPRESS* (later, *Hampshire Express*, 1865–1868; the *Amherst Record*, 1868–1953), first published in September 1844, was the weekly Amherst* newspaper read by the Dickinson family; references to Edward* and Austin* dotted its pages, and ''Miss Emily E. Dickinson'' was listed 27 August 1857 as one of the ''candid and impartial judges'' of rye and Indian bread for the 1857 Hampshire Agricultural Fair. Dickinson mentioned the *Express* in letters* and once pasted a poem cut from its pages in the back of her Bible.*

The *Express* aimed ''to improve the general welfare and prosperity, and the moral and intellectual improvement of the community'' under the successive editorships of Samuel Nash (1844–1848), Homer A. Cook (1848–1849), J. R. Trumbull (1849–1856), Homer Bliss (1856), John H. Brewster (1856–1857), Pliny H. White (1857–1858), John H. Brewster (1858–1859), J. H. M. Leland (1859), Henry A. Marsh (1859–1867), J. L. Skinner (1867–1868), C. C. Storrs and H. M. McCloud (1868–1871), McCloud (1871–1877), McCloud and John E. Williams (1877–1879), and John E. Williams (1879–1890). Alongside regular columns on ''Washington Correspondence,'' ''New England News,'' and ''The Legislature'' were columns devoted to agriculture, inspiration, wit and humor, local news, advertising, fiction, and local poetry. ''Amherst Matters'' regularly reported on Amherst Academy,* Mt. Holyoke Female Seminary,* Amherst College,* and the Massachusetts Agricultural College,* as well as ''Personal Gossip'' ranging from charges of adultery, theft, and drunkenness to notes on the many small miracles of daily life in a country town—orioles returning or the flowering of Mary Hitchcock's night blooming cereus. There were produce and gardening tips (later called ''Science''* and ''Religious Intelligence''); exotica (''Sir Walter Scott's First Love,'' ''Marie Antoinette's Last Days,'' ''Russian Drowsky Drivers,'' ''Fishing in China,'' ''Divorces in Roumania,'' ''Women Who Don't Wash,'' ''Does the Dog Reason?'' ''Do Insects Talk?'' ''The Religious Card Player,'' ''A Learned Canary''); practical advice (''The Use and Abuse of the Bath,'' ''Kissing the Dead''); and a constant commitment to wit and humor in columns such as ''Scrapbasket,'' ''Paragrams,'' ''Wit and Wisdom,'' ''Scissorings,'' ''All Sorts,'' and ''Sunbeams'' (recalling Dickinson's humor* column in the school paper *Forest Leaves* at Amherst Academy). The *Express* regularly reported lectures by distinguished people (including Henry Ward Beecher, Frederick Douglass, R. W. Emerson,* Mark Twain, Edward Hitchcock,* Bronson Alcott) and printed high-minded articles on the mind, the value of study, ''Gleanings from Great Thinkers,'' inspirational topics (''This Life a Pilgrimage,'' ''Immortality of Goodness''), and religious revivals.* For several years the tragedies of the Civil War* dominated the paper, succeeded by acerbic columns on woman suffrage, female lobbyists, and temperance issues. The *Express* assumed the centrality of Amherst as "foremost in educational matters and for beauty in natural scenery" and delighted in the town's quaint and curious ways: "We are fond of queer old things and ways, and therefore we would not have the Amherst College Bell ring in a simple prosaic manner; we like its ancient and fantastic tune. But it is queer" (20 September 1877). (*See*: Bibliography for Books and Reading)

Joan Kirkby

HAMPSON, ALFRED LEETE (1890–1952)   From 1923, Hampson joined Martha Dickinson Bianchi* in preparing Emily Dickinson collections for the press. He shared Madame Bianchi's love of church music and European travel and brought typing, filing, and other organizational skills to the Dickinson legacy during summers at the Evergreens.* He answered much of Bianchi's correspondence and helped inventory the poems. The first Dickinson text Hampson assisted in producing was *Life and Letters* (1924).* For *The Complete Poems* (1924)* he created the new headings. He typed the manuscript for *Further Poems* (1929)* and did some research and typing for the centenary *Poems* (1930).* He also edited *Poems for Youth* (1934) and did most of the work on *Unpublished Poems* (1935).* Madame Bianchi made Hampson her literary executor following Mabel Todd's* public announcement in 1929 that she held hundreds of unpublished poems. On Bianchi's death in 1943, Hampson inherited her copyrights and all of the Emily Dickinson papers and mementos then kept in the Evergreens. From 1944 onward, librarian William McCarthy assisted Hampson in completing an inventory of the materials and arranging their sale to Bianchi's cousin, the Wall Street lawyer Gilbert Montague, who bought them for $40,000 and gave them to Harvard. The Dickinson copyrights, along with the right to refuse permission to reprint, became the property of Mary Landis,* Bianchi's friend, who married Hampson in 1947. The most extensive published source dealing directly with Hampson is Maravene Loeschke's carefully researched *The Path Between: An Historical Novel of the Dickinson Family of Amherst* (Columbia, MD: C. H. Fairfax, 1988).

RECOMMENDED: "Alfred L. Hampson." Obituary. *New York Times* 13 May 1952: 23–24; Emily Dickinson Publication Papers, Houghton Library, Harvard University; Elizabeth Horan, "Mabel Loomis Todd, Martha Dickinson Bianchi, and the Spoils of the Dickinson Legacy" and "To Market: The Dickinson Copyright Wars."

Elizabeth Horan

HAMPSON, MARY LANDIS (1894–1988)   was the last major figure to preside over the Evergreens* and the Dickinson family legacy. Her chance meeting with Martha Dickinson Bianchi* at the National Arts Club in New York City in the early 1930s became a memorable landmark in her life.

Daughter of Mary Rosenbaum Landis and Charles K. Landis, Jr., Mary had lived in Vineland, New Jersey, and summered at Sea Isle City. In 1918 she graduated from Smith College, majoring in zoology, and during the following two years studied at the College of Physicians and Surgeons of Columbia University. Subsequently, she turned to ophthalmology and assisted two prominent ophthalmologists in teaching Columbia University medical students.

In 1947 Mary Landis married Alfred Leete Hampson,* Martha Bianchi's literary collaborator, who had inherited the Evergreens and the family's collection of Emily Dickinson papers in 1943. Aware of Madame Bianchi's concern for the ultimate disposition of her aunt's manuscripts, Mary Hampson and her husband undertook an extensive review of the holdings, categorizing and annotating them. The poet's papers, books, and personal possessions were sold by Alfred Hampson to Gilbert H. Montague, who donated them in the early 1950s to Harvard's Houghton Library.

The Hampsons continued living at the Evergreens, maintaining the house and its furnishings as if they were preserved in amber. After Alfred died in Paris in 1952, Mary returned to a residence that, by the terms of Bianchi's will, was threatened with demolition on her death. In her own will, she bequeathed Bianchi's papers to Brown University and set up the Martha Dickinson Bianchi Trust for preservation of the Evergreens as a cultural and study center. Following Mary Hampson's death, the Hampshire Probate Court on 29 January 1990 decreed that her will should prevail. Thus, the house should not be razed.

RECOMMENDED: *Alumnae Biographical Register*, 1871–1935. Smith College Archives; Will of Mary Landis Hampson, 14 November 1980. Hampshire County Registry of Probate. Northampton, MA.

Mary Elizabeth Kromer Bernhard

HANDWRITING   The handwritten manuscript is a mirror of ink or pencil; in Dickinson's holographs two broad scriptural styles, two "hands," one for rough copy drafts, another for fair copy drafts, reflect two different moments in the compositional process. The small, often slurred hand Dickinson used when first jotting down rough drafts of poems and messages remained constant throughout her life: the "scribble writing" of the late 1850s persisted into the 1880s. The hand she used in her fair copies, however, changed dramatically over the course of her lifetime. The traditional division of Dickinson's fair copy handwriting into three periods, though ultimately arbitrary, has assisted scholars in hypothesizing a working chronology for her largely undated writings; this periodization schema has, in turn, led to a clearer delineation of the boundaries of her style periods. In the manuscripts of the 1850s, Dickinson's handwriting is small and flowing, upper- and lowercase letters are readily distinguishable, and most letters within words are linked. The legibility of the early script suggests that Dickinson was modeling her hand after the exemplary hands of penmanship copybooks or, perhaps, imitating the exactness of print. In the 1860s, a period of profound poetic experimentation, Dickinson's calligraphy ceased to be simply recursive: the fixed alphabetic forms characteristic of the 1850s were abandoned, the alignment of words on the page grew irregular, and the extreme slant of the pen strokes gives the impression of a writer working under intense pressure. Finally, in the 1870s, the handwriting of the fair copy draft evolved again. Dickinson's writing reached its maximum size in the mid-1870s, and the unlinking of letters, begun in the 1860s, was nearly complete, giving the manuscripts a new feeling of spaciousness. In these years, poetry and prose manuscripts became virtually indistinguishable. At the end of the decade, Dickinson abandoned her pen for a pencil; the loose, broken handwriting of the 1880s revealed increasing physical weakness. Several narratives—biographical* and artistic—emerge and intersect to account for these scriptural evolutions. Early scholars suggested that abrupt adaptations in Dickinson's handwriting may have corresponded to changes in her vision or paralleled shifts in psychic equilibrium. More recently, scholars have analyzed Dickinson's resistance to the economy of mechanical reproduction and focused on the relationship between her messages and her medium, calling, finally, for a *poetics* of handwriting. (*See*: Editorial Scholarship; Johnson; Ward)

RECOMMENDED: Susan Howe, *The Birth-mark*; Thomas H. Johnson, "Establishing a Text: The Emily Dickinson Papers"; Martha Nell Smith, *Rowing in Eden: Rereading Emily Dickinson*; Theodora Ward, "Characteristics of the Handwriting" in *Poems*.

Marta Werner

HARPER'S NEW MONTHLY MAGAZINE came to the Dickinson household from January 1851. Though Lavinia* called it "my usual magazine," Jack Capps has shown Dickinson's direct use of material from *Harper's*. Published in New York by G. W. Curtis (1853–1892), *Harper's* included engravings, essays, literary notices, and poetry, drawing on material previously published in British periodicals (*London Times, Chamber's Edinburgh Journal, Punch*). There were a few contributions from writers like Thackeray, Dickens,* Kingsley, and De Quincey. *Harper's* printed articles of tangential literary interest ("Peculiar Habits of Authors," "Epigrams and Epigrammatists," "Samples of Fine English," "Letters and Letter-Writing," "Lack of Poetry in America," "Have Great Poets Become Impossible") as well as more exotic articles. Pieces of general human interest included "Climate and Character," "Disagreeable People," "Does the Dew Fall," "Dreams," "Force of Fear," "Hours with the Dead," "Pleasures of Illness," "A Day in a Lunatic Asylum," "Memory and Its Caprices," "Morbid Impulses," "Use of the Passions," "Somnambulism," "Vampires," "Ventriloquism," "What Women Talk About," "Whims of Great Men," and "Wits of the Pulpit." Manners and mores of foreign lands were featured in "Life in Abyssinia," "Australian Life," "Buccaneers of the Spanish Main," "Caravan Journeys in Asia," "Funeral Rites in Ceylon," "Feet-Washing in Munich," "Ghosts and Sorceresses of India," "Public Executions in England," "Religion, Love and Marriage in Italy," "Royal Amusements in Java," "The Transylvanians," "The Turk at Home," "Water-

Cure Life in Europe,'' and "Wolf Nurses in India.'' (*See*: Bibliography for Books and Reading)

RECOMMENDED: Mark Bauerlein, "The Meaning of Emily Dickinson's Social Withdrawal.''

Joan Kirkby

HAVEN, JOSEPH and MARY and their children were residents of Amherst* from 1850 to 1858 while the Reverend Haven (1816–1874) taught moral philosophy and metaphysics at Amherst College.* Many parties and gatherings were held at the Haven home, some of which Dickinson attended. The Havens also frequently called at the Dickinson household. Rev. Professor Haven performed the July 1856 marriage ceremony of Austin* and Susan Dickinson.* Emily Dickinson corresponded frequently and intimately with Mary Haven when the family relocated after Professor Haven accepted a position in Chicago in 1858.

RECOMMENDED: *Life*; *Years*.

Kathryn Balteff

HAWTHORNE, NATHANIEL (1804–1864) Like Dickinson, Hawthorne drew on the vocabulary of Calvinism and Congregationalism* for his meditations on sin and redemption, doubt and faith,* and the confrontation with an inscrutable, immaterial reality. Scholars have long identified Hawthorne as an influence on Dickinson and continue to trace their profound intellectual and linguistic* connections. Dickinson probably never read *The Scarlet Letter*, but scholars confirm that she knew *Mosses from an Old Manse* and *The House of the Seven Gables*, and her references in letters attest to her recognition of Hawthorne's literary significance. They also suggest that she associated Hawthorne's fiction with absence and loss. In one of many letters to Austin* during his residence in Boston, Dickinson wrote that, in her loneliness, she was reminded of *The House of the Seven Gables'* elderly spinster Hepzibah, who longingly waited for her brother, Clifford, to return. Dickinson quickly added that she did not "mean that you are *him*, or that Hepzibah's *me* except in a relative sense, only I was reminded'' (L62). In June 1864, writing to Higginson* from Cambridge,* she marked Hawthorne's passing in a letter concerned with illness and injury, both Higginson's and her own. Dickinson wrote to Elizabeth Holland* that her mother, in her decline, "reminds one of Hawthorne's blameless Ship— that forgot the Port'' (L542). Hawthorne himself never wrote of such a ship; rather, Cotton Mather had included this legend in *Magnalia Christi Americana*. Dickinson may have seen Longfellow's* mention of the "Phantom Ship'' in his 1837 review of Hawthorne's *Twice-Told Tales* in the *North American Review*. After Higginson sent Dickinson a copy of his *Short Studies of American Authors*, she commented ambiguously that Hawthorne "appalls, entices'' (L622). Her interest in Hawthorne seems never to have dimmed: in 1882, Dickinson wrote to Thomas Niles,* an editor for Roberts Brothers,* to ask about the status of James Russell Lowell's planned work on Hawthorne. (*See*: Gothicism; Romanticism)

RECOMMENDED: *Letters*; *Life*; Jack L. Capps, *Emily Dickinson's Reading*; Karl Keller, *The Only Kangaroo among the Beauty: Emily Dickinson and America*; Jerome Loving, *Emily Dickinson: The Poet on the Second Story*.

Catherine Carr Lee

HEALTH AND MEDICAL HISTORY   Recent speculation by teams of biographers* and physicians provides divergent diagnoses of Dickinson's two major physical crises and leaves open questions about how emotional pressures may have influenced the poet's physiological symptoms. On several occasions, she referred to variations of "nervous prostration," which in today's climate might be termed a form of depression. Yet the only elements of Emily Dickinson's medical history documented with any certainty are her visits to Boston ophthalmologist Henry Willard Williams during the summers of 1864 and 1865 and the kidney failure that apparently caused her death in 1886.

Richard Sewall and Martin Wand suggest that Dickinson's consultations with Dr. Williams may have been due to exotropia, a misalignment of the eyes; whereas Polly Longsworth and Norbert Hirschhorn propose an inflammatory condition known as iritis/uveitis as a more likely diagnosis. In any case, Williams' treatment for Dickinson included bandages over the eyes to restrict exposure to light. Several Dickinson letters from 1863 indicate that her symptoms had become acute, and James Guthrie speculates that she may have been experiencing serious difficulty with vision* as early as summer 1862. Longsworth and Hirschhorn also question her attending doctor's diagnosis of Bright's disease* as the cause of her death and the sickness of two and a half years that preceded it; their research spotlights severe primary hypertension as the condition that probably proved fatal.

RECOMMENDED: James Guthrie, " 'Before I got my eye put out': Dickinson's Illness and Its Effects on Her Poetry"; Norbert Hirschhorn and Polly Longsworth, " 'Medicine Posthumous': A New Look at Emily Dickinson's Medical Conditions"; Martin Wand and Richard B. Sewall, " 'Eyes be Blind, Heart be Still': A New Perspective on Emily Dickinson's Eye Problem."

Charles M. Erickson and Marianne Erickson

HEAVEN   Since heaven is virtually synonymous with Dickinson's "Flood subject" of immortality* (L319), the terms "heaven," "paradise," "eternity," and "Eden" pervade Dickinson's poetry and letters.* Her approach to the subject of heaven incorporates aspects of both Christian and Romantic* thought, and her poems about heaven range in tone from cynicism to awe as she wavers between skepticism and faith.*

Rejecting Calvinist orthodoxy, Dickinson scorned the conception of heaven as an afterlife reward for the denial of earthly life: "Who has not found the Heaven—below—/ Will fail of it above—" (P1544). Like William Blake,* she believed that heaven is as "vast—as our Capacity" to conceive it, and "As fair—as our idea" (P370). Thus "Paradise is of the option" (P1069). But like Blake, she also understood that all humans are born both "infinite to Venture" and "Finite—to fail" (P847). Heaven has become an "interdicted Land" (P239), for fallen human perception is relative, unable to apprehend any heaven without its prior loss: "The Heaven hath a Hell—/ Itself to signalize—" (P459). Eden is "that old-fashioned House" we live in without ever "suspecting" what it is "Until we drive away" (P1657). Dickinson rebelled against the built-in losses of such an existence: "What Comfort was it Wisdom—was—/ The spoiler of Our Home?" (P965).

Some of Dickinson's poems about heaven are based on her concept of "Compound Vision," a spiritual state in which fallen perception is overcome by "Light—enabling Light" so that "The Finite" becomes "furnished / With the Infinite" (P906). In this spiritual state one may glimpse heaven; and although Dickinson remained at times profoundly skeptical, her poems and letters include many affirmations of a visionary* faith in heaven as an eternal "Zone whose even Years / No Solstice interrupt—" (P1056). The description of heaven in P1056 accords with that given in the Bible*; for a seasonless "Zone," whose "Sun constructs perpetual Noon," is a Zone where "there shall be no night" (*Rev.* 21.23–25, 22.5) and where in the pure and uninterrupted illumination of absolute Truth (P836), all earth's mysteries are solved. (*See*: God; Religion)

RECOMMENDED: Charles R. Anderson, *Emily Dickinson's Poetry: Stairway of Surprise*; Jane Donahue Eberwein, *Dickinson: Strategies of Limitation*; Robert Weisbuch, *Emily Dickinson's Poetry*.

Rosa Nuckels

HERBERT, GEORGE (1593–1633)   English poet and country parson whose best-known work is *The Temple*, a collection of poems published after his death. Like Dickinson's work, much of Herbert's poetry deals with a variety of meditative spiritual themes, from "Faith"* to "Affliction." By Dickinson's time, many of Herbert's poems had been converted into church hymns,* and his work enjoyed renewed popularity. She could have been exposed to Herbert through a number of sources. The Dickinson family library contained copies of several large anthologies, including Griswold's *Sacred Poets of England and America* and Chamber's *Cyclopedia of English Literature*, both of which contained Herbert's work. Additionally, Sue Dickinson* owned an 1857 edition of *The Poetical Works of George Herbert*, and pencil markings in the "Church Porch" section are probably attributable to Emily. Two marked lines in particular are notable, since they appear to highlight the theme of self*-examination found in Dickinson's own writing: "Dare to look in thy chest; for 'tis thine own; / And tumble up and down what thou find'st there."

Herbert's poem "Matins" also was reprinted in the 28 October 1876 *Springfield Republican.** Emily must have read this version, as Sue Dickinson later discovered a handwritten copy of its middle stanzas among her sister-in-law's papers. Sue assumed it was Emily's own work since she had altered Herbert's punctuation to match her own characteristic style. Subsequently, these stanzas were published as Dickinson's in the first edition of *Bolts of Melody*,* and the error was not corrected until the second edition.

Millicent Todd Bingham's* oversight in attributing Herbert's work to Dickinson demonstrates the stylistic similarities between the two poets. Dickinson's wit, her reliance on colloquial* language and unusual imagery, and her experimentation with stanza and rhyme* have prompted critics to draw comparisons between her work and the seventeenth-century metaphysical poets in general. While it is difficult to determine the extent to which Dickinson was inspired by Herbert, their similarities of style and theme suggest that she was influenced by him and possibly found in him a kindred spirit. (*See*: Books and Reading; Linguistic and Stylistic Approaches)

RECOMMENDED: *Life*; Jack Capps, *Emily Dickinson's Reading*; George Herbert. *The Complete English Poems*. Ed. John Tobin. London: Penguin, 1992; Benjamin Lease, *Emily Dickinson's Readings of Men and Books*; Dorothy Huff Oberhaus, ''A Reading of Emily Dickinson.''

Kimberly Markowski

HIGGINSON, THOMAS WENTWORTH (1823–1911)   was a central figure in Dickinson's life and career. He was widely known as a Unitarian* minister, an ardent abolitionist, an advocate of spiritualism* and woman's* rights, and a colonel of the first regiment of black soldiers during the Civil War.* Higginson was also a highly regarded poet and essayist, a prolific contributor to the *Atlantic Monthly*.* His nature* essays and a pivotal piece entitled ''Letter to a Young Contributor'' (affirming the need for spiritual independence in time of war) had an electrifying effect on Dickinson. On 15 April 1862, for one of the few times in her life, she wrote an unsolicited letter to a stranger—enclosing four poems. One of the poems she sent to Higginson, ''Safe in their Alabaster Chambers—'' (P216),* reinforces his earlier portrayal of orthodox Christian belief as ''a gloomy sleep of ages and an incredible resurrection to end it.'' Dickinson had found a kindred spirit. He was not, however, totally so. What she did not know was that Higginson was at war with himself.

In late 1861, Higginson had spent hours in the fields surrounding Worcester watching insects* and birds* and recorded in his field book, ''I burn with insatiable desire to penetrate their consciousness.'' He proclaimed in his diary that his longing to take part in the war must give way to his personal responsibilities to his invalid wife, that this war was not for him. He delivered lectures to the Worcester Natural History Society and wrote a series of nature studies for *The Atlantic*. In his ''Letter to a Young Contributor'' (written in January and published in April 1862), he meditated on ''the trivialities of war'' and on his belief that ''war or peace, fame or forgetfulness can bring no real injury to one who has formed the fixed purpose to live nobly day by day.''

But this view of war suddenly changed. Union forces were being routed at

Shenandoah Valley and were in retreat all across the Potomac. In early August, Higginson made new living arrangements for his wife and obtained official authority to serve as captain of a company of men. In his urgent call for recruits (printed in the *Worcester Spy*), Higginson posed a challenge to the young men of his town: "What will you say to your children's children when they say to you, 'a great contest was waged between Law and Disorder, Freedom and Slavery, *and you were not there?*'" Soon after, he was offered and accepted a colonelcy of the First South Carolina Volunteers, a new regiment of freed slaves.

Higginson had responded promptly to each of Dickinson's letters.* When there was long silence, she conveyed her concern: "Did I displease you, Mr Higginson? But wont you tell me how?" (L274). An explanation was provided by notices about Higginson's military activities in the *Springfield Republican*.* She responded to what she read there with an extraordinary letter (L280). In it, she informed her friend that "War feels to me an oblique place—" and conveyed her deep concern for his survival. She extended to him an invitation rarely offered to anyone ("Should there be other Summers, would you perhaps come?"). She did not customarily pray but now included him "when service is had in Church, for Our Arms." His recent *Atlantic* essay moved her to the thought "that the 'Supernatural,' was only the Natural, disclosed—." This idea is elaborated in a two-line poem incorporated into the text: "Not 'Revelation'— 'tis—that waits, / But our unfurnished eyes—" (P685) and in an enclosed longer poem, "The Soul unto itself" (P683). A postscript sums up the intimations of immortality* and mortality in Higginson's essay and in the war he was now confronting: "I trust the 'Procession of Flowers' was not a premonition—."

Julia Ward Howe's "Battle Hymn of the Republic," sung to the tune of "John Brown's Body," became a rallying cry for Union soldiers and a stirring evocation of what seemed to many a holy war. Martial imagery was pervasive in the Bible* and church hymns* Dickinson grew up with; it is present in her numerous commemorative poems, such as "Bless God, he went as soldiers" (P147). With the coming of the war, the imagery darkens. "It feels a shame to be Alive—" (P444), written after the son of the president of Amherst College* was killed in action at Newbern, pays tribute to the heroic dead and evokes startling and grotesque images (corpses stacked up like dollars, an enormous pearl of life dissolved in a horrid bowl). When Higginson was seriously injured on the battlefield, Dickinson sent a message conveying her concern and incorporating the closing lines of a poem that deals disturbingly with the precariousness of everyday existence: "That after Horror—that 'twas *us*—" (L282; P286).

Their correspondence continued to the end of her life. Higginson preserved all of the seventy-one letters Dickinson sent him, along with 102 enclosed poems. He left vivid accounts of his two visits to the Homestead* and kept a record of her many pungent remarks (L342a and L343b). Her last letter to him, written a few days before she died, is a ten-word inquiry about *his* health.

Higginson was both moved and disturbed by the unconventional power of her poems and utterances. One of the striking sayings that he had reported to his wife after a visit ("If I feel physically as if the top of my head were taken off, I know *that* is poetry*. . . . Is there any other way?") made a lasting impression. Two decades later, Higginson compared Dickinson to William Blake* in words that echo hers: "When a thought takes one's breath away, who cares to count the syllables." His breath was taken away because Higginson himself was both a fastidious counter of syllables and a passionate admirer of Thoreau.* From the outset, Dickinson made it clear to her "Preceptor" that she could and would never correct her "spasmodic" gait and unconventionalities. They understood each other, were different from each other, were very much in need of each other.

Higginson published widely and encouraged other writers to do likewise. But he also recognized the ways in which publication* and publicity curb creativity. In his "Letter to a Young Contributor," Higginson quoted Goethe's observation that "if a person once does a good thing, society forms a league to prevent his doing another." He understood that a rare temperament like Dickinson's required privacy. He also understood her method of "publishing" hundreds of poems by enclosing them in hundreds of letters to friends and relatives—poems that could never have been written for impersonal public display. (Dickinson turned to Higginson to shield her from the requests of those asking to print her poems.)

After her death, Higginson coedited Dickinson's *Poems* (1890),* predictably smoothing away colloquialisms* and metrical unconventionalities to make them more accessible to the readers of his day. He was not surprised by the excitement and curiosity Dickinson's book aroused. "One result of this glare of publicity," Higginson wrote in 1891, "has been the constant and earnest demand by her readers for further information in regard to her."

Very early in their correspondence, Dickinson had told Higginson that "If fame* belonged to me, I could not escape her—" (L265). In his *Short Studies of American Authors* (1880), Higginson paid tribute to Thoreau's unpublished diary ("there is nothing finer in literary history") and summed up Thoreau's stature in words that seem to echo that trenchant comment: "There is no fame more permanent than that which begins its real growth after the death of an author, and such is the fame of Thoreau." Such would be the fame of Dickinson. (*See*: "An Open Portfolio"; *Out-Door Papers*)

RECOMMENDED: Karen A. Dandurand, "Why Dickinson Did Not Publish"; Tilden G. Edelstein. *Strange Enthusiasm: A Life of Thomas Wentworth Higginson*. New Haven: Yale University Press, 1968; Benjamin Lease, *Emily Dickinson's Readings of Men and Books*; Barton Levi St. Armand, *Emily Dickinson and Her Culture: The Soul's Society*; Anna Mary Wells. *Dear Preceptor: The Life and Times of Thomas Wentworth Higginson*. Boston: Houghton Mifflin, 1963.

Benjamin Lease

HILLS, HENRY (1833–1896) **and MARY**   Henry Francis Hills entered his father Leonard's successful straw hat business (L. M. Hills and Sons) in 1852.

He and his wife (Mary Adelaide Spencer) had a residence in New York and spent summers in Amherst.* Their large Victorian house still stands next door to the Homestead.* Thus the Hillses and the Dickinsons exchanged visits, notes (seasonal greetings or sympathy), and gifts (flowers* and cakes). Henry once wrote to his wife, "I think that Emily & the other Dickinsons are *true* friends" (*Years* 2:293). Austin's friendship was especially evident when he took over the Hills company to save it from ruin. Their children were Samuel (who died young), Mary, Caroline, and Leonard Dwight, the latter of whom became Lavinia Dickinson's* legal and financial adviser.

RECOMMENDED: *Letters*; *Years*.

Masako Takeda

HISTORICISM is a critical approach formalized in the 1980s under the rubric "New Historicism," and it distinguishes itself from traditional historical study in two ways. First, following post-Heideggerian hermeneutics and Frankfort school neo-Marxism, it stresses the subjective or ideological nature of our sense of the past: we tend to see only what our interested standpoint permits. Second, in line with structuralism, it sees history as a semiotic field, a text, in which literary and nonliterary phenomena interweave. From this perspective, historicism becomes "cultural poetics," the analysis of powerful but often unacknowledged systems of meaning that link literature to other art forms, disciplines, and social enterprises.

In Dickinson studies, history gives way to historicism as a result of the poet's extraordinary privacy. To the extent that she recused herself from public concerns, we lack decisive evidence of her engagement with the religion,* sexual mores, political and social events, and literary trends that surrounded her. In the wake of Richard Sewall's scrupulous diffidence regarding the interpretation of uncertain facts, historical scholars like Barton Levi St. Armand are led to construct implicitly historicist models of the cultural fabric into which she was woven. Robert McClure Smith exemplifies the methods of the New Historicism consciously applied. The trust of such studies and, indeed, of most important Dickinson scholarship is that her poems and letters*—their lexicon of ideas, tastes, and strategies—engage her times in a coherent manner even when her biography* remains silent.

The theory underlying the New Historicism is additionally important to Dickinson studies because it reinforces the feminist* agenda of freeing our view of history from male and heterosexist prejudices. From a feminist perspective, for example, the search for "Master"* leads not merely to a particular lover* but to the complex experience of gender in which, as a nineteenth-century female, Dickinson participated.

Because of inconclusive biographical data, because Dickinson's voice,* "the Columnar Self"* that speaks her poems (P789), is both female and sexually ambivalent, and because her business is "Circumference"* rather than confession (L268), the methods of historicism are central to Dickinson studies. In the absence of telling documentary evidence, scholars must negotiate rather than determine the meaning of her life and oeuvre. (*See*: Cultural Studies; Philosophical Approaches; Poststructuralist Approaches)

RECOMMENDED: Robert McClure Smith, *The Seductions of Emily Dickinson*; Barton Levi St. Armand, *Emily Dickinson and Her Culture: The Soul's Society*.

Bryan C. Short

HITCHCOCK, EDWARD (1793–1864)   was a geologist and educator, teaching various sciences* at Amherst College.* He was born in Deerfield, Massachusetts, and as a boy worked as a farmer, carpenter, and surveyor. Self-educated, he studied at night, nearly ruining his health and eyesight. He was principal of Deerfield Academy from 1815 to 1818 and minister of the Congregational* church there from 1821 to 1825. Before ordination, Hitchcock studied at the Yale Theological Seminary, where he also enjoyed studying chemistry in Benjamin Silliman's laboratory. In 1825 he accepted the chair of chemistry and natural history at Amherst College. He left the college for a while, taking geological commissions, but returned to serve as its capable and influential president from 1845 to 1854. As a field geologist, Hitchcock had an international reputation, and it is said that he watched over the college's transformation from a center of Congregational study to one of scientific education. However, Conrad Wright points out in his introduction to a recent reprint of *The Religion of Geology* that "in his own mind, he was a minister," trying to reconcile what was written in the Scriptures with what he had discovered or learned in his scientific studies. As professor of natural theology and geology, Hitchcock encouraged religious commitment among students and fostered a campus culture of revivalism.

Most of his lectures were published in books, among them *A Catalogue of Plants Growing without Cultivation in the Vicinity of Amherst College* (1829) and *Elementary Geology* (1841), which were textbooks at Mount Holyoke* Seminary when Emily Dickinson studied there; she also read *The Religion of Geology* (1851) and *Religious Lectures on Peculiar Phenomena in the Four Seasons* (1853). Among her seven letters mentioning Hitchcock, Dickinson once wrote, "When Flowers* annually died and I was a child, I used to read Dr Hitchcock's Book on the Flowers of North America. This comforted their Absence—assuring me they lived" (L488) in reference to his *Religious Lectures*, in which he discussed the Resurrection, as well as to *A Catalogue of Plants*. Although Dickinson did not always agree with what Hitchcock said, he greatly influenced her and her poetry.* As Sewall says, he taught her "how to look at nature and what to look for" (*Life* 356–57). She actually incorporated many arguments from his lectures as well as scientific knowledge such as chemical and geologic lore into many of her poems. Sometimes she tried to find her own solutions to problems, such as the Resurrection, by adapting Hitchcock's arguments as well as by applying her own scientific knowledge. His daughter Catharine (1828–1911), called Kate, was one of Emily's friends until she married in 1852; his son Edward, Jr., was Austin Dickinson's* lifelong intimate, and his youngest daughter, Jane, was Lavinia Dickinson's* best friend until she married and left Amherst in 1864. Emily is known to have corresponded with all members of the Hitchcock family.

RECOMMENDED: *Life*; Edward Hitchcock. *The Religion of Geology and Its Connected Sciences*. 1852. New York: Regina Press, 1975; Carlton Lowenberg, *Emily Dickinson's Textbooks*; Dirk J. Struik. *Yankee Science in the Making*. New York: Collier, 1962; Cynthia Griffin Wolff, *Emily Dickinson*.

Hiroko Uno

HOLLAND, ELIZABETH CHAPIN (1823–1896)   was central to the small group of friends and readers with whom Emily Dickinson kept in close contact through shared letters* and poems. In fact, between 1854 and 1886 Dickinson sent more letters and poems to Elizabeth, whom she frequently addressed as "Sister" or "Little Sister" (L412, for instance), than to any other single reader outside the immediate family circle with the exception of T. W. Higginson.* Very little biographical information about Elizabeth Chapin Holland exists. Scanty details must be culled from brief and infrequent mentions in biographies of Josiah Gilbert Holland,* whom she married in 1845. Most accounts emphasize her physical appearance and her roles as supportive spouse and nurturer of the couple's three children (Annie, Kate, and Theodore) and, later, their numerous grandchildren. Typical is a brief pen portrait found in Harriette Merrick Plunkett's laudatory 1895 biography *Josiah Gilbert Holland* (New York: Scribner's). On the strength of a miniature portrait painted around the time of her marriage, Plunkett describes Elizabeth "with a fair complexion, a rosy bloom, a pair of remarkably frank and fearless bluish-gray eyes, and a wealth of soft brown hair. She was of medium height, but looked fairly petite beside the tall and stalwart figure of her husband."

Dickinson's letters to Elizabeth Holland demonstrate that she overcame much of her natural reticence and took unusual risks with this correspondent. Daring to think aloud, she confided her joys, worries, doubts, and disappointments more freely in this epistolary friendship* than in most other correspondences. Yet most Dickinson biographers and critics have dismissed her friendship with Elizabeth Holland as a superficial exchange of domestic* news between female friends and have chosen to focus, instead, on how Elizabeth's husband might have hindered or helped the poet's attempts to publish* her poetry or have assumed that Dickinson wrote to them primarily as a pair. Although she met Josiah Holland before knowing his wife, Dickinson actually sent very few "union letters" to the couple, a fact highlighted in a November 1866 letter to Elizabeth that offered stringent reproof to those who send joint letters: "A mutual plum is not a plum," she complained (L321). After 1865 she most often chose to address Elizabeth alone and usually asked her friend to pass along cordial greetings to her husband and children.

Dickinson's correspondence with Elizabeth Holland contains much more than idle chatter or sharing of domestic details; these letters served two important and intimately connected purposes. First, this relationship helped satisfy the poet's need for a network of close, sympathetic female friends she could sustain and comfort with her words.* In addition, she shared many of her poetic aspirations and inspirations with Elizabeth Holland. (*See*: Ward)

RECOMMENDED: *Life*, ch. 25; Harriette Merrick Plunkett. *Josiah Gilbert Holland*. New York: Scribner's, 1895; Stephanie A. Tingley, " 'My Business is to Sing': Emily Dickinson's Letters to Elizabeth Holland''; Theodora Van Wagenen Ward, Introduction, *Letters to Dr. and Mrs. Josiah Gilbert Holland*.

Stephanie A. Tingley

HOLLAND, JOSIAH GILBERT (1819–1881)   was a prominent newspaper editor and author. Holland spent his early work years as a minister and then a doctor. In 1846 he turned to journalism and joined the staff of the *Springfield Republican** (as coeditor with Samuel Bowles*) in 1849.

Emily Dickinson met Holland in August 1851, almost two years before her first visit to the Holland home in Springfield, Massachusetts, at a reception held in her father's parlor to celebrate his receipt of an honorary A.M. from Amherst College.* Even before this meeting, Edward Dickinson* and his daughters had long enjoyed Holland's lively essays in the *Republican*, and Emily knew of Holland's attempts to discover, encourage, and publish* new writers; more particularly, she admired his commitment to promoting the work of women* writers. According to Dickinson's biographer* Cynthia Griffin Wolff, however, she was uncomfortable with Holland's conservative ideas about appropriate subject matter and style for poetry, particularly for the work of "lady poets." The ambivalence seemed to be mutual, for Holland's granddaughter Theodora Ward* reports that "Dr. Holland is quoted as having said that Emily's verse was too ethereal for publication" (*Letters* 25). In any case, despite his considerable literary connections, at some point Emily Dickinson apparently decided that he could not, or would not, help her with her attempt to publish her poetry.* Most letters Thomas H. Johnson* lists as having been written to "The Hollands" in Appendix III of his 1958 edition of Dickinson's letters* were actually addressed solely to Josiah's wife, Elizabeth Chapin Holland.* (*See*: Scribner's)

RECOMMENDED: *Life*, ch. 25; Karl Keller, *The Only Kangaroo among the Beauty: Emily Dickinson and America*; Harry Houston Peckham. *Josiah Gilbert Holland in Relation to His Times*. Philadelphia: University of Pennsylvania Press, 1940; Harriette Merrick Plunkett. *Josiah Gilbert Holland*. New York: Scribner's, 1895; Theodora Van Wagenen Ward, Introduction, *Letters to Dr. and Mrs. Josiah Gilbert Holland*.

Stephanie A. Tingley

HOLLAND, SOPHIA (1828–1844)   A childhood friend and classmate of Dickinson, Holland was born in Belchertown, Massachusetts. Along with parents Seneca and Fanny Holland, Sophia moved with her five siblings to Prospect Street, Amherst,* at age four. From 1841, Dickinson's first year at Amherst

Academy,* Holland studied classics and French and continued to do so until her death.* Although unrelated to J. G. Holland,* Sophia's family heritage is nonetheless important: Perez Dickinson (Sophia's maternal grandfather) and Samuel Fowler Dickinson* (Emily's paternal grandfather) were brothers. Thus, these friends were second cousins as well as classmates.

On 29 April 1844, after visiting the bedside of typhoid-stricken Holland, Dickinson witnessed the death of her friend, who was buried at West Cemetery. At the time, Dickinson was sent by her parents to stay with her Aunt Lavinia Norcross* in Boston.* It is evident that Emily was affected by this deathbed scene, which she described two years later in a letter to Abiah Root* (L11). Several critics speculate that this experience of early loss affected Dickinson in various ways, causing both deep depression and her struggle with religion.*

RECOMMENDED: *Life*; Bettina L. Knapp, *Emily Dickinson*.

Michelle Tice

HOME, AS SUBJECT   The use of "home" in Dickinson's work may be metaphysical, religious,* biographical,* or any combination thereof. Known as the poet who rarely left her "Father's ground," as she phrased it (L330), Dickinson may have used "home" in an effort to impart order to her world and thus control it.

Although this complex image should be evaluated for its use in individual poems and letters,* the assertion "Nature* is a Haunted House—but Art—a House that tries to be haunted" (L459A) reflects the poet's need to structure and enclose metaphysical thoughts within familiar, graspable images. Likewise, "One need not be a Chamber—to be Haunted—" (P670) begins with the image of a home that symbolizes the self* in order to delve fully into the dissolution of consciousness.*

According to New England orthodoxy in the nineteenth century, "home" was often used as a way to describe conventional notions of heaven,* where God* the Father welcomed the elect.* Dickinson frequently used "home" as a way to challenge this divine domesticity* by asserting that the temporal nature of an earthly home underlies its special meaning, as in "Forever—is composed of Nows—" (P624).

While much psychoanalytic criticism has been written about Dickinson's supposed agoraphobia, little in her poetry* suggests such personal anxiety involving her home. However, Dickinson rarely, if ever, used "home" in a conventional nineteenth-century domestic sense. In fact, although consolation literature by female writers abounded during Dickinson's lifetime, "home" for Dickinson did not correspond to this discourse, which proposed that the home should be created and then watched over by the mother as moral center of the family. (*See*: Philosophical Approaches; Psychological Approaches; Sentimentalism; Women's Culture)

RECOMMENDED: Aliki Barnstone, "Houses within Houses: Emily Dickinson and Mary Wilkins Freeman's 'A New England Nun' "; Robin Riley Fast. " 'The One Thing

Needful': Dickinson's Dilemma of Home and Heaven''; Thomas Foster, ''Homelessness at Home: Placing Emily Dickinson in (Women's) History''; Jean McClure Mudge, *Emily Dickinson and the Image of Home*; Jim Philip, ''Valley News: Emily Dickinson at Home and Beyond.''

Amy J. Pardo

THE HOMESTEAD   The Dickinson family Homestead is located at 280 Main Street in Amherst.* The poet was born and lived for all but fifteen years of her life in this Federal-style brick house, built in 1813 under the supervision of her paternal grandfather, Samuel Fowler Dickinson.* Although Samuel Dickinson lost title to the house in 1828, he continued living there with his wife and daughters. In 1830, Edward Dickinson,* Samuel's eldest child and Emily's father, bought half the property for $1,500 and moved in with his wife and infant son. In 1833, he sold his share of the Homestead to John Leland and Nathan Dickinson, who already held the deed to his father's half. David Mack,* who bought the house from them, moved in after Samuel Fowler Dickinson's household moved to Ohio. The Edward Dickinsons lived as tenants in the eastern side of the house for seven years of Emily's childhood until Emily was nine. In 1840, her family moved to a generous white clapboard dwelling on North Pleasant Street, adjacent to the village burial ground. With David Mack's death in 1854, Edward Dickinson paid $4,000 for the entire property, which consisted of the house and outbuildings, two and a half acres on the north side of the highway, and a meadow of eleven and a half acres south of the highway to the County Road (now College Street). In May 1855, Edward Dickinson advertised locally, seeking ''a skilful Mason who will lay Brick and Stone, and plaster and whitewash in the best manner'' (*Years* 1:332). Among the renovations several new rooms were added along with a cupola, a large veranda with long French doors on the west side, and Italianate marble mantels about the fireplaces in the double parlor. All repairs were said to have cost ''over five thousands.'' In the following year, Edward Dickinson built a house next door, to the west, for his son and new daughter-in-law, Susan Huntington Gilbert,* which they named ''the Evergreens.''*

   During the last twenty years of her life, Emily Dickinson rarely if ever left the contiguous Dickinson properties, which are set back from the street with a tall hemlock hedge affording additional privacy. From her second-story bedroom, the poet could view the Holyoke Range and Pelham Hills. Two windows of her bedroom face south toward Main Street; the other two face west toward the Evergreens. In the conservatory at the house's southeast corner she grew a wide range of the flowers* and herbs so often named in her poetry.* To the north of the house stood a great barn with room for a carriage, sleigh, and harness rooms, stalls for two horses and two cows, and a toolhouse with a room for the hired man on the second floor. Although the Dickinsons hired help, Emily had a range of regular chores; throughout her adult life she regularly baked bread, cake, and gingerbread. The downstairs pantry was one of the places

where the poet wrote, according to her cousin Louisa Norcross.* From 1875 to
1882, Lavinia* and Emily nursed their paralytic, bedridden mother in this house.
When Emily Dickinson died in 1886, her coffin was carried out the back door
by the Irish hired men who worked the Dickinson grounds. Following Lavinia
Dickinson's death in 1899, Martha Dickinson* became the sole owner of the
Homestead, which she termed "the Mansion" in her correspondence. She sold
the house in 1915 to Rev. Harvey Parke, rector of the Episcopal Church. Priscilla
Parke sold it to Amherst College,* the current owner, in 1965. It was designated
a National Historical Site in 1963. Since 1977 the neighborhood has been on
the National Register as the Dickinson Historic District. In 1996, Amherst College ceased using the Homestead for faculty housing and appointed its first
curator trained in historical preservation. Portions of the Homestead, including
the poet's bedroom and gardens,* are open to visitors, by previous appointment.
(*See*: Domesticity; Funeral; Home; Kelley; Maher)

RECOMMENDED: Mary Elizabeth Kromer Bernhard. "Priscilla Park and a Magnetic
House." *Emily Dickinson International Society Bulletin* 8, 2 (1996): 6–7; "The Dickinson Homestead, Amherst, Massachusetts." Amherst, MA: Amherst College, 1991;
Polly Longsworth, *The World of Emily Dickinson*; Jean McClure Mudge, *Emily Dickinson and the Image of Home*.

Elizabeth Horan

HOWELLS, WILLIAM DEAN (1837–1920)   Dickinson's respect for Howells' novels was posthumously reciprocated by his important review of *Poems*
(1890),* a review that established parameters for critical assessments of the poet
in the 1890s. Dickinson's comments about *The Undiscovered Country* (1880)
and *A Fearful Responsibility* (1881) during their serialization in *Scribner's
Monthly** reveal a thorough familiarity with the fiction of the nation's leading
champion of Realism* in literature. But it was as editor of the *Atlantic Monthly**
and as an essayist for the *North American Review* and *Harper's Monthly** that
Howells would become an influential molder of late-nineteenth-century literary
taste. In the course of his insightful *Harper's* review, Howells discussed Dickinson's personality, speculated on the probable cause of her isolation,* drew
comparisons with Emerson,* Blake,* and Heine, and presented a number of her
best poems, including "How many times these low feet staggered—" (P187)
and "I died for Beauty—" (P449). Howells observed that the poems "will
form something like an intrinsic experience with the understanding reader of
them" and prophetically asserted that they constitute "a distinctive addition to
the literature of the world" (Buckingham 74, 78). (*See*: Critical Reception)

RECOMMENDED: *Letters*; Willis J. Buckingham, ed., *Emily Dickinson's Reception
in the 1890s: A Documentary History*; William Dean Howells, "The *Poems of Emily
Dickinson*."

Robert McClure Smith

HOWLAND, WILLIAM (1822–1880)   Although Emily Dickinson sent her
1852 verse valentine,* "Sic transit gloria mundi" (P3),* to this Amherst Col-

lege* tutor and student in her father's law office, Howland was her sister's suitor rather than the poet's. Lavinia's* diary reports frequent visits from "Tutor" Howland (among other gentlemen callers), and the entry for 8 October 1851 raises interesting conjectures: "Tutor Howland spent afternoon here. Bowdoin called *twice*, Howland escaped *narrowly*. Received offer of *marriage" (Years* I:216). Howland later practiced law in Lynn, Massachusetts. His brother George also frequently joined the social set that gathered at classmate Austin Dickinson's* Pleasant Street house during his years at the college.

RECOMMENDED: *Letters*; *Years*; *Life*.

Jane Donahue Eberwein

HUMOR   Dickinson's range of appreciation for the vital importance of having fun extends variously and significantly beyond her long-recognized wry wit and clever quips. An integral part of the profundity Dickinson offers in her interrogations of life-and-death matters is the comic slant with which she apprehends all of experience, from the mundane to the marvelous. Often Dickinson's humorous remarks inject a bit of levity into quotidian trials. When her nephew Ned* suffers a hornet's sting, Aunt Emily sends a cheering note: "You know I never liked you in those Yellow Jackets" (L511). To her Norcross cousins,* Dickinson describes her rather severe "Aunt Libbie" critically but with a light-hearted turn to make her remark socially acceptable: "The trees stand right up straight when they hear her boots, and will bear crockery wares instead of fruit, I fear. She hasn't starched the geraniums yet, but will have ample time" (L286). Her humor is not limited to domestic relationships of the "women's* sphere" but sometimes ironically deflates the self-important patriarchal institutions denying women full citizenship; thus the Fourth of July is a holiday when "Little Boys are commemorating the advent of their Country" (L650; Smith 76–77). Humor is a way Dickinson has of fending off the disappointments of sociopolitical and cultural constrictions. For her, "the expression of freedom [is] laughter," and wit "provides the detachment from convention which allows her an identity separate" from that which customary religious, social, and political commitments "demand" (Walker 63).

To reimagine, destabilize, and subvert the order of things, Dickinson employs multitudinous strategies. Often she teases, posing as a child,* ingenue, or provincial hick in order to utter a sexual woman's intense desires with a maturity that acknowledges anxieties over appendant issues of identity and power. In "He fumbles at your Soul" (P315), the "lover? Muse? God? Death?" figure or representative of "sex, creativity, salvation, or dying," the poem's "all-powerful force" is himself a tease, stunning by degrees (Juhasz 52–53). Sometimes Dickinson's comedy is black, extravagant, campy, even grotesque. In poems like "A still—Volcano—Life" (P601) and "I've dropped my Brain—My Soul is numb—" (P1046), Dickinson "literally deconstructs the female body,* littering pieces of it around the landscape of her mind" (Miller 118). Through humor, her most frequently anthologized poems likewise display sociability and generosity. The speaker of "I'm Nobody! Who are you?" (P288) "conspiratorially invites the reader* to share in deflating authority figures"; and "though drunk on life rather than on liquor," the speaker of "I taste a liquor never brewed—" (P214) "is still a drunk, another stock comic type from Falstaff to W. C. Fields" (Oberhaus 119).

Like other bards and prophets,* Dickinson knew that the comic or humorous is no less serious than the tragic. She also knew that the heights and depths of human existence could never be climbed, would never be plumbed, without a humorous attenuation to the world. In her scriptures, then, she added a beatitude noticeably missing from Jesus' rather grave dicta: "Blessed are they that play, for theirs is the kingdom of heaven" (L690). (*See*: Cartoons; Currier)

RECOMMENDED: Sandra M. Gilbert, "The Wayward Nun beneath the Hill: Emily Dickinson and the Mysteries of Womanhood"; Suzanne Juhasz, Cristanne Miller, and Martha Nell Smith, *Comic Power in Emily Dickinson*; Barbara Mossberg, *Emily Dickinson: When a Writer Is a Daughter*; Dorothy Huff Oberhaus, "Dickinson as Comic Poet"; Nancy Walker, "Emily Dickinson and the Self: Humor as Identity."

Martha Nell Smith

HUMPHREY, HEMAN (1779–1861)   As president of Amherst College* (1823–1845), Humphrey was a foremost representative of the religious* orthodoxy that institution had been founded to defend. Influenced by a conversion experience at age twenty and educated for the ministry at Yale College, Humphrey used both pulpit and presidency to promote revivals* and missions. He participated actively in the six "seasons of awakening" that occurred under his administration at Amherst.

Humphrey helped to shape the religious and moral character of the students by personally counseling them and providing weekly instruction in the Westminster Catechism. He also organized and served as first pastor of a separate church on campus for regular worship. In addition, Humphrey was closely associated with the First Church,* heading the council that installed Aaron Colton* as pastor and acting as a pulpit supply. His funeral addresses honored local dignitaries such as Mary Lyon.*

RECOMMENDED: Edward Hitchcock. *Reminiscences of Amherst College*. Northampton, MA: Brigman and Childs, 1863; Heman Humphrey, *Valedictory Address Delivered at Amherst College*. Amherst, MA: J. S. & C. Adams, 1845; W. S. Tyler. *History of Amherst College during Its First Half Century, 1821–1871*. Springfield, MA: Clark W. Bryan, 1873.

Rowena Revis Jones

HUMPHREY, JANE T. (1829–1908)   Daughter of Dr. Levi H. Humphrey of Southwick, Massachusetts, Jane was one of Dickinson's earliest friends.* She probably came to Amherst to attend the academy and lived with the Dickinsons. In her 1842 first letter to Jane (L3), Emily mentioned fun "jumping into bed when you slept with me.'' The next contact was at college. Somewhat older than Emily, Jane graduated from Mount Holyoke Female Seminary* at the end of Emily's year there (1848). She became preceptress of Amherst Academy* in 1848–1849, then taught school in Ohio, Washington, Georgia, and at Lawrence Academy in Groton, Massachusetts. In 1858, Jane Humphrey married William Wilkinson, a harness manufacturer of Springfield. The couple resided in Southwick.

Six letters* written by Dickinson to Jane Humphrey survive. After the one written in 1842, there is a break in the exchange followed by a sequence of five important letters between 1850 and 1855. Fragments were published in George F. Whicher's *This Was a Poet* (1938), whole texts in Johnson's *Letters.**

During the future poet's formative period, Jane seems to have provided her friend with moral and emotional support. Letters to Jane, often high-spirited and humorous,* are less moody than those to Abiah Root.* Emily indulged her rebellious strain and talent for satire. She gave vent to impatience with oppressive domesticity* and with Amherst's atmosphere of revivalism*: ''The path of duty looks very ugly indeed. . . . I dont wonder that good angels weep—and bad ones sing songs'' (L30); ''I am standing alone in rebellion, and growing very careless'' (L35). She yielded to the delight of exercising her imaginative conceits and style. In the striking epistle of April 1852 (L86), Dickinson seems to be figuring herself in a scene from *David Copperfield*; she also paints an elaborate, sentimental* picture of herself in the ''death-of-a-virgin'' pose. With a view to such passages, Jane Humphrey may be regarded as Emily's most important literary correspondent before Susan Gilbert.* Moreover, as in the letters to Sue, the stylistic flourishes displayed for Jane tend to be accompanied by intense declarations of affection. The last extant letter to Jane (L180), highly emotional in tone, lacks the aura of finality pervading the conclusion of the exchange with Abiah Root.

Thus, in the correspondence with Jane Humphrey, Emily Dickinson was trying to establish who she was or even who she was going to be (*Life* 390–99). Not only did she dare to voice openly her rebellion and criticism of her milieu, but she seemed consciously to have used letters to Jane as opportunity for imaginative exercises and stylistic practice.

RECOMMENDED: *Letters*; *Life*; *Years*.

Agnieszka Salska

HUMPHREY, LEONARD (1824–1850)   Dickinson praised Humphrey as her ''excellent Principal'' while she was enrolled at Amherst Academy* 1846–1847 (L14) and afterward counted him among her friends.* Apparently well acquainted among his peers in the village, he came with a companion to pay Dickinson a ''delightful'' visit during her year at Mount Holyoke* (L20). Having graduated at the head of his class from Amherst College* in 1846, he returned 1848–1849 to earn an advanced degree and afterward was appointed tutor. Humphrey's early death* in November 1850 elicited characteristic responses of bereavement and melancholy from his "scholar" (L39, 86).

RECOMMENDED: *Years*; *Amherst College Biographical Record*. 1973.

Rowena Revis Jones

HUNTINGTON, FREDERICK DAN   An 1839 Amherst College* graduate, Huntington was one of the many educated and articulate people who were part of Susan* and Austin Dickinson's* circle of friends during the years when they entertained widely. Huntington was professor of moral philosophy at Harvard before he changed from Unitarianism* to Episcopalianism and became bishop of central New York. Emily Dickinson's father gave her a copy of Huntington's book, *Christian Believing and Living*, in 1860. Huntington's letter to Lavinia* after Emily's death described his impression of a woman "hardly more terrestrial than celestial" (*AB* 197). (*See*: Catholicism)

RECOMMENDED: *AB*; *FF*; *Life*.

Janet McCann

HYMNS, INFLUENCE OF   Dickinson's prosody was rooted in, but not dominated by, hymn stanzas. Sufficiently familiar with hymns to quote and paraphrase particular texts (P3, 112, 168), she appropriated hymn forms for purposes beyond their conventional uses for prayer,* praise, and exhortation.

She used standard hymn meters often and irreverently to explore loss, faith,* and eternity, sometimes to exalt poetry.* "I reckon—when I count at all—" (P569), "My life closed twice before its close" (P1732), and many other poems use common meter, which consists of alternating lines of eight and six syllables (8-6-8-6). Known in secular contexts as ballad stanza, common meter is usually rhymed *abab* or *abcb* in hymnals. Short meter—two six-syllable lines followed by one of eight syllables, then a fourth of six syllables (6-6-8-6), customarily rhymed *abab* or *abcb*)—is the prosodic structure of "I've seen a Dying Eye" (P547), which contradicts the evangelical ideal of holy dying, and "I never saw a Moor—" (P1052), which affirms faith in the poet's imagination. Occasionally, as in P205 and 1510, she experimented with long meter (8-8-8-8, rhymed *abab* or *aabb* by most hymnists). She also employed sevens and sixes (7-6-7-6, usually *abab* or *abcb* in hymns)—for instance, in P686 and 757—and common particular meter (8-8-6-8-8-6, *aabccb*), as in P106 and 722. In each pattern she enriched texture, varied tempo, and modulated tone with deliberate metrical variation (sometimes, as in P166 and 727, mixing hymn meters) and unpredictable, semantically appropriate short lines (P234).

Conventional hymnody sets up expectations for exact rhyming* but tolerates eye rhyme (*home, come*), consonantal rhyme (*tongue, song*), and vowel rhyme (*rise, tide*). Dickinson adapted the *abcb* rhyme pattern common in hymns for virtuoso sound effects (P214, 444). Her trademark compression* may reflect her hymn-singing experience: hymnists clip syllables to maintain regularity; she culled words to distill meanings.

Although her reading encompassed a variety of lyrics,* many critics focus on her complex relation to master hymnist Isaac Watts.* Neither disciple nor captive, she departed at will from the four- and six-line stanzas predominant in hymnals. Hymnody prefers end-stopped lines and demands self-contained stanzas; she made increasing use of enjambment during her most productive years. Such independence prompts scholars to ponder line breaks in her manuscripts and inquire whether or when the stanza was her poetic unit. Textual editors* have had to make decisions about line placement and stanza division. "Of all the Souls that stand create—" (P664), for example, has been printed as three quatrains and as a block of twelve lines.

There are parallels with hymns in Dickinson's syntax,* word* choices, metaphors,* and dashes.* In these categories, as in metrics and rhyme, she experimented more boldly. Her idiom was colloquial, but she did not follow Watts and his imitators in restricting herself to vocabulary and syntax immediately accessible to a mass audience. With dashes and quotation marks she pursued expressive effects beyond the reach of hymnody.

The hymn paradigm also informs explorations of Dickinson's themes, tone, and beliefs. She used language and tropes with homiletic resonances to comment on evangelical Protestant pieties such as Sabbath-keeping (P324),* early rising (P112), and beelike busyness (P1533); to protest God's* treatment of humans (P476, 1201); and to question Calvinist dogma. "This World is not Conclusion" (P501) admits in common meter that we cannot be certain of immortality.* "The Road to Paradise is plain" (P1491), an ironic reworking of Watt's "Broad is the road that leads to death," leaves hymn stanzas behind as it confronts the doctrine of election.* Drawing out the potentials of traditional forms, she "sang" in her own way. (*See*: Linguistic and Stylistic Approaches; Music; Musical Settings; "The Yellow Rose of Texas")

RECOMMENDED: Carlton Lowenberg, *Musicians Wrestle Everywhere: Emily Dickinson and Music*; Timothy Morris, "The Development of Dickinson's Style"; David T. Porter, *The Art of Emily Dickinson's Early Poetry*; Barton Levi St. Armand, *Emily Dickinson and Her Culture: The Soul's Society*.

Mary DeJong

I

"I cannot live with You—" **(P640)**   expresses an agonized passion so strong that it renounces the possibility of physical union for the lovers or salvation for the speaker. Johnson* dates the poem as having been written in 1862, and it appears in semifinal draft in Fascicle* 33 (Appendix A). Dickinson included several textual variants*: "consequence" for "excellence" in line 35 and "exercise" or "privilege" for "Sustenance" in line 49. First published in the 1890 *Poems,** the lyric* was titled "In Vain" by Mabel Loomis Todd.* Todd changed "broke" to "broken" in line 10 and, more significantly, deleted one of the poem's major paradoxes by changing "meet" to "keep" in line 45. By changing "White" to "pale" in line 49, Todd also altered Dickinson's metaphor* of the Eucharist at the poem's end.

One of Dickinson's most famous love* poems, it is sometimes considered part of her "Master"* series. Criticism focuses on the poem's complex use of paradox and its series of negations, which make the impossible love possible, even if the lovers must "meet apart." Images and diction blend the domestic* with the divine: the sexton's chalice is compared to a cup "Discarded of the Housewife." The poem conflates marital/sexual life with Christian life and rebirth; "life" for the speaker is not the divine life of the Lord's Supper but instead life with her beloved. In some of the poem's most quoted lines, the speaker argues that she cannot "rise—with You—/ Because Your Face / Would put out Jesus'."* As a result, the poem is often cited as an example of Dickinson's unorthodox Christianity. Wolff calls the poem an "anti-tale of salvation" (419) because the narrative structure moves through life, communion, death,* and resurrection. The lyric comes full circle in the final stanza as the white wafer of the Eucharist is replaced by "that White Sustenance—/ Despair." Cameron analyzes the communion metaphor to show that the "White Sustenance" embodies the speaker's lover*; possessing it, the speaker can also have her lover, even though she cannot be with him.

RECOMMENDED: *Poems*; Sharon Cameron, *Choosing Not Choosing: Dickinson's Fascicles*; Judith Farr, *The Passion of Emily Dickinson*; Gail Donohue, "Lyric Voice: 'I cannot live with You—' "; Inder Nath Kher, *The Landscape of Absence*; Cynthia Griffin Wolff, *Emily Dickinson*.

Denise Kohn

"I felt a Funeral, in my Brain" (P280)   articulates a state of consciousness* that follows literally the stages of a funeral* rite: the mourners tread, the service is conducted, the pallbearers carry the casket, the church bells ring. Even the "Plank in Reason" that breaks in the final stanza may refer to the literal plank placed across the grave* to hold the casket before it is lowered into the ground. If we follow the poem's stages in this way, then it might depict a kind of Poe-esque* premature burial, given that the speaker describes events from inside the casket. The "knowing" that is finished in the final stanza would presumably be consciousness.

When the poem was first published in *Poems* (1896),* its final stanza was omitted, perhaps because the stanza focuses on the end of knowing. However, the poem admits of the possibility that there is one type of knowing (probably based in reason) that has ended in order to make way for another kind (perhaps nonrational) that can begin with the suggestive last word, "then—." Indeed, if "I felt a Funeral, in my Brain" is examined with the poem immediately following in Fascicle* 16, we might see a complementary pair concerning the theme of cognition (Appendix A). " 'Tis so appalling—it exhilirates—" (P281), occupying with P280 the fascicle's center position, seems to derive a kind of excitement from returning once more to the first kind of knowing.

Most often, P280 is understood as representing a state of mind or consciousness rather than a literal funeral. It has been seen as describing, among other states, repression (a kind of burial), dread (in which rational knowing is obliterated), spiritual crisis* (feeling trapped in the incessant treading of the congregation), and a sort of writer's block (where sense almost breaks through, but numbness and silence prevail). Sounds in this poem have often been noted, especially the repetition of "treading—treading" and "beating—beating" and the paratactic "And"s that begin six of the last eight lines. In addition P280 establishes its rhythm and coherence with many "when"s and "then"s. While preventing closure, the rhythm lends punch to the final and suspenseful "then—."

Some critics try to find evidence for Emily Dickinson's biography* in this poem, with Garbowsky seeing its action as a "figurative" funeral that creates a metaphor* for the agoraphobic panic attack. Cody, on the other hand, reads the poem as spoken by Dickinson herself in describing how a plank in reason broke to give way to what he argues was mental illness; in fact, Cody anchors a large part of his argument on this poem. Another possible reading sees this poem as fulfilling a common fantasy in our society, the impossible witnessing of one's own funeral. Mark Twain, of course, made fictive use of this possibility in *Tom Sawyer*. Dickinson, too, employed this strange point of view, but hers is a harrowing rather than a comic fantasy, for the poem denies sight of grieving relatives, the comfort of an elegy,* or a resolution. (*See*: Gothicsm; Psychological Approaches)

RECOMMENDED: *Poems*; Paula Bennett, *Emily Dickinson: Woman Poet*; Sharon Cameron, *Lyric Time: Dickinson and the Limits of Genre*; John Cody, *After Great Pain: The Inner Life of Emily Dickinson*; Maryanne M. Garbowsky, *The House without the Door: A Study of Emily Dickinson and the Illness of Agoraphobia*; Cynthia Griffin Wolff, *Emily Dickinson*.

Daneen Wardrop

"I heard a Fly buzz—when I died—" (P465)   offers Dickinson's response to the question, What is it like to experience death*? For the narrator, the final moments of life are interrupted by the mundane buzzing of a fly, demonstrating Dickinson's unique twist on the old familiar deathbed scene. This poem was probably composed around 1862, and the manuscript was placed in Fascicle* 26 (Appendix A). It was not published until 1896, when it debuted in the third series of *Poems by Emily Dickinson.** The poem appeared under the title "Dying," and several words were altered by editor Mabel Loomis Todd*: "In the Room" in line 2 became "round my form," "around" in line 5 became "beside," "firm" in line 6 became "sure," "the Room" in line 8 became "his power," and "be" in line 10 became "I." Line 11 was completely altered to read "Could make assignable,—and then." The poem was not correctly printed until 1945 in *Ancestors' Brocades.*

Jack Capps has identified two potential sources from which Dickinson could have drawn inspiration for this poem. The first is Elizabeth Barrett Browning's* *Aurora Leigh*, which she read and admired greatly. Book VI of this work in particular contains imagery involving dimming light and a buzzing fly. The second source may have been a contemporary poem by Florence Vale entitled "Are we almost there?" which Dickinson praised in an early letter to Abiah Root.* This poem portrays a dying girl poised between life and death. In an experience similar to the narrator's in Dickinson's poem, the loss of vision* marks the final moment before death.

"I heard a Fly buzz" has sparked much critical discussion since its first publication.* Much of this has centered on imagery, especially the emphasis on light and color (e.g., the "Blue" buzz of the fly). The insect's* symbolic importance has also been debated, along with the poem's emphasis on seeing versus hearing. Finally, the poem has been examined for what it reflects about Dickinson's views of mortality, death, and the possibility of an afterlife. The ambiguity of its final line continues to encourage varied interpretation and discussion. (*See*: Immortality; Vision)

RECOMMENDED: *Poems*; Jack Capps, *Emily Dickinson's Reading*; Joseph Duchac, *The Poems of Emily Dickinson: An Annotated Guide to Commentary Published in English, 1890–1977* and *The Poems of Emily Dickinson: An Annotated Guide to Commentary Published in English, 1978–1989*; Cynthia Griffin Wolff, *Emily Dickinson*.

Kimberly Markowski

"I like a look of Agony" (P241)   captures a fleeting moment when the speaker of the poem witnesses a breakdown of the boundaries between body* and mind. The speaker presumes that a dichotomy between body and mind frames everyday experience, collapsing only at the moment of death,* when the mind's activity is inscribed on the surface of the body. For the speaker, then, a person's death becomes the ultimate index of truth because it initiates this fusion of external and internal. The "I" also discovers in the "look of Agony" evidence of another's interior space hitherto obscured through "sham." Irony pervades the poem; the speaker's search for unquestionable truth and proof of others' interiority is realizable only in the moment of another's death.

The original fascicle* version of P241 provides ways of viewing it distinct from mechanical reproductions (Appendix A, Fascicle 16). Unlike other published volumes of Dickinson's poems, the *Manuscript Books** show how Dickinson positioned the poem between "Tie the Strings to my Life, My Lord" (P279) and "I felt a Funeral, in my Brain" (P280).* Taken together, these poems can be read as the representation of death from three different perspectives: before death (P279), at the very moment of death (P241), and after death (P280). Another variation from printed forms is evident in the second stanza. Dickinson originally transcribed this stanza as five lines, the first two of which read "The Eyes glaze once and—/ That is Death—." The drama of death's appearance is heightened by the separation of the two lines. All printed versions of the poem, however, merge these two lines into one and reduce the second stanza to four lines. The fascicle version of this poem, then, provides critical insight into why Dickinson bound particular poems together and how she intended poems to be published.*

The poem, unpublished during Dickinson's lifetime, first saw print in *Poems* (1890),* edited by Thomas Wentworth Higginson* and Mabel Loomis Todd.* Higginson gave his own flourish to the poem by entitling it "Real," despite Dickinson's own refusal to title* her poems in manuscript form. At the time of its appearance, critics, most notably William Dean Howells,* interpreted the poem as reflecting a Puritan* tradition both in its theme of the pursuit of truth in signs and in its economy of words.* The poem has since been cited frequently as evidence of the influence Dickinson's historical* context had on her imagery and language use. Popular renderings of death in American culture and biblical* representations of Jesus'* agony on the cross are both understood to have inflected Dickinson's treatment of death within the poem. Criticism of the poem has often focused on her deviation from traditional rhyme* schemes, her creation of an imagined poetic persona, and her interest in realms beyond the self* such as the afterlife and the subjectivity of others. (*See*: Critical Reception; Editorial Scholarship)

RECEPTION: *Poems*; Christopher E. G. Benfey, *Emily Dickinson and the Problem of Others*; Willis J. Buckingham, ed., *Emily Dickinson's Reception in the 1890s: A Documentary History*; David T. Porter, *The Art of Emily Dickinson's Early Poetry*; Barton

Levi St. Armand, *Emily Dickinson and Her Culture: The Soul's Society*; Robert Weis-buch, *Emily Dickinson's Poetry*.

H. Jordan Landry

"I taste a liquor never brewed—" (P214)   Perhaps composed in 1860, this poem appears as the opening poem in Fascicle* 12 (Appendix A). It was first published in the *Springfield Daily Republican** in May 1861, with intrusive editorial* changes for the sake of conventional rhyme* and metaphor.* The manuscript's original reading for stanza 1, l. 3 is "Vats upon the Rhine," and for stanza 4, l. 4 it is "Leaning against the—Sun—"; Johnson* accepts both of Dickinson's alternatives, though he prints it in *Complete Poems, 1960** with these lines above. It has been read as having sources in Keats,* Thoreau,* and, most significantly, Emerson*—both in his poem "Bacchus" and his essay "The Poet." One of Dickinson's most admired nature* poems, its speaker may be one of nature's creatures or the poet herself. In either case, as elsewhere in her work, a transcendental* experience of some kind is evoked. The poem is suf-fused with the language of alcohol and inebriation, creating an extended meta-phor that situates the speaker, if it *is* Dickinson, in the otherwise conventionally shameful position of a drunken woman, but transformed here by humor* and hyperbole into a context of power, will, and accomplishment.

RECOMMENDED: *Poems*; Cecil D. Eby, " 'I taste a liquor never brewed': A Variant Reading"; Suzanne Juhasz, *The Undiscovered Continent: Emily Dickinson and the Space of the Mind*; Genevieve Taggard, *The Life and Mind of Emily Dickinson*.

Haskell Springer

THE IMITATION OF CHRIST   Thomas a Kempis (1380–1471), a German ecclesiastic, presented this pithy but passionate four-part text as a meditation offering advice on the spiritual life. In poetic Latin prose, Thomas both excitedly and colloquially* urged the reader to live like Jesus* with love and service to others. The Dickinson library included 1857 and 1876 editions in English trans-lations.

Although Dickinson and Thomas shared Christianity as a source and some of Thomas' concerns overlapped those of neo-Puritan* Amherst,* Dickinson's writing showed selective influences of his book's content and form. She shared his sense of mission and its object, the soul; Dickinson, like Jesus,* declared that her "business is to love" (L269). Like Dickinson, Thomas stressed the soul's need for privacy. He taught that Christians should endure a life of sacrifice and trial, the way of the cross that Dickinson called the "Scarlet way" (P527). Thomas' last section contemplates Holy Communion, offering a cluster of im-ages that Dickinson explored in depth. The third chapter, "On Inward Conso-lation," features long dialogues between Christ and "The Disciple," whom Christ calls "my son." Several Dickinson poems open gender in this dramatic dialogue format between two figures (one Christ-like) who are male, female, or nongendered. Thomas ended many of his Christ/disciple dialogues with a lyrical and clarifying prayer*; Dickinson's poems often read like prayers.

Dickinson loved the world—especially nature,* home,* family, and friends*—too much to "die to the world" (59). She feared the self's* dissolution and resisted the concept of obedience that Thomas advised. However, she contemplated the complexities of these matters. *The Imitation* may have helped to clarify her purpose in life to write poetry* that explores the nature of God* and creation. In Thomas, Dickinson found a congenial soul inspired by the words and spirit of Christ, who visited both writers "with trial and with consolation" (94). (*See*: Bible; Books and Reading; Religion)

RECOMMENDED: *Life*; Dorothy Huff Oberhaus, *Emily Dickinson's Fascicles: Method and Meaning*; Thomas a Kempis. *The Imitation of Christ*. Trans. Leo Sherley-Price. Harmondsworth: Penguin, 1952.

Joanna Yin

IMMORTALITY   The term and its adjective emerge in fifty-five poems and appear throughout Dickinson's letters.* Influenced both by the liberal theologies her tutor Benjamin Newton* promoted and by her father's New England Calvinism, her attitude toward spiritual immortality combined belief, doubt, denial, irony, and curiosity. Dickinson associated the term not only with eternity but also with material life and death.* She repeatedly expressed her concern and, on occasion, her boredom with the subject of her own salvation by pointing to the limited attainability of, and knowledge about, immortality. Thus, according to L752a, its existence cannot be proven; in P800 it is the privilege of a few; in P1289 it seems restricted to youth. In P1646, by contrast, it is but "A bland uncertainty."

Sometimes Dickinson connected immortality with what she found on earth. In L619, earth is "but a Nest, from whose rim we are all falling" into what is presumably immortality; in P1234 "Mortality's Ground Floor / Is Immortality—"; and in P1748, immortality is a divine secret buried deep into a volcano. In these examples, the poet seems to mock and doubt the concept and value of immortality, but many poems and letters* in which Dickinson occasionally personified immortality also represent a serious and sometimes distinctly affirmative treatment of the subject. Some critics consequently hold that in Dickinson's lexicon, immortality is always a positive term that signifies subliminal and empowering uncertainty. While that position is arguable, scholars unanimously agree that Dickinson's work displays an undying curiosity about what she called "the Flood subject" (L319). Some critics have related Dickinson's ambivalent feelings about immortality to the presence or absence of death within the circle of her loved ones at a given time. Others have concentrated on her concern with poetic (im)mortality. Although Dickinson resisted public exposure of herself and her work, it could be argued that she actively sought worldly, poetic immortality by leaving behind an impressive creative legacy, the discovery of which she was evidently not particularly determined to prevent. (*See*: Circumference; Faith; Fame; God; Time)

RECOMMENDED: *Letters*; *Poems*; Jane Donahue Eberwein, "Immortality and the Shape of a Poet's Career"; Gary Lee Stonum, *The Dickinson Sublime*.

Sylvia Henneberg

INSECTS Dickinson's insects—from bee to beetle, butterfly, caterpillar, centipede, chrysalis, cocoon, cricket, fly, glowworm, gnat, leech, midge, moth, spider—are an important part of, and clue to, the world of her poetry.* Most occur only a few times, but the bee appears on 124 occasions, the butterfly 49, the fly, cricket, and gnat 12, 11, and 10. They fulfill natural* rhythms and processes, mark change, and resonate with human concerns and aspirations.

The question is often, What here is tradition, what innovation? Dickinson's gender assignment is particularly intriguing, though her intention remains perhaps less obvious. Her bee was "he," yes; but idiomatic expectations of female identity for her spinning and weaving "Spider" yield to identification of this artisan as "Himself" (P1138). Her metaphors* drew imaginatively on insects for analogies to human emotional states—likening "Suspense" to "the Gnat that mangles men" (P1331) and anguish to "A Small Leech—on the Vitals—" (P565).

Her butterfly can be exotic, even exalted in its "Numidian / Assumption Gown" (P1387, 1244). Her bee, with one clover, conjures up a "prairie" (P1755). Yet both creatures recognize the worth of the simple flower* Dickinson salutes as nature's "Purple Democrat" (P380). Her bee embodies "Liberty" (P661), but affection for the bee "dazzled" by summer's plenty may be tempered by distaste for a self-absorbed chauvinist fumbler (P727). "Babbles the Bee in a stolid Ear" (P216), but her fly of P465* is less unfeeling than simply alive.

Dickinson's "minor Nation" of crickets elegizes the seasonal* transition it "celebrates," and it appears in subtle, telling relation both to the "Beauty" that is "nature's fact" (P1775) and the "Nature [that] is Harmony" (P668). Yet only for the butterfly does the poet become "I": "My Cocoon tightens—Colors teaze—" (P1099). Dickinson's teleological argument takes this metamorphosis as its norm for achieved potential, that power of "Equal Butterfly" that confers sudden, liberating perspective on the "Universe" (P129).

Anthropocentric humor* may grate. The keynote, however, is fellow-feeling with "Bloom and Bees" fulfilling their "Oriental Circuit" (P813), as well as "the Gnat" holding up "His Cup for Light" (P1000). Dickinson's "Entomology" remains humane, the tenor and pitch of its notes true (P1128). (*See*: Flowers; Garden)

RECOMMENDED: Charles R. Anderson, *Emily Dickinson's Poetry: Stairway of Surprise*; Jane Donahue Eberwein, *Dickinson: Strategies of Limitation*; Barton Levi St. Armand, *Emily Dickinson and Her Culture: The Soul's Society*.

James Fegan and Haruko Kimura

ISOLATION   When Dickinson pointed to the door of her room and whispered exultantly to her niece of ''freedom, Matty!'' she sounded a theme not only of her life but of her poetry* (*FF* 66). Solitude, or loneliness, enabled Dickinson's astonishing artistic output and served as a frequent theme. It is ''The Maker of the soul'' (P777) and is often interpreted through domestic* metaphors* of door, chamber, or room. These sometimes gothic* interiors can represent the terrifying struggle of confronting one's own consciousness*—a ''lonely Place'' (P1323), the ''Cavern's Mouth'' (P590), or dangerous chambers and corridors (P670) that reveal ''Assassin hid in our Apartment.'' Elsewhere we find loneliness of the grave* (P529) or heaven* (P405). Other poems create eerie landscapes devoid of human presence such as ''This Consciousness that is aware'' (P822), which embarks on what Eberwein calls ''the private pilgrimage of an isolated soul'' (82).

Dickinson's isolation was likely the deliberate choice, as Rich points out, of one who recognized her own genius. Charting the dimensions of the mind and the richness of her mental life conferred a God-like power and enabled her to encounter the greater forces of God,* immortality,* and spirit. She often conveyed the grandeur of her task, employing the royal ''we.'' In P789, the ''Columnar Self'' yields ''Conviction—That Granitic Base—/ Though None be on our Side—.'' Poems 1695 and 306 celebrate ''The Soul's Superior instants'' or ''polar privacy.'' In P383, ''Exhiliration—is within.'' P1354 tells us the population of the mind is ''One—.'' Privacy confers an inner liberty that necessitates holding oneself ''aloof'' (P1092) and shunning what is public (P998). Dickinson would not be ''shut . . . up in Prose'' (P613) by the wider world. She preferred to ''dwell in Possibility''—''A fairer House'' providing the necessary conditions for her literary genius (P657). (*See*: Friendship; Renunciation)

RECOMMENDED: *Poems*; Christopher Benfey, *Emily Dickinson and the Problem of Others*; Jane Donahue Eberwein, *Dickinson: Strategies of Limitation*; Suzanne Juhasz, *The Undiscovered Continent*; Adrienne Rich, ''Vesuvius at Home: The Power of Emily Dickinson''; R. Bruce Ward, *The Gift of Screws: The Poetic Strategies of Emily Dickinson*.

Terry Blackhawk

J

JACKSON, HELEN MARIA FISKE HUNT (1831–1885)   The daughter of
Nathan Welby Fiske,* Amherst*-born Jackson met Dickinson during childhood
and again in 1860 during a visit to the Homestead* with her first husband, Major
Edward B. Hunt, before becoming her literary friend and correspondent in the
1870s. After the premature death of her husband (1863) and son (1865), Jackson
embarked on a professional career as "H. H.," writer of popular didactic poetry
and fiction. Publication of two critiques of U.S. Indian policy (*A Century of
Dishonor* [1881] and the novel *Ramona* [1883–1884]) won her acclaim as the
greatest American woman* writer by her contemporaries.

In 1866 Thomas Wentworth Higginson,* her mentor, stylistic model, and
fellow boarder at a literary boardinghouse in Newport, Rhode Island, introduced
Jackson to Dickinson's poetry*; two unmailed envelopes in Dickinson's handwriting* suggest that a correspondence between the two women was initiated
around 1868. With a large part of that exchange missing, Dickinson's first surviving note to Jackson is a congratulatory poem upon her second marriage to
William S. Jackson of Colorado (1875). It evoked Jackson's enthusiastic reply,
"You are a great poet" (L444, 444a), and marked the beginning of her repeated
attempts to induce Dickinson to publish*: "it is a wrong to the day you live in,
that you will not sing aloud." The ensuing correspondence traces a literary
friendship* based on exchange of works, mutual recognition, and friendly competition: Dickinson commented admiringly on *Ramona* and more ambivalently
on Jackson's poetry* (remarking to Higginson in L622, "Mrs Jackson soars to
your estimate lawfully as a Bird"), while Jackson, having received P1465, complained that Dickinson's mastery thwarted her own creative efforts, "[f]or which
I am inclined to envy, and perhaps hate you" (L601a). While Dickinson's few
surviving letters* to Jackson are characterized by a rare absence of "posing,"
combined with an exceptional tolerance for her friend's requests for explications,

Jackson's correspondence suggests a continuous interest in her friend's "portfolios of verses" (L937a), a growing understanding of her obscurities ("Part of the dimness must have been in me," L476c), as well as attention to technical aspects ("I like your simplest and [most direct] lines best"). At the same time, however, their epistolary exchange highlights fundamentally different attitudes toward the literary marketplace: whereas Dickinson failed to understand Jackson's reasons for publication, all of Jackson's letters written between 1876 and 1878 as well as her two personal visits (1876 and 1878) constituted attempts to persuade Dickinson to contribute anonymously to *A Masque of Poets*,* an endeavor that eventually succeeded in 1878 with Jackson's submission of P67 ("Success is counted sweetest").* Her wish to be made Dickinson's "literary legatee & executor" (L937a) was thwarted by her premature death from cancer. Dickinson's dedicatory elegies,* as well as her condolatory letters to William Jackson ("Helen of Troy will die, but Helen of Colorado, never," L1015), Thomas Niles,* Samuel Bowles, Jr., and Higginson illustrate how deeply Jackson's death* affected her.

Critics and reviewers of the 1890s developed a special interest in the Jackson–Dickinson friendship. The celebrated author's enthusiasm for Dickinson's poetry was employed as a marketing strategy by Mabel Loomis Todd,* who included an autographed copy of L937a in her preface to *Poems* (1891).* In addition, a brief journalistic debate (later disproved) flared up over the question to what extent Jackson's novel *Mercy Philbrick's Choice* (1876) and her short story "Esther Wynn's Love-Letters" (published pseudonymously under "Saxe Holm"* in 1871) were modeled on Dickinson's life. Subsequent critical reception generally recognizes Jackson as the only contemporary (apart, perhaps, from Ben Newton*) to have recognized Dickinson's significance fully. (*See*: Critical Reception)

RECOMMENDED: *Letters*; *Life*; Susan Coultrap-McQuin. "Very Serious Literary Labor: The Career of Helen Hunt Jackson." *Doing Literary Business: American Women Writers in the Nineteenth Century*. Chapel Hill: University of North Carolina Press, 1990; Betsy Erkkila, *The Wicked Sisters: Women Poets, Literary History, and Discord*; Thomas H. Johnson, *Emily Dickinson: An Interpretive Biography*.

Marietta Messmer

JAMESON, MARIETTE FRANKLIN Mariette Jameson moved with her lawyer husband (later, Amherst postmaster), John, from Boston* to Amherst* in 1875, settling into the house opposite the Dickinson Homestead*; she faithfully recorded what happened in the two Dickinson households in her letters to her son John Franklin Jameson, a professor of history at Johns Hopkins University. From the language of her letters, it can be deduced that Jameson was an educated woman who showed commonsensical good nature. Thus on one occasion she sent something to eat to Maggie Maher,* the Irish household helper of the Dickinsons, when she was ill with typhoid fever, and at another time she disapproved of slander directed against Susan Gilbert Dickinson* by members

of the Amherst community. Once, the Dickinson sisters even called this friend
the "angel of the neighborhood" (*Years* 2:453). Mariette Jameson also attended
Emily Dickinson's funeral,* of which she gave a detailed description in a 23
May 1886 letter. Two notes by Emily Dickinson to her have survived, one as
late as 24 April 1886.

RECOMMENDED: *Letters*; *Years*.

Jutta Fraunholz

JAPANESE RESPONSES TO DICKINSON   Why is Emily Dickinson a
well-known poet in Japan? It is perhaps because her concerns (such as nature,*
death,* and immortality*) are universal and familiar at once to the Japanese,
who have been accustomed for fifteen centuries to read haiku or Tanka (short
poems) that have symbolic connotations similar to hers.

The first brief introduction of Emily Dickinson to Japan was made by Matsuo
Takagaki in 1927; in 1931 Bunsho Jugaku wrote the first article on her nature
poems, appreciating her as a Blakean* mystic. In 1940 Motoshi Karita contributed toward a better understanding of Dickinson by writing a magazine essay
on her. Toshikazu Niikura, the founding president of the Emily Dickinson Society of Japan (EDSJ), published the first book on her in 1962 and another
comprehensive study in 1989.

The 1960s was a significant decade, when the basic study of Dickinson began
with translations of her poems by Tamotsu Nakajima and Kikuo Kato. The
1970s showed a gradual and steady increase in study of Dickinson and in her
popularity, but the 1980s represented a glorious achievement in Dickinson studies in Japan: EDSJ was founded with its annual *EDSJ Newsletter* in 1980, and
almost twenty books on Dickinson were issued in that decade. Amy Horiuchi
discovered Zen traits in her, Masao Nakauchi examined her metaphors,* and
Akira Kawano investigated her color imagery, while Michiko Iwata wrote a
biography* of Dickinson as a martyr to love* and poetry* (1982). Tsuyoshi
Omoto has maintained an annual bibliography of Japanese Dickinson studies
since 1986.

For the Dickinson centennial year, Tamaaki Yamakawa, second president of
EDSJ and author of several books on her, coedited *After a Hundred Years:
Essays on Emily Dickinson*. Also in 1986, when seventeen members of EDSJ
participated in three international celebrations in the United States, a represen-
tative of Japanese Dickinsonians, T. Niikura, gave a special lecture at the Folger
Library centennial conference in Washington, D.C. That same year, EDSJ spon-
sored a series of lectures by guest speakers Ruth Miller and Richard Sewall in
Tokyo.

More recently, Hiroko Uno published *Emily Dickinson Visits Boston* (1990)
and translated two books on Dickinson with collaborators. In doctoral dissertations at Hiroshima University, Takao Furukawa studied her poetics (1990),
and Katsuhiko Inada inquired into her strategies for immortality (1991). Masako
Takeda, who translated love poems and letters of Dickinson and read papers at

the 1992 Emily Dickinson International Society conference in Washington, published a 1996 volume of translations.

Dickinson has been honored in the performing arts as well as through scholarship in Japan. A famous actress, Tetsuko Kuroyanagi, acted Emily Dickinson in Amherst for an Asahi Television film (1980), and Tsuyoshi Chiba translated *The Belle of Amherst* by William Luce and directed the one-woman play (1991). (*See*: Asian Responses; Dramatic Representations; Visual Arts, Responses)

RECOMMENDED: Takao Furukawa, *The Poetics of Emily Dickinson*; Tsuyoshi Omoto, *Emily Dickinson in Japan: A Bibliography: 1927–85*; Hiroko Uno, *Emily Dickinson Visits Boston*; Tamaaki Yamakawa, et al., *After a Hundred Years: Essays on Emily Dickinson*.

Takao Furukawa

JENKINS, REV. JONATHAN LEAVITT and SARAH   Minister of the First Church* in Amherst* from 1867 to 1877, Rev. Jenkins, his wife (Sarah Maria Eaton), and their children were close friends of the entire Dickinson family even after they left Amherst. Jenkins, among Emily's favorite ministers, received strong support of her father and brother in the construction of a modern First Church building across the street from the Homestead.* According to MacGregor Jenkins,* his father interviewed Emily in 1873 at Edward Dickinson's* insistence and declared her theologically "sound." The Jenkinses, who named one of their sons Austin Dickinson Jenkins, received affectionate letters* from the poet along with occasional flowers,* pussy willows, a sketch, and two poems to Mrs. Jenkins (P1352 and 1391) and one to their daughter Sally* (P1521) during their years in Amherst and after their move to Pittsfield. Dickinson's sense of losing friends and neighbors, whom she once addressed as "my Mr. and Mrs Clergyman, with confiding love" (L423), is especially evident in letters to Mrs. Jenkins at the time of their move (L501, 506, 520). After Jenkins's farewell sermon, Dickinson wrote to Elizabeth Holland* of the cost of loving their clergyman (L492). Rev. Jenkins officiated at her parents' funerals* in 1874 and 1882, at her nephew Gilbert's* in 1883, and at her own in 1886.

RECOMMENDED: *Letters*; *Life*; *Years*; MacGregor Jenkins, *Emily Dickinson: Friend and Neighbor*.

Jean Carwile Masteller

JENKINS, MACGREGOR and SALLY   MacGregor and Sally Jenkins were the children of Jonathan and Sarah Jenkins,* neighbors of the Dickinson family between 1866 and 1877, when Jonathan Jenkins served as pastor of the First Church* at Amherst.* MacGregor and Sally would have been approximately eight and eleven years old in 1877, when their family moved to Pittsfield. MacGregor Jenkins' memoir, *Emily Dickinson: Friend and Neighbor*, offers a charming if romanticized glimpse of Dickinson as she impressed him at a young age. By his accounts, he ("Mac") and Sally ("Did") and their friends were surprised during games of pirates and gypsies, for example, by Dickinson's lowering a basket of gingerbread loaves, each topped with a flower.* He also records various notes she left the children. (*See*: Black Cake; Fiction)

RECOMMENDED: *Letters*; MacGregor Jenkins, *Emily Dickinson: Friend and Neighbor.*

Daneen Wardrop

JESUS Dickinson's attitude towards Jesus apparently underwent substantial change over time. In early letters to Abiah Root* and Jane Humphrey* she mourned her incapacity to accept Jesus as bearer of heavenly grace and his lack of love for her. She attributed the love* her friends and sister developed for Jesus to womanly maturity and wisdom, placing it in contrast to her own penchant for risk taking and love for the world. The demand she sensed to accept Jesus was partly fed by mystic thought and partly by the spirit of revivalism* around her. At the time, love for Jesus was associated with peace and womanly* submission, to which she could not yield.

However, from letters to T. W. Higginson,* Elizabeth Holland,* and Mary Hills* dated 1877 (the year Susan Dickinson* gave her a copy of Thomas a Kempis' *The Imitation of Christ**), it appears that Dickinson came to accept Jesus more and more. Closer examination of her work reveals that she all along rejected the heavenly* aspect of Jesus, which could be blotted out by a single human face: "Your Face / Would put out Jesus'—" (P640). Her eventual convictions are summed up in a letter to Mrs. Henry Hills: "When Jesus tells us about his Father, we distrust him. When he shows us his Home, we turn away, but when he confides to us that he is 'acquainted with Grief,' we listen, for that also is an Acquaintance of our own" (L932). Only when Dickinson discovered human qualities in Jesus did faith* overcome doubt. (*See*: God; Religion)

RECOMMENDED: *Letters*; *Years*; Jane Donahue Eberwein, *Dickinson: Strategies of Limitation*; Dorothy Huff Oberhaus, " 'Tender Pioneer': Emily Dickinson's Poems on the Life of Christ"; Virginia H. Oliver, *Apocalypse of Green: A Study of Emily Dickinson's Eschatology*; Cynthia Griffin Wolff, *Emily Dickinson.*

Jutta Fraunholz

JEWELS play a subordinate but nonetheless significant role among Dickinson's image patterns, functioning as part of a larger network of images that attribute value to intangibles through references to items of material worth (precious metals, mines and mining sites such as "Ophir," rare crystals and minerals such as chrysolite, and so on). All the well-known jewels appear in her poems— amethysts, diamonds, emeralds, garnets, opals, pearls, rubies, sapphires, and so on—with pearls being the gem of choice. Complicating this picture, however, is the fact that often these jewel references are used as much for their color as for their value per se, as, for example, "topaz" in P697 and "Sapphire" in P291. Alternatively, Dickinson may deploy jewels to connote permanence, as in an "Amethyst remembrance" (P245). One of Dickinson's most striking uses of jewel imagery occurs in P1397, where "Opal" captures the peculiarly fresh and evanescent quality of air following an electrical storm. Here the emphasis falls not only on the gem's multiple colors but on their shifting quality. Such a metaphor* superbly exemplifies Dickinson's ability to give precise expression to sensory experience through transference from one sense realm to another, or synesthesia. Finally, Dickinson incorporates jewel images in a larger network of female sexual imagery that pervades her writing. "Pearl," in particular, appears to take on resonance as a clitoral image in poems such as P213 and P452 (*See*: Flowers; Lesbian Approaches).

RECOMMENDED: *Poems*; Rebecca Patterson, *Emily Dickinson's Imagery.*

Paula Bennett

JOHNSON, THOMAS HERBERT (1902–1985) Dickinson's best-known and most respected twentieth-century editor* made the poems available for the first time in a form as close as possible to the poet's own intentions. Having already opened the way for discussion of early American poetry through a 1938 collection of Puritan* writing, coedited with Perry Miller, and a 1939 edition of Edward Taylor's poetry (which he had discovered in Yale University's Sterling Memorial Library), Johnson also gained early renown for his work with Robert E. Spiller, Willard Thorp, and Henry Seidel Canby as editors of the *Literary History of the United States* (1948). He was then selected in 1950 to take advantage of Harvard University's acquisition of Dickinson's literary estate by editing her manuscripts. He would eventually complete a scholarly biography* of Dickinson and edit some nine volumes of her writings. Johnson later extended his influence over our understanding of literary history by writing *The Oxford Companion to American History* (1966).

Johnson's three-volume variorum edition of *The Poems of Emily Dickinson,** which was the most accurate and complete collection when it appeared in 1955, aimed at making her poetry available just as she wrote it. To do this, Johnson (assisted by Theodora Ward* and Jay Leyda) included all 1,775 poems—most taken from the manuscripts—along with all known textual variants,* arranged in as close to chronological order as possible. The edition introduces conjectural dates of composition based on studies of handwriting* and paper and assigns a number to each poem (numbers that have since become the standard means of referring to Dickinson's poems, since she left most untitled). Johnson condensed these three volumes into his 1960 *Complete Poems of Emily Dickinson.** In spite of his intent to present Dickinson as she was, Johnson was restrained by the limitations of printing, which can never exactly duplicate handwritten characters. In addition, Johnson chose to normalize Dickinson's spelling in *Complete Poems.*

Johnson's 1958 three-volume edition of some 1,045 of *The Letters of Emily Dickinson** (compiled with Theodora Ward) made available for the first time all of her known correspondence in unexpurgated form. Again, accurately dating the letters* was a particularly difficult aspect of the edition. Johnson's detailed and sensitive biographical introduction to the letters demonstrates his deep understanding of Dickinson as poet and woman. His *Emily Dickinson: An Interpretive Biography* (1955) was one of the most widely translated works on Dickinson and remained the standard critical biography of the poet until Richard Sewall published his two-volume 1974 *Life*.

Following his death on 3 January 1985, Johnson was remembered through a memorial unit that appeared in *Dickinson Studies*,* a fact that further emphasizes his importance to twentieth-century understanding of the poet. Richard Sewall recalled that Johnson's editions began a thirty-year swell of interest in Dickinson, while Frederick Morey referred to Johnson as "the leading Dickinson scholar of his generation" and "the most prolific and well-known Dickinson scholar around the world" (9). Also in this issue scholars Toshikazu Niikura and Tamaaki Yamakawa commented on Johnson's importance to Dickinson studies in Japan,* citing his editions as the sources of the best Japanese translations. In addition, Brita Lindberg-Seyersted of Norway and Rev. Niels Kjær of Denmark celebrated Johnson's importance to Scandinavian* studies of Dickinson. (*See*: Franklin; Todd)

RECOMMENDED: Willis J. Buckingham, "Emily Dickinson's 'Lone Orthography' "; Ralph W. Franklin, *The Editing of Emily Dickinson: A Reconsideration*; "Johnson, Thomas Herbert (1902–1985)." *Contemporary Authors*. 124. Ed. Hal May and Susan M. Trosky. Detroit: Gale, 1988: 240–41; Niels Kjær, ed. "Thomas Herbert Johnson Memorial Unit (27 April 1902–3 Jan. 1985)." *Dickinson Studies* 62, 1 (1987): 3–18 and Addendum *Dickinson Studies* 65, 1 (1988): 25–26.

Jennifer Hynes

K

KEATS, JOHN (1795–1821)   It is possible that Emily Dickinson never read this English poet. Current evidence shows no Keats volume among the Dickinson books at Harvard, nor does any copy belonging to her family seem to exist elsewhere. Colonel Higginson* had mentioned Keats in the article that prompted Dickinson to contact him initially, and Thomas Johnson* noted that the "Endymion" quotation in her L1034 (1886) appeared in Higginson's "The Life of Birds."* Dickinson mentioned Keats twice more. In L261, she might have been trying to impress Higginson by showing she had read his essay; in L1018, she compared Helen Hunt Jackson* to Keats by means of eulogy.

Two Dickinson poems, "I died for Beauty—but was scarce" (P449) and "Beauty—be not caused—It Is—" (P516), are reminiscent of Keats' "Ode on a Grecian Urn." P449 states of Beauty and Truth that "Themself are One," which echoes "Beauty is truth, truth beauty." In P516, Beauty "ceases" if chased, implying that it becomes something other than Beauty if the viewer feels a need to pursue it. P1434, "Go not too near a House of Rose—," may have its foundation in Keats' "Ode on Melancholy." (*See*: Romanticism)

RECOMMENDED: *Poems*; *Letters*; Ernest Fontana, "Dickinson's 'Go not too near a house of rose.' "

Marcy L. Tanter

KELLEY, THOMAS (1833?–1920)   Employed as a workman by Edward Dickinson,* Kelley comforted Emily Dickinson when Judge Otis Lord* became fatally ill (L752) and was chosen by the poet as her chief pallbearer. Kelley emigrated in 1854 from Killurney, Parish Temple-etney, County Tipperary, Ireland. In 1855 he married Mary Maher (1825–1909), elder sister of Dickinson domestic servant Margaret Maher.* They settled at Kelley Square, adjacent to the Amherst* train depot and Dickinson meadow, where they raised eight children. Some of their children ran errands for Emily, and two of three houses in the family compound at Kelley Square were purchased from Edward Dickinson.* (*See*: Funeral)

RECOMMENDED: Jay Leyda, "Miss Emily's Maggie"; Aífe Murray, "Kitchen Table Poetics: Maid Margaret Maher and Her Poet Emily Dickinson."

Aífe Murray

KELLOGG, ELIZA   A close acquaintance of the Dickinson family, Eliza M. Kellogg married Amherst* businessman (and school superintendent from 1868 to 1871 and 1885 to 1887) Hanson Leland Read on 25 November 1851. Dickinson attended the wedding, but eventually her sole contact with Eliza appears to have been by letter.* The Reads' two young sons, William (aged twenty-one) and Samuel (aged eleven) drowned on 26 December 1873 in a tragic skating accident at Adams Pond, Amherst (see letters 404 and 426).

RECOMMENDED: *Letters*.

Marianne Erickson

KIMBALL, BENJAMIN (b. 1850)   The son of Otis and Lucy Sarah Kimball, he was a cousin of Otis P. Lord* and executor of Lord's estate upon his death in 1884. Dickinson wrote and requested Kimball's remembrances of Lord as a "kinsman," she being "only his friend"* (L967). She thanked him for his response: "Your noble and tender words of him were exceedingly precious—I shall cherish them" (L968). Dickinson's two letters* to Kimball, along with the poems she enclosed (e.g., P1599 and 1638) indicate her strong feelings for Judge Lord. Kimball practiced law in Boston,* where he lived with his wife, Helen Manning Simmons.

RECOMMENDED: *Letters*; *Life*.

Carolyn Kemp

L

LATIN AMERICAN RESPONSES TO DICKINSON   With the exception
of George Monteiro's detailed survey of translations and criticism in Portuguese,
the bibliography on Latin American responses to Dickinson is far from complete. Even so, there is reason to believe that an ample public in Latin America
has read her work, primarily in translation. Among writers fluent in English who
have indicated respect for Emily Dickinson's work, Mexican poet Octavio Paz
used the prologue to the English version of his book on Sor Juana to mention
Dickinson as one of five great women writers of the Western Hemisphere. Chilean Nobel laureate Gabriela Mistral annotated all of the Emily Dickinson poems
in her personal copy of the Spanish-language edition of Allen Tate and John
Peale Bishop's anthology of U.S. poetry. There are good reasons to think that
contemporary poets, the Nicaraguan Ernesto Cardenal and Chilean Nicanor Parra
(both intensely engaged with U.S. literature), respond to Dickinson: their writing
shares Dickinson's epigrammatic and often comic style, engagement with religious* themes, and concern with New World locales. Among women writers,
Silvina Ocampo, Argentine writer of fantastic short stories and herself a famous
semirecluse, and the contemporary Chilean–U.S. poet Marjorie Agosin have read
and been influenced by Dickinson's work, which shares their fascination with
the contradictions of gender identity.

   Probable influence aside, actual translations into Spanish and Portuguese provide the most reliable index to Dickinson's reputation in Latin America. Such
translations, only sporadically noted in bibliographies, most often appear in
widely circulating, somewhat ephemeral forms of magazines and newspaper
literary supplements. The popularity and respectability of literature in translation
have enabled many major writers to earn part of their living as translators. Such
was the case with Juan Ramón Jiménez, a key Spanish poet who relocated to
Puerto Rico after the Spanish civil war. Jiménez produced the earliest known

translations of Dickinson into Spanish, probably in conjunction with his bilingual Puerto Rican wife, Zenobria Camprobí, who likewise collaborated in his influential translations of Tagore. Jiménez and Camprobí were driving forces behind the magazine *Asomante*, published in Puerto Rico, which in the 1940s and 1950s became a major Spanish-language venue for Emily Dickinson criticism by, for instance, renowned U.S. translator Harriet de Onís and noted Spanish scholar Carmen Bravo Villasante. Another important translator of Dickinson has been the Mexican writer and diplomat Rosario Castellanos, as Ahern points out.

Dickinson has been among the most widely read U.S. poets in Portuguese. Monteiro's 1971 article on Brazil's Emily Dickinson lists some forty-six items, and in 1982, he reviewed the work of Jorge de Sena, whose translations of Dickinson into Portuguese numbered eighty poems. Buckingham lists significant collections of Dickinson translations probably circulating in Latin America as of 1970: fifty-three poems translated by Mario Manent, published in Barcelona in 1957 and twice reprinted, and a 1946 collection of sixty-seven poems published in Mexico. Buckingham's and Myerson's listings suggest that Dickinson's poems have received more attention in Latin America than her letters,* which remain little known. This could change as the diffusion of U.S. literature grows. (*See*: Canadian Responses)

RECOMMENDED: Maureen Ahern, ed. and trans. *A Rosario Castellanos Reader*. Austin: University of Texas Press, 1988; Willis J. Buckingham, *Emily Dickinson: An Annotated Bibliography*; Ana María Fagundo Guerra, "The Influence of Emily Dickinson on Juan Ramón Jiménez' Poetry"; Elizabeth Horan, "Emily Dickinson, Gabriela Mistral, y sú publico"; George Monteiro, "Brazil's Emily Dickinson" and "Jorge de Sena's Dickinson"; Joel Myerson, *Emily Dickinson: A Descriptive Bibliography*.

Elizabeth Rosa Horan

LAVINIA   Dickinson, Lavinia Norcross

LEGAL IMAGERY   Dickinson's poetry reveals a skeptical attitude toward both God's* and man's laws, employing legal diction to capture various ways society uses law to limit and deny power.

Massachusetts Puritans* dating back to John Winthrop had deployed legal tropes to describe their relationship with God. They thought of themselves as enrolled in a covenant whose terms ruled that God would sustain them if they obeyed the law but would wreak swift revenge if they betrayed their contract. Puritan use of legal rhetoric implied the fusion of secular and sacred; it was geared to imposing political and spiritual control on forces of individualism. By contrast, Dickinson used legal imagery to assert independence and called on her Puritan inheritance to provide a liberating rhetoric.*

In P251, Dickinson's Eve-like persona eyes forbidden fruit. She realizes that climbing the fence to get coveted berries violates God's law. Although children have a natural desire and ability to climb the fence, if a girl should climb over, her apron (a symbol of her gender) would be "stained," and "God would certainly scold!" God has a double standard. His unfair and repressive restrictions limit female behavior.

Dickinson's father, a successful Amherst* lawyer, dominated his household. In P273, Dickinson's Father in Heaven, under the guise of an attorney, uses a satchel to carry the deeds of "Dedicated" lives. Pulling the "Belt" around his briefcase and closing the "Buckle" so that none will be lost, he extinguishes the intrinsic significance of the individual self* by enclosing it in the satchel with other indefinable "Dedicated" lives.

Resisting annihilation, Dickinson shaped a language to challenge patriarchal authority. P116 threatens to summon her state's Chief Justice to help her file a lawsuit against God. In P430, Dickinson's speaker transforms the world with her linguistic power, bequeathing beauty and value. Her "word of Gold" "Dowered—all the World—." As poetic creator, she wrests power from those in authority. P699 presents itself as a legal document (an offer to sell country property to an owlish judge), which justifies the poet as capable of transacting business.

Dickinson's poetry develops, in part, as a reaction to external authority. She appropriates an alternative power by writing from the perspective of an alienated consciousness* and using legal language as a weapon against limitation and orthodoxy. Only after the reader senses the ambiguity* of her images, will their ironic, gendered possibilities be recognized. (*See*: Feminist Approaches)

RECOMMENDED: *Life*; Joanne Feit Diehl, " 'Ransom in a Voice': Language as Defense in Dickinson's Poetry"; James R. Guthrie, "Law, Property, and Provincialism in Dickinson's Poems and Letters to Judge Otis Phillips Lord"; Rebecca Patterson, *Emily Dickinson's Imagery*.

Deborah Dietrich

LESBIAN APPROACHES TO DICKINSON   Rebecca Patterson, writing in 1951, was the first biographer* to suggest that Dickinson's poetry reflected sexual feelings for a woman, Kate Anthon.* Patterson's theory aroused little serious interest until John Cody's 1971 psychobiography, in which he too discussed evidence in Dickinson's writing indicating that she probably had a strong emotional attachment to other women. In a 1977 article, Lillian Faderman analyzed Dickinson's letters to Sue Gilbert* to demonstrate their homoerotic content and to suggest how Dickinson's erotic* interest in women was reflected in her poetry.*

A number of more recent biographers and critics have observed Dickinson's homoeroticism as it appears in her verse. In a 1993 study, Martha Nell Smith goes so far as to claim that even the "Master"* letters may have been written to a woman, postulating that Dickinson disguised the lesbian nature of her love by dressing a woman up in masculine pronouns. However, it was more likely that Dickinson did not see herself as a "lesbian" (a sexual identity that became a fixed category only through the writings of sexologists in the late nineteenth century) but rather that she viewed her passionate love for other women in the context of "romantic friendship,"* which appears to have been a widespread and socially accepted institution in her day.

Regardless of how Dickinson may have explained her homoerotic feelings to herself, her writing leaves no doubt of its existence. Her homoerotic poetry appears to span the length of her literary career, from one of her first poems, written in 1854, "I have a Bird in spring" (P5), to one of her very late ones, written in 1883, "To see her is a Picture—" in its third variant (P1568). On the whole, Dickinson's homoerotic poems, like her heteroerotic ones, depict love that has been frustrated. In many of the homoerotic poems some circumstance has snatched the other woman away from the speaker. In "Her sweet Weight on my Heart a Night" (P518) and "Frigid and sweet Her parting Face—" (P1318) the beloved inexplicably slips away. Several poems that employ a bird* metaphor depict the female beloved as flying away: for example, "I have a Bird in spring" (P5) and "It did not surprise me—" (P39). In still other poems the female beloved is stolen away by someone else (P452, 631).

Despite her inevitable loss of the other woman in these poems, the speaker frequently swears undying devotion and even "idolatry." In "Precious to Me— She still shall be—" (P727) the speaker vows to love the beloved "Though She forget the name I bear." In "The Lady feeds Her little Bird" (P941), though the beloved deigns to nurture the lover less and less often, the lover (a female bird) nevertheless continues "on Her yellow Knee / [to] Fall softly, and adore." Such idolatry, which the beloved of these poems sometimes merits and often does not, intensifies the lover's pain. (*See*: Eroticism; Lovers; Psychological Approaches)

RECOMMENDED: Paula Bennett, *Emily Dickinson: Woman Poet*; John Cody, *After Great Pain: The Inner Life of Emily Dickinson*; Lillian Faderman, "Emily Dickinson's Letters to Sue Gilbert"; Rebecca Patterson, *The Riddle of Emily Dickinson*; Martha Nell Smith, *Rowing in Eden: Rereading Emily Dickinson*.

Lillian Faderman

LETTERS   The extant part of Dickinson's correspondence to date includes nearly 1,200 letters and prose fragments addressed to more than ninety known correspondents and constitutes the poet's only surviving creative output apart from her poetry.* The first selection of letters was published in Thomas Wentworth Higginson's* *Atlantic Monthly** introduction to his correspondence with Dickinson (1891), followed by Mabel Loomis Todd's* two editions of selected letters (1894 and 1931) and Thomas H. Johnson's* 1958 edition of all texts available until then. To this corpus, Richard B. Sewall's edition of *The Lyman Letters* (1965) added seven "snatches" offering glimpses into Dickinson family life, which had been copied by Joseph Lyman* from his correspondence with the poet. The recent resurfacing of an additional letter and several missing manuscripts suggests the possibility of further discoveries, as the extant material constitutes only a small fraction of Dickinson's actual correspondence: some epistolary exchanges are missing entirely (her letters to Benjamin Newton* and Charles Wadsworth*), while others show substantial gaps (the correspondence with Susan Gilbert* for two years after her marriage in 1856 and the exchange with Josiah* and Elizabeth Holland* between 1862 and 1865). In addition, Johnson was unable to place any letters in the year 1857. With few exceptions, only the Dickinson side of each correspondence survives, as Lavinia* burned her sister's private papers upon the poet's death. In some instances, Dickinson's original autographs were mutilated (the letters to Susan Gilbert) or destroyed by their recipients (the Norcross correspondence), and print editions thus had to rely on Todd's or the addressee's own transcripts.

From the 1860s onward, letters became Dickinson's preferred medium of social interaction (often with people whom she had never met), thus enabling her to establish a wide range of recipient-specific epistolary relationships on her own terms. As the letter writer of the Dickinson household, the poet maintained ties with Amherst College* graduates, clergymen, and family members (her brother Austin,* her cousins Louise* and Frances Norcross,* her nephew Ned*) and, upon births and deaths, sent congratulatory and condolatory notes to Amherst* neighbors. In addition, Dickinson formed warm epistolary friendships,* as she did with the Hollands, and conducted erotically* charged exchanges with her sister-in-law Susan as well as—until their marriages—some of her or Sue's schoolmates (Jane Humphrey,* Abiah Root,* Catherine Scott Turner Anthon*). The epistolary medium also allowed Dickinson to discuss and disseminate her poetic work. She enclosed poems in her correspondences with eminent men of letters, writers, and editors, including Higginson, Helen Hunt Jackson,* Samuel Bowles,* and Thomas Niles*; Susan Gilbert provided critical feedback on several versions of P216 ("Safe in their Alabaster Chambers," L238).*

Dickinson's letters have primarily been studied as biographical* documents, with critical interest concentrating on elucidating the poet's relationship to individual correspondents and identifying the recipient of the so-called Master* letters (three unfinished and most likely unmailed drafts written between 1858 and 1861, suggestive of an intense and unrequited erotic relationship). In addition, the "poetic" quality of Dickinson's correspondence has sparked stylistic comparisons with her poems. The frequency of dashes,* internal rhymes,* passages of metrical prose, the integration of verse lines into letters, and the practice of mailing poems as letters all tend to challenge a strict generic differentiation between Dickinson's poetry and her prose. Moreover, she enclosed newspaper clippings and cutouts from the family Bible* and other books; drew cartoons* and animated passages of letters (turning o's into faces that look back at the reader); and included dried flowers* as means of communication. Such intertextual aspects illustrate the playful and artistic nature of Dickinson's correspondence and suggest how her letters can contribute to a more diversified and complementary understanding of the poet. (*See*: *New Poems*)

RECOMMENDED: *Letters*; Suzanne Juhasz, "Reading Emily Dickinson's Letters"; Cristanne Miller, "A Letter Is a Joy of Earth: Dickinson's Communication with the

World''; Agnieszka Salska, "Dickinson's Letters"; Martha Nell Smith, "The Poet as Cartoonist."

Marietta Messmer

LETTERS OF EMILY DICKINSON (1894)   Known as the first edition of Dickinson's letters,* this was a publication in two volumes, collected and edited by Mabel Loomis Todd,* following the publication of *Poems** in 1890 and 1891. It was also the first book issued about Dickinson, prepared at the request and with the authorization of Austin* and Lavinia Dickinson.*

The book was divided into thirteen chapters, listing Dickinson's letters in sets of various addressees. While Todd abandoned the idea of general chronology, she nevertheless kept to the temporal succession of letters within each set. The letters were preceded by the general introduction, in which Todd described eloquently the circumstances leading to their collection and publication, as well as by short introductions to each chapter. A good many passages regarded as either insignificant or embarrassing to relatives then living were left out at the request of both Austin and Lavinia Dickinson. These were listed in Appendix I of the second edition published in 1931.

Since Dickinson did not keep a diary, the letters were the only prose available to her readers; their publication offered a rare insight into her private world, thus providing a much needed context for her poems.

RECOMMENDED: *AB*; Mabel Loomis Todd, Introduction to *Letters of Emily Dickinson* (1931).

Danuta Piestrzyńska

LETTERS OF EMILY DICKINSON (1931)   The 1931 edition of *Letters of Emily Dickinson*, published by Harper and Brothers, was edited by Mabel Loomis Todd.* Todd, who had been the mistress of Dickinson's brother Austin,* was entrusted by him and Lavinia* to edit and publish the poet's letters in 1894. Todd claimed in her 1931 preface that her motivation in issuing another edition of the letters was that the "Emily legend" had been "revamped" to suit the taste of the times, and "Emily herself [had] all but vanished in the process." Todd may have been moved to these statements by Martha Dickinson Bianchi's* 1924 publication of *The Life and Letters of Emily Dickinson.**

It is true that Bianchi created an image of her aunt as something of a 1920s flapper, claiming, for example, that Dickinson "had quite a spicy affair with a young law student in her father's office" (*LL* 70). However, Todd's motivation may have been not simply to correct such concocted images of the poet but also to assert her own primacy as Dickinson's literary representative over Bianchi, who was, after all, the daughter of Todd's despised rival, Susan Gilbert Dickinson.* Like the 1894 edition, Todd's later volume expunges all references to Susan, though Susan was (as Bianchi's book makes clear) one of Emily's most important correspondents.

Todd's claim that it was Lavinia and Austin who requested "that I omit certain passages, references to a relative then living" is a patent attempt to mask her animosity toward her rival. Though Susan had died in 1913, Todd asserted in this collection that she would "continue to respect their wishes."

The second edition of Dickinson's letters contains all material from the 1894 collection, restores a number of deleted passages, and adds several new letters. Todd makes no pretense to thoroughness in this volume, stating in her preface, "Several other groups of unpublished letters now known to exist are not included." The value of Todd's publication has been superseded by Thomas Johnson's* more complete three-volume collection, *The Letters of Emily Dickinson.**

RECOMMENDED: *Letters*; *LL*; *Letters of Emily Dickinson*. Ed. Mabel Loomis Todd (1931).

Lillian Faderman

THE LETTERS OF EMILY DICKINSON (1958)   This three-volume collection, edited by Thomas H. Johnson* and Theodora Ward* and published by Harvard University Press, was the first complete edition of all the letters* and prose fragments that the poet was known to have written at the time. It was intended as a companion to the 1955 variorum edition of *The Poems of Emily Dickinson** and the interpretive biography* issued in the same year. The editors' goal in preparing this collection was to round out the total picture of the poet's life and work, thus bringing to conclusion the task of editing the entire canon of Dickinson's poetry* and prose begun in 1950. Since very few letters have been discovered subsequently, this publication maintains its status as the most authoritative edition of Dickinson's prose.

The nearly 1,200 letters and prose fragments are numbered and arranged chronologically, with the earliest known letter dated April 1842. Johnson grouped the letters in sections by years, each section introduced with summary background information. Following each letter is information on the manuscript location, publication history, particulars regarding enclosures or addressing, and explanatory notes regarding the content and recipient of the letter. Most of the letters derive from Dickinson autographs, while about a quarter come from transcripts or previous publications. Approximately a hundred letters were published for the first time in this book.

Johnson's introduction stresses the importance of the letters as (auto)-biographical information that portrays Dickinson's artistic and psychic development. He views the letters both as "self-portraits" (xxi) and as a "conveyance for her poems" (xx). He attributes their value as literature to their artistic, poetic qualities as well as their expression of the poet's "acute sensitivity" and "unique personality" (xv, xxi). The fact that letters were the mature Dickinson's "sole means of escape from a self-elected incarceration" heightens their urgent poignancy (xix). These volumes include photographs of Dickinson family and friends as well as facsimiles of letters showing the fascinating evolution of the poet's handwriting* style and presentation. A few surviving letters Dickinson received from recognized literary figures such as Helen Hunt Jackson,* Thomas

W. Higginson,* and editor Thomas Niles* are published in the collection to offer responses to the poet's work by her contemporaries.

Unlike earlier collections by Mabel Loomis Todd* and Martha Dickinson Bianchi,* all Dickinson autographs appear here in their entirety, with previously omitted passages restored. Johnson makes note of passages that were erased or apparently altered by persons other than the author. In these volumes and in the 1986 *Emily Dickinson: Selected Letters* drawn from them, Johnson contributed greatly toward making the poetry, prose, and life of Emily Dickinson available to a wider audience relatively free of the familial and adversarial editorial hindrances that marked earlier editions of letters and poems. (*See*: Editorial Scholarship; *New Poems*)

RECOMMENDED: *Letters*; *Emily Dickinson: Selected Letters*; David Higgins, *Portrait of Emily Dickinson: The Poet and Her Prose*; Sarah Wider, "Corresponding Worlds: The Art of Emily Dickinson's Letters."

Carolyn Kemp

THE LIFE AND LETTERS OF EMILY DICKINSON (1924)   Various factions vied for the rights to publish the work and the authority to define the life of Emily Dickinson after her death. The publication of *The Life and Letters of Emily Dickinson* is no exception. Edited by the poet's niece, Martha Dickinson Bianchi,* it combines excerpts from Dickinson's letters* with Bianchi's reminiscences about her aunt's life, emphasizing familial intimacies. The first section, "Life," is an anecdotal biography* drawn, Bianchi said in her foreword, "from family letters hitherto withheld, deathless recollections, and many sentences overheard from her [Dickinson's] own lips." The second part, "Letters," chronologically arranges selections of material Dickinson sent to correspondents.

Bianchi's editing of *The Life and Letters* followed Mabel Loomis Todd's* *Letters* (1894),* which had effectively excised the presence of Susan Gilbert Dickinson,* Emily Dickinson's sister-in-law, Bianchi's mother, and the wife of Todd's lover—William Austin Dickinson.* Bianchi maintained that she published this book to establish "Sister Sue's" importance in Dickinson's life and to her work. She also claimed her desire to "submit Emily's work to the final judgment of others, and her life, as far as it concerns others, as a beautiful inspiration" (103).

However, Bianchi, believing in her own supreme and unquestionable authority as the only living heir of Dickinson's property, felt no compunction against taking from Todd's work without crediting her source. She used excerpts from letters not in her possession that had appeared previously only in Todd's edition. For these and other editorial licenses, Morris Schappes accused her of shoddy scholarship. He found numerous inaccuracies in Bianchi's reproduction of texts and mistakes in dates, contentions that subsequent scholars have supported. Likewise, biographer Richard Sewall finds little new or of value in Bianchi's work. Yet *The Life and Letters* remains significant for restoring Susan's presence, although Lillian Faderman follows Rebecca Patterson in arguing that Bianchi's editing was designed to hide the homosocial nature of the poet's friendship with her sister-in-law. Overall, the intimate glimpse Bianchi provided into family life, despite its obvious bias, offers useful information, as Jay Leyda's documentary approach demonstrated. (*See*: Editorial Scholarship; Lesbian Approaches)

RECOMMENDED: *Life*; *LL*; *Years*; Lillian Faderman, "Emily Dickinson's Letters to Sue Gilbert"; Elizabeth Horan, "Mabel Loomis Todd, Martha Dickinson Bianchi, and the Spoils of the Dickinson Legacy"; Morris U. Schappes, "Errors in Mrs. Bianchi's Edition of Emily Dickinson's *Letters*."

Jeanne E. Clark

LIND, JENNY The Swedish singer's two-year tour of the United States—"a combination of craftsmanship and hype unequaled in American musical history, orchestrated by none other than P. T. Barnum" (Reynolds)—drew the Dickinson family (except for Austin*) to Northampton on the night of 3 July 1851. L46, to Austin, records the poet's reaction: "take some notes from her 'Echo'—the Bird* sounds from the 'Bird Song' and some of her curious trills, and I'd rather have a Yankee." Except for a demonstration at Boston's* Chinese Museum in 1846 and a band concert in 1853 (L13, 118), this was the only performance by a professional musician that Dickinson was ever to hear. (*See*: Hymns; Music; Musical Settings)

RECOMMENDED: *Letters*; David S. Reynolds. *Walt Whitman's America: A Cultural Biography*. New York: Knopf, 1995.

Jonathan Morse

LINGUISTIC AND STYLISTIC APPROACHES The complexities of Dickinson's language and style have encouraged a variety of critical responses. Early reviewers dismissed her abbreviated syntax* and neologisms as simply ungrammatical; later critics justified them as stylistic deviations. Dickinson's seemingly arbitrary capitalization* and use of the dash,* the existence of textual variants,* and the question of line breaks all compound the problem of rendering Dickinson's poetry into print and of providing an adequate textual analysis. Linguistic and stylistic analyses have followed both the development of twentieth-century theoretical approaches and the progression of Dickinson editions.* T. H. Johnson's* *The Poems of Emily Dickinson*,* for example, with its regularization of the poetic line, suggests a closer approximation to the hymn* meters of Dickinson's Congregational* upbringing than R. W. Franklin's* *The Manuscript Books of Emily Dickinson*ion* would indicate. Whereas traditional grammarians judge Dickinson's poetry ungrammatical, transformational-generative approaches have noted her feature violations and the multirecoverable deletions of her structural style, and cognitive linguists have argued for a conceptual metaphor* approach and the recognition of a grammar of discourse. Scholars have identified Dickinson's adroit manipulation of Latinate and Germanic vocabulary, the subtleties of her irregular rhymes,* the ambiguities* of her elliptical style, the taut conciseness of the syntactic and phonetic pun, and her indeterminacy of reference. Dickinson's eclectic mix of colloquialism* and formality, her experiments with poetic form and meter, her idiosyncratic uses of morphology and the subjunctive mood distinguish her from other nineteenth-century poets, placing her firmly in the ranks of modernist poets. (*See*: Compression; Disjunction; Metonymy; Oxymoron; Slantness)

RECOMMENDED: Sirkka Heiskanen-Mäkelä, *In Quest of Truth: Observations on the Development of Emily Dickinson's Poetic Dialectic*; Brita Lindberg-Seyersted, *The Voice of the Poet: Aspects of Style in the Poetry of Emily Dickinson*; Cristanne Miller, *Emily Dickinson: A Poet's Grammar*; David Porter, *Dickinson: The Modern Idiom*; Judy Jo Small, *Positive as Sound: Emily Dickinson's Rhyme.*

Margaret Freeman

LONGFELLOW, HENRY WADSWORTH (1807–1882)   His popular, public, and uniquely profitable career shows by contrast why Dickinson's diametrically different writing was solitary and private. Coupled with Romantic,* Victorian, and even Puritan* values, Longfellow's traditional poetics and (easily satirized) sentimental* morality appealed then to worldwide audiences—including the Dickinson household—but now seem dated, while her "Verse is alive" (L260) and timeless.

Longfellow helped Americans define themselves as literary artists, readers, and citizens of an emerging nation. As professor of modern languages (Bowdoin, 1829–1835; Harvard, 1836–1854), he taught Spanish, Italian, French, German, and Scandinavian. Translating Dante's *Divine Comedy* and other works, he introduced European values and literature to new generations even while establishing American literary traditions. More popular than Tennyson and Browning,* he is the only American honored in Westminster Abbey's Poets' Corner.

Longfellow's most memorable works added mythic, legendary dimensions to a past lamented for its paucity of actual and symbolic ruins. Narrative poems like the immensely successful *Song of Hiawatha* (1855), *The Courtship of Miles Standish* (1858), and *Tales of a Wayside Inn* (1863) and *Evangeline: A Tale of Acadie* (1847) romanticize historical situations and characters. Dickinson's family owned, and she read, many of these. Although Emerson's* ideas reverberate more strongly through Dickinson's work, Capps finds that she relied more often on Longfellow's words. For example, she quoted Miles Standish's " 'John Alden' " and " 'Priscilla' " (P357), signifying Longfellow's poetic characters rather than mere historical figures.

Longfellow's prose also influenced Dickinson. Sewall's *Life* repeats Higginson's story that Austin* smuggled Longfellow's 1848 novel *Kavanagh* "into the house despite Mr. Dickinson" (163). Several Dickinson letters* and poems refer to *Kavanagh*'s overall romanticism, its sentimental poet Adolphus Hawkins, and its schoolgirls Alice and Cecilia, whose mutual love resembled that of young Dickinson and Susan Gilbert.* An 1851 letter to Sue (L56) contrasts poetry* and pedestrian prose, mentioning Longfellow's *Golden Legend* sitting majestically among grammar texts. Loosely based on Faust stories, *Legend* was the first published section of *Christus, a Mystery*, the trilogy Longfellow considered his greatest work. Admiring if not venerating Longfellow in her youth, Dickinson later became more sure of her own poetry and his flaws. Dickinson read and wrote about her era's most popular poet, but simultaneously rebelled—in her life and art—against traditions he epitomized. (*See*: Books and Reading)

RECOMMENDED: Jack L. Capps, *Emily Dickinson's Reading 1836–1886*; Richard Sewall, ''Emily Dickinson's Books and Reading''; Cecil B. Williams. *Henry Wadsworth Longfellow*. Boston: Twayne, 1964.

Susan Kurjiaka

LOOMIS, EBEN JENKS and MARY WILDER   Mabel Todd's* parents visited the Homestead* in 1884. Dickinson's notes during and after their call indicate that she felt kindly toward the Loomises but shrank from a personal interview. Sharing his son-in-law's scientific* interests (though without David Todd's academic credentials), Loomis served from 1850 to 1900 as a clerk in the Nautical Almanac, Washington, D.C. The Loomises raised their daughter in a lively social and cultural atmosphere. Later, when their granddaughter Millicent Todd (Bingham)* spent extended vacations with them in Washington,* Mrs. Loomis expressed disapproval of Mabel's relationship with Austin Dickinson.*

RECOMMENDED: *Letters*; *Life*; Polly Longsworth, *Austin and Mabel: The Amherst Affair and Love Letters of Austin Dickinson and Mabel Loomis Todd* and ''Millicent Todd Bingham (1880–1968).'' *Emily Dickinson International Society Bulletin* 6, 2 (1994): 4+.

Jane Donahue Eberwein

LORD, OTIS PHILLIPS (1812–1884)   was for years the closest friend of Edward Dickinson.* Prior to his appointment to the Massachusetts Supreme Court (1875–1882), he was a lawyer, a politician, and a judge in the Superior Court. He also was in love with Emily Dickinson, and she was in love with him. Many questions have been raised about Dickinson's romantic attachments. Otis Phillips Lord, however, is the only known male recipient of her passionate love* letters. Only fifteen of her letters* survive from their voluminous correspondence, some only fragments, some heavily censored (probably by Austin*).

Lord graduated from Amherst College* in 1832, when Dickinson was only two years old. He helped found the first college literary society. After earning a law degree from Harvard, he practiced law and held political office as state representative in 1847–1848 and 1853–1854 (speaker in 1854) and state senator in 1849. About the time of his appointment to the Superior Court (1859), he became a close friend of Edward Dickinson and a welcomed visitor in the Dickinson home. The two men shared conservative political views and were leaders of the Whig* Party.

When Emily Dickinson and Lord started corresponding is unknown. The earliest surviving letters, dated about 1878 by Thomas Johnson,* are love letters apparently written only months after the 10 December 1877 death of Lord's wife of thirty-four years, Elizabeth Farley. Several writers suggest that strong attraction existed before Mrs. Lord's death (Guthrie, Wolff, Walsh). Dickinson's claim, "I have done with guises" (L559), supports this theory. Walsh argues at some length that Lord was the intended recipient of the "Master"* letters and that Lord was Dickinson's frequent private visitor when she was in Boston* for eye treatment (1864–1865).

Guthrie's valuable article on Dickinson and Lord points out that the poem "The Judge is like the Owl" (P699), dated 1863, is "overtly flirtatious" and "makes an implicit claim to the intellectual respect and the romantic prerogatives due to a grown woman" (31). Guthrie's analysis of Dickinson's rhetorical* patterns in poems and letters written for Lord offers many insights into the playfulness of their passion. He points out that their facetious stances and legal* metaphors* often deal with serious issues: potential marriage,* extent of sexual activity she would grant before marriage, her possible relocation to his home in Salem (27). How close they came to marriage is unknown. Emily Dickinson's attachments to her home,* the opposition of Abbie Farley* (Lord's niece and heir), and the illnesses both suffered in the 1880s were all hindrances. Lord died suddenly in 1884, two years before Dickinson. At her funeral,* wrote T. W. Higginson,* Lavinia* put in the coffin "two heliotropes . . . 'to take to Judge Lord' " (*Years* 2:475). (*See*: Lovers)

RECOMMENDED: *Life*; *Years*; James Guthrie, "Law, Property and Provincialism in Dickinson's Poems and Letters to Judge Otis Phillips Lord"; John Evangelist Walsh, *The Hidden Life of Emily Dickinson*; Cynthia Griffin Wolff, *Emily Dickinson*.

Ronald Palosaari

LOVE, AS SUBJECT   Dickinson's assurance "That Love is all there is, / Is all we know of Love" (P1765) suggests both the infinite scope of "love" and its ultimate unknowability. Dickinson's poems resist attempts to categorize references to love or to assign specific addressees. Instead, they open up wider readings of both the love poems and the kinds of love they represent. Dickinson crossed boundaries of religion,* gender, and family along with poetry's own traditions.

Research on nineteenth-century women* poets reveals that "love" was a sanctioned subject with expected metaphors,* images, and addressees: love poems were to be heterosexual, lyrical,* romantic, often spiritually uplifting, and full of nature's* more delicate wonders. However, Dickinson did not write within these conventions, despite early and systematic editorial* efforts to mold public perceptions of her work.

Early editors arranged Dickinson's poetry by traditional subjects such as "love," "nature,"* and "life" and assigned such titles as "Renunciation"* or "The Wife." The "love" sections collected poems that seemingly addressed a male subject. When a few of Dickinson's most erotic* poems (many of them arguably written to a woman) were included, they appeared in "sanitized" versions, as Martha Nell Smith points out with regard to "Wild Nights" (P249). Punctuation was also normalized, as in "I'm 'wife'—I've finished that—" (P199). When early editions remove the quotation marks around "wife," the ironic tone disappears, obscuring the way Dickinson interrogates the wifely role and, indeed, the very love associated with it.

Love is no small, containable thing in Dickinson's poetry; it is, instead, "all." As such, love occupies many different categories, and Dickinson presented multiple kinds of love, often in the same poem: love as myth; forbidden love; love as paradise; and love as Calvary. In Dickinson's treatment of love, it often becomes both the vehicle and tenor of metaphor.* For example, in P491 love as Jesus* becomes the vehicle for expressing the possibility of immortality* as well as the even more far-reaching imperative to live. Love becomes multiple, operating as part of the larger metaphor of life's infinitude. Love cannot finally be fixed in Dickinson's poetry. Not an end in itself, love is a tool—and Poem is its name—something that can be transmuted for excavating, explaining, and embracing the world. (*See*: Dash; Lovers; Marriage; Poetry)

RECOMMENDED: Martha Nell Smith, *Rowing in Eden: Rereading Emily Dickinson*; Cheryl Walker, *The Nightingale's Burden: Women Poets and American Culture before 1900*.

Jeanne E. Clark

LOVERS, SPECULATION ABOUT   Dickinson's reclusive habits and personal idiosyncrasies spurred Amherst gossip about possible lovers such as George Gould,* whose courtship was supposedly forbidden by her father, and John Langdon Dudley,* who married her cousin. Other men from Amherst College* and her father's law office have been mentioned as possible suitors, notably Benjamin Newton.* Publication of Dickinson's writing intensified speculation, as readers discovered eroticism* in many poems, in the three letter drafts addressed to "Master,"* and in letters to certain women.

Lavinia Dickinson* dismissed notions that her sister's life had been devastated by romantic tragedy, asserting simply that Emily "was always watching for the rewarding person to come" (Bingham, *Home* 413). Yet Martha Dickinson Bianchi* responded to public curiosity by relating in *The Life and Letters of Emily Dickinson* a romantic story she claimed to have heard from her mother, Susan,* about Emily's passion for a married man and her noble renunciation* of that love. Whether Bianchi believed this story about Charles Wadsworth* or told it to deflect attention from other attachments she knew about but preferred to conceal remains a question. Other candidates for Dickinson's "Master" include Samuel Bowles,* editor and family friend, and Otis Phillips Lord,* to whom she may have become engaged long after writing most of her "love" poems. Persuasive but mutually contradictory cases have been made for all these possible lovers, and it may be that the poet experienced a succession of infatuations rather than one life-transforming passion. What these stories share, however, is assumption of the poet's longing for some forbidden person. These are sentimental* tales of secret devotion, earthly sacrifice, hope for heavenly* union, and resignation to a life whose adventures could only be internal. It is the story Barton St. Armand distills as Dickinson's private myth of "the Romance of Daisy* and Phoebus."

Editorial* developments have fostered conjecture. Mabel Loomis Todd* and T. W. Higginson* featured a category of "Love" poems in each of their collections. Thomas Johnson's* chronologically arranged editions with biographically* oriented annotation encouraged readers to search out a hidden autobiographical narrative while pointing attention toward both Newton and Wadsworth. More recently, R. W. Franklin's* reconstruction of the poems' original fascicle* arrangements prompted Ruth Miller to argue for Bowles as the object of Dickinson's devotion, while leading William Shurr to elaborate a story of hidden commitment to Wadsworth. Biographers, however, have failed to support the romantic narratives readers tend to draw from Dickinson's lyrics,* which may well reflect the poet's tendency to adopt the voice* of some "supposed person" (L268) rather than engage in confessional writing.

RECOMMENDED: Jane Donahue Eberwein, *Dickinson: Strategies of Limitation*; Judith Farr, *The Passion of Emily Dickinson*; Ruth Miller, *The Poetry of Emily Dickinson*; Barton Levi St. Armand, *Emily Dickinson and Her Culture: The Soul's Society*; William Shurr, *The Marriage of Emily Dickinson*.

Jane Donahue Eberwein

LYMAN, JOSEPH BARDWELL (1829–1872)   was a school friend of Austin Dickinson* who became Emily's friend and correspondent and one of Lavinia's* suitors. Although most of his correspondence with the Dickinsons has been lost, Lyman copied parts of seven letters from Emily Dickinson and quoted from two others. In letters to the woman he married, he made many references to the family, especially Lavinia and Emily.

Curiously, as Sewall demonstrates in *The Lyman Letters*, Lyman's appreciation of Emily was consistently stronger than for Lavinia, whom he had once considered marrying. Lyman was inspired by Emily Dickinson's character and intellect but puzzled by some of her attitudes. He predicted in 1858 that she would never marry but added that she would be a "most true & devoted" wife if she did (*Ly* 67). In an 1858 letter, he referred to Emily Dickinson as a superior housekeeper to Vinnie, although the younger sister eventually took charge of practical household matters. Later, Lyman and his wife collaborated on a book, *The Philosophy of Housekeeping*, which suggests his interest in such skills.

In a sketch of Emily Dickinson found among his papers after his death, Lyman refers to her "very firm strong little hands absolutely under control of the brain" and her "mouth made for nothing & used for nothing but uttering choice speech, rare thoughts, glittering, starry misty figures, winged words" (*Ly* 69). His emphasis in his letters on Vinnie's sweet kisses serves to contrast his views of these sisters. Even so, as late as May 1854, three years after he left New England and a sorrowing Vinnie for the South, Lyman wrote to his mother that he was still considering marriage to Vinnie. Lyman's surviving letters are valuable as well for their descriptions of the Dickinson household. Although some later critics proffer negative views of the Dickinsons' home life, Lyman, who spent long visits with that family, referred to "that charming second home of mine in Amherst"* (*Ly* 1). He clearly approved of all members of that household, although it remains unclear if he ever visited them again.

In 1858, Lyman, by then a law school graduate and resident of New Orleans, married Laura Baker of Nashville, Tennessee. His successful legal career was interrupted by the Civil War,* during which he served as a noncombatant in the Confederate army. Afterward, he moved to New York to become a journalist. He died at age forty-three, survived by his widow and six of their seven children.
RECOMMENDED: *Life*; *Ly*.

Ronald Palosaari

LYON, MARY (1797–1849)   Mary Lyon founded Mount Holyoke Female Seminary* in 1837, ten years before Emily Dickinson enrolled as a student. Lyon's vision of an institution devoted to the higher education of women was a lifelong one. After a hardscrabble youth in Buckland, Massachusetts, she traveled across rural New England pursuing an education, including one year (1818) spent studying at Amherst Academy.* In her early twenties she began a series of teaching assignments and boarded during the summer of 1823 with Orra and Edward Hitchcock,* whereupon the three became devoted friends. While teaching at Ipswich Female Seminary, Lyon along with mentor Zilpah Grant proposed founding a new institution, a New England Female Seminary, but was disappointed in good men's fear of "greatness in women." In 1833 Lyon spent the summer traveling and studying educational reform. She returned to New England committed to the idea of a seminary and spent a large part of the next several years almost single-handedly raising funds. The seminary opened in South Hadley, Massachusetts, with eighty young women. Edward Hitchcock continued to be a stalwart supporter and served as lecturer in anatomy in the 1840s. An energetic (some would say driven) woman, Lyon believed women were entirely capable of pursuing higher education and, indeed, were entitled to it. Creating an environment conducive to introspection and privacy was critical to Lyon, who was forty before she lived in a room by herself. In fact, her initial architectural recommendation for the seminary building included individual rooms for each student, arguing that solitude was essential to "most serious persons of reflection." Lyon also was a woman bent on religious* questioning. She did not join the church until she was twenty-six, older than most of her contemporaries. A central tenet in Lyon's life was that individuals expressed God's will by exploring their talents to the fullest. Higher education for women, in this view, made spiritual sense to her: women were making use of God's* gifts to them by expanding and then using their minds in the world.

The intersection of Mary Lyon's life with Emily Dickinson's came just as the poet's literary life was beginning and Lyon's life as an educational pioneer was ending. Dickinson's year at the seminary marked the virtual end of the poet's apprenticeship; soon she would begin writing poems. For Mary Lyon, 1847–1848 was her last full year of teaching. Early in 1849, suffering from influenza and erysipelas, she died at the seminary. (*See*: Revivalism; Women's Culture)

RECOMMENDED: Anne Edmonds. *A Memory Book: Mount Holyoke College, 1837–1987*. South Hadley, MA: Mount Holyoke College, 1988; Arthur C. Cole. *A Hundred Years of Mount Holyoke College*. New Haven: Yale University Press, 1940; Elizabeth Green. *Mary Lyon and Mount Holyoke: Opening the Gates*. Hanover, NH: University Press of New England, 1979.

Martha Ackmann

LYRIC   Dickinson's poetry* fulfills many generic expectations of the lyric. Traditionally, the lyric is a brief poem that emphasizes subjective and interior reality as opposed to the negotiation between personal and social reality. Spatial and temporal categories are often blurred or ambiguous (as in "I heard a Fly buzz—when I died—," P465,* where the speaker's disclosure works in tension with her dying). The lyric is generally nonnarrative and offers itself without causal necessity; it lives, for the most part, within the present, within a moment rescued from the flow of time. It suggests intimacy and vital presence. The subject of the lyric often deals with the desire for some kind of transcendence coupled with a consciousness of mortality; many of Dickinson's poems reveal a grappling with the lyric concerns of temporality and transience.

John Stuart Mill described the action of lyric poetry as speech in overheard soliloquy. The locus of the overheard becomes accentuated in Dickinson because of the intensely private nature of her work. In nineteenth-century America, the lyric was a marginalized genre: it did not answer to the needs of epic grandeur and social affirmation. The lyric was perceived as a "female" practice. Through her use of the compressed space of the lyric, Dickinson was able to infuse the diminutive with her ample, large-scale meditations. The lyric—domestic, private, contained—allowed her to focus on the particulars of her own experience without the order and coherence demanded by the novel, essay, or epic poem.

Her primary lyric predecessors were Keats* and the Brownings,* but Dickinson's lyric mode was mostly self-taught; she did not abide by traditional theories. Her versifying is widely regarded as highly innovative, her unconventional lyricism described self-reflexively in her often-quoted response to Thomas Wentworth Higginson*: "You think my gait 'spasmodic'—I am in danger—Sir—/ You think me 'uncontrolled'—I have no Tribunal" (L265). The "spasmodic" and "uncontrolled" aspects of her work underscore the carefulness of her craft and her controlled deviation from traditional forms. Her meters, usually iambic or trochaic, derive almost exclusively from English hymnology.* Edward Dickinson* owned copies of Isaac Watt's* *Christian Psalmody* and *The Psalms,*

Hymns, and Spiritual Songs, works that influenced Dickinson in her training in prosody. One of her major contributions to the lyric, however, lies in her re-fashioning of the hymn and her combining of different metrical patterns, often for ironic effect. Her syntax* rarely conforms to the quatrain when she uses it, and her rhymes* are often inexact. She frequently turns to imperfect and "feminine" rhymes and varies the rhyming pattern in a given poem. If her "Business" is "Circumference"* (L268), she uses her limitations to exact various freedoms. In light of Franklin's* edition of her *Manuscript Books*,* grouping of her poems into sequences suggests alternate readings of the boundaries of her lyrics and the lyric poem in general. Her notation of meaning through various kinds of dashes,* along with the word* variants she so often provides, contributes to a multiplicity of readings of her poems. (*See*: Music; Women's Culture)

RECOMMENDED: Sharon Cameron, *Lyric Time: Dickinson and the Limits of Genre* and *Choosing Not Choosing: Dickinson's Fascicles*; Margaret Dickie, *Lyric Contingencies: Emily Dickinson and Wallace Stevens*; Gudrun M. Grabher, "Dickinson's Lyrical Self"; Thomas H. Johnson, "The Poet and the Muse: Poetry as Art."

Susan McCabe

M

MACK, DAVID (1778–1854)   Born at Middlefield, Massachusetts, and educated at Windsor Hill Academy, he was prominent at Middlefield as merchant, town clerk, representative at the General Court, and general of militia. He was a major of militia at the Boston* alert in 1814. In 1834 Mack moved to Amherst,* where he served as trustee of both Amherst Academy* and Amherst College.* At Amherst he was a merchant, a deacon at the First Church* (Congregational*), and a justice of the peace. Mack married three times, and his six children were born at Middlefield. He bought the Dickinson Homestead* after Samuel Fowler Dickinson's* financial collapse, occupying the west side of the house from 1834 to 1840 while Edward Dickinson's* young family lived in the east side.

RECOMMENDED: *Years*; James Avery Smith. *Families of Amherst, Massachusetts.* Unpublished typescript, 1984, and *Records of West Cemetery at Amherst, Massachusetts.* Amherst: Official records of the town engineer.

James Avery Smith

MACK, REBECCA (1814–1899)   The daughter of Ephraim Robins, she was born Rebecca A. Robins, also known as Henrietta. She married Samuel Ely Mack in 1841. They had three daughters, born at Amherst* in 1842, 1843, and 1845. They were living in Amherst as late as October 1847, perhaps in the Dickinson Homestead* with her father-in-law, General David Mack.* By 1848 they had relocated to Cincinnati, Ohio, and were living at Covington, Kentucky, in 1850. Rebecca Mack, whose hospitality to Amherst young people prompted the poet to recall her as "the Angel of Childhood" (L939), was one of the few visitors Dickinson welcomed in 1884.

RECOMMENDED: *Letters*; James Avery Smith. *Families of Amherst, Massachusetts.* Unpublished typescript, 1984.

James Avery Smith

MADNESS, AS SUBJECT   Perhaps no poems in Dickinson's works elicit more varied responses than those treating madness as their theme. Many critics have focused on establishing biographical* proof of psychotic episodes in Dickinson's life in response to the vivid and accurate descriptions of the stages of mental breakdown in such poems as "I felt a Funeral, in my Brain" (P280),* "I felt a Cleaving in my Mind—" (P937), and "It was not Death, for I stood up" (P510). Many of these poems describe a shattering psychological* moment for the speaker; the descent into madness is variously likened to a ritualistic New England funeral* (P280), imagined as the complete rupture of coherent, linear thought (P937) and portrayed as a chilling episode of catatonic immobility (P510, 1046). The parameters within which scholars began to search for biographical counterparts to these poems were initiated by Thomas Higginson's* description of Dickinson as a "partially cracked" poet (L481n) and were fortified both by her own reference to "a terror . . . I could tell to none" (L261) and by her increasing reclusivity and eccentricity in later life. However, many recent critics view the powerful language of these poems as testimony to her ability to overcome such debilitating moments; as Adrienne Rich states, "she had to possess the courage to enter, through language, states which most people deny or veil with silence" (176).

Dickinson handled the theme of madness with a lighter touch in a few other poems: "I think I was enchanted" (P593); "Much Madness is divinest Sense—" (P435)*; and "A little Madness in the Spring" (P1333). (*See*: Gothicism)

RECOMMENDED: John Cody, *After Great Pain: The Inner Life of Emily Dickinson*; Paul J. Ferlazzo, *Emily Dickinson*; Sandra M. Gilbert, and Susan Gubar, *The Madwoman in the Attic*; Adrienne Rich, "Vesuvius at Home: The Power of Emily Dickinson."

Mary Jane Leach-Rudawski

MAHER, MARGARET (1841–1924)   was employed at the Homestead* as maid-of-all-work for thirty years (1869–1899). Called "Maggie" by the Dickinsons, she was a skilled nurse who tended to family members in both houses. Emily Dickinson stored her fascicles* in Maher's trunk and may have asked her to burn these upon the poet's death. Maher was assigned to do general housework for Mabel Loomis Todd* while Todd prepared the first volume of poems for press. Dickinson's daguerreotype*—disliked and discarded by the family—was saved by Margaret Maher and made available by her when the first volume of poems went to press. Maher's brother-in-law was Dickinson employee Thomas Kelley.* Maher, her three siblings, and their parents emigrated by the mid-1850s from Parish Killusty, County Tipperary, Ireland. Prior to her Homestead tenure, she was employed by the Boltwood family. She never married and is buried with her brother Thomas and their parents in St. Mary's Cemetery, Northampton.

RECOMMENDED: Jay Leyda, "Miss Emily's Maggie"; Aífe Murray, "Kitchen Table Poetics: Maid Margaret Maher and Her Poet Emily Dickinson."

Aífe Murray

MANUSCRIPT BOOKS   Handsomely boxed and crisply printed by Harvard's Belknap Press, Ralph W. Franklin's* two-volume 1981 edition of *The Manuscript Books of Emily Dickinson* provided revolutionary new ways to read most of the poems in facsimiles of the pages on which Dickinson presented herself to the world. His volumes include an introduction that explains his means of reconstituting so many hitherto dispersed pages of books and sets, complete indexes for cross-referencing poems, and eleven separate appendixes (of various sequences, missing sheets, repeated poems, and other oddities). They primarily reproduce all forty extant "fascicles"* and all fifteen "sets" or preliminary groupings. To restore what had been disarranged by Dickinson's earliest editors, Franklin used Mabel Loomis Todd's* lists, the dating of Theodora Ward* and Thomas H. Johnson,* and "primary" evidence from the "manuscripts themselves," including handwriting,* paper markings, and stains. Readers who compare manuscript poems with those in the Johnson variorum will note significant differences in lineation, but the greater value lies in seeing poems placed by the poet herself in proximate positions.

Franklin's 1967 *Editing* and his articles prepared readers for a revisioning of the poet's work; his lengthy introduction and subsequent essay helped to shape readers' interpretations of Dickinson's craftsmanship. On one hand, he argued that she may have stopped binding groupings in 1864 after six years of the practice because she had "survived the crisis and drive" of personal need; on the other hand, he said that with her survival from whatever crisis* claimed her, her sense of vocation "to leave an organized legacy for the world" declined (*Manuscript Books* xii). Although the latter comment suggests Franklin's acceptance of Dickinson as a self-conscious editor, he later asserted that "the fascicles are, simply, poems copied onto sheets of stationery and, without elaboration, bound together" and that "they were private documents copied for her own uses" that "served Dickinson as her workshop" ("The Dickinson Fascicles" 4, 16–17).

Franklin's position notwithstanding, *The Manuscript Books* have become the means by which scholars have found significant patterns within the fascicles. Although reading them cannot substitute for seeing the delicate papers in the Houghton vaults, *The Manuscript Books* remain the most accessible unmediated way to read Dickinson in her own context. (*See*: Editorial Scholarship)

RECOMMENDED: Ralph W. Franklin, "The Dickinson Packet 14—and 20, 10, and 26," *The Editing of Emily Dickinson: A Reconsideration, The Manuscript Books of Emily Dickinson*, and "The Emily Dickinson Fascicles."

Eleanor Elson Heginbotham

MARRIAGE   The celibate Dickinson portrayed marriage as a state of communion with the other—person or God*—resembling the eternal bliss of heaven.* As Cynthia Griffin Wolff demonstrates in her critical biography,* the voice* of the wife or bride* is one that Dickinson adopted to describe her experience authoritatively. The wife's voice explains what it is like to suffer and love.* While the actual lives of married women often appeared to Dickinson depressing and enervating, and these observations found their way into her poems, for the most part she represented marriage itself as the ideal union and role. Marriage is a state of being that involves a true merging of identity.

Some poems suggest a mystic marriage between the speaker and an unidentified human lover,* and at other times the mate seems to be God or Death* or both. Frequently, Dickinson made the common metaphysical equation between union of lovers and union with God, but she took the unusual perspective of having the human relationship outshine the divine.

P246 is a thumbnail sketch of a blissful human union. Although the word "marriage" is not used, the marriage relationship is implied, and the heavenly merges with the human. "Forever at His side to walk—" the speaker proposes; she will be "Blood of His Blood—/ Two lives—One Being—now—." After such a life, she concludes heaven will be simply a matter of unmediated understanding: "Just finding out—what puzzled us—/ Without the lexicon!"

From the other side of the equation, P817 compares marriage with union with God, this time with heavenly marriage as tenor and earthly marriage as vehicle of the metaphor.* "Given in Marriage unto Thee / Oh thou Celestial Host—" the speaker begins, and concludes that only this Marriage, not being earthly, will endure: "Other Betrothal shall dissolve—."

Other poems examine the nature of the sacrament of marriage. P1072 compares the extreme state of the speaker who is "The Wife—without the Sign!" with the condition of ordinary women, married conventionally to ordinary men. This theme is picked up again in P1737, in which the suggestion to "Rearrange a 'Wife's' affection" is answered with a resounding negative: "When they dislocate my Brain!" The unacknowledged spouse has learned more of love and pain from her position than traditional "Wifehood" could teach. To be "wife" was death, rebirth, and renewal, the marriage with God a mirror image of the fullest human union.

RECOMMENDED: *Poems*; Jerome Loving, *Emily Dickinson: The Poet on the Second Story*; Cynthia Griffin Wolff, *Emily Dickinson.*

Janet McCann

MARTHA, MATTIE   Bianchi, Martha Dickinson

MARVELL, IK (Donald Grant Mitchell, 1822–1908)   is chiefly remembered as the author of the best-selling volumes *Reveries of a Bachelor* (1850) and its sequel, *Dream Life* (1851). During the early 1850s, *Reveries* was particularly popular with Emily Dickinson, her brother and sister, and her friend and future sister-in-law Susan Gilbert.* Mitchell's books may best be described as loosely organized sketchbooks on such topics as time and eternity, marriage* versus the solitary life, religious faith* and organized religion,* past and present, the satisfactions of home* and family, letter* writing, and dreams. Marvell's main character, the Bachelor-Dreamer, blends romantic,* sentimental* musings on abstract topics with witty, often wickedly subversive comments critical of contemporary society and its values. Dickinson's enthusiasm for *Reveries* caused her to name her dog Carlo* after the Bachelor's dog. She provided some indication of this book's impact on her own writing in an 1851 letter to Susan: "If you were only here—perhaps we would have a 'Reverie' after the form of 'Ik Marvel,' indeed I do not know why it would'nt be just as charming as of that lonely Bachelor, smoking his cigar. . . . We will be willing to die Susie—when such as *he* have gone, for there will be none to interpret these lives of our's" (L56). The influence of Marvell's style is most evident in its effect on both the style and tone of Dickinson's personal correspondence. (*See*: Books and Reading)

RECOMMENDED: *Letters*; Wayne R. Kime, *Donald G. Mitchell*. Boston: Twayne, 1985; Ik Marvell, *Dream Life: A Fable of the Seasons*. New York: C. Scribner, 1851, and *Reveries of a Bachelor: Or, a Book of the Heart*. New York: Baker and Scribner, 1850.

Stephanie A. Tingley

THE MASCULINE ROLE   is equated with dominance, agency, and spatial freedom in Dickinson's poetry. Like the "man of noon" in her letter to Susan Gilbert* (L93), for whom flowers* yearn, even though he "scathes" them, the masculine figure represented in her poetry* inspires female desire despite his threatening the female body* with death, violation, and spatial constriction. This image of potent masculinity's ability to control the woman emotionally and physically articulates Dickinson's anxiety about nineteenth-century gender roles that allot agency to the man and demand willing compliance from the woman. "He put the Belt around my life—" (P273) exemplifies the frightening constriction the masculine can impose on the woman's life.

Yet power available in poetic inspiration is also posited as masculine. In "To my small Hearth His fire came—" (P638), the infiltration of a masculine presence into the home* leads to ecstasy and the breakdown of restrictive boundaries. This transcendence initiated by the masculine is commensurate with a key goal of Dickinson's poetics: the attainment of "Possibility" (P657). By casting the poetic muse as masculine and occasionally speaking herself in male voices* such as boy or earl, Dickinson both conveyed her conception of the powerful, active force driving creativity and disguised her own claim to such power.

Poetic ambiguity* is heightened with the masculine role. "He fumbles at your Soul" (P315) is a paradigmatic example of the ambiguity infused into the masculine since the "He" can be read variously as death,* God,* or a male lover.* Dickinson structures this nexus of associations with the masculine—as destructive threat, as creative promise, and as elusive signifier—in order to create deep resonances with this figure and to promote a number of diverse responses to it. (*See*: Feminist Approaches; Women's Culture)

RECOMMENDED: Joanne A. Dobson, " 'Oh, Susie, it is dangerous': Emily Dickinson and the Archetype of the Masculine"; Adrienne Rich, "Vesuvius at Home: The Power of Emily Dickinson."

H. Jordan Landry

A MASQUE OF POETS   was published by Roberts Brothers* in 1878 as the fourteenth (and final) volume in its first "No Name Series" of books. This popular series (which included thirty-five novels and two volumes of verse between 1877 and 1887) was a marketing bonanza: all works were published anonymously, and part of the fun was guessing who the author of each title might be. *A Masque of Poets* is one of the most famous volumes in the series because of the many important writers who contributed its seventy-one poems: Amos Bronson and Louisa May Alcott; Thomas Bailey Aldrich*; Ellery Channing; Mary Mapes Dodge; James T. Fields; Richard Watson Gilder; Helen Hunt Jackson*; Sidney Lanier; George Parsons Lathrop (who edited the volume); Rose Hawthorne Lathrop; James Russell Lowell; Louise Chandler Moulton; Christina Rossetti; Bayard Taylor; Celia Thaxter; Henry David Thoreau*; and J. T. Trowbridge. The book sold well: printings of 1,500 and 500 copies were done in November 1878, and another 90 in April 1894, plus an additional 500 copies in the "Red Line Edition" (so called because the text on each page is within a single-rule red border) in November 1878.

Dickinson's "Success" (P67),* later collected in *Poems* (1890),* appeared on p. 174. The poem was contributed to the volume by Helen Hunt Jackson, who had been trying for two years to get Dickinson to send in some verses herself. In the guessing game that followed publication* of the book, Dickinson's poem was most often assumed to be the work of Ralph Waldo Emerson.*

RECOMMENDED: Aubrey L. Starke, "An Omnibus of Poets." *Colophon: A Quarterly for Book Lovers*, part 16 (Mar. 1934): unpaged; Madeleine B. Stern and Daniel Shealy. "The No Name Series." *Studies in the American Renaissance* (1991): 375–402.

Joel Myerson

MASSACHUSETTS AGRICULTURAL COLLEGE   A land grant institution founded in 1865 following the passage of the Morrill Act, it is now the University of Massachusetts. After much debate and competition from other towns, Amherst* was chosen as site of the college, located north of the town center. It was the first institution in New England to claim a much-contested focus on the education of farmers. Edward Dickinson* was an early supporter.

In its early days, prominent Amherst College* professors lectured at the college, including Dr. Edward Hitchcock, Jr., L. Clark Seelye, Ebenezer Snell, and B. K. Emerson, all of whom were connected to the Dickinson family. Sculptor

Daniel Chester French,* son of Henry Flagg French, first president of the college, was also an acquaintance of the family. (*See*: Greenough)
RECOMMENDED: *Letters*; *Life*; L. B. Caswell. *Brief History of the Massachusetts Agricultural College*. Springfield, MA: F. A. Bassette, 1917.

Erika Scheurer

"MASTER"   Dickinson wrote three long, anguished love* letters* and at least seven poems to someone she called "Master." The identity of Master has been the subject of intense speculation, the two most frequently cited candidates being Samuel Bowles,* whom Dickinson clearly admired, and Rev. Charles Wadsworth,* whom she called "My closest earthly friend" and "my shepherd from 'Little Girl'hood" (L765, 766). The case for Wadsworth, detailed by William Shurr, Vivian Pollak, and Benjamin Lease, rests upon clues that Master was a married, distant, religious authority; Dickinson's frequent references to "Calvary," which was the name of Wadsworth's church; remarks in the poet's correspondence with Wadsworth's longtime intimate, James D. Clark* of Northampton, and James' brother Charles* indicating an intimacy between pastor and poet; and correspondences between upheavals in Dickinson's emotional life and crises* in Wadsworth's life. The case for Bowles, elaborated by Judith Farr and Ruth Miller, relies upon parallels between the Master letters and the letters and poems Dickinson sent to Bowles. Farr demonstrates the Master letters' indebtedness to Charlotte Brontë's* *Jane Eyre* and their resemblance to letters Brontë wrote to Constantin Heger (whom she called Master), and she compares Bowles to Rochester, citing his magnetic attractiveness for women and his powerful personality.

The first letter ("I am ill," L187), written in ink with a few penciled deletions, probably dates from the spring of 1858. It apparently responds to a letter received from Master complaining both that he had been ill and that he did not understand her "flowers,"* presumably her poems. There has been some disagreement about the dating of the two subsequent letters, written in the "Daisy"* voice. Based on an analysis of changes in Dickinson's handwriting,* R. W. Franklin* suggests that the letter most desperate in tone ("Oh, did I offend it—" L248), which Johnson* places third and dates in early 1862, is actually the second, written in early 1861. In this letter, written in heavily edited pencil, Daisy abjectly worries that she has offended Master, longs for a task to accomplish for him, begs him to teach her what she has done wrong, fantasizes about kneeling at his knee, begs him to punish her rather than banish her, pleads that he take her into his life, and promises that she will be his "best little girl." The remaining letter ("If you saw a bullet hit a Bird," L233) has been dated to the first half of 1861, possibly in the summer; it is in ink, heavily corrected in pencil. In a series of rapidly changing voices*—melodramatic, factual, childish,* reminiscent—the letter openly confesses the speaker's passion. Daisy remembers that she had asked Master for "Redemption" but had forgotten "the Redemption in the Redeemed," and she wishes that she could have "the

Queen's place" with Master at night, or that they could walk together in the meadow. The close of the letter urges him to come to New England, to Amherst,* that summer, so that they might look upon each other's face. *The Master Letters of Emily Dickinson*, ed. R. W. Franklin, discusses the revised dating and includes loose facsimiles of these letters.

Some critics disparage what they see as disproportionate attention paid to Master, or they claim that Master was a woman. Commenting upon "If you saw a bullet hit a Bird," Martha Nell Smith notes that in the phrase "if I had the Beard on my cheek—like you," the last two words are penciled in above the line, so the original thought could easily have been addressed to a woman. Susan Howe has suggested in *My Emily Dickinson* that the Master letters are prose exercises playing with allusions to Dickens'* *David Copperfield*, in which Steerforth refers to "Master" Davy as "Daisy" and in which "Little Em'ly" writes Davy disjointed, pleading letters after eloping with Steerforth. (*See*: Lovers; Lesbian Approaches)

RECOMMENDED: Judith Farr, *The Passion of Emily Dickinson*; Benjamin Lease, *Emily Dickinson's Readings of Men and Books*; Vivian R. Pollak, *Dickinson: The Anxiety of Gender*; William Shurr, *The Marriage of Emily Dickinson: A Study of the Fascicles*; Martha Nell Smith, *Rowing in Eden: Rereading Emily Dickinson*.

Marianne Noble

MATHER, RICHARD HENRY (1834–1890)   Graduate of Amherst College* in 1857 and a teacher at Williston Seminary from 1857 to 1858, Mather studied at Berlin University in Germany in 1858–1859 before earning his M.A. at Amherst College in 1860. From 1859 to 1890, he taught Greek and German there. He and his family resided on the south side of Main Street just across from the Evergreens.* His pride was the Mather Art Collection at the college. His first wife was Lizzie Carmichael of Geneva, New York. They married in 1858, and she died in 1877. In 1881, he married Ellen A. Mather of Cleveland, Ohio, who in 1895 was still living as a widow in Amherst in the house on Main Street. Dickinson exchanged neighborly notes and remembrances with this household, including Lizzie Mather's mother, Elizabeth Carmichael.*

RECOMMENDED: Charles F. Carpenter and Edward W. Morehouse. *The History of the Town of Amherst*. Amherst, MA: Carpenter and Morehouse, 1896; *Amherst College Biographical Record*. Amherst, MA, 1963; *Beers Atlas of Hampshire County*. 1873; James Avery Smith. *Records of West Cemetery at Amherst, Massachusetts*. Amherst, MA: unpublished typescript, 1984; *Amherst Directory*. 1895.

James Avery Smith

METAPHOR   is the dominant trope of Dickinson's figurative language, and Dickinson's poetic language is predominantly figurative. To speak of the forms and functions of metaphor in Dickinson's poetry is a way of speaking about her poetry* writ large. To read Dickinson is to encounter the mystery, precision, and transformative power of these phrases: they are responsible for much of what thrills and challenges in her poetry.

Metaphor means, in Greek, to carry across: it is a figure of speech in which a word or phrase that ordinarily designates one thing is used to designate another. Metaphor says that x is y ("My life had stood—a Loaded Gun"*) or that x acts "y-ily" (My Life had stood), or that something is an xy ("a Vesuvian face" [P754]). This carrying across or yoking causes a new state or condition or entity to come into being, one not literally true. The relation of x to y creates z, so that x(life)/y(gun) produces a drama, a narrative transpiring within the sudden new world of z.

Metaphoric transfer may be understood as an implicit comparison, evoking analogy: my life is like a loaded gun. Or as one thing conceived as representing another, evoking symbolism: my life represented by a loaded gun. Metaphor is one of the four master tropes (the others being metonymy,* synecdoche, and irony). Metaphor has kinship with synecdoche—presenting a part for a whole or the whole for the part (gun for life). But it is also like metonymy—one thing used to substitute for another with which it is closely associated (gun for life? an association surprising yet revelatory).

Commentators on Dickinson often place the focus of their analysis on one or another of these aspects of metaphor—analogical, synecdochal, metonymic— because to understand the processes of metaphor making aids us in understanding her thought. But there is considerable overlap in these definitions, for Dickinson's metaphors operate by establishing relations between like and like, like and different; they make substitutions across lines of contiguity and distinctiveness. They bring into prominence subordinate rather than ordinate qualities (what aspects of volcanoes are facial?); they link abstract (life) with concrete (gun); they embed one metaphoric transfer within another: "And do I smile, such cordial light / Upon the Valley glow—/ It is as a Vesuvian face." Thus it helps to look not only at what they bring into relation but at the relationality that is their primary activity. The yoking of elements with very little verbal explanation of how these things become contiguous or equivalent (metaphors formed through parataxis and hypotaxis, as Cristanne Miller demonstrates) is characteristic. The dash* that creates the loaded gun metaphor could signal the copula "is," or a comma could suggest an appositional phrase.

The result is analogy or equivalence where none had been before: similarity, contiguity out of difference, distinction. When a life is said to be a loaded gun, its subsequent actions have a significance that would not exist if the writer were speaking literally of lives *or* of guns. The meaning of the concluding lines, "For I have but the power to kill, / Without—the power to die—" can be calculated only by understanding power, murder, and death* in terms of the life/gun gestalt. Thus while Dickinson's metaphors contribute significantly to the oft-observed compression* and omission* that make her poetry so elusive, at the same time, they continually make new meanings, virtually out of thin air. (*See*: Ambiguity; Syntax)

RECOMMENDED: Roland Hagenbüchle, "Precision and Indeterminacy in the Poetry of Emily Dickinson"; Suzanne Juhasz, "Adventures in the World of the Symbolic: Emily Dickinson and Metaphor" and *The Undiscovered Continent: Emily Dickinson and the Space of the Mind*; Cristanne Miller, *Emily Dickinson: A Poet's Grammar*; Robert Weisbuch, *Emily Dickinson's Poetry*.

Suzanne Juhasz

METONYMY Dickinson's abundant use of this trope of contiguity forms microcosms of her poetic enterprise. In metonymies of modifier for modified, effect for cause, tool for its function, concrete for abstract, and container for contained, she explores the grand by means of the common, the ambiguous* within the certain, and the intimate within the public. For example, in the metonymy "the rare Ear" (P842), by substituting the physical body* part for its function, she anticipates a dialectical relationship—"Ear" for a listener. Metonymy can either enact a poetic compression* or create an explosion of the poetic subject. Critics have posited many theoretical interpretations of Dickinson's poetics based on their understanding of her use of metonymy as either a compression or expansion.

Dickinson's metonymies enact a poetic compression by means of containing multiple referents. In the metonymy of modified for modifier—"How the old Mountains drip with Sunset" (P291)—all the possible attributes of closing day are compressed into the word "Sunset." In a metonymy of effect for cause—"The Morning after Wo—" (P364), the causes of woe become possible referents for the effect itself. Hagenbüchle notes that "the 'cause' must be inferred from the 'effect,'" because a specific referent for any particular metonymic trope is not supplied in the poem. He sees this as metonymy's inherent indeterminacy. It necessitates a loss of the actual referent because it is "accompanied by a concurrent weakening of the organizing center of the mind"; "this power of imagination is dearly paid for by the . . . loss of the actual object" (36–37).

Miller claims that the indeterminacy created by metonymic compression is related to Dickinson's position as a nineteenth-century woman* poet. Because metonymy allows "veiled or disguised statement" that might otherwise be censored from public discourse, the compression of metonymy is of the suppressed within the publicly acknowledged (111).

The indeterminacy of Dickinson's metonymies also functions as an expansion, for rather than concealing or denying meaning, metonymy creates new relationships in and through language. Stonum views this as an element of her affective poetics, which "stimulate responses in the reader (rather) than . . . instruct the reader's imagination" (90). The indeterminacy created by metonymy may "allude to an experience . . . that remains veiled throughout the poem." With her "affective metonymy," Dickinson seeks to "arouse fascination" and create a "rhetorical solicitation of her own readers."

Dickie explores the relational use of metonymic expansion by focusing on the contiguity of language itself. Through metonymies—"In tender—solemn Alphabet" (P263)—language becomes an object of touch rather than sight; language "gets printed and translates invisible plights into tangible form. Hands hold onto such keepsakes" (52). The trope of metonymy reveals Dickinson's "interest in the power of language to bind together, to strengthen links between the self* and the other" and is thus Dickinson's "effort to retain a hold on this world."

Metonymic expansion not only functions between poetic voice* and reader but also within language itself. Dickinson's most striking metonymic usage magnifies relationships within a poetic event by means of tropes that make a singular poetic subject multiple. In the metonymies of P341* ("The Nerves sit ceremonious . . . / The stiff Heart . . ."), in which the sites of emotion are used for the emotions themselves, Dickinson makes her subject multiple by giving each site agency; relations are enacted within a single self.* In the synesthesia of P465* ("With Blue—uncertain stumbling Buzz—"), Dickinson expands her subject by using metonymies of modifier for the modified; each attribute of the "Fly" is in a distinct relation to the "I" of the poem. Metonymic expansion is about enacting relationships both in, and by means of, language. (*See*: Metaphor; Reader-Response Approaches; Rhetorical Approaches)

RECOMMENDED: Margaret Dickie, *Lyric Contingencies: Emily Dickinson and Wallace Stevens*, ch. 3; Roland Hagenbüchle, "Precision and Indeterminacy in the Poetry of Emily Dickinson"; Cristanne Miller, *Emily Dickinson: A Poet's Grammar*; Gary Lee Stonum, *The Dickinson Sublime*.

Lynne EFM Spear

MONTAGUE, GEORGE and SARAH   The eldest brother in the Montague family, George (1804–1893) left Amherst* shortly after graduating from the academy. He returned in 1866 with his second wife, Sarah Seelye, and served as the treasurer of the Massachusetts Agricultural College* from 1867 to 1884. A few pieces of the frequent correspondence from Dickinson to her cousin George still survive in copy. Sarah Montague was present at the Homestead* at the time of Dickinson's death.

RECOMMENDED: *Life*; *Years*.

Kathryn Balteff

MONTAGUE, HARRIET and ZEBINA   Although Dickinson is said to have had continual correspondence with these favorite cousins, no surviving letters have been found. Brother and sister enjoyed entertaining in the Montague home located across from the two Dickinson residences on Main Street. Both were seen as oddities in Amherst's* social circles, however, and they seldom ventured out. Zebina became paralyzed in the 1830s and was confined to their home, while Harriet was an outcast from the First Church* community due to an unspecified sin committed in 1845. Like Dickinson, neither Harriet nor Zebina ever married. Zebina frequently penned both historical and comedic articles for the local press. It is noteworthy that Zebina's closest friend outside Amherst was former classmate Otis Phillips Lord,* Dickinson's lover* in later years.

RECOMMENDED: *Life*; *Years*.

Kathryn Balteff

MOUNT HOLYOKE FEMALE SEMINARY   Emily Dickinson attended Mount Holyoke in 1847–1848 after completing her studies at Amherst Academy.* At sixteen she was among the youngest students, entering the first of three classes or academic levels and later being promoted to the middle. During her year, 235 students were enrolled; an equal number were denied admission. As with most colleges of the day, the curriculum placed heavy emphasis on science.* Dickinson shared a room with her cousin, Emily Norcross,* and found the environment generally pleasing.

The seminary, like many colleges, conducted revivals,* and students were identified in relation to their profession of faith*: those who had professed, those who hoped to, and those who were "no hopers." Dickinson was among eighty "no hopers" when she entered; by the end of the term in August only twenty-nine remained, including the poet.

Dickinson most seriously considered professing her faith in January 1848, when she joined sixteen other students who felt an "uncommon anxiety" and met with Mary Lyon* in the principal's room. The next day the poet wrote a letter* with a significant postscript: "There is a great deal of religious interest here and many are flocking to the ark of safety. I have not yet given up to the claims of Christ, but trust I am not entirely thoughtless on so important & serious a subject" (L20). At that point Dickinson made a decision about a profession of faith that influenced the rest of her life. She chose to continue questioning.

Dickinson did not return to the seminary for a second year. Scholars have speculated that homesickness, a dull curriculum, or an oppressive religious* atmosphere influenced her decision. Looking at Dickinson within the context of other students at the seminary is revealing. Out of 115 students who entered with Dickinson, 23 returned. Prevailing cultural attitudes argued that women did not need higher education. Since Dickinson did not appear to be headed for teaching or missionary work (the two occupations Mount Holyoke alumnae usually pursued) and did not financially need to earn an independent living, another year at the seminary may have seemed needless. No matter why Dickinson left, Mount Holyoke's most significant legacy for her was its belief that women had a right and an obligation to pursue an intellectual life. (*See*: Jesus; Women's Culture)

RECOMMENDED: Christopher Benfey, "Emily Dickinson's Mount Holyoke"; Sydney McLean, "Emily Dickinson at Mount Holyoke"; Anna Mary Wells, "Emily Dickinson, 1849."

Martha Ackmann

MRS. BANGS' BOARDINGHOUSE   Dickinson stayed at this Cambridge-port boardinghouse in 1864 and 1865 while being treated for her eye disorder. Deborah Bangs and her daughter ran the establishment, which was located one mile from Harvard College. Bangs may have been familiar to the Dickinsons, as her late husband once served, as did Edward Dickinson,* as representative to the General Court. Dickinson's primary reason for staying at Mrs. Bangs', however, was that her cousins, Louisa* and Frances Norcross,* also resided there. Boardinghouse life required that Dickinson forgo considerable privacy. In her letters* the poet occasionally called her Cambridge* residence a "Wilderness," "Prison," and "Jail" (L293, 290). Yet she also called Mrs. Bangs and her daughter "very kind" (L293) and admitted she found friends there. Dickinson's two stays marked the longest time she spent as an adult away from home.* After she returned from Mrs. Bangs' Boardinghouse, Dickinson never again left Amherst. (*See*: Byron)

RECOMMENDED: Martha Ackmann, "The Matrilineage of Emily Dickinson"; Mark Peel, "On the Margins: Lodgers and Boarders in Boston, 1860–1900." *The Journal of American History* 72 (1986): 813–34; Hiroko Uno, *Emily Dickinson Visits Boston.*

Martha Ackmann

"Much Madness is divinest Sense—" **(P435)**   dates from about 1862 and appears in Fascicle* 29 (Appendix A). It was first published in *Poems* (1890)* with one alteration: "prevails" for "prevail" in l. 5. This poem's social satire on the "Majority" (whose numerousness is emphasized by the plural "prevail") attacks its lack of discernment about individual behavior, as well as the fear of difference that leads it to define disagreement as insanity. The opening may be parallel to Melville's "man's insanity is heaven's sense" (*Moby-Dick*). The "discerning Eye" that sees through society's "Madness"* is certainly the poet's and, implicitly, belongs to certain other naysayers as well. (*See*: Gothicism; Isolation; Psychological Approaches; Vision)

RECOMMENDED: Ronald Wallace, *God Be with the Clown: Humor in American Poetry.* Columbia: University of Missouri Press, 1984: 102–3.

Haskell Springer

MUSIC, AS SUBJECT   Dickinson began musical training at a young age, and it became an integral part of her life and poetry.* Her interest in music was first noticed by her Aunt Lavinia Norcross* at the age of two and one half. She later began piano and singing lessons that continued through her year at Mount Holyoke,* where she practiced piano daily and sang in at least one of the academy's two choirs. Although Dickinson possessed an extensive personal music portfolio, she did not restrict her playing to printed melodies. She was known to improvise on the piano late into the night; and, as Sewall observes, Dickinson's "fondness for music . . . was to develop into a considerable talent" (*Life* 326). The full impact of music on her life can be seen only by examining her letters* and poems, which are laden with references to her fellowship with, and interpretations of, music and melody. There are numerous poems mentioning music in general as well as bird*songs and specific melodies of instruments such as cornets and bells. For Dickinson, music was vital and alive and a vehicle that could rise above the circuit world and beyond circumference.* (*See*: Hymns; Musical Settings; "The Yellow Rose of Texas")

RECOMMENDED: *Life*; Carlton Lowenberg, *Musicians Wrestle Everywhere: Emily Dickinson and Music*; Judy Jo Small, *Positive as Sound: Emily Dickinson's Rhyme*.

Kathryn M. Balteff

MUSICAL SETTINGS   There are more than 1,400 musical settings of Emily Dickinson's words by over 250 composers, mostly American, of approximately 675 of her poems and letters.* These settings include solo songs; duets; choral works for women, men, and mixed choruses; and orchestral works with singers, with narrations, and even with ballet music.

The two most frequently set poems are "I'm Nobody! Who are you?" (P288) and "Wild Nights—Wild Nights!" (P249)—at least twenty-nine settings each! Other poems with more than twenty known settings are "Because I could not stop for Death—" (P712),* "I never saw a Moor—" (P1052), "I taste a liquor never brewed—" (P214),* "If I can stop one Heart from breaking" (P919), and "There's a certain Slant of light" (P258).*

As a form of interpretation, musical settings are as valid as verbal discussion. Even settings that may violate one's sense of the poem's truth nonetheless offer the listener a unique experience that, in turn, opens some new possibilities to the reader. Three settings of "I taste a liquor never brewed—" provide a good example. Arthur Farwell wrote one between 1938 and 1941 that is a strophic setting with fairly regular meter but an angular and somewhat disjunct melody; the piano part is texturally thick. Gordon Getty, composer of the ambitious song cycle *The White Election* (1982), set this poem to a melody resembling an early American drinking song. It has two melodically identical verses and simple chordal harmonies supported by a minimal piano part. A third setting by John Duke (1975) is through-composed and reels drunkenly through a series of keys and musical ideas with a feeling of being drunk on life.

The first musical setting appeared ten years after Dickinson's death; Etta Parker's "Have you got a Brook in your little heart" (P136) was published in 1896, followed the next year by Clarence Dickinson's (no relation) setting of six Dickinson poems, including "Have you got a Brook" and "I taste a liquor never brewed—." During the first half of the twentieth century, a trickle of new musical settings included music by Ernest Bacon (over forty-five songs), Arthur Farwell (thirty-nine songs), Vivian Fine (fourteen settings), and Elliott Carter.

Since the publication of Aaron Copland's *Twelve Poems of Emily Dickinson* in 1951, probably the best-known settings of her poetry, there has been a torrential flood of composition that continues today. Some are settings of a single poem, and others are loosely related song groups, while still other song cycles attempt to illustrate passages in Dickinson's life. Composers include Robert Baksa (fourteen songs); Samuel Barber (one choral setting of "Let down the Bars, Oh Death—," P1065); Roger Bourland (three books of madrigals for women's choruses); Robert Chauls (*Of Great Men and Death*, a cycle for tenor and piano); Gloria Coates (two song cycles and more); Sharon Davis; John Duke (ten songs); Gordon Getty (*The White Election*); Juliana Hall (fourteen songs); John Harbison; Martin Kalmanoff (twenty songs); Otto Luening; Henry Mollicone; Alice Parker; Thomas Pasatieri; George Perle; Vincent Persichetti; Daniel Pinkham; Ned Rorem; Paul Schwartz; Elam Sprenkle; Leo Smit (*The Ecstatic Pilgrimage: Five Song-Cycles for Mezzo-Soprano and Piano*, eighty songs written between 1988 and 1989); Clare Shore; Louise Talma; Robert Starer; and George Walker.

Almost every combination of voices and instrumentation has been used by composers to interpret or reflect on Emily Dickinson's meaning. As might be expected, most settings are for solo female voice (soprano or mezzo-soprano) and piano. There are also settings for baritones and basses, but not many for tenor. There are settings for any of these voices with small ensembles such as string quartets, brass quintets (Elam Sprenkle), woodwind ensembles (Thomas Pasatieri), voice with solo instruments and piano, and voice with electronic tape. Varied choral settings also have been written for women's, men's, children's, and mixed choruses, some performed a cappella and others accompanied by a single instrument, a small ensemble, or a full orchestra.

There have also been several musical theater pieces based on Emily Dickinson's poetry that used parts of poems and letters. Hunter Johnson wrote the music for Martha Graham's ballet *Letter to the World*, which incorporated a narrator among the dancers. *Rendezvous of Light*, a very effective "music theater drama" for soprano, clarinet, cello, and piano, composed by Mark Lanz Weiser and first presented in 1994, uses text from letters as well as original monologue material written by Peter Krask.

Availability of this enormous body of musical settings varies; while much has been published, a great deal is still in manuscript in the hands of the composers. Recordings of the Copland songs and some others are extant commercially, and there are archival recordings of first performances, again through the composers. (*See*: Dance Responses; Dramatic Representations; Fiction; Hymns; Music; Visual Arts)

RECOMMENDED: Michael Hovland, *Musical Settings of American Poetry: A Bib-*

liography. Westport, CT: Greenwood Press, 1986; Carlton Lowenberg, *Musicians Wrestle Everywhere: Emily Dickinson and Music*; Kristina Melcher, ed. *Schwann Opus: The Reference Guide to Classical Music*. Santa Fe, NM: annual editions; Maryann Sewell, "Rendezvous of Light."

Maryann Sewell

"My Life had stood—a Loaded Gun—" (P754)   is perhaps the most discussed and debated of all Dickinson poems. The poem lends itself to such extensive discourse because it epitomizes her technique of the "omitted center."* What is this poem about? Adrienne Rich sees P754 as "the central poem in understanding Dickinson." However, the poem is essentially hermetic, and it would be more plausible to suggest that it functions as a kind of Rorschach test: all interpretations of it may be seen to reveal more about the interpreter's interests than the undebatable "truth" of Dickinson's meaning.

Rich herself suggests that it is a poem about ambition. Sharon Cameron sees it as a poem in which fury has grown larger than life. Lillian Faderman argues that it is a poem that illustrates Dickinson's ambivalence toward heterosexuality. Joanne Dobson reads it as a poem about the explosive potential of speech. But, in fact, it is impossible to construe with certainty any interpretation of "My Life had stood—a Loaded Gun."

To make observations about the nature of the poem's imagery, its tropes of woods and hunters and guns, is far less problematic. Several critics, such as Vivian Pollak and Ellin Ringler-Henderson, agree that P754 is "the most American poem Dickinson ever wrote," a sort of "Natty Bumppo" poem replete with nineteenth-century American novelistic images—forests, hunting partners, the protector and the defended.

It is also interesting to note the choices Thomas Johnson* made in construing the poem's text from the variants—choices that most anthologies accept. Johnson cites four variant words in the poem: "the—" for "in," line 5; "low" for "Deep," line 16; "harm" for "stir," line 18; and "art" for "power," line 23. Johnson's choices of "stir" over "harm" and "power" over "art" render the foes of the Master* somewhat less clearly deserving of the vengeance of the gun's "Yellow Eye" or "emphatic Thumb" and the speaker's deadliness in her service of the Master more out of her control. The action of the poem is thus even more sinister in Johnson's rendition than it might be were other choices of variants made.

"My Life had stood—a Loaded Gun—" was written about 1863 and placed by Dickinson in Fascicle* 34 (Appendix A). In 1929, it was first published in the *London Mercury* and then included in *Further Poems of Emily Dickinson*,* edited by Martha Dickinson Bianchi* and Alfred Leete Hampson.* (*See*: Ambiguity; Metaphor; Textual Variants)

RECOMMENDED: Paula Bennett, *My Life a Loaded Gun: Female Creativity and Feminist Poetics*; Sharon Cameron, "A Loaded Gun: Dickinson and the Dialectic of

Rage''; John Cody, *After Great Pain: The Inner Life of Emily Dickinson*; Joanne Dobson, Lillian Faderman, and Ellin Ringler-Henderson, "Discussions of 'My Life had stood— a Loaded Gun' ''; Adrienne Rich, "Vesuvius at Home: The Power of Emily Dickinson.''

Lillian Faderman

N

NATURE Dickinson won recognition as a nature poet even in her lifetime, as newspaper editors demonstrated by titling* poems "October," "Sunset," and "The Snake"; and all three editions of the 1890s included sections on "Nature." Readers felt comfortable with subject matter typically chosen by other nineteenth-century women* poets and by Romantics* generally. Dickinson's poems treat flowers,* birds,* insects,* animals, seasons,* and times of day, usually from a domestic* perspective reflecting observations in the garden* and home* conservatory or from the Homestead* windows. She included bats, moles, and fossils in those observations, however, as well as conventionally poetic creatures, and let her imagination summon such exotic natural phenomena as tigers, volcanoes, and prairies.

Among cultural influences contributing to Dickinson's interest in nature was the women's tradition of botanical drawing that encouraged detailed representation of familiar specimens. Another was science* education at Amherst Academy* and Mount Holyoke,* under the influence of Edward Hitchcock* and his geological discoveries. Christian lessons Hitchcock drew from the sciences also taught Dickinson to think of nature as complementing biblical* revelation.

Dickinson, who referred to her poems as "flowers," often sent verse or prose celebrations of nature to friends. Beyond that, she sometimes employed poetry* to distill the essence of one or another natural being, as in the series of bird poems she exchanged with Helen Hunt Jackson.* What may be most distinctive in her treatment of nature, however, is a tendency to focus on transitional points in natural cycles: sunrises, a particular slant of late afternoon winter light, or Indian summer. She wrote of buried bulbs with their promise of renewal, of butterflies bursting from cocoons, but also of flowers yielding to frost. Thus poems classified by editors as dealing with "Nature" can generally be read equally well as speculations on "Time and Eternity." In using nature imagery

to probe death's* mysteries and the prospect of immortality,* however, Dickinson avoided easy assurances, either the sentimentally* romantic ones of feminine verse or the Christian ones she had been taught to expect. Nature, to her,
remained a "mystery," a "haunted house," and a force that was both exquisitely dear and radically strange (P1400). (*See*: Critical Reception; Women's
Culture)

RECOMMENDED: *Life*; Paula Bennett, *Emily Dickinson: Woman Poet*; Jane Donahue
Eberwein, *Dickinson: Strategies of Limitation*; Jean Mudge, *Emily Dickinson and the
Image of Home*; Cynthia Griffin Wolff, *Emily Dickinson*.

Jane Donahue Eberwein

NED   Dickinson, Edward (nephew)

NEW CRITICAL APPROACHES   John Crowe Ransom, whose call for an
"ontological" critic in his essay "The New Criticism" (1941) would give the
movement its name, was only one among its leading practitioners to write important essays on Dickinson's poetry. The American New Critics' innovative
methodology of interpretation and evaluation, which emphasized close examination of the text with little regard for the biographical* or ideological circumstances in which it was produced, found a useful experimental ground in a
formally complex poetry relatively untouched by a significant critical history.

The new explicative techniques pioneered by Ransom, Tate, Blackmur, and
others uncovered an Eliotian, or at the very least protomodernist, Dickinson
whose syntactic* duplicities and ironic reserve veiled a thinker of considerable
eschatological sophistication. In so doing, the New Critics surpassed a previous
cultish criticism informed and inspired by speculation about the poet's biography
and established the formal evaluative criteria that would assure Dickinson's later
canonization as a key figure in American Romanticism.*

Allen Tate's essay "Emily Dickinson" also provides an effective demonstration that the New Criticism, as applied by its most skilled practitioners, was far
from rigidly ahistorical. Arguing that Dickinson's poetry mediates a larger societal friction caused by an emergent Transcendentalism* confronting a declining Puritanism,* Tate acknowledges that literature is always a social and cultural
activity; thus he provides a model for later culture-based readings of the poet.
Indeed, more generally, the New Critics establish the basic critical parameters
within which Dickinson's poetry is still read. Charles Anderson's groundbreaking book, the first detailed study of the poetry and an exemplification of applied
New Criticism, provides touchstone readings of individual poems with which
later critical studies establish qualified agreement or necessary divergence.

But the poet and the New Criticism also establish a more complex dialectical
relation: each provides an effective analysis of the other's formal weaknesses.
The accessibility of Dickinson's poems to New Critical aesthetics also helps
definitively expose the limitations of those aesthetics, foregrounding the necessary exclusions and repressions that facilitate any rigorously text-based close

reading. The most obvious analytical blindness is the New Critics' inability to confront adequately the significance of Dickinson's gender. This elision directly impacts their reception of the poet insofar as essays that critique "biographical" readings are often themselves notable for a condescension contoured, however unconsciously, by biographical circumstance. Remarks like Blackmur's "[I]t sometimes seems as if in her work a cat came at us speaking English" (180) or Tate's observation that our "moral image" of the poet is that of "a dominating spinster whose every sweetness must have been formidable" (201) demonstrate the ease with which New Critical gallantry toward "Miss Dickinson" so often deteriorated into a revelatory sexism. (*See*: Feminist Approaches; Historicism; Reader-Response)

RECOMMENDED: Charles R. Anderson, *Emily Dickinson's Poetry: Stairway of Surprise*; R. P. Blackmur, "Emily Dickinson's Notation" and "Emily Dickinson: Notes on Prejudice and Fact"; John Crowe Ransom, "Emily Dickinson: A Poet Restored"; Allen Tate, "Emily Dickinson."

Robert McClure Smith

NEWMAN, ANNA DODGE (1846–1887)   was one of five children who became wards of Dickinson's father after the deaths of their parents in 1852. The youngest two girls, Anna and Clarissa,* lived at the Homestead* with the Dickinsons from 1853 until 1858, when they moved next door to the Evergreens*; they lived there with Austin's* family for eleven years. In 1864, the sisters visited Dickinson while the poet was in Cambridgeport, Massachusetts. When Clara married on 14 October 1869, she and Anna left Amherst.* Their relationship with their guardian remained significant; Anna sought and received Edward Dickinson's* consent when she married George H. Carleton (3 June 1874). The correspondence between Emily and the Newman cousins continued. The last and only known letter to Anna was in 1884, expressing thanks for pictures of her children (L925). The last trace is Lavinia's* report to Anna on Dickinson's health* in 1885.

RECOMMENDED: *Years*; Polly Longsworth. *The World of Emily Dickinson.*

Masako Takeda

NEWMAN, CLARISSA BADGER (1844–1920)   In 1853, Dickinson announced to her brother at Harvard, "The Newman family are coming" (L106). Clara and her sister Anna,* ages nine and seven, had been orphaned the year before. These children of Edward Dickinson's* sister became his wards and lived at the Homestead* for the next five years before moving next door to the Evergreens.* According to Clara's document entitled "My Personal Acquaintance with Emily Dickinson," they seemed to prefer the Homestead, although there may be some bias in their report of Austin's* and Sue's* household. Clara married Sidney Turner, 14 October 1869, and left Amherst* with Anna. Dickinson mentioned the ceremony to Perez Cowan* (L332). Clara wrote to Dickinson often (L339), but only two of Dickinson's letters to her survive.

RECOMMENDED: *Life*; Millicent Todd Bingham, *Emily Dickinson's Home.*

Masako Takeda

NEWMAN, MARK HASKELL (1806–1852) **and MARY** (1809–1852) Born in Andover, Massachusetts, Mark Newman was residing there in 1828, when he married Mary Dickinson of Amherst*; she was the daughter of Samuel Fowler Dickinson* and Lucretia Gunn* and sister of Edward Dickinson.* They lived in Andover through 1838, where five of their children were born, and three died. In 1830 he was taxed for horses and carriages at Amherst as a nonresident. Newman operated the Amherst Book Store but by 1850 was a publisher in New York City. When both Newmans died in 1852, Edward Dickinson became guardian of nieces Anna* and Clarissa.*

RECOMMENDED: *Life*; James Avery Smith. *Families of Amherst, Massachusetts.* Amherst, MA: Unpublished typescript, 1984.

James Avery Smith

NEW POEMS OF EMILY DICKINSON (1993) Perhaps the most controversial contribution to Dickinson studies in the last twenty years, William Shurr's *New Poems of Emily Dickinson* (coedited with Anna Dunlap and Emily Grey Shurr) has drawn critical responses with as much force as a nineteenth-century Amherst* Sunday drew Congregationalists.* What has prompted the passionate responses is Shurr's claim that, hiding among the camouflage of prose in the three volumes of Dickinson's "highly charged" letters,* there lurk exactly 498 short texts that can and should be excavated and read entirely on their own as "new *poems.*" To this end, Shurr has plucked various passages from the letters and reformatted them into five categories: prose-formatted poems, riddles, workshop materials, juvenilia, and epigrams. There are also a chapter on metrics and a bibliographical essay.

Shurr's primary justifications for his project rest on the notion that, throughout her letters, Dickinson willingly blurred boundaries between poetry* and prose. Grounding his argument on Dickinson's habit of unraveling lines of her letters to weave into separate poems, Shurr suggests that his experiment is sanctioned as well as predicted by Dickinson's own editorial* practices. Moreover, he maintains that the editor must recognize "the poem's changing life in human society," a transgressive concept borrowed from Jerome McGann that not only enables but encourages the editor to modify the text in response to "perceived needs" of the contemporary audience.

Publication of this book raises a number of provocative questions such as the privileging of the poem over the letter and the murky business of authorial intention. Most important, perhaps, concerns have been raised about the cultural, historical, literary, and gender politics of converting private prose letters written by a woman into public lyric* poems that have been reformatted by a team headed by a man. (*See*: Editorial Scholarship; *Letters* [1958])

RECOMMENDED: Margaret Dickie, "Dickinson in Context"; Vivian R. Pollak. Rev. of *New Poems of Emily Dickinson*. Ed. William Shurr. *American Literature* 66 (1994): 602–3.

Dean Rader

NEWTON, BENJAMIN FRANKLIN (1821–1853)   One of Dickinson's most important friends in her early adulthood, Newton was a law student in her father's office from 1847 to late 1849. Dickinson described him as "a gentle, yet grave Preceptor, teaching me what to read, what authors to admire, what was most grand or beautiful in nature, and that sublimer lesson, a faith in things unseen, and in a life again, nobler, and much more blessed—" (L153). At other times she called him tutor or master,* regarding him as an older brother. Most important, however, he was the first person to encourage Dickinson as a writer. Shortly before his death* Dickinson sent him, apparently for the first time, some of her poems for praise and criticism. In a letter to Thomas W. Higginson* in 1865 she wrote about Newton: "My dying Tutor told me that he would like to live till I had been a poet, but Death was much of Mob as I could master— then" (L265). Newton was her literary and spiritual guide; they were both interested in modern literature and disliked orthodox religion.* In 1850, after Newton had moved to Worcester, Massachusetts, he sent her a copy of Ralph Waldo Emerson's* *Poems*. Dickinson corresponded with Newton from the time he moved from Amherst* until his death,* 24 March 1853, but none of their correspondence has survived. Nine months after his death she wrote to his minister, Rev. Edward Everett Hale,* to ask about Newton's last hours (L153).

RECOMMENDED: *Life*; Cynthia Griffin Wolff, *Emily Dickinson*.

Lena Koski

NILES, THOMAS (1825–1894)   was born in Boston,* where he attended the Boston Latin School. He began working at the Old Corner Bookstore in 1839, where he met William D. Ticknor and James T. Fields; he then worked for the publishing arm of the business, William D. Ticknor and Company, which became Ticknor and Fields in 1854. When the popular James R. Osgood was hired in 1855, the more reticent Niles saw that the new man was favored over him, and he resigned. He became a partner in an undistinguished stationery and bookselling company, which failed during the panic of 1857.

Niles joined Roberts Brothers* in 1863 and was universally credited with making the firm a success: he imported the best English books, expanded the Christmas trade, arranged for work with the best printers in Boston, began selling books in series, and established successful personal relations with authors published by the firm (including Louisa May Alcott, whose *Little Women* he was personally responsible for publishing). He married the owner's half sister in 1866, and in 1872 he was made a full partner in the company. Niles died in

Italy of a heart attack while on his first vacation in thirty years. Roberts Brothers survived only four years without him.

Dickinson had corresponded with Niles, even sending him poems. After T. W. Higginson* had unsuccessfully approached Houghton Mifflin about publishing *Poems* (1890),* Mabel Loomis Todd* and David Todd took the manuscript to Niles. He was not impressed by the poetry, especially after receiving an unenthusiastic reader's report from the poet Arlo Bates,* and he offered to publish only a small edition, with Lavinia Dickinson* paying for the plates. After the critical and commercial success of *Poems*, he redrew the contract in Lavinia's favor and actively pursued and promoted further volumes of Dickinson's poems and letters.* He never regretted his decision to publish her. (*See*: Publication)

RECOMMENDED: Raymond L. Kilgour. *Messrs. Roberts Brothers Publishers*. Ann Arbor: University of Michigan Press, 1952.

Joel Myerson

"Nobody knows this little Rose—" (P35)   Early publications of this poem, itself a wandering "pilgrim," include appearances in the *Springfield Republican** (1858); in *Youth's Companion* (1891) as "A Nameless Rose"; and in *Bolts of Melody** (1945), where it was number eighty-three in the "My Pageantry" section. Divided in early publications into three quatrains, the two existing manuscripts of twelve undivided lines actually differ from each other only in punctuation and the lineation of the final lines.

The culmination of Fascicle* 1, this poem shares a page with "Garlands for Queens, may be—" (P34), which ends with nature* "ordain[ing]" a rose (Appendix A). It brings the twenty-two-poem cycle, more full of flowers* than any other, to a fitting finish, repeating the trinitarian imagery of Bee, Butterfly, and Breeze of the opening, "The Gentian weaves her fringes—" (P18).

Metonymic* of the poem or the fascicle or the poet herself, the Rose (subject in at least fifty poems) in this case is removed from nature to be "lift[ed] up" to the addressee, whether that addressee might be Mary Bowles,* as Wolff believes, or God,* as Budick holds. Plucked from nature, this Rose violates the natural order in its use by the poet either for solace or as symbol of the enterprise upon which she is embarking (the fascicles). It is "easy" for the little Rose to die, but not the poem that, as Dickinson will later say, expresses or distills the flower's essence. The poem's opening word works two ways: no ordinary people may know the Rose; but the poet, who in P288 calls herself "Nobody," surely does.

RECOMMENDED: E. Miller Budick, *Emily Dickinson and the Life of Language: A Study in Symbolic Poetics*; Karen Dandurand, "Another Dickinson Poem Published in Her Lifetime"; Dorothy Huff Oberhaus, *Emily Dickinson's Fascicles: Method and Meaning*; Cynthia Griffin Wolff, *Emily Dickinson*.

Eleanor Elson Heginbotham

NORCROSS, BETSEY FAY (1777–1829)   First wife of Joel Norcross,* mother of Emily Norcross Dickinson,* Betsey Norcross was the daughter of

Sally Fairbanks Fay and Jude Fay. In a world made up of a prominent husband and a houseful of children, Betsey managed her large establishment in Monson, Massachusetts, effectively and with sensitivity. Yet her friends, as well as family, were crucial to her. Although described as "retiring in her disposition," she was "alive to the affections and sufferings of others" and actively involved in charitable work. Betsey grieved over the loss of four of her nine children: Eli and Nancy, who did not survive childhood, and Austin and Hiram, who lived into their twenties. Emily had been consistently supportive of her mother, whose health was precarious prior to the Norcross–Dickinson marriage in 1828. With the deaths of her older brothers, Mrs. Dickinson became the eldest of the surviving children: William Otis, Lavinia,* Alfred, and Joel Warren.* At the urgent request of her mother in early September 1829, she hurried to Monson with young Austin.* No sooner did they arrive than Betsey died on the fifth, more than a year before her granddaughter, Emily Dickinson, was born. (*See*: Genealogy)

RECOMMENDED: *Years*; Mary Elizabeth Kromer Bernhard, "Portrait of a Family: Emily Dickinson's Norcross Connection"; The Reverend Alfred Ely. Obituary of Betsey Fay Norcross. *Hampden Journal and Advertiser* 16 Sept. 1829.

Mary Elizabeth Kromer Bernhard

NORCROSS COUSINS   Frances and Louisa

NORCROSS, EMILY (1828–1852)   Daughter of Amanda Brown and Hiram Norcross, Emily shared a room with the poet when the cousins attended Mount Holyoke Female Seminary.* Orphaned at age eight, she lived with her Norcross grandparents and attended Mount Holyoke from 1845 to 1848, where she attracted the attention of principal Mary Lyon,* who noted that she "devoted considerable time" to music (Mary Lyon to Susannah Fitch, 17 September 1848, Mount Holyoke College Archives). Following graduation, Norcross accepted a teaching position in Ohio, becoming the first woman in the Norcross family to be financially independent. Her career cut short by illness, however; she died in Monson of tuberculosis.

The cousins' year together in 1847–1848 was marked by intimacy, intellectual immersion, and religious* questioning. Dickinson was quite fond of Emily and called her an "excellent room-mate" (L18). Like the poet, Norcross took the pursuit of an intellectual life seriously, lamenting that she was so hurried, she did not have adequate time for reading and reflection. The cousins also wrestled with the decision to join the church. Norcross debated a year before joining in 1847 and expressed regret, but not condemnation, that at Mount Holyoke the poet had decided to continue questioning.

RECOMMENDED: Martha Ackmann, "The Matrilineage of Emily Dickinson"; Mary Elizabeth Kromer Bernhard, "Portrait of a Family: Emily Dickinson's Norcross Connection."

Martha Ackmann

NORCROSS, FRANCES (1847–1896)   Frances Norcross and her older sister Louisa* were Dickinson's much-esteemed "little cousins" whom the poet admitted into her circle of intimates. The Norcrosses visited the poet regularly and maintained a twenty-seven-year correspondence with Dickinson that is distinguished by its candor and expansiveness. Dickinson's letters* to the Norcrosses reveal that the poet frequently turned to them for emotional comfort as well as for advice on reading and news of cultural events. The letters to the Norcrosses are important because they provide a record of Dickinson's psychological, intellectual, and social life and also because they demonstrate that Dickinson valued her cousins' intelligence and their respect for her privacy —two qualities the poet deemed critical in those she selected as her literary audience.

Frances Norcross lived with her sister her entire life, eventually settling with her in Concord, where she became involved in the town's artistic and political activities. Frances acted in plays, participated in Bronson Alcott's School of Philosophy, raised money for the education of women and minorities, and was a longtime member of the Saturday Club.

In 1884 Frances accepted a position as a librarian at the Harvard Divinity School. Although women were rarely hired for such positions, Frances worked for a decade, helping to expand the library and implement a new cataloging system. Books* were central to Frances Norcross' life; her obituary noted that she was " 'actively interested in anything of a literary nature.' " The most important literary involvement of Frances Norcross' life began in 1891, when Mabel Todd* asked her to contribute poems Dickinson had shared with the cousins for *Poems, Second Series*. Frances, taking the lead role for the sisters, was deeply torn. She did not need convincing that the poems had literary quality, yet she felt she would compromise the poet's privacy by allowing them to be published. She was persuaded to become involved with the project when she met with Thomas Wentworth Higginson,* whom she knew Dickinson had trusted and who had agreed to coedit the volume. When Todd again appealed to the cousins for their help in compiling a volume of Dickinson letters, Frances felt further pressed. She was reluctant to become involved with the project since Todd alone was editing the 1894 volume. Todd and Frances Norcross, two strong-willed women, struck a compromise. Norcross would share letters with Todd under three conditions: the sisters were not to be identified; they would keep the original letters and give Todd handwritten copies; and they retained the right to excise portions of the letters to protect the privacy of the poet, themselves, and other persons mentioned. Todd accepted the cousins' terms grudgingly, complaining, "They had the most intimate letters from Emily, but they wouldn't let anybody put their eyes on them. . . . They were such geese" (*AB* 238). Frances Norcross' commitment to preserving Dickinson's privacy frustrated Todd, and even today scholars wish they had Dickinson's original and unexcised letters to these cousins. Yet without the Norcross cousins' respect for the poet, the candid letters might not have been written at all. (*See*: Women's Culture)

RECOMMENDED: *AB*; *Life*; Martha Ackmann, "The Matrilineage of Emily Dickinson."

Martha Ackmann

NORCROSS, JOEL (1776–1846)   Civic leader, conspicuously successful entrepreneur, and ardent advocate of improved educational facilities in Monson, Massachusetts, Joel Norcross was the father of Emily Norcross Dickinson.* Born in Sturbridge, Joel was the first of six children of Sarah Marsh Norcross and William Norcross. After his parents' move to Monson in 1777, he was followed by Amos, Sarah (Flynt), Betsy (Packard), William, and Erasmus. On the death of their eminent father in 1803, Joel assumed a primary role, endorsed by his mother and the family at large. His was a cohesive, enterprising family that joined forces on both social and business levels. Widespread maladies, especially "consumption," within and without the Norcross family, greatly increased familial unity.

Joel Norcross, sharp-minded and astute, began his commercial career in his father's general store but later became a major figure in the Monson textile industry. He was a founder and major stockholder in the Hampden Cotton Manufacturing Company, one of the promoters and builders of the Petersham and Monson Turnpike from the Connecticut line to New Hampshire, and stockholder and director of the Western Railroad (in Massachusetts). He employed many farmhands in the raising of sheep, cattle, grain, and hay and was a large landholder who bought, sold, and built houses for investment. Active in the Congregational* Church, he also served for many years as county commissioner, as Monson coroner, and twice as selectman.

Norcross was in the forefront of the founders of Monson Academy, the coeducational institution that opened in 1806 as an area educational and cultural center. From its initial organization in 1804 to 1846, he served as a trustee. He was probably the academy's largest contributor, with gifts of more than $7,000.

Emily Norcross Dickinson remained close to her father even after her mother, Betsey's,* death and his second marriage to Sarah Vaill* in 1831. Conservative politically and socially, Joel Norcross and Edward Dickinson* were mutually congenial. On Joel's death, Emily became a beneficiary, while Dickinson and Alfred Norcross were named executors of the estate. (*See*: Genealogy)

RECOMMENDED: Mary Elizabeth Kromer Bernhard, "Portrait of a Family: Emily Dickinson's Norcross Connection"; Charles Hammond. *Discourses, and Speeches Delivered at the Celebration of the Semi-Centennial Anniversary of Monson Academy*, 18–19 July 1854. New York: John A. Gray, 1855; Joel W. Norcross. "The History and Genealogy of the Norcross Family." Unpublished manuscript. 2 vols., 1882. New England Genealogical Society, Boston.

Mary Elizabeth Kromer Bernhard

NORCROSS, JOEL WARREN (1821–1900) Norcross was the poet's youngest uncle. Born in Monson, he lived for a time with the Dickinsons while attending Amherst Academy* and before moving to Boston* to enter business. Norcross' successful importing firm suffered financial losses during the Civil War,* and he was forced to close. During the war his wife, Lamira, died of tuberculosis, leaving him with two young children, William and Anna. In 1866 he married the family's housekeeper, Maggie Gunnison, and the couple had one daughter, Edith. The marriage was unhappy, at least according to his children. Anna reported that Maggie "threw tantrums," and descendants suspect that some of the poet's letters* may have been destroyed, as Maggie disdained anything connected to her husband's family.

During the 1880s Norcross devoted himself to two passions: travel and genealogy.* He visited his children in California and assembled an impressive two-volume genealogy of the Norcross and Fay families that is now housed at the New England Historical and Genealogical Society. Energetic, ambitious, opinionated, risk-taking, vain, Joel stood in his generation of Norcrosses as the maverick whose substantial ego amused more than irritated Emily Dickinson.

RECOMMENDED: *Life*; David Porter, *Dickinson: The Modern Idiom.*

Martha Ackmann

NORCROSS, LAVINIA (1812–1860) **and LORIN** (1808–1863) Lavinia Norcross, sixth child of Betsey Fay* and Joel Norcross* and Emily Norcross Dickinson's* bright-minded sister, had a profound influence on young Emily Dickinson's aesthetic development. This aunt's special relationship to her niece resulted in a rich understanding that obviously spurred the future poet's creative interests. Lorin Norcross, called Loring, was Lavinia's husband, son of Joel Norcross' brother William and Orril Munn Norcross. Lavinia and Lorin were matched in warmth of personality and vulnerability.

Seven years younger than her sister Emily, Lavinia was demonstrative, winsome, and sympathetic; yet she could be archly independent. This definitive quality is evident in her descriptive, even colorful writing. Her commitment to the natural world was passionate. Like Emily Norcross Dickinson, she attended Monson Academy and studied at the Herrick School in New Haven (1830). Even during the Norcross–Dickinson courtship, Edward Dickinson looked on young Lavinia as "intelligent and interesting," sending her a gift when she was seriously ill (Pollak 202).

Lavinia helped manage the Norcross household in Monson after her mother's death in 1829 for the man she described as "an affectionate father whose worth we can never realize." Joel Norcross' second marriage in 1831 was traumatic for her, and she wrote to her sister, "What shall I call her? Can I say Mother? Emily you may depend I want to be with you" (*Years* 1:16). Yet she accepted Sarah Vaill* graciously as a stepmother, maintaining close familial ties.

The eldest of three children, Loring had just turned five when his father died in 1813. Because Joel Norcross was appointed guardian of his brother's children, and Orril Norcross married a second time in 1816, Loring became an active participant in life at his uncle's house. He was a student at Monson Academy in the family tradition, then began his career as a clerk before moving to Southbridge, and finally to Boston, where he became a dry goods commission merchant.

Lavinia stunned the Dickinsons in the spring of 1833 by indicating her intention to marry Loring "whether it be right for cousins to marry or no" (*Years* 1:23). Though she had "many sorrowful hours," she concluded, "If I love him, it is sufficient." Aware of the family's negative reaction to a marriage of close relatives, Lavinia persisted; yet she confided in Emily that Edward had told her she was "crazy." The wedding took place on 4 November 1834. Opposition soon faded, and Lavinia realized that even Edward Dickinson "would not miss of seeing us if he had to walk 6 miles" in Boston where they settled. Initially, the couple boarded with Loring's sister, Betsy, and her husband, Matthew Wood. The brothers-in-law engaged in business jointly for a time, and Loring became active as a member of the Boston School Board and secretary of the Massachusetts Temperance Union. Their first child, Lavinia, born 13 December 1837, lived only to age four, dying 19 May 1842. A second daughter, Louisa,* had been born 20 January 1842, followed by Frances Lavinia,* 4 August 1847. The children were the focus of their congenial, hospitable parents, who experienced financial reverses when Loring's business failed in the mid-1850s.

From earliest childhood, Emily Dickinson was drawn to her Aunt Lavinia, who was physically delicate but imaginatively vigorous. After Lavinia Dickinson's* birth in 1833, small Emily spent several weeks in Monson. Her aunt reported that the wild thunderstorm en route from Amherst to Monson frightened her niece. But now "she is so happy here she must not go yet," and she "gets more rides than she did at home" and plays "moosic" on the piano. On Emily's return to Amherst,* Lavinia wrote her sister, "You must not let her forget me" (*Years* I: 21–23).

After moving to Boston, Lavinia wrote vivid letters describing lavish soirees or gorgeous flowers, indicating "this will be for Emily's benefit." The exchanges of visits between Dickinsons and Norcrosses simply increased rapport and affection. More than that, however, Emily Dickinson made extended visits on her own. Her melancholy mood triggered by Sophia Holland's* death* vanished after a month with Aunt Lavinia and her family in 1844. She spent a month with them in 1846, stimulated by Boston's* cultural and educational sights.

The death of Aunt Lavinia in 1860 of "consumption" was a searing experience for Emily. She wrote her sister, "it is dark and strange to think of summer afterward!" (L217). After Loring died 17 January 1863, Loo and Fanny became indispensable in Emily Dickinson's firmament.

RECOMMENDED: *Letters*; *Years*; Millicent Todd Bingham, *Emily Dickinson's Home: Letters of Edward Dickinson and His Family*; Vivian R. Pollak, *A Poet's Parents: The Courtship Letters of Emily Norcross and Edward Dickinson*; Dickinson Papers, Houghton Library, Harvard University.

Mary Elizabeth Kromer Bernhard

NORCROSS, LOUISA (1842–1919)   Daughter of Lavinia* and Loring Norcross,* Louisa—as Dickinson observed—was "one of the ones from whom I do not run away" (L199). Louisa and her younger sister, Frances,* spent their early years with their parents in Boston* and, after their deaths in the 1860s, lived with relatives in Monson, Connecticut, and Wisconsin. Loo and Fanny returned to Massachusetts and settled in Mrs. Bangs' Boardinghouse,* where Dickinson lived with them in 1864 and 1865. Eventually the sisters moved to Concord, living out the rest of their lives immersed in a variety of intellectual and political activities. Louisa described herself in the 1904 *Woman's Journal* as "an ardent crusader for women, a whole-souled suffragist, and a lover of every progressive 'ism.' "

Among the activities both sisters participated in was the Concord Saturday Club, a small group devoted to the study of literature whose members included Louisa May Alcott, William Ellery Channing, Ralph Waldo Emerson,* and Robertson James. In addition to studying published literature, the club was committed to first readings of well-known writers or those of "too personal a character for general publication." Although no definitive record exists indicating Loo and Fanny Norcross shared their cousin's poetry with the group, it is possible they may have. Clearly, the Norcrosses' involvement in elite literary circles in Concord demonstrated that Dickinson could have pursued through them another avenue toward publication* if she had wanted.

Both sisters were aware that Dickinson was serious about poetry. The poet shared with them at least twenty-five poems, and during the poet's lifetime they knew that Dickinson corresponded with Thomas Wentworth Higginson.* Loo also reported observing Dickinson compose her verse. She wrote, "I know that Emily Dickinson wrote most emphatic things in the pantry, so cool and quiet, while she skimmed the milk; because I sat on the footstool behind the door, in delight, as she read them to me. The blinds were closed, but through the green slats she saw all those fascinating ups and downs going on outside that she wrote about" (Scharnhorst 485).

During Louisa Norcross' later years she stayed at home in Concord while Frances worked in Cambridge.* Their relationship as sisters closely resembled Emily Dickinson's with Lavinia* in the reciprocal way each took care of the other. The closeness Dickinson felt for Loo and Fanny likely was rooted in the poet's belief that they understood both her need for privacy and her commitment to poetry.* Dickinson also believed Loo understood her ambition. Writing in 1859, Dickinson declared, "I have known little of you, since the October morning when our families went out driving, and you and I in the dining-room decided to be distinguished. It's a great thing to be 'great,' Loo, and you and I might tug for a life, and never accomplish it, but no one can stop our looking on, and you know some cannot sing, but the orchard is full of birds, and we all can listen. What if we learn, ourselves, some day!" (L199).

RECOMMENDED: *Life*; Martha Ackmann, "The Matrilineage of Emily Dickinson"; Gary Scharnhorst, "A Glimpse of Dickinson at Work."

Martha Ackmann

NORCROSS, SARAH VAILL (1788–1854)   The second wife of grandfather Joel Norcross,* Sarah Vaill Norcross was respected by the Dickinsons but ultimately regarded as an outsider. The Vaills were acquainted with the Norcrosses. Sarah's brother was a friend of Joel's and one of the founding trustees of Amherst College*; years later Sarah's niece taught the poet to play the piano. Yet in 1830, when Joel Norcross declared his intentions to marry Sarah Vaill, his daughter, Lavinia Norcross,* was not entirely pleased. In fact, Lavinia, especially conscious that the announcement came a little more than a year after Betsey Fay Norcross'* death, termed the event "father's calculations." Sarah's letters to the Dickinsons nonetheless reveal a warm and affectionate woman. After grandfather Joel died, she continued to visit in Amherst.* Commenting on her stepgrandmother's austerity, Emily wrote, "I'd as soon think of popping fire crackers in the presence of Peter the Great!" (L130).

RECOMMENDED: Martha Ackmann, "The Matrilineage of Emily Dickinson"; Mary Elizabeth Kromer Bernhard, "Portrait of a Family: Emily Dickinson's Norcross Connection."

Martha Ackmann

O

_____

"OMITTED CENTER" In 1960 Jay Leyda observed that "a major device of Emily Dickinson's writing, both in her poems and in her letters,* was what might be called the 'omitted center' " (*Years* 1:xxi). Instead of some reference to the document's occasion, setting, or concrete subject, Leyda noted that her writings regularly provide us with "the riddle, the circumstance too well known to be repeated . . . , the deliberate skirting of the obvious."

Leyda's phrase quickly became a byword, naming a widespread sense that Dickinson trafficked to an unusual degree in mystery, avoidance, and circumlocution. Moreover, the phrase described something more than a style Dickinson practiced occasionally, as became fully clear once complete editions* of the poems and letters were available. Again and again she wrote texts that conspicuously failed to identify the contexts they themselves presumed as central. In private letters such a practice might pass without comment, for it could be supposed that the letter's addressee understood what the letter did not specify. Yet Dickinson did the same thing in hundreds of poems.

Often, as when Dickinson's speaker tells us she felt a funeral in her brain, we are provided with no location for the speaker's whereabouts and no sure referent for the speaker's condition. Death,* madness,* external trauma, or internal turmoil? We cannot say, although P280 seems to be about little else than that for which it refuses to provide scene or circumstance.

The more pressingly a poem invokes a narrative context, the more flagrant the omitted center. Whereas "I felt a Funeral, in my Brain"* can be ascribed to a generalized speaker and hence to the allegorical "scenelessness" Robert Weisbuch analyzes, Dickinson also wrote dozens of poems alluding to what seem specific, acutely experienced events that have taken place before the moment of the poem's utterance. Yet such poems never identify the persons involved, locate the events invoked, or let us know quite what story has been presupposed. Nor, despite occasional proposals to the contrary, do such poems contribute as pearls to some necklace of coherently sequenced poems.

Rhetorically,* Dickinson's omissions have both power and charm, but they can also frustrate. In response some commentators have tried to write in what they believe the poems themselves erased—a fictive* or autobiographical context that would locate Dickinson's writings within an intelligible story. Others take the absences as deliberate and positive signs, for example, as ones that express epistemological, theological, or psychological* gaps that the poems can then be said to thematize. Neither approach has been fully satisfactory. (*See*: Ambiguity; Compression)

RECOMMENDED: *Years*; Robert Weisbuch, *Emily Dickinson's Poetry*.

Gary Lee Stonum

"AN OPEN PORTFOLIO"   Thomas Wentworth Higginson* composed this essay (also known as "The Outlook") in late July 1890 after receiving proofs of *Poems by Emily Dickinson** from Roberts Brothers*; it was placed as a promotional article in the *Christian Union*. Higginson situated Dickinson's poetry within Ralph Waldo Emerson's* "Poetry of the Portfolio," a "department of poetry" not originally intended for publication.* In "The New Poetry" (*The Dial* 1840), Emerson praised a new democratic "revolution in poetry" that was raising the literary importance of "the portfolio over the book." Writing privately freed writers from critical scrutiny and encouraged the "easy and unpremeditated translation of their thoughts and feelings into rhyme." Higginson argued similarly that, although Dickinson's poetry was "[w]ayward and unconventional in the last degree; defiant of form, measure, rhyme,* and even grammar," her reticence to print and her relative social seclusion suggested that she was not willfully neglectful of literary convention but simply following "an exacting standard of her own" (293). "An Open Portfolio," rewritten for his Preface to *Poems* (1890),* provided readers with a preview of fourteen edited poems and drew comparisons with the popular poetry of British poet Jean Ingelow and New Hampshire author Celia Thaxter. He compared Dickinson favorably to William Blake* to downplay critical preoccupation with apparent technical faults: "When a thought takes one's breath away, who cares to count the syllables?" (*See*: Critical Responses)

RECOMMENDED: Ralph Waldo Emerson. "New Poetry." *The Dial* 1 (Oct. 1840): 221–32; Thomas Wentworth Higginson. "An Open Portfolio." *Christian Union* 42 (25 Sept. 1890): 392–93.

Nancy Johnston

OUT-DOOR PAPERS   Thomas Wentworth Higginson's* *Out-Door Papers* (Boston: Ticknor and Fields, 1863) includes several important nature* essays published in the *Atlantic Monthly** and seems to have played a vital role in drawing Dickinson closer to him. In a letter to his wife, Higginson mentioned seeing this book on a table in the Homestead* living room, where he first met the poet (L342a). Dickinson paid special attention to one of its essays, "The Procession of the Flowers,"* in L280, sent to him during the Civil War*; she again showed great gratitude to him as his "Scholar" in commenting on this book in L458. (*See*: Books and Reading)

RECOMMENDED: *Life*; Barton Levi St. Armand, *Emily Dickinson and Her Culture: The Soul's Society*; Benjamin Lease, *Emily Dickinson's Readings of Men and Books.*

Midori Kajino Asahina

OXYMORON   is a figure of speech in which two words commonly thought of as opposites are juxtaposed, as in Dickinson's phrase "uncertain certainty" (P1411). The joining of these words results in a compressed* paradox. Dickinson's poetry usually allows for two potential responses from the reader to any one oxymoron: a reconciliation of the two terms as one word becomes absorbed into the other or the maintenance of the two terms in balanced and oppositional relationship. The first response demands a deconstruction of binary oppositions so that, for example, the two terms in a phrase like "an Honor honorless" (P713) might be collapsed as the adjective "honorless" serves to redefine the concept of "Honor," sparking new associations with this supposed virtue. Dickinson encouraged such a reading because it leads to a rupturing of traditional definitions of "Honor" and, thereby, initiates a revitalization of the word.* The second potential response refuses to reconcile the two terms and instead maintains an uneasy tension between them by focusing more on the compact riddle within "an Honor honorless." An emphasis on the elusiveness of the riddle's solution works to retain the full ambiguity* and contradiction available in the phrase. Ultimately, Dickinson delighted in the oxymoron because of these dual possibilities inherent in its form and probably intended the oxymoron to produce both these effects—ambiguity and deconstruction of oppositions—which are crucial to her poetics.

Dickinson frequently employed the oxymoron to question traditional social conventions such as gender roles and religious* beliefs and to express uncertainty about the ability to possess absolute knowledge. For example, she described the possibility of God's* coming for the soul as a "fond Ambush" (P338), linking care and violence, nurturance and destruction. Such a phrase conjoins positive and negative meanings, thereby destabilizing conventional Puritan* notions of God while simultaneously resisting the substitution of a new finite definition in place of the traditional one. The jarring interplay of words, paradigmatic of Dickinson's use of oxymoron, attempts to illuminate not the knowable but the ineffable and the unsayable. The concomitants of opposites evident in the oxymoron urge a fluid movement between a number of newly realized meanings rather than a static embrace of some final, singular meaning. In this way, the oxymoron allows for the discovery of personal meaning in poetic language.

Hawthorne* and the Bible* have been cited as influences on Dickinson's development of the oxymoron as a central facet of her style. Dickinson's relationship to a feminist* aesthetic has also been explored through analysis of the oxymoron in her poetry. A critical debate among Dickinson scholars focuses on whether the oxymoron is part of an intentional feminist linguistic* style designed to undermine patriarchal language or is simply a standard figure of speech within poetic language and wielded as such by Dickinson.

RECOMMENDED: Marvin K. L. Ching. "Interpreting Meaningful Nonsense." *Linguistic Perspectives on Literature*. Ed. Marvin K. L. Ching, Michael C. Haley, and Ronald F. Lunsford. London: Routledge, 1980: 319–27; Beth Maclay Doriani, *Emily Dickinson, Daughter of Prophecy*; Karl Keller, *The Only Kangaroo among the Beauty: Emily Dickinson and America*; Brita Lindberg-Seyersted, *The Voice of the Poet: Aspects of Style in the Poetry of Emily Dickinson*; Wendy Martin, "Emily Dickinson."

H. Jordan Landry

P

PHELPS, ELIZABETH STUART (Ward) (1844–1911)   Phelps was the author of many popular novels, among them *The Gates Ajar* (1868), *The Story of Avis* (1877), and *The Silent Partner* (1871). Although there is no record that Dickinson was acquainted with her, Leyda speculates that a letter from Dickinson to Louise Norcross* refers to this reformer: "Of Miss P—I know but this, dear. She wrote me in October, requesting me to aid the world by my chirrup more. Perhaps she stated it as my duty, I dont distinctly remember, and always burn such letters, so I cannot obtain it now. I replied declining. She did not write to me again—she might have been offended, or perhaps is extricating humanity from some hopeless ditch" (L380). St. Armand compares major themes in Dickinson's poetry with Phelps' depiction in *The Gates Ajar* of inflexible Calvinism in conflict with a domestic* heaven.* Like Dickinson, Phelps was influenced by *Aurora Leigh* and referred to this poem throughout *The Story of Avis*. (*See*: Sentimentalism; Women's Culture)

RECOMMENDED: *Letters*; *Years*; Elizabeth Stuart Phelps. *Chapters from a Life.* Boston: Houghton Mifflin, 1896; Barton Levi St. Armand, *Emily Dickinson and Her Culture: A Soul's Society.*

Dorothy Z. Baker

PHILOSOPHICAL APPROACHES   Emily Dickinson's poetry is so packed with abstract words and big ideas that some critics have wondered where those ideas came from and whether or not they are valid as philosophical concepts. Allen Tate's 1932 essay was an early but still influential attempt to relate Dickinson's poetry to a systematic body of thought. Tate argued that Dickinson came of age at a perfect time for a poet: when one set of theological and intellectual traditions, those of Puritan* New England, were on the wane, and another set, those of the Godless and money-driven "Gilded Age," were not yet firmly established. According to Tate, Dickinson had the advantage of dwelling in the great New England intellectual tradition of sermons, hymns,* and Bible* reading without being imprisoned within it. Tate claimed that ideas of God* and fate and knowledge were, for her, "momently toppling from the rational plane to the level of perception" (208).

Dickinson's acute attention to the processes of perception has occupied more recent critics of various philosophical persuasions. Yvor Winters, in an essay suggestively titled "Emily Dickinson and the Limits of Judgment" (1938), praised Dickinson for those poems in which she acknowledged the limits of human knowledge. "It is possible," he wrote admiringly of poems like "Our journey had advanced—" (P615), "to solve any problem of insoluble experience by retreating a step and defining the boundary at which comprehension ceases" (290). In his readings of "Kantian" poems like "To hear an Oriole sing" (P526), phenomenological critic Charles Anderson gives close attention to Dickinson's treatment of issues of skepticism and of access to things of this world through sight and hearing. Philosophical skepticism (the denial that our senses give us accurate access to the world) is also a major concern of Christopher Benfey's book, *Emily Dickinson and the Problem of Others*. Benfey borrows ideas from philosophers such as Ludwig Wittgenstein and Stanley Cavell to probe Dickinson's "responses" to skepticism, her sense, in several key poems, that our deepest relation to the world is less one of scientific* knowledge than an intimacy she calls "nearness" (as in "A nearness to Tremendousness—," P963). A particularly ambitious attempt to draw philosophical implications from Dickinson's poetry is Sharon Cameron's *Lyric Time*, in which she argues that Dickinson's poetry makes innovative use of time and shows a sophistication about "being in the world" that rivals Martin Heidegger's. Cameron also returns us to those big abstractions Dickinson so loves, especially in her "definition poems." (*See*: Poststructuralist Approaches; Religion)

RECOMMENDED: Charles Anderson, *Emily Dickinson's Poetry: Stairway of Surprise*; Christopher Benfey, *Emily Dickinson and the Problem of Others*; Sharon Cameron, *Lyric Time: Dickinson and the Limits of Genre*; Allen Tate, "Emily Dickinson"; Yvor Winters. *In Defense of Reason: Primitivism and Decadence, a Study in American Experimental Poetry*. New York: Swallow Press and William Morrow, 1947.

Christopher Benfey

POE, EDGAR ALLAN (1809–1849)   died when Dickinson was eighteen, leaving behind important poetry, fiction, criticism, and literary theory. Dickinson's fascination with death* and psychic* terror resembles Poe's, and her emphasis on poetic affect and the "music"* of poetry are consistent with his literary theories. These similarities, though, may derive from Romantic*–Victorian culture rather than from Poe's direct influence. His reputation had plummeted by the time Dickinson told Higginson,* "Of Poe, I know too little to think" (L622).

Yet she certainly knew some of Poe's works, which were widely reprinted in periodicals. A literary group she attended as a young woman probably read and discussed Poe. When she thanked a friend for sending a gift of a "pearl," an "onyx," and an "emerald" (L171), she may have referred to a book by Poe, spelling his name acrostically. Most tellingly, she quoted from "Annabel Lee" in an 1858 letter: "The 'Kingdom by the Sea' never alters, Joseph, but the 'children' do" (*Ly* 52). (*See*: Books and Reading; Gothicism; Popular Culture)

RECOMMENDED: *Ly*; Jack L. Capps, *Emily Dickinson's Reading, 1836–1886*; Judy Jo Small, *Positive as Sound: Emily Dickinson's Rhyme*; Barton Levi St. Armand, *Emily Dickinson and Her Culture: The Soul's Society.*

Judy Jo Small

***POEMS BY EMILY DICKINSON* (1890)**   The first collection of Dickinson's poetry* to appear in print introduced 116 poems and launched the poet's critical* reputation. Published posthumously on 12 November 1890, the volume received immediate critical acclaim and such excellent sales (nearly 1,500 copies in the initial three printings) that the publisher, Roberts Brothers,* engaged editors* Thomas Wentworth Higginson* and Mabel Loomis Todd* for a second series of *Poems.**

Soon after Dickinson's death, her sister Lavinia* found a box of manuscript poems that she offered to her sister-in-law Susan Dickinson* with a plan for their publication.* Unsatisfied, perhaps, with Sue's progress, Lavinia approached Dickinson's literary friend Higginson to discuss the possibility of editing* a volume. His diaries confirm that he visited Sue and Austin Dickinson* in September 1886 and spoke with Lavinia about the project later the same year. Although Higginson declined to take on the entire project, especially the selection and transcription of more than 700 poetry manuscripts, he promised to examine a copy text. Lavinia solicited as copyist Mabel Loomis Todd, a friend and Amherst* neighbor, who, by November 1889, hand-copied and typed the manuscripts and categorized them into A-B-C lists according to her estimate of their suitability for publication. From her selection, Higginson chose 199 poems and arranged them into thematic categories: Life, Love,* Nature,* and Time and Eternity.

Houghton Mifflin of Boston, Higginson's own publisher, was approached in April or May of 1890 but declined to publish the unknown poet. The second choice was Roberts Brothers, which had included Dickinson's "Success is counted sweetest" (P67)* in an anthology of anonymous verse, *A Masque of Poets** (1878). House reader Arlo Bates* admired some of Dickinson's poetry and recommended that the firm produce a small collection, insisting strongly that the proposed volume be reduced by half and carefully edited. Higginson and Todd bowed to his selection of ninety poems but insisted the collection include an additional dozen he had discarded, among them "I shall know why— when Time is over—" (P193), "I died for Beauty—but was scarce" (P449), and "Safe in their Alabaster Chambers—" (P216).* While the editors adamantly defended Dickinson's poetic methods, they nevertheless conceded that her poems should conform to conventional literary standards. In all but a few poems, they added titles,* dropped capitalization,* modernized spelling, removed interlineal markings and textual variants,* erased elongated dashes,* altered line and stanza divisions, and replaced diction with possible synonyms. Although accounts of the editing procedure have blamed Higginson more often than Todd for liberal editing, their journal entries and correspondence indicate shared decisions.

RECOMMENDED: *AB*; R. W. Franklin, *The Editing of Emily Dickinson: A Reconsideration*; Joel Myerson, *Emily Dickinson: A Descriptive Bibliography*.

Nancy Johnston

POEMS BY EMILY DICKINSON, SECOND SERIES (1891) The second volume of Dickinson's poetry edited by Thomas Wentworth Higginson* and Mabel Loomis Todd* introduced 192 poems and a facsimile of "There came a Day at Summer's full" (P322). The unanticipated success and favorable sales of the first volume of *Poems** convinced the editors to honor Dickinson's original poetic form and methods, which had not deterred her readers. Higginson wrote to Todd about the editing, insisting: "Let us alter as little as possible, now that the public's ear is opened" (*AB* 127); however, much of the poetry was amended to reform her unusual punctuation and syntax.* Lavinia Dickinson* also requested that some of her favorites be included in the new volume, the preface of which (written by Todd) is noteworthy for its detailed descriptions of editorial* procedures. Willis Buckingham notes that *Poems* (1891) garnered much the same enthusiastic critical reception* as the first volume, an exception being a March 1891 review in *Scribner's Monthly** that debated whether Dickinson's eccentric form diminished her poetic thought.

RECOMMENDED: *AB*; Willis J. Buckingham, ed., *Emily Dickinson's Reception in the 1890s*; R. W. Franklin, *The Editing of Emily Dickinson: A Reconsideration*; Joel Myerson, *Emily Dickinson: A Descriptive Bibliography*.

Nancy Johnston

POEMS BY EMILY DICKINSON, THIRD SERIES (1896) The third in a three-volume series published by Roberts Brothers* and edited by Mabel Loomis Todd* introduced 166 new poems. The preliminary selection from approximately 700 Dickinson manuscripts was completed by 16 July 1891, but the new volume was delayed so that Todd could edit a selection of Dickinson's letters.* Thomas Wentworth Higginson,* previously a coeditor with Todd on *Poems* (1890)* and *Poems* (1891),* was by now in his early seventies and did not wish to undertake a third volume. Although Todd was left to do the editorial* work alone, R. W. Franklin* offers textual evidence to suggest that many of the included poems had already been jointly edited with Higginson during preparation for earlier volumes. Todd, who had sole editorial responsibility, may have deferred to his indirect influence when she kept many of Higginson's distinctive Latin titles* for Dickinson's untitled manuscripts. As in the previous two volumes, she continued the editorial practice of smoothing syntax,* correcting rhyme,* regularizing grammar, and standardizing punctuation.

Poems (1896), reviewed with much less enthusiasm than the previous two volumes, sold only about 2,000 copies. Uninformed by his Aunt Lavinia* of the forthcoming publication, Dickinson's nephew Ned* was outraged by a negative *New York Tribune* review that he believed exposed the family to public scorn. No further volumes of poetry were edited by Todd with the family's consent. (*See*: Critical Reception; Dash)

RECOMMENDED: Willis J. Buckingham, *Emily Dickinson's Reception in the 1890s*; R. W. Franklin, *The Editing of Emily Dickinson: A Reconsideration*; Polly Longsworth, *Austin and Mabel: The Amherst Affair and Love Letters of Austin Dickinson and Mabel Loomis Todd.*

Nancy Johnston

POEMS BY EMILY DICKINSON (1937)   After the third series of poems was published under Mabel Todd's* direction in 1896, a legal quarrel between her and Lavinia Dickinson* over a strip of land led to division of the manuscripts between Mabel and Lavinia. Lavinia's collection of poems was passed on to Susan Dickinson,* the poet's sister-in-law, and then to her niece, Martha Dickinson Bianchi,* who published them in a series of editions, culminating in *Poems by Emily Dickinson* (1937),* edited by Bianchi with Alfred Leete Hampson* and published by Little, Brown and Company. Bianchi had published *The Single Hound** (collecting poems Emily apparently sent Susan) in 1914 and then *The Complete Poems* (1924)* and *Further Poems* (1929)*; another "complete" edition appeared in 1930. Still more poems emerged in *Unpublished Poems* (1935),* edited with Hampson. The 1937 *Poems* brought together these issues with the three nineteenth-century editions.

The first portion of the volume divides into the four sections designated in prior editions: Life, Love,* Nature,* Time and Eternity. *Further Poems* and *Unpublished Poems* constitute the two last sections. There is no attempt at chronological ordering. Bianchi's introduction reveals some critical insight into Dickinson; she writes, for example, "Her spontaneity in words pries under accepted usage or sets fire to it" (vii). Johnson's introduction to *The Poems* (1955)* notes that while Bianchi felt no need to alter rhyme* and meter for greater smoothness, she and Hampson "created irregularities to enhance the notion of quaintness" (xlvii–iii). Since Bianchi never mastered Dickinson's handwriting,* various misreadings persist in the 1937 edition. For example, in P475, Bianchi reads "Hemlocks" as "hundreds." (*See*: Editorial Scholarship)

RECOMMENDED: *Poems*; R. W. Franklin, *The Editing of Emily Dickinson: A Reconsideration.*

Susan McCabe

THE POEMS OF EMILY DICKINSON: CENTENARY EDITION (1930)   Despite the fact that this collection, edited by Martha Dickinson Bianchi* and Alfred Leete Hampson,* compiled all of the known extant Dickinson poems, it is impossible to attribute much, if any, of the pageantry surrounding Emily Dickinson's centenary in 1930 to Little, Brown's publication of *The Poems of Emily Dickinson*. Bianchi intended to supersede the wildly popular *Further Poems of Emily Dickinson* (1929)* with a comprehensive compilation of nearly 800 poems that included the first three volumes of *Poems* as well as those in *The Single Hound*,* *Further Poems*, and one poem that appears for the first time: "Fitter to see Him, I may be" (P968). She also composed a new eight-page introduction to commemorate this "authoritative" edition. However, where Bianchi's introduction to the *Further Poems* focuses on the depth and significance of the poems, her introduction for the *Centenary Edition* tends to lionize the mythology and morality of Dickinson the person, a tendency of Dickinson studies in the 1930s.

Only in retrospect, when we reexamine the aura surrounding Dickinson in that decade, does the *Centenary Edition* assume its rightful place in the Dickinson canon. Amid the pomp of her centenary and the obsession with the figure of Dickinson, this collection remains important precisely because it redirects our attention to the staggering intensity and profundity of Dickinson's poems, without which the Dickinson persona shines less brightly.

RECOMMENDED: Elizabeth Horan, "To Market: The Dickinson Copyright Wars"; Klaus Lubbers, *Emily Dickinson: The Critical Revolution*; Joel Myerson, *Emily Dickinson: A Descriptive Bibliography*; Rev. of *The Poems of Emily Dickinson*, ed. Martha Dickinson Bianchi. *Saturday Review of Literature* 6 Dec. 1930: 443.

Dean Rader

THE POEMS OF EMILY DICKINSON (1955)   In 1937 R. P. Blackmur complained, "The disarray of Emily Dickinson's poems is the great obvious fact about them as they multiply from volume to volume—I will not say from edition to edition, for they have never been edited" (Franklin 116). In 1955, sixty-five years after the first selection by Mabel Loomis Todd* and Thomas Wentworth Higginson,* Harvard University Press brought order to the corpus by publishing Thomas H. Johnson's* variorum in three magisterial volumes.

Its title deserves to be quoted in full: *The Poems of Emily Dickinson, including Variant Readings Critically Compared with All Known Manuscripts*. Johnson's straightforward purpose—"to establish an accurate text of the poems and to give them as far as possible a chronology" (lxi)—was, in fact, a pioneering labor, and his edition immediately became the only one acceptable for scholarship. As Johnson's texts established themselves, the variorum was supplemented by the one-volume *Complete Poems*,* an inexpensive reading edition without textual variants* or apparatus, and then by *Final Harvest*, a selection containing 576 of the 1,775 *Complete Poems*.

To read some of the reviews of the 1955 edition is to realize how distant an era Johnson worked in. Louise Bogan, for instance, envisioned Johnson's Dickinson as a history-free creature of the text: "a woman of timeless genius . . .

[w]orking alone, without a vigorous culture to back her up, [who] nevertheless became, within limits, a self-determined woman who made choices—rather than the pathetic recluse of the legend—and an artist who more often than not was right the first time'' (179). In a New Critical* non sequitur, Bogan went on to conclude: ''Emily Dickinson never completely escaped from her Romantic* and late-Puritan* inheritance; women poets today have a greater variety of both technical means and material to draw upon.''

On the other hand, Jay Leyda's careful analysis anticipated future criticism to an astonishing degree. Though his word for the edition as a whole was ''magnificent,'' Leyda called attention to two ''flaws in principle'': inconsistency in deciding which texts should be called verse and which should be called prose and an attempt to key the chronology of some poems to events in the life of Charles Wadsworth*: ''The tendency to read the poems as autobiography should be combatted not reinforced by the editor'' (245).

In 1967, R. W. Franklin* discovered a disconcerting connection between those two flaws. ''The principle of editing that a text exactly represent the author's final intention is inadequate, since finality cannot be established,'' says Franklin at the end of *The Editing of Emily Dickinson*. ''[But] if one attempts, with a biographical* concern, to approach the poet through her works, one must have those works exactly as she left them. . . . [The] editor [of Emily Dickinson], in trying to avoid the twin pitfalls of arbitrariness and relativism, . . . will have to struggle with editorial and critical principles even to the limits of ontology and epistemology'' (142–43). In Baltimore a year before that, Jacques Derrida had read his paper ''Structure, Sign, and Play in the Discourse of the Human Sciences,'' introducing the revolutionary word ''*déconstruction*.'' The time had clearly come to rethink Johnson's methods. As of 1997, Franklin is reediting the manuscripts.

But Johnson's edition will always remain the foundation of modern Dickinson scholarship. Anticipating its eventual supersession, Leyda understood its place in literary history. ''I don't believe there is a higher honor for a work,'' he concluded, ''than to be regarded as a beginning'' (245). (*See*: Editorial Scholarship)

RECOMMENDED: Louise Bogan. ''The Poet Dickinson Comes to Life.'' *The New Yorker* 8 Oct. 1955: 190–91; R. W. Franklin, *The Editing of Emily Dickinson: A Reconsideration*; Thomas H. Johnson, ed., *The Complete Poems of Emily Dickinson, Final Harvest: Emily Dickinson's Poems*, and *The Poems of Emily Dickinson*; Jay Leyda. Rev. of *The Poems of Emily Dickinson*. Ed. Thomas H. Johnson. *New England Quarterly* 29 (1956): 239–45.

Jonathan Morse

POETIC TRIBUTES   If Hart Crane famously invoked the poet in ''To Emily Dickinson'' from ''The Bridge'' as ''O sweet, dead Silencer,'' one would hardly know it by the number of twentieth-century homages the Amherst* poet has inspired. From improbable trysts to visits to the Homestead,* from incorporation of lines from letters* and poems to an entire volume of poetry traceable to Dickinson's elusive "Master* Letters," American poets enter into commerce with Dickinson in ways that are surprising, engaging, sometimes ironic, often highly contemporary and original.

In *The Only Kangaroo among the Beauty*, Karl Keller quotes in full John Burdett Payne's "Emily and Walt, Walt and Emily," a poem rendering an imaginary missed meeting between Whitman* and Dickinson in New York. It begins by describing crosstown buses heading toward and away from an open poetry reading and thus cleverly encapsulates Keller's distinction between these two poets: the public Whitman, on his way to participate in the reading and leaning out the bus window to invite Dickinson, and the private Dickinson, purposefully riding in the other direction. In Payne's vividly etched story, each thinks lovingly of the other (263).

Donald Hall's "The Impossible Marriage" with its apt first sentence ("The bride* disappears") projects the nuptials of these two progenitors of American poetry with humor and lasciviousness. When the bride is returned to the altar, the groom has "withdrawn to the belltower with the healthy young sexton / from whose comradeship we detach him with difficulty." Hall concludes with more appropriated diction from both poets, and, like Payne, cross-fertilizes their roles: "—O pale, passionate / anchoret of Amherst! O reticent kosmos of Brooklyn!"

"Emily Dickinson and Gerard Manley Hopkins" in Madeline DeFrees' *Magpie on the Gallows* employs subtle, funny *ottava rima* to posit a surprisingly fruitful shipboard romance between Dickinson and the English Jesuit poet. But the cruise failed, as did their affair, which DeFrees records primarily in Dickinson's own language.

In Sandra Gilbert's *Emily's Bread*, the poet offers deft portraits of nineteenth- and twentieth-century women.* The "Emily" of the title invokes Dickinson and Brontë, both prized more for their baking skills than their poetic achievements during their lifetimes. "Emily's Bread" begins, "Inside the prizewinning blue-ribbon loaf of bread, / there is Emily, dressed in white, / veiled in unspeakable words." "The Emily Dickinson Black Cake* Walk" celebrates Dickinson's various roles and names in her household and creative life: baker, Uncle Emily, Emilie. In "A Book of Days" from Martha Collins' *The Arrangement of Space*, part 6 is titled "*Emily Dickinson: 1830–1886*" and begins by invoking the objects in Dickinson's room. The ending is especially powerful: "For us it goes the other way: / the deep green cave, the flesh / of love, the wings / of the white election—."

Other poets identify with the poet's geographical place through their visits to the Homestead on Main Street in Amherst.* Richard Wilbur writes "Altitudes" from *Things of This World* in two contrasting sections. The first describes a church in Rome, its ornate structure appropriate to its audience. Wilbur speculates about the distance between the Roman cathedral and Dickinson's father's house, the sun pouring through small windows for her alone, the birds* in the trees, "And a wild shining of the pure unknown / On Amherst." Marianne Boruch's "For Emily Dickinson," Charles Wright's "Visiting Emily Dickinson," and Amy Clampitt's "Amherst" describe these poets' impressions of local landmarks as ways of connecting with the poet. As Adrienne Rich states in "I am in Danger—Sir—," "you . . . chose to have it out at last / on your own premises." By contrast, James Schevill asserts in "Emily Dickinson" that "She made an asylum of poetry."

Three distinctive poetic sequences deserve close reading. Part II of Kashmiri poet Agha Shahid Ali's *A Nostalgist's Map of America*, which uses P1463 as an epigraph and repeated reference, includes the title poem and "In Search of Evanescence." Part 9, written using Dickinsonian lines and dashes,* envisions an American town called "Evanescence." It includes lines to a friend who had announced in the previous poem that he was dying. David Graham's book *Magic Shows* offers an impressive eight-section suite, "How Straight Up Is Curved: Homage to Emily Dickinson," each section using a Dickinson first line. Lynda Hull's posthumously published collection, *The Only World*, includes her "Suite for Emily," a devastating portrait of a childhood friend who was suffering from AIDS and in jail for heroin use. Hull invokes the nineteenth-century Emily and weaves her language and stance into this deadly frame.

Lucie Brock-Broido's entire volume *The Master Letters* comprises poems derived from the syntax* and imagery of Dickinson's prose and poetry.* The changes Brock-Broido renders in the combination of prose poems, sonnets, and couplets are remarkable, intricately tuned and shaped. In *Where Divinity Begins*, Deborah DeNicola has a sequence called "The Passion of Emily" about various mythological and historical women. "I Dream the Passion of Emily," too, is "after The Master Letters." The speaker dreams of lifting Dickinson off "her alabaster cross," saying she knows "what was sacrificed // for the poems tied / in fascicles,* disinterred / from the father's house. // I lift her fallen hand / read the palm, / infinity's pencil, / promise of circumference* // yet to come." This promise in the Dickinson body of work is one that poets will continue to explore with appreciation and wonder. (*See*: Dance Responses; Dramatic Representations; *Emily Dickinson International Society Bulletin*; Fiction; Musical Settings; Poets, Influence on; Visual Arts)

RECOMMENDED: Lucie Brock-Broido. *The Master Letters*. New York: Knopf, 1995; Ellen Davis. Rev. of *The Master Letters* by Lucie Brock-Broido. *Emily Dickinson International Society Bulletin* 8, 1 (May, June 1996): 11; Marguerite Harris, ed. *Emily Dickinson: Letters from the World*. New York: Cymric Press, 1970; Stephanie A. Tingley, "Sandra Gilbert and Emily Dickinson."

Ellen Davis

POETRY, AS SUBJECT   It would not be erroneous to say that almost all of Dickinson's poems are about poetry, in one way or another. Some, ostensibly about topics as diverse as oils, opera, birds,* and carpentry, can also be read analogically as references to poetry. However, there is a group of poems in which "poetry" or words directly associated with it, like "word,"* "poet," and "publication,"* are literally identified as subject. These include "To pile like Thunder to it's close" (P1247), "A Word dropped careless on a Page" (P1261), "I think I was enchanted" (P593), "It would never be Common— more—I said—" (P430), "A Word made Flesh is seldom" (P1651), "This Was a Poet—It is That" (P448),* "The Poets light but Lamps—" (P883), "I would not paint—a picture—" (P505), "Publication—is the Auction" (P709), and "Silence is all we dread" (P1251).

From such poems we learn about Dickinson's perceptions of poetry—its utter importance, its overwhelming power. To deal a "word of Gold" is to dower "all the World" (P430). Poetry is so powerful that it conquers time: "A Word that breathes distinctly / Has not the power to die" (P1651); it "hath an Element / Like Deity—to keep—" (P593). Poetry is "extra-ordinary": the sense that poets distill from ordinary meanings is, at the very least, "amazing" (P448), at the most, a "Divine Insanity" (P593); Poetry produces fear and awe as well as inspiration, transformation, or "Ransom" (P1251): despair, when "Infection in the sentence breeds" (P1261); even a form of death,* for like love,* like God,* none can "see" it and "live" (P1247). This kind of power, in fact, is consistently portrayed as equaling or even challenging God's. The equation of poetry with God makes these poems among Dickinson's boldest. But it is poetry that is godlike, not poets; "The Poets light but Lamps—/ Themselves—go out—" (P883). Dickinson is reticent about the poet, with whom she never directly identifies and whom she sometimes disowns altogether: "Nor would I be a Poet—" (P505). Perhaps this is the other side of the grandiosity of her claims for the art that is, by virtue of performance, hers. Indeed, some of her statements find a certain relief in contrariety. Silence may be "all we dread" (P1251), but sometimes, as opposed to the "paltry melody" of speech, it is "beautiful" (P1750).

RECOMMENDED: everything on Dickinson

Suzanne Juhasz

POETS, INFLUENCE ON   Dickinson established, along with Walt Whitman,* the urgency of individual voice* and innovative method, touchstones of American poetry.* If Whitman has been perceived as more influential than Dickinson, two major factors need consideration. First, the full extent of her originality in terms of poetic method was not recognized until Thomas H. Johnson's* 1955 edition; the nature and extent of her influence have been, in part, shaped by the edition available to a poet at a particular period. Contemporary poets have been in a better position than the moderns to appreciate Dickinson's influence because of greater textual and biographical* information. Second, in spite of many shared concerns, Dickinson divides with Whitman along gender lines; she has primarily been a precursor for female poets. Dickinson has left, however, a wide and varied legacy.

Modern Poets. Even though Dickinson's formal inventions were not fully available to the generation of poets immediately following the posthumous publication of her poems, her poetics struck them as original and defiant. Her particular handling of thematic concerns of mortality and isolation* likewise had a significant impact. William Dean Howells,* commenting on the roughness of the poems, recommended Dickinson to Stephen Crane in the 1890s. Her ironic mode seemed fitting, at least to Howells, for the emerging generation. The compact and abstract aspect of her poems, their emphasis on tough paradox and ambiguity,* would seem to suit them for the climate fostered by T. S. Eliot and his "New Critical"* followers. But although her work possesses qualities of economy and fragmentation admired, for example, by William Carlos Williams, he, like most other male modernists, favored Whitman over Dickinson. Robert Frost nevertheless called her "the greatest woman *writer* in the history of the world" and, indeed, ranked her among the top three American poets; he admired her unflinching concern with death* and spiritual doubt in the face of it (Keller 309). Critical of what he considered her occasional carelessness with form, he could appreciate the controlled playfulness of her verse. Amy Lowell, with Frost, was among Dickinson's first major supporters, regarding her not only as a foremother in her poem "The Sisters" but as an exemplar for the imagist movement. Dickinson's often startling images and compressed* presentation would continue, partly through Lowell's mediation, to influence other women poets, among them Harriet Monroe and Edna St. Vincent Millay. Lowell exulted in the poet's daring stance and reflected Dickinson's departure from metrics and exact rhyme* in her own experiments with cadence. Dickinson's appropriate yet idiosyncratic word* choices from a variety of lexicons along with her eliding of syntactical* connectives inflected Marianne Moore's eccentric poetics. Louise Bogan has noted Dickinson's influence on moderns as beyond our capacity to appreciate fully in its reshaping of diction, versification, and perception itself; for Bogan and others, she was a mystical poet. For Hart Crane, she epitomized *the* American dilemma that he summarized in his "To Emily Dickinson": "You who desired so much—in vain to ask—/ Yet fed your hunger like an endless task" (Keller 308).

Contemporary Poets. The exploration of interior states and the primacy of subjectivity manifest in poetry after World War II brought Dickinson's influence to the forefront. Poets dissatisfied with the legacy of Eliot's "impersonal theory of art" turned to poetry of greater personal scope. Robert Lowell's *Life Studies*, in its emphasis upon solitude and alienation, owes some of its derangement to Dickinson. Elizabeth Bishop shares in her predecessor's interrogation of orthodoxy, religious* and otherwise. Many of her poems reveal a kindred use of unresolvable paradox, irony, and uncertainty. Theodore Roethke refers to her privileging of the unconscious over the rational, and Dickinson's use of riddling language in compact stanzas emerges in his own, her spiritual questions contributing to his longer meditations. Allen Ginsberg declares Dickinson an important early influence: one sees her trace in his short visionary poems of dissonant but visible musicality.* Sylvia Plath's dense imagery, its volcanic force in portraying conflicts between the creative and the domestic,* seems informed by Dickinson's idiom. In her wry, exultant examination of death,* Stevie Smith is also marked by Dickinson's unremitting reflection upon annihilation: "Drowning is not so pitiful / As the attempt to rise" (P1718) possibly haunts Smith's "Not Waving but Drowning."

Contemporary poets often foreground visionary* aspects of her work: Anthony Hecht sees a "religious seriousness" rather than the reticence often ascribed to her (Farr 162); Richard Wilbur remarks upon Dickinson's sincerity and integrity in excavating the most difficult states of psychic* turmoil. Charles Wright declares, "Emily Dickinson is the only writer I've ever read who knows my name, whose work has influenced me at my heart's core, whose music is the music of songs I've listened to and remembered in my very body" (*Halflife*, University of Michigan Press, 1988). Dickinson can be felt in his mastery of the lyric* moment, suspended, mysterious, riveting. Charles Simic often pairs the abstract with the concrete, the mundane with the cosmic; in very short poems, he manages to produce great conflations of proportion, a tactic of Dickinson's. He refers to her (rather than to Whitman) as a pillar in American art and, comparing her with his other hero, Joseph Cornell, praises her as "without precedent, eccentric, original, and thoroughly American" (*Dime-Store Alchemy: The Art of Joseph Cornell*, Ecco, 1992). Along with her subjects, Dickinson's inventive poetic methods are also invoked: A. R. Ammons, using a similarly abstract vocabulary, uses the colon in a way akin to Dickinson's dash.*

Adrienne Rich, influenced by Dickinson in all her incarnations in print, perceives the poet as gifted with ability to register extreme psychic states and as a figure of female empowerment. Dismissing the "mythology" of Dickinson as pathological, she puts forth instead a woman of great integrity and will, who "chose / silence for entertainment, / chose to have it out at last / on [her] own premises" ("I am in Danger—Sir," *Necessities of Life: Poems 1962–1964*, Norton, 1966). Such a revised reading of Dickinson has influenced a generation of feminist* poets.

Dickinson's defiant iconoclasm becomes a pervasive impulse, yielding not only a feminist recuperation of the poet but also a postmodern one, a perspective emphasizing her dynamic language use and the instability of concepts of identity and knowledge. The autonomy of self embraced by Rich is refracted in the focus on linguistic* subversions. Drawn to Dickinson's disruption of conventional narrative, Alice Fulton revels in the poet's unpredictable, intellectually charged puns and conceits. Heather McHugh's *Hinge and Sign* (Wesleyan, 1995) recalls Dickinson's language play as, defiant and irreverent, it interrogates identity. McHugh is equally compelled by the breakages and sutures represented by the dash. Susan Howe, prominent language poet, seems likewise influenced by Dickinson's textures of unlikely grammar and volatile syntax.*

Many women poets currently influenced by Dickinson explicitly assert their conscious alliance. Mebdh McGuckian, contemporary Irish poet, in her coded, cryptic language and her dense, shifting metaphors,* also bears Dickinson's imprint. As McGuckian's "The Most Emily of All" elliptically records, "a sentence clings tighter / because it makes no sense"; her control of a verse permeated by wild, fluid reversals shows Dickinson's influence (*Marconi's Cottage*, 1991). Lucie Brock-Broido's *The Master Letters* "echo formal & rhetorical* devices from Dickinson's work," as she puts it (Knopf, 1995). Lynda Hull's "Suite for Emily" epitomizes her debt to Dickinson: she inherits the often rough and razor-painful occupying of extreme mental states. With the somewhat incongruous pairing of urban terrors with her quotations from Dickinson, Hull concentrates on mortality and worldly transience, as when she elegizes*: "What heaven she found she made. / And so did we, worlds that sear, consume—earthly / delirious" (*The Only World*, Harper, 1995). Lynn Emanuel's *The Dig* includes a homage poem to Dickinson in which she imagines being the dead poet (University of Illinois Press, 1992). Other poems take on the posthumous position reminiscent of many Dickinson speakers; even as Emanuel imagines the moment of dying, she affirms an earthly ecstasy.

Overall, some of Dickinson's qualities continue to exert great influence: (1) her combination of the highly intellectual with the emotional; (2) her unresolvable tension between an allegorical reading of the world and a concrete one, oscillating between perspectives of the cosmic and of the mundane; (3) her suspension of closure; (4) her play with form, grammar, and syntax; (5) her subversion of set categories and limits, including those of gender; and (6) her attention to the large concerns of ontology and epistemology within lyric confines. (*See*: Philosophical Approaches; Poetic Tributes)

RECOMMENDED: Betsy Erkkila, "Dickinson and Rich: Toward a Theory of Female Poetic Influence"; Paul J. Ferlazzo, *Critical Essays on Emily Dickinson*; Alice Fulton, "Her Moment of Brocade: The Reconstruction of Emily Dickinson"; Anthony Hecht, "The Riddles of Emily Dickinson"; Karl Keller, *The Only Kangaroo among the Beauty: Emily Dickinson and America*; David Porter, *Dickinson: The Modern Idiom*.

Susan McCabe

POPULAR CULTURE REPRESENTATIONS   Nonscholarly representations of Dickinson began before scholarship existed on this formidable poet. As reported by Mabel Loomis Todd,* her reputation as a recluse was the talk of Amherst.* Unfortunately, for some, that reputation still overshadows the poet's work. Susan Dickinson* attempted to salvage her sister-in-law's reputation at the time of her death by declaring in an obituary published in the *Springfield Republican** that "as she passed on in life, her sensitive nature shrank from much personal contact with the world, and more and more turned to her own large wealth of individual resources for companionship" (*Years* 2:473).

Since Higginson's* pronouncement on Dickinson as a "half-cracked poet-ess," popular culture depictions of her have flourished in their (mis)-representations of the poet as a mad* agoraphobic who dressed only in white. Rivaled solely by Edgar Allan Poe's* own undeserved reputation as an alcoholic drug addict/pedophile, Dickinson's notoriety remains within the late nineteenth century's view of her as a spinster who dispensed poems with her baking. The Tony Award-winning Julie Harris portrayed her as an addled old maid whose excellence in cookery ranks with her poetic achievement in William Luce's play, *The Belle of Amherst* (1976). In between snippets of verse and letters,* Dickinson recites her recipe for black cake* to the audience. Norman Rosten's 1969 attempt to capture Dickinson onstage, *Come Slowly, Eden*, is also preoccupied with her baking talents. In this play, history is abandoned as Lavinia* conspires with Higginson after Dickinson's death to rummage through the poet's personal belongings, occasionally picking up letters and poems to read aloud to the audience. Appearing only in the play when her words need rationalization, Dickinson is stereotyped as a love*lorn poet, preoccupied with nature* and dominated by her father. Thus two major popular culture representations of Dickinson virtually equate her literary brilliance with her baking talent. Other popular culture representations of Dickinson exist, such as various children's biographies, fictitious* biographies, T-shirt images, and cartoons. (*See*: Dramatic Representations)

Amy J. Pardo

POSTAGE STAMP　Designed by Bernard Fuchs after the daguerreotype,* the U.S. postage stamp honoring Dickinson was issued at Amherst,* Massachusetts, on 28 August 1971. The stamp presents a multicolored portrait of Dickinson against a greenish background. Beneath the image are printed her name, the series title "American Poet," and the eight-cent value. The Scott number for the stamp is 1436.

RECOMMENDED: Scott Standard Postage Stamp Catalogue, 1997. 148th ed. Sidney, OH: Scott, 1996.

Jonnie Guerra

POSTSTRUCTURALIST APPROACHES　Two varieties of poststructural-ism have left their mark on Dickinson studies. One, which can loosely be called deconstructive, focuses on the propensity for signification to run wild in Dickinson's poems. The other, which can more strictly be called feminist,* examines the gender issues in this unruly proliferation of meaning and their implications for the poet's identity and mission. In both varieties language is regarded less as an instrument than a power in its own right, one capable of organizing human wishes in its own image. The poems are thus often read as allegories of language and its vicissitudes more than as articulations of the poet's vision.*

Dickinson would seem to invite such approaches, for like poststructuralist theorists she is clearly interested in the perils, possibilities, and paradoxes that language can lead to when pushed to the limit. In one poem she writes of "internal difference, / Where the Meanings, are—" (P258). Her lines anticipate a basic premise of structuralism and poststructuralism, the claim that meaning arises not from the linguistic* sign (which an author chooses and to that extent necessarily determines) but from differences among signs (hence, from the global or systemic aspect of language, which no one commands).

One consequence of this claim is that meaning cannot easily be circumscribed or secured. Differential relations stop nowhere, so as a process signification is potentially limitless. Such proliferation, if understood as a blessing, might prove to be the "Circumference"* that poets disseminate in P883. Understood as baleful, it might prove to be the ominously "undeveloped Freight" that the "delivered syllable" in P1409 threatens to convey.

David Porter takes the second view in *The Modern Idiom*, ironically the most thoroughly deconstructive reading of Dickinson extant. The irony is that he is hostile to poststructuralist ideas and seeks to police literary language for the excesses and indeterminacies that deconstruction usually celebrates. A more sympathetic view is taken by Sharon Cameron, who sees profundity rather than bafflement in Dickinson's most explosive or enigmatic poems. She also finds in them several of the main themes of poststructuralist theory—particularly the gulf between presence and representation and the centrality of mourning both to the need for representation and to the experience of temporality.

Another frequent concern of poststructuralism has been figural language, especially the patterns of thinking associated with different tropes and also the cognitive status of figurality in general. Roland Hagenbüchle was the first Dickinson critic to pursue this concern, arguing that her tropes are more often metonymic* than metaphoric* (depending on relations of nearness, roughly speaking, rather than those of likeness) and, hence, less easily assimilable to some overall unity. Her wildness is a stylistic choice, in other words, one that exploits an inherent potential of language.

Poststructuralist feminism* has most interestingly developed the implications of Dickinson's use of figures. Margaret Homans argues that Dickinson associates all figural language with the feminine, specifically with Eve, whereas literal language belongs with Adamic naming, that is, the masculine. Although Eve's language may be more wayward than the one God* ordained Adam to speak, it provides the opening within an otherwise patriarchal tradition for a specifically woman's poetry. Homans makes the case for Dickinson as distinctively a woman poet on the grounds of literary theory, rather than the more common biographical* or historical* grounds.

Homans bases part of her argument on Lacanian psychoanalysis,* from which Mary Loeffelholz draws more directly but more pessimistically. Within Lacan's labyrinthine theory the endless chains of signification not only obey what he calls the Law of the Father but arise specifically from prohibitions and misrecognitions that this law dictates. Loeffelholz reads Dickinson as intuitively sensing the double binds that Lacan stresses and accordingly engaging with masculine literary authority in a much more ambivalent and self-divided fashion than most feminist critics discern. (*See*: Philosophical Approaches)

RECOMMENDED: Sharon Cameron, *Lyric Time: Dickinson and the Limits of Genre*; Roland Hagenbüchle, "Precision and Indeterminacy in the Poetry of Emily Dickinson"; Margaret Homans, *Women Writers and Poetic Identity: Dorothy Wordsworth, Emily Brontë, and Emily Dickinson*; Mary Loeffelholz, *Dickinson and the Boundaries of Feminist Theory*; David Porter, *Dickinson: The Modern Idiom*.

Gary Lee Stonum

PRAYER   As with most thematic clusters of poems, Emily Dickinson adopted many poses in her poems on prayer. In this she resembled certain seventeenth-century metaphysical poets, whose work she may have known and with whom she has sometimes been compared. Her voices range from despair, as in "At least—to pray—is left—is left—" (P502), to worship, as in "My period had come for Prayer—" (P564). They include the childlike* pose of "Of Course—I prayed—" (P376) and an appeal to the "Madonna dim" from "a Nun" (P918). The "Apparatus" of prayer, as outlined in "Prayer is the little implement" (P437), appears unwieldy despite its apparent simplicity: to gain attention "Where Presence—is denied them," supplicants "fling their Speech . . . in God's* Ear." The process is complete, it seems, only "If then He hear—." Most of Dickinson's personae fail in their attempts to reach God's* ear. In "I meant to have but modest needs—" (P476), for example, the speaker seeks God in prayer only to be mocked for believing the promise of Matthew 7:7: "Ask, and it shall be given you; seek, and ye shall find; knock, and it shall be opened unto you." This promise figures prominently in Dickinson's treatment of prayer in both poems and letters.* As early as 1853, she suggested that the promise that prayers will be answered "t'was only a blunder of Matthew's" (L133). Thirty years later she offered a similar assessment in berating a friend: "You are like God. We pray to Him and He answers 'No.' Then we pray to Him to rescind the 'no,' and He don't answer at all, yet 'Seek and ye shall find' is the boon of faith"* (L830). (*See*: Bible; Herbert; Prophecy; Religion)

RECOMMENDED: Sally Burke. "A Religion of Poetry: The Prayer Poems of Emily Dickinson"; Steve Carter, "Emily Dickinson and Mysticism"; Jane Donahue Eberwein, *Dickinson: Strategies of Limitation*; Dorothy Huff Oberhaus, " 'Engine against th' Almightie': Emily Dickinson and Prayer"; Shira Wolosky, *Emily Dickinson: A Voice of War*.

Emily Seelbinder

PROPHECY   Understood as a truth-telling and visionary* mode, prophecy in the antebellum years deeply interested New Englanders, including Emily Dickinson. She and her contemporaries encountered it both as oratory and as literature, most notably by Ralph Waldo Emerson,* Henry David Thoreau,* and Walt Whitman,* but also by preachers, political speakers, and others. The imminence of the Civil War* encouraged a rhetoric* of apocalypse as orators often questioned the purity of the nation and spoke of the war as God's* judgment. Surrounded by a host of orators and self-proclaimed prophets, Dickinson responded with a wisdom literature of her own making. She drew on the prophetic tradition she knew best, the Judeo-Christian one, to claim both religious* and poetic authority.

Prophecy forms the center of Transcendentalist* poetics. According to Emerson, the poet's office consists of articulating the spiritual facts of earthly existence, with the effect of emancipating humanity through the poet's sublime* vision. But the Romantic* idea of the poet as prophet derives from classical and biblical models. Prophecy forms the largest body of writings in the Bible*—those of the Old Testament prophets as well as John's Book of Revelation in the New Testament—and also forms the largest body of poetry in the Scriptures. Along with the wisdom literature of the Bible (e.g., the Book of Proverbs), these writings may be the most significant single rhetorical influence on Dickinson's art. Indeed, the Judeo-Christian prophetic tradition more broadly defined as including Scripture as well as the evangelical preaching of Dickinson's day (which extended the scriptural prophetic tradition into contemporary times) profoundly informed Dickinson's art, even as she drew on it to challenge aspects of evangelical dogma.

The notion of prophecy thus links many of Dickinson's contexts—historical,* literary, rhetorical, religious—and, in fact, clarifies how Dickinson probably saw her own art. We hear her prophetic voice particularly in the proverbial statements that usually open her poems. But her poetry of prophecy goes beyond that to express the stance, style, structures, and themes of Judeo-Christian prophets. Understanding Dickinson's poetry as prophecy explains her choice of "slantness"* or indirection as a poetic technique, as she, like the scriptural prophets, positioned herself on the margins of her community yet directed her words to it. Like Isaiah and Christ before her, she spoke to "those who have ears to hear" and seemed to write her poetry out of an inner compulsion to speak truth.

Prophecy as poetry also helps to explain the spoken quality of Dickinson's verse and Dickinson's choice of song for her poetry: the most notable female prophet of the Bible, Miriam, is known for having sung her prophecy rather than offered a jeremiad. The struggle to find and manipulate a rhetorical form through which to express a religious vision links Dickinson to other American women "prophets" who were disallowed the public platform because of cultural constraints against women's public prophetic speech: Anne Hutchinson, Harriet Beecher Stowe,* Sarah Grimke, and possibly the myriad female devotional poets of Dickinson's day. Indeed, in that time, a number of influential women spoke to women's special predilection to prophesy—not only Margaret Fuller but also the conservatively religious Lydia Maria Child and Sarah Josepha Hale. In the context of female oratory, male preaching, romantic poetry, and the Scriptures, Dickinson crafted her own understanding of the female seer who condemns superficiality and hypocrisy but also consoles, sings, and wonders, adjusting the terms of faith* to a new vision of spirituality. (*See*: Hymns; Women's Culture)

RECOMMENDED: Beth Maclay Doriani, *Emily Dickinson, Daughter of Prophecy*; Murray Roston. *Prophet and Poet: The Bible and the Growth of Romanticism*. Evanston, IL: Northwestern University Press, 1965.

Beth Maclay Doriani

PSYCHOLOGICAL APPROACHES Psychoanalytic theorists fashion systems for understanding how internal psychic processes mesh with external social environments to produce individuals and culture. Modifying and elaborating upon ideas inherited from Sigmund Freud about the psychic processes that produce metaphor* and metonymy,* processes of mourning and transference, and mechanisms of desire, psychoanalytic theorists are expanding Dickinson studies.

Scholars interested in how Dickinson retools language to register a subversive female identity often begin with Jacques Lacan's and Julia Kristeva's adaptations of Freud's oedipal theory. The oedipal complex is the process whereby preverbal children part from the mother and exchange the pleasures of undifferentiated bodily union with her for the social legitimacy of the paternal realm. Here, the individual, assuming a gendered social position, is initiated into the laws and language of the patriarchal culture—the language that, purportedly, cannot render women's subjectivity but can render women only as objects of patriarchal fantasies. The following applications of psychoanalytic theories to "I think I was enchanted" (P593), a poem that invites speculation because it potentially presents a girl's account of inheriting an alternative transformative language from a maternal realm rather than a paternal one, explore ways of using the oedipal paradigm to understand Dickinson's life in language.

A classical Freudian analyst like Cody might read P593 as a forbidden fantasy of returning to the "dark" and "enchant[ing]" state of original physical ("felt") unity with the mother. A Lacanian critic, however, might interpret the fused "read[ing]" and feeling of the "Foreign Lady" as indicating that, having entered language, the narrator can never regain direct access to the mother but can only attempt to regain her through language that delivers nothing but endless signs of her desire. Alternatively, Hogue cites Kristeva to interpret P593 as a poem performing Dickinson's "maternal" poetics of indeterminacy. Hogue argues that whenever the poet uses the organizing structures of language to master an experience at the expense of its complexity, she or he reenacts the oedipal scenario: the chaotic experience of union with the mother's body exchanged for the safety of the linguistic* power to master experience. She sees Dickinson creating a poetry of multiple meanings in her refusal to sacrifice the many-dimensional preoedipal mother in exchange for singularity of meaning. Inasmuch as the "witness[ing]" but not "explain[ing]" narrator opposes her inherited poetics of "Witchcraft" (associated with women and bodies) to critique patriarchal religion* implicitly, she can be interpreted as potentially recounting the story of her reception of a maternal, bodily poetics from a woman.

Juhasz, using a relational psychoanalytic perspective, argues that children don't gain language at the expense of their mothers but instead negotiate specific, mutual linguistic meanings with the mother, meanings that may reorder the terms of the dominant culture. For Juhasz, P593's narrator might be a young woman who inscribes her maternally negotiated symbolic meanings onto dominant cultural meanings. She brings her idiosyncratic discourse into dialogue with prevailing discourse through pairs of opposing terms ("San[ity]"/"Insanity") and metaphors that perform her ability to assign different meanings to cultural terms and even to reverse social hierarchies; "meanest Tunes" become "Titanic Opera" in this narrator's contradictory system. (*See*: Browning, Elizabeth; Feminist Approaches; Madness; Poststructuralist Approaches)

RECOMMENDED: John Cody, *After Great Pain: The Inner Life of Emily Dickinson*; Cynthia Hogue, *Scheming Women: Poetry, Privilege, and the Politics of Subjectivity*; Suzanne Juhasz, "Adventures in the World of the Symbolic: Emily Dickinson and Metaphor."

Robin E. Calland

PUBLICATION, ATTITUDES TOWARD   "Publication—is the Auction / Of the Mind of Man—" (P709), Dickinson stated unequivocally. In her third letter to Thomas Wentworth Higginson,* she said, "I smile when you suggest that I delay 'to publish'—that being foreign to my thought, as Firmament to Fin—" (L265). Dickinson's disclaimer of a desire to publish has been seen by many twentieth-century critics as the bitter resignation of one prevented by the blindness of her contemporaries from achieving the fame* she deserved—and, they assume, the fame she certainly wanted. But, in fact, her ideas about publication were not idiosyncratic; in choosing not to publish, she carried out in practice attitudes expressed by many of her contemporaries, Higginson among them. Dickinson put off publication indefinitely by casting Higginson in the role of her "Preceptor" and herself in that of his "Scholar," adopting the stance that in asking his help, she irrevocably declared herself to hold the "Barefoot-Rank" of unpublished poet (L265).

Only ten of Dickinson's poems were published in her lifetime, to our present knowledge (Poems 3,* 35,* 214,* 216,* 228,* 137,* 130,* 324,* 67,* and 986* in order of first appearance from 1852 to 1866). Not one of these publications was initiated by her. In several cases, there is evidence poems reached editors through third parties. When she at least tacitly consented to publication, as in the *Drum Beat*,* she did so because she could not refuse to aid a particular cause (e.g., L676).

Dickinson chose not to publish to avoid the demands made on successful authors, demands that would have taken her time, her privacy, and what Higginson called in his April 1862 "Letter to a Young Contributor" the writer's "seclusion . . . and therefore [her] unconsciousness." She chose not to publish to keep her poems "alive"—a concern reflected in her first request to Higginson (L260) and directly linked to her need to delay publishing. For this poet, who often went back to revise poems written years before, every poem was potentially a work in progress. As this sense of process gave life to her poems, it was essential to keep them within her own control where she could freely—and privately—revise them. For Dickinson, while there was life, there was the possibility of revision. It was inevitable that her poems would not be published until after her death. (*See*: "An Open Portfolio"; Dickinson, Susan; Fascicles; Women's Culture)

RECOMMENDED: Karen Dandurand, "Dickinson and the Public" and "Why Dickinson Did Not Publish"; Joanne Dobson, *Dickinson and the Strategies of Reticence*; Martha Nell Smith, *Rowing in Eden: Rereading Emily Dickinson.*

Karen Dandurand

PURITAN HERITAGE   Dickinson's family traces back to Nathaniel Dickinson, a seventeeth-century Puritan settler of early Amherst.* In the nineteenth century Amherst was a conservative pocket of neo-Puritanism. The discourse of her Puritan heritage deeply informed Dickinson's life and the concerns and rhetoric* of her poems.

Rejecting a vindictive God* and his exclusive heaven,* Dickinson worked against the Calvinist tenets of reprobation and unconditional election.* She preferred the Calvinist concept of grace, which undergirded her Romantic* celebration of life and the ecstatic stance of many of her speakers. She never stopped yearning for a loving God and a just heaven.

Dickinson's religious* heritage also gave her the methods of self-examination and interpretation required of the Puritan spiritual pilgrimage. Puritans were encouraged to evaluate their daily behavior in diaries that recorded their progress toward perfection in God. Clergy also showed their congregations how to read the word for signs of God's favor. Dickinson examined this Puritan semiology to see how theocrats generated meaning in a system of signs that reflected political and social constructs; she created verbal constructs to empower her own poetic meaning.

Further, Puritanism left a rhetorical* legacy. Puritans were required to read the Bible* as a guide for living. With its deep capacity for analogy and treasure of stirring narratives, especially the metanarrative of the journey toward paradise regained, the Bible provided a source of power and drama for Dickinson's poems. In addition, the traditional Puritan sermons that Dickinson heard in the First Church* used logical construction, colloquial* diction, vivid imagery, and urgent tone; Dickinson liberally used these rhetorical techniques.

Dickinson attacked the Puritan view of women as subordinate to men, exemplified in her prominent father and submissive mother. She examined patterns of power in the fabric of Puritan discourse, where man is subordinate to God, and woman is subordinate to man, and created poems that envision more egalitarian gender relations. With poems representing the full spectrum of females from abject to omnipotent, her corpus can be read as a field on which old Puritan arguments and new arguments of Emersonian* self-reliance engage each other.

Dickinson's Puritan heritage gave her the great themes of her poetry*: the nature of God, men, women, life, death,* and "the Flood subject" of immortality* (L319). It also gave her a passion for words* and logic to grapple with these subjects in ways that restructured the old Puritan polarities of active man/ passive woman, good/evil, spirit/flesh, elect/damned, life/death, and mortal/immortal. Dickinson opened these closed categories to multiple possibilities and brought to this work the drama that her Puritan ancestors brought to the constant struggle between good and evil. (*See*: Congregationalism; Faith; Prayer; Prophecy)

RECOMMENDED: Beth Maclay Doriani, *Emily Dickinson, Daughter of Prophecy*; Jane Donahue Eberwein, " 'Graphicer for Grace': Emily Dickinson's Calvinist Language" and *Dickinson: Strategies of Limitation*; Rowena Revis Jones, "The Preparation of a Poet: Puritan Directions in Emily Dickinson's Education"; Dorothy Huff Oberhaus, *Emily Dickinson's Fascicles: Method and Meaning*.

Joanna Yin

R

READER-RESPONSE THEORY is a mode of inquiry into the tripartite exchange between the reader, writer, and text. The reader's subjective engagement with the text and the ways the formal properties of the text elicit particular responses from the reader are cornerstones of this theoretical model. Reader-response critics also analyze the text to discern traces of the author or the author's attitude toward reading, the message inscribed by the author, and the cues transmitted to the reader for decoding purposes.

Gary Lee Stonum's *The Dickinson Sublime* is inflected by the rhetorical* approach, which explores how the author's construction of the text transmits meaning to, and produces intended effects in, the reader. For Stonum, the romantic* sublime—an experience of intense emotion that disrupts normal modes of consciousness*—is repeatedly thematized in Dickinson's poems and reflects her commitment to evoking an affective response from readers. Dickinson's anxiety about power and the traditional definition of poet as master results in her creation of an aesthetic that privileges multivalency and thereby encourages multiple forms of reader-response.

In ''The Big Tease,'' Suzanne Juhasz also draws on the rhetorical approach, particularly the concept that within an individual text are inscribed traces of both an image of an ideal reader capable of best realizing the meaning of the text and of the author capable of writing it. According to Juhasz, Dickinson's position within a patriarchal society freights the reader/writer with danger: Dickinson's desire to disrupt accepted meanings while attracting an ideal reader who appreciates her linguistic* deviance is threatened by the reader who expects traditional definitions of words* and a conventional woman poet inscribed within the text. Dickinson negotiates the potential threat the reader poses through ''tease,'' a movement between invitation to, and resistance of, the reader.

Semiotic, phenomenological, and feminist* versions of reader-response are woven together to forge a theory on Dickinson in *Rowing in Eden: Rereading Emily Dickinson* by Martha Nell Smith. The phenomenological approach is concerned with the process by which the individual reader brings the text to life, the semiotic approach is interested in the text itself as a cluster of signifiers and the way they convey meaning, and feminism adds to both these modes of inquiry the issue of women's relationship to language. Crucial to Smith's own theory are the conception of Dickinson's poems as generating endless interpretations and her revelation that each reading of Dickinson is shaped by the ideological, historical,* and social position of the reader. Outlining a history of readers' strategies of reading, mutilating, and editing* Dickinson's manuscripts in order to produce particular acceptable versions of Dickinson—as heterosexual, as a conventional poet, as a "true woman"—Smith warns against the pursuit of an authoritative reading of Dickinson. Such a goal is antithetical to Dickinson's poetic style, which, through its privileging of indeterminacy, resists monolithic readings and promotes each reader to the position of an active producer of meaning.

These three practitioners of reader-response theory move Dickinson studies in a new direction by reframing ways to look at such familiar issues as Dickinson's negotiation of power and the uniqueness of her poetic style and by initiating original inquiries into Dickinson's stance toward the reader and her reader-centered aesthetics. All three critics excavate the ways in which Dickinson's unique style—the dashes,* textual variants,* obscured referents, and indeterminate language—favors multiplicity and encourages the reader to make active choices. Such theories implicitly critique New Critical* values that posit the text as a hermetically sealed object of study and argue for a new approach to Dickinson that highlights her concern with the process of reading. Also privileged in these readings is a call for literary criticism to respond to Dickinson by using theory that mirrors the values inherent in her own poetics.

RECOMMENDED: Suzanne Juhasz, "The Big Tease"; Martha Nell Smith, *Rowing in Eden: Rereading Emily Dickinson*; Martin Orzeck, and Robert Weisbuch, eds., *Dickinson and Audience*; Robert McClure Smith, *The Seductions of Emily Dickinson*; Gary Lee Stonum, *The Dickinson Sublime*.

H. Jordan Landry

REALISM   is a broad term referring to those works that, in opposition to idealized or romanticized modes of literature, strive for verisimilitude in depicting nature,* life, and the world. The term also refers to the American Realistic period, a literary movement coming into prominence at the close of the Civil War* and maintaining its dominance in American letters until the turn of the century. While this movement is most often associated with novelists such as William Dean Howells* and Mark Twain, the poet Walt Whitman* is recognized as contributing to a democratic style and subject matter that also commented on current social and political structures and events.

The literary movement with which Dickinson is commonly associated is Romanticism,* and only on rare occasions is she linked with Realism. In *Emily Dickinson and Her Culture*, Barton Levi St. Armand argues that Dickinson's poetry reflects her culture but not with the "economy of plot and realism of description" that characterize Realism (97). He emphasizes her "literary conservatism" after the Civil War and asserts that while Realism was replacing Romanticism, "Dickinson remained a romantic."

Yet Dickinson's poetry also demonstrates some key characteristics associated with Realism. First, her descriptions possess a detailed accuracy in rendering her environment, especially nature. Examples of realistic nature poems include "A Bird* came down the Walk—" (P328) and "A narrow Fellow in the Grass" (P986).* Another characteristic of Realism found in her poetry is its engagement with political, social, and historical events. For instance, Dickinson wrote a number of Civil War poems, such as "They dropped like Flakes—" (P409), "It feels a shame to be Alive—" (P444), and "My Triumph lasted till the Drums" (P1227).

While Dickinson's poetry includes certain traits of Realism, her opinion of realist writers remains fraught with mysterious ambivalence. She cryptically noted, "of Howells and [Henry] James, one hesitates" (L622). Howells, who rejected Romanticism and almost exclusively reserved his accolades for Realists, apparently recognized realist qualities in her poetry because he placed Dickinson among those few Americans whose writing represented a "distinctive" contribution to world literature.

RECOMMENDED: Elissa Greenwald, "Dickinson among the Realists"; William Dean Howells, "The Poems of Emily Dickinson"; Donald Pizer, ed. *The Cambridge Companion to American Realism and Naturalism: Howells to London*. Cambridge: Cambridge University Press, 1995; Barton Levi St. Armand, *Emily Dickinson and Her Culture: The Soul's Society*; Shira Wolosky, *Emily Dickinson: A Voice of War*.

Mary Carney

RELIGION AND RELIGIOUS CRITICISM   Though Emily Dickinson may not fit the traditional mold for a religious person, she was clearly fascinated by religious matters, and she explored such matters from differing, sometimes contradictory points of view. Many critics have explored and attempted to codify Dickinson's religious perspective. Much has been made of her assertion to Higginson* that her family was "religious" but she herself was not (L261), of her apparent practice of keeping the Sabbath by "staying at Home" (P324),* of her correspondence with several clergymen and her obvious interest in good preaching, and of her many statements expressing both belief and unbelief in poems, letters,* and biographical* anecdote. She has been claimed as both Catholic* and Protestant, Calvinist and anti-Calvinist, firm believer and lifelong skeptic. She has been identified as a mystic, an antinomian, and an existentialist. Some critics argue that she rejected the religious practices of her day or at least seriously questioned them. Others counter that she was always a deeply religious person or that she gradually became one as her life progressed. Still others assert that her "religion" was poetry.* There is often evidence in Dickinson's life and work both to confirm and to disprove these critical positions. Adding to the difficulty for critics is Dickinson's fondness for ambiguity* and paradox as well as her use of voices* that appear to contradict each other when poems on similar subjects—including poems collected by the poet herself into the fascicles*—are compared side by side. While Dickinson's belief system may be impossible to codify, her exploration of religious subjects is rich and diverse. As the following bibliography demonstrates, religious criticism of Dickinson is rich and diverse as well. (*See*: Faith; Philosophical Approaches; Prophecy; Puritan Heritage)

RECOMMENDED: Nadean Bishop, "Queen of Calvary: Spirituality in Emily Dickinson"; Jane Donahue Eberwein, "Emily Dickinson and the Calvinist Sacramental Tradition"; Rowena Revis Jones, " 'A Royal Seal': Emily Dickinson's Rite of Baptism"; Douglas Novich Leonard, "Emily Dickinson's Religion: An 'Ablative Estate' "; Elisa New, "Difficult Writing, Difficult God: Emily Dickinson's Poems beyond Circumference"; Dorothy Huff Oberhaus, *Emily Dickinson's Fascicles: Method and Meaning*; Virginia H. Oliver, *Apocalypse of Green: A Study of Emily Dickinson's Eschatology*; Regina Siegfried, "Bibliographic Essay: Selected Criticism for Emily Dickinson's Religious Background."

Emily Seelbinder

RENUNCIATION, AS SUBJECT AND STRATEGY   While the term "renunciation" is only explicitly addressed in a single poem (P745), it is a concept at the core of understanding Dickinson's life and work. Some degree of deferment or yearning is a common theme in Dickinson's poems, and the language thrives under her mastery of anticipation, possibility, and unquenched desire. As she states in her manifesto on the subject, "Renunciation—is a piercing Virtue—." For Dickinson, it was a virtue; by renouncing most social and intimate encounters, she retained absolute control over her emotional life and relationships and conserved intellectual and emotional resources for her writing. For example, P640 begins with the dilemma: "I cannot live with You—/ It would be Life—/ And Life is over there—/ Behind the Shelf." The final stanza provides her solution: "So We must meet apart—/ You there—I—here—/ With just the Door ajar." "Meet[ing] apart" was the poet's strategy to maintain relationships under her control while keeping acquaintances and close friends* interested in her.

In form, content, and language, Dickinson's writing evidences what Juhasz terms "a pattern that informs her life and work . . . renunciation transformed" (252). Dickinson's poetic form is radically concise, to the point of risking meaning. Poetic content often centers on what is deferred and the paradoxical conditions for its fulfillment (P754). In language, her poems use atypical grammar and syntax* and create negations to expand potential meanings, for example, "stopless," "threadless," "noteless," along with frequent use of "not."

Dickinson's acts of renunciation are most often viewed as deliberate and voluntary strategies designed to enable her development as an artist. From a feminist* perspective, renunciation has historically played a part in a woman's desire to be a writer. To conserve resources for her art, Dickinson selectively renounced social norms and the opinion of others (even while seeking it out) and belittled the value of publication,* while taking steps to preserve her poems for posterity.

"Renunciation—is the Choosing / Against itself—/ Itself to justify / Unto itself—" (P745). To venture into the intensity of language that characterizes her poems, Dickinson required the utmost control of her emotional and creative responses, supported by the physical security afforded by her home.* (*See*: Isolation; Linguistic and Stylistic Approaches; Women's Culture)

RECOMMENDED: Suzanne Juhasz, "Renunciation Transformed, the Dickinson Heritage: Emily Dickinson and Margaret Atwood"; Carolyn Kemp, " 'No' Is the Wildest Word: Emily Dickinson and the Poetics of Refusal"; Garry M. Leonard, "The Necessary Strategy of Renunciation: The Triumph of Emily Dickinson and the Fall of Sylvia Plath"; Heather Thomas, "Emily Dickinson's 'Renunciation' and Anorexia Nervosa."

Carolyn Kemp

REPETITION   is fundamental to all poetry, even though Marianne Shapiro declares in *The New Princeton Encyclopedia of Poetry and Poetics* that "pure repetition does not exist" (1036). As a device for highlighting similarity and difference, it is vital to Dickinson's poetic style, structure, meaning, and dynamic effects.

Syntactic* repetition is prominent as an ordering principle in her verse. Parallelism frequently structures whole poems, as in "Poor little Heart!" which progresses by parallel lines beginning each stanza: "Proud little Heart! . . . Frail little heart! . . . Gay little Heart—" (P192). Still more often, parallelism links sequential parts, as in "It was not Death . . . / It was not Night . . . / It was not Frost . . ." (P510). Anaphora, repetition at the beginning of successive lines, abounds, as does polysyndeton, repetition of conjunctions. Refrains appear only occasionally (e.g., P301). At their most effective, symmetrical syntactic structures provide a base upon which interesting variations are woven (Lindberg-Seyersted 212–13).

Reiteration of single words or phrases, fairly common in Dickinson's practice, performs several significant functions. It may add emphasis, as in "Wild Nights—Wild Nights!" (P249), or register hesitation, as in "Because—because if he should die" (P205), or enhance other moods. Dickinson is particularly fond of repeating a word* to call attention to its diverse meanings. Her unusual repetitions of pronouns can dramatize profound mysteries, as, for example, in the lines "Renunciation—is the Choosing / Against itself—/ Itself to justify / Unto itself—" (P745), which force the reader* to ponder differences within what is superficially the same. Similarly, in "Because I could not stop for Death—/ He kindly stopped for me—" (P712),* the recurrence of the verb "stop" foregrounds equivocal definitions that intensify the poem's rich central paradox.

Phonic repetitions are particularly important to Dickinson's art; repeated units of prosodic organization such as meter, line, and stanza also characterize her poetry throughout her career. Recurrent formal metric patterns establish expectations against which she counterpoints sometimes striking rhythmic deviations. Likewise, within a framework where rhymes* sound at predictable intervals, unexpected types and locations of rhyme produce a variety of expressive effects. Alliterative repetitions link works and add texture and emphasis. Strangest of all, puns tease out semantic differences that underlie identical sounds, as in the homonyms in the line "Some schism in the Sum—" (P1569). (*See*: Linguistic and Stylistic Approaches)

RECOMMENDED: Carroll D. Laverty, "Structural Patterns in Emily Dickinson's Poetry"; Brita Lindberg-Seyersted, *The Voice of the Poet: Aspects of Style in the Poetry of Emily Dickinson*; Cristanne Miller, *Emily Dickinson: A Poet's Grammar*; Judy Jo Small, *Positive as Sound: Emily Dickinson's Rhyme*.

Judy Jo Small

REVIVALISM   Dickinson's 1846–1850 letters to Abiah Root* and Jane Humphrey,* with their anxious probing into the writer's religious* condition, demonstrate the early impact upon her of the Second Awakening, a series of revivals that rippled through the Connecticut Valley* from the 1790s through the mid-1800s. In the First Church,* Amherst,* three "awakenings" took place during the term of Aaron Colton* alone, and another under the ministry of Edward Strong Dwight.* Repeated seasons of revival were recorded meanwhile at Amherst College,* and, in 1847–1848 at Mount Holyoke* Mary Lyon* used measures common to early nineteenth-century revivalism to help effect "hopeful conversions." Consistent with revivalism throughout the valley, her regimen was orderly and without emotional display, involving periodic self-examination as to one's spiritual state, "inquiry" meetings for the troubled or impenitent, and special days for fasting and prayer.*

At the core of this revivalism lay the continued insistence of the pro-revivalist Edwardsean, or "New Divinity," school of theology prevailing in mid-nineteenth-century Amherst upon the immediacy of an inward operation of "grace." It supported appeals for an instantaneous "Change of Heart" (L678) and placed greater weight upon human consent, so that individuals could be challenged to convert.

Dickinson herself never testified to a conscious change in her relation to God.* Her canon, however, not only echoes the phraseology of revivalist hymns* and sermons but also conveys a persistent longing for the same spiritual assurance as her schoolmates professed who had responded affirmatively to Christ's "call." (*See*: Edwards; Election; Faith; Jesus)

RECOMMENDED: Joseph Conforti, *Jonathan Edwards, Religious Tradition, and American Culture*. Chapel Hill: University of North Carolina Press, 1995; Elizabeth Alden Green. *Mary Lyon and Mount Holyoke: Opening the Gates*. Hanover, NH: University

Press of New England, 1979; Heman Humphrey. *Revival Sketches and Manual.* New York: American Tract Society, 1859.

Rowena Revis Jones

RHETORICAL APPROACHES TO DICKINSON   Rhetoric is the art of persuasion. Whereas literary criticism measures discourse against aesthetic criteria, rhetoric asks how it achieves a calculated effect on its audience. The two disciplines overlap: beauty can be convincing, and persuasiveness beautiful. In the Western tradition, literature and rhetoric are more often distinguished on the basis of goals and motives than the expressive techniques they employ.

Helen McNeil best states the case for a rhetorical approach to Dickinson: "Despite her chosen distance from public discourse, Dickinson wrote rhetorically—that is, she used devices which are meant to argue and convince" (7). Well educated for her day, Dickinson received a thorough grounding in rules, strategies, and devices suitable to letters* and poems as well as more formal writing. Her schooling made a rhetorical approach to composition natural to her.

Rhetorical studies of Dickinson fall into three groups. The first argues with McNeil that Dickinson's works were rhetorically conceived. Unwilling to enter the literary marketplace, she wrote not to delight but to prove her point and induce her reader to share her brilliant, slantwise* observations. Such studies include Brita Lindberg-Seyersted's treatment of "aspects of style" in Dickinson's poems.

A second and larger group of rhetorically oriented approaches to Dickinson explores the bearing of rhetorical topics like figure, syntax,* and voice* on Dickinson's work. These approaches show her verse to be coherent and meaningful—effective communication—rather than bemusingly lovely. Dorothy Huff Oberhaus' analysis of "method and meaning" in the fascicles* offers a good example.

The third group reads Dickinson's poems through a reconstruction of their rhetorical situation. Hundreds are, after all, letters addressed to particular interlocutors. Judith Farr's and Martha Nell Smith's discussions of the Emily–Sue* relationship lie at the center of scholarly interest in Dickinson as correspondent. Her poems are counters in a network of intense and even passionate relationships. Rhetorical analysis considers the worldly contexts of her work.

Given the sophistication of her education, the overlap between her verse and her letters, ongoing interest in her relationships, and the explosion of rhetorical criticism in the second half of the twentieth century, rhetorical approaches to Emily Dickinson bear important fruit. Indeed, the strong and pointed voice that rhetorical analysis attributes to her has helped efface the earlier view of Dickinson as a frightened escapee from the life of her day. (*See*: Linguistic and Stylistic Approaches; Prophecy; Reader-Response Theory)

RECOMMENDED: Judith Farr, *The Passion of Emily Dickinson*; Brita Lindberg-Seyersted, *The Voice of the Poet: Aspects of Style in the Poetry of Emily Dickinson*;

Helen McNeil, *Emily Dickinson*; Dorothy Huff Oberhaus, *Emily Dickinson's Fascicles: Meaning and Method*; Martha Nell Smith, *Rowing in Eden: Rereading Emily Dickinson.*

Bryan C. Short

RHYME is a pervasive feature of Dickinson's poetry. Almost all of her poems are rhymed, and the rhymes usually appear at predictable intervals as in conventional syntactic* patterns. Her innovative use of partial ("inexact," "near," "slant"*) rhymes, however, constitutes a major extension of English prosodic technique, and it has substantially influenced modern poetry. Critics long debated the value of these partial rhymes; early editors "corrected" them, and many readers have found fault with them. But Dickinson has helped create the taste by which she has come to be judged; manipulations of rhyme are now understood to be indispensable to poetic art.

About half of Dickinson's rhymes are conventional, full ("exact") rhymes (syllables with identical medial vowel and final consonant sounds, e.g., *reach/ speech*). Of the partial rhymes, a large proportion are consonantal rhymes (syllables with different medial vowels, e.g., *Grace/Price*) or unaccented rhymes (where one or both syllables receives less than full stress, e.g., *me/Divinity*). A few assonantal rhymes (e.g., *green/dream*) and identical rhymes (e.g., *Sow/so*) appear as well. Though some poems contain full rhymes exclusively or partial rhymes exclusively, Dickinson commonly mixes both types. The expanded range of possible rhyme words and sounds, in conjunction with readers' expectations, enables great flexibility of effect.

Aesthetically, the interest of dissonance and the allure of strange chromaticism are added to the pleasures of euphony. One of Dickinson's most powerful tools is the sudden surprise of an unexpected rhyme (as in the final line of "Apparently with no surprise," P1624). She also achieves enchanting effects with acoustic textures composed of intricately nuanced rhymes (as throughout P893, "Drab Habitation of Whom?").

Structurally, rhyme serves as an acoustic marker of line ends and other units of equivalence shaping stanzas and poems. Thus the chime of Dickinson's end rhymes provides a recurrent signal of an underlying structural stability. Even so, the play of her rhymes, especially the characteristic deviations from conventional rhyme patterns, contributes to the formal modulations and disruptions (e.g., in the middle stanza of "After great pain, a formal feeling comes—" P341*). Full rhyme and partial rhyme also play a role in poetic closure or lack of closure.

Since the sound of words is experienced along with their intellectual content, rhyme assumes a semantic function as well. As Dickinson employs it, the phonic value of rhyme interacts with lexical significance to guide readers'* inferences, participate in ingenious twists of wit (e.g., the homonymic rhyme of "The Spirit is the Conscious Ear," P733), and indicate subtleties of tone that are inseparable from meaning. (*See*: Disjunction; Hymns; Linguistic and Stylistic Approaches; Poets, Influence on; Repetition)

RECOMMENDED: Thomas H. Johnson, *Emily Dickinson: An Interpretive Biography*; Brita Lindberg-Seyersted, *The Voice of the Poet: Aspects of Style in the Poetry of Emily Dickinson*; Timothy Morris, "The Development of Dickinson's Style"; David T. Porter, *The Art of Emily Dickinson's Early Poetry*; Judy Jo Small, *Positive as Sound: Emily Dickinson's Rhyme*.

Judy Jo Small

ROBERTS BROTHERS (1863–1898)   was a Boston* firm that published over 1,300 works, including many by its two most famous authors: Louisa May Alcott and Dickinson. The firm, which specialized in photographic albums, grew out of a company established by two brothers who had emigrated from England, Lewis and Austin Roberts. Austin left the firm in 1863, when it branched into bookselling. Thomas Niles* joined it in the same year. He had worked with the distinguished Boston publisher Ticknor and Fields, and he put his knowledge to use by greatly expanding the firm's list of publications. In 1872, Niles was made a full partner. Roberts Brothers published many of the best writers of the late nineteenth century, including Lydia Maria Child, Edward Everett Hale,* Lafcadio Hearn, Helen Hunt Jackson,* Joaquin Miller, William Morris, Christina Rossetti, A. C. Swinburne, Walt Whitman,* Oscar Wilde, and many of the later Transcendentalists.* Niles' death in 1894 deprived the firm of its most important person, and the company was bought out by Little, Brown in 1898.

Dickinson's "Success" (P67)* had been published in Roberts' *A Masque of Poets*￼ in 1878. The Todds* approached Niles about *Poems* (1890),* which he published with reluctance. All were delighted with the book's success, and Roberts Brothers continued to publish Dickinson until the firm was sold: *Poems* (over 9,000 copies in nineteen printings), *Poems: Second Series*￼ (nearly 6,500 copies in ten printings), *Letters*￼ (2,500 copies in two printings), and *Poems: Third Series*￼ (2,000 copies in two printings). After Little, Brown purchased Roberts Brothers, they kept all three series of *Poems* in print through the 1920s and added new titles on their own; not until *Bolts of Melody*￼ in 1945 was Dickinson published in America by another firm. (*See*: Critical Reception; Publication)

RECOMMENDED: Raymond L. Kilgour. *Messrs. Roberts Brothers Publishers*. Ann Arbor: University of Michigan Press, 1952; Joel Myerson, *Emily Dickinson: A Descriptive Bibliography*.

Joel Myerson

ROMANTICISM   invites debate; long after the Civil War* hastened the end of American Romanticism (ca. 1810–ca. 1865), its influence continues. Common characteristics link "Romantic" writers and other artists—theme, style, subject matter, focus, and philosophy. Although the movement was gradual, transoceanic, and controversial, meaningful if not absolute parameters help define this cultural revolution that powerfully influenced the "temper of the times" in which Emily Dickinson reached poetic maturity. She responded to its rule-breaking, democratic, freedom-loving, experimental, and passionate dynamic but also felt the contrarieties that made Romanticism a powerful force for despair as well as optimism.

American Romanticism followed the English movement by ten to twenty years, just as English Romanticism followed German Romantic thought. Although culminating in the nineteenth century, Romanticism's reaction against neo-classicism and that movement's reliance on reason began earlier. The American Revolution partly fueled Romanticism through new democratic and individualistic ideals, but also the convulsions of the French Revolution and resultant European upheavals fostered the beginnings of modern art, music, politics, religion,* and philosophy.* Emily Dickinson, writing much poetry* during the Civil War—but certainly committing herself to poetry the decade before—was by philosophy, taste, lifestyle, and influences attuned to these elements that traditionally define Romanticism.

"The Soul selects her own Society—" (P303)* witnesses to Dickinson's intense individualism: her commitment to Romantic trust in the ability, nobility, sanctity, and worth of the individual, above—and often in opposition to—community, institution, doctrine, and even religious faith.* Beginning with Goethe's Werther, through Cooper's Leatherstocking and Byron's* Manfred, to Thoreau's* Walden pilgrim and Whitman's* solitary singer, Romantics often celebrated and occasionally mourned the isolated* self* asserting itself against other powers. The iconoclastic self might possess divinity within, limiting the need for ministers and dogma (and obviously incurring the Establishment's wrath). Revolutionary idealism fueled reform movements in education, law, woman's and slaves' rights, prisons, and other areas.

Romanticism's foregrounding of emotion, intuition, and imagination as ways for the soul to achieve knowledge found expression in "The Soul has Bandaged moments—" (P512), among other Dickinson poems. In probing emotional extremes, she called upon Romantic epistemologies of the inner "psychological" self and explored the movement's concept of the imagination. ("Psychology," derived from the Greek word for soul, is itself a Romantic neologism that reached America by way of Emerson* and the German thought he derived from Coleridge and Carlyle.*) Explanations for the ways the imagination works moved from the Enlightenment's emphasis on scientific* materialism to a more spiritualized notion of heart, soul, and imagination. "Pure" reason and logic seemed "cold" and inhumane in the Transcendentalists'* critique of the Unitarian* Church and in the sentimentalized* "religion of the heart" that challenged Calvinist rigidities.

Romantic appreciation of nature* found expression in Dickinson's responses to flowers,* birds,* insects,* the garden,* storms, and volcanoes. Like Wordsworth and the Transcendentalists,* she saw nature as emblematic and symbolic:

a layered text to be read and understood, an organic metafiction. Descriptions of its untamed excesses and beauties became sublime* for Romantic writers, who saw nature as possessing inherent and changeless—but paradoxically ever-changing—qualities that could be awe-inspiring for the Poet/Seer. Romantics exalted nature itself and the rural and pastoral life as subjects for painting, poetry,* and other philosophical or artistic work. Wordsworth's and Coleridge's *Lyrical Ballads* (1798) celebrated these ideas, as did Emerson's *Nature* (1836), which Dickinson and other American Romantics found inspirational.

Dickinson "reckon[ed]" that poets' imaginations encompass "All" (P632, 569)—including the gothicism,* orientalism, medievalism, and fascination with wildness, ruins, luxury, primitivism, mythology, foreignness, and other revelations of imaginative possibility that fascinated the Romantics. She responded to the movement's inclination toward hyperbole, paradox, and opposition as means of describing and symbolizing the workings of the imagination. Romantics embraced the strange and new, the common and ordinary; they explored irrational, subliminal, supernatural, and dream states. Coleridge, Emerson, and Whitman discussed "contrarieties" and "multieties" that the mind and self contain. Thoreau examined Walden's blending of both muck and the infinite, fish and stars. In form, Romantic literature expressed the inclusiveness of the movement's vision.* Poets abandoned traditional forms, experimented with those the previous century had neglected, invented new ones, and developed innovative, figurative language rather than using stylized, "poetic" diction.

Dickinson, in her solitary work, studied the great Romantics, experienced the passions sweeping through the movement, and translated many of these dispositions into poetry, while retaining skepticism and ironic distance so that her poetry "transcends" Romanticism yet is rooted firmly within it. (*See*: Historicism; Realism; Visual Arts)

RECOMMENDED: M. H. Abrams. *The Mirror and the Lamp: Romantic Theory and the Critical Tradition.* New York: Oxford University Press, 1953; Harold Bloom. *Emily Dickinson: Modern Critical Views.* New York: Chelsea House, 1985; Joanne Feit Diehl, *Dickinson and the Romantic Imagination*; Cynthia Griffin Wolff, "Dickinson's Use of the Romantic Grotesque."

Susan Kurjiaka

ROOT, ABIAH PALMER   Born in 1830, the daughter of Deacon Harvey Root of West Springfield, Massachusetts (Feeding Hills), Abiah came to Amherst* to stay with her cousins, the Palmers, while studying at Amherst Academy* for one year. Johnson* gives the dates of her Amherst year as 1843–1844; Leyda says she arrived there in June 1844. "Biah" Root became one of Dickinson's closest friends and a member of "the five" circle mentioned in L11. Besides Abiah Root and Emily Dickinson, the group included Abby Wood,* Harriet Merrill, and Sarah Tracy* (*Life* 380). Eight years later, Dickinson recalled her first impressions of Abiah Root: "with the utmost equanimity you ascended the stairs, bedecked with dandelions, arranged, it seemed, for curls.

I shall never forget that scene, if I live to have gray hairs, nor the very remarkable fancies it gave me then of you'' (L91).

In the same letter Abiah is described as ''dignified,'' and the tone of Emily's letters to her consistently indicates that even as a girl Miss Root was serious-minded and sensitive. She must also have appreciated Emily's writing talent, for she saved her part of their correspondence and made it available for Mabel Loomis Todd's* 1894 edition of *Letters** (cf. Introduction to *Letters*, 1931, and *Ancestors' Brocades*). Letters to Abiah Root are the only surviving part of what almost certainly was a larger body of correspondence with ''the five.''

For the winter of 1845–1846 Abiah transferred to Margaret Campbell's School in Springfield, but Emily's letters make it clear that she visited Amherst intermittently between late summer 1847 and spring 1854. There are twenty-two letters to Abiah Root written between February 1845 and summer 1854 (most published in *Letters*, 1894 and 1931). The sequence belongs to Dickinson's most important youthful correspondence. Letters to Abiah are warm, often highly emotional, and reflective. They show little of Dickinson in her rebellious or satirical moods. Instead, they offer glimpses of the depth and intensity of her religious* concerns as the poet-to-be struggled for honest self*-definition. At the height of the girls' intimacy, Dickinson discussed with Abiah her spiritual anxieties and decisions against the background of revivalism* at school and in the community. As more and more of those close to her made public profession of faith* and joined the established church, and as the female friends* of her youth prepared to enter adult lives of useful work, family responsibilities, and institutionalized piety, Emily's letters to Abiah evidence a growing sense of isolation.* Occasionally, they show Dickinson consciously demonstrating her stylistic dexterity (see especially L31).

The correspondence ended just before Abiah's marriage to Rev. Samuel Strong as Dickinson declined her friend's invitation to visit. Telling Abiah not to expect her because ''I'm so old fashioned, Darling, that all your friends would stare'' (L166), the future poet registered an early intuition of her singular status as ''the only Kangaroo among the Beauty.'' This famous phrase from an 1862 letter to Higginson* (L268) captures in more aesthetic terms the youthful insight that closed, on a note of finality, her correspondence with Abiah Root.

The dynamic of Emily Dickinson's friendship with Abiah foregrounds a process through which the poet was learning her difference. In the course of the relationship, two exactly contemporary and once-intimate young women drifted apart emotionally and intellectually as Abiah progressed into adulthood along the path conventionally prescribed for young women of her social standing and education. Emily Dickinson, on the other hand, grew aware that her needs were different. At the end of their contact, Dickinson seemed able to accept her isolating, ''old fashioned'' condition and refused to continue the relationship on a purely social basis.

RECOMMENDED: *AB*; *Letters*; *Life*; *Years*; R. W. Franklin, ''Emily Dickinson and Abiah Root: Ten Reconstructed Letters.''

Agnieszka Salska

THE ROUND TABLE   Cousins Henry and Charles Humphreys Sweetser*
launched this New York literary weekly in December 1863 only to suspend
publication the following July in reaction to high wartime paper costs. On 12
March 1864, however, the journal published Dickinson's "My Sabbath"
(P324).* Whether she herself submitted the poem to Charles Sweetser, an Amherst* neighbor from childhood, or whether someone else did remains uncertain.
Despite Edward Dickinson's* encouraging note to the editors when *The Round
Table* resumed publication in 1865, Charles Sweetser quickly turned his atten-
tion to other projects.

RECOMMENDED: *Years*; Robert Scholnick. " 'Don't Tell! They'd Advertise': Emily
Dickinson in the *Round Table.*" *Periodical Literature in Nineteenth Century America.*
Ed. Kenneth M. Price and Susan Belasco Smith. Charlottesville: University Press of
Virginia, 1995: 166–83.

Jane Donahue Eberwein

S

"Safe in their Alabaster Chambers—" **(P216)**   takes a chilling perspective on the difference between death* and life by highlighting the torpor of the entombed elect* as they await "Resurrection." This poem became one of Dickinson's first publications,* appearing in the 1 March 1862 issue of the *Springfield Republican.** It was among four poems (with P318, 319, and 320) that she sent the next month, in modified form, to T. W. Higginson* with her introductory letter* (L260). Emily's 1861 discussion of various drafts of this poem (L238) with Susan Dickinson* offers revealing insight into the poet's artistic workshop and the editorial* advice she received. Sue's tribute to the opening stanza ("I always go to the fire and get warm after thinking of it") suggests that this interchange may have influenced the poet's definition of poetry* as the force that "makes my whole body so cold no fire ever can warm me" (L342a).

Yet this remains an especially open-ended poem, copied variously into Fascicles* 6 and 10 as a two-stanza work in which virtually the same opening lines get matched with either of two alternative conclusions: one sentimentally contrasting the numbness of the dead with the laughing exuberance of ongoing biological life and the other icily matching their condition against immensities of astronomical and historical drama (Appendix A). Another version, adopted for *Poems* (1890),* includes all three stanzas as one poem. Modern anthologies generally follow Thomas Johnson* in presenting both two-stanza options in recognition of the fact that no holograph evidence shows the poet herself blending three stanzas of this poem. Rather, she experimented with three different lines of development from the opening stanza. The third option, beginning "Springs—shake the sills—", appears only in her exchange with Susan. "Safe in their Alabaster Chambers—" has received widespread critical attention for its imagery ("Soundless as dots—on a Disc of Snow—"), its revelation of Dickinson's composing method, its value as an indication of her relationships with both Sue and Higginson as literary mentors, and the insight it offers into the poet's attitudes toward death and immortality.*

RECOMMENDED: Charles R. Anderson, *Emily Dickinson's Poetry: Stairway of Surprise*; Ruth Miller, *The Poetry of Emily Dickinson*; Martha Nell Smith, *Rowing in Eden: Rereading Emily Dickinson*; Robert Weisbuch, *Emily Dickinson's Poetry*; Cynthia Griffin Wolff, *Emily Dickinson*.

Jane Donahue Eberwein

SAND, GEORGE (1804–1876) Dickinson's knowledge of foreign authors was not impressive, and George Sand (pen name of Aurore Dudevant) appears to have been the only French author she read, and that in translation. Judging by the fragmentary evidence of her letters,* Dickinson must have held Sand in high regard, possibly as a role model for herself, both as woman and as writer. Although Sand's name is mentioned only once, Dickinson paired her with Elizabeth Barrett Browning* in a letter to Louise* and Frances Norcross* (L234) that salutes both Sand and Barrett Browning as "women, now, queens, now!" While it has been suggested that Dickinson's own childhood traumas may have prompted "They shut me up in Prose—" (P613), reference in this letter to Sand's traumatic experiences as a child who " 'must make no noise in her grandmother's bedroom' " raises the possibility that the poem may also have been occasioned by both Sand's and Barrett's experiences as "victims of tyranny and restraint." (*See*: Books and Reading)

RECOMMENDED: *Letters*; Elizabeth Phillips, *Emily Dickinson: Personae and Performance*; George Frisbie Whicher, *This Was a Poet: A Critical Biography of Emily Dickinson*.

Danuta Piestrzyńska

SANFORD, JOHN ELIOT (1830–1907) Sanford graduated from Amherst College* as valedictorian in 1851 and was a frequent caller in the Dickinson home during his college days and later while studying law with Edward Dickinson.* Although Sanford frequently escorted Lavinia Dickinson* to social events, he seems to have been more interested romantically in Emily's friend Mary Warner,* who rejected him. In 1852, he was reported engaged to Ann Fiske of Amherst,* but his marriage to Emily White of Taunton, Massachusetts, occurred in 1856 after he set up his legal practice there. He was a trustee of Amherst College from 1874 until his death. As a close friend of Austin Dickinson,* Sanford made a six-week private trip to St. Louis and New Orleans with the poet's brother in 1887.

RECOMMENDED: *Life*; *Years*.

Midori Kajino Asahina

"SAXE HOLM" Evidence that Emily Dickinson's local literary reputation began even during her lifetime emerged in newspaper speculation about authorship of stories her friend Helen Hunt (Jackson)* wrote for *Scribner's** under the pseudonym Saxe Holm. Although stylistic traits quickly led readers to identify Hunt as probable author, morbid and unworldly qualities noted in "Esther Wynn's Love-Letters" and succeeding tales distinguished them from Hunt's other fiction, and Hunt herself refused to acknowledge this series as her own. Suspecting a collaborator, the author of an anonymous 25 July 1878 article in the *Springfield Republican** pointed to Amherst* as the likely home of this supposed coauthor, characterized as the reclusive daughter of a prominent family. Four days later, a follow-up in the *Springfield Union* even raised the name "Dickinson." This brought a quick rejoinder from Samuel Bowles,* who put an end to public rumors by asserting that "we happen to *know* that no person by the name of Dickinson is in any way responsible for the Saxe Holm stories."

RECOMMENDED: *Life*; *Years*.

Jane Donahue Eberwein

SCANDINAVIAN RESPONSES TO DICKINSON   Three years before editing* *The Complete Poems of Emily Dickinson*,* Thomas H. Johnson* served as visiting professor of American literature at Denmark's University of Copenhagen. That visit introduced university-educated Danes to Dickinson thirty-two years before Poul Borum first translated some of her poems into Danish. Norwegian professor Brita Lindberg-Seyersted has also cited Johnson as a major force behind her understanding of, and love for, Dickinson's work. In a paper delivered at the "New England Poetry" conference in Helsinki in 1981, Finnish scholar Sirkka Heiskanen-Mäkelä traced the evolution of Dickinson studies in Finland. Heiskanen-Mäkelä states that while Dickinson has generally become known in English to those Finns with a command of that language, Swedish-speaking Finns had access to her work in the 1920s and 1930s, when she aroused much interest in Sweden. The earliest known Finnish print item mentioning Dickinson is a 1934 review of her poetry, and the first Finnish essay on her was published in 1948. After a burst of popularity in the 1950s, spurred by the work of the late scholar and translator Helvi Juvonen, Finnish interest in Dickinson has fallen. There is currently no Emily Dickinson Society in Finland nor interest in forming one, and the country's two major Dickinson scholars, Sirkka Heiskanen-Mäkelä and Kaarina Halonen, have been unable to interest publishers in their new translations of poems. One of the difficulties Finns face lies in the translation of Dickinson: the Finnish language's entire linguistic* structure, syntax,* metrics, and phonology differ radically from those of English. Dickinson has fared better in Denmark, where the Reverend Niels Kjær has become a spokesperson for Dickinson and operates the Emily Dickinson Center. In 1993, Kjær donated to the International People's College in Denmark his entire collection of Dickinson books and periodicals. Kjær reports that Dickinson is firmly established in Denmark and that Dickinson books have been followed by plays, concerts, a ballet, and a "talking" book of her poetry. (*See*: French-Language

Responses; German-Language Responses; Slavic-Language Responses; Visual Arts, Responses)

RECOMMENDED: Sirkka Heiskanen-Mäkelä, "Emily Dickinson in Finland"; Niels Kjær, "Collecting Dickinson: The Emily Dickinson Collection, Denmark"; Brita Lindberg-Seyersted, "The Theme of Death in Emily Dickinson's Poetry" and *The Voice of the Poet: Aspects of Style in the Poetry of Emily Dickinson*; Per Winther, "On Editing Emily Dickinson."

Susan Biscella

SCIENCE   Dickinson drew on scientific and technological vocabulary to a greater extent than other poets of her time. Her use of scientific language may have been influenced by her wide reading, by courses at Amherst Academy* and Mount Holyoke,* or by Edward Hitchcock,* Amherst's self-described "geological theologian." Dickinson often employed technical terms in the least technical arenas, and frequently used science to counter or intensify religious* or emotional subjects. " 'Faith,''* she declared, "is a fine invention" (P185). Newton's *Principia* describes heaven* (P1295); the law of the conservation of matter assuages grief (P954). Yet Dickinson was skeptical toward science, satirizing its "Savans" (P100) and critiquing its penchant to categorize and define. P1241 advises the "Scientist of Faith" (a likely allusion to Hitchcock) not to let "Revelation / By theses be detained." Scientific dogma pales against poetic epiphanies. "By intuition, Mightiest Things / Assert themselves—and not by terms" (P420). In P415 scientists bow to natural eclipses but cannot face the sudden emotional or spiritual eclipse that "Reverses Nature," rendering "Jehovah's Watch . . . wrong."

"To know" (her most frequent verb) was primary to Dickinson; and if science's answers were insufficient (P433) or invasive (P443), experiment was nevertheless essential (P1073). According to Diehl, Dickinson "maintains that the only truth . . . depends upon what one discovers by oneself. Living and dying thus assume the status of an experiment" (184). Consciousness* is a cosmic experiment (P822); God* and death* conduct experiments (P300, 550). From manuscript substitutions for "whole Experiment of Green" (P1333), Anderson concludes that Dickinson saw nature* as "a process by which essential truths are searched out and proved in particular experiments" (80). The "Scarlet Experiment" of P861 bears this out. To "Split the Lark" yields blood, poetry,* sacrifice, and song—a far different truth than its "Sceptic Thomas" would have predicted. Embellishing her wit, scientific language gave Dickinson a tool to deflate the pompous, control the painful, and pose questions of being and knowing. (*See*: Philosophical Approaches)

RECOMMENDED: *Life*; Charles R. Anderson, *Emily Dickinson's Poetry: Stairway of Surprise*; Joanne Feit Diehl, *Dickinson and the Romantic Imagination*; William Howard, "Emily Dickinson's Poetic Vocabulary."

Terry Blackhawk

SCRIBNER'S MONTHLY   Edited by Dickinson's longtime friend Dr. J. G. Holland,* *Scribner's Monthly* came to the Dickinson household from its first issue in November 1870. Dickinson often mentioned the journal, writing to Elizabeth Holland* in 1881 that "The Neighborhood are much amused by the 'Fair Barbarian' and Emily's Scribner is perused by all the Boys and Girls" (L689). *Scribner's* was an illustrated journal primarily devoted to literature and literary topics; the decorative and fine arts; cultural institutions ("The New Museum in Rome," "The London Theatres," "The Art Schools of Philadelphia"); colleges and universities (including Bowdoin, Harvard, Princeton, Smith); and high-minded travel to metropolitan cultural centers such as Benares, London, Moscow, New York, Philadelphia, and San Francisco or notable landscapes such as Yellowstone or Yosemite. There was also an Editorial Department with regular columns: "Topics of the Time" (e.g., republicanism in Europe, sex and wages, social taxes, the woman* question); "The Old Cabinet" (with items like "Winter Exhibition of the National Academy," discussions of friendship,* sentiment*); "Home* and Society" (fashion, stationery, dining, middle-age travel); "Books and Authors at Home and Abroad"; "Culture and Progress Abroad and at Home." The extensive literary sections featured stories, including those by Hans Christian Anderson, Rebecca Harding Davis, Julian Hawthorne, "Saxe Holm,"* Harriet Prescott Spofford,* Ivan Turgeneiff; poetry by William Cullen Bryant, Alice Cary, James T. Fields, T. W. Higginson,* Sidney Lanier, Louise Chandler Moulton, Elizabeth Stuart Phelps,* Christina Rossetti, Rose Terry, Celia Thaxter; serialized fiction by Frances Hodgson Burnett, George Cable, Bret Harte, J. G. Holland, William Dean Howells,* Henry James, Jules Verne; and literary essays such as "A Day with the Brownings at Pratolino," "Reminiscences of Charlotte Brontë,"* "A Breakfast with Alexandre Dumas," "The Homes and Haunts of Emerson,"* "In and Out of London with Dickens,"* "On the Reading of Newspapers," "Recent Women Poets," "Dante Gabriel Rossetti," "Spiritual Songs from the Pen of Novalis," "The Shakespeare* Death Mask," and "Charles Algernon Swinburne." (*See*: *Atlantic Monthly*; Books and Reading bibliography; *Harper's*; *Springfield Republican*)

Joan Kirkby

SEASONS   We value Dickinson's seasonal poems for their particularity, their "certain Slant of light" (P258), their individual but universal response to life. Under her cultivation, "Winter" (in poetry, as in life) can be "as arable as Spring" (P1707). Her seasons are earth's, and more. The exultant " '*There* is no more snow!' " of the May-June P22 resonates powerfully—both with childhood surprise and with the "there was no more sea" of *Revelation* 21, 1. Many of her seasonal references have an undertone of a "summer of the just" or sacrament. Her seasons mark human loss and pain in differing modes, midsummer's all-but-joyous "leaned into Perfectness" (P962) contrasting with "Winter's silver Fracture" (P846).

Mentions of summer predominate overwhelmingly (145 references, plus 2 for midsummer and 1 summertime), with 30 for winter, 29 for spring, and 15 for autumn/fall. Dickinson mentioned every month but December in poems, though only March, April, May, and June occur frequently. The church year manifests itself only occasionally, with references to Christmas and perhaps to Lent.

Both conventional and idiosyncratic elements appear in these poems, which link Dickinson's fascination with both nature* and time.* "June day," alone, would be ordinary, but "June Noon/January Night" excites interest (P592). "September's Baccalaureate" (P1271) offers intriguing oxymoron.* "June" may occur with summer or stand alone, for itself or the season.

Yet it would be misleading, perhaps, to think of Dickinson as "a haiku poet" for her focus on seasons. Her cast of thought was one of contrast, cycle, and process that often involved speculation into Christian promises of immortality* overcoming death.* She was particularly attuned to transitions—both observed and intuited. For Dickinson, "Summer into Autumn slips"—imperceptibly (P1346). She responded especially to the year's "magical frontier[s]" (P1764). Thinking of summer as having "two Beginnings" in June and October, she prized the later one, which felt "graphicer for Grace" (P1422). Her "Autumn" could be gloriously weird, as in the dramatically pictorial and painful P656. In her subtle seasons we have the year's, earth's, life's plenty—perhaps even God's* fullness. (*See*: Bible; Elegy; Visual Art, as Influence)

RECOMMENDED: Paul J. Ferlazzo, *Emily Dickinson*; Greg Johnson, *Emily Dickinson: Perception and the Poet's Quest*; Cynthia Griffin Wolff, *Emily Dickinson*.

James Fegan and Haruko Kimura

SEELYE, ELIZABETH and JULIUS HAWLEY (1824–1895)   An 1849 graduate of Amherst College,* Seelye studied at Auburn Theological Seminary and at Halle, Germany, before being ordained pastor of the First Dutch Reformed Church of Schenectady, New York (1853–1858). He then moved to Amherst* as professor of mental and moral philosophy at Amherst College. Seelye served from 1874 to 1877 as a member of Congress from Massachusetts. An active citizen, he promoted concrete sidewalks, a gas company, and a water supply system in Amherst. He was president of the college from 1877 to 1890 and pastor of the college church from 1877 to 1892. His wife, born Elizabeth Tillman James, died in 1881. Their home was on College Street, just to the south of the edifice of the First Congregational Church.* It was probably his association with Austin Dickinson* in civic affairs that entitled Professor Seelye to serve as honorary pallbearer for the poet. (*See*: Funeral)

RECOMMENDED: Charles F. Carpenter and Edward W. Morehouse. *The History of the Town of Amherst.* Amherst, MA: Carpenter and Morehouse, 1896; *Amherst College Biographical Record.* Amherst, MA, 1963; *Beers Atlas of Hampshire County.* 1873; *Amherst Directory.* 1869; James Avery Smith. "Inscriptions of Wildwood Cemetery, Amherst, MA." Unpublished manuscript, 1975.

James Avery Smith

SELF, AS THEME   Dickinson's poetry suggests that the self is ultimately uncontainable in language and incommensurate with socially determined discourses. Many of Dickinson's speakers represent selves who enjoy varying degrees of liberation from the identities imposed by social discourse. From the child* angered by the constraints of adult roles in "I'm ceded—I've stopped being Their's—" (P508), to the bride* seeking fulfillment through social conformity in "A Wife—at Daybreak I shall be—" (P461), to the regal speaker of "Mine—by the Right of the White Election!" (P528), Dickinson engages her readers* in dramas of self-discovery. The self she offers through her poems and letters* astonishes us as much with its capacity for surrender to social forces as by its power to challenge even God* in its assertion of personal authority.

At the same time, Dickinson's poems repeatedly examine the ease with which speakers are swept into totalizing discourses that erase knowledge of a prior, uncontainable selfhood. As "We lose—because we win—" (P21) demonstrates, speakers constantly struggle to retain consciousness* of a self that antedates entry into the discourses that define the self historically. The "Gamblers" in this poem resume play because they "recollect" that the rules defining them as winners or losers acquire authority only through their assent. The poem tells us that recognizing our assent to the rules—the social discourse that defines us—can free us from containment within these and that playing such games with the self is always a gamble. In this poem as throughout the works, Dickinson presents the self as a dynamic entity paradoxically inside and outside language and, as a result, perennially in tension between opposing forces. (*See*: Philosophical Approaches)

RECOMMENDED: Margaret Dickie, *Lyric Contingencies: Emily Dickinson and Wallace Stevens*; Mary Loeffelholz, *Dickinson and the Boundaries of Feminist Theory*; Helen McNeil, *Emily Dickinson*; Martha Nell Smith, *Rowing in Eden: Rereading Emily Dickinson*; Gary Lee Stonum, *The Dickinson Sublime*.

Paul Crumbley

SENTIMENTALISM   Although sentimental values are, in many respects, alien to Dickinson's poetic and personal sensibility, her poetry and life conform in intriguing ways to sentimental culture. Typically, nineteenth-century sentimentality idealized an "angel in the house": a pure, passionless, moral, gentle, loving woman selflessly devoted to domesticity,* children, and religious* values. This idealized woman had no personal anger (though she might indignantly protest social cruelty), no personal ambition apart from her desire to be a good wife, mother, and housekeeper, and no desire to upset the status quo. Dickinson's white dress, her reluctance to leave her domestic space, her love of flowers,* and her devotion to family cooking are all in keeping with the "angel in the house" stereotype, which was familiar to her from the sentimental fiction and poetry that she frequently read. L85, for example, mentions "The Light in the Valley," "Only," and "A House upon a Rock," and though her description of them as "sweet and true" books about "pure little lives, loving God,* and their parents, and obeying the laws of the land'' is derisive, the letter* itself is quite sentimental: "Will you be kind to me, Susie*? I am naughty and cross, this morning, and nobody loves me here . . . and yet it is'nt anger—I dont believe it is, for when nobody sees, I brush away big tears with the corner of my apron, and then go working on.''

Early poems frequently feature the typical sentimental vision of life as sadly beautiful: we see the domestic joys that dead* people miss, scenes in which saving news arrives too late to rescue a dying person, or pathetic scenes in which victims pitifully but beautifully ascend to their maker. Other features of Dickinson's poetry* that mirror sentimental concerns are her focus on smallness, limitation, and deprivation as sources of pleasure and empowerment; her emphasis upon the role of suffering lover; her deliberate avoidance of publication*; her focus on vulnerability; and her valuation of the home* as bastion of security, warmth, and value in opposition to a corrupting and crass economic sphere. Dickinson's use of the "little girl'' voice, or the "Daisy''* persona, is another aspect of her sentimentality that indicates what the poet may have derived from sentimental discourse. Like many sentimental authors, she found in the child role* a means of expressing anger without recrimination and erotic* desire without transgressing sexual taboos. Images of marriage* in her poetry and letters also conform to sentimental ideals, though they may convey a veiled, ironic critique of marriage. (*See*: Women's Culture)

RECOMMENDED: Joanne Dobson, *Dickinson and the Strategies of Reticence: The Woman Writer in Nineteenth-Century America*; Jane Donahue Eberwein, *Dickinson: Strategies of Limitation*; Karen Sanchez-Eppler, *Touching Liberty: Abolition, Feminism, and the Politics of the Body*; Barton Levi St. Armand, *Emily Dickinson and Her Culture: The Soul's Society*; Cheryl Walker, *The Nightingale's Burden: Women Poets and American Culture before 1900*.

Marianne Noble

SHAKESPEARE, WILLIAM (1564–1616) Perhaps out of respect for Edward Hitchcock's* concerns about the Bard's "libertine'' ways that undercut his "splendid moral sentiments,'' neither Amherst Academy* nor Mount Holyoke Female Seminary* assigned Shakespeare's works among textbooks Emily Dickinson studied (*Life* 353). Yet she had ample opportunity to share her enthusiasm with friends.* She belonged to a Shakespeare Club that met to read his plays, and she probably attended some public readings, though no fully staged performances. From age fourteen until her last months, she employed allusions to Shakespeare in her letters,* demonstrating confidence that friends would catch such references. The Dickinson collection of family books now at Harvard's Houghton Library shows that she had access to two complete sets of Shakespeare as well as several individual books and the concordance that was Judge Lord's* gift to her in 1877. Penciled markings in the poet's hand and other evidence of appreciative use show that she valued these books. Although Dickinson enjoyed Shakespeare from girlhood, he apparently meant even more to her after the optical crisis she endured in the early 1860s, when she was denied access to books in order to save her eyes; she reported to Joseph Lyman* how she "flew to the shelves and devoured the luscious passages" on her return from Cambridge (*Ly* 76). "Why is any other book needed," she asked Higginson* (L342b), by way of accounting for her choice of Shakespeare, who evidently represented for her all dramatic and poetic possibilities.

A striking feature of Dickinson's response to Shakespeare is her tendency to refer to him as a contemporary, someone still very much alive and part of her life. "While Shakespeare remains," she wrote to Higginson, "Literature is firm" (L368). Congratulating Helen Hunt Jackson* on *Ramona*, she wished "Would that like Shakespere, it were just published" (L976). His plays introduced memorable characters into her life and, perhaps more stimulatingly, the awareness of dramatic conflict even within seemingly ordinary affairs. " 'Hamlet' to Himself were Hamlet—/ Had not Shakespeare wrote—," she observed (P741). Macbeth's amazement when Birnam Wood came to Dunsinane served to express her own sense of the marvelous when Higginson visited Amherst or Elizabeth Holland* sent arbutus from New York. Benjamin Lease calls attention to the "imagery of sacred royalty" she drew from Shakespeare's histories to communicate her sense of poetic vocation (37). Judith Farr demonstrates a pattern of allusion to *Antony and Cleopatra* by which the poet identified herself with Antony and Susan Dickinson* with Cleopatra enacting their private tragedy. Farr also sees in Dickinson's references to Shakespeare's sonnet sequence parallels with the poet's own attraction to a gentleman (Samuel Bowles*) and a dark lady (Susan). To Susan, Dickinson wrote a few years before she died, "With the exception of Shakespeare, you have told me of more knowledge than any one living—" (L757).

Dickinson quoted Shakespearean phrases throughout her poems and letters, often adapting his words to fit a new circumstance or rewording them slightly, as readers do who quote from memory. She called on a wide range of plays for references, including *As You Like It, Coriolanus, King Lear, Romeo and Juliet*, and *Othello*. Often, she blended these allusions with references to the Bible* and favorite poets. Beyond quotation, she alluded more subtly to Shakespeare, as when "mail from Tunis" (P1463) recalls *The Tempest* (II, i, 246–48).

Yet critics feel Shakespeare's influence even more strongly in the lively experimental qualities of Dickinson's own language than in overt or subtle quotations. According to Anderson, Shakespeare furnished her with "clues for . . . resurrection" of a poetic language that had flattened in her America (32). Lease numbers Shakespeare among "catalysts to release Dickinson's distinctive voice and vision*" (35), while Sewall likens the Yankee poet to the Elizabethan playwright in terms of shared capacity "to refresh the language and create a genuinely new music"* (*Life* 708). Perhaps Dickinson herself said it best: "he has had his Future who has found Shakespeare—" (L402). (*See*: Books and Reading)

RECOMMENDED: *Life*; Charles Anderson, *Emily Dickinson's Poetry: Stairway of Surprise*; Jack L. Capps, *Emily Dickinson's Reading 1836–1886*; Judith Farr, *The Passion of Emily Dickinson*; Benjamin Lease, *Emily Dickinson's Readings of Men and Books*.

Jane Donahue Eberwein

"Sic transit gloria mundi" (P3)   is the first of ten poems known to have been published in Dickinson's lifetime. It appeared in the *Springfield Republican** on 20 February 1852, with the comment: "A VALENTINE. The hand that wrote the following amusing melody to a gentleman friend of ours, as 'a valentine,' is capable of writing very fine things, and there is certainly no presumption in entertaining a private wish that a correspondence, more direct than this, may be established between it and the Republican." It is not known who sent this poem to the editor.

The purpose of valentine* exchanges was to surprise the recipient while keeping up banter. Comic valentines with grossly exaggerated expressions were in fashion in the 1850s. There were two sorts of comic caricature: the abusive and the genial. Dickinson's is the latter type. This second valentine poem of hers consists of seventeen quatrains. It is the longest of her early poems, with conventional rhyme,* meter, and punctuation. It deals with death* or separation in an unrestrained, rapid, and satirically pedantic manner. There is no coherent message except in the last three stanzas, where the speaker-author secretly expects that the recipient, William Howland* (then a tutor at Amherst College*), will be able to take a joke and mourn her fictive* death. Surely, he hides between lines. In this way, she burlesques a profession of romantic valentine friendship.*

In lines parodying political oratory, Dickinson's speaker fills the roles of soldier, patriot, politician, nature*-lover, parent, Eve, and devoted friend. But she basically poses as a precociously wise student. The poem's bombastic humor,* puns, clichés, homilies, Scots dialect, and Latin adages call to mind some of Dickinson's favorite books: *Peter Parley*, a very popular reader for schoolchildren of the time, Isaac Watts'* *Divine and Moral Songs*, Ik Marvel's* *Reveries of a Bachelor*, and Robert Burns' poetry. She mimics many literary sources to create new expressions, though the results are eclectic, and the connotations of words* and images cannot be clearly understood because they are so freewheelingly connected, line by line, that logical progression becomes nonsensical. Yet Dickinson's gifts for sharp satire and ambivalent expression are already glimpsed in this poem.

RECOMMENDED: Martha Winburn England, "Emily Dickinson and Isaac Watts: Puritan Hymnodists"; Vivian R. Pollak, "Emily Dickinson's Valentines"; David T. Porter, *The Art of Emily Dickinson's Early Poetry*; Judy Jo Small, *Positive as Sound: Emily Dickinson's Rhymes*; John Emerson Todd, *Emily Dickinson's Use of the Persona*.

Michiko Iwata

THE SINGLE HOUND: POEMS OF A LIFETIME (1914)   This collection introduced 142 poems, most of them drawn from the stock of brief, codelike message-poems sent by Emily to Susan Dickinson* between 1858 and 1886. Although Susan had copied many of these poems for personal use, they were not published until a year after her death, when Martha Dickinson Bianchi* presented *The Single Hound* "as a memorial to the love of those 'Dear, dead Women' " (vi). Bianchi's editorial* authority derived less from her expertise as a textual or Dickinson scholar than from her close familial ties to the poet, and the personal nature of the editorial* enterprise is reflected in her haphazard presentation of the documents: no attempt was made to arrange the poems chronologically or to compare poems printed here with variants published by Mabel Loomis Todd,* and several poems included were of uncertain provenance. Moreover, since Sue transcribed almost one-quarter of the poems her daughter included in the volume, it is not always clear whether Bianchi was preparing copy from the original manuscripts, many of which have been lost, or from her mother's transcripts. In spite of Bianchi's minimal and, in places, misleading editorial apparatus, the texts of Dickinson's poems are refreshingly accurate. More important, Bianchi's edition constitutes an early record of the friendship* between Susan and Emily Dickinson that had been obscured by Todd's control over Dickinson's papers. Notably, Bianchi restored Dickinson's loving poem to Sue, "One Sister have I in our house" (P14), the only other autograph of which was inked over by Austin Dickinson* in an attempt to excise his wife's name from his sister's writing.

RECOMMENDED: Martha Dickinson Bianchi, ed. *The Single Hound: Poems of a Lifetime*. Boston: Little, Brown, 1914; Elizabeth Horan, "To Market: The Dickinson Copyright Wars"; Martha Nell Smith, *Rowing in Eden: Rereading Emily Dickinson*.

Marta Werner

SLANTNESS   Dickinson used the word "slant" and its variants in six poems, two of which are among her most famous. Poems such as "Tell all the Truth but tell it slant—" (P1129)* and "There's a certain Slant of light" (P258)* express a poetic philosophy* of revelation gained through indirection and the unexpected. Slantness might be seen as the poet's toolbox: oxymoron,* oblique description, and familiar words* used in unusual contexts made a structure through which Dickinson orchestrated her readers' epiphany. "Success in Circuit lies," she wrote, indicating that the description of context and circumference* is more useful than direct portraiture in making new again the familiar and in revealing gradually to an audience truths that would otherwise blind.

As usual, Dickinson's poetry presents a paradox: slantness is both the condition of seeing something from a new perspective and the means through which that perspective is gained. Poem 310 shows slantness as the state of heightened awareness gained after turmoil ("Give Avalanches—/ And they'll slant—"), while "There's a certain Slant of light" describes it as an element of the natural world bringing about that heightened awareness. This paradox makes the slantness trope a knot of performance, nature,* poem, revelation, and existence, so intertwined as to leave the core a mystery.

Dickinson's use of slant also reveals her belief in the enormous power of poetry* as a performative tool for revelation. The speaker of "Tell all the Truth" acts as a mediator and translator of truth and image that would otherwise blind the reader.* Her task as she sets it out here is to turn the astonishing revelations of her unique vision,* through indirection, into their most effective and instructive form: the poem. The strange and momentarily frightening syntax* of "As Lightning to the Children eased" is resolved by the line "With explanation kind," as if to exemplify the oxymoron "dazzle gradually." The poet allows us the moment of unsettled feeling—a moment of slantness—before resolution, using unconventional word order to delay explanation and thus mimicking the experience of the frightened child.*

Richard Sewall brings this philosophy into the context of Dickinson's biography*: "with willful cunning and surely with an artist's skill, she avoided direct answers to the major questions" (*Life* 3). She regarded and revealed the truth of her existence so metaphorically* that, despite hundreds of scholars' research efforts, we still know little of Dickinson's "true" life. (*See*: Linguistic and Stylistic Approaches; Philosophical Approaches)

RECOMMENDED: *Life*; Suzanne Juhasz, Cristanne Miller, and Martha Nell Smith, *Comic Power in Emily Dickinson*; David Porter, *The Art of Emily Dickinson's Early Poetry* and *Dickinson: The Modern Idiom*.

Sara Eddy

"Some keep the Sabbath going to Church—" (P324)   Marked by its set of contrasting images that cluster around "Church" and "Home,"* this poem was prominent in Dickinson circles in the nineteenth century. Dickinson sent it (with three other poems) to T. W. Higginson* in July 1862; placed it as the final poem in Fascicle* 9 (Appendix A); and gave it to two people, one of whom was a member of the Sweetser family who published it in *The Round Table** on 12 March 1864 as "My Sabbath." It appeared as "A Service of Song" in *Poems* (1890).* This activity was followed by a dearth of critical attention.

"Church" and "Home" and the subsequent sets of images bring together several large questions that Dickinson explored in other writing. In the poem, the speaker celebrates a church ritual in an orchard with a bobolink as sexton, one who sings instead of tolling a bell. In this pleasant scene, "God* preaches, a noted Clergyman—," and the speaker finally claims that this setting constitutes a heaven* she can enjoy throughout her life rather than "getting to" the heaven of traditional religious* beliefs. The poem reveals Dickinson's delight in a natural setting, her preference for earth and this life, her rejection of institutionalized religion and its practices, and her general distrust of ministers and their dogmatism.

The speaker's tone is playful throughout the poem, almost filled with wonder at the beauty of nature*; in the comparison of nature in this setting with things of heaven, she actually divinizes the earth. But this playful tone of the speaker is in sharp contrast to Dickinson's irony at the core of the poem. In tone, what Dickinson does not state is very clear: that the rites of organized religion are not aesthetically or religiously efficacious, even that they are negative; that the ministers and their sermons are not relevant to the life she knows and lives; that ministers and their congregations would probably not choose the simple message and lightly exercised authority of the deity as characterized in this poem; and that heaven as an ''eternal reward'' for life is inadequate, especially when a heaven configured differently can be experienced throughout a lifetime. Seen in this way, the poem becomes a powerful critique of nineteenth-century institutional religion and a clear example of, among many things, Dickinson's independence of accepted thought and belief. (*See*: Congregationalism; Faith)

RECOMMENDED: Beth Maclay Doriani, *Emily Dickinson, Daughter of Prophecy*; Dorothy Huff Oberhaus, *Emily Dickinson's Fascicles: Method and Meaning*; Gary Lee Stonum, *The Dickinson Sublime*.

Susan Rieke

SPIRITUALISM, AS INFLUENCE   Beginning in the 1850s and throughout Dickinson's lifetime, a spiritualist movement swept through America and England. Orthodox Christianity, with its central belief in a grand resurrection of the dead in some unknowable future, was giving way to the belief that the dead surround us as invisible but accessible presences. Among the many admired by Dickinson who attended seances were Barrett Browning,* Ruskin, and Higginson.* Dickinson's dramatic response to Higginson's *Atlantic** essay, ''Letter to a Young Contributor,'' was occasioned, in part, by its references to an afterworld, to ''some other realm of existence'' free of ''earth's evanescent glories'': as a counterpart of Higginson's satiric summation of orthodox belief (''a gloomy sleep of ages and an incredible resurrection to end it''), Dickinson enclosed her ''Safe in their Alabaster Chambers—''* (L260; P216).

Though never committed to any ideology, Dickinson was drawn to spiritualism; its influence is reflected in numerous poems. Notable for vivid representations of spiritual manifestations and clairvoyance are ''Alone, I cannot be—'' (P298), ''They put Us far apart—'' (P474), ''This World is not Conclusion'' (P501), and ''I see thee better—in the Dark—'' (P611). Dickinson's ''Called back,''* a two-word message to her Norcross* cousins written during the last days of her life, echoes the title of a popular novel that dwells on spectral visions* and the redemptive power of love* (L1046).

RECOMMENDED: Ann Braude. *Radical Spirits: Spiritualism and Women's Rights in Nineteenth-Century America.* Boston: Beacon Press, 1989; Russell M. Goldfarb and Clare R. Goldfarb. *Spiritualism and Nineteenth-Century Letters.* Rutherford, NJ: Fairleigh Dickinson University Press, 1978; Howard Kerr. *Mediums, and Spirit-Rappers, and Roaring Radicals: Spiritualism in American Literature, 1850–1900.* Urbana: University of Illinois Press, 1972; Benjamin Lease, *Emily Dickinson's Readings of Men and Books*;

Barton Levi St. Armand, "Emily Dickinson and the Occult: The Rosicrucian Connection" and "Veiled Ladies: Dickinson, Bettine, and Transcendental Mediumship."

Benjamin Lease

SPOFFORD, HARRIET PRESCOTT (1835–1921)   A near contemporary of Emily Dickinson, Harriet Prescott Spofford, born in Calais, Maine, wrote lyrical, haunting fiction that was acclaimed during her lifetime by such critics as Elizabeth Stuart Phelps,* W. D. Howells,* Henry James, and Thomas Wentworth Higginson.* In fact, Higginson acted as "preceptor" to Spofford as well as to Dickinson. He vouched for Spofford to James Russell Lowell, editor of the *Atlantic Monthly*,* who doubted a woman could have written the story she submitted in 1858. Higginson may also have recommended Spofford's work to Dickinson. In an April 1862 letter, she apparently responded to a query from him about Spofford's short story "Circumstance," in which a frontier woman sings through the night in order to charm and thus save herself from a panther called an "Indian devil." Dickinson wrote, "I read Miss Prescott's 'Circumstance,' but it followed me, in the Dark—so I avoided her—" (L261). Clearly, though, Dickinson did not avoid Harriet Prescott Spofford, as she demonstrated in this note to her sister-in-law: "You stand nearer the world than I do, Susan. Send me everything she [Spofford] writes." Dickinson also claimed to Sue* that Spofford's writing was "the only thing I ever read in my life that I didn't think I could have imagined myself!"—high praise, indeed (*FF* 28). Late in life, Spofford would praise Dickinson's poetry,* almost certainly unaware that Dickinson had esteemed Spofford's own work. (*See*: Gothicism; Women's Culture)

RECOMMENDED: *Letters*; *Life*; Barton Levi St. Armand, *Emily Dickinson and Her Culture: The Soul's Society*; Harriet Prescott Spofford. *"The Amber Gods" and Other Stories*. Ed. Alfred Bendixen. New Brunswick: Rutgers University Press, 1989.

Daneen Wardrop

THE *SPRINGFIELD REPUBLICAN* was "next in importance to the Bible* in determining the mental climate of Emily Dickinson's formative years," according to biographer George Whicher. Founded as a weekly in 1824 by Samuel Bowles (1797–1851), a former proprietor of the *Hartford Times* and a seventh-generation New Englander, the *Republican* achieved its greatest fame under the editorship of Bowles' son Samuel* (1826–1878), a close friend of the Dickinson family. In 1844, at age eighteen, he persuaded his father to let him begin a daily edition, the first in Massachusetts outside Boston.* A morning paper from late 1845, the *Republican* reached Amherst* on the afternoon train and was delivered by the postal carrier.

The paper's name derived from the Democratic-Republican (later, simply, Democratic) Party, but by 1835 the editor had shifted allegiance to the recently formed Whig* Party, of which Edward Dickinson* was a longtime active member. In 1855, with the disintegration of the Whigs, the younger Bowles declared the *Republican* independent of party, a position maintained through the remainder of its history, although it generally supported policies and candidates of the Republican Party, formed in 1854.

The *Republican*'s editorial independence frequently aroused ire in many homes, including probably Emily Dickinson's. Nevertheless, its circulation exceeded that of any New England paper outside Boston, and it had subscribers nationwide. Under the second Bowles it became, in Horace Greeley's words, "the best and ablest country journal ever published on this continent." Its aim was to present "the fruit of all human thought and action" and to be "the daily nourishment of every mind" (1/4/51).

In an age of verbosity, the *Republican* was widely admired for the conciseness of its news and editorial writing and for its strong and progressive stands on a wide array of local, state, and national issues, although it was conservative on some social issues, including woman* suffrage. In the century's great sectional crisis, it strongly opposed slavery but until 1861 advocated a solution that would preserve the union; after secession it fully supported prosecution of the union war effort and the abolition of slavery.

Through its reputation for boldness and innovation, the *Republican* attracted outstanding men (and a few women) to its editorial staff and became known as a "school of journalism" before such schools existed formally. Among its "alumni" were another Dickinson friend, Dr. Josiah G. Holland* (later a founder of *Scribner's**), founders of the *New York Sun* and *Wall Street Journal*, and editors of several major newspapers.

Emily Dickinson, who read the *Republican* "every night" (L133), found in it not only political news and opinion but informative reports on developments in art, literature, religion,* science,* and many other topics of contemporary interest. Bowles' vivid reports on his extensive travels probably influenced Dickinson's images of Europe and of her own expanding country.

In her extant correspondence, Dickinson's most frequent comments on the *Republican* deal with reports of activities by members of her circle of friends*— births, marriages, illnesses, deaths, travels. L133 to the Hollands, for example, notes that "*The Republican* seems to us like a letter from you, and we break the seal and read it eagerly." She also expresses appreciation for its "sprightly" accounts of freak accidents (L133) and refers to its literary columns, edited by Josiah Holland and Frank Sanborn (L402, 974).

The *Republican*'s literary offerings included short fiction, poetry (mostly indifferent and often anonymous), and humorous* sketches that may have helped form Dickinson's sense of the comic. It published seven Dickinson poems, almost certainly without her prior knowledge: P3 (1852),* P35 (1858),* P214 (1861),* P216 (1862),* P137 and P228 (1864),* and P986 (1866).* All appeared anonymously and some with alterations she found objectionable (L316). Such editorial* tamperings may have led Dickinson to refuse later publication offers and to declare publication* "the Auction / Of the Mind" (P709). Her rejection of an offer by "Two Editors of Journals" (L261) may refer to Bowles and Holland.

Dickinson corresponded several times with the paper's third editor, Samuel Bowles (1851–1915), in 1880 congratulating him on his "noble perpetuation of [his father's] cherished 'Republican' " (L651). On 17 May 1886, the paper reported Dickinson's final illness and the next day carried Susan Dickinson's* tender obituary for her sister-in-law, probably the first appearances there of her name. Although the *Republican* may have influenced Dickinson's decision to withhold her poetry from publication, it undoubtedly succeeded in giving "daily nourishment" to her remarkable mind.

RECOMMENDED: Richard Hooker. *The Story of an Independent Newspaper: One Hundred Years of the* Springfield Republican, *1824–1924.* New York: Macmillan, 1924; George S. Merriam. *The Life and Times of Samuel Bowles.* 2 vols. New York: Century, 1885; George Frisbie Whicher, *This Was a Poet: A Critical Biography of Emily Dickinson.*

Georgiana Strickland

STEARNS, FRAZAR AUGUSTUS (1840–1862)   This friend of Austin Dickinson* fell on 14 March 1862 at the Battle of Newbern, North Carolina, a Union victory. A first lieutenant in the Massachusetts Infantry, twenty-first Regiment, he was eulogized in *Adjutant Stearns* by his father, William Augustus Stearns.* In a letter to Samuel Bowles,* Dickinson commented that "Austin is chilled— by Frazer's [*sic*] murder—" (L256). Whereas Austin paid $500 for an alternate to take his place when drafted, Frazar was ready to give his life, perhaps in response to spiritual anguish he felt in common with Emily. Although he did make a confession of faith* at age twelve, the decision troubled him the rest of his life, perhaps predisposing him to the typhoid fever that required a recuperative sea voyage to Bombay. As St. Armand comments, Frazar's willingness "to die in battle for the greater glory of the Union cause assured an escape from the prison-house world of the New England theology while it promised salvation through suffering and justification through death" (111). Emily commemorated Frazar in a poem (P690), originally sent as a letter to Bowles (L257), and mentioned him in three letters to her Norcross* cousins (L245, 255, 362). (*See*: Civil War; Death)

RECOMMENDED: Phyllis Lehrer. "Frazar Stearns: A Young Man with a Promise." *Amherst Record* 5 May 1982: 15–16; Barton Levi St. Armand, *Emily Dickinson and Her Culture: The Soul's Society*; William Augustus Stearns. *Adjutant Stearns.* Boston: Massachusetts Sabbath School Society, 1862; Shira Wolosky, *Emily Dickinson: A Voice of War.*

Michael Strysick

STEARNS, REBECCA ALDEN FRAZAR and WILLIAM AUGUSTUS were Amherst* community leaders. A graduate of Harvard (1827) and Andover Theological Seminary (1831), William Augustus Stearns was appointed the fourth president of Amherst College* in 1854, moving there from church ministry in Cambridgeport, Vermont. The couple's son Frazar* was killed in battle during the Civil War, and Stearns eulogized him in a memorial volume titled *Adjutant Stearns*. Rebecca Stearns became a correspondent of Dickinson's in the 1870s, around the time of her husband's death.* Dickinson sent her a total of nine letters,* two of which contained short poems (P1338 and 1368), the most notable being a stanza written on 8 June 1876 after the death of President Stearns (L463).

RECOMMENDED: Barton Levi St. Armand, *Emily Dickinson and Her Culture: The Soul's Society*; William Augustus Stearns. *Adjutant Stearns*. Boston: Massachusetts Sabbath School Society, 1862; William S. Tyler. *A History of Amherst College during the Administration of Its First Five Presidents, from 1821 to 1891*. New York: F. H. Hitchcock, 1895.

Michael Strysick

STODDARD, ELIZABETH DREW (1823–1902)   Although, as far as we know, Dickinson never met this poet and novelist, the two were joined in the mind of Thomas Wentworth Higginson.* After meeting Dickinson in her Amherst* home in August 1870, Higginson wrote to his wife of the visit: "[I]f you had read Mrs. Stoddard's novels you could understand a house where each member runs his or her own selves" (L342a). Indeed, all three of Stoddard's novels describe families composed of individuals who seem to lead separate existences with private emotional lives. A striking example is *The Morgesons* (1862), Stoddard's most autobiographical novel, in which the heroine, Cassandra Morgeson—an outgoing, outspoken woman who struggles against the restraints of conventional womanhood—is not understood by her family, including her elfish, temperamental, artistic, isolated younger sister Veronica.

As Lawrence Buell and Sandra Zagarell point out, biographical* similarities united Stoddard and Dickinson as daughters of prominent, middle-class Massachusetts families. After their early educations at the best local girls' schools, both attended female seminaries: Stoddard went to Wheaton, while Dickinson attended Mount Holyoke.* Both women rebelled against social expectations, using writing to express dissatisfaction with conventional ideals of female purity, piety, domesticity,* and submissiveness. (*See*: Isolation; Women's Culture)

RECOMMENDED: Lawrence Buell and Sandra A. Zagarell. Introduction to *The Morgesons and Other Writings, Published and Unpublished* by Elizabeth Stoddard. Philadelphia: University of Pennsylvania Press, 1984; James Henderson Matlack. "The Literary Career of Elizabeth Barstow Stoddard." Diss., Yale University, 1967; Elizabeth Stoddard. *Poems*. Boston: Houghton Mifflin, 1895, *Temple House*. New York: G. W. Carlton, 1867, and *Two Men: A Novel*. New York: Bunce and Huntington, 1865.

Jennifer Hynes

STOWE, HARRIET BEECHER (1811–1896)   Emily Dickinson was familiar with the work of Harriet Beecher Stowe, a popular author known for her advocacy novels *Uncle Tom's Cabin* (1852) and *Dred* (1856) and for her domestic* and local color novels, among them *The Minister's Wooing* (1859) and *The Pearl of Orr's Island* (1862). In a letter to her brother, Dickinson commented that her father gave her "quite a trimming" for reading *Uncle Tom's Cabin*, claiming that modern books could not compare to the classics (L113). A play based on that novel was staged in Amherst* in 1854. Dickinson may have met Stowe in 1872 in Amherst, where Stowe spent the summer months visiting her daughter, Georgianna May, wife of Henry F. Allen, the Episcopal rector. During that summer, Susan Dickinson* entertained Stowe and her brother, Henry Ward Beecher. Keller compares Dickinson and Stowe in their use of "millennializing typology" for the purpose of accepting, challenging, and transforming Puritan* thought (111). (*See*: Books and Reading; Women's Culture)

RECOMMENDED: *Letters*; *Years*; Karl Keller, *The Only Kangaroo among the Beauty: Emily Dickinson and America*; Cynthia Griffin Wolff, *Emily Dickinson*.

Dorothy Z. Baker

THE SUBLIME   By contrast to the beautiful, an aesthetic mode that is inherently pleasing, the sublime always admixes the fearful or threatening. Traditionally, it has been understood as the category of experience through which divinity's terrible majesty is apprehended, and this is how Dickinson often regarded it. She most often characterized her response to the sublime as "awe," which, like "agony," "astonishment," "transport," and several other favorite terms, names the "tremendousness" of experiencing God* as absolute and transcendent.

The field of aesthetics includes all forms of experience, not just artistic ones, so the sublime is by no means exclusively an artistic category. Nevertheless, it has since antiquity chiefly designated those features of poetry that are exceptional, excessive, or otherwise inexplicable by the rules of art. More important, it represents the poetic in terms not of compositional features but of effects on the reader,* especially intensities of sensation or feeling. Dickinson echoed precisely this understanding in a famous declaration to Colonel Higginson*: "If I read a book [and] it makes my whole body so cold no fire ever can warm me I know *that* is poetry. If I feel physically as if the top of my head were taken off, I know *that* is poetry" (L342a).

Not only was the sublime thus arguably the essence of poetry* for Dickinson, but it also provided a structure that organized many of her poems and many of the experiences they engage. According to a number of modern accounts deriving from Kant's *Critique of Judgment*, there are three phases to the sublime: (1) a normative phase prior to encountering tremendousness, in which the mind feels more or less adequate to the objects in its world and able to understand them; (2) a traumatic phase, in which the fearful encounter with some numinous object disrupts the mind's capacities and hence its confidence; and (3) a reactive phase, in which the mind restores or enlarges itself by imitating or identifying with, and thus sublimating, the power that had precipitated the trauma.

All three phases may be detected in such poems as "At Half past Three, a single Bird" (P1084) and "A little Madness in the Spring" (P1333), but Dickinson more typically lingered on the traumatic phase. It has been argued that her poetry is based on a singularly hesitant sublime in which the lure of empowerment in the reactive phase is indefinitely postponed, and Dickinson's speaker remains poised on the border between time and immortality,* unwilling to commit herself unreservedly to identification with a numinous power she often understands as patriarchal.

No evidence exists to suggest that Dickinson had any direct knowledge of Kant, Edmund Burke, or the other Enlightenment thinkers who helped revive an interest in the sublime. Her awareness could have come from reading in the poetic tradition that ran from Milton through Wordsworth and beyond, and it may also have drawn upon her familiarity with the painting and art criticism of her day. Judith Farr and others have explored her knowledge of Thomas Cole and his successors in the Hudson River school, and Farr has noted the possibility that Dickinson picked up Burke's ideas from John Ruskin's *Modern Painters*. One link to a specific discourse about the sublime is the importance of landscape, especially extreme landscapes featuring mountains, deserts, volcanoes, storms, and maelstroms. On the other hand, by the middle of the nineteenth century, such images of the sublime had become romantic* commonplaces, for which Dickinson would have needed no special source. (*See*: Visual Arts)

RECOMMENDED: Judith Farr, *The Passion of Emily Dickinson*; Gary Lee Stonum, *The Dickinson Sublime*.

Gary Lee Stonum

"Success is counted sweetest" (P67)   was first published by the *Brooklyn Daily Union* in 1864 although Dickinson had transcribed it into her fifth fascicle* around 1859 (Appendix A). It reappeared (with editorially* altered text) in *A Masque of Poets** (1878), after repeated requests by compiler Helen Hunt Jackson.* Of the three autograph copies, two date from 1859, and one from 1862; they contain variations in capitalization* and punctuation, but the major difference among them is that only one is divided into stanzas. Criticism has seen Dickinson as asserting, variously, "the perception of value won through deprivation" (Whicher 202), "the *superiority* of . . . anguished comprehension to mere possession" (Wilbur 57), the dignity (Sherwood)—or the inutility (Homans)—of suffering. With an inversion of common logic, the poem claims, directly or ironically, that those who are denied "Victory" actually understand it better than those who experience it. Its context may have been the Civil War.* (*See*: Civil War; Dash; Oxymoron; Publication)

RECOMMENDED: Margaret Homans, *Women Writers and Poetic Identity: Dorothy Wordsworth, Emily Brontë, and Emily Dickinson*; William R. Sherwood, *Circumference and Circumstance: Stages in the Mind and Art of Emily Dickinson*; Richard Wilbur, "Sumptuous Destitution"; George Frisbie Whicher, *This Was a Poet: A Critical Biog-*

raphy of Emily Dickinson; Shira Wolosky, "Emily Dickinson's War Poetry: The Problem of Theodicy."

Haskell Springer

SUE, SUSIE, or SUSAN Dickinson, Susan Huntington Gilbert

SWEETSER, CATHERINE DICKINSON (1814–1895) **and JOSEPH A**. (1808–1874?)   The firstborn in the Homestead,* Catherine (or Catharine) was the sixth child of Samuel Fowler* and Lucretia Gunn Dickinson.* She grew up in Amherst,* attending Amherst Academy.* In 1833, after a brief stay with her sister Mary, she joined her parents in Ohio. In 1835 she returned east to marry Joseph Sweetser, formerly associated with his brother Luke* in Amherst but by 1834 a New York businessman. Outwardly their marriage was successful: they had eight children, and Joseph's business prospered. However, a memorandum Catherine wrote on their twenty-fifth anniversary shows ambivalence, and there was discord in the late 1860s over their daughter Mary's marriage to her cousin Charles Sweetser, which Joseph refused to sanction. Joseph's unsolved disappearance in 1874 posed a unique challenge to Dickinson as writer of consolation letters (L408). Other letters* also offer sympathy for Aunt Katie's losses (L338, 478) or thank her for sympathy extended (L828, 952). The letters reflect a shared love of flowers* and interest in gardening.* Of eleven extant letters, only the earliest is to Joseph (L190); all others are to Catherine alone.
RECOMMENDED: *Letters*; Millicent Todd Bingham, *Emily Dickinson's Home*.

Karen Dandurand

SWEETSER, CHARLES HUMPHREYS (1841–1871)   Orphaned at age seven, Charles Sweetser was adopted by his uncle Luke Sweetser* and raised with his similarly dislocated cousin, Abby Wood.* He graduated from Amherst College* in 1862 and began a promising career in journalism, working first for the *Springfield Republican** and then with papers in Chicago, St. Paul, and Brooklyn. In 1864 he established *The Round Table*,* a literary journal that published Dickinson's poem "Some keep the Sabbath going to Church—" (324)* as "My Sabbath." Dickinson and Sweetser may have corresponded about this publication,* but no letters* have been found. Sweetser married his cousin Mary Newman Sweetser (Edward Dickinson's* niece) in 1867 but died soon after of tuberculosis. The *Springfield Republican*'s obituary called him a man of rare enthusiasm and high ambition but also stressed that the world would call his career a failure because of his frequent ill health and lack of business experience.
RECOMMENDED: *Life*; *Years*.

Sara Eddy

SWEETSER, J. HOWARD and NELLIE   John Howard Sweetser (1835–1904) was the only child of Luke Sweetser,* a leading Amherst* figure. The household, which included orphaned cousins, was located behind the Dickinson family homes. Howard left Amherst College* to become a large mercantile wholesaler in New York and married Lucy Cornelia Peck in 1860. The couple and their children (Alice, Howard, and "Nettie") spent summers in Amherst at the Sweetser family home. Dickinson often wrote to Nellie and sent flowers* and cakes.

RECOMMENDED: *Letters*; *Years*.

Masako Takeda

SWEETSER, LUKE (1800–1882) **and ABBY** (ca. 1806–1882)   Born at Athol, Massachusetts, Luke Sweetser reached Amherst* in 1820–1821 as a student at Amherst Academy* and clerk in the Amherst store. He and his brother Joseph bought the store "Sweetser, Cutler and Co." in 1824. A successful merchant, Sweetser served as selectman, justice of the peace, and representative to the General Court (1847–1849). Like Edward Dickinson,* he was an active promoter of the Amherst and Belchertown Railroad, which in 1850 had the depot just east of the Dickinson Homestead.* Sweetser supported education and agriculture and was active in banking. His wife, Abby T. Munsell, was born in New York State. Their two children were born at Amherst, and she died there three months after Luke's death. This was the lady Dickinson characterized as rolling "down the lane to church like a reverend marble" (L339). (*See*: Wood)

RECOMMENDED: *Letters*; Charles F. Carpenter and Edward W. Morehouse. *The History of the Town of Amherst.* Amherst, MA: Carpenter and Morehouse, 1896; James Avery Smith. *Families of Amherst, Massachusetts.* Amherst, MA: Unpublished typescript, 1984 and *Records of West Cemetery at Amherst, Massachusetts.* Amherst: Official records of the town engineer.

James Avery Smith

SWETT, ANNA JONES NORCROSS (1856–1939)   Dickinson's first cousin, Anna was the daughter of Lamira Jones and Joel Warren Norcross.* After her mother died, Anna visited for a while in 1864 at Mrs. Bangs' Boardinghouse* during the time the poet was being treated for her eye disorder. Anna Norcross married Lewis Swett in 1877, and the couple had one son, Louis. Anna's only grandchild, Sylvia Swett Viano, recalled that her grandmother reported visiting the poet frequently in Amherst* and would recount vivid stories of observing Dickinson "talk poetry." Viano reported, "My grandmother said Dickinson would open the window or the curtains and say poetically what she saw outdoors in the garden* or a bird* or whatever it was. My grandmother stood in awe . . . to hear this going on" (Ackmann 123).

RECOMMENDED: *Years*; Martha Ackmann, " 'I'm Glad I Finally Surfaced': A Norcross Descendent Remembers Emily Dickinson."

Martha Ackmann

SYNTAX   Dickinson's syntax tends to follow one of three patterns: the paratactic juxtaposition of short sentences without connective explanation; the hypotactic exploration of complex sentences; and the use of contrast to link short statements through repeated negation or the use of conjunctions. All three patterns suggest the individual person or psyche in moments of relationship more than they do universal or ultimate principles of order or connection.

Parataxis most strikingly typifies Dickinson's syntax, giving her verse its characteristic compression* and ellipticism. For example, "Title divine—is mine!" (P1072) proceeds almost entirely through the juxtaposition of parallel exclamations, requiring the reader's interpretation to gain coherence. Lines 2–5 read, "The Wife—without the Sign! / Acute Degree—conferred on me—/ Empress of Calvary! / Royal—all but the Crown!"; the rest of the poem is similarly paratactic. As this example shows, parataxis is closely linked to Dickinson's use of syntactic and rhetorical* parallelism. Such disjunctive* or parallel linking of ideas does not provide thematic coordination. While often regarded as childlike in tone, parataxis (which characterizes large sections of the Bible*) tends to give Dickinson's poetry an elevated and emotionally charged quality.

Syntactic deletion functions as an extreme form of parataxis, causing the reader to fill in not only transitions between sentences and commonly deleted function words but often primary sentence-internal connectors. For example, the final stanza of "It was not Death, for I stood up" (P510) compares the unnamed "It" to "Chaos" then modifies "Chaos" ambiguously,* "Without a Chance, or Spar—/ Or even a Report of Land—/ To justify—Despair." Because the link between chaos and despair is primarily metaphorical* and parallel rather than causal or otherwise logically specified, the link between "Despair" and "It" or the speaker's state is even more difficult to determine with confidence. Syntactic doubling creates similar difficulties in referentiality and connection.

In contrast, hypotactic syntax allows Dickinson to specify the relations that juxtaposition only implies, although syntactic deletion, inversion, and the highly figurative quality of Dickinson's language prevent even largely hypotactic poems from establishing more than temporary or tenuous connections. An excellent example of hypotaxis occurs in "To pile like Thunder to its close" (P1247), where each line depends on the distinctions that precede it, and where conjunctive or logical connectors like "then," "while," "both and neither," and "either" abound.

Repeated assertion and negation, or description and contrast, give Dickinson's poems an impulsive quality, as though the speaker were just working out a thought or feeling. Equally important, Dickinson uses repeated negation definitionally to indicate states too ephemeral or difficult to define positively—as in "It was not Death, for I stood up" (P510). The conjunction "but" functions similarly. In "Robbed by Death—but that was easy—" (P971) or " 'Twas awkward, but it fitted me—" (P973) or "Unfulfilled to Observation—/Incomplete—to Eye—/But to Faith—a Revolution" (P972), contrasting conjunctions give Dickinson's verse an argumentative, colloquial,* and unsettled quality.

Dickinson's syntax also contains many informal elements: contractions; intimacy signals (e.g., you know, well, you see); tag questions addressed to the reader* ("Hav'nt You," P700); idiomatic repetitions (as in "And I—Could I stand by" in P640); and use of speech fragments. Together with the features mentioned before, these make Dickinson's poems characteristically colloquial and speechlike.

There are some inversion of word order in Dickinson's poems and some highly complex syntax. Its primary difficulties occur through deletion and juxtaposition, however, rather than through the complexities of the syntax itself. (*See*: Linguistic and Stylistic Approaches; "Omitted Center"; Repetition)

RECOMMENDED: Brita Lindberg-Seyersted, *The Voice of the Poet: Aspects of Style in the Poetry of Emily Dickinson*; Cristanne Miller, *Emily Dickinson: A Poet's Grammar* and "Dickinson's Language: Interpreting Truth Told Slant"; David Porter, *The Art of Emily Dickinson's Early Poetry*.

Cristanne Miller

T

"Tell all the Truth but tell it slant—" **(P1129)**   was written about 1868, drafted in pencil on a scrap of stationery. In 1945, the poem appeared in *Bolts of Melody*,* edited by Mabel Loomis Todd* and Millicent Todd Bingham* with text arranged as two quatrains.

In "Tell all the Truth but tell it slant—," the speaker/poet suggests that indirection in language will protect readers by easing the impact. The speaker's maternal image is underscored by reference to readers as children who need shielding from the lightning's dazzle. For Dickinson, truth is internal and cannot be stated directly. It is realized in a web of images that constitutes the poem's statement. Dickinson's poetic communication depends on a circuitous or symbolic way of speaking. "My Business is Circumference,"* she wrote to Higginson* (L268). Because Dickinson omitted* the center and concentrated instead on effects, her readers* are able to identify with emotion whether or not they share its cause. To the extent that readers fill in the blanks, they participate with the poet in the making of the poem.

In the middle-class community from which Dickinson came, women's* discourse was culturally monitored. Dickinson adopted strategies of indirection in order to express forbidden feelings obliquely. By gradually revealing abstract truth to her readers, the poet protected not only her readers but herself as well. She did not have to take responsibility for conveying frightening or nonconforming truth. By keeping "Truth" at a safe metaphorical* distance, she allowed only readers capable of understanding the opacity of her language to comprehend her meaning. Only as readers are able to penetrate her meaning will they be able to grasp the difficult truths that her writing conveys.

Dickinson's veiled mode of articulation has many aspects: disjunction,* omission of subject identification, compressing* enigmatic metaphor.* Her intent is not to conceal but to reveal gradually to those who can understand. (*See*: Philosophical Approaches; Slantness)

RECOMMENDED: Daniel R. Barnes, "Telling It Slant: Emily Dickinson and the Proverb"; Beth Maclay Doriani, *Emily Dickinson, Daughter of Prophecy*; Karl Keller, "Notes on Sleeping with Emily Dickinson."

Deborah Dietrich

TEXTUAL VARIANTS in which two or more words, phrases, or stanzas are left to stand as alternates for each other appeared in the manuscript books as early as 1859. By the twelfth fascicle* (1861), their proliferation amounted to a primary compositional practice by which Dickinson emphasized the meaning-making process involved in both writing and reading texts. Her practice was to interlineate the variant above or below the word in question or to "footnote" it, using crosslike asterisks positioned near the word to link it to its variant, which is often found at the bottom of the poem. While one word occupies a position within the poem, and the variant stands somewhere outside it, a hierarchized choice is not implied; Dickinson regularly incorporated variants and created new ones in the poems she sent to friends* in letters.* Indeed, variants proliferated at every stage of the composition process, from rough draft and fascicle copying, through writing out copies for friends, to marking the fascicle copies in pencil sometimes decades later. A chief editorial* difficulty has been to cope with the many versions of poems Dickinson produced using variants and with the question of whether or not they are to be taken as altogether distinct poetic acts. Thomas H. Johnson's* three-volume variorum edition, *The Poems of Emily Dickinson*,* subordinates variants, drafts, and versions sent in (or as) letters below a representation of a complete and numbered poem.

While, in some instances, variant wordings have no appreciable effect upon the poem, in most cases the variants directly complicate meaning. In P527, for example, the last three lines are crucially altered by our inability to rank variants. The sacrament is described as "Patent, every drop, / With the Brand [Stamp] of the Gentile Drinker / Who indorsed [enforced] the Cup—." Is the "Gentile," Jesus,* merely a human salesman endorsing his product, or is his persuasiveness more violent, inexorable in his aspect as the Godhead? The variants both prompt and refuse the choice. The reader cannot "complete" the poem without depriving it of its vitality in the contradiction; the poem, in turn, sustains the reader* indefinitely in the act of making meaning. The variants embody imaginative relationship; they thus formally incarnate the core concern of Dickinson's poetry.* (*See*: Ambiguity; Linguistic and Stylistic Approaches; *Manuscript Books*; Words)

RECOMMENDED: *AB*; *Poems*; Sharon Cameron, *Choosing Not Choosing: Dickinson's Fascicles*; Ralph W. Franklin, *The Manuscript Books of Emily Dickinson*; Susan Howe, "These Flames and Generosities of the Heart: Emily Dickinson and the Illogic of Sumptuary Values."

Melanie Hubbard

"The Brain—is wider than the Sky—" (P632) Written about 1862 and copied by Dickinson into Fascicle* 26, it has only one textual variant*: l. 3, contain/include (Appendix A). It was first published in *Poems* (1896)* as "The Brain." Though the subject of consciousness* is introduced in stanza 1, the poem's theme is the brain's infinity—which it elucidates by comparing it sequentially to the sky, the sea, and God,* using the lexical fields of measurement and capacity. While the first two stanzas claim the mind's superiority to matter, the last seems to assert that the mind and the idea of God are indistinguishable.

RECOMMENDED: *Poems*; Suzanne Juhasz, *The Undiscovered Continent: Emily Dickinson and the Space of the Mind*; Inder Nath Kher, *The Landscape of Absence: Emily Dickinson's Poetry*.

Haskell Springer

"The Bustle in a House" (P1078) First published in *Poems* (1890),* this is distinguished from many Dickinson poems by the plainness of its diction, admirably deploying generic language of time,* distance, and loss in three disyllabic words tellingly placed within its eight lines. In this poem of a shared, general condition, the articles are exactly right: the general truth of "*The* Bustle," the anonymous particularity of "*a* House," no "a" before "Death."* The absence of repetition* except for the poem's four "*the*'s," enhances the effect of its use of resonant resemblance. The moving wordplay* underlying the metaphor* "Sweeping up the Heart" is inescapable, but the domestic "hearth" is also evoked by the chain "Death," [dearth], "Earth," with the "Earth" ending the poem's first stanza so movingly because, perhaps unconsciously, rearranged as the "Heart" that ends the first line of the second. The tie of "earth" and "heart[h]" knits the stanzas at the level of human sympathy and solidarity. Here, too, Dickinson uses triangulation ("*Enacted upon Earth*" and "*Eternity*") to join the whole. The metaphors preceding "Eternity" are domestic* ones, in keeping with her *American Dictionary*,* which cited *Isaiah* 57, 15, "the high and lofty One that inhabiteth eternity." Interestingly, a lesser poem of domestic death (P389) uses "rustle." That poem has more detail but less weight. P1078 is even enhanced by what is missing. The statement and sympathy are universal; no dead person is present nor any describable persona. The working of the elided relative ("which" or "that") may be "too deep for tears."

This poem's sympathy, response, and maturity are universal. Central, however, is the statement that the "Love"* that is "put away" is for, belongs to, a particular person. The domestic imagery of its metaphors makes it very much one of Dickinson's poems on women's* condition.

The suggestion that there is more convention than conviction in the poem's "Until Eternity" may originate in preconceptions today's reader* so often brings to Emily Dickinson. The poem's paradox (we do love then and later; the mechanical bustle and the putting away are not evidence of the contrary) is a mature and wise perception. There is undoubtedly an element of consolation in the poem's statement. That perception and mechanism are valid, whether or not there is heavenly* reunion. "Until Eternity" was a consolation made available to the poet by the language and culture of her community (of those she may, in part, have sought to console). (*See*: Elegy; Immortality)

RECOMMENDED: Thomas W. Ford, *Heaven Beguiles the Tired: Death in the Poetry of Emily Dickinson*; Elizabeth Phillips, *Emily Dickinson: Personae and Performance.*

James Fegan and Haruko Kimura

"The Soul selects her own Society—" (P303)   According to Duchac's bibliography, the first published study of this poem reads the image of the kneeling emperor as proof that "the secluded one thought well of herself," while the third (1944) claims that the phrase "Valves of her attention" is a "precise scientific* reference . . . to the valve of the brachiopod."

That is, "The Soul selects her own Society—" has occasioned some typical junk Dickinsoniana: psychobiographical fantasies and silly attempts at worrying poetry into prose. But classical New Criticism* has served the poem well. The sensitive readings of Mark Van Doren (*Introduction to Poetry*, 1951) and Denis Donoghue (*Connoisseurs of Chaos*, 1965) have valuable things to teach about language, and David Porter has helped us hear how "the poem ends with a decisive sound that belies its utter indefiniteness" (64).

In general, however, the most productive readings of this poem have been those that establish it in a context. George Monteiro, for example, has demonstrated that its imagery is closely linked to Emerson's* essay "Friendship," as "I taste a liquor never brewed" (P214)* is to "The Poet"; Robert M. Luscher has established a thematic connection with another, now unfamiliar Emerson essay, "Spiritual Laws." Building on an independent discovery of the link with "Friendship," Jonathan Morse has claimed a general significance for such discoveries of historical* intertextuality. Their effect on readers'* sense of meaning, says Morse, is analogous to the change in an artistic canon when it receives the impact of a new work of art.

A different sort of discovery is the countercontextualization of Sharon Cameron's *Choosing Not Choosing*. Beginning with the observation that Dickinson criticism has "stressed . . . the separation of any given utterance from a decipherable situation that it could be said to represent," Cameron postulates a Dickinson whose fascicles* represent an ongoing deconstruction of all fixed intertextual relationships (3 n.2). "The Soul selects her own Society—" is one of Cameron's key examples, and in her hands it is a powerful one. It helps us understand, for instance, why that anapestic 1944 phrase "the valve of the brachiopod" is silly: because it comes to us from a dead language of fixed meanings that can never represent Dickinson's endlessly deferred coherence. (*See*: Appendix A, Fascicle 20)

RECOMMENDED: Sharon Cameron, *Choosing Not Choosing: Dickinson's Fascicles*; Joseph Duchac, *The Poems of Emily Dickinson: An Annotated Guide to Commentary Published in English, 1890–1977*; Robert M. Luscher, "An Emersonian Context of Dickinson's 'The Soul selects her own Society' "; George Monteiro, "Dickinson's Select Society"; Jonathan Morse, "History in the Text"; David Porter, *Dickinson: The Modern Idiom.*

Jonathan Morse

"There's a certain Slant of light" (P258)   is the middle poem of Fascicle* 13 and was published in the first edition of Dickinson's verse, *Poems* (1890)* (Appendix A). From the fascicle version to this early printed version, three word changes were made. The second line was changed to "On winter afternoons"; Johnson* claims that this was for the sake of regularizing the meter, but curiously, other trimeter lines that are short a syllable were left unchanged. Johnson also claims that the word "heft" was changed to "weight" "to protect the author from the taint of provincialism" (xlv). The indeterminacy of the line "None may teach it—Any—" was removed in the 1890 version by printing "None may teach it anything."

This poem explores the relation between the external natural* world and internal psychic* experience. It begins by defining the light in terms of a human experience of that light: the manifestation of the "Heavenly* Hurt" is "internal difference." In the relation between the external and the internal, the poem suggests concealed merit or authenticity of the internal self* ("Where the Meanings, are—"), which is found throughout Dickinson's poems.

Numerous critics have written about this poem, generally to focus on contextualizing the internal experience of the "Slant of light." Anderson sees this as "her finest poem on despair" and claims that "winter sunlight is simply the over-image of despair, inclosing the center of suffering" (215–16). Monteiro, by contrast, reads the natural phenomenon of the poem as a more hopeful figurative structure. He claims that, by connecting "light" with "heft," Dickinson employs a Puritan* idea from *Corinthians II*: the "Biblical* idea of glory ('light') has the literal meaning of weight." Thus "Sunlight on a winter afternoon provided the poet with one of her direct experiences of Divinity" (Item 13). Cameron moves even further from the poem's physical world by focusing on the "apocalyptic" experience suggested by the vocabulary of *Revelation.* Through its connection with the "Seal Despair—," "light" is "scour[ed]" of "its traditional associations with life" and creates a *figura* predictive of the death* at the poem's end. In this poem, "literal reality permanently assumes those metaphoric* characteristics that seemed initially intended only to illuminate it"; light as a *figura* of death becomes "saturated in the terms of its own figuration" (101–3).

The poem can also be read as an event occurring in the realm of language, without symbolic referents. Throughout it, personified agents enact ineffable effects: "Shadows—hold their breath—." In the final stanza, when the "light" goes, the presence of the listening "Landscape" fades into the abstract "Distance / On the look of Death—." The qualities of light that remain can be described only with the distance of the simile. Dickinson gives the external world agency, and this natural world becomes the agent acting on the human "we" of the poem; thus this poem enacts a connection in language between nature and human emotional experience. (*See*: Poststructuralist Approaches; Vision)

RECOMMENDED: Charles R. Anderson, *Emily Dickinson's Poetry: Stairway of Surprise*; Sharon Cameron, *Lyric Time: Dickinson and the Limits of Genre*; Margaret H. Freeman, Gudrun M. Grabher, and Roland Hagenbüchle, eds., " 'There's a certain Slant of light': Swedish, Finnish, Chinese, Japanese, Yiddish"; George Monteiro, "Dickinson's There's a Certain Slant of Light"; Barton Levi St. Armand, *Emily Dickinson and Her Culture: The Soul's Society*.

Lynne EFM Spear

"These are the days when Birds come back—" (P130)   Dickinson's 1859 poem about a speaker who knows better but longs to interpret the warmth and light of Indian summer as signs that winter and death* will not arrive was published* in 1864 and again in 1890. Dickinson herself may have contributed it to *Drum Beat*,* a Civil War* fund-raising magazine, which published the poem anonymously as "October" on 11 March 1864. After Dickinson's death, the poem surfaced in three slightly different versions—one in Fascicle* 6 (Johnson's* official version); another written in pencil around 1859; and one copy of the first two stanzas done around 1883 (Appendix A). In 1890, Todd* and Higginson* called the poem "Indian Summer" when including it in *Poems by Emily Dickinson.**

Critics are drawn to the tension between the experienced aspect of the speaker who pronounces Indian summer a sham and the credulous aspect that interprets the season* as a sign of Nature's* promise of immortality,* akin to Jesus'* promise at the Last Supper. In the first line, the undeceived aspect of the speaker who knows the sordid truth about "these" kinds of "days" immediately acquaints readers with her conflicting desire to accept Indian summer at face value. She tricks readers* into believing the poem is about spring when "Birds come back." Until the fourth stanza, the speaker increasingly acknowledges the power of the self who would misinterpret seasonal cues. She shifts from blaming Nature for constructing "old—old sophistries," to blaming the perceiver who "mistake[s]" the "blue and gold." When she employs apostrophe ("Oh fraud"), she does not establish mutuality between herself and Nature but exposes the hopelessness of her desire that Nature would recognize her with a ceremony ensuring her immortality.

Critics generally agree that the speaker invokes Christian sacrament knowing the impossibility of Nature's ever extending immortality; however, they disagree about why she does so. Anderson indicates that, in the face of almost certain death,* the speaker submits to her desire in order to experience a " 'last Communion' between her critical mind and her yearning heart" (149). Wolff suggests that the "Last Communion in the Haze" is the poet's opportunity to accompany the reader through the painful discovery of the impossibility of obtaining reciprocity with Nature (307–9). Finally, Budick believes Dickinson invokes Christian ritual in the context of inexorable natural death to indict prevailing theologies for reducing the landscape to a false system of divine signs that undermine faith* (54). (*See*: Birds; Religion)

RECOMMENDED: E. Miller Budick, *Emily Dickinson and the Life of Language: A Study in Symbolic Poetics*; Karen Dandurand, "New Dickinson Civil War Publications"; Jane Donahue Eberwein, "Emily Dickinson and the Calvinist Sacramental Tradition"; Cynthia Griffin Wolff, *Emily Dickinson.*

Robin E. Calland

"This is my letter to the World" (P441)   was probably written early in 1862. Dickinson included the poem with nineteen others in Fascicle* 24 (Appendix A). In *Poems* (1890),* Higginson* and Todd* placed this poem on a separate leaf just after the table of contents and before the first page of poems.

The poem represents the poet/speaker as a letter* writer. She is sending her letter out "to the World," into the public sphere, and as a consequence, she runs the risk of being misunderstood or condemned for her nonconforming ideas. Instead of taking responsibility for creating the message, she claims to be a conveyor of the news of the original speaker, Nature.* Dickinson emphasizes the link between "News" and "Nature" by placing both words on the same poetic line, capitalizing* them, and stressing their alliteration. By emphasizing their connection, the poet further detaches the poem's persona from information she relates.

If in stanza 2, "Hands" is a synecdoche for God,* Dickinson is suggesting that God's hands, although invisible, are committed to an inevitable design. This mysterious design is the source of the message Nature tells with "tender Majesty." Here Dickinson suggests that Nature's tenderness and authority surpass the mysteries of God's design, for the infinite is only supposed because it remains invisible, whereas Nature is actual and can be apprehended through the senses.

The poem's metaphor* of the poet as intimate writer of messages aptly characterizes Dickinson's work. Dickinson's life of isolated* artistic creativity encouraged her extraordinary awareness of the natural world and her dependence on written correspondence to communicate with those she could not see in person. There are many stylistic similarities between her poems and letters. For example, the language in both is compressed,* metaphorical,* and disjunctive.* In some of her letters, she switched from prose to verse midsentence. Dickinson was a prolific correspondent, and her "letters to the world" gave her an opportunity to self-publish many of her poems, while protecting her personal life from public scrutiny. (*See*: Publication)

RECOMMENDED: *Life*; *Poems*; Cristanne Miller, *Emily Dickinson: A Poet's Grammar.*

Deborah Dietrich

"This was a Poet—It is That" (P448)   Copied into Fascicle* 21 about 1862 (Appendix A), the year after Elizabeth Barrett Browning's* death,* the quatrains of this remarkable, if stunningly slant,* declaration of aesthetic principles were published in *The Poems of Emily Dickinson: Centenary Edition** (1930) and subsequent collections as eight-line stanzas. When Eberwein speaks of the "concentrated passion" of "This was a Poet" and its "compression of narrative" (138), she alerts readers to attend to the complexity of images (from botany, perfumery, poetry,* and much else) as well as of grammar.

The "chopped language . . . image heaped uncomfortably upon image" (Budick 128) and ambiguity* of pronoun referentiality underscore the profound dissonances in the poem. Miller, for example, notes "the ambivalence between admiration and ironic disdain" of the speaker for her own art (122); Pollak observes the narrator's exploration of "the alien underworld of the female psyche . . . at odds with her extravagant tributes to the poet as invulnerable superman" (232).

Using Emersonian* language to describe the actions and characteristics of the "superman" (the verbs—"Distills," "Arrested," "Entitles"—are all in Emerson's "The Poet"), Dickinson signals her complexity with the apparently confused series of changing pronouns, "This," "It," and "That." The ambiguity of antecedents, of particular interest to Cristanne Miller and to E. Miller Budick, draws the reader into the speaker's attempts at defining the undefinable: the method, effect, and value of the poet who, echoing and significantly altering the hymn,* punningly produces "amazing sense / From ordinary Meanings."

Although, as Cynthia Wolff points out, this is Dickinson's "most famous poem about the poet" (532), it is rarely discussed in terms of its placement in a fascicle full of images of doors ("I Years had been from Home," P609) and closed compartments ("In falling Timbers buried—" and "I died for Beauty," P614, 449). Dickinson has, in fact, placed "They shut me up in Prose—" (P613) on the left-hand page facing "This was a Poet"; the two resonate against each other contextually, underscoring Dickinson's distinctions between the world of prose and that of poetry. In the first, on the left, the speaker is "shut up"; on the right, the poet is the *dis*closer. On the left, the poet chafes at being "still": on the right, the poet is the *dis*tiller (the homophone of which suggests that the poet destabilizes what the stolid world of prose decrees). On the left, the metaphoric bird is "lodged . . . for Treason—in the Pound"; on the right, the poet "arrests" the "familiar species" for all time. On the left, the world attempts "Captivity"; on the right, the poet is triumphantly "Himself—to Him—a Fortune—/ Exterior—to Time." (*See*: Feminist Approaches; *Manuscript Books*)

RECOMMENDED: E. Miller Budick, *Emily Dickinson and the Life of Language*; Charles R. Anderson, *Emily Dickinson's Poetry: Stairway of Surprise*; Jane Donahue Eberwein, *Dickinson: Strategies of Limitation*; Cristanne Miller, *Emily Dickinson: A Poet's Grammar*; Vivian Pollak, *Dickinson: The Anxiety of Gender*.

Eleanor Elson Heginbotham

THOREAU, HENRY DAVID (1817–1862)   A key figure in American Transcendentalism,* Thoreau was considered by T. W. Higginson* one of "our most original authors"; and it has been argued that if Higginson was Dickinson's literary preceptor, Thoreau was Higginson's. Born in Concord, Massachusetts, where he spent most of his life, Thoreau attended Harvard and then was irregularly employed in his family's pencil business, as schoolteacher, and as surveyor. Disenchanted with social constraints, Thoreau went to Walden Pond on 4 July 1845 in order to live simply and "deliberately" in a cabin for over two years, an experience he recorded in his best-known work, *Walden* (1854). The book critiques America's emphasis on business, technology, and material success, while proclaiming that a renewal of life is possible through the elimination of superfluities and an immersion in nature.*

The kinship between Dickinson and Thoreau seems close. According to an anecdote, her future sister-in-law Sue* quoted Thoreau when she was first introduced to Emily; Dickinson's recognition of those lines is said to have sealed their friendship.* One may assume her thorough acquaintance with Thoreau's work. The Dickinson library included copies of his *Letters to Various Persons* and *A Week on the Concord and Merrimack Rivers* as well as two copies of *Walden* (one of them marked) that dated from the middle 1860s (although she may have read the book earlier). She must also have been familiar with Thoreau's essays that appeared in the *Atlantic** in 1862 as well as his *Cape Cod*, since she asked in an 1866 letter to Sue and Austin* during their seashore vacation, "Was the Sea cordial? Kiss him for Thoreau" (L320). He is also mentioned in a letter of 1881 (L691).

Both writers use the journey, accompanied by a close examination and careful description of the minute phenomena of nature, as an emblem for a personal quest; both assess values similarly and apply Yankee economics to spiritual growth; and both were elevated into the canon of American literature in the 1930s. (*See*: Books and Reading; Emerson)

RECOMMENDED: *Life*; Thomas Wellborn Ford, "Thoreau's Cosmic Mosquito and Dickinson's Terrestrial Fly"; Robert A. Gross, "Lonesome in Eden: Dickinson, Thoreau, and the Problem of Community in Nineteenth-Century New England."

Josef Raab

TIME, AS SUBJECT   In a poem from about 1862, Dickinson wrote "Some—Work for Immortality—/ The Chiefer part, for Time—" (P406), lines that pursue the mystery of time by investigating the canceling out of time that eternity, immortality,* and infinity represent. St. Armand states flatly that, "like most romantics,* Dickinson was obsessed with the idea of time," making clear that she "collapsed time into a sundial rather than into a clock" (277). The temporal delineations made by Dickinson derived from those found in nature*: the four quarters of a day, the four cycles of the sun, as well as the four seasons.* These organic divisions allowed that while time always moves forward, it does so at various speeds in a kind of counterpoint. The oppositions time presented—noon/

midnight, sunrise/sunset, east/west—were crucibles through which the excess of time—eternity, immortality, infinity—could be resolved. Indeed, if it were not for the temporal opposition of the finite and the infinite, neither element could be understood, a point Dickinson made when writing, "Time feels so vast that were it not / For an Eternity— / I fear me this Circumference* / Engross my Finity—" (P802).

Patterson suggests that Dickinson exploited the symbolic potential of time to the fullest and that these temporal distinctions, along with their corresponding associations with color, seasons, and emotions, "unified the poetry* of her major period, making of it a more respectable body of work than the faulty and too often trivial fragments in which it is customarily presented" (181). St. Armand connects her poetic world with the prophetic* poetry of William Blake,* describing Dickinson's temporal delineations as creating a "mystic day." He presents a table of how the four sun cycles of sunrise, noon, sunset, and midnight correspond to Dickinson's symbolic seasonal, human, Christian, spiritual, psychological,* color, floral,* geographical, and religious* cycles (317). (*See*: Death)

RECOMMENDED: Rebecca Patterson, *Emily Dickinson's Imagery*; Georges Poulet, *Studies in Human Time*. Baltimore: Johns Hopkins University Press, 1956; Barton Levi St. Armand, *Emily Dickinson and Her Culture: The Soul's Society*.

Michael Strysick

TITLING OF POEMS   Currently, common practice is to refer to Dickinson's poems either by the number assigned by Thomas Johnson* or by the poem's first line. However, Dickinson did supply titles to 24 of the 1,775 poems she wrote, 21 of them poems that she wrote for, and sent to, friends.* They are as follows: " 'Navy' Sunset" (P15); "Whistling under my window" (P83); "Baby" (P227); "Snow" (P311); "Thunderstorm" (P824); "Country Burial" (P829); "My Cricket" (P1068); "A Bluebird" (P1395); "Epitaph" (P1396); "A Gale" (P1397); "Word to a Friend" (P1398); "A Portrait of the Parish" (P1407); "Humming-Bird" (P1463); "Blue Bird" (P1465); "The Oriole" (P1466); "Christ's Birthday" (P1487); "Cupid's Sermon" (P1509); "A Pebble" (P1510); "My Country's Wardrobe" (P1511); "The Bumble Bee's Religion" (P1522); and "Sunset" (P1622). In all but two cases, the title was included in the letter that accompanied the poem. The exceptions are " 'Navy' Sunset" and "Baby," where the title appeared on the same sheet as the poem itself. Dickinson titled only three poems she bound into packets: "Snow Flakes" (P36); "Pine Bough" (P161); and "Purple" (P776). The fact that Dickinson was more likely to provide titles for poems composed for a specific person or occasion and the relatively small number of poems that were titled at all suggests that she considered the actual naming of her poems somewhat cosmetic.

The few poems that did manage their way into print during Dickinson's lifetime were also given titles, although it is unclear whether these were supplied by Dickinson, the editors, or a collaboration of parties. Considering the problems she encountered with the editorial* process, it seems most likely that titles were supplied by editors. These poems are as follows, given in order of publication* with the name of the text in which the poem appeared: "A Valentine" (P3),* *Springfield Daily Republican**; "To Mrs.—, with a Rose" (P35),* *Springfield Daily Republican*; "The May-Wine" (P214),* *Springfield Daily Republican*; "The Sleeping" (P216),* *Springfield Daily Republican*; "My Sabbath" (P324),* *The Round Table**; "Sunset" (P228),* *Springfield Daily Republican*; "The Snake" (P986),* *Springfield Daily Republican*; and "Success" (P67),* *A Masque of Poets*. (*See*: "Omitted Center")

RECOMMENDED: *Poems*; Cynthia Griffin Wolff, *Emily Dickinson*.

Kimberly Markowski

TODD, MABEL LOOMIS (1856–1932)   "Emily is called in Amherst* 'the myth,' " wrote Mabel Loomis Todd, a newcomer in town, just before she was invited to the Homestead* to play the piano and sing for the unseen poet (*Life* 217). Without ever glimpsing her, Todd entered Dickinson's home often during her last three years of life, and the two exchanged flowers* and notes. Todd sang, played music,* and painted flowers for the poet, receiving flowers and poems in return. The arms-length acquaintance stimulated Todd's appreciation for her gifted neighbor and set the stage for posthumous publication* of the poetry.*

Todd was nearly twenty-five when she arrived in Amherst with her husband, David Peck Todd, appointed professor of astronomy at Amherst College* in 1881. A pretty, vivacious woman with limpid brown eyes and bewitching mouth, Mabel possessed musical talent and artistic skills such as the quiet, pious villagers had not met before in a female. Socially charming, unusually egocentric, she made herself the center of attention wherever she went.

Mabel was the only child of Eben J. and Mary Wilder Loomis* of Washington, D.C.* Her father's job as clerk of the Nautical Almanac Office and his avocations of amateur naturalist and poet gave his family some access to scientific* circles. Mrs. Loomis, daughter of a New England Congregational* minister, was a colorful talker and outspoken moralist, ingenious at making ends meet. Mabel grew up in boardinghouses, adapting herself to the public and private faces required. During the early 1870s she attended Georgetown Female Seminary and afterward took piano and voice lessons at the New England Conservatory of Music in Boston and taught herself to paint botanical studies. Growing up, she wrote and occasionally published stories and essays, emulating her father. In 1876 she married David Todd, a protégé of astronomer Simon Newcomb.

Two years after Dickinson's death, in February 1888, Lavinia* brought a carton of her sister's poems to Todd and begged her to get them published, for Todd had begun to place travel articles and stories in popular magazines. By then Mabel was locked into dramatic relations with the family, having entered a clandestine love affair with Austin Dickinson* in the autumn of 1882. Condoned by David Todd, the affair was tacitly accepted by Vinnie and Emily but had aroused wrath in Austin's wife, Sue,* and her children. Since Vinnie first asked Sue to publish Emily's poetry, then turned secretly to Mabel in a frustrated desire for action, the editing* of Dickinson's life work was doomed to adversity from the start. Its story has been detailed, omitting all mention of the love affair, in Millicent Todd Bingham's *Ancestors' Brocades: The Literary Debut of Emily Dickinson* (1945).

Enlisting the collaboration of Thomas Wentworth Higginson,* Dickinson's literary mentor in Boston,* Todd devoted much of the next nine years to the careful transcription, selection, and editing of three volumes of Dickinson's poems. They were published by Roberts Brothers* as *Poems by Emily Dickinson,* Series I, II, and III, in 1890, 1891, and 1896, respectively. While recognizing Todd's and Higginson's heroic work in rescuing Dickinson's poetry from probable oblivion and creating publishable texts from her highly unfinished manuscripts, critics today often fault the editors' high-handed categorizing of Dickinson's verse, their "smoothing" of rhymes* and meters, their adding of titles,* and other editorial sins committed in an attempt to bring the poet's unorthodox style into line with nineteenth-century tastes. In 1894 Todd also published *The Letters of Emily Dickinson,* having rounded up, with Lavinia's help, many of the poet's correspondents.

The counsel of Dickinson's brother and sister gives authority to what Todd wrote and said about the poet as she aided public reception of the poetry by writing book columns, lecturing, and encouraging reviewers (including William Dean Howells*) to treat the poems favorably. At Austin's death in 1895, however, Mabel's relations with Lavinia turned adversarial. The Todd–Dickinson lawsuit of 1898 appeared to be a dispute over a bit of land Austin intended to deed to the Todds and that Vinnie claimed was obtained by fraud. Yet unspoken jealousies, fears, hatreds, and vindictiveness were all behind the court and local moral censure that came down upon the Todds.

Publicly humiliated, Todd boxed away the mass of Dickinson manuscripts still in her possession. She turned to other writing and to extensive lecturing about the astronomical voyages she took with David all over the world. Extraordinarily active, Todd started local chapters of the Daughters of the American Revolution (DAR) and the Womans' Club and established the Amherst Historical Society. In 1913 she suffered a stroke from which she never fully recovered, bringing an end to her writing and lecturing career. In 1917 she moved to Cocoanut Grove, Florida, dividing her time thereafter between that home, Matsuba, and a summer camp at Hogg Island, Maine. David's behavior grew increasingly bizarre after 1913. He was institutionalized from 1922 until his death in 1939, a situation that caused Mabel enormous anguish.

In 1931, after Sue Dickinson's daughter Martha Dickinson Bianchi* had published several books of poetry and biography* about her aunt, usurping poems to which Todd claimed title, Mabel was goaded into reissuing an enlarged version of *The Letters of Emily Dickinson.* Before she died of a stroke the following year, Todd extracted from her daughter Millicent the promise to publish all Dickinson materials stored away in 1898. It cost Millicent twenty-three years and much travail and bitterness to bring out a new book of Dickinson's poems and three biographical volumes.

Eventually, Harvard acquired title to the poems and letters* Bianchi had inherited, and Amherst College received the Dickinson manuscripts and family papers that were in Todd's possession (although Harvard holds title to the former). Other Dickinson materials, including photographs, were given by Bingham to Yale when she bequeathed that institution the love letters exchanged by her mother and Austin Dickinson, the only part of her mother's archive she could not bring herself to publish. (*See*: Critical Reception)

RECOMMENDED: *AB*; *Life*; Polly Longsworth, *Austin and Mabel: The Amherst Affair and Love Letters of Austin Dickinson and Mabel Loomis Todd.*

Polly Longsworth

TRACY, SARAH SKINNER (1828–1916)   One of Dickinson's four closest Amherst Academy* friends* (the "five" she designated in L11 to Abiah Root*), Tracy was born in Tretmont, Vermont, and stayed with cousins only to attend Amherst Academy during the year 1844–1845. Although little is known of Tracy in her youth, except that her mother died when she was eight, some information can be inferred from Dickinson's writing. In a poem to Elbridge Bowdoin,* Dickinson mentioned Tracy as one of six "comely maidens" (P1). Dickinson also depicted Tracy as the "Virgil" of the group of childhood friends, attesting to her peaceful disposition. According to various scholars, ambiguity exists about Tracy's name. It is possible that Dickinson purposely referred to her as "Sarah S." to avoid confusion with other Sarahs attending the academy. Marriage* is not what ended Tracy and Dickinson's relationship, as it did with other childhood friends, for Tracy never married. She was a dutiful daughter who returned to live with her father in Beverly, Massachusetts, where she spent the rest of her life. Tracy and Dickinson's last known correspondence was in 1851.

RECOMMENDED: *Life*; *Years*.

Michelle Tice

TRANSCENDENTALISM   was a movement of philosophical* idealism and a special kind of Romanticism* that reached its height in New England in the 1840s. Led by Ralph Waldo Emerson* and Henry David Thoreau,* Transcendentalists reacted against eighteenth-century empiricism and asserted the supremacy of mind over matter, defending intuition as a guide to truth. However, they did not produce an organized philosophical system. Transcendentalism stood for self*-expression and bolstered American ideas of individualism, self-reliance, the worth of common humanity, the equality of races and sexes, and the interdependence of the natural world and its human inhabitants. The movement, rooted in American Unitarianism,* combined the antiformalism of European idealism with an interest in Oriental mysticism. Since the Transcendentalists believed that the senses can recognize only representations or symbols, they valued consciousness* over experience (or history). According to Transcendentalism, nature* is benevolent and compassionate toward the individual, permitting her to use it for her profit and instruction and allowing her to read its innermost meanings. Nature will yield its spiritual significance to the perceptive observer who can pursue and rise above its symbolic clues and thus come face-to-face with Nature's Cause (God* or the Oversoul).

Emily Dickinson grew up with these Transcendental ideas and never wholly discarded them, although, by 1862, when she started to write her major poetry,* Transcendentalism had declined considerably. Until then, writers like Emerson, Thoreau, Hawthorne,* and Melville had all asserted the existence of a transcendent reality and had deemed it the task of literature to reveal this higher realm. However, the realism* that followed romanticism was more concerned with everyday experience. Dickinson wrote in between those two traditions. She read the works of the leading Transcendentalists (including some Theodore Parker and William Ellery Channing), and it seems that she had already absorbed the movement's central features by the early 1850s. Both T. W. Higginson* and Austin Dickinson* (in his younger years) were strongly influenced by the movement. Like the Transcendentalists, Dickinson sought a transcendent knowledge and rejected system and argument in favor of intuition. But while Transcendentalism addressed an impersonal higher reality, Dickinson, rooted in latter-day Puritanism,* addressed a personal God directly and questioned his authority. Moreover, her Nature is more treacherous and unpredictable, providing only transitory moments of ecstasy or insight. Although the natural world may sometimes convey a feeling of safety, this will be followed by hostility. While the Transcendentalists believed that they could read and understand the symbolic significance of nature, it was thoroughly ambivalent for Dickinson. She could not share the movement's moral idealism: while the Transcendental writers found a justification for evil, Dickinson took agony to be the price paid for each moment of ecstasy.

Some of Dickinson's nature poems restate Transcendentalist attitudes about the mystical bond between man and nature and nature's ability to reveal to man truths about humankind and the universe. But this is a small part of her poetry. Most of her work is not in the Transcendental mood: some poems affirm an unbreachable separation between man and nature; others merely show delight in the variety and spectacle of nature. She substituted passing insights and ambivalence for the Transcendentalists' orphic vision* and assurances. (*See*: Historicism)

RECOMMENDED: Paul J. Ferlazzo, "Emily Dickinson"; Clark Griffith, *The Long Shadow: Emily Dickinson's Tragic Poetry*; Hyatt H. Waggoner, "Emily Dickinson: The Transcendent Self"; Cynthia Griffin Wolff, *Emily Dickinson*.

Josef Raab

TUCKERMAN, EDWARD (1817–1886) **and SARAH ELIZA SIGOURNEY CUSHING** (1832–1915)   Amherst* residents, the Tuckermans were Dickinson's close friends,* as evidenced by their extensive correspondence. Edward Tuckerman joined the Amherst College* faculty in 1855, first in history, then botany. Especially intimate with Sarah, Dickinson regularly included poems in letters* to her, among them "Brother of Ophir" (P1366C), "Go not too near a House of Rose—" (P1434), "A Route of Evanescence" (P1463), "The Robin is a Gabriel" (P1483), "We shall find the Cube of the Rainbow" (P1484), "Not seeing, still we know—" (P1518), "The Dandelion's pallid tube" (P1519), "The stem of a departed Flower" (P1520), "Sweet Pirate of the heart" (P1546), "How slow the Wind—" (P1571), "We wear our sober Dresses when we die" (P1572), and "To try to speak, and miss the way" (P1617). Dickinson's final correspondence with Sarah was a poetic sympathy note on the death* of her husband, two months before Dickinson's death in 1886 (L1035).

RECOMMENDED: *Letters*; *Years*.

Dorothy Z. Baker

TUCKERMAN, FREDERICK (1857–1929) **and ALICE GIRDLER COOPER** (1857–1932)   The Frederick Tuckermans were Amherst* residents and friends* of Emily Dickinson. An early historian of Amherst College,* Frederick Tuckerman wrote *Amherst Academy*: A New England School of the Past, 1814–1871*. Although he was the son of poet Frederick Goddard Tuckerman of Greenfield, only eighteen miles from Amherst, there is no evidence of a relationship between Dickinson and the poet. Frederick Tuckerman was also the nephew of Edward Tuckerman, professor at Amherst College. Alice Tuckerman was one of five children born to Mr. and Mrs. James Sullivan Cooper, Amherst residents friendly with the Dickinsons. Dickinson wrote notes of congratulation to the Tuckermans on the birth of their first child (L903, 904).

RECOMMENDED: *Letters*; Eugene England. *Beyond Romanticism: Tuckerman's Life and Poetry*. Provo, UT: Brigham Young University Press, 1991; Frederick Tuckerman. *Amherst Academy: A New England School of the Past, 1814–1871*. Amherst, MA: Printed for the trustees, 1929.

Dorothy Z. Baker

U

UNITARIANISM   Although vigorously opposed by the orthodox Congregationalists* who prevailed in Dickinson's Amherst* and not present as a denomination there before 1898, Unitarianism nevertheless exerted a distinct presence
in the poet's life, not only through the Dickinson family library but also through
such close friends as Samuel Bowles* and Thomas Wentworth Higginson.* On
at least one occasion, the poet sought consolation from a prominent Unitarian
clergyman, Edward Everett Hale.*

Describing themselves as "liberal Christians," Unitarians constituted an increasingly controversial faction within New England Congregationalism during
the early decades of the nineteenth century. Antirevivalist,* they represented a
long drift, given impetus in the aftermath of the Great Awakening, toward
greater reliance on reason and historical analysis in biblical* interpretation, along
with an emphasis on moral culture and one's own role in the redemptive process.
Unitarians tended as a group to reject the doctrines of election* and innate
depravity and to regard Jesus* Christ as subordinate, rather than equal, to God*
the Father.

The liberal-orthodox debate contributed significantly to a persistent religious*
tension in Dickinson's poems. Following the liberal lead, she professed not to
"respect 'doctrines' " (L200) and rejected outright those asserting original sin
and an Atonement intended to expiate sin or satisfy divine justice. Instead, she
focused on human potential and presented Calvary as an archetype for her own
redemptive suffering. Like the Unitarians, she stressed Christ's humanity. Re-
vealingly, when Dickinson's poems were first published, it was the Unitarian
press that reviewed them most favorably.

RECOMMENDED: Rowena Revis Jones, " 'A Taste for 'Poison': Dickinson's Departure from Orthodoxy''; David Robinson. *The Unitarians and the Universalists*. Westport, CT: Greenwood Press, 1985.

Rowena Revis Jones

UNPUBLISHED POEMS OF EMILY DICKINSON (**1935**)   was the third selection of Dickinson poems edited by Martha Dickinson Bianchi,* daughter of Susan Dickinson,* Emily's sister-in-law. It was prepared with the assistance of Alfred Leete Hampson.* *Unpublished Poems* was a companion piece to *Further Poems* (1929)* in that most of its selections derived from manuscripts bequeathed by Lavinia* to Susan and then by Susan to Martha. After publishing three volumes of selected poems and three ostensibly comprehensive collections, Bianchi willed the manuscripts to Hampson. Later, the manuscripts were sold to Harvard University, reedited, and included in Johnson's* 1955 variorum edition of *The Poems.**

Unpublished Poems includes 131 poems, all but a handful written between 1860 and 1870. Its editorial policy features large-scale but not complete normalization of Dickinson's punctuation and capitalization.* Stanzas are sometimes separated or combined, and lines divided or collapsed in a process of formal regularization. Generally, the most accessible or grammatically transparent among textual variants* are chosen. Occasional words are changed or misquoted, and in several cases stanzas are omitted. Rough thematic groupings (flowers,* dreams, graveside* reflections) appear within the collection, but no overall organizational principle is evident.

Unpublished Poems included fewer of the verses responsible for Dickinson's modern reputation than the earlier Bianchi collections. However, it contains such revealing poems as "We grow accustomed to the Dark—" (P419), "Exhiliration—is within—" (P383), and "They shut me up in Prose—" (P613). Also notable are the lovely tribute to Elizabeth Barrett Browning,* "I think I was enchanted" (P593), the exquisitely descriptive "A slash of Blue—" (P204), and the wryly witty "The Flower must not blame the Bee—" (P206). (*See*: Editorial Scholarship)

Bryan C. Short

V

VALENTINES   The exchange of valentines within the United States is directly related to the celebration of St. Valentine's Day in England and, like that secular English tradition, is rooted in springtime mating rituals. Evolving over the centuries, the practice of exchanging valentines probably originated with a drawing of lots among middle- and lower-class unmarried men and women in the seventeenth and eighteenth centuries; matched lots were held to be an omen of a pair's possible marriage. By the mid-nineteenth century in America, the holiday had reached its height, helped along by growing consumerism spurred by the Industrial Revolution. Premade valentines with bits of clichéd verse became overwhelmingly popular modes of romantic expression. When critics deplored the practice of such mass-marketed sentiment,* a handbook for writing one's own verse appeared: the *Sentimental Valentine Writer for Both Sexes* (Philadelphia, 1845).

During Emily Dickinson's lifetime, two types of valentines were popular: the traditional, sentimental token of expression and the satiric jest. The jest may be either genial, as it appears to be in Dickinson's efforts, or quite abusive, serving misogynist interests by satirizing the unmarried woman as an "old maid." Since this holiday allowed women's desire to be made public, particularly on leap years, the satiric jest may have developed in an effort to undermine women's burgeoning power in mating rituals.

The valentine "Awake ye muses nine, sing me a strain divine" (P1) is the first known poem composed by Dickinson. Written in 1850 and addressed to Elbridge Bowdoin,* her father's law partner, the verse teasingly urges Bowdoin to choose among several young ladies, including Emily herself, who is referred to without name as "she with *curling hair.*" The only other verse valentine Dickinson is known to have written, " 'Sic transit gloria mundi' " (P3),* appeared in the *Springfield Republican* * on 20 February 1852, a leap year. Although also a jest, this poem is unusual since its satirical thrust is political and not sentimental; it pokes fun at phallocentric events from the discovery of gravity to the American Revolution. A nonverse valentine apparently written by Dickinson and addressed to George Gould* appeared in an 1850 issue of *The Indicator*, a student publication he edited; it consists of religious and classical allusions as well as current events (L34). (*See*: Humor)

RECOMMENDED: Vivian R. Pollak, "Emily Dickinson's Valentines"; Leigh Eric Schmidt. "The Fashioning of a Modern Holiday: St. Valentine's Day, 1840–1870." *Winterthur Portfolio: A Journal of American Material Culture* 28 (1993): 209–45.

Amy J. Pardo

VINNIE or VINNY Dickinson, Lavinia Norcross

VISION   Eyesight and insight and the relationships between these two kinds of seeing were vital concerns of Emily Dickinson throughout her life, for these two kinds of seeing provided the stimulus and the means for her poetic creativity. While still a young woman, she underwent extensive treatment for an eye condition, probably exotropia, that doubtless raised in her the fear of blindness. The lengthy treatment period included severe restrictions on the use of her eyes, thereby fostering her growing intellectual concern with the process and range of human perception. This experience may have been connected with the personal crisis* that led to her overflowing productivity in the early 1860s, but the circumstances of this crisis and any connections to her eye condition may never be fully explained.

Seeing "New Englandly" (P285), Dickinson delighted in the beauty of nature* and observed Amherst* village life from a distance. But she increasingly resorted to another perspective that she called "Compound Vision" (P906), by which she assumed an imaginary vantage point outside the temporal world. From this visionary perspective she wrote many of her poems exploring love,* loss, death,* and immortality*; she also explored the distortions and limitations of human perception and language in the fallen world.

Although she remained at times profoundly skeptical, she gradually developed a personal vision of Christianity that critics have alternately described as mystical or metaphysical. Aware of her impending death, she wrote a farewell note containing the simple message "Called back"* (L1046), apparently confirming her final position of faith* in God* and immortality. The visionary quality of her thought has led some critics to compare her to such figures as St. Teresa of Avila, George Herbert,* and William Blake.* (*See*: Health; Religion; Science)

RECOMMENDED: James R. Guthrie, "Measuring the Sun: Emily Dickinson's Interpretation of Her Optical Illness"; Greg Johnson, *Emily Dickinson: Perception and the Poet's Quest*; William Mulder, "Seeing 'New Englandly': Planes of Perception in Emily Dickinson and Robert Frost"; Hiroko Uno, "Optical Instruments and 'Compound Vision' in Emily Dickinson's Poetry"; Martin Wand and Richard B. Sewall. " 'Eyes be Blind, Heart be Still': A New Perspective on Emily Dickinson's Eye Problem."

Rosa Nuckels

VISUAL ART, AS INFLUENCE   The primarily visual quality of Dickinson's language had myriad cultural and personal wellsprings, but the key formal influence was probably the English critic John Ruskin, whose applications of religious* aesthetics to landscape art she studied intently. In poem after poem—in her "landscapes so lone" (L176)—Dickinson plumbed God's* power and mystery and the Ruskinian view of nature as the veil that both obscures and reveals. She translated issues of faith* and art into poems of light and dark, creating tonal dramas of earth and sky. A typically enigmatic image, "Sunset that screens, reveals—" (P1609), suggests this affinity with landscape painters.

Naturalist art movements cited as influences on Dickinson include the Hudson River painters, the luminists, and the Pre-Raphaelites, some of whom were avidly collected by Austin* and Susan Dickinson.* Works of American painters Asher B. Durand and John F. Kensett, for example, were literally next door to Dickinson, easily accessible as fuel for her idiosyncratic Romantic* imagination. Their light- and color-saturated canvases are evoked in lines like "There's a certain Slant of light" (P258)* and "Like Mighty Foot Lights—burned the Red" (P595). With Dickinson as with the painters, nature's "curtain" (night, death*) eternally vied with the sun, with revelation. Her visual imagination transformed the radical realism of Pre-Raphaelite landscapes into a radical power of the eye to observe and the ear to listen, a divine power. Their brilliant sunset colors—crimsons, purples, and magentas—were hers, too, held against light's inscrutable dazzle. The ecstasy of poetic moments like "Mail of ices" (P666) and "the Snow / From Polar Caskets" (P375) is electrified with the Romantic* (and Christian) paradox of light as both specter and protector.

Dickinson's letters* and poems, often punctuated with sketches, tell the story of her love for visual art. Her familiarity with contemporary thought in art circles in America and abroad was secured by the many books and periodicals delivered to her door. She shared the Victorian view that linked painting with poetry* ("Those Boys and Girls, in Canvas" [P499]). Dickinson's dashes,* lineation, and diction ("A slash of Blue—/ A sweep of Gray—" [P204]) conjure the kinetic brushstrokes of J.M.W. Turner, whose art Ruskin extolled in *Modern Painters*. Her picturing of lightning as "The Doom's electric Moccasin" (P1593) reflects Ruskin's notion of storm cloud and lightning as God's judgment yet comes to us through a vision* that remains uniquely her own. (*See*: Visual Art Responses)

RECOMMENDED: Judith Farr, "Dickinson and the Visual Arts" and *The Passion of Emily Dickinson*; Barton Levi St. Armand, *Emily Dickinson and Her Culture: The Soul's Society*.

Rebecca Emlinger Roberts

VISUAL ART RESPONSES   Beginning with Marsden Hartley's essay tribute to Dickinson in *Adventures in the Arts* (1921), the poet has been a source of inspiration to numerous visual artists in the United States. Especially during the second half of the twentieth century, projects undertaken in Dickinson's honor

have been diverse. They range from visual representations based on the daguerreotype* and illustrated editions of the poetry, to paintings, photographs,
sculptures, and installations that interpret Dickinson's life and/or poems in innovative ways. Often the adaptations involve provocative connections between
the artist's visual imagery and Dickinson's own words* and figural strategies.

Most notable among the artists influenced by Dickinson is American assem-
blage artist Joseph Cornell, who commemorated the poet in "box constructions." Cornell used collage, painted interiors, grids, and arrangements of small
objects to create an iconography of absence, the distinguishing signature for his
boxes and a theme that links his work to Dickinson's. Art historians Dore Ash-
ton, Carter Ratcliff, and Dickran Tashjian have demonstrated Cornell's strong
identification with the poet and analyzed the meaning of the boxes he dedicated
to her.

A number of contemporary women artists have produced works that celebrate
Dickinson as a symbol of female creativity and inspiring role model. Judy Chicago chose Dickinson as one of thirty-nine guests for *The Dinner Party*. The
place setting that honors the poet is designed with a lace motif that symbolizes
the repressiveness of the cultural milieu in which Dickinson struggled to find
her voice. Carla Rae Johnson's lectern series includes one for Dickinson that
memorializes the poet as Vesuvius. Ann Kowaleski's art quilts feature dancing*
imagery to portray the spiritual connection that exists between Dickinson and
other women artists, whatever their field. Aífe Murray and Barbara Penn explore
Dickinson's creativity within the context of female domesticity* generally. Murray's work foregrounds the poet's relationships with the Irish women servants
employed by the Dickinson family; Penn's develops associations between the
artist's own grandmother, a woman she never knew, and Dickinson, whose life
remains an enigma.

Recent works by other visual artists—Lesley Dill, Roni Horn, and Paul Katz,
to name a few—use individual Dickinson texts as an integral part of their own
imagery. In particular, Lesley Dill has created over a hundred sculptures and
mixed media pieces that blend lines or a complete Dickinson poem with images
of enlarged body parts or empty clothing. Dill's work, like Dickinson's, explores
the contraries of human experience—between inner and outer, spirit and flesh,
pleasure and despair—and does so with wit, imagination, and humor.*

The first major exhibition devoted to visual art inspired by Dickinson's life
and work was organized by Susan Danly and presented at the Mead Art Museum
at Amherst College* in spring 1997. Although the show represented U.S. artists
exclusively, Dickinson has attracted the attention of artists in other countries as
well. Danish artist Frank Hammershoj has created fourteen oil paintings in response to individual Dickinson poems. These were part of the stage setting for
a production of *The Belle of Amherst* that toured Denmark in 1991. For Mariko
Hagiwara of Japan, Dickinson's poems have provided the source of inspiration
for abstract expressionist paintings. Since 1992, Hagiwara's works have been

regularly exhibited at the Tokyo Metropolitan Art Museum. (*See*: Dramatic Responses; Fictive Responses; Musical Settings)

RECOMMENDED: Susan Danly, *Language as Object: Emily Dickinson and Contemporary Art*; Jonnie Guerra, "Dickinson Adaptations in the Arts and the Theatre."

Jonnie Guerra

VOICE   Critical approaches to Dickinson's voice can be divided into two general categories: (1) a literal view of voice as unified, connected to orality, and belonging to the poet and (2) a poststructuralist* emphasis on the poet's multiple voices as created personae. In the first approach, scholars examine the individualizing, speechlike qualities of Dickinson's writing, her colloquialism,* and New England regionalisms. Also important are accounts of the poet's reading her work aloud and her own positive valuations of voice and orality (e.g., "You know I have a vice for voices—" [PF19]). In the second approach, scholars separate the voice from the poet herself, taking seriously Dickinson's assertion that "When I state myself, as the Representative of the Verse—it does not mean—me—but a supposed person" (L268). Some identify the various personae that Dickinson creates in her poems and letters (e.g., voices of bard, bride,* girl or boy child,* lover, queen, and the dead). Others connect Dickinson's fragmented, often contradictory voices to her gender, positing a dominant voice that remains distinctly female. (*See*: Fictionality)

RECOMMENDED: *Letters*; Erika Scheurer, " 'Near, but remote': Emily Dickinson's Epistolary Voice."

Erika Scheurer

W

WADSWORTH, CHARLES (1814–1882)   Dickinson referred to this minister of the Arch Street Presbyterian Church in Philadelphia as "My closest earthly friend" and "My Shepherd from 'Little Girl'hood'' (L765 and 766). On a family trip to Washington* in early 1855, the Dickinson sisters stayed with the Coleman* family, congregants of the Arch Street Church; during her visit, Dickinson heard Wadsworth preach and almost certainly met him. In the following years, the Colemans mailed copies of his sermons, and there developed an intense relationship between the poet and the minister. Wadsworth visited her at the Homestead* in March 1860, and there is persuasive evidence that Dickinson asked him to call again during the summer of 1861; his second visit to the Homestead did not take place, however, until August 1880.

The spring and summer of 1861 brought crisis* for both the minister and the poet. Wadsworth, though an unyielding Union supporter, believed that slavery was not in itself a sin in God's eyes, that America's greatest sin had been the wicked and hypocritical assaults "launched against our Christian brethren of the South" (Lease 11–12). Shortly after the firing on Fort Sumter, forty-seven southern presbyteries severed their relationship with their governing body in Philadelphia. Wadsworth's position became increasingly precarious at the Arch Street Church, and he eventually accepted an invitation to preside over Calvary Church, San Francisco—a church founded by his close friend William Anderson Scott (a southerner whose congregants would not support his ardent secessionist sympathies).

What must have been an extensive Dickinson–Wadsworth correspondence is missing. Surviving among Dickinson's papers is a single, solicitous, pastoral note, undated and unsigned (in Wadsworth's handwriting and bearing an embossed crest "C W"); in it, the minister conveys his distress at "the affliction which has befallen, or is now befalling you" and urges her to write, "though it be but a word" (L248a). Also among her papers are three impassioned draft letters addressed to a man she calls "Master."* Reading these in light of Wadsworth's crisis and impending move may well illumine many details in the second and third of these "Master letters" (redated by R. W. Franklin* as having been written in "Early 1861" and "Summer 1861").

After Wadsworth's death (on 1 April 1882), Dickinson provided numerous accounts of the minister in letters to her closest friends* (L750, L765, L801) and to Wadsworth's friends, the Clark brothers. James D. Clark* initiated the correspondence with a letter and an enclosed volume of the dead minister's sermons (L766). Over a four-year period, Dickinson responded with twenty-one letters,* the last of them sent during her final days (L1040). In her letters, Dickinson characterized Wadsworth as both "a 'Man of sorrow' " and someone capable of "inscrutable roguery" (L776, 1040). Others who knew him well gave support to Dickinson's view of the minister while adding details that establish them as kindred spirits.

A fellow-minister praising Wadsworth's pulpit oratory used terms that could equally apply to the poet's compressed* power; he called special attention to how Wadsworth distilled into a single sentence the equivalent of a laborious argument (Lease 9). Mark Twain, who often attended services at Calvary Church, left a vivid record of the minister's deadpan humor: "Dr. Wadsworth never fails to preach an able sermon; but every now and then, with an admirable assumption of not being aware of it, he will get off a firstrate joke and then frown severely at any one who is surprised into smiling at it" (*Years* 2:112). At Wadsworth's funeral, one of the speakers remarked on his inability to interact with other ministers "without painful and exhausting physical effort" (Lease 26–27) and further observed how this seclusiveness gave his sermons a concentration and lofty power they might not otherwise possess ("He spoke out like a Hebrew prophet* whom his lofty theme was enough to satisfy, and to whom it was unknown whether men heard or did not hear").

Throughout her life and career, Dickinson responded deeply to this "Shepherd" and his distinctive mingling of awe and play. Wadsworth's presence is most clearly reflected in such poems as "There came a Day at Summer's full" (P322), "I went to Heaven—" (P374), "Me—come! My dazzled face" (P431), "Title divine—is mine!" (P1072), and "The Spirit lasts—but in what mode—" (P1576). (*See*: Lovers; Religion)

RECOMMENDED: *Years*; William Dusinberre, *Civil War Issues in Philadelphia, 1856–1865*. Philadelphia: University of Pennsylvania Press, 1965; Benjamin Lease, *Emily Dickinson's Readings of Men and Books*; Vivian R. Pollak, "After Calvary: The Last Years of Emily Dickinson's 'Dearest Earthly Friend' "; Barton Levi St. Armand, *Emily Dickinson and Her Culture: The Soul's Society*.

Benjamin Lease

WARD, THEODORA VAN WAGENEN (1890–1974) This granddaughter of Emily Dickinson's close friends Josiah* and Elizabeth Holland* spent thirty-five years as a Dickinson scholar, both as an editor* of the poem and letter manuscripts and as a biographer.* In 1951 Ward published a collection of Dickinson's correspondence with her grandparents, in which she worked to demonstrate how important the Hollands (particularly Elizabeth) were to Emily Dickinson and to redress what she believed was benign neglect of the significance of the couple's thirty-five-year friendship with the poet. She persuasively argued that her grandmother, in particular, was central to Dickinson's select circle of friends.* Ward's 1961 collection of biographical essays, *The Capsule of the Mind*, is noteworthy for her sensitivity to, and empathy for, the challenges, choices, and limitations life in nineteenth-century Amherst* offered Emily Dickinson as a woman* artist. Most will remember her, however, as the person who assisted Thomas H. Johnson* with the daunting task of collecting, dating, ordering, and editing the Harvard collections of Dickinson's *Poems* (1955)* and *Letters* (1958).* Both of the Ward-authored appendixes to *Poems* have profoundly influenced Dickinson scholarship since 1955, particularly her illustrated essay "Characteristics of the Handwriting," an expansion and revision of her observations about the Holland letter manuscripts that traces and documents changes in Dickinson's handwriting* from 1850 to her death in 1886. Together with study of the paper upon which Dickinson wrote her poems and letters, these physical details from the manuscripts were used to establish a chronology that, although tentative, has profoundly affected the ways in which subsequent critics have written about the development of Dickinson's style and the shape of her poetic career.

RECOMMENDED: Stephanie A. Tingley. "The Contributions of Theodora Van Wagenen Ward." *Emily Dickinson International Society Bulletin* 8, 1 (1996): 2+; Theodora Van Wagenen Ward, *Letters to Dr. and Mrs. Josiah Gilbert Holland* and *The Capsule of the Mind: Chapters in the Life of Emily Dickinson*.

Stephanie A. Tingley

WARNER, MARY (1830–1903) A childhood friend* of Emily Dickinson, Warner was born in Medford, Massachusetts. In 1844, she moved to Amity Street in Amherst* when her father, Aaron Warner, accepted a position as professor of rhetoric at Amherst College.* In 1847, Dickinson's last year at Amherst Academy,* Warner studied in the classical program. Earlier, she studied with private tutors, which is possibly why she was not part of Dickinson's special group of "five," the friends she named in a letter to Abiah Root* (L11). Like Emily Fowler,* Abby Wood,* and Susan Gilbert,* Warner was a part of the religious* revival,* joining the Amherst College church in June 1850 by profession of faith.* Although she remained in Amherst all her life, Warner and Dickinson did not remain close friends beyond their twenties. On 13 August 1861, despite being courted earlier by Austin Dickinson,* Warner married Edward Payson Crowell, a professor of Latin at Amherst College. The friends' correspondence was then limited to sporadic poem-letters of condolence. On 9 March 1903, Mrs. Crowell died and was buried in West Cemetery, Amherst.

Her thirty-three-page scrapbook of poems and newspaper articles survived and is in Brown University's Manuscript Collection.

RECOMMENDED: Annie L. Crowell. "Emily Dickinson—an Heritage of Friendship." *Mount Holyoke Alumnae Quarterly* 29 (Feb. 1946): 129–30; Barton Levi St. Armand, *Emily Dickinson and Her Culture: The Soul's Society.*

Michelle Tice

WASHINGTON, D.C.   For three weeks from mid-February to early March 1855, Emily and Lavinia Dickinson* visited their father, then a congressman, in the nation's capital. It was Emily's only trip out of Massachusetts. The sisters stayed at the Willard Hotel, toured the National Gallery, and traveled by boat to Mount Vernon, where, Dickinson recorded, they visited George Washington's tomb. Letters to Susan Gilbert* and Elizabeth Holland* document Dickinson's travel impressions and homesickness (L178, 179).

RECOMMENDED: *Letters*; *Life*; *Years*; Katharine Zadravec, "Emily Dickinson: A Capital Visitor."

Jonnie Guerra

WATTS, ISAAC (1674–1748)   An English nonconformist clergyman, Watts was best known for his hymns* and metrical versions of the Psalms of David. His collection of verses for children, *Divine and Moral Songs*, was used to inculcate values. Well into the 1800s his lyrics* were standard texts for Anglo-American evangelical Protestant worship and religious instruction. Familiar with his prosody, figurative language, and precepts, Dickinson occasionally quoted, paraphrased, and parodied Watts (P3, 112; L521, 542). She often challenged orthodoxy in hymnlike forms whose rich metrical texture, innovative rhyming,* and ironic complexity departed from Watts. (*See*: Music)

RECOMMENDED: Martha Winburn England, "Emily Dickinson and Isaac Watts, Puritan Hymnodists"; Judy Jo Small, *Positive as Sound: Emily Dickinson's Rhyme*; William E. Stephenson, "Emily Dickinson and Watts's Songs for Children"; Shira Wolosky, "Rhetoric or Not: Hymnal Tropes in Emily Dickinson and Isaac Watts."

Mary DeJong

WEBSTER, DANIEL (1782–1852)   was born in Salisbury, New Hampshire, the son of a poor farmer. After graduating from Dartmouth College, he was admitted to the bar and rose rapidly as both a lawyer and Federalist Party (later, Whig*) leader. Unequaled as an orator, he exerted great influence on constitutional law both as congressman from Boston and senator from Massachusetts but was disappointed in his presidential ambitions. Serving repeated terms as secretary of state and senator, Webster championed the interests of the Northeast and nationalism, achieving important legislative compromises with John C. Calhoun and Henry Clay.

Edward Dickinson* was among Webster's staunchest political supporters and one of his delegates at the 1852 national Whig Convention in Baltimore. A letter from his college-student daughter to Abiah Root,* congratulating her friend on meeting Webster, shows Emily Dickinson's admiration for this New England hero (L21). When she wrote to Susan Gilbert* in June 1852 that she wished she could join her father as a delegate in Baltimore, however, she was probably showing more desire for reunion with her friend (then teaching there) than political commitment. Still, there is no evidence that any of the Dickinsons lost faith in Webster, as Massachusetts abolitionists typically did, when his support for the Compromise of 1850 subordinated antislavery feeling to preservation of the Union. (*See*: Cultural Studies; Historicism)

RECOMMENDED: *Life*; Irving H. Bartlett, *Daniel Webster*. New York: Norton, 1978; Maurice G. Baxter. *One and Inseparable: Daniel Webster and the Union*. Cambridge: Harvard University Press, 1984.

Peter Holloran

WEBSTER, NOAH (1758–1843)   This Connecticut native served in the American Revolution after graduating from Yale in 1778 but exerted a more revolutionary effect on his country through the philological labors to which he devoted the rest of his life. Webster's spelling books, grammar, and dictionaries established national standards of orthography, pronunciation, and usage. Although his *American Dictionary of the English Language** (1828) and its many subsequent abridgments exposed him to complaints about provincialisms and innovations, Webster's dictionaries far outsold Joseph Worcester's competing works—especially in schools across the country. By the middle decades of the nineteenth century, Webster was acknowledged as America's preeminent lexicographer and, by extension, "the Schoolmaster of Our Republic."

Emily Dickinson, who treasured her 1844 family lexicon, would have known of Webster also as an Amherst* citizen (1812–1824): collaborator with Samuel Fowler Dickinson* in founding both Amherst Academy* and Amherst College,* communicant of the First Church,* and grandfather of her schoolmate Emily Fowler.* The "quiet Christianism" Webster promoted through his definitions and examples of usage supported the evangelical culture that permeated Connecticut Valley* institutions in her youth.

RECOMMENDED: Richard Benvenuto, "Words within Words: Dickinson's Use of the Dictionary"; Rowena Revis Jones, "The Preparation of a Poet: Puritan Directions in Emily Dickinson's Education"; "Reply to an Attack on Webster's Dictionaries" (pamphlet collection from the library of Edward Hitchcock: Amherst College Library, Special Collections); Cynthia Griffin Wolff, *Emily Dickinson*.

Jane Donahue Eberwein

WHIG PARTY   This American political party, prominent from 1834 to 1856, was founded by opponents of Andrew Jackson's Democratic policies. Whigs supported Henry Clay's American System, advocating a strong federal government that had a unifying effect on the nation. Members of the Massachusetts party tended to be conservative, elite, antiexpansionist, and antislavery. However, because the first concern of Whigs was national and party unity and because of their unwavering respect for property rights and the Constitution, staunch northern Whigs resisted alienating southern Whigs in the years before the Civil War.* The issue of slavery eventually led to the dissolution of the party, with radical abolitionists breaking off to form the Free-Soil and Republican Parties.

Following his father, Edward Dickinson* was a die-hard Whig, as was Otis Lord.* Although both opposed slavery, they followed Daniel Webster* in valuing Whig ideals of unity above the activist abolitionist stance (held by T. W. Higginson* and, much later, Samuel Bowles*). Dickinson was active in all levels of Whig politics. When he was a representative to Congress in 1853, the first meeting to form the Republican Party was held in his rooms after the passage of the Kansas-Nebraska Bill. Edward Dickinson, however, refused to abandon the Whigs. (*See*: Cultural Studies; Historicism; *Springfield Republican*)

RECOMMENDED: Millicent Todd Bingham, *Emily Dickinson's Home*; Kinley J. Brauer. *Cotton versus Conscience: Massachusetts Whig Politics and Southwestern Expansion, 1843–1848*. Lexington: University Press of Kentucky, 1967; Betsy Erkkila, "Emily Dickinson and Class"; George S. Merriam. *The Life and Times of Samuel Bowles*. 2 vols. New York: Century, 1885.

Erika Scheurer

WHITMAN, WALT (1819–1892)   Whitman wrote only one book of poetry, *Leaves of Grass*, first published in 1855 but then reissued frequently in a lifelong process of addition and revision until the final "deathbed" edition of 1891–1892. He is known for his concentration on the diversity of U.S. working people; his attention to a kind of spirituality based on the ecstasies of the material world, including the body*; and his celebration of the self,* especially in the long poem "Song of Myself." In terms of style, Whitman is immediately recognized for his cataloging and long, aggrandized lines.

The two most discussed American poets of the nineteenth century, Whitman and Dickinson can be an odd pair to consider together. Her lines are as cryptic and compacted as his are expansive and seemingly accessible. Dickinson claimed that she had never read Whitman but "was told that he was disgraceful—" (L261), perhaps an ironic comment given the number of questionably decorous poems she herself wrote. An illuminating contrast of the two poets can be found by looking at "I'm Nobody! Who are you?" (P288) next to section 24 of "Song of Myself," which begins "Walt Whitman, an American, one of the roughs, a kosmos" (50). Whitman identifies the self, "a kosmos," by claiming the universe, while Dickinson's claim for the self, a "Nobody," is actually a vehement disclaimer. Both poets' claims for the self, however, are audacious.

Actually, some of their similarities are striking. Several critics have examined Whitman and Dickinson together, notably Karl Keller, who offers four rubrics under which to consider the two poets: "American Erotic,"* "American High," "Coping in America," and "Corrupting America." He concentrates on the

Americanness of each poet and celebrates the more outrageous facets of each writer's work. In a book-length study, Agnieszka Salska has discussed their Emersonian* leanings.

While Whitman promoted his work assiduously, and Dickinson declined to publish*, neither poet was fully appreciated by contemporaries. We can look at Thomas Wentworth Higginson* as just one example of the time's prevailing taste. He is famous for his probable dissuading of Dickinson from publishing,* but he was no more visionary a critic when it came to Whitman. Higginson said of Whitman: "It is no discredit to Walt Whitman that he wrote 'Leaves of Grass,' only that he did not burn it afterwards" (Keller 253). Both Whitman and Dickinson held firmly to styles of writing not understood or accepted in their time—Whitman with his almost prosy lines, and Dickinson with her slant* rhymes.* Both appeared to approach their work as a kind of ongoing portfolio; we can see this in Whitman's progressive revisioning of his one book and in Dickinson's continued revisioning of her fascicles.* Whitman and Dickinson are largely understood to be the forebears of modern American poetry. (*See*: Critical Reception; Poetic Tributes; Poets, Influence on; Realism; Romanticism)

RECOMMENDED: *Life*; Karl Keller, *The Only Kangaroo among the Beauty: Emily Dickinson and America*; Agnieszka Salska, *Walt Whitman and Emily Dickinson: Poetry of the Central Consciousness*; Walt Whitman. *Complete Poetry and Collected Prose.* New York: Library of America, 1982; Cynthia Griffin Wolff, *Emily Dickinson.*

Daneen Wardrop

WHITNEY, MARIA (1830–1910)   A close friend of Samuel Bowles* and his wife's distant relative, Whitney was a guest/housekeeper for the Bowleses during Mary's* pregnancies and depressions in the 1860s and 1870s. She knew Emily Dickinson through Austin* and Susan Dickinson.* Emily Dickinson wrote to Whitney mainly after Samuel Bowles' death, seeking consolation for grief caused by the loss of their mutual friend.* Whitney was also acquainted with the Norcross cousins, especially Louise Norcross,* with whom she corresponded and visited occasionally. By the time of Bowles' death in 1878 she had left for Smith College, where she became a language professor.

RECOMMENDED: *Life*; Judith Farr, *The Passion of Emily Dickinson.*

Lena Koski

WOMEN'S CULTURE   in nineteenth-century America changed greatly in many spheres: sociopolitical, technological, economic, philosophic, scientific. Women's lives, so strictly regulated in 1800, were radically different in 1900 (even before suffrage in 1920). Today, theories abound linking physical and mental breakdowns common to women of that time to thwarted intellectual and creative dreams.

A fundamental division in women's culture is reflected in the dichotomies, contradictions, and riddles of Emily Dickinson's life and poetry. Whereas the sphere of culture dictated by men and their institutions limited women to domesticity,* however broadly defined, women developed a countervailing culture for themselves in reaction against that male sphere. Dickinson's life and writing reflect both her renunciation of patriarchal "women's culture" and, paradoxically, her participation in aspects of it, even though she produced poetry* that transcends gender, sphere, and century.

In the male-defined gender spheres of the time (necessarily accepted and even enforced by women as well as men), public realms—including politics, law, commerce, intellectual endeavor (and its prerequisite, education)—were for men only. Not thought physically, emotionally, or intellectually "sturdy" enough for public life, women were thought "unnatural" if not pursuing "normal" outlets of marriage,* family, and domestic duties. The Victorian "True Woman" (exemplar of natural, noble femininity) was domestic (concerned with home and family), submissive (obedient and self-denying), pure (virtuous and proper), and pious (spiritual and regenerate).

A counterculture developed as women writers and activists, unable to live fully within patriarchal culture, redefined women's roles. Early in the century, women's novels, drama, and poetry outsold men's. A woman could stay properly at home and write from her own romantic and domestic experiences. Even the movement to educate women came from a perceived need for moral instruction of boys: Who better than their mothers? But improved educational opportunities increased women's participation in the "outside" world. When Emma Willard, Catharine Beecher, and Mary Lyon* founded early important "female seminaries" in Troy, New York (1821), Hartford, Connecticut (1823), and South Hadley, Massachusetts (1836), they did so for a combination of intellectual and spiritual motives; thus when Dickinson attended Lyon's Mount Holyoke* (1847–1848), she found religious* conversion still the most important subject. In the 1840s, Margaret Fuller produced the first woman's rights document in America (*Woman in the Nineteenth Century*), and the 1848 Seneca Falls Convention began the organized women's movement. In the 1850s, Harriet Beecher Stowe* wrote the most influential book of the century, *Uncle Tom's Cabin*, and "Fanny Fern" was the highest paid columnist—a fact advertised for shock value. Women's activism in reforms plus the devastation of Civil War* weakened other proscriptions. Susan B. Anthony, Elizabeth C. Stanton, and others demanded public roles and opportunities, including legal and economic reforms, graduate and professional education, and the political and literary voices necessary to speak for the marginalized.

Dickinson subscribed to some aspects of the conventional domestic culture associated with women, and she carried out chores expected of ladies in her socioeconomic class, even though she remained single and childless. She lived at home, nursed an ailing mother, tended her garden,* baked award-winning bread, and supported her extended family's emotional life through letter* writing. But simultaneously she rebelled, pursuing self*-definition and creating another life cocooned within patriarchally defined domesticity—retreating deeply into "home"* (both literally and figuratively) to protect and enable her poetry.

Her dual response was not accidental: she wrote Higginson* that her father "buys me many Books—but begs me not to read them—because he fears they joggle the Mind" (L261). Not having to marry to survive, Emily Dickinson was in a select group of women who could avoid writing for the marketplace yet still prosper. For many others, the limitations of the marketplace were the limitations of their lives. What happened to the 1890 *Poems by Emily Dickinson** shows what happened to women during the entire century: her work was prettified, toned down, conventionalized, and regularized. In spite of this attempt to domesticate her, readers recognized her inherent genius, and she invaded, if not dominated, the patriarchal space of "Great Writer," redefining American poetry. No submissive, genteel "poetess" or "lady writer": "This was a Poet—" (P448). (*See*: Cultural Studies; Sentimentalism)

RECOMMENDED: Sandra Gilbert, "The Wayward Nun beneath the Hill"; Sandra Gilbert and Susan Gubar, *The Madwoman in the Attic*; Mary Kelley. *Private Woman, Public Stage: Literary Domesticity in Nineteenth Century America*. New York: Oxford University Press, 1984; Charlotte Nekola, " 'By Birth a Bachelor': Dickinson and the Idea of Womanhood in the American Nineteenth Century"; Cheryl Walker, *The Nightingale's Burden*.

Susan Kurjiaka

WOOD, ABBY MARIA (1830–1915)   One of Dickinson's four closest Amherst Academy* friends (along with Harriet Merrill, Abby Root,* and Sarah Tracy*), Abby Wood was singled out in an 1845 letter* to Abiah as "our particular friend, and the only particular friend among the girls" (L8). From the age of three, when her father died, Abby grew up near the Dickinsons in the home of Luke and Abby Sweetser.* Emily's letters to Abby trace a story of lives growing in different directions from cheerful girlhood intimacy through a period of quiet estrangement to renewed, mature friendship.* A deacon's niece, Abby joined the First Church* in the revival* of 1850, prompting Dickinson's observation that "she makes a sweet, girl christian" but also her declaration that "I am one of the lingering *bad* ones" (L36). Despite frequent ill health as a young woman, Abby married the Reverend Daniel Bliss, an Amherst College* graduate, and left with him in 1855 for lifelong missionary service in Syria, where they founded the Syrian Protestant College in Beirut (now the American University of Lebanon). From there, the Blisses sent remembrances that included plant specimens for Emily Dickinson's herbarium and cedar wood from which the pulpit of Amherst's new First Church* was carved. Revisiting Amherst* in 1873, Mrs. Bliss refused to be deterred from renewing early ties by the aura of "mystery" already surrounding her friend; "I saw that the Flake was on it" (P1267) is thought to be Dickinson's response to their reunion.

Emily's astounded report to Austin* about lengthy letters exchanged between Abby Wood and Eliza Coleman* documents this friend's penchant for writing, and there is no doubt that the two of them corresponded while Emily was at Mount Holyoke,* and Abby either with her mother in Athol or her husband in

Syria. Not one of these letters has appeared, however, so knowledge of their friendship rests mainly on early letters to Abiah Root. This attachment may have had at least indirect influence on Dickinson's publishing* history, as Abby's cousin Charles Humphreys Sweetser,* who grew up with her as another "orphan" in Luke Sweetser's household, printed "Some keep the Sabbath going to Church—" (P324)* in an 1864 issue of *The Round Table.*

RECOMMENDED: *Letters*; *Life*; *Years*; Jane Donahue Eberwein, "Amherst's Exotic Pulpit: A Possible Dickinson Contribution?"

Jane Donahue Eberwein

WORDS   Dickinson's love for words was intense and personal, uniting all the interests of her life. She grew up in New England during a period of heightened interest in language as the Transcendentalists* were drawing on European Romanticism* and the Higher Criticism of the Bible* to challenge old assumptions and to propose new theories about human perception and about the origin and processes of language. Against this background of theological and secular investigations into the nature of language, Dickinson privately mined lexical resources to write poetry unprecedented in its economy and compression.*

So personal was her philology that in her poetry* and letters* she frequently personified linguistic* or literary constructs. For example, in P1126 she represented words as "Candidates" for election* to a poem. Her first letter to T. W. Higginson* asked him to judge whether her verse "breathed" (L260), and her next told him that for several years her lexicon had been her "only companion" (L261). To her, books were "Kinsmen of the Shelf" (P604). The Bible* was the single most important book in her life, and Revelation was perhaps her favorite among its books. "There is a word" (P8) echoes Revelation 1:16–18. Poems 1039, 1587, and 1651, taken together, suggest that she conceived of her poetry in sacramental terms, linking her poetics to St. John's teachings about the gift of language through the divine Word Incarnate, or *Logos* (John 1. 1–18). (*See: American Dictionary*; Webster, Noah)

RECOMMENDED: *Life*; Philip F. Gura. *The Wisdom of Words: Language, Theology, and Literature in the New England Renaissance*. Middletown, CT: Wesleyan University Press, 1981; Roland Hagenbüchle, "Sign and Process: The Concept of Language in Emerson and Dickinson"; Cynthia L. Hallen and Laura M. Harvey, "Translation and the Emily Dickinson Lexicon"; Cristanne Miller, "Terms and Golden Words: Alternatives of Control in Dickinson's Poetry."

Rosa Nuckels

Y

<hr>

"THE YELLOW ROSE OF TEXAS"   is a popular American folk song first printed in 1858. A widespread academic myth, intended as a joke, holds that "all of Emily Dickinson's poems can be sung to the tune of 'The Yellow Rose of Texas.' " This misconception trivializes her poetry,* which exhibits far more metric and strophic variation than any one tune can encompass.

The metric structure of the song is roughly similar to that of many Dickinson poems. Its form is "ballad meter," a stanza of four lines each having four (or three) stresses and rhyming *abcb* or *abab*. Dickinson shows a propensity for this verse design, but exceptions abound (e.g., P341, 390, 553, 680, 745, 1340).

Ballad meter (especially the variety alternating lines of four stresses and lines of three stresses) has been since the Middle Ages a mainstay of English popular poetry, the source of the meters of Protestant hymns,* and an important influence on literary poetry. Folk tunes have powerfully shaped the meter: "The four pulse beats of the normal musical phrase are a fundamental fact of Western folk music and of much Western art music" (Bronson 73).

Consequently, a huge body of English tetrameter verse (e.g., Lovelace's "To Lucasta, Going to the Wars" or Wordsworth's "A Slumber Did My Spirit Seal") can be sung to countless tunes, among them not only "The Yellow Rose of Texas" but also "Barbara Allen," "Auld Lang Syne," "Amazing Grace," "I Dreamt I Dwelt in Marble Halls," "Maryland, My Maryland," "America the Beautiful," "I Want to Hold Your Hand," and "One Hundred Bottles of Beer on the Wall."

Dickinson's art extended the capacities of this vital metrical paradigm. A preexisting tune overrides the natural verbal rhythms of her poetic texts and distorts their proper emphases and pauses. Even when the music's* rhythm is closely aligned with that of an individual poem, significant poetic features are sacrificed. The mood of "The Yellow Rose of Texas" is, of course, totally out of keeping with everything Dickinson ever wrote. (*See*: Musical Settings; Watts)

RECOMMENDED: T. V. F. Brogan. "Ballad Meter." *The New Princeton Encyclopedia of Poetry and Poetics*. Ed. Alex Preminger and T. V. F. Brogan. Princeton, NJ: Princeton University Press, 1993: 1–25; Bertrand H. Bronson, et al. "Ballad." *The New Grove Dictionary of Music and Musicians*. Ed. Stanley Sadie. Vol. 2. London: Macmillan, 1980: 70–76; Thomas H. Johnson, *Emily Dickinson: An Interpretive Biography*; David T. Porter, *The Art of Emily Dickinson's Early Poetry*.

Judy Jo Small

Appendix A
Fascicle Listings of Dickinson Poems

These listings follow R. W. Franklin's findings as detailed in *The Manuscript Books of Emily Dickinson* (1981). The number preceding each poem's opening line is that assigned by Thomas H. Johnson. Dates refer to Franklin's estimate of when Dickinson copied these poems into a particular fascicle and may not reflect the date of composition.

FASCICLE 1 (about 1858)

18	The Gentian weaves her fringes—
6	Frequently the woods are pink—
19	A sepal, petal, and a thorn
20	Distrustful of the Gentian—
21	We lose—because we win—
22	All these my banners be.
23	I had a guinea golden—
24	There is a morn by men unseen—
323	As if I asked a common alms—
25	She slept beneath a tree—
7	The feet of people walking home
26	It's all I have to bring today—
27	Morns like these—we parted—
28	So has a Daisy vanished
29	If those I loved were lost
30	Adrift! A little boat adrift!
31	Summer for thee, grant I may be
32	When Roses cease to bloom, Sir,

33   *Oh* if remembering were forgetting—

 4   On this wondrous sea—Sailing silently—

34   Garlands for Queens, may be—

35   Nobody knows this little Rose—

FASCICLE 2 (about 1858)

   8   There is a word

   9   Through lane it lay—thro' bramble—

  15   The Guest is gold and crimson—

  36   I counted till they danced so

  37   Before the ice is in the pools—

  38   By such and such an offering

  39   It did not surprise me—

  40   When I count the seeds—

 147   Bless God, he went as soldiers,

  56   If I should cease to bring a Rose

  14   One Sister have I in the house—

1730   ''Lethe'' in my flower,

  57   To venerate the simple days

1729   I've got an arrow here.

  41   I robbed the Woods—

  42   A Day! Help! Help! Another Day!

  43   Could live—did live—

  44   If she had been the Mistletoe

  10   My wheel is in the dark!

  45   There's something quieter than sleep

  46   I keep my pledge.

  47   Heart! We will forget him!

  48   Once more, my now bewildered Dove

  17   Baffled for just a day or two—

FASCICLE 3 (about 1858–1859)

  58   Delayed till she had ceased to know—

  89   Some things that fly there be—

  90   Within my reach!

  91   So bashful when I spied her!

92   My friend must be a Bird—

93   Went up a year this evening!

94   Angels, in the early morning

95   My nosegays are for Captives—

96   Sexton! My Master's sleeping here.

97   The rainbow never tells me

98   One dignity delays for all—

88   As by the dead we love to sit,

99   New feet within my garden go—

903 I hide myself within my flower

11   I never told the buried gold

49   I never lost as much but twice,

50   I hav'nt told my garden yet—

51   I often passed the village

12   The morns are meeker than they were—

52   Whether my bark went down at sea—

53   Taken from men—this morning—

13   Sleep is supposed to be

54   If I should die,

55   By Chivalries as tiny,

FASCICLE 4 (about 1859)

134 Perhaps you'd like to buy a flower,

135 Water, is taught by thirst.

136 Have you got a Brook in your little heart,

137 Flowers—Well—if anybody

138 Pigmy seraphs—gone astray—

83   Heart not so heavy as mine

139 Soul, Wilt thou toss again?

140 An altered look about the hills—

141 Some, too fragile for winter winds

142 Whose are the little beds, I asked

143 For every Bird a Nest—

85   "They have not chosen me—" he said—

144 She bore it till the simple veins

81   We should not mind so small a flower—

145   This heart that broke so long—
146   On such a night, or such a night,

FASCICLE 5 (about 1859)

66   So from the mould
110   Artists wrestled here!
67   Success is counted sweetest
111   The Bee is not afraid of me.
112   Where bells no more affright the morn—
68   Ambition cannot find him.
113   Our share of night to bear—
114   "Good night," because we must!
86   South Winds jostle them—
69   Low at my problem bending,
115   What Inn is this
116   I had some things that I called mine—
117   In rags mysterious as these
118   My friend attacks my friend!
70   "Arcturus" is his other name—
119   Talk with prudence to a Beggar
120   If this is "fading"
121   As Watchers hang upon the East—
84   Her breast is fit for pearls,
122   A something in a summer's Day
71   A throe upon the features—
72   Glowing is her Bonnet,
123   Many cross the Rhine
124   In lands I never saw—they say
125   For each extatic instant

FASCICLE 6 (about 1859)

73   Who never lost, are unprepared
74   A Lady red—amid the Hill
126   To fight aloud, is very brave—
127   'Houses'—so the Wise Men tell me—
128   Bring me the sunset in a cup,
75   She died at play,

129   Cocoon above! Cocoon below!

76   Exultation is the going

77   I never hear the word "escape"

130   These are the days when Birds come back—

131   Besides the Autumn poets sing

216   Safe in their Alabaster Chambers—

78   A poor—torn heart—a tattered heart—

132   I bring an unaccustomed wine

133   As Children bid the Guest "Good Night"

79   Going to Heaven!

80   Our lives are Swiss—

FASCICLE 7 (about 1859)

59   A little East of Jordan,

148   All overgrown by cunning moss,

100   A science—so the Savans say,

101   Will there really be a "Morning"?

102   Great Caesar! Condescend

103   I have a King, who does not speak—

104   Where I have lost, I softer tread—

149   She went as quiet as the Dew

105   To hang our head—ostensibly—

106   The Daisy follows soft the Sun—

60   Like her the Saints retire,

61   Papa above!

107   'Twas such a little—little boat

62   "Sown in dishonor"!

150   She died—*this* was the way she died.

63   If pain for peace prepares

108   Surgeons must be very careful

64   Some Rainbow—coming from the Fair!

109   By a flower—By a letter—

65   I cant tell you—but you feel it—

FASCICLE 8 (about 1860)

165   A *Wounded* Deer—leaps highest—

152   The Sun kept stooping—stooping—low!

166   I met a King this afternoon!

167   To learn the Transport by the Pain—

168   If the foolish, call them *"flowers"*—

169   In Ebon Box, when years have flown

170   Portraits are to daily faces

171   Wait till the Majesty of Death

172   'Tis so much joy! 'Tis so much joy!

173   A fuzzy fellow, without feet,

174   At last, to be identified!

175   I have never seen 'Volcanoes'—

153   Dust is the only Secret—

176   I'm the little "Heart's Ease"!

177   Ah, Necromancy Sweet!

154   Except to Heaven, she is nought.

170   Pictures are to daily faces

178   I cautious, scanned my little life—

179   If I could bribe them by a Rose

180   As if some little Arctic flower

FASCICLE 9 (about 1860)

186   What shall I do—it whimpers so—

187   How many times these low feet staggered—

188   Make me a picture of the sun—

269   Bound—a trouble—

215   What is—"Paradise"—

155   The Murmur of a Bee

156   You love me—you are sure—

162   My River runs to Thee—

189   It's such a little thing to weep—

190   He was weak, and I was strong—then—

191   The Skies cant keep their secret!

192   Poor little Heart!

193   I shall know why—when Time is over—

194   On this long storm the Rainbow rose—

157   Musicians wrestle everywhere—

195   For this—accepted Breath—

196   We dont cry—Tim and I,

158   Dying! Dying in the night!

197   Morning—is the place for Dew—

198   An awful Tempest mashed the air—

199   I'm "wife"—I've finished that—

200   I stole them from a Bee—

201   Two swimmers wrestled on the spar—

202   My Eye is fuller than my vase—

203   He forgot—and I—remembered—

204   A Slash of Blue! A sweep of Gray!

205   I should not dare to leave my friend,

206   The Flower must not blame the Bee—

324   Some—keep the Sabbath—going to church—

FASCICLE 10 (about 1860–1861)

230   We—Bee and I—live by the quaffing—

231   God permits industrious Angels—

232   The *Sun—just touched* the Morning—

233   The Lamp burns sure—within—

163   Tho' my destiny be Fustian—

207   Tho' I get home how late—how late—

208   The Rose did caper on her cheek—

209   With thee, in the Desert—

185   Faith is a fine invention

210   The thought beneath so slight a film—

318   I'll tell you how the Sun rose—

159   A little Bread—a crust—a crumb—

160   Just lost, when I was saved!

211   Come slowly—Eden!

212   Least Rivers—docile to some sea.

270   *One Life* of so much Consequence!

234   You're right—"the way is narrow"—

216   Safe in their Alabaster Chambers—

235   The Court is far away—

236   If *He dissolve*—then—there is *nothing—more*—

237   I think just how my shape will rise—

224   I've nothing else—to bring, You know—

FASCICLE 11 (about 1861)

283   A Mien to move a Queen—

284   The Drop, that wrestles in the Sea—

285   The Robin's my Criterion for Tune—

243   I've known a Heaven, like a Tent—

223   I came to buy a smile—today—

287   A Clock stopped—

288   I'm Nobody! Who are you?

245   I held a Jewel in my fingers—

244   It is easy to work when the soul is at play—

286   That after Horror—that 'twas *us*—

240   Ah, Moon—and Star!

317   Just so—Christ—raps—

246   Forever at His side to walk—

221   It cant be "Summer"!

247   What would I give to see his face?

1737   Rearrange a "Wife's" affection!

248   Why—do they shut Me out of Heaven?

249   Wild Nights—Wild Nights!

250   I shall keep singing!

251   Over the fence—

FASCICLE 12 (about 1860)

214   I taste a liquor never brewed—

161   A feather from the Whippowil

181   I lost a World—the other day!

182   If I should'nt be alive

183   I've heard an Organ talk, sometimes—

184   A transport one cannot contain

185   "Faith" is a fine invention

293   I got so I could hear his name—

263   A single Screw of Flesh

264   A Weight with Needles on the pounds—

217   Father—I bring thee—not Myself—

265   Where Ships of Purple—gently toss—

266   This—is the land—the Sunset washes—

294   The Doomed—regard the Sunrise

225   Jesus! thy Crucifix

267   Did we disobey Him?

295   Unto like Story—Trouble has enticed me—

296   One Year ago—jots what?

297   It's like the Light—

298   Alone, I cannot be—

273   He put the Belt around my life—

274   The only Ghost I ever saw

275   Doubt Me! My Dim Companion!

276   Many a phrase has the English language—

321   Of all the Sounds despatched abroad—

514   Her smile was shaped like other smiles—

353   A happy lip—breaks sudden—

FASCICLE 13 (about 1861)

289   I know some lonely Houses off the Road

252   I can wade Grief—

253   You see I cannot see—your lifetime—

254   "Hope" is the thing with feathers—

255   To die—takes just a little while—

256   If I'm lost—now—

257   Delight is as the flight—

219   She sweeps with many-colored Brooms—

290   Of Bronze—and Blaze—

258   There's a certain Slant of light,

228   Blazing in Gold—and

259   Good Night! Which put the Candle out?

260   Read—Sweet—how others—strove—

261   Put up my lute!

322   There came a Day—at Summer's full—

262   The lonesome for they know not What—

291   How the old Mountains drip with Sunset

325   Of Tribulation, these are They,

292   If your Nerve, deny you—

FASCICLE 14 (about 1861)

319   The maddest dream—recedes—unrealized—

277   What if I say I shall not wait!

240   Ah, Moon—and Star!

278   A Shady friend—for Torrid days—

271   A solemn thing—it was—I said—

272   I breathed enough to take the Trick—

238   Kill your Balm—and it's Odors bless you—

239   "Heaven"—is what I cannot reach!

7   The feet of people walking home

582   Inconceivably solemn!

422   More Life—went out—when He went

423   The Months have ends—the Years—a knot—

424   Removed from Accident of Loss

299   Your Riches—taught me—Poverty.

583   A Toad, can die of Light—

332   There are two Ripenings—

584   It ceased to hurt me, though so slow

310   Give little Anguish,

       (poems unknown?)

FASCICLE 15 (about 1862)

410   The first Day's Night had come—

411   The Color of the Grave is Green—

414   'Twas like a Maelstrom, with a notch,

580   I gave myself to Him—

415   Sunset at Night—is natural—

419   We grow accustomed to the Dark—

420   You'll know it—as you know 'tis Noon—

421   A Charm invests a face

577   If I may have it, when it's dead,

412   I read my sentence—steadily—

416   A Murmur in the Trees—to note—

417   It is dead—Find it—

418   Not in this World to see his face—

581   I found the words to every thought

413   I never felt at Home—Below—

578   The Body grows without—

579   I had been hungry, all the Years—

FASCICLE 16 (about 1862)

327   Before I got my eye put out—

607   Of nearness to her sundered Things

279   Tie the Strings to my Life, My Lord,

241   I like a look of Agony,

280   I felt a Funeral, in my Brain,

281   'Tis so appalling—it exhilirates—

282   How noteless Men, and Pleiads, stand,

242   When we stand on the tops of Things—

445   'Twas just this time, last year, I died.

608   Afraid! Of whom am I afraid?

446   He showed me Hights I never saw—

FASCICLE 17 (about 1862)

348   I dreaded that first Robin, so,

505   I would not paint—a picture—

506   He touched me, so I live to know

349   I had the Glory—that will do—

507   She sights a Bird—she chuckles—

350   They leave us with the Infinite.

508   I'm ceded—I've stopped being Their's—

509   If anybody's friend be dead

510   It was not Death, for I stood up,

511   If you were coming in the Fall,

351   I felt my life with both my hands

352   Perhaps I asked too large—

328   A Bird, came down the Walk—

512   The Soul has Bandaged moments—

513   Like Flowers, that heard the news of Dews,

FASCICLE 18 (about 1862)

495   It's thoughts—and just One Heart—

337   I know a place where Summer strives

496   As far from pity, as complaint—

338   I know that He exists.

497   He strained my faith—

339   I tend my flowers for thee—

498   I envy Seas, whereon He rides—

499   Those fair—fictitious People—

500   Within my Garden, rides a Bird

340   Is Bliss then, such Abyss,

341   After great pain, a formal feeling comes—

501   This World is not Conclusion.

342   It will be Summer—eventually.

343   My Reward for Being, was This.

344   'Twas the old—road—through pain—

502   At least—to pray—is left—is left—

503   Better—than Music! For I—who heard it—

FASCICLE 19 (about 1862)

333   The Grass so little has to do,

334   All the letters I can write

326   I cannot dance upon my Toes—

425   Good Morning—Midnight—

585   I like to see it lap the Miles—

426   It dont sound so terrible—quite—as it did—

427   I'll clutch—and clutch—

428   Taking up the fair Ideal,

429   The Moon is distant from the Sea—

430   It would never be Common—more—I said—

431   Me—come! My dazzled face

432   Do People moulder equally,

433   Knows how to forget!

586   We talked as Girls do—

587   Empty my Heart, of Thee—

588   I cried at Pity—not at Pain—

336   The face I carry with me—last—

FASCICLE 20 (about 1862)

1725   I took one Draught of Life—

1761   A train went through a burial gate,

364   The Morning after Wo—

524   Departed—to the Judgment—

525   I think the Hemlock likes to stand

365   Dare you see a soul at the "White Heat?"

526   To hear an Oriole sing

301   I reason, Earth is short—

527   To put this World down, like a Bundle—

366   Although I put away his life—

367   Over and over, like a Tune—

670   One need not be a Chamber—to be Haunted—

302   Like Some Old fashioned Miracle—

303   The Soul selects her own Society—

368   How sick—to wait—in any place—but thine—

528   Mine—by the Right of the White Election!

369   She lay as if at play

370   Heaven is so far of the Mind

FASCICLE 21 (about 1862)

609   I—Years had been—from Home—

610   You'll find—it when you try to die—

611   I see thee better—in the Dark—

447   Could—I do more—for Thee—

612   It would have starved a Gnat—

613   They shut me up in Prose—

448   This was a Poet—It is That

614   In falling Timbers buried—

449   I died for Beauty—but was scarce

450   Dreams—are well—but Waking's better,

451   The Outer—from the Inner

174   At last—to be identified—

452   The Malay—took the Pearl—

453   Love—thou art high—

615   Our journey had advanced—

616   I rose—because He sank—

454   It was given to me by the Gods—

FASCICLE 22 (about 1862)

652   A Prison gets to be a friend—

314   Nature—sometimes sears a Sapling—

479   She dealt her pretty words like Blades—

480   "Why do I love" You, Sir?

481   The Himmaleh was known to stoop

482   We Cover Thee—Sweet Face—

653   Of Being is a Bird

654   A long—long Sleep—A famous—Sleep—

655   Without this—there is nought—

656   The name—of it—is "Autumn"—

657   I dwell in Possibility—

483   A Solemn thing within the Soul

658   Whole Gulfs—of Red, and Fleets—of Red—

484   My Garden—like the Beach—

659   That first Day, when you praised Me, Sweet,

485   To make One's Toilette—after Death

660   'Tis good—the looking back on Grief—

486   I was the slightest in the House—

487   You love the Lord—you cannot see—

488   Myself was formed—a Carpenter—

489   We pray—to Heaven—

315   He fumbles at your Soul

1076   Just Once! Oh Least Request!

FASCICLE 23 (about 1862)

712   Because I could not stop for Death—

759   He fought like those Who've nought to lose—

713   Fame of Myself, to justify,

678   Wolfe demanded during Dying

760   Most she touched me by her muteness—

761   From Blank to Blank—

762   The Whole of it came not at once—

763   He told a homely tale

764   Presentiment—is that long Shadow—on the Lawn—

765   You constituted Time—

766   My Faith is larger than the Hills—

714   Rests at Night

715   The World—feels Dusty

767   To offer brave assistance

768   When I hoped, I recollect

316   The Wind did'nt come from the Orchard—today—

716   The Day undressed—Herself—

717   The Beggar Lad—dies early—

769   One and One—are One—

770   I lived on Dread—

FASCICLE 24 (about 1862)

311   It sifts from Leaden Sieves—

595   Like Mighty Foot Lights—burned the Red

1712   A Pit—but Heaven over it—(missing)

1710   A curious Cloud surprised the Sky,

602   Of Brussels—it was not—

603   He found my Being—set it up—

604   Unto my Books—so good to turn—

605   The Spider holds a Silver Ball

598   Three times—we parted—Breath—and I—

599   There is a pain—so utter—

600   It troubled me as once I was—

601   A still—Volcano—Life—

596   When I was small, a Woman died—

441   This is my letter to the World

442   God made a little Gentian—

343   My Reward for Being—was This—

597   It always felt to me—a wrong

443   I tie my Hat—I crease my Shawl—
       (completion of P1712)
       (completion of P443)

606   The Trees like Tassels—hit—and swung—

444   It feels a shame to be Alive—

FASCICLE 25 (about 1862)

371   A precious—mouldering pleasure—'tis—

532   I tried to think a lonelier Thing

533   Two Butterflies went out at Noon—

304   The Day came slow—till Five o'clock—

1053   It was a quiet way—

372   I know lives, I could miss

373   I'm saying every day

305   The difference between Despair

374   I went to Heaven—

375   The Angle of a Landscape—

683   The Soul unto itself

534   We see—Comparatively—

376   Of Course—I prayed—

529   I'm sorry for the Dead—Today—

530   You cannot put a Fire out—

531   We dream—it is good we are dreaming—

1727   If ever the lid gets off my head

1739   Some say good night—at night—

535   She's happy, with a new Content—

536   The Heart asks Pleasure—first—

FASCICLE 26 (about 1862)

628   They called me to the Window, for

669   No Romance sold unto

465   I heard a Fly buzz—when I died—

674   The Soul that hath a Guest,

629   I watched the Moon around the House

1181   When I hoped—I feared—

630   The Lightning playeth—all the while—

631   Ourselves were wed one summer—dear—

466   'Tis little I—could care for Pearls—

632   The Brain—is wider than the Sky—

467   We do not play on Graves—

312   Her—last Poems—

633   When Bells stop ringing—Church—begins—

468   The Manner of it's Death

469   The Red—Blaze—is the Morning—

634   You'll know Her—by Her Foot—

470   I am alive—I guess—

1067   Except the smaller size—

635   I think the longest Hour of all

329   So glad we are—a stranger'd deem

471   A Night—there lay the Days between—

FASCICLE 27 (about 1862)

389   There's been a Death, in the Opposite House,

554   The Black Berry—wears a Thorn in his side—

307   The One that could repeat the Summer Day—

561   I measure every Grief I meet

562   Conjecturing a Climate

396   There is a Languor of the Life

397   When Diamonds are a Legend,

398   I had not minded—Walls—

399   A House upon the Hight—

390   It's Coming—the postponeless Creature—

308   I send Two Sunsets—

391   A Visitor in Marl—

392   Through the Dark Sod—as Education—

393   Did Our Best Moment last—

555   Trust in the Unexpected—

394   'Twas Love—not me—

556   The Brain, within it's Groove

557   She hideth Her the last—

395   Reverse cannot befall

558   But little Carmine hath her face—

559   It knew no Medicine—

560   It knew no lapse, nor Diminution—

FASCICLE 28 (about 1862)

564   My period had come for Prayer—

402   I pay—in Satin Cash—

565   One Anguish—in a Crowd—

335   'Tis not that Dying hurts us so—

566   A Dying Tiger—moaned for Drink—

567   He gave away his Life—

568   We learned the Whole of Love—

403   The Winters are so short—

569   I reckon—when I count at all—

404   How many Flowers fail in Wood—

405   It might be lonelier

406   Some—Work for Immortality—

570   I could die—to know—

571   Must be a Wo—

572   Delight—becomes pictorial—

FASCICLE 29 (about 1862)

FASCICLE 30 (about 1862)

521   Endow the Living—with the Tears—

538   'Tis true—They shut me in the Cold—

539   The Province of the Saved

540   I took my Power in my Hand—

541   Some such Butterfly be seen

542   I had no Cause to be awake—

543   I fear a Man of frugal Speech—

379   Rehearsal to Ourselves

544   The Martyr Poets—did not tell—

550   I cross till I am weary

386   Answer July—

551   There is a Shame of Nobleness—

552   An ignorance a Sunset

553   One Crucifixion is recorded—only—

387   The Sweetest Heresy received

388   Take Your Heaven further on—

FASCICLE 31 (about 1862)

306   The Soul's Superior instants

537   Me prove it now—Whoever doubt

377   To lose one's faith—surpass

378   I saw no Way—The Heavens were stitched—

522   Had I presumed to hope—

523   Sweet—You forgot—but I remembered

362   It struck me—every Day—

363   I went to thank Her—

672   The Future never spoke—

359   I gained it so—

360   Death sets a Thing significant

361   What I can do—I will—

380   There is a flower that Bees prefer—

381   A Secret told—

382   For Death—or rather

383   Exhiliration—is within—

545   'Tis One by One—the Father counts—

546   To fill a Gap

547   I've seen a Dying Eye

384   No Rack can torture me—

548   Death is potential to that Man

385   Smiling back from Coronation

549   That I did always love

FASCICLE 32 (about 1862)

455   Triumph—may be of several kinds—

617   Dont put up my Thread & Needle—

456   So well that I can live without—

618   At leisure is the Soul

457   Sweet—safe—Houses—

619   Glee—The great storm is over—

620   It makes no difference abroad—

621   I asked no other thing—

622   To know just how He suffered—would be dear—

623   It was too late for Man—

624   Forever—is composed of Nows—

625   'Twas a long Parting—but the time

626   Only God—detect the Sorrow—

458   Like Eyes that looked on Wastes—

459   A Tooth upon Our Peace

460   I know where Wells grow—Droughtless Wells—

627   The Tint I cannot take—is best—

461   A Wife—at Daybreak—I shall be—

462   Why make it doubt—it hurts it so—

463   I live with Him—I see His face—

464   The power to be true to You,

FASCICLE 33 (about 1862)

636   The Way I read a Letter's—this—

637   The Child's faith is new—

472   Except the Heaven had come so near—

638   To my small Hearth His fire came—

639   My Portion is Defeat—today—

473   I am ashamed—I hide—

640   I cannot live with You—

641   Size circumscribes—it has no room

474   They put Us far apart—

642   Me from Myself—to banish—

475   Doom is the House without the Door—

313   I should have been too glad, I see—

476   I meant to have but modest needs—

643   I could suffice for Him, I knew—

644   You left me—Sire—two Legacies—

477   No Man can compass a Despair—

FASCICLE 34 (about 1862 or 1863)

645   Bereavement in their death to feel

646   I think To Live—may be a Bliss

647   A little Road—not made of Man—

649   Her Sweet turn to leave the Homestead

650   Pain—has an Element of Blank—

651   So much Summer

648   Promise This—When You be Dying—

478   I had no time to Hate—

754   My Life had stood—a Loaded Gun—

710   The Sunrise runs for Both—

755   No Bobolink—reverse His Singing

756   One Blessing had I than the rest

690   Victory comes late—

757   The Mountains—grow unnoticed—

758   These—saw Visions—

711   Strong Draughts of Their Refreshing Minds

993   We miss Her—not because We see—

675   Essential Oils—are wrung—

FASCICLE 35 (about 1863)

692   The Sun kept setting—setting—still

693   Shells from the Coast mistaking—

694   The Heaven vests for Each

733   The Spirit is the Conscious Ear.

734   If He were living—dare I ask—

695   As if the Sea should part

668   "Nature" is what We see—

735   Upon Concluded Lives

736   Have any like Myself

680   Each Life Converges to some Centre—

696   Their Hight in Heaven comforts not—

697   I could bring You Jewels—had I a mind to—

698   Life—is what we make it—

699   The Judge is like the Owl—

1142 The Props assist the House—

700   You've seen Balloons set—Hav'nt You?

689   The Zeros taught Us—Phosphorus—

701   A Thought went up my mind today—

673   The Love a Life can show Below

702   A first Mute Coming—

703   Out of sight? What of that?

704   No matter—now—Sweet—

737   The Moon was but a Chin of Gold

738   You said that I "was Great"—one Day—

739   I many times thought Peace had come

FASCICLE 36 (about 1863)

982   No Other can reduce Our

788   Joy to have merited the Pain—

269   Bound a Trouble—and Lives will bear it—

789   On a Columnar Self—

790   Nature—the Gentlest Mother is,

720   No Prisoner be—

259   Good Night—Which put the Candle out?

721   Behind Me—dips Eternity—

671   She dwelleth in the Ground—

722   Sweet Mountains—Ye tell Me no lie—

723   It tossed—and tossed—

724   It's easy to invent a Life—

791   God gave a Loaf to every Bird—

725   Where Thou art—that—is Home—

726   We thirst at first—'tis Nature's Act—

792   Through the Straight Pass of Suffering

727   Precious to Me—She still shall be—

665   Dropped into the Ether Acre—

666   Ah, Teneriffe—Receding Mountain—

793   Grief is a Mouse—

728   Let Us play Yesterday—

729   Alter! When the Hills do—

FASCICLE 37 (about 1863)

679   Conscious am I in my Chamber,

740   You taught me Waiting with Myself—

705   Suspense—is Hostiler than Death—

741   Drama's Vitallest Expression is the Common Day

706   Life, and Death, and Giants—

742   Four Trees—upon a solitary Acre—

707   The Grace—Myself—might not obtain—

743   The Birds reported from the South—

744   Remorse—is Memory—awake—

745   Renunciation—is a piercing Virtue—

746   Never for Society

708   I sometimes drop it, for a Quick—

747   It dropped so low—in my Regard—

748   Autumn—overlooked my Knitting—

667   Bloom upon the Mountain stated—

709   Publication—is the Auction—

749   All but Death, can be Adjusted—

750   Growth of Man—like Growth of Nature—

751   My Worthiness is all my Doubt—

752   So the Eyes accost—and sunder

753   My Soul—accused me—And I quailed—

FASCICLE 38 (about 1863)

794   A Drop fell on the Apple Tree—

795   Her final Summer was it—

796   Who Giants know, with lesser Men

797   By my Window have I for Scenery

730   Defrauded I a Butterfly—

731   "I want"—it pleaded—All it's life—

876   It was a Grave, yet bore no Stone

798   She staked her Feathers—Gained an Arc—

799   Despair's Advantage is achieved

800   Two—were immortal twice—

801   I play at Riches—to appease

732   She rose to His Requirement—dropt

802   Time feels so vast that were it not

803   Who Court obtain within Himself

804   No Notice gave She, but a Change—

686   They say that "Time assuages"—

681   On the Bleakness of my Lot

805   This Bauble was preferred of Bees—

806   A Plated Life—diversified

807   Expectation—is Contentment—

FASCICLE 39 (about 1863)

(poems unknown)

771   None can experience stint

772   The hallowing of Pain

773   Deprived of other Banquet,

774   It is a lonesome Glee—

775   If Blame be my side—forfeit Me—

776   The Color of a Queen, is this—

677   To be alive—is Power—

777   The Loneliness One dare not sound—

676   Least Bee that brew—

778   This that would greet—an hour ago—

779   The Service without Hope—

718   I meant to find Her when I came—

780   The Truth—is stirless—

719   A South Wind—has a pathos

781   To wait an Hour—is long—

782   There is an arid Pleasure—

783   The Birds begun at Four o'clock—

784   Bereaved of all, I went abroad—

785   They have a little Odor—that to me

786   Severer Service of myself

682   'Twould ease—a Butterfly—
787   Such is the Force of Happiness—

FASCICLE 40 (about 1864)

827   The Only News I know
961   Wert Thou but ill—that I might show thee
962   Midsummer, was it, when They died—
902   The first Day that I was a Life
963   A nearness to Tremendousness—
964   "Unto Me?" I do not know you—
965   Denial—is the only fact
966   All forgot for recollecting
903   I hide myself—within my flower,
904   Had I not This, or This, I said,
905   Between My Country—and the Others—
906   The Admirations—and Contempts—of time—
907   Till Death—is narrow Loving—
908   'Tis Sunrise—Little Maid—Hast Thou
967   Pain—expands the Time—
968   Fitter to see Him, I may be
969   He who in Himself believes—
970   Color—Caste—Denomination—
909   I make His Crescent fill or lack—
971   Robbed by Death—but that was easy—
972   Unfulfilled to Observation—

Appendix B
Major Archival Collections for Dickinson Research

AMHERST COLLEGE, THE EMILY DICKINSON COLLECTION

This extensive manuscript collection, contributed by Millicent Todd Bingham and housed in the Robert Frost Library, features six bound fascicles, unbound fascicle sheets, and poem and letter drafts that had been in the possession of Mabel Loomis Todd. Along with Harvard's Houghton Library collection, this is one of two primary repositories of Dickinson's manuscripts. A feature of Amherst's Emily Dickinson Collection is the famous daguerreotype portrait. Other highlights include a lock of the poet's hair and an early silhouette. The card catalog documenting this collection was prepared by Jay Leyda. Access to the poet's manuscripts is necessarily restricted because of their fragility; researchers are asked to work with xerox or microfilm copies. (Microfilm copies of the Amherst College collection are also available for use at about sixty other institutions in the United States, Canada, Japan, and several European countries.)

Hours: 9:00 A.M. to noon and 1–4 P.M. Monday through Friday.

See: Lancaster, John. "Dickinson Libraries: The Amherst College Collection." *Emily Dickinson International Society Bulletin* 2.2 (Nov./Dec. 1990): 7.

Access: Write to Curator of Special Collections, Amherst College Library, Amherst College, Amherst, MA 01002–5000. Telephone (413) 542–2299. Fax (413) 542–2692.

BOSTON PUBLIC LIBRARY, THE DICKINSON/HIGGINSON PAPERS

Primarily an archive for Thomas Wentworth Higginson's papers, this collection features seventy-three of Emily Dickinson's letters to her friend, literary mentor, and editor. Also included are forty-two autograph poems and a few transcriptions made by Mabel Loomis Todd. Todd's letters to Higginson regarding their joint editing task are also available for use by researchers.

Hours: 9:00 A.M. to 5:00 P.M. Monday through Friday.

See: Monti, Laura V. "The Dickinson/Higginson Papers: Boston Public Library." *Emily Dickinson International Society Bulletin* 5.1 (1993): 13.

Access: Write to the Rare Books and Manuscripts Department, Boston Public Library,

700 Boylston Street, Boston, MA 02117. Telephone (617) 536–5400, extension 425. Fax (617) 536–7758. Appointment necessary.

BROWN UNIVERSITY, THE MARTHA DICKINSON BIANCHI COLLECTION

Donated to Brown University under terms of Mary Landis Hampson's will, this collection assembles papers and books from the Evergreens, home of Austin and Susan Dickinson and their daughter Martha Dickinson Bianchi. Its materials, still being cataloged, are of particular interest to scholars interested in Susan Dickinson and Madame Bianchi.

Hours: 9:00 A.M. to 5:00 P.M. Monday through Friday. Access to the Bianchi Collection is by appointment only.

See: Brown, Mark N. "Dickinson Libraries: The Brown University Library Collection." *Emily Dickinson International Society Bulletin* 7.1 (May/June 1995): 8–9.

Access: Write to Curator of Manuscripts, The John Hay Library, Brown University, Box A, Providence, RI 02912. Telephone (401) 863–2146.

HARVARD UNIVERSITY: THE HOUGHTON LIBRARY

The base of this collection is the Dickinson papers, books, and objects bequeathed by Martha Dickinson Bianchi to Alfred Leete Hampson; these were purchased by Gilbert H. Montague, a Harvard alumnus, who donated them in 1950 in memory of his wife, Amy Angell Collier Montague. It includes fascicles, manuscripts of other Dickinson poems and letters, family papers, and selected books from the Homestead. Associated papers include Martha Dickinson Bianchi's editorial papers. Holdings are partially documented in "Dickinson Papers, Lists, and Notes," but readers should consult the following article for a fuller description of holdings and a complete list of inventories and guides. Access to the poet's manuscripts is necessarily restricted because of their fragility; researchers are directed, instead, to facsimile and photostatic reproductions and slides.

Hours: 9:00 A.M. to 5 P.M. Monday through Friday; 9:00 A.M. to 1:00 P.M. Saturday. Visits to the Emily Dickinson Room must be arranged in advance.

See: Falsey, Elizabeth. "Dickinson Libraries: The Houghton Library Collection, Harvard University." *Emily Dickinson International Society Bulletin* 3.1 (May/June 1991): 3–4.

Access: Write to The Houghton Library, Harvard University, Cambridge, MA 02138 or call (617) 495–2449. Fax (617) 495–1376.

THE DICKINSON ELECTRONIC ARCHIVES PROJECT

The Dickinson Electronic Archives Project will present each of Dickinson's ninety-nine correspondences and all of her ungathered poems, drafts, and fragments by reproducing high-quality images of the manuscripts themselves with diplomatic, line-for-line transcriptions. Links will be made between and among texts (poetic and epistolary) with the same lines and/or with similar holographic strategies, and the entire database will be searchable for a wide variety of readerly interests. Access will be greatly expanded so that common readers can act as virtual editors, and experts will greatly benefit from many readers' bringing questions and especial interests to examination of documents previously accessible to only a few. Preservation of the documents themselves will also be facilitated in that the electronic medium enables readers to view all these manuscript characteristics without handling the originals themselves.

See: Smith, Martha Nell. "The Importance of a Hypermedia Archive of Dickinson's Creative Work." *The Emily Dickinson Journal* 4.1 (1995): 75–85 and "A Hypermedia Archive of Dickinson's Creative Work, Part II: Musings on the Screen and the Book." *The Emily Dickinson Journal* 5.2 (1996): 18–25.

Access: In order to cultivate audiences, the Collective will maintain a limited, free, and open Web site at http://jefferson.village.virginia.edu/dickinson/

THE JONES LIBRARY, INC., SPECIAL COLLECTIONS, AMHERST

The public library of Amherst, Massachusetts, the Jones Library features its Emily Dickinson Collection, which combines characteristics of a scholarly research center and a public exhibition area. Charles Green, then director of the Jones Library, began the collection in 1924. Steadily augmented by both purchases and gifts, the collection now includes first editions, scholarly writings, translations, and artwork as well as some manuscript poems and letters that the library makes available to scholars. A recent addition to the library provides improved exhibit space for books, paintings, and memorabilia. Other special collections on Amherst town history provide further support for Dickinson-related research.

Hours: Monday through Friday, 10:00 A.M. to 5:00 P.M.; Saturday 11:00 A.M. to 5:00 P.M.

See: Lombardo, Daniel. "Dickinson Libraries: The Jones Collection." *Emily Dickinson International Society Bulletin* 3.2 (Nov./Dec. 1991): 3; Bernhard, Mary Elizabeth Kromer. "The Jones Library Dickinson Exhibit." *Emily Dickinson International Society Bulletin* 5.1 (May/June 1993): 1–2.

Access: Write to Curator of Special Collections, The Jones Library, Inc., 43 Amity St., Amherst, MA 01002 or call (413) 256–4090.

THE UNIVERSITY OF NEBRASKA-LINCOLN, THE LOWENBERG COLLECTION

Recognized as "the finest Dickinson research collection outside of New England," this archive makes available to scholars the remarkable collection of Dickinson books and materials assembled by Carlton and Territa Lowenberg and donated to the University of Nebraska in 1992. It includes editions of Dickinson's work (no manuscripts), books in which her poems appear, photographs, church and town histories, materials demonstrating interest in Dickinson around the world, and documentation of local culture. Particularly notable are Carlton Lowenberg's collections of textbooks from the poet's time and of musical settings of Dickinson poems. Complete inventory information should be available on the Internet by 1998. The inventory for the portion of the collection located in Special Collections may be viewed at the following URL on the Internet: http://www.unl.edu/spec/lowenberg/emily.html, and inventory for books may be viewed at http://iris.unl.edu by selecting the UNL & Schmid Law Library Catalog, selecting KEYWORD, and typing in LOWENBERG COLLECTION to review the 3,000+ catalog records.

Hours: Portions of the collection located in Special Collections at Love Library and at the Music Library are available from 8:00 A.M. to 5:00 P.M Monday through Friday.

The portion located in the circulating collection at Love Library is available all hours that the main library is open.

See: Johnson, Kathleen. "The Lowenberg Collection: The University of Nebraska-Lincoln." *Emily Dickinson International Society Bulletin* 6.1 (May/June 1994): 10+; Lowenberg, Carlton. "Emilyana: 'Gathered from many wanderings.' " *Emily Dickinson International Society Bulletin* 6.2 (Nov./Dec. 1994): 1+.

Access: Write to University Libraries, 201AE Love Library, University of Nebraska-Lincoln, Lincoln, NE 68588–0410 or call 402–472-2553.

YALE UNIVERSITY, THE TODD-BINGHAM ARCHIVE

This collection features the papers of Mabel Loomis Todd and Millicent Todd Bingham and, therefore, provides material of special interest to those studying Dickinson's editing history, inquiring into the roles of these women who played such key roles in representing the poet to the public, or curious about Amherst social life from Mrs. Todd's perspective. An extensive photographic collection supplements print and manuscript materials. Those contemplating research in the Manuscripts and Archives Reading Room need two pieces of identification, one of them with a photograph.

Hours: Open Monday through Friday, 8:30 A.M. to 4:45 P.M. except for holidays and the Christmas holiday period.

See: Schiff, Judith Ann. "The Todd-Bingham Archive, Yale University Library." *Emily Dickinson International Society Bulletin* 4.1 (May/June 1992): 5+.

Access: Write to the Reference Archivist, Manuscripts and Archives, 150 Sterling Memorial Library, 120 High St., New Haven, CT 06520 or call (203) 432–1744.

Bibliography

In addition to books and articles cited within this encyclopedia, there is a wealth of scholarship for the reader to explore. Invaluable guides in this process are Willis J. Buckingham's *Emily Dickinson: An Annotated Bibliography*, which lists scholarship in other languages as well as English, Karen Dandurand's *Dickinson Scholarship: An Annotated Bibliography 1969–1985*, and ongoing Modern Language Association (MLA) international bibliographies both in print form and on CD-ROM.

PRIMARY SOURCES

Bianchi, Martha Dickinson. *Emily Dickinson Face to Face: Unpublished Letters with Notes and Reminiscences by Her Niece*. Boston: Houghton Mifflin, 1932.

———. *The Life and Letters of Emily Dickinson*. Boston: Houghton Mifflin, 1924.

Bingham, Millicent Todd. *Emily Dickinson: A Revelation*. New York: Harper & Brothers, 1954.

———. *Emily Dickinson's Home: Letters of Edward Dickinson and His Family*. New York: Harper & Brothers, 1955.

Dickinson, Emily. *The Complete Poems of Emily Dickinson*. Ed. Martha Dickinson Bianchi. Boston: Little, Brown, 1924.

———. *The Complete Poems of Emily Dickinson*. Ed. Thomas H. Johnson. Boston: Little, Brown, 1960.

———. *Emily Dickinson's Letters to Dr. and Mrs. Josiah Gilbert Holland*. Ed. Theodora Van Wagenen Ward. Cambridge: Harvard University Press, 1951.

———. *Emily Dickinson: Selected Letters*. Ed. Thomas H. Johnson. Cambridge: Harvard University Press, Belknap Press, 1986.

———. *Final Harvest: Emily Dickinson's Poems*. Ed. Thomas H. Johnson. Boston: Little, Brown, 1961.

———. *Further Poems of Emily Dickinson*. Withheld from Publication by her Sister Lavinia. Ed. Martha Dickinson Bianchi and Alfred Leete Hampson. Boston: Little, Brown, 1929.

———. *A Letter*. Amherst, MA: Friends of Amherst College Library, 1992.

———. *Letters of Emily Dickinson.* Ed. Mabel Loomis Todd. 2 vols. Boston: Roberts Brothers, 1894.

———. *Letters of Emily Dickinson.* Ed. Mabel Loomis Todd. New York: Harper and Brothers, 1931.

———. *The Letters of Emily Dickinson.* Ed. Thomas H. Johnson and Theodora Ward. 3 vols. Cambridge: Harvard University Press, Belknap Press, 1958.

———. *The Manuscript Books of Emily Dickinson.* Ed. R. W. Franklin, 2 vols. Cambridge: Harvard University Press, Belknap Press, 1981.

———. *The Master Letters of Emily Dickinson.* Ed. R. W. Franklin. Amherst, MA: Amherst College Press, 1986.

———. *New Poems of Emily Dickinson.* Ed. William H. Shurr, Anna Dunlap, and Emily Grey Shurr. Chapel Hill: University of North Carolina Press, 1993.

———. *Poems (1890–1896) by Emily Dickinson* (facsimile of 1890, 1891, and 1896 volumes; introduction by George Monteiro). Gainesville, FL: Scholars' Facsimiles & Reprints, 1967.

———. *Poems by Emily Dickinson.* Ed. Mabel Loomis Todd and T. W. Higginson. Boston: Roberts Brothers, 1890.

———. *Poems by Emily Dickinson: Second Series.* Ed. T. W. Higginson and Mabel Loomis Todd. Boston: Roberts Brothers, 1891.

———. *Poems by Emily Dickinson: Third Series.* Ed. Mabel Loomis Todd. Boston: Roberts Brothers, 1896.

———. *Poems by Emily Dickinson.* Ed. Martha Dickinson Bianchi and Alfred Leete Hampson. Boston: Little, Brown, 1937.

———. *Poems for Youth.* Ed. Alfred Leete Hampson. Boston: Little, Brown, 1934.

———. *The Poems of Emily Dickinson: Centenary Edition.* Ed. Martha Dickinson Bianchi and Alfred Leete Hampson. Boston: Little, Brown, 1930.

———. *The Poems of Emily Dickinson including Variant Readings Critically Compared with All Known Manuscripts.* Ed. Thomas H. Johnson. 3 vols. Cambridge: Harvard University Press, Belknap Press, 1955.

———. *The Single Hound: Poems of a Lifetime.* Ed. Martha Dickinson Bianchi. Boston: Little, Brown, 1914.

———. *Unpublished Poems of Emily Dickinson.* Ed. Martha Dickinson Bianchi and Alfred Leete Hampson. Boston: Little, Brown, 1935.

REFERENCE WORKS

Buckingham, Willis J., ed. *Emily Dickinson: An Annotated Bibliography: Writings, Scholarship, Criticism, and Ana 1850–1968.* Bloomington: Indiana University Press, 1970.

———. *Emily Dickinson's Reception in the 1890s: A Documentary History.* Pittsburgh: University of Pittsburgh Press, 1989.

Capps, Jack L. *Emily Dickinson's Reading 1836–1886.* Cambridge: Harvard University Press, 1966.

Dandurand, Karen. *Dickinson Scholarship: An Annotated Bibliography 1969–1985.* New York: Garland, 1988.

Duchac, Joseph. *The Poems of Emily Dickinson: An Annotated Guide to Commentary Published in English, 1890–1977.* Boston: G. K. Hall, 1979.

———. *The Poems of Emily Dickinson: An Annotated Guide to Commentary Published in English, 1978–1989*. New York: G.K. Hall, 1993.

Leyda, Jay. *The Years and Hours of Emily Dickinson*. 2 vols. New Haven: Yale University Press, 1960.

Longsworth, Polly. *The World of Emily Dickinson*. New York: Norton, 1990.

Lowenberg, Carlton. *Emily Dickinson's Textbooks*. Ed. Territa A. Lowenberg, Carla L. Brown. Lafayette, CA: N.p., 1986.

———. *Musicians Wrestle Everywhere: Emily Dickinson and Music*. Berkeley, CA: Fallen Leaf Press, 1992.

Myerson, Joel. *Emily Dickinson: A Descriptive Bibliography*. Pittsburgh: University of Pittsburgh Press, 1984.

Rosenbaum, S. P., ed. *A Concordance to the Poems of Emily Dickinson*. Ithaca, NY: Cornell University Press, 1964.

BIOGRAPHIES

Cody, John. *After Great Pain: The Inner Life of Emily Dickinson*. Cambridge: Harvard University Press, Belknap Press, 1971.

Johnson, Thomas H. *Emily Dickinson: An Interpretive Biography*. Cambridge: Harvard University Press, Belknap Press, 1955.

Pollitt, Josephine. *Emily Dickinson: The Human Background of Her Poetry*. New York: Harper & Brothers, 1930.

Sewall, Richard B. *The Life of Emily Dickinson*. 2 vols. New York: Farrar, Straus, & Giroux, 1974.

———. *The Lyman Letters: New Light on Emily Dickinson and Her Family*. Amherst: University of Massachusetts Press, 1965.

Taggard, Genevieve. *The Life and Mind of Emily Dickinson*. New York: Knopf, 1930.

Ward, Theodora. *The Capsule of the Mind: Chapters in the Life of Emily Dickinson*. Cambridge: Harvard University Press Belknap Press, 1961.

Whicher, George Frisbie. *This Was a Poet: A Critical Biography of Emily Dickinson*. New York: Scribner's, 1938.

Wolff, Cynthia Griffin. *Emily Dickinson*. New York: Knopf, 1986.

CRITICAL BOOKS, ARTICLES, AND DISSERTATIONS

Ackmann, Martha. "Biographical Studies of Emily Dickinson." *The Emily Dickinson Handbook*. Eds. Roland Hagenbüchle, Cristanne Miller, and Gudrun Grabher. Amherst: University of Massachusetts Press, 1998.

———. " 'I'm Glad I Finally Surfaced': A Norcross Descendent Remembers Emily Dickinson." *Emily Dickinson Journal* 5, 2 (1996): 120–26.

———. "The Matrilineage of Emily Dickinson." Diss., University of Massachusetts, 1988.

Aiken, Conrad. "Emily Dickinson and Her Editors." *Yale Review* 18 (1929): 796–98.

Anderson, Charles R. *Emily Dickinson's Poetry: Stairway of Surprise*. New York: Holt, Rinehart, and Winston, 1960.

Anderson, Peggy. "The Bride of the White Election: A New Look at Biblical Influence on Emily Dickinson.'' *Nineteenth-Century Women Writers of the English-Speaking World*. Ed. Rhoda B. Nathan. New York: Greenwood, 1986: 1–11.

Baker, Dorothy Z. "*Ars Poetica/Ars Domestica*: The Self-Reflexive Poetry of Lydia Sigourney and Emily Dickinson." *Poetics in the Poem: Critical Essays on American Self-Reflexive Poetry*. Ed. Dorothy Z. Baker. New York: Peter Lang, 1997: 69–89.

Barker, Wendy. *Lunacy of Light: Emily Dickinson and the Experience of Metaphor*. Carbondale and Edwardsville: Southern Illinois University Press, 1987.

Barnes, Daniel R. "Telling It Slant: Emily Dickinson and the Proverb." *Genre* 12 (1979): 219–41.

Barnstone, Aliki. "Houses within Houses: Emily Dickinson and Mary Wilkins Freeman's 'A New England Nun.' " *Centennial Review* 28 (1984): 129–45.

Bauerlein, Mark. "The Meaning of Emily Dickinson's Social Withdrawal." *Emily Dickinson Journal* 5, 2 (1996): 72–77.

Benet, Laura. *The Mystery of Emily Dickinson*. New York: Dodd, Mead, 1974.

Benfey, Christopher E. G. *Emily Dickinson and the Problem of Others*. Amherst: University of Massachusetts Press, 1984.

———. "Emily Dickinson's Mount Holyoke." *Five Colleges, Five Histories*. Ed. Ronald Story. Amherst: Five Colleges and Historic Deerfield, 1992. 29–48.

Bennett, Paula. "Critical Clitoridectomy: Female Sexual Imagery and Feminist Psychoanalytic Theory." *Signs: Journal of Women in Culture and Society* 18 (1993): 235–59.

———. *Emily Dickinson: Woman Poet*. Iowa City: University of Iowa Press, 1990.

———. *My Life a Loaded Gun: Female Creativity and Feminist Poetics*. Boston: Beacon Press, 1986.

———. "The Pea That Duty Locks: Lesbian and Feminist-Heterosexual Readings of Dickinson's Poetry." *Lesbian Texts and Contexts: Radical Revisions*. Ed. Karla Jay and Joanne Glasgow. New York: New York University Press, 1990. 104–25.

Benvenuto, Richard. "Words within Words: Dickinson's Use of the Dictionary." *ESQ: A Journal of the American Renaissance* 29 (1983): 46–55.

Bernhard, Mary Elizabeth Kromer. "Portrait of a Family: Emily Dickinson's Norcross Connection." *New England Quarterly* 60 (1987): 363–81.

Bingham, Millicent Todd. *Ancestors' Brocades: The Literary Debut of Emily Dickinson*. New York: Harper & Brothers, 1945.

Bishop, Nadean. "Queen of Calvary: Spirituality in Emily Dickinson." *University of Dayton Review* 19 (1987–1988): 49–60.

Blackmur, R. P. "Emily Dickinson's Notation." *Outsider at the Heart of Things: Essays by R. P. Blackmur*. Ed. James T. Jones. 1956. Urbana: University of Illinois Press, 1989. 178–88.

———. "Emily Dickinson: Notes on Prejudice and Fact." *The Recognition of Emily Dickinson: Selected Criticism since 1890*. Eds. Caesar R. Blake and Carlton F. Wells. 1937. Ann Arbor: University of Michigan Press; Toronto: Ambassador, 1964: 201–23.

Blake, Caesar R., and Carlton F. Wells, eds. *The Recognition of Emily Dickinson: Selected Criticism since 1890*. Ann Arbor: University of Michigan Press; Toronto: Ambassador, 1964.

Bloom, Harold, ed. *Emily Dickinson: Modern Critical Views*. New York: Chelsea House, 1985.

Bogus, S. Diane. "Not So Disparate: An Investigation of the Influence of Elizabeth Barrett Browning on the Work of Emily Dickinson." *Dickinson Studies* 49, 1 (1984): 38–46.

Buckingham, Willis J. "Emily Dickinson's Dictionary." *Harvard Library Bulletin* 25 (1977): 489–92.

———. "Emily Dickinson's 'Lone Orthography.' " *Papers of the Bibliographical Society of America* 75 (1981): 419–35.

———. "Poetry Readers and Reading in the 1890s: Emily Dickinson's First Reception." *Readers in History: Nineteenth-Century American Literature and the Context of Response.* Ed. James L. Machor. Baltimore: Johns Hopkins University Press, 1993. 164–79.

Budick, E. Miller. *Emily Dickinson and the Life of Language: A Study in Symbolic Poetics.* Baton Rouge: Louisiana State University Press, 1985.

Buell, Janet W. " 'A Slow Solace': Emily Dickinson and Consolation." *New England Quarterly* 62 (1989): 323–45.

Burbick, Joan. "Emily Dickinson and the Economics of Desire." *American Literature* 58 (1986): 361–78.

Burke, Sally. "A Religion of Poetry: The Prayer Poems of Emily Dickinson." *Emily Dickinson Bulletin* 33, 1 (1978): 17–25.

Bzowski, Frances. " 'Half Child—Half Heroine': Emily Dickinson's Use of Traditional Female Archetypes." *ESQ: A Journal of the American Renaissance* 29 (1983): 154–69.

Cady, Edwin H., and Louis J. Budd. *On Dickinson: The Best from* American Literature. Durham, NC: Duke University Press, 1990.

Cameron, Sharon. *Choosing Not Choosing: Dickinson's Fascicles.* Chicago: University of Chicago Press, 1992.

———. " 'A Loaded Gun': Dickinson and the Dialectic of Rage." *PMLA* 93 (1978): 423–37.

———. *Lyric Time: Dickinson and the Limits of Genre.* Baltimore: Johns Hopkins University Press, 1979.

Carter, Steve. "Emily Dickinson and Mysticism." *ESQ: A Journal of the American Renaissance* 24 (1978): 83–95.

Cary, Cecile W. "*The Mill on the Floss* as an Influence on Emily Dickinson." *Dickinson Studies* 36, 2 (1979): 26–39.

Catel, Jean. "Emily Dickinson: Essai d'analyse psychologique." *Revue Anglo-Américaine* 2 (1925): 394–405.

Chaichit, Chanthana. "Emily Dickinson Abroad: The Paradox of Seclusion." *The Emily Dickinson Journal* 5, 2 (1996): 162–68.

Chase, Richard. *Emily Dickinson.* New York: William Sloane Associates, 1951.

Crosthwaite, Jane. "The Way to Read a Letter: Emily Dickinson's Variation on a Theme by Charlotte Brontë." *American Transcendental Quarterly* 42 (1979): 159–65.

Crumbley, Paul. *Inflections of the Pen: Dash and Voice in Emily Dickinson.* Lexington: University Press of Kentucky, 1997.

Dandurand, Karen. "Another Dickinson Poem Published in Her Lifetime." *American Literature* 54 (1982): 434–37.

———. "Dickinson and the Public." *Dickinson and Audience.* Ed. Martin Orzeck and Robert Weisbuch. Ann Arbor: University of Michigan Press, 1996. 255–77.

———. "New Dickinson Civil War Publications." *American Literature* 56 (1984): 17–27.

———. "Why Dickinson Did Not Publish." Diss., University of Massachusetts, 1984.

Danly, Susan. *Language as Object: Emily Dickinson and Contemporary Art*. Amherst: University of Massachusetts Press, 1997.

Decker, William Merrill. " 'A Letter Always Seemed to Me like Immortality': The Correspondence of Emily Dickinson." *ESQ: A Journal of the American Renaissance* 39 (1993): 77–104.

Delphy, Francoise. *Emily Dickinson*. Paris: Didier, 1984.

Dickie, Margaret. "Dickinson in Context." *American Literary History* 7 (1995): 320–33.

———. *Lyric Contingencies: Emily Dickinson and Wallace Stevens*. Philadelphia: University of Pennsylvania Press, 1991.

Diehl, Joanne Feit. *Dickinson and the Romantic Imagination*. Princeton: Princeton University Press, 1981.

———. "Emerson, Dickinson, and the Abyss." *English Literary History* 44 (1977): 683–98.

———. " 'Ransom in a Voice': Language as Defense in Dickinson's Poetry." *Feminist Critics Read Emily Dickinson*. Ed. Suzanne Juhasz. Bloomington: Indiana University Press, 1983. 156–75.

Dobson, Joanne. *Dickinson and the Strategies of Reticence: The Woman Writer in Nineteenth-Century America*. Bloomington: Indiana University Press, 1989.

———. " 'Oh, Susie, it is dangerous': Emily Dickinson and the Archetype of the Masculine." *Feminist Critics Read Emily Dickinson*. Ed. Suzanne Juhasz. Bloomington: Indiana University Press, 1983: 80–98.

Dobson, Joanne, Lillian Faderman, and Ellin Ringler-Henderson. "Discussions of 'My Life had stood—a Loaded Gun." *Women's Studies* 16, special issue (1989): 117–48.

Donohue, Gail. "Lyric Voice: 'I cannot live with You—.' " *Dickinson Studies* 46, bonus issue (1983): 3–7.

Doreski, William. " 'An Exchange of Territory': Dickinson's Fascicle 27." *ESQ: A Journal of the American Renaissance* 32 (1986): 55–67.

Doriani, Beth Maclay. *Emily Dickinson, Daughter of Prophecy*. Amherst: University of Massachusetts Press, 1996.

Eberwein, Jane Donahue. "Amherst's Exotic Pulpit: A Possible Dickinson Contribution?" *Dickinson Studies* 65, 1 (1988): 37–42.

———. *Dickinson: Strategies of Limitation*. Amherst: University of Massachusetts Press, 1985.

———. "Dickinson's Local, Global, and Cosmic Perspectives." *The Emily Dickinson Handbook*. Ed. Roland Hagenbüchle, Cristanne Miller, and Gudrun Grabher. Amherst: University of Massachusetts Press, 1998.

———. "Doing Without: Dickinson as Yankee Woman Poet." *Critical Essays on Emily Dickinson*. Ed. Paul J. Ferlazzo. Boston: G. K. Hall, 1984. 205–23.

———. "Emily Dickinson and the Calvinist Sacramental Tradition." *Emily Dickinson: A Collection of Critical Essays*. Ed. Judith Farr. 1987. Upper Saddle River, NJ: Prentice-Hall, 1996. 89–104.

———. " 'Graphicer for Grace': Emily Dickinson's Calvinist Language." *Studies in Puritan American Spirituality* 1 (1990): 170–201.

———. "Immortality and the Shape of a Poet's Career." *University of Dayton Review* 19, 1 (1987–1988): 5–17.

———. " 'Siren Alps': The Lure of Europe for American Writers." *Emily Dickinson Journal* 5, 2 (1996): 176–82.

Eby, Cecil D. " 'I Taste a Liquor Never Brewed': A Variant Reading." *American Literature* 36 (1965): 516–18.

England, Martha Winburn. "Emily Dickinson and Isaac Watts: Puritan Hymnodists." *Critical Essays on Emily Dickinson*. Ed. Paul J. Ferlazzo. 1965. Boston: G. K. Hall, 1984. 123–31.

Erkkila, Betsy. "Dickinson and Rich: Toward a Theory of Female Poetic Influence." *American Literature* 56 (1984): 541–59.

———. "Emily Dickinson and Class." *American Literary History* 4 (1992): 1–27.

———. "Emily Dickinson on Her Own Terms." *The Wilson Quarterly* 9 (1985): 98–109.

———. *The Wicked Sisters: Women Poets, Literary History, and Discord*. New York: Oxford University Press, 1992.

Faderman, Lillian. "Emily Dickinson's Letters to Sue Gilbert." *Massachusetts Review of Literature, the Arts, and Public Affairs* 18 (1977): 197–225.

Fagundo Guerra, Ana María. "The Influence of Emily Dickinson on Juan Ramón Jiménez' Poetry." Diss., University of Washington, 1967.

Farr, Judith. "Dickinson and the Visual Arts." *The Emily Dickinson Handbook*. Ed. Roland Hagenbüchle, Cristanne Miller, and Gudrun Grabher. Amherst: University of Massachusetts Press, 1998.

———. *The Passion of Emily Dickinson*. Cambridge: Harvard University Press, 1992.

———, ed. *Emily Dickinson: A Collection of Critical Essays*. Upper Saddle River, NJ: Prentice-Hall, 1996.

Fasel, Ida. "Called Back: A Note on Emily Dickinson." *Iowa English Yearbook* 8 (1963): 73.

Fast, Robin Riley. " 'The One Thing Needful': Dickinson's Dilemma of Home and Heaven." *ESQ: A Journal of the American Renaissance* 27 (1981): 157–69.

Fast, Robin Riley, and Christine Mack Gordon, eds. *Approaches to Teaching Dickinson's Poetry*. New York: Modern Language Association, 1989.

Ferlazzo, Paul J. *Emily Dickinson*. Twayne U.S. Authors Series. Indianapolis: Bobbs-Merrill, 1976.

———. "Emily Dickinson." *The Transcendentalists: A Review of Research and Criticism*. Ed. Joel Myerson. New York: Modern Language Association, 1984. 320–27.

———, ed. *Critical Essays on Emily Dickinson*. Boston: G. K. Hall, 1984.

Finch, A. R. C. "Dickinson and Patriarchal Meter: A Theory of Metrical Codes." *PMLA* 102 (1987): 166–76.

Fontana, Ernest. "Dickinson's 'Go not too near a House of Rose.' " *Dickinson Studies* 68, 2 (1988): 26–29.

Ford, Thomas W. "Emily Dickinson and the Civil War." *University Review* 31 (1965): 199–203.

———. *Heaven Beguiles the Tired: Death in the Poetry of Emily Dickinson*. University: University of Alabama Press, 1966.

———. "Thoreau's Cosmic Mosquito and Dickinson's Terrestrial Fly." *New England Quarterly* 48 (1975): 487–504.

Foster, Thomas. "Homelessness at Home: Placing Emily Dickinson in (Women's) History." *Engendering Men: The Question of Male Feminist Criticism*. Ed. Joseph A. Boone and Michael Cadden. New York: Routledge, 1990. 239–53.

Franklin, Ralph W. "The Dickinson Packet 14—and 20, 10, and 26." *Papers of the Bibliographical Society of America* 73 (1979): 348–55.

———. *The Editing of Emily Dickinson: A Reconsideration*. Madison: University of Wisconsin Press, 1967.

———. "The Emily Dickinson Fascicles." *Studies in Bibliography* 36 (1983): 1–20.

———. "Emily Dickinson to Abiah Root: Ten Reconstructed Letters." *Emily Dickinson Journal* 4, 1 (1995): 1–43.

Freeman, Margaret H., Gudrun Grabher, and Roland Hogenbüchle, eds. " 'There's a certain Slant of light': Swedish, Finnish, Chinese, Japanese, Yiddish." *The Emily Dickinson Journal* 6, 2 (1997): 38–72.

Frye, Northrop. "Emily Dickinson." *Fables of Identity: Studies in Poetic Mythology*. New York: Harcourt, Brace, & World, 1963. 193–217.

Fulton, Alice. "Her Moment of Brocade: The Reconstruction of Emily Dickinson." *Parnassus: Poetry in Review* 15, 1 (1989): 9–44.

Furukawa, Takao. *The Poetics of Emily Dickinson*. Tokyo: Kenkyusha, 1992.

Garbowsky, Maryanne M. *The House without the Door: A Study of Emily Dickinson and the Illness of Agoraphobia*. London and Toronto: Associated University Press, 1989.

Gelpi, Albert J. *Emily Dickinson: The Mind of the Poet*. Cambridge: Harvard University Press, 1965.

Gerlach, John. "Reading Dickinson: Bolts, Hounds, the Variorum, and Fascicle 39." *Emily Dickinson Journal* 3, 2 (1994): 78–99.

Gilbert, Sandra M. "The Wayward Nun beneath the Hill: Emily Dickinson and the Mysteries of Womanhood." *Feminist Critics Read Emily Dickinson*. Ed. Suzanne Juhasz. Bloomington: Indiana University Press, 1983. 22–44.

Gilbert, Sandra, and Susan Gubar. *The Madwoman in the Attic: The Woman Writer and the Nineteenth-Century Literary Imagination*. New Haven: Yale University Press, 1979.

Grabher, Gudrun R. "Dickinson's Lyrical Self." *The Emily Dickinson Handbook*. Eds. Roland Hagenbüchle, Cristanne Miller, and Gudrun Grabher. Amherst: University of Massachusetts Press, 1998.

———. *Emily Dickinson: Das transzendentale Ich*. Heidelberg: Carl Winter Universitätsverlag, 1981.

Greenwald, Elissa. "Dickinson among the Realists." *Approaches to Teaching Dickinson's Poetry*. Ed. Robin Riley Fast and Christine Mack Gordon. New York: MLA, 1989. 164–69.

Griffith, Clark. *The Long Shadow: Emily Dickinson's Tragic Poetry*. Princeton: Princeton University Press, 1964.

Gross, Robert A. "Lonesome in Eden: Dickinson, Thoreau, and the Problem of Community in Nineteenth-Century New England." *Canadian Review of American Studies* 14 (1983): 1–17.

Guerra, Jonnie. "Dickinson Adaptations in the Arts and the Theatre." *The Emily Dickinson Handbook*. Ed. Roland Hagenbüchle, Cristanne Miller, and Gudrun Grabher. Amherst: University of Massachusetts Press, 1997.

Guthrie, James R. " 'Before I got my eye put out': Dickinson's Illness and Its Effects on Her Poetry." *Dickinson Studies* 42, 1 (1982): 16–21.

———. "Law, Property and Provincialism in Dickinson's Poems and Letters to Judge Otis Phillips Lord." *Emily Dickinson Journal* 5, 1 (1996): 27–44.

————. "Measuring the Sun: Emily Dickinson's Interpretation of Her Optical Illness." *ESQ: A Journal of the American Renaissance* 41 (1995): 239–55.

Hagenbüchle, Roland. *Emily Dickinson: Wagnis der Selbstbegegnung*. Tübingen: Stauffenberg, 1988.

————. "Precision and Indeterminacy in the Poetry of Emily Dickinson." *ESQ: A Journal of the American Renaissance* 20 (1974): 33–56.

————. "Sign and Process: The Concept of Language in Emerson and Dickinson." *ESQ: A Journal of the American Renaissance* 25 (1979): 137–55.

Hagenbüchle, Roland, Cristanne Miller, and Gudrun Grabher. *The Emily Dickinson Handbook*. Amherst: University of Massachusetts Press, 1998.

Hallen, Cynthia L., and Laura M. Harvey. "Translation and the Emily Dickinson Lexicon." *Emily Dickinson Journal* 2, 2 (1993): 130–46.

Harris, Susan. "Illuminating the Eclipse: Dickinson's 'Representative' and the Marriage Narrative." *Emily Dickinson Journal* 4, 2 (1995): 44–61.

Hart, Ellen Louise. "The Elizabeth Whitney Putnam Manuscripts and New Strategies for Editing Emily Dickinson's Letters." *Emily Dickinson Journal* 4, 1 (1995): 44–74.

————. "The Encoding of Homoerotic Desire: Emily Dickinson's Letters and Poems to Susan Dickinson, 1850–1886." *Tulsa Studies in Women's Literature* 9 (1990): 251–72.

Hecht, Anthony. "The Riddles of Emily Dickinson." *Emily Dickinson: A Collection of Critical Essays*. Ed. Judith Farr. 1986. Upper Saddle River, NJ: Prentice-Hall, 1996. 149–62.

Heginbotham, Eleanor E. "Dwelling in Possibilities: The Fascicles of Emily Dickinson." Diss., University of Maryland, 1992.

Heiskanen-Mäkelä, Sirkka. "Emily Dickinson in Finland." *Higginson Journal of Poetry* 8 (1974): 18–19.

————. *In Quest of Truth: Observations on the Development of Emily Dickinson's Poetic Dialectic*. Jyväskylä: Jyväskylän Yliopisto, 1970.

Henneberg, Sylvia. "Neither Lesbian nor Straight: Multiple *Eroticisms* in Emily Dickinson's Love Poetry." *Emily Dickinson Journal* 4, 2 (1995): 1–19.

Higgins, David. *Portrait of Emily Dickinson: The Poet and Her Prose*. New Brunswick, NJ: Rutgers University Press, 1967.

Hirschhorn, Norbert, and Polly Longsworth. " 'Medicine Posthumous': A New Look at Emily Dickinson's Medical Conditions." *New England Quarterly* 69 (1996): 299–316.

Hogue, Cynthia. *Scheming Women: Poetry, Privilege, and the Politics of Subjectivity*. Albany: State University of New York Press, 1995.

Holland, Jeanne. "Scraps, Stamps, and Cutouts: Emily Dickinson's Domestic Technologies of Publication." *Cultural Artifacts and the Production of Meaning: The Page, the Image, and the Body*. Ed. Margaret J. M. Ezell and Katherine O'Brien O'Keeffe. Ann Arbor: University of Michigan Press, 1994. 139–81.

Homans, Margaret. " 'Syllables of Velvet': Dickinson, Rossetti, and the Rhetoric of Sexuality." *Feminist Studies* 11 (1985): 569–93.

————. *Women Writers and Poetic Identity: Dorothy Wordsworth, Emily Brontë, and Emily Dickinson*. Princeton: Princeton University Press, 1980.

Horan, Elizabeth. "Emily Dickinson, Gabriela Mistral, y sú publico." Santiago, Chile, *Academia* 13–14 (1986): 189–204.

———. "Mabel Loomis Todd, Martha Dickinson Bianchi, and the Spoils of the Dickinson Legacy." *A Living of Words: American Women in Print Culture*. Ed. Susan Albertine. Knoxville: University of Tennessee Press, 1995: 65–93.

———. "To Market: The Dickinson Copyright Wars." *Emily Dickinson Journal* 5, 1 (1996): 88–120.

Howard, William. "Emily Dickinson's Poetic Vocabulary." *PMLA* 72 (1957): 225–48.

Howe, Susan. *My Emily Dickinson*. Berkeley, CA: North Atlantic Books, 1985.

———. "Part Two: Childe Emily to the Dark Tower Came." *Code of Signals: Recent Writings in Poetics*. Ed. Michael Palmer. Berkeley, CA: North Atlantic, 1983. 196–218.

———. "These Flames and Generosities of the Heart: Emily Dickinson and the Illogic of Sumptuary Values." *The Birth-Mark: Unsettling the Wilderness in American Literary History*. Hanover, NH: University Press of New England, 1993. 2–26.

Howells, William Dean. "The Poems of Emily Dickinson." *Critical Essays on Emily Dickinson*. Ed. Paul J. Ferlazzo. 1891. Boston: G. K. Hall, 1984: 31–36.

Hughes, Gertrude Reiff. "Subverting the Cult of Domesticity: Emily Dickinson's Critique of Women's Work." *Legacy: A Journal of American Women Writers* 3, 1 (1986): 17–28.

Jenkins, MacGregor. *Emily Dickinson: Friend and Neighbor*. Boston: Little, Brown, 1930.

Johnson, Greg. *Emily Dickinson: Perception and the Poet's Quest*. Tuscaloosa: University of Alabama Press, 1985.

Johnson, Thomas H. "Establishing a Text: The Emily Dickinson Papers." *Studies in Bibliography* 5 (1952–1953): 21–32.

———. "The Poet and the Muse: Poetry as Art." *Emily Dickinson: A Collection of Critical Essays*. Ed. Richard B. Sewall. 1955. Englewood Cliffs, NJ: Prentice-Hall, 1963. 70–77.

Jones, Rowena Revis. "Edwards, Dickinson, and the Sacramentality of Nature." *Studies in Puritan American Spirituality* 1 (1990): 225–53.

———. "The Preparation of a Poet: Puritan Directions in Emily Dickinson's Education." *Studies in the American Renaissance* (1982): 285–324.

———. "A 'Royal Seal': Dickinson's Rite of Baptism." *Religion and Literature* 18 (1986): 29–51.

———. "A Taste for 'Poison': Dickinson's Departure from Orthodoxy." *Emily Dickinson Journal* 2, 1 (1993): 47–64.

Juhasz, Suzanne. "Adventures in the World of the Symbolic: Emily Dickinson and Metaphor." *Feminist Measures: Soundings in Poetry and Theory*. Ed. Lynn Keller and Cristanne Miller. Ann Arbor: University of Michigan Press, 1994. 139–62.

———. "The Big Tease." *Comic Power in Emily Dickinson*. Austin: University of Texas Press, 1993. 26–62.

———. "Reading Emily Dickinson's Letters." *ESQ: A Journal of the American Renaissance* 30 (1984): 170–92.

———. "Renunciation Transformed, the Dickinson Heritage: Emily Dickinson and Margaret Atwood." *Women's Studies: An Interdisciplinary Journal* 12 (1986): 251–70.

———. *The Undiscovered Continent: Emily Dickinson and the Space of the Mind*. Bloomington: Indiana University Press, 1983.

————, ed. *Feminist Critics Read Emily Dickinson*. Bloomington: Indiana University Press, 1983.

Juhasz, Suzanne, Cristanne Miller, and Martha Nell Smith. *Comic Power in Emily Dickinson*. Austin: University of Texas Press, 1993.

Keller, Karl. "Notes on Sleeping with Emily Dickinson." *Feminist Critics Read Emily Dickinson*. Ed. Suzanne Juhasz. Bloomington: Indiana University Press, 1983. 67–79.

————. *The Only Kangaroo among the Beauty: Emily Dickinson and America*. Baltimore: Johns Hopkins University Press, 1979.

Kemp, Carolyn. " 'No' is the Wildest Word: Emily Dickinson and the Poetics of Refusal." M.A. thesis, New College of California, 1990.

Khan, Salamatullah. "Emily Dickinson on Death." *Indian Responses to American Literature*. Ed. C. D. Narasimhaiah. Manipal, India: Manipal Power Press, 1967.

Kher, Inder Nath. *The Landscape of Absence: Emily Dickinson's Poetry*. New Haven: Yale University Press, 1974.

Kirkby, Joan. "Dickinson Reading." *Emily Dickinson Journal* 5, 2 (1996): 247–54.

————. *Emily Dickinson*. New York: St. Martin's, 1991.

Kjær, Niels. "Collecting Dickinson: The Emily Dickinson Collection, Denmark." *Emily Dickinson International Society Bulletin* 6, 2 (1994): 3.

Knapp, Bettina L. *Emily Dickinson*. New York: Continuum, 1989.

Laverty, Carroll D. "Structural Patterns in Emily Dickinson's Poetry." *Emerson Society Quarterly* 44, 3 (1966): 12–17.

Lease, Benjamin. *Emily Dickinson's Readings of Men and Books: Sacred Soundings*. New York: St. Martin's, 1990.

Leonard, Douglas Novich. "Emily Dickinson's Religion: An 'Ablative Estate.' " *Christian Scholar's Review* 13 (1984): 333–48.

Leonard, Garry M. "The Necessary Strategy of Renunciation: The Triumph of Emily Dickinson and the Fall of Sylvia Plath." *University of Dayton Review* 19, 1 (1987–1988): 79–90.

Leyda, Jay. "Miss Emily's Maggie." *New World Writing*. Third Mentor Selection. New York: New American Library, 1953. 255–67.

Lilliedahl, Ann. *Emily Dickinson in Europe: Her Literary Reputation in Selected Countries*. Washington, DC: University Press of America, 1981.

Lindberg-Seyersted, Brita. *Emily Dickinson's Punctuation*. Oslo: American Institute, University of Oslo Press, 1976.

————. "The Theme of Death in Emily Dickinson's Poetry." *Studia Neophilogica: A Journal of Germanic and Romance Languages and Literature* 34 (1962): 269–81.

————. *The Voice of the Poet: Aspects of Style in the Poetry of Emily Dickinson*. Cambridge: Harvard University Press, 1968.

Loeffelholz, Mary. "The Compound Frame: Scenes of Emily Dickinson's Reading." Diss., Yale University, 1986.

————. *Dickinson and the Boundaries of Feminist Theory*. Urbana: University of Illinois Press, 1991.

————. "Etruscan Invitations: Dickinson and the Anxiety of the Aesthetic in Feminist Criticism." *Emily Dickinson Journal* 5, 1 (1996): 1–26.

Loeschke, Maravene. "Challenges of Portraying Emily Dickinson in William Luce's Play *The Belle of Amherst*." *Emily Dickinson Journal* 2, 2 (1993): 124–29.

Lombardo, Daniel. "What the Dickinsons Read." *Tales of Amherst*. Amherst, MA: Jones Library, 1986.

Longsworth, Polly. *Austin and Mabel: The Amherst Affair and Love Letters of Austin Dickinson and Mabel Loomis Todd*. New York: Farrar, Straus, & Giroux, 1983.

———. " 'Was Mr. Dudley Dear?': Emily Dickinson and John Langdon Dudley." *Massachusetts Review* 26, 3 (1985): 360–72.

Loving, Jerome. *Emily Dickinson: The Poet on the Second Story*. Cambridge: Cambridge University Press, 1986.

Lubbers, Klaus. *Emily Dickinson: The Critical Revolution*. Ann Arbor: University of Michigan Press, 1968.

Luscher, Robert M. "An Emersonian Context of Dickinson's 'The Soul selects her own Society.' " *ESQ: A Journal of the American Renaissance* 30 (1984): 111–16.

Martin, Wendy. *An American Triptych: Anne Bradstreet, Emily Dickinson, Adrienne Rich*. Chapel Hill: University of North Carolina Press, 1984.

———. "Emily Dickinson." *Columbia Literary History of the United States*. Ed. Emory Elliott. New York: Columbia University Press, 1988. 609–26.

Maurois, Andre, "Emily Dickinson, Poétesse et Recluse." *Revue de Paris* 60 (Nov. 1954): 1–13.

McGann, Jerome. "Emily Dickinson's Visible Language." *Emily Dickinson Journal* 2, 2 (1993): 40–57.

McLean, Sydney R. "Emily Dickinson at Mount Holyoke." *New England Quarterly* 7 (1934): 25–42.

McNeil, Helen. *Emily Dickinson*. London and New York: Virago-Pantheon, 1986.

Messmer, Marietta, "Dickinson's Critical Reception." *The Emily Dickinson Handbook*. Eds. Roland Hagenbüchle, Cristanne Miller, and Gudrun Grabher. Amherst: University of Massachusetts Press, 1998.

Miller, Christanne. "Dickinson's Experiments in Language." *The Emily Dickinson Handbook*. Ed. Roland Hagenbüchle, Cristanne Miller, and Gudrun Grabher. Amherst: University of Massachusetts Press, 1998.

———. "Dickinson's Language: Interpreting Truth Told Slant." *Approaches to Teaching Dickinson's Poetry*. Ed. Robin Riley Fast and Christine Mack Gordon. New York: Modern Language Association, 1989. 78–84.

———. *Emily Dickinson: A Poet's Grammar*. Cambridge: Harvard University Press, 1987.

———. "The Humor of Excess." *Comic Power in Emily Dickinson*. Austin: University of Texas Press, 1993. 103–40.

———. " 'A Letter is a Joy of Earth': Dickinson's Communication with the World." *Legacy: A Journal of American Women Writers* 1 (1986): 29–39.

———. "Terms and Golden Words: Alternatives of Control in Dickinson's Poetry." *ESQ: A Journal of the American Renaissance* 28 (1982): 48–62.

Miller, Ruth. *The Poetry of Emily Dickinson*. Middletown, CT: Wesleyan University Press, 1968.

Mock, Michele. "Partnership in Possibility: The Dialogics of his efficient daughter Lavinia and his poetess daughter Emily." *Emily Dickinson Journal* 6, 1 (1997): 68–88.

Monteiro, George. "Brazil's Emily Dickinson: An Annotated Check List of Translations, Criticism, and Reviews." *Emily Dickinson Bulletin* 18 (1971): 73–78.

———. "Dickinson's Select Society." *Dickinson Studies* 39, 1 (1981): 41–43.

————. "Dickinson's 'There's a certain Slant of light.' " *The Explicator* 31, 2 (Oct. 1972): item 13.

————. "Jorge de Sena's Dickinson." *Luso Brazilian Review* 19 (1982): 23–29.

Morey, Frederick L. "Two Major Sources: Emblems and *Aurora Leigh*." *Dickinson Studies* 45, 1 (1983): 43–45.

Morris, Adalaide K. "Two Sisters Have I: Emily Dickinson's Vinnie and Susan." *Massachusetts Review* 22 (1981): 323–32.

Morris, Timothy. "The Development of Dickinson's Style." *American Literature* 60 (1988): 26–41.

Morse, Jonathan. "History in the Text." *Texas Studies in Literature and Language* 24 (1982): 329–46.

————. "Memory, Desire, and the Need for Biography: The Case of Emily Dickinson." *The Georgia Review* 35 (1981): 259–72.

Mossberg, Barbara Antonina Clarke. *Emily Dickinson: When a Writer Is a Daughter.* Bloomington: Indiana University Press, 1982.

Mudge, Jean McClure. *Emily Dickinson and the Image of Home.* Amherst: University of Massachusetts Press, 1975.

————. "Emily Dickinson and 'Sister Sue.' " *Prairie Schooner* 52 (1978): 90–108.

Mulder, William. "Seeing 'New Englandly': Planes of Perception in Emily Dickinson and Robert Frost." *New England Quarterly* 52 (1979): 550–59.

Mulqueen, James E. "Is Emerson's Work Central to the Poetry of Emily Dickinson?" *Emily Dickinson Bulletin* 24, 2 (1973): 211–20.

Murray, Aífe. "Kitchen Table Poetics: Maid Margaret Maher and Her Poet Emily Dickinson." *Emily Dickinson Journal* 5, 2 (1996): 285–96.

Nekola, Charlotte. " 'By Birth a Bachelor': Dickinson and the Idea of Womanhood in the American Nineteenth Century." *Approaches to Teaching Dickinson's Poetry.* Ed. Robin Riley Fast and Christine Mack Gordon. New York: Modern Language Association, 1989. 148–54.

New, Elisa. "Difficult Writing, Difficult God: Emily Dickinson's Poems beyond Circumference." *Religion and Literature* 18, 3 (1986): 1–27.

Nickell, Joe. "A Likeness of Emily?: The Investigation of a Questioned Photograph." *Emily Dickinson International Society Bulletin* 5, 2 (1993): 1+.

Oberhaus, Dorothy Huff. "Dickinson as Comic Poet." *Approaches to Teaching Dickinson's Poetry.* Ed. Robin Riley Fast and Christine Mack Gordon. New York: MLA, 1989. 118–23.

————. *Emily Dickinson's Fascicles: Method and Meaning.* University Park: Pennsylvania State University Press, 1995.

————. " 'Engine against th' Almightie': Emily Dickinson and Prayer." *ESQ: A Journal of the American Renaissance* 32 (1986): 153–72.

————. "In Defense of Sue." *Dickinson Studies* 48, bonus issue (1983): 1–25.

————. "A Reading of Emily Dickinson." *"Like Season'd Timber": New Essays on George Herbert.* Ed. Edmund Miller and Robert DiYanni. New York: Peter Lang, 1987. 345–68.

————. " 'Tender Pioneer': Emily Dickinson's Poems on the Life of Christ." *American Literature* 59 (1987): 341–58.

Oliver, Virginia H. *Apocalypse of Green: A Study of Emily Dickinson's Eschatology.* New York: Peter Lang, 1989.

Omoto, Tsuyoshi. *Emily Dickinson in Japan: A Bibliography, 1927–85.* Tokyo: Senshu University Press, 1986.

Orzeck, Martin, and Robert Weisbuch, eds. *Dickinson and Audience*. Ann Arbor: University of Michigan Press, 1996.

Paglia, Camille. *Sexual Personae: Art and Decadence from Nefertiti to Emily Dickinson*. New Haven: Yale University Press, 1990.

Patterson, Rebecca. "Emily Dickinson's 'Double' Tim: Masculine Identification." *Critical Essays on Emily Dickinson*. Ed. Paul J. Ferlazzo. 1971. Boston: G. K. Hall, 1984. 167–75.

———. *Emily Dickinson's Imagery*. Ed. Margaret H. Freeman. Amherst: University of Massachusetts Press, 1979.

———. *The Riddle of Emily Dickinson*. Boston: Houghton Mifflin, 1951.

Peeck-O'Toole, Maureen. "Lyric and Gender." *Dutch Quarterly Review of Anglo-American Letters* 18 (1988): 319–29.

Peng, Temple. "Singing Along with Great Masters." *Beijing Review*. North American ed. (Apr. 1990): 36–37.

Petrino, Elizabeth A. " 'Feet so precious charged': Dickinson, Sigourney, and the Child Elegy." *Tulsa Studies in Women's Literature* 13 (1994): 317–38.

Philip, Jim. "Valley News: Emily Dickinson at Home and Beyond." *Nineteenth-Century American Poetry*. Ed. A. Robert Lee. Totowa, NJ: Barnes and Noble, 1985. 61–79.

Phillips, Elizabeth. *Emily Dickinson: Personae and Performance*. University Park: Pennsylvania State University Press, 1988.

Pollak, Vivian R. "After Calvary: The Last Years of Emily Dickinson's 'Dearest Earthly Friend.' " *Dickinson Studies* 34, 1 (1978): 13–18.

———. *Dickinson: The Anxiety of Gender*. Ithaca, NY: Cornell University Press, 1984.

———. "Emily Dickinson's Valentines." *American Quarterly* 26 (1974): 60–78.

———, ed. *A Poet's Parents: The Courtship Letters of Emily Norcross and Edward Dickinson*. Chapel Hill: University of North Carolina Press, 1988.

Porter, David T. *The Art of Emily Dickinson's Early Poetry*. Cambridge: Harvard University Press, 1966.

———. *Dickinson: The Modern Idiom*. Cambridge: Harvard University Press, 1981.

Ransom, John Crowe. "Emily Dickinson: A Poet Restored." *Emily Dickinson: A Collection of Critical Essays*. Ed. Richard B. Sewall. 1956. Englewood Cliffs, NJ: Prentice-Hall, 1963. 88–100.

Rao, C. Vimala. "The Poetry of Emily Dickinson." *Indian Response to American Literature*. Ed. C. D. Narasimhaiah. Manipal, India: Manipal Power Press, 1967.

Rich, Adrienne. "Vesuvius at Home: The Power of Emily Dickinson." *On Lies, Secrets, and Silence: Selected Prose 1966–1978*. 1976. New York: Norton, 1979. 157–83.

Rosenthal, M. L., and Sally M. Gall. "Emily Dickinson's Fascicles." *The Modern Poetic Sequence: The Genius of Modern Poetry*. New York: Oxford University Press, 1983. 45–73.

Sahal, N. "Emily Dickinson on Renown." *Banasthali Patrika* 4 (1968): 83–85.

St. Armand, Barton Levi. *Emily Dickinson and Her Culture: The Soul's Society*. Cambridge: Cambridge University Press, 1984.

———. "Emily Dickinson and the Occult: The Rosicrucian Connection." *Prairie Schooner* 51 (1977–1978): 345–57.

———. "Veiled Ladies: Dickinson, Bettine, and Transcendental Mediumship." *Studies in the American Renaissance* (1987): 1–51.

———. " 'Your Prodigal': Letters from Ned Dickinson, 1879–1885." *New England Quarterly* 61 (1988): 358–80.

Salska, Agnieszka. "Dickinson's Letters." *The Emily Dickinson Handbook*. Ed. Roland Hagenbüchle, Cristanne Miller, and Gudrun Grabher. Amherst: University of Massachusetts Press, 1998.

———. "Emily Dickinson's Letters: The Making of a Poetics." *Crossing Borders: American Literature and Other Artistic Media*. Ed. Jadwiga Maszewska. Warszawa: PWN, 1992.

———. *Walt Whitman and Emily Dickinson: Poetry of the Central Consciousness*. Philadelphia: University of Pennsylvania Press, 1985.

Sanchez-Eppler, Karen. *Touching Liberty: Abolition, Feminism, and the Politics of the Body*. Berkeley: University of California Press, 1993. Ch. 4.

Sands, Margaret. "Re-Reading the Poems: Editing Opportunities in Variant Versions." *Emily Dickinson Journal* 5, 2 (1996): 139–47.

Savinel, Christine. *Emily Dickinson et la grammaire du secret*. Lyon: Presses Universitaires de Lyon, 1993.

Schappes, Morris U. "Errors in Mrs. Bianchi's Edition of Emily Dickinson's *Letters*." *American Literature* 4 (1933): 369–84.

Scharnhorst, Gary. "A Glimpse of Dickinson at Work." *American Literature* 57 (1985): 483–85.

Scheurer, Erika. " 'Near, but remote': Emily Dickinson's Epistolary Voice." *Emily Dickinson Journal* 4, 1 (1995): 86–107.

Scholnick, Robert. " 'Don't Tell! They'd Advertise': Emily Dickinson in the *Round Table*." *Periodical Literature in Nineteenth-Century America*. Ed. Kenneth M. Price and Susan Belasco Smith. Charlottesville: University Press of Virginia, 1995. 166–82.

Sewall, Richard B. "Emily Dickinson's Books and Reading." *Emily Dickinson: A Collection of Critical Essays*. Ed. Judith Farr. 1974. Upper Saddle River, NJ: Prentice-Hall, 1996. 40–52.

———. "Science and the Poet: Emily Dickinson's Herbarium and 'The Clue Divine.' " *Harvard Library Bulletin*, n.s. 3, 1 (1992): 11–26.

———, ed. *Emily Dickinson: A Collection of Critical Essays*. Englewood Cliffs, NJ: Prentice-Hall, 1963.

Sewell, Maryann. "Rendezvous of Light." *Emily Dickinson International Society Bulletin* 6, 2 (1994): 10+.

Sherwood, William R. *Circumference and Circumstance: Stages in the Mind and Art of Emily Dickinson*. New York: Columbia University Press, 1968.

Shurr, William H. *The Marriage of Emily Dickinson: A Study of the Fascicles*. Lexington: University Press of Kentucky, 1983.

Siegfried, Regina. "Bibliographic Essay: Selected Criticism for Emily Dickinson's Religious Background." *Dickinson Studies* 52, 2 (1984): 32–53.

Simpson, Jeffrey E. "The Dependent Self: Emily Dickinson and Friendship." *Dickinson Studies* 45, 1 (1983): 35–42.

Small, Judy Jo. *Positive as Sound: Emily Dickinson's Rhyme*. Athens: University of Georgia Press, 1990.

Smith, Martha Nell. "Dickinson's Manuscripts." *The Emily Dickinson Handbook*. Eds. Roland Hagenbüchle, Cristanne Miller, and Gudrun Grabher. Amherst: University of Massachusetts Press, 1998.

———. "The Poet as Cartoonist." *Comic Power in Emily Dickinson*. Austin: University of Texas Press, 1993: 63–102.

———. *Rowing in Eden: Rereading Emily Dickinson*. Austin: University of Texas Press, 1992.

Smith, Robert McClure. *The Seductions of Emily Dickinson*. Tuscaloosa: University of Alabama Press, 1996.

Staub, Michael E. "White Moth and Ox: The Friendship of Emily Dickinson with Helen Hunt Jackson." *Dickinson Studies* 68, 2 (1988): 17–25.

Stephenson, William E. "Emily Dickinson and Watts's Songs for Children." *English Language Notes* 3 (1966): 278–81.

Stonum, Gary Lee. *The Dickinson Sublime*. Madison: University of Wisconsin Press, 1990.

Tate, Allen. "Emily Dickinson." *Collected Essays*. 1932. Denver: Alan Swallow, 1959. 197–213.

Thomas, Heather Kirk. "Emily Dickinson's 'Renunciation' and Anorexia Nervosa." *American Literature* 60 (1988): 205–25.

Tingley, Stephanie A. "The Contributions of Theodora Van Wagenen Ward." *Emily Dickinson International Society Bulletin* 8, 1 (1996): 2+.

———. " 'My Business is to Sing': Emily Dickinson's Letters to Elizabeth Holland." *Dickinson and Audience*. Ed. Martin Orzeck and Robert Weisbuch. Ann Arbor: University of Michigan Press, 1996. 181–99.

———. "Sandra Gilbert and Emily Dickinson." *Emily Dickinson International Society Bulletin* 6, 1 (1994): 1–3.

Todd, John Emerson. *Emily Dickinson's Use of the Persona*. The Hague: Mouton, 1973.

Uno, Hiroko. *Emily Dickinson Visits Boston*. Kyoto: Yamaguchi, 1990.

———. "Optical Instruments and 'Compound Vision' in Emily Dickinson's Poetry." *Eibungaku Kenkyu: Studies in English Literature* 64, 2 (1988): 227–43.

Waggoner, Hyatt H. "Emily Dickinson: The Transcendent Self." *Criticism* 7 (1965): 297–334.

Walker, Cheryl. *The Nightingale's Burden: Women Poets and American Culture before 1900*. Bloomington: Indiana University Press, 1982.

Walker, Nancy. "Emily Dickinson and the Self: Humor as Identity." *Tulsa Studies in Women's Literature* 2, 1 (1983): 57–68.

Walsh, John Evangelist. *The Hidden Life of Emily Dickinson*. New York: Simon and Schuster, 1971.

———. *This Brief Tragedy: Unraveling the Todd-Dickinson Affair*. New York: Grove Weidenfeld, 1991.

Wand, Martin, and Richard B. Sewall. " 'Eyes be Blind, Heart be Still': A New Perspective on Emily Dickinson's Eye Problem." *New England Quarterly* 52 (1979): 400–406.

Ward, R. Bruce. *The Gift of Screws: The Poetic Strategies of Emily Dickinson*. Troy, NY: Whitston, 1994.

Wardrop, Daneen. *Emily Dickinson's Gothic: Goblin with a Gauge*. Iowa City: University of Iowa Press, 1996.

Waugh, Dorothy. *Emily Dickinson Briefly*. New York: Vantage, 1990.

Weisbuch, Robert. *Emily Dickinson's Poetry*. Chicago: University of Chicago Press, 1975.

Wells, Anna Mary. "Emily Dickinson, 1849." *Dickinson Studies* 73 (1990): 23–30.

Werner, Marta L. *Emily Dickinson's Open Folios: Scenes of Reading, Surfaces of Writing*. Ann Arbor: University of Michigan Press, 1995.

Wider, Sarah. "Corresponding Worlds: The Art of Emily Dickinson's Letters." *Emily Dickinson Journal* 1, 1 (1992): 19–38.

Wilbur, Richard. "Sumptuous Destitution." *Emily Dickinson: A Collection of Critical Essays*. Ed. Judith Farr. 1960. Upper Saddle River, NJ: Prentice-Hall, 1996. 53–61.

Winther, Per. "On Editing Emily Dickinson." *American Studies in Scandinavia* 11 (1979): 25–40.

Wolff, Cynthia Griffin. "[Im]pertinent Constructions of Body and Self: Dickinson's Use of the Romantic Grotesque." *Emily Dickinson: A Collection of Critical Essays*. Ed. Judith Farr. 1993. Upper Saddle River, NJ: Prentice-Hall, 1996. 119–29.

Wolosky, Shira. *Emily Dickinson: A Voice of War*. New Haven: Yale University Press, 1984.

———. "Emily Dickinson's War Poetry: The Problem of Theodicy." *Massachusetts Review* 25 (1984): 22–41.

———. "Rhetoric or Not: Hymnal Tropes in Emily Dickinson and Isaac Watts." *New England Quarterly* 61 (1988): 214–32.

Yamakawa, Tamaaki, et al. *After a Hundred Years: Essays on Emily Dickinson*. Kyoto: Apollon-sha, 1988.

Zadravec, Katharine. "Emily Dickinson: A Capital Visitor." *Emily Dickinson: Letter to the World*. Washington, DC: Folger Shakespeare Library, 1986. 27–33.

Index of Poems Cited

Poems are listed in Thomas H. Johnson's numerical order (roughly chronological) for ease of identifying those cited within the text only by number. Complete listings of all 1,775 titles, alphabetically arranged, may be found at the back of Johnson's editions of *The Poems of Emily Dickinson* and *The Complete Poems of Emily Dickinson*. **Bold type** indicates a separate entry on this poem. For further insight into these and other Dickinson poems, readers should consult Joseph Duchac's *The Poems of Emily Dickinson: An Annotated Guide to Commentary Published in English*, the first volume of which covers criticism of particular poems from 1890–1977, while the second covers 1978–1989.

General Index

Page numbers in **bold type** refer to main entries in the encyclopedia.

Camprobí, Zenobria, 172
Canadian responses to Dickinson, **39–40**
capitalization, 4, **40–41**, 51, 93, 179, 225, 285
Capps, Jack, 17, 18–19, 135, 156, 180
Cardenal, Ernesto, 171
Carlo, **41**, 69, 192
Carlyle, Thomas, 36, **41–42**, 80, 252
Carman, Bliss, 39
Carmichael, Elizabeth, **42**, 195
Carter, Elliott, 202
cartoons, **42–43**, 67, 175, 235
Cary, Cecile, 99
Castellanos, Rosario, 172
Catel, Jean, 118, 119
Catholicism, **43–44**, 81, 245
Celan, Paul, 124
Chaichit, Chanthana, 11
Channing, William Ellery, 292
Chauls, Robert, 202
Chiba, Tsuyoshi, 165
Chicago, Judy, 299
Chickering, Joseph Knowlton, **44**, 75
Child, Lydia Maria, 11, 238, 251
child role, 3, **44**, 67, 107, 110, 149, 237, 262, 263, 300
China, responses to ED, 11
Christ. *See* Jesus
circle imagery, **45**, 101; "Circumference," 19, 24, **45–46**, 201, 288; cycles, 287–88; and poetics, 142–43, 187, 236, 279
Civil War, **46–47**, 132, 238, 251, 305–6, 308; effect on associates of ED, 56, 139–40, 185, 214, 220, 255, 271, 272, 301; and Ed poems, 49, 89, 245, 274
Clampitt, Amy, 230
Clark, James and Charles, **47–48**, 194, 302
Coates, Gloria, 202
Cody, John, 23, 155, 173, 239
Cole, Thomas, 274
Coleman, Eliza M., **48**, 89–90, 309
Coleman, Lyman and Maria, **48**, 117, 301
Coleman, Olivia, 48, 99
Coleridge, Samuel Taylor, 97, 252, 253
Collins, Martha, 229
colloquialism, **49–50**, 139, 153, 241; in

poems, 116, 283; as stylistic device, 86, 180, 238, 277–78, 300
Colton, Aaron Merrick, **50**, 90, 127, 150, 248
Colton, Sara Philips, **50**
Come Slowly, Eden, 235
Complete Poems of Emily Dickinson (1924), 16, **50–511**, 120, 133, 226
Complete Poems of Emily Dickinson (1960), **51–52**, 158, 167, 227
compression, 9, **52–53**, 152, 196, 197, 220, 232, 277, 279, 286, 310
Congregationalism, 7, **53–54**, 73, 114, 143, 213, 294
Connecticut Valley, **54–55**, 59; characteristics, 6, 43, 53, 90, 248, 305; institutions, 7–8, 8–9, 114, 199
consciousness, as theme, **55–56**, 56, 65, 101, 161, 243, 259, 292; in poems, 146, **155–56**, 262, 281, 283–84
Conway, Hugh (John Frederick Fargus), 38
Cooper, Abigail, **56**
Cooper, James Fenimore, 252
Copland, Aaron, 202
copyright issues, 20. *See also* Harvard University
Cornell, Joseph, 233, 299
Cowan, Perez Dickinson, **56**, 208
Crane, Hart, 21, 24, 228, 232
crisis: biographical, 2, 71, 137, 190, 264, 297, 301; and poetics, **56–57**; psychological or spiritual, 155–56, 189, 194–95
critical approaches to ED, 58–59. *See also* biographical scholarship; editing; feminism; historicism; linguistic and stylistic approaches; New Critical approaches; philosophical approaches; post-structuralist approaches; psychological approaches; reader-response approaches; religious approaches; rhetorical approaches
critical reception, 227, 227–28, 300; of the 1890s, 13, **57–58**, 148, 163, 224–26, 251, 294
Crosthwaite, Jane, 34
cultural studies, **58–59**

About the Contributors

Martha Ackmann teaches women's studies at Mount Holyoke College and is coeditor of *Legacy: A Journal of American Women Writers*. She is completing a study of Dickinson's Norcross relatives.

Midori Ando, who wrote many essays on Emily Dickinson for Japanese bulletins and magazines, is best known to English-language readers for her essays on "Eroticism in Emily Dickinson's Poetry" and "Emily Dickinson's Vision of 'Circumference' and Death from a Japanese Perspective."

Midori Kajino Asahina, Associate Professor at Keio University and an executive member of the Emily Dickinson Society of Japan, was a visiting scholar at the University of Massachusetts, Amherst, in 1990. She is particularly interested in Dickinson's nature writing.

Dorothy Z. Baker teaches nineteenth-century American literature at the University of Houston, where she is an Associate Professor. She recently edited *Poetics in the Poem: Critical Essays on American Self-Reflexive Poetry*, to which she contributed an essay on Lydia Sigourney and Emily Dickinson.

Kathryn Balteff, a graduate assistant at Oakland University, is an accomplished musician as well as a reader of poetry.

Christopher Benfey teaches at Mount Holyoke College. He is the author of *Emily Dickinson and the Problem of Others* (1984) as well as *The Double Life of Stephen Crane* (1992).

Paula Bennett, Associate Professor of English at Southern Illinois University, Carbondale, is an authority on women's poetry in the nineteenth century. She has written two books on Dickinson: *My Life a Loaded Gun: Female Creativity and Feminist Poetics* and *Emily Dickinson: Woman Poet*.

Mary Elizabeth Kromer Bernhard, independent scholar and Amherst resident, is the author of "Portrait of a Family: Emily Dickinson's Norcross Connection" as well as other articles and reviews.

Susan Biscella taught as a graduate assistant at Youngstown State University. She now devotes herself to family duties and writing in New Waterford, Ohio.

Terry Blackhawk, poet and teacher, studied Dickinson under the auspices of a National Endowment for the Humanities Teacher-Scholar award. She has taught in the Detroit public schools and at Madonna University in Michigan.

Robin E. Calland is a graduate student in English at the University of Colorado, Boulder.

Mary Carney is a doctoral candidate at the University of Georgia and specializes in American literature.

Monica Chiu, Assistant Professor at the University of Wisconsin–Eau Claire, specializes in Asian American literature and has complementary interests in feminist theory, women's studies, cultural studies, American literature from 1865 to 1900, and literature and medicine.

Alisa Clapp-Itnyre wrote her dissertation at the University of Illinois on music as cultural discourse in works of Victorian novelists. Author of articles on Gaskell and Anne Brontë, she teaches at De Pauw University.

Jeanne E. Clark is a Ph.D. candidate in English literature at Arizona State University, writing her dissertation on Dickinson's "Prison Poetics." Her *Ohio Blue Tips* won the University of Akron Poetry Prize in 1997.

Paul Crumbley, Assistant Professor of English at Utah State University, is the author of *Inflections of the Pen: Dash and Voice in Emily Dickinson*.

Karen Dandurand, Associate Professor of English at Indiana University of Pennsylvania, is a founding editor of *Legacy: A Journal of American Women Writers*. Her *Dickinson Scholarship: An Annotated Bibliography 1969–1985* and her articles on Dickinson are greatly appreciated by her fellow scholars.

Ellen Davis writes poetry and reviews. She lives in the Boston area with her husband, the artist Don Aquilino.

Mary DeJong, Associate Professor of English and women's studies at Pennsylvania State University–Altoona, has published widely on women's engagement in nineteenth-century American hymnody.

Deborah Dietrich is an Assistant Professor of English at California State University–Fullerton. She is working on a study of early American women's travel narratives.

Beth Maclay Doriani, Associate Professor of English at Northwestern College, studies the intersection of gender, religion, and language. Author of *Emily Dickinson, Daughter of Prophecy*, she is now preparing a book on nineteenth-century women's protest literature.

William Dow is an Adjunct Assistant Professor of English at the American University of Paris, where he teaches American and comparative literature. He has published articles in the fields of American nineteenth-century literature and twentieth-century fiction in French and American journals.

Jane Donahue Eberwein, author of *Dickinson: Strategies of Limitation*, is Professor of English at Oakland University. She is especially interested in Dickinson's relationship to the tradition of imaginative literature grounded in New England Puritanism.

Sara Eddy, like Dickinson a native of Amherst, continues work on her doctoral dissertation in English at Tufts University.

Charles M. Erickson practices dentistry in Fremont, Michigan. Though his interest in Dickinson was forced upon him by his marriage to a Dickinson scholar, he is up to the task and finds her as meticulous a poet as he is a dentist.

Marianne Erickson teaches in the departments of comparative literature and German at Washington University in St. Louis. She is currently completing her dissertation on translation theories applied specifically to the poetry of Dickinson, Rilke, and Milosz. Her articles and translations have appeared in various literary and medical journals.

Lillian Faderman of California State University at Fresno has written or edited numerous books on ethnic literatures and lesbianism. Notable among these are *Surpassing the Love of Men: Romantic Friendship and Love between Women from the Renaissance to the Present* and *Chloe plus Olivia: An Anthology of Lesbian Literature from the Seventeenth Century to the Present*.

Judith Farr, poet and scholar, is Professor of English at Georgetown University. Her recent novel, *I Never Came to You in White*, provides an imaginative complement to *The Passion of Emily Dickinson*.

James Fegan, English-born and Cambridge-educated, has been teaching English language and literature in Japan for many years. He is a Professor at Waseda University in Tokyo.

Jutta Fraunholz recently completed her doctoral dissertation on Emily Dickinson's "Tomes of Solid Witchcraft" at the Free University of Berlin. She has studied in England as well as the United States and is currently at work on a comparison between the aesthetics of Greek antiquity and those of modernism.

Margaret Freeman, founding president of the Emily Dickinson International Society, teaches at Los Angeles Valley College. Her interest in linguistic approaches to poetry led to her central role in the translation project that began at the 1991 Washington conference and recently culminated in a special issue of *The Emily Dickinson Journal*.

Takao Furukawa, Professor of English at Okayama University, is president of the Emily Dickinson Society of Japan and editor-publisher of the poetry magazine *Shimyaku*. Author of *The Poetics of Emily Dickinson*, he has won awards for eleven volumes of poetry written under the pen name Takao Ona.

Jonnie Guerra is Dean of the College at Randolph-Macon Woman's College. She directed the 1992 conference "Translating Emily Dickinson into Language, Culture, and the Arts" and currently serves as vice president of the Emily Dickinson International Society.

Sahoko Hamada, coeditor of *Selected Poems of Emily Dickinson*, is an Associate Professor at Seisen Junior College, Shiga, Japan.

Ellen Louise Hart of Cowell College at the University of Santa Cruz is energetically engaged in editorial scholarship. With Martha Nell Smith, she is co-editing *The Book of Susan and Emily Dickinson*.

Eleanor Elson Heginbotham, Assistant Professor of English at Concordia College, St. Paul, has taught in Liberia, Vietnam, Indonesia, and Maryland. Having written her dissertation at the University of Maryland on a selection of the fascicles, she is working toward publication of a book.

Sylvia Henneberg, a graduate student at the University of Georgia, is writing her dissertation on late poems of Adrienne Rich. Her interest in American women writers has already resulted in articles on Dickinson and Rich.

Peter C. Holloran is the author of *Boston's Wayward Children* (1994) and secretary of the New England Historical Association. He received his Ph.D. in history from Boston University and is an Assistant Professor of history at Northeastern University.

Elizabeth Horan, Assistant Professor of English at Arizona State University, has published enlightening articles on Dickinson's publication and editorial history. She also studies Latin-American women writers.

Melanie Hubbard recently completed her dissertation, "Sacrament of the Word: Emily Dickinson's Material Practice in the World of Print," at Columbia University.

Jennifer Hynes earned her Ph.D. at the University of South Carolina with a dissertation dealing with networking among nineteenth-century women writers. She has taught at West Virginia University and is currently preparing a volume of the work of Elizabeth Stoddard.

Michiko Iwata of Kyoto is an active member of the Emily Dickinson Society of Japan. She participated in the Washington Innsbruck conferences.

Nancy Johnston teaches English at York University, Toronto. She pursues interests in Dickinson, Higginson, and nineteenth-century publishing history as well as textual criticism.

Rowena Revis Jones, Professor Emerita of English at Northern Michigan University, was among the first to use Johnson's editions of the poems and letters for her 1960 dissertation (Northwestern University). Her studies of the poems in the context of their New England religious tradition are much valued by Dickinson scholars.

Suzanne Juhasz, author of *The Undiscovered Continent: Emily Dickinson and the Space of the Mind* and editor or coauthor of other Dickinson books, is a founding board member of the Emily Dickinson International Society and editor of *The Emily Dickinson Journal*. She is Professor of English at the University of Colorado.

Carolyn Kemp is a writer, mother, and Dickinson aficionado who works as a marketing manager at a software company in Boston. She serves as coeditor of the poetry magazine RE*MAP, making good use of her M.A. in poetics.

Haruko Kimura, Professor at St. Marianna University School of Medicine, holds degrees from Tsuda College and the University of Tokyo. She has also studied at Brandeis University and at Radcliffe College's Bunting Institute.

Joan Kirkby, who writes on both Australian and American literature, is Associate Professor of English and cultural studies at Macquarie University in Australia. She is engaged in an ambitious book project that entails reading everything Emily Dickinson read.

Denise Kohn is a graduate student at the University of Houston, where she focuses on nineteenth-century English and American literature. She has published articles on Jane Austen and Anthony Trollope.

Lena Koski is a researcher with the Department of English at Abo Akademi University, Turku, Finland. She wrote her 1992 master's thesis on Dickinson and fame and is completing a licentiate thesis titled "Dickinson and Deviance."

Susan Kurjiaka, Assistant Professor at Florida Atlantic University, has recently returned from a year's teaching assignment in Warsaw, Poland, as a Fullbright fellow. Although a Hawthorne scholar, she reports that she teaches Dickinson's poetry in almost every class.

H. Jordan Landry is a graduate student in English literature and a part-time instructor at the University of Colorado at Boulder.

Mary Jane Leach-Rudawski, a doctoral candidate at the University of Minnesota, is interested in American poetry—especially that of the Modernist period and the Harlem Renaissance.

Benjamin Lease, Professor Emeritus at Northeastern Illinois University, is best known for *Emily Dickinson's Readings of Men and Books: Sacred Soundings.* He was the originating editor of the *Emily Dickinson International Society Bulletin* "Scholars" series.

Catherine Carr Lee, who teaches at the University of Texas at Dallas, is combining her scholarly interests in the language of the Salem witchcraft confessions, nineteenth-century American culture, representations of women's sexuality, and Nathaniel Hawthorne in a book project dealing with Hawthorne and witchcraft.

Daniel Lombardo is the curator of Special Collections at the Jones Library in Amherst, Massachusetts, where he is responsible for historical and literary collections, including those of Emily Dickinson, Robert Frost, and Julius Lester. He is the author of *Tales of Amherst: A Look Back* (1986), *A Directory of Craftsmen in the Connecticut Valley of Massachusetts before 1850* (1987), and *A Hedge Away: The Other Side of Emily Dickinson's Amherst* (1997).

Polly Longsworth, author of *Austin and Mabel* and *The World of Emily Dickinson*, is preparing a new biography of the poet.

Kimberly Markowski is pursuing a Ph.D. at West Virginia University. Her interests focus on nineteenth-century American women writers and representations of immigrant experience in turn-of-the-century American literature.

Jean Carwile Masteller, Professor of English at Whitman College, teaches American literature and American studies. She has published work on many nineteenth-century authors and is currently at work on a study of popular fiction for workingwomen and on women's reading groups in the 1890s.

Susan McCabe, author of *Elizabeth Bishop: Her Poetics of Loss* (1994), is Assistant Professor in modern and contemporary American poetry at Arizona State University.

Janet McCann, Associate Professor of English at Texas A & M, is the author of *Looking for Buddha in the Barbed Wire Garden* and *Wallace Stevens Revisited: The Celestial Possible.*

Marietta Messmer, who recently completed her doctoral study at York University in Canada with a disseration on "Reconstructing Dickinson's Epistolary Subject Positions," has returned to Germany to accept a research and teaching appointment at the Georg-August-Universtät, Göttingen.

Cristanne Miller, third president of the Emily Dickinson International Society, chairs the English Department at Pomona College. Citations throughout this book demonstrate the invaluable contributions of *Emily Dickinson: A Poet's Grammar*.

Michele Mock, Assistant Professor at the University of Pittsburgh, Johnstown campus, is managing editor for *Legacy: A Journal of American Women Writers*.

Jonathan Morse, Professor of English at the University of Hawaii at Manoa, writes about twentieth-century literature, the theory of literary history, and Emily Dickinson. He is the author of *Word by Word: The Language of Memory*.

Aífe Murray, a San Francisco poet, artist, and independent scholar, is working on a cross-disciplinary study of silence and voice as figured in the story of the Dickinson servants and their poet employer. Titled *Kitchen Table Poetics*, her forthcoming book will highlight the relationship of maid-of-all-work Margaret Maher and Emily Dickinson.

Joel Myerson, Carolina Research Professor of American Literature at the University of South Carolina, is well known as editor, bibliographer, and scholar in the field of nineteenth-century American literature. Among his Dickinson publications are *Emily Dickinson: A Descriptive Bibliography* (1984) and a supplement to it in the *Emily Dickinson Journal* (1995).

Marianne Noble, Assistant Professor at American University in Washington, D.C., is writing a book on masochistic imagery in sentimentality. She has published articles on Harriet Beecher Stowe, Susan Warner, and Emily Dickinson.

Rosa Nuckels, who recently completed doctoral study at the University of North Texas, is the author of "The Belle of Amherst Meets the Madame de Sade of Criticism" in *CCTE Studies* (1994).

Marisa Anne Pagnattaro is a Ph.D. candidate at the University of Georgia. Also an attorney, she is interested in depictions of justice in American literature.

Ronald Palosaari teaches at Augsburg College in Minneapolis.

Amy J. Pardo earned her Ph.D. from the University of Alabama in 1996 with a dissertation entitled " 'Out of the Attic': The Gothic Mode in the Poetry of Emily Dickinson and Christina Rossetti." When not at work on a literary travel guide to the Southeast, she is adapting the dissertation manuscript for publication.

Danuta Piestrzyńska of Georgia State University, a specialist in English poetry of the late nineteenth and early twentieth centuries, has translated Dickinson letters into Polish.

Josef Raab, Assistant Professor of American studies at the Catholic University of Eichstätt, Germany, is the author of *Elizabeth Bishop's Hemisphere* (1993) and articles on Dickinson, Bishop, and aspects of American popular culture. He is currently working on a study of Chicano literature.

Dean Rader is completing a book entitled *Linking Society and Desire: Wallace Stevens and the Modern Lyric* and coediting with Brian Clements *Western Tongues: An Anthology of Twentieth-Century Poetry in Translation.* He is Assistant Professor of English at Texas Lutheran University.

Susan Rieke is an Associate Professor of English at Saint Mary College in Leavenworth, Kansas. In addition to writing two books of poetry, she has published articles on Walt Whitman and Emily Dickinson.

Rebecca Emlinger Roberts, poet, provided editorial assistance with this encyclopedia while completing graduate study in English at Oakland University. She now teaches rhetoric there.

Agnieszka Salska, Professor of American literature at Poland's University of Lodz, has been translating Dickinson's poetry into Polish and is now doing the same for Galway Kinnell's. She is the author of *Walt Whitman and Emily Dickinson: Poetry of the Central Consciousness.*

Erika Scheurer, Assistant Professor of English at the University of St. Thomas in St. Paul, has published on composition theory and pedagogy as well as on Dickinson's epistolary voice.

Emily Seelbinder is Associate Professor of English at Queens College in Charlotte, North Carolina, where she specializes in nineteenth-century American literature and African-American literature.

Maryann Sewell, soprano, is on the voice faculty at Montgomery College in Rockville, Maryland. She frequently performs musical settings of Emily Dickinson poems.

Bryan C. Short, Professor of English at Northern Arizona University, has published widely on American literature and rhetorical theory, and is completing a book on Dickinson's rhetoric.

Judy Jo Small, author of *Positive as Sound: Emily Dickinson's Rhyme*, is Associate Professor of English at North Carolina State University.

James Avery Smith has been town engineer of Amherst, Massachusetts, since 1971. A graduate of Drexel University, he was ordained to the Presbyterian ministry in 1967 and is a clergyman in the United Church of Christ. He teaches voice at Westfield State College.

Martha Nell Smith, Associate Professor of English at the University of Maryland, is developing a hypermedia archive for Dickinson textual study. She is well known for *Rowing in Eden: Rereading Emily Dickinson.*

Robert McClure Smith, author of *The Seductions of Emily Dickinson*, is Assistant Professor of English at Knox College.

Lynne EFM Spear is a graduate student in the Department of English at the University of Colorado at Boulder. She is editorial assistant for the *Emily Dickinson Journal* and coordinator of the EDIS Web Site.

Haskell Springer is Professor of English at the University of Kansas. His most recent publication is *America and the Sea: A Literary History.*

Gary Lee Stonum, author of *The Dickinson Sublime*, is Professor of English at Case Western Reserve University.

Georgiana Strickland of the University Press of Kentucky provides laudable service to the Dickinsonian community by editing the *Emily Dickinson International Society Bulletin.*

Michael Strysick is working on a book-length project, "Feudal America: Literature, Community, and the Politics of Social Reform." He teaches English at Davidson College.

Masako Takeda is the author of *From Japan to Amherst: My Days with Emily Dickinson* and has edited and translated Dickinson's letters and poems into Japanese.

Marcy L. Tanter recently completed her doctoral study at the University of Massachusetts with a dissertation on Dickinson.

Michelle Tice graduated with an M.A. in English from Youngstown State University in June 1996. She is interested in researching American women writers, including women poets, working-class women, and women journalists from the nineteenth century.

Stephanie A. Tingley, Associate Professor of English at Youngstown State University, has been especially interested in Dickinson's correspondence with Elizabeth and Josiah Holland. She is completing a book on Emily Dickinson's letters.

Hiroko Uno, author of several Dickinson-related articles as well as *Emily Dickinson Visits Boston*, is Professor of English at Shiga University.

Daneen Wardrop, Assistant Professor of English at Western Michigan University, is the author of *Emily Dickinson's Gothic: Goblin with a Gauge*; she is currently working on Whitman and Dickinson.

Marta L. Werner is Assistant Professor of English at Georgia State University. She is the author of *Open Folios: Scenes of Reading, Surfaces of Writing* and is currently preparing an electronic edition of Dickinson's fragments.

Joanna Yin teaches English at the University of Hawaii. She is interested in the thematic and rhetorical influences of Puritan discourse on Dickinson's poems. Currently, she is working on the mathematics of Dickinson.

ISBN 0-313-29781-9